The Holy Monk and the Spirit Woman

Xuemo

Translated by J. C. Cleary

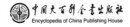
中国大百科全书出版社
Encyclopedia of China Publishing House

First Edition 2018

ISBN 978-7-5202-0279-4

Copyright © 2018 by Xuemo

Published by Encyclopedia of China Publishing House

Fuchengmen Beidajie No.17, Xicheng District , Beijing, China

Tel:(86)10-88390739

http://www.ecph.com.cn

E-mail:limoyun2008@sina.com

Printed by Global Oriental (Beijing) Printing Co Ltd

Contents

Introduction

Esoteric Hidden Treasure

1 The Secret History of Khyungpo

The *Secret History of Khyungpo* has existed all along by means of a certain mystical method, which people call "secret treasure."

The secret treasures include treasures in the form of texts, treasures in the form of sacred objects, and treasures in the form of teachings. Treasures in the form of texts means the texts of the sutras. Treasures in the form of sacred objects means ritual implements, relics of eminent monks and teachers of great virtue, and so on. The relics of the Tantric dakini Vajravarahi (Diamond Sow) discovered by the author are a classic treasure in the form of a sacred object. In different forms, these secret treasures are preserved in the forms of the five elements—earth, water, fire, air, and space.

The most miraculous among the secret treasures are treasures in the form of consciousness. Treasures in the form of consciousness are one kind of treasures in the form of teachings. When circumstances were not favorable and there was no way to transmit them widely, certain kinds of mantras and teaching methods and other cultural materials were hidden by the buddhas and bodhisattvas or spirits, hidden deep within the consciousness of certain people, so that the transmission of them would not be lost. Then, when the circumstances were ripe, under the impetus of a certain kind of spiritual power, they flow forth again from the minds of those who hold these treasures of consciousness.

The *Secret History of Khyungpo* thus belongs to the category of treasures in the form of consciousness. It takes the spiritual quest of Khyungpo Naljor and preserves it in a certain mysterious place. At a certain moment in time many years ago, I encountered it.

In that instant, I suddenly thought of Khyungpo Naljor. I very much wanted to know his Path to experiencing enlightenment. When we speak of those people who are seek freedom, what is more meaningful is in fact not the outcome, but rather the process of overcoming the self and reaching the Other Shore of freedom. I very much wanted to know what kind of life and process of practice Khyungpo Naljor, who had been an ordinary man, had gone through so that he became a sage.

At this point, I relied on a realm of experience that goes beyond nature, that goes beyond the distinctions of time and space, and I reached the place I wanted to reach. At that time, I had undergone many years of cultivating the Great Mudra of Light, and I had already broken through the barriers, and my discriminating mind had begun to merge with the realm of light. In that kind of boundless clear light, I began to pray and observe. Soon I saw a point of light—it was like a firefly fluttering around on a dark night. At the beginning, it moved back and forth, seeming to be there for an instant, and then seeming to be gone. Later it came to rest, and it was like a star in the night sky, fixed in one spot. At that point I was observing it in the midst of clear emptiness. Before long, the point of light changed into the light of a candle. At first, the candlelight was swaying, but gradually the brightness opened up, and finally the light radiated out in all directions. At this point, I saw a candlestick, and I also saw a hand lifting the candlestick. Following along from the hand to the arm, and I saw the whole body of the person holding up the candlestick. An old man with a penetrating vision was looking right at me. He was very lean. He told me that he was Khyungpo Naljor. I felt this was strange, because the Khyungpo Naljor depicted in the tangka paintings was a fat lama. But he told me that the real Khyungpo Naljor was a gaunt old man. He told me that the form I was seeing was how he looked as a one-hundred-forty-eight-year-old man.

So in this manner, in this realm of light, we managed to communicate. I inquired about his past, I heard his story, and I asked him everything about himself. Many years later, when I mentioned this story to a disciple of the tenth Panchen Lama, he laughed mysteriously. He said I should not take this as a dream.

One day that old man set out a book before my eyes — this was the *Secret History of Khyungpo*. The pages of this book seemed to have already yellowed with age. He opened it to the first page. I earnestly read it. Every night I could read through several dozen pages. The days passed, and I read through this book and finished it. A person who had experienced enlightenment told me that this book was written using dakini scripts. In this respect, it is very similar to Milarepa's *Songs of Enlightenment*. The story goes that the book we are familiar with as the Milarepa's *Songs of Enlightenment* was passed on by an adept from the dakini scripts.

Over time I came to understand clearly all the content set forth in this book. Later on I came to thoroughly understand all the esoteric meanings that lay behind the text in this book.

Still later, the frost of dualism truly melted away in the light of wisdom, and all the barriers between the old man and me were gone. From this time on, I no longer had to use this text, and I could communicate with this wise old man.

As they say in the practice of yoga, I was in accord with this old man.

This "being in accord" is a very meaningful phrase. It is a little like people transmitting data over the internet. He presses "send" and I press "receive" and the transmission of the message begins from this.

What is transmitted between that old man and me, besides the contents of this book, also includes something called "experiencing the light."

Thus, at a certain point, my vessel of wisdom was filled up, and this book was born by it pouring out.

This then is the origin of the present book.

Professor Chen Xiaoming of Peking University has called this kind of writing "comprehending past lives."

He said:

Xuemo's works are obviously not the same ... It's like tasting a story in a dream that completely disarranges the present logic, and goes beyond the boundaries of the present space and time at will. What is called "comprehending past lives" means comprehending the outcome of one's whole fate — that is, everything is within the calculation of fate. It is something that can see through fate, and has a serene spirit.

The narrator himself is a spirit within the programming of the calculations of fate. He is a ghostly auxiliary who can calculate fate. He loves this movement of fate, he stays close to this movement of fate — this is comprehending past lives.

The Professor also said:

Xuemo uses his sincerity for religion, and his experiences come near to the extreme limits of life. Thus there is a sort of intoxication of the spirit in the body, a kind of madness in the manner of Dionysius, the god of wine ... This kind of work also is like a kind of spell, a kind of final mantra. Only by using this spell-like writing can he give forth his own inner life experience — experience facing death ... The meaning of comprehending past lives lies in this: only such extreme writing can reveal the basic substance of contemporary writing.

(from Chen Xiaoming, How Can Literature Be Free: From Culture to Religion; from the lecture on Xuemo's Curses of Xixia)

When I saw the passages above, I exclaimed: Professor Chen has good insight!

In the time when critics have been alienated, someone like Professor Chen Xiaoming is really very hard to find. Mr. Chen, being full of so many contemporary terms and influences, has still not been cut off by the times from his spiritual wisdom.

This is right. In reality I have gone through a kind of supernatural writing process. I have experienced "that kind of pure Dharma bliss that never for a moment leaves me." I have merged into "that realm that is bright and empty as the sky, pure as the ocean, without waves or ripples, without clouds, like a dream or an illusion, a mind without obstructions." "When I write there are no words in my mind, it is bright and empty as the sky, empty and spiritual to the limit, yet I am able to let all sorts of writings flow out from within inherent nature." (from *The Great Mudra of Light: the Heart of Real Practice*)

But I do not cling to this, because according to the standards of what is called "the Supreme Truth," everything in this world is an illusion. That is to say, the basic substance of all things and appearances is in reality all illusory transformation. It is like something in a memory.

In all the activities of humankind, except for memories, we cannot find any real substance that does not change.

Yet those memories dissolve away, like yellow dogs running away in a dust storm—it is very hard for us to catch them.

However, because the present book appears, those many historical memories will certainly become just the opposite, and last forever.

This is the meaning of Xuemo being alive.

2 The Transmission of the Light

After passing on information for many years, the old man Khyungpo Naljor had handed on to me all the wisdom and the light of his realization. This kind of story always appears in the tales of the warrior-heroes. All the great heroes, at the moment of danger, can take their entire wealth of inner strength, and pass it along to their disciples. This of course is a narrative device for such stories. But in yoga, such stories of transmission really happen. This is very similar to the transmission of a certain program between two computers online.

This is the power of being in accord.

If there is no accord, then there is no yoga. The real meaning of yoga is being in accord. Being in accord with an advanced teacher is the key for all the esoteric teachings.

Here I will use an example that you can take in. You can consider the wise teacher as a computer equipped with many programs of wisdom. I am like a computer on another network. My faith in him and my karmic links with him are data lines. As long as these three things are fully prepared, then it is possible to guarantee that the "data" of wisdom will be transmitted between us. Although outsiders will never be able to put together these high-level programs, after going through a long training process, they may be able to use them. Similarly, though the author's wisdom is simple and crude, because there has been this process of transmission after being in accord, I am able for this reason to have the wisdom and ability offered by these "programs."

In the yoga system of the Great Mudra, this is called "the Great Mudra of Light." It is only because I have obtained these "programs" of wisdom written by these great teachers over the ages, that my life has realized an upward course. It is only because this experience, this light was transmitted, that my writings are called the system of "the Great Mudra of Light."

In fact, later on, it was already very hard for me to distinguish myself from this old man. It was also very hard for me to distinguish myself from the Five Great Diamonds I practiced and followed him as tutelary deities. In yoga, they often use one expression to describe this: "without duality, without difference."

Later on, at the Ta'er Monastery in Qinghai, I invited a virtuous teacher to attest to the fact that I merged with the experiential realm of clear light to write. He said: At this time, there is no duality and no difference between you and the Five Great Diamonds.

The German philosopher Martin Buber in *I and Thou* wrote of this kind of accord:

> *The world of It is set in the context of space and time.*
>
> *The world of Thou is not set in the context of either of these.*
>
> *The particular Thou, after the relational event has run its course, is bound to become an It.*
>
> *The particular It, by entering the relational event, may become a Thou.*

— translated by Ronald Gregor Smith (New York: Charles Scribner's Sons, 1958), p. 33.

This is another explanation of "without duality, without difference."

Besides this, you also can read the very detailed explanations of "without duality, without difference" which I give in my books *The Great Mudra of Light: the Heart of Real Practice* and *The Great Mudra of Light: Real Practice, Sudden Entry.*

Therefore, you can understand this book in four ways:

1. It is a kind of record of a completed interview from when I and "he" had not yet reached the stage "without duality and without difference."

2. It is in fact my own esoteric journey of soul.

3. You can still take it as the words of a novelist, a different kind of spiritual novel.

4. You can also take it as a kind of symbol.

Chapter 1

A Choice of Fate

Xuemo: "Honored Master, what I am most concerned about, is what happened after your first 'betrayal' — please permit me to use this word; your many friends in the original Bon teaching also understand it this way. In your life, that was the first most crucial decision point. The reason that I can know you today is because you make this choice. I have heard that this event brought about major repercussions, and their evil spirits and poisonous dragons were sent at you to punish you. Can you please explain what you went through?"

1　The Bloody Knife that Drew the Horizon

That's right. That was the first time in my life that I faced hardship and danger.

Bonpo is the original religion of Tibet, with a history longer than Buddhism, and great influence. It has its own body of tradition and culture. As for that, I will go on and introduce it to you later.

I do not like the expression "betrayal." In fact, my behavior was simply a manifestation of the working of causal conditions. Even now, I still consider Bonpo to be an excellent religion, as great and profound as Buddhism. On this point, I agree with what you say. You say that all religions are different sides of the fabric of truth. This is correct. The Buddha himself said: "All good teachings are the Buddha Dharma." They have higher and lower levels, differences in concepts, but they do not necessarily differ in value. Different medicines are suitable for different sicknesses. We cannot say which kind of medicine is right and which is wrong. What is a good medicine is relative to the disease.

The year when I formally left Bonpo, I was just twenty-eight years old. Hey, that was the best age of my life. I had left childhood behind, and I had the maturity of an adult. I had the passion of a donkey, and the courage of a bull. I had the wisdom of a teacher, and everything I needed to command people's respect. At that age I was the sun, and wherever I went, there were countless admiring eyes. Ha, ha—and of course there were quite a few girls with passion in their eyes.

Do you like it when I talk like this? I do not like it when you take me for some great consummate master. I just hope you take me as a friend... That's right, a friend.

Although you are my disciple in the transmission of mind, still, fundamentally, we are one substance. When I talk with you, it is still as if I am talking to myself.

So then, let us talk freely, okay?

You ask how the Bonpo guardian spirits punished me? This is a good question.

I' ll tell you. The eyes of that very beautiful girls I first encountered — that was the first adverse circumstance created by the guardian spirits. At that time, I was at the "burning drill" age you speak of in your book *Desert Rites.*

My dreams too were colored pink. You should not by any means think that I was a natural born holy man. I wasn't, I was not a natural born holy man. I too felt greed and anger, I felt afflictions, and even more, I had a yearning for carnal love.

In those days, in my dreams, that very pretty woman always appeared. Her name was Lamu, which in Tibetan means "heavenly woman." She was just eighteen, and extremely beautiful. When she sang Tibetan songs, it was like a lark singing. Her face when she smiled was like a snow lotus opening. Her two eyes, so full of affection, were the first agents sent by the guardian spirits to punish me.

Because she was there, my life was full of so much torment.

You may not know it, but at many moments when my mind was wavering, I even thought of returning to lay life.

But every time I thought of returning to lay life, there appeared before my eyes an even more beautiful woman.

She was Niguma.

Once Niguma appeared, Lamu no longer attracted me. Perhaps in the Buddhist scriptures you have read this story: A monk was in love with his own beautiful wife. One day the Buddha took him up to heaven, and as soon as he saw the heavenly women, the devis, the monk immediately discovered that his wife had become ugly. At that moment in my life, I felt the same way.

Every time, as soon as Niguma appeared, the appeal of that pretty woman faded out.

Wanting to search for Niguma became an important reason for me to leave the Bonpo religion.

2 The Cry of Pain That Resounded through Heaven and Earth

It's true. When I left Bonpo, I really hurt the feelings of a lot of Bonpo people.

From their point of view, this was not just a great loss; more than that, it was a major loss of face. This too is understandable. There is no religion that would be willing for its leading teacher to go off and join another religion. Later on there were some people who considered what I had done as "forsaking the darkness for the light." Naturally, they can take it this way. But you must realize, that my real aim was to find Niguma.

At that time, the urgency in my mind was no less strong than that of someone who is first in love being concerned about his beloved… Let me tell you a secret: a lot of times, so-called religious feeling is in fact the same kind of excitement as worldly emotion. Isn't that so?

At that time, there certainly appeared many fearful symptoms.

That day, I heard many Bonpo guardian spirits all wailing. At first I thought it was really someone crying. Later I discovered the sound of crying gradually got louder, and the sound penetrated heaven and earth, like demons crying and wolves howling, a frightful sound, but also incomparably solemn. This is because, as I listened to that so-called wailing sound, I also heard the sound of a sea conch being blown that shook heaven and earth. In many traditional explanations, this sound of a sea conch symbolizes resounding worldwide fame.

Later on, I finally did win fame in the world. In the history of Buddhist culture, I was made into a figure who cannot be ignored. Of course, right now, except in the history books and among the disciples who inherited my teachings, many people no longer know who I was. No matter how great one's fame, fundamentally it is still like a cloud passing by. You should not have any regrets. This is the way it is. When you went to Nanmu county before and inquired about me, nobody knew me. Among the historical and cultural figures on their official website, there is no introduction to me. It's not important. In different times, among different people, there is always a different focus. What you are saying is correct: even if everyone in the whole world knows you, when this crop of people is gone, you will still be a stranger to the next crop of people.

There is nothing that can be done about this. No matter what it is, everything goes through four processes: birth, development, decay, and dissolution. No matter how famous, or no matter how high one's social position, or no matter how wealthy one is—everyone goes through this.

Nevertheless, while I was in the world, throughout Tibet, if there was anyone who did not know of me, that person would be ridiculed by others as uncultured and ignorant.

That morning as I was listening to the sound of wailing filling the sky, I also heard the sound of the conch shell. This was a long-drawn-out sound that penetrated heaven and earth—it cut across the vast sky and pierced through from one end to the other. That sound shook the leaves on the trees all around with a reverberating sound. It was like an air defense alert would be later. Even if you thought you were in a dream, that sound would be able to penetrate your eardrums and make you wake up. When you first lectured about the Great Mudra of Light, didn't you hear that kind of sound? At that time, you and the people in the audience all heard this kind of sound penetrating the sky. The great flow created by that sound rolled across the sky with unstoppable force. It was surging on, extending without end, resounding through the endless blue firmament.

To me, that sound was the sea conch of wisdom waking up the world. At that moment I felt certain that, no matter how corrupt and unworthy people say this world is, that pure and clear correct perception can always resound through the sky of history just like the sound of the sea conch penetrating space.

That morning, even though I heard the sound of the sea conch, I did not know that later I would become famous, and I did not know that I would become the teacher of a generation. You spoke correctly when you said that the road ahead is dark. It truly is. Everything in human life is really unknown, and it is always changing. When your mind changes, your choices change, and then your course in human life also changes.

At that time I certainly did not know what kind of difficulties or dangers lay ahead for me. I went so far as to be prepared to die at any time. The Buddha said that human life can be over from one breath to the next. If this breath goes out, and cannot come back in, then I die. At the time I did not know it then, but later I would end up living a hundred and fifty years.

That morning, when that sound started, I thought it was a monk in the temple blowing the sea conch. There was only Tashi who also heard the wailing of the guardian spirits. Those spirits guarding the teaching are worldly guardians, meaning that they have not yet awakened to empty inherent nature. They do not know that, no matter whether it is Buddhism or Bonpo, both are just a bridge leading to the truth, and nothing more. They also do not know that, in many of its teachings, Bonpo has absorbed many things from Buddhism. This is because many years ago, there were people who took Buddhist scriptures that had been changed in appearance and buried them in the ground, and later these became the "hidden treasures" of Bonpo. This is why, of the things they believe in, a great many are in reality Buddhist things.

One day in the future, you will see that in the teachings of Bonpo, there are many things that in fact are Buddhist teachings with the terminology changed. At that time you will join the Buddhist discussion forum organized for Sichuan province, and you will organize a forum for the Shangpa Kagyu culture, and you will see a Bonpo forum. Those scholars in fact have already taken Bonpo teachings and created a Buddhist culture. Bonpo also has concepts of great perfect enlightenment, and the transformation of the enlightened ones into rainbows, and it also has many rituals that can benefit people.

But when I was twenty-eight, I certainly did not know such things. Of course, those guardian spirits did not know these things either. They just cared about names and forms. Once they heard I was leaving Bonpo, they came out with the wailing that sounded like a sea conch. After that, they began to take advantage of circumstances, and accepting certain ritual instructions, they began to launch attacks at me.

With these Bonpo guardian spirits, with their extremely heavy discriminating minds, taking the lead and joining in, many unfortunate things started to happen around me. For example, one morning I discovered that the water supply had changed into filthy blood. This gave forth a horrible stench. This was the stench of a thousand-year-old cesspool. If you are interested, if you go west to the most marginal land of agricultural villages, if you are lucky, you may see a hemp pit. This is a storage pit where they specialize in composting hemp, so it forms a pool of black water, and the stench is beyond compare. When the water came out, it smelled just like this. Nevertheless, although I recognized this as a weird occurrence, I was not afraid. At that time, because I was seeking Niguma, I was prepared to lay down my life at any time.

In my eyes, abandoning the darkness for the light was the greatest good fortune. Of course I later discovered that the light and the dark are, in reality, the discriminating minds of worldly people.

The second weird occurrence was that the banner in front of the temple gate was suddenly snapped by a wild wind. On the banner were written various kinds of inscriptions, mostly containing prayers for good fortune and for warding off disaster. As it turned out, the inscriptions on the banner could not even protect their own flagpole.

At this same time, whenever I had a careless moment, I was always seeing those guardian spirits appear with their angry looks. Their heads were as big as mountains, their eyes were like suns, and when they opened their mouths to breath in, the sky flowed into their mouths like liquid.

There were countless nights when these guardian spirits appeared in my dreams. They showed their fangs, and made rumbling laughing sounds. These sounds were actually the howls which a teaching master makes when subduing demons. They really took me for a demon. This is a very interesting phenomenon. Have you discovered it yet? In this world, there are always people who think that those whose outer appearance is different from their own are really demons. In your novel *Curses of Xixia*, some people think Na A Jia is a wise man, and some people think he is a demon. Which is correct? Both are. Many people who are called demons by worldly people might in fact be the greatest people of wisdom.

In my dreams, I was really afraid that these Bonpo guardian spirits might kill me. They spewed out black vapor at me. You know, black is the only color that the death-dealing magic has. Thus, in my dreams, there was a large rock pressing on my chest, and there was muddy water all around me, and in the muddy water there were countless poisonous insects. There were spiders, scorpions, centipedes, and toads. Just like the guardian spirits, they were all spitting out black poisonous vapors at me. In these black poisonous vapors more insects came to life, and it was like this, endlessly writhing.

I saw a female demon with a head the size of a bushel basket, with long sharp protruding fangs, many meters long. Time and again she pierced my body with her fangs. The strange thing was, in the dream, I was really feeling pain. Every time her fangs went into my body, I felt a pain piercing my heart and lungs. When she pulled her fangs out, my body went back to its original condition.

I was having dreams like this every night.

However, in the midst of these dreams, sometimes I could remember Niguma. As soon as I prayed to her, she would appear.

Her body was like a rainbow, overflowing with countless lights. These lights became liquid, and flowed forth, and inundated the poisonous vermin.

In many dreams, I would call out, "Niguma, my mother." But Niguma just smiled at me. She did not say a word. I often wanted to talk to her, but she did not say anything. One time, she drew a line in the sky, and I immediately saw a spiritual design, one man and one woman joined together. You too have seen this design. People call this the Vajra.

At that time, I still did not now what the Vajra (Diamond) was. I did not like the Vajra.

I only liked Niguma.

In my mind Niguma was a beautiful female spirit or goddess.

3 The Black Dragon Method of Slaying

Later I finally came to know that the choice I had made to leave
Bonpo had provoked the enmity of some conservatives in the Bonpo
religion, and a few among them had already begun to launch very
severe black magic spells against me. They drew a three-cornered
mandala, and provided a lot of poisons, because these guardian spirits
like to eat poisonous things. Among all the spells they employed,
the most severe was the black dragon method for slaying. This black
dragon was a poisonous dragon in a deep pond. He had no good
thoughts, and whoever gave him good things to eat, he would help. He
was very much like those fearsome assassins among humans who can
be bought for money. Yes, this is the kind you wrote about in *Curses of
Xixia.*

On the third day that they were using their spells, I saw there was
a huge black dragon following me. He looked very much like a black
tornado. By this point, my body already bore the traces of poisoning. I
was always itching. I did not know whether this was really due to being
poisoned, or it was psychosomatic. If I had really been poisoned, then I
might get a kind of sickness called leprosy. At that time, we called this
kind of sickness the dragon disease.

To tell the truth, I was terrified.

I was very afraid that I had already caught leprosy. I had seen
people suffering from leprosy whose noses had disintegrated or who
had had their eyes blinded, and I had seen strange creatures who had
lost all four limbs. In those days, we would take those sick people
away deep into the mountains and forests, take them and segregate
them, to live and die on their own. In some remote villages, there were
even people who would burn people with leprosy to death, in order to

prevent the poison from spreading. If I got infected with this sickness, not only would I not be able to spread the teaching—even my life would be hard to preserve.

I had not thought that the people in Bonpo who had treated me extremely well would now have this kind of animosity against me, just because I wanted to leave Bonpo.

I discovered that this black dragon was following me all the time, spewing black vapor on to my body. It was very much like that kind of tornado you have seen, swirling up, piercing the sky. On the dragon's head there were two eyes like two lamps.

Luckily, I knew a few methods of defense, and I visualized diamond clubs like arrows flying out of my heart chakra on all sides, forming a giant defensive screen all around my body, like a shell, protecting me inside. On those diamond clubs were unquenchable fierce fires, and every time I visualized the fiery screen, that black dragon would move a bit farther away.

He was very afraid of me. If he did not pay attention to everything in front of him, that fire of wisdom could burn him. This is the secret of the Realm of Reality—all things are just made by mind. In fact, in the eyes of the black dragon, that fire which I was visualizing was as frightening as a real fire.

The protective circle that I was visualizing was very strong and solid. It was only because of this factor that the poisonous dragon did not directly take my life.

I knew that those followers wanted to kill me before I left Bonpo, and this way, Bonpo could avoid an embarrassing incident. This is because, seen from any angle, if some one who is to be a teaching master choses to leave Bonpo, it will always become a negative influence on Bonpo. All these unlucky signs were the doing of those guardian spirits who had not awakened to the empty inherent nature.

Only later did I realize that, in my life, what was creating adverse conditions for me then was not only the Bonpo guardian spirits — even more adverse conditions came from somewhere else. Many years later, a certain dakini called Sukhasiddhi told me that the source of these adverse conditions was the discriminating mind. The aim of all forms of cultivation is to wipe away the discriminating mind. The discriminating mind brings conflict, brings afflictions, draws forth false thoughts. For this reason, in all the scriptures, empty inherent nature is said to be "without the discriminating mind."

A thousand years ago, on the morning that water source turned to filthy blood, in the sky there appeared a blood-red strip of sky. It extended from the southern sky to the northern sky, as if someone had taken a sword and cut the sky in half. When I came out of my door, I saw a lot of people looking at it. They were craning their necks as if they had been hung by their palates on a formless fish hook. From the lips of some of the people came sounds of oohs and ahs. As they saw me pass by, they grew silent. Ever since they had heard the tell that I was leaving Bonpo, many of the people had been looking at me strangely.

That red strip of sky on the horizon emitted a light that pierced the eye — the light gave forth a golden hue, and splashed in all directions. Many years later, when I told this to a great teacher from India, he told me: "This golden-colored light symbolized that you will have endless good fortune, and your wealth and power will be very great. That blood-red strip of sky along the horizon symbolized that you will become a dazzling being in the firmament of history."

But at the time when I saw this red strip of sky, I just felt that my mind was surging with a feeling I had never experienced before. The people there were looking at me strangely. I heard the sound of footsteps coming from behind me, and I knew it was Tashi. Ever since I had revealed my intention to leave Bonpo, Tashi had been very agitated. Tashi was the strongest believer in Bonpo.

Tashi overtook me with a few quick steps, and blocked my Path. He looked at me with a challenge in his eyes. Tashi had been my greatest supporter. He had always thought that I was the person who could revitalize Bonpo. He was always telling people stories about the unusual signs that accompanied my birth. He always said: "He is born like unfinished raw material to be master of the teaching: when he is born, he is like masters in embryonic form; only bodhisattvas in the eighth stage are like this." I was always against all of this. I did not like other people boasting about me to my face. Once they boasted, I was not free. But I did understand Tashi. Tashi called himself a mastiff, and he only knew one tent. Many of my disciplines had been pulled in by Tashi. Tashi took Bonpo as his reason for living. He was a person who would cut off his head for Bonpo.

Tashi said, "If you are going to leave Bonpo, I would rather you die."

I mildly said, "I would rather die, but I still have to leave Bonpo."

4 The Firelight of the Death-Dealing Mandala

At this night, I was still feeling a very ominous and dangerous sign. It first appeared in dreams. I would dream that a spiral of dark mud rose from the earth, engulfing me. Everything in the dream was very dark and depressing, and there was not a bit of light. That black dragon trailing behind me was still spewing poison, and that poison vapor it spewed out always covered me. But even if it was in a dream, the defensive ring I visualized was still very strong and solid, and this way the poisonous dragon could not do anything to me.

When I awoke, I felt a large rock pressing down on my chest, and later on, I was still hearing great howling sounds in the night sky. Later a consummate master from India said that the howling was not only from the Bonpo guardian spirits, but also the descendants of the demon king Mara. Because I had appeared in the world, the demon king would lose quite a few of his retinue.

Although in my mind I was not afraid, these sounds were eerie. It was very hard for me to go to sleep. For more than ten years, I had consistently studied the Bonpo scriptures. At the beginning, I focused on this with complete enthusiasm. I happily mastered many scriptures. But as I delved deeper, I had more and more doubts. One day my friend Samdan came to visit. Samdan loved to read the Buddhist scriptures, and when he saw me studying the Bonpo texts, he laughed and said: "These texts look very much like they were copied from the Buddhist scriptures." I remember that it was at this moment that my faith in Bonpo began to waver.

After I returned home, I asked my father where the Bonpo texts came from. My father said they were transmitted by Shenrab Miwo (traditionally considered the founder of Bonpo). I also asked from where Shenrab Miwo got this line of transmission of the teachings. My father could not answer. Then I thought: actually, Bonpo does not come from sacred India. From this the seeds of doubt were planted.

Only later did I find out that, just when I was waking up from the dream, Tashi and several other men were in a secluded place above the Bonpo temple practising some death-dealing magical techniques. The mandala for these deadly arts has a three-cornered shape. Tashi had written down his wishes on a piece of paper for making pledges. His idea was that if I persisted in betraying the Bonpo religion, he would call upon the guardian spirits to slay me. The men had supplied some black hemp and other such things, and some blue flowers picked in the mountain valleys. They were chanting a spell handed down from a thousand years ago. The story goes that this spell had already slain countless people. In Tashi's view, this spell would become a rope, and it would emerge from their mouths like a moving black snake, and wrap itself around my neck.

At this moment I woke up from my dream in alarm. After I woke up, I still felt a giant rock pressing down on my chest, and it felt as if a rope was wrapped tightly around my neck. As in the dream, a rock and mud slide in were still pressing down on my body. According to the traditional accounts, this dream symbolized that the local guardian spirits were angry. Local guardian spirits are a kind of earth spirit. In the Bonpo guidelines for group offerings, the local guardian spirits are earth gods who must be given offerings. Perhaps in the discriminating minds of the local guardian spirits, my leaving Bonpo was a clear act of religious betrayal.

The local guardian spirits I am talking about have two kinds. One kind is similar to the earth spirits, and one kind are protectors of the religion. They are non-humans, or yakshas. Strictly speaking, the yakshas are a kind of powerful demons. Of course, you could understand them as occult powers or occult things. In the teachings I passed on to you later, there are many procedures for setting these occult powers in motion. In general there are four categories of such procedures.

One kind is called "methods of increasing." They are used especially for setting in motion those occult powers of increase: they can make you get rich or add to your merit and rewards.

One kind is called "methods of stopping." They use the power of restful extinction in the universe to put to rest your afflictions and troubles.

One kind is called "methods of reconciling." They are used to aid the power of love in the universe to enable people to respect and love you, and let you have a great ability to conciliate and win people over.

What Tashi was employing are the "death-dealing methods." They use spiritual means to set in motion occult power that functions to wreck or destroy, in order to achieve their goal — for example, to destroy my physical body and my health and so on.

You must realize that there are infinite occult powers in the universe, divided into different frequencies and wave lengths, which can produce different functional powers. When you use a special form to mobilize these occult powers, you can achieve your aim, whether it is to end disasters, or to increase them, whether it is to reconcile, or to slay.

These four — methods of increasing, stopping, reconciling, and slaying — are the four fundamental abilities sought by many of those who cultivate yoga.

I got up and left the house. The moon in the sky was bright, and the dark mountains cast their jagged shadows. The wind was blowing and swept across my face, refreshing and cool.

Looking toward the distant mountains, I thought of a dream I had had when I was little. I almost suspect that this was not a dream. In ordinary dreams you cannot make out colors, because when you are asleep the part of our brains that controls colors is in a state of restful sleep. What I went into was a scene full of light. In the dream, I was invited into a holy place by five girls. There was a woman there who was very familiar, as if we had known each other for a long time. The woman took a book, a book with a vivid red cover, with Sanskrit written on it. At that time, I still could not recognize Sanskrit. In the book there was a group of men. Absentmindedly, I heard someone introduce them by saying, these are the Five Great Diamonds.

Though my somnolent mind was filled with wonder, I did not ask any questions, because every time I started to think of one, I could hear a voice giving an explanation. This voice did not come from any throat, but came from the spirit of my inherent mind. It told me this was my past life. I was not clear whether this voice was saying "past life" or "mission in life" — in my eyes, these two expressions are both the same.

The woman smiled warmly and took this book and put it into my breast. I remember immediately feeling a great joy filling the heavens.

That woman told me her name was Niguma.

I clearly remember her face: she was bright as the moon; she had a light and graceful presence like a pure breeze; she was precious as a beautiful flow; she radiated a warmth like the sun in springtime. That face made a deep imprint on my life. In inadvertent moments, I can often see her.

Niguma, my Niguma!

I still remember this dream. I did not tell anyone about it. I thought to myself: in this lifetime, I must surely find this woman. I thought that maybe she was my mother in a previous lifetime.

I had this dream when I was eight years old. At that time, I had already begun to lecture on the Bonpo scriptures, and I had become known near and far as a spiritual child prodigy. Every time I finished lecturing on a scripture, people would all give me many offerings. This was the norm. But I was not interested in the things that were so fine in the eyes of the ordinary lay people. I kept remembering that dream. Sometimes Niguma would still appear in my dreams. She was always looking at me from far away, and she was still smiling warmly like that. I was always able to sense compassionate waves emanating from her body. I very much wanted to get close to her, but she was always so far away from me.

At that time, I thought that maybe if I thought about something by day, then I would dream about it at night.

But one night a month later, Niguma again appeared in my dream. This time she came close. I could see that there was an eye on her forehead. That eye emitted a gentle light, like moonlight, which could shine into my mind. I remember the woman saying, "I have waited for you a long time—why haven't you come?" This voice did not come from the throat, but from the spirit of inherent mind.

I thought, she is surely my mother from a past life. I gazed at the moonlight, and felt that the moonlight itself had become that woman. I thought: no matter what happens, I must go find her.

At that time, I certainly did not know that in a remote mountain valley, a fire mandala intended to kill me was blazing up. A bunch of Bonpo guardian spirits with their discriminating minds were beginning to extend their fangs and claws toward me.

5 Guardian Spirits Extending Their Fangs and Claws

When I saw that bunch of guardian spirits extending their fangs and claws, most of them were mountain spirits, and also dragon spirits. In the Bonpo scriptures, there are many verses to the dragon spirits. They eat the soft tissue around people's mouths, then reveal their evil appearance. They would appear from time to time in my dreams. Some of them spewed forth water, some spewed forth fire. Some were in human bodies with snakes' tails. No matter whether their appearances were distinct or not, they all had frightening shapes. That frightening quality was mostly something I felt, and not something I saw with my eyes. They entered my bones like a cold wind on a winter morning. They ran wild, and invaded every cell in my body—into those fresh living cells there pored a kind of sticky glue. In some people's lives, this makes them weak and sluggish—it was this kind of thing. Many people, once they have been infested by this kind of thing without being aware of it, drift along from then on, and never again have any interest in life or motivation to keep going.

On this particular day, this sticky slime launched an attack on me. I came up with one single thought: "Okay then, that's it, a person is just a bug infesting the earth, what's the use of all this hard work?" At this the sticky slime said: "That's right, you are already famous far and wide; all you have to do is while away the time, and your fame will surely spread through the world. Why do you have to come up this dissatisfied state of mind? Do you know? Right now you can borrow the power of Bonpo, without making any effort yourself, and everything will go as it should and follow the Path of least resistance. If you start having a different idea about how your future will ultimately turn out, you are really an ignoramus."

I thought, "That's right, isn't it? A human life lasts no more than a hundred years, what's the use of struggling?"

This way I would stop making an effort, and abandon my idea of leaving Bonpo to search for the real truth. Before long, I would be a teaching master. I was quite famous, and everyone had heard of me. I had mountains of offerings presented to me, and a storehouse full of gold and silver as big as a barn full of cow dung. In the future my disciples would be like the cattle and sheep of ten thousand families covering the mountains and fields. Some years on, when I was dying, when I was on the brink of death, I would discover that in reality I had no understanding, because I had been unable to relinquish so many things, like the temple buildings, like the gold and silver, like my favorite little disciple, like my snuff bottle ...

At that moment I finally realized that the so-called liberation that I had been searching for my whole life was in reality a picture of a cake painted on a wall. Later, when I died, my spiritual consciousness would be like a kite with a broken string, drifting this way and that, and would not be able to find the route it ought to follow.

This is the way it is. Your life will end. I heard the voice of a woman.

At this I started crying, and when the sound of the crying came forth from my throat, I woke up.

I thought: lucky it was a dream.

6 A Father's Tears

Early in the morning, I went to see my father, and told him what I was thinking. Although I already had planned to leave Bonpo, I still had not directly spoken of it with my father. My father was a master of the Bonpo teaching, a very dignified man. My father had a kind of unexplainable spiritual power in him. The story went that my father was able to ride a drum up into the sky. Quite a few people said they had seen this, but I never had. Father only let me study the scriptures. Father said: Although the esoteric techniques of the teaching are useful, you just wanted to make Bonpo truly flourish, and it was necessary to start out from the scriptures. If you do not read what has been handed down through the generations, this is not the techniques of the teaching. There have been so many people who were experts in the techniques of the Bonpo teaching, but they are all dead, and all that is left for this lifetime is the written culture.

I knew what my father said was right. Since Padmasambhava had come to Tibet several centuries before, Bonpo had suffered many blows, but the solid and strong vital energy of Bonpo had never been damaged, and the Bonpo culture had entered deeply into people's minds. Bonpo has a large number of scriptures. Though some of these scriptures are thought by people to be just the Buddhist scriptures under another guise, in fact Bonpo itself has a vastly different culture than Buddhism. My reputation had come from expounding these Bonpo scriptures.

My father took this important mission to make Bonpo flourish and put it on my shoulders.Father said: The flourishing of a religious sect is not a matter of how many followers it has, but of how its written culture flourishes. This is because, no matter how many followers there may be, this will all be blown away with the winds of the time, whereas the written culture can be handed down. Under my father's guidance, I had become a famous learned scholar in Bonpo.

Therefore, when he heard me say that I wanted to leave Bonpo, at first my father was shocked, and then he got angry.

My father very rarely got angry. Bonpo considers anger to be a major affliction that is to be counteracted and controlled. So my father's attendant Yeshe was shocked as he saw my father now. Later, he told me he had never seen my father's temper like this.

My father was shaking and he said: As long as I am breathing, you had better not do this, alright?

My father's eyes were overflowing with tears. Even though Tashi had reported this matter to him before, he had not taken it to heart. I had always been very diligent, and when I studied the Bonpo scriptures I went without sleep and neglected to eat. He did not believe I could really leave Bonpo.

In those years, more and more people were leaving Bonpo. Although the Bonpo scholars said that their own religion was older than Buddhism, still, there were many people abandoning it. There was nothing that could be done about it. In those years, more and more people were going to India to collect Buddhist scriptures and seek the Buddhist teachings. Every one of these students who came back could build up a big reputation in his local area, and every one with a reputation could attract a large group of disciples. Although the number of people who believed in Bonpo was not small, the trend was toward decline. My father had not thought that his own son too would leave him.

Father was silent for a long time. Then he said: "You must think about it more. No matter what they say, Bonpo is still something precious handed down from our ancestors. If you want to understand it fully, then stay in Bonpo. If you cannot understand it fully, then wait till after I am dead, then do what you want."

I went out silently. It was an unbearable feeling. It was clear to me that my father was truly angry. I loved my father very much. But to believe in this thing Bonpo — once I had doubts, then it lost its meaning.

I let out a long sigh.

I thought: I love my father, but I love truth even more.

7 Tashi's Threats

Tashi had told a lot of people about my plan. They all came to try to advise me not to leave Bonpo. Among them there were some very learned ones and geshes (professors of Divinity). The level of learning among Bonpo geshes is very high, and even Buddhist monks respect them very much. The three parts of the Bonpo Canon — scriptures, codes of rules, and commentaries — are very broad and deep, and unless you are an old man who has plumbed the depths of the scriptures, it is very hard to know their innermost secrets. They did not quote scriptures to me, because they knew full well that what they understood, I also understood, and what I did not understand, they did not understand either. When I had asked them some questions, I had always managed to frighten them. This is because there are some questions that people were asking Sakyamuni Buddha two thousand years ago, and even the Buddha had kept silent and not answered.

The geshes were trying to get to me emotionally, telling me to think of my father's reputation. There was something unspeakable, both emotionally and logically, for the son of a Bonpo master to end up leaving Bonpo and joining another religion. I too had thought of this. Thus the geshes understood that although they made every effort, with many things, all they could do was go along with the course of events.

Tashi was still making those covert threats, and all I did was give a slight smile.

Tashi had been my strongest supporter, and earlier on, when some people attacked me, he had helped me. But when I decided to leave Bonpo, he was the one who was most eager to use death-dealing methods to kill me. Before, in my eyes, he was the person closest to me, and he was the first person to know what was on my mind. Later I often lamented that the one who hurts you is often the one who knew you best.

Maybe Tashi thought that, compared to the loss of face for Bonpo, my physical body was not that important. Then too, he might have thought that with these death-dealing methods, at the same time they killed the person, they would also deliver the slain person from this world. As far as I was concerned, wouldn't this be a kind of compassion?

There were three people with Tashi who worked together to put these death-dealing methods into action. All of them were considered accomplished practitioners of Bonpo. Besides Tashi, each of the other men also had his own motives.

Pema Nam was a young man just a bit less well known than me, and he too wanted to be a master of the Bonpo teaching. Every time he saw people giving offerings to me, his mind was filled with jealousy. Verbally he catered to Tashi, and on the surface he was doing this for Bonpo, but in reality, he was acting to realize his own ambitions. Pema Nam was an eloquent speaker, and he had read many books. Whenever he spoke, he was very eloquent, but unfortunately he lacked attainment in experiencing enlightenment. Because he had not done much work at the level of the true nature of mind, his verbal eloquence had not made him detached from greed, anger, and ignorance. At the fire mandala for the death-dealing methods, he both chanted spells and visualized me being burned to cinders by the fire from the fire mandala. He looked ahead to the vacant teaching position that would be left behind after my death. That teaching position looked ordinary enough, but once he occupied it, then he would have limitless glory. In the eyes of the people of that area, a teaching master is a personage like a heavenly spirit.

Though each had his own motives, the other two men working against me were both sincerely devoted to Bonpo. They of course believed that by killing me, they would certainly avoid a humiliation for Bonpo.

The fire on the fire altar in that remote mountain valley burned for seven days and seven nights.

8 The Power of Spells and Adverse Causal Factors

I do not want to speak about whether or not the death-dealing methods were effective or not. I did not die, and from this point of view, it is clear that the spells did not achieve their objective. But I really did become sick. I developed a fever, and was in a stupor for many days. I felt as if my spirit was being torn to shreds, and everything around me faded out. It was even more like being drenched in a dirty muddy downpour, with everything all sticky and foul-smelling both inside and out.

There were many moments when I felt that I had already died, and had gone to hell. The hell I entered was not like in the traditional stories. My hell was filled with mud and muck, filled with bloody filth, filled with the anguished cries and curses of sinners. I did not see demons with ox heads or horse faces, and I did not see King Yama. I just felt as if I were groveling in the mud, and I could not see the light of the sky. I did not know which direction was which, and I could not find my way home. Everything before my eyes was pitch black, and I could not see anything that could be called light.

Sometimes I was being burned by fierce flames, sometimes I tumbled into an icy pit. Sometimes I was thrown onto a mountain of swords, and felt the pain of my heart being pierced with ten thousand arrows. Sometimes I was thrown into a giant grinding mill and my soul and physical body were being ground up by the sharp teeth extending from its two rotors. Sometimes my soul really flew away. I turned into powder, and was swirled around by the wind of karma. I felt that the universe itself was filled with numberless swirling eddies. Time and again those swirling eddies seized me and carried me off.

I do not know how long I was sick. During that time I had no concept of time or space. All I remember is that when I woke up, I found out that my father was ill. My father's illness was very serious. He was not far from the brink of death. My father opened his dry eyes and looked at me, with his eyes full of expectations.

Some people said my father was dying in my place. Relying on his power as an accomplished master, he had taken the full brunt of the power of those evil spells that had been launched at me, and from this, he achieved perfect peace and died. However, I knew that my father had already been sick before with some kind of heart disease. I thus suspected that perhaps he had been stricken because of my decision to leave Bonpo. No matter whether my father took on the power of the spells in my place, or if it was my decision to leave Bonpo that hit him, I felt that my father's death was linked to me.

This became a pain point in my life that I would not dare touch.

Some people say that the power of the spells of these death-dealing methods, though not enough to endanger my life, nevertheless did create a major adverse causal factor in my life. They did indeed mobilize many adverse occult powers that followed me as I lived through a lifespan of more than a hundred years. Later on, there was always dissension among my followers, and some say that this was connected to the adverse causal factors created by the Bonpo guardian spirits.

The day before I truly woke up, I had a dream. I dreamed that the sky was full of the power of the spells, and they were like yellow sand swirling in the sky, wrapping around me. Later I discovered a woman. She was like a lantern on a dark night coming from far away. The nearer the lantern came, the bigger it got, and it became brighter and brighter. The force of the spells that was like yellow sand on my body gradually dissolved away. What happened was like a bright light driving away a dark night.

As I looked on in a trance, the lantern in that woman's hand seemed like what you call a black hole in the universe, and the endless power of the spells was sucked into the black hole.

You know, of course, that the woman was Niguma.

Respectfully following the arrangements made by my father as he approached death, without waiting until I had really recovered my health, the Bonpo elders conducted a ceremony.

Half holding me up, half supporting me, they let me occupy the master's seat.

In this fashion, I inherited my father's position as a master of the teaching.

9 Having No Choice but to Occupy the Master's Seat

That day had been picked by a renowned Bonpo master as an auspicious day, and all the Bonpo temples in the area had been thoroughly cleaned. The believers joyously sang and laughed and talked. In the area I had a very lofty reputation. I had begun to lecture on the teachings when I was thirteen years old. When lecturing, I could cite from more than seven hundred scriptures, and people praised me as a spiritual prodigy. When I succeeded to the position of a master of the teaching, it could be said that people's expectations were focused on me.

That morning I woke up very early. My state of mind was complicated. On one hand, I was very satisfied with the congregation's trust in me. On the other hand, I also felt a certain heaviness, because ultimately my heart was not in Bonpo. My intention was already set: sooner or later I would leave Bonpo, and go to India. In the normal course of thing, in religious groups in general, who knows how many ugly situations develop due to struggles to take over controlling power within the religion. Yet the strange thing was that, in Bonpo, I had won unified support from top to bottom. Although Pema Nam also wanted to be the religious leader, this was just a thought. He struggled against me, but he did not have sufficient caliber. I often hoped that there could be someone that everyone believed in, who would come and take my place as a master of the teaching, so that I could go off to India without anything to hold me back. But many venerable figures were very forcefully urging me to take the position. I understood that all people need something to rely on psychologically, and often it is not important whether or not the entity they rely on is real—all that is necessary is that the believers accept that he exists. Just as people in general are willing to take an image made of clay and think of it as a real deity, they need there to really be a teaching master in the teacher's seat. As for what that teaching master is actually really like, that is a separate matter. What people need is that "teaching master" in their minds. It doesn't matter if what they are worshipping is a dog's tooth—as long as they take it as a sacred relic, then they will accordingly have the benefits of worshipping a sacred relic.

I saw in the distance a house with a canopy over it, hung with prayer flags and five-colored banners. Although it says in some books that Buddhism defeated Bonpo, in the lives of the common people, the power of Bonpo was still very great. Because Bonpo had many practical techniques, like casting horoscopes, and driving away demons, it was able to eliminate many real psychological afflictions for the common people. Very often, the ordinary folk blurred the boundary between Buddhism and Bonpo. Thus when I was installed as a Bonpo master, many people who believed in Buddhism also hung out their prayer flags. In all the houses they heated pine branches and fragrant things over slow fires in their stoves, and the unique clear scent of pine branches filled the mountain valley.

When the time came, the Bonpo monks and a great crowd of people from near and far gathered around the temple. They were wearing their holiday finery, and clustered together on the road on both sides of the temple.

The ceremony for assuming the teaching master's seat began, and the sounds of drums and cymbals and horns were heard. The solemn atmosphere was striking. Under the direction of those in charge of the ceremony, I presented the ritual offering of a piece of silk known as the *hada* to the generations of Bonpo patriarchs, and I heard the Bonpo monks begin singing a long song, with its simple sincere sound seeming to reach to the heavens. I seemed to see the generations of patriarchs smiling at me — they seemed to be entrusting me with the Bonpo scriptures. Suddenly my mind was filled with guilt, and I felt that somehow I could not face them. Though I had studied so many Bonpo scriptures, in the depths of my heart, they had never produced any faith. According to what it says in religious teachings, if there is no faith generated, then all forms of cultivation are meaningless. At this point I thought, even though I have no faith at all, yet I lecture on the teachings to so many believers — isn't this a bit deceptive?

After I offered the *hada*, the multitude of monks began to chant the scriptures — they were praying that the Bonpo teaching should last forever, and blessing the new master of the teaching. I received the *hadas* offered by the noble guests who had come to the place. They all sincerely wished me good fortune and long life, and gave me gifts, and I in turn gave presents to them.

10 Eyes Misty with Tears

After the ceremony for assuming the teaching master's seat was concluded, the crowd of believers, who had come from near and far, held horse races and archery contests. These competitions took place on a flat expanse of land at the foot of the mountain. With the honor guard and drum squad and attendants and guards clustered around me, I went to the competition ground to take part in the festivities.

The joyous atmosphere of the horse races filled my heart with an emotion that is hard to describe. For the horse races, the people first divided into small groups, and from each small group one was picked as the winner. Then they held a second round to decide the competition. When the first group's horses charged out from the starting line, the sound of the cheering from the onlookers sounded like thunder. The riders cheered too. The dust kicked up by the horses' hooves went everywhere, and covered the race course like a hazy veil.

Though the general atmosphere was joyous, to me it still seemed like being in a dream. This was because I knew that everything before my eyes would soon pass away, and we could not keep anything. Our activities could not leave the slightest trace, and our lives would flow away to no one knows where. At that point, I had a moment of anxiety. I was tired of all this noise, tired of all these empty illusions that were like flowers reflected in a mirror or the moon reflected in the water. I felt that I myself had become a pool of impermanence, in which countless bubbles were bursting and disappearing, while countless bubbles were forming. In each one I was dying, and in each one I was also being reborn. I developed a strong urge to leave.

Thus it was, after showing myself one more time, I returned to the temple.

When the ceremony for assuming the teaching master's seat was finished, I felt that my mind was absolutely empty. My father was gone. Though my father's health had not been good, I still thought his departure was connected to me. I understood that my father had received a major blow. Because he had raised me to become the Bonpo teaching master, he had expended a lot of mental effort. I remember that from the time I could understand things, my father was teaching me to do recitations, teaching me to do visualizations, teaching me the common rituals, and directing me to study all kinds of Bonpo scriptures. I remember my father smiling with delight the day I first went up to the podium to lecture on the scriptures. My father was very kind, and he never berated me. In my father's eyes, his son was truly a sage who had come again. Besides the fact that I was born in an easy delivery so no blood was shed, this was also because my horoscope birth sign was the four tigers, and this is the sign of great nobility. My father strongly believed that because of my birth, Bonpo would flourish. Many times the flourishing of a religion is due to a great personage coming into the world. My father saw Bonpo as more important than his life. His hope was that, in the hands of this son, Bonpo would become the great religion lighting up Tibet, as it had been centuries earlier.

But I had broken my father's heart. When my father departed, he could no longer speak, and in fact he had no need to speak. He had already said everything before his eyes closed. I heard and understood that message. I knew my father hoped I would take back what I had said before. In that instant, I was with my father on the brink of death. But Niguma appeared there in my mind too, and I even heard her talking to me. Then I heaved a long long sigh.

Just as I was sighing, the fire of my father's life was extinguished. His pupils dilated. I even forgot to say a prayer according to the Bonpo style. It was as if I had been hit by a thunderbolt. After quite a while, I kept saying again and again, as if I had gone crazy: I have no father!

I no longer have my father! My tears gushed out, and I had a strange blockage in my chest.

My father's attendant Yeshe took me off to one side.

Before long, I heard the geshes vigorously chanting the scriptures. I felt that the sky had gone gray as ash.

11 Passion for Life Gone Away

Not long after my father's passing, I gave a lecture on a scripture. The one I lectured on was the *Dolnyi Kelsang*. This is a famous scripture that is called a hidden treasure, a *terma*. In the history of Tibet, there have been many scriptures that were preserved in the form of *terma*. These are the same sort as those Buddhist scriptures that were unearthed in your hometown of Dunhuang from the Mogao Caves. In order to avoid having the scriptures destroyed in the great disasters and upheavals that would destroy Buddhism, some people of knowledge took the scriptures and hid them away. According to the way they were hidden away, there are the ones that were hidden in the ground, the ones that were hidden in water, the ones that were hidden on cliffs or in caves in cliffs … In all, there are six forms of these hidden treasures: earth, water, fire, air, space, and consciousness.

Dolnyi Kelsang is a treasure of consciousness. This means it was hidden away in the depths of human consciousness. According to the Bonpo explanation, when a certain scripture might be difficult to pass on in the event of natural disasters or man-made calamities, that religion's deities or saints can hide the scripture in the depths of their own consciousness or the consciousness of other people. Many years later, when the sky has cleared, with the support of some esoteric spiritual power, these treasures of consciousness can be revealed again by being written out or recited. The people who do this might be Bonpo masters, or they might be illiterate herdsmen. The one who bestowed the hidden treasure and the one who dug it up might be the same person, or they might be separated by many generations. The scripture I was lecturing on this time, *Dolnyi Kelsang*, was a hidden treasure of consciousness scripture handed down from a man called Tulku Dolnyi.

According to the explanation of the ancients, words flow out from a bright emptiness, and in reality this is the manifestation of the Dharmakaya of the buddhas and bodhisattvas making use of the written word. I can understand this explanation very well.

The first time I lectured on the scriptures with the status of a teaching master, many people had come to hear me with high expectations. Unexpectedly, on this occasion when I lectured on the scriptures, I did not have the least enthusiasm. Many people thought this was the original incident that brought sorrow to my father. I was the only one who knew that I already had major doubts about the Bonpo religion. In my eyes, these so-called scriptures that came from the treasures of consciousness could not be put on the same level as the Buddhist scriptures, which were clearly passed down by people with the eye for the truth. Though I clearly understood this, in a different sense, the treasures of consciousness were scriptures from deep in the memory. I did not even know that almost all the scriptures of the early period of Buddhism were all transmitted from memory. But this thread of doubt was being woven into a giant screen, and this became a big barrier between me and Bonpo that could not be pushed aside.

There was nothing to do about it.

When you lose faith in something, your enthusiasm for life can quietly go away. If you very much respect a person, and then suddenly suspect that he might be mediocre, or even contemptible, you are sure to have this kind of fall. When that kind of bond dissolves, it is like the tide going out: it cannot be pulled back. I even had doubts about my father approving me as a teacher—this was the most deadly thing. I was thinking: if the thing that I have pursued my whole life cannot bring me self-confidence and peace of mind, what is the meaning of this kind of belief?

Looking at the offerings of the faithful piled up, I was depressed and unhappy. I saw clearly that these offering could not change anything. If I was ignorant, these offerings could not make me understand clearly. If I was troubled, these offerings could not make me cool and calm. I was seeking the truth, and these offerings could not lead me to the Path. I was looking for three meals a day, and a few clothes to wear every year, and this mountain of offerings, to me, was just a decoration.

I wanted to look for something I had not been able to find in all these months and years.

But the more deeply I studied it day after day, the more doubts I had about Bonpo. Although there were some truths in it, the obscure transmission of Bonpo had already cast a shadow in my mind that I could not wipe away. The line of transmission from teacher to disciple is the life of the esoteric teaching. If there is no transmission, then there is no esoteric teaching. Every time I lectured on the scriptures, I could never speak of the doubts that were in my mind. Nevertheless, these seeds of doubt gradually took root—they began to sprout and flower and bear fruit. The result was to make it that I was no longer the energetic practitioner I had been in the past. I began to think about questions I had never thought about before.

I began to come into contact with some Buddhist scriptures. I discovered that what I had entered into was a whole world, an incomparably vast and profound world. Though I had not yet glimpsed the whole thing, the dazzling light that hit my eyes woke me up. I could even acknowledge that the most refined parts of Bonpo could have come from Buddhism. Every time I lectured on the Bonpo scriptures, even though I tried hard to speak of the special excellence of the Bonpo teaching in very strong language, I myself discovered I had no confidence in this. In all the times I lectured on the Bonpo scriptures, I never belittled Buddhism. I went so far as to ignore the reaction of Tashi and others like him, and time after time I praised the great scope and depth of the Buddhist system. Even the stupidest person could see my zeal for Buddhism had already clearly outstripped my love for Bonpo.

Tashi's aversion to me had already become public. He hoped that a teaching master could spread the Bonpo religion. From his own personal experience, Tashi had verified the special excellence of the Bonpo teaching, and because Tashi had a deep faith in Bonpo, his faith had become the most powerful guarantee. From what I heard, there were still several men who continued to employ the death-dealing methods against me, and among them the most fanatical was Pema Nam. Pema Nam poured out invective against me, and he incited quite a few die-hard Bonpo believers against me. Although they did not dare to make trouble publicly, out in the remote mountain valleys the fires on the mandala of death-dealing methods again blazed up. Some people again employed curses, and buried black cattle horns and other such defensive items in certain places where I often went.

In many absent-minded moments I could see dangerous apparitions. For example, I always could see those mountain spirits or dragons, appearing in the guise of giant scorpions. They wriggled along, filling the sky and covering the earth. Sometimes they showed their fangs and claws; sometimes they opened their mouths wide, wanting to suck out my vital essence. They were like waves washing over me, wave after wave, never stopping. Whenever one of these times came, I always felt that my chest was constricted and my heart was pounding. I knew that all of this was because I was too concerned with such rituals. In times past, I heard tell that such rituals had taken away the lives of many who were slain by them. It was precisely all these stories I had heard about this — that had created this great pressure on me. Only many years later did I understand that all these ominous signs of misfortune and danger in reality were coming from my own mind.

But before I clearly understood the nature of mind, fearsome black clouds were spread all across the sky of my life. During those days, I could not see the sun. No, if someone told me there was a sun, this was only something I was yearning for in the future. I could never forget Niguma, and I could never forget the prediction that a great accomplished teacher called Amoga had made about me. He said my fundamental teacher was Niguma. He said I would found a religious lineage called Shangpa Kagyu and I would have more than a hundred thousand disciples. In my eyes, what he said was a prediction, and it was not as if he had drawn up a blueprint for my life. Later on, the course of my life really did fulfill that plan.

Among all those dangerous signs, the one that for me was impossible to forget, was that mass of scorpions writhing around filling the sky and covering the earth. This almost became an image I could not get rid of. Later on, when I was wounded or attacked by petty people, I would always think of those scorpions.

Throughout my life, petty people like that bunch of scorpions were the nightmare I could not get away from. Whether it was when I left Bonpo, or when I was seeking the Dharma later on, or even when I had many disciples, I always could feel drops of spit flying at me. I was always being vilified by people. This is because I always appeared to be—note that I say "appeared to be" and not "really was"—very outstanding. No matter whether it was in Bonpo, or later in India, or even later when I had a group of followers, I was always like the sun striking the eyes of worldly people. Wherever I went, I was always someone who could not be ignored. That's why many people always took me as their rival and attacked me. Little did they know that in the eyes of a wise person, the behavior of petty people is as ridiculous as ants trying to shake a tree.

When I was wrapped up in a depressed mood as if covered with a black cloud, I felt that I was very isolated. You always say that when a man transcends, he cannot but be lonely. You may be right. But in those days I discovered that this isolation which wrapped around me had become physical, almost tangible. Those people who had treated me well before now all became mouths spewing isolation at me. In their looks, in their unspoken feelings, in every silent hint, they were saying I was preposterous and did not know good from bad. In their eyes, abandoning such a good teaching master was not right, and now I wanted to go off without rhyme or reason to some unknown destination—this was really a farce.

I felt myself enclosed in a many-layered formless net, and though it was formless, it was still very strong and tenacious. It was like a fishnet imbued with a tough, pliable power. It was like glass—it was solid, though it let the light through. It was like a net in the sky that was present everywhere. It cut me off from the world, and wanted to make me suffocate and die.

Though a Bonpo teaching master is looked upon with real favor and glory, this glory is as natural as a long beard on a man well along in years. This is regarded as wealth and good fortune, this is the formless bequest fashioned for us over a thousand years by generations of masters. In Tibet, Bonpo is more ancient than Buddhism, and it has influenced the ancestors of the Tibetan people more directly, and long ago soaked into the "field of the storehouse consciousness" of the people. Of course, you could also call this "the collective unconscious." This is a term that only appeared in the last millennium. This is really a great formless asset, enough for me to go through life without sorrows or worries.

In the eyes of many people, anyone who would abandon these riches is no different than a fool or a madman.

It's not that I didn't know this, but I thought, in human life, apart from the needs of the physical body, there is also something more important. It is an ability that goes beyond the physical body, and the material plane, and the conventional world. It is the reason I am living, and it is the meaning of life. In other words, it was for this purpose that I came into this world.

I thought: Give Bonpo to the people who love Bonpo and let them go believe in it. As for me, I will go seek the woman who calls me to be concerned with the deeper level of life.

I could never forget that name: Niguma.

12 The Bequest of the Spiritual Secret

One day when I was still a boy, my mother told me about the bequest of the spiritual secret. My mother said that in a dream, she had seen a woman, and she was very beautiful. That woman was always looking at her and smiling. Mother said that the woman's smile was clear and bright, and would send out waves like halos. As these waves of light washed over her, she felt that the ordinary world of mortals was transformed into the Pure Land.

After my mother told me this story, that night I dreamed of this woman. She said to me, in the future, no matter when, or no matter what things appeared, all I had to do was chant "Niguma Khyenno" and she would help me attain what I hoped for.

In my dreams, I witnessed her saying this countless times.

In one particular dream, I encountered countless demons. They bared their fangs and rushed at me. I knew that my young body could not fill these huge mouths, so I cried out "Niguma Khyenno!" At that instant, Niguma appeared. Those fangs immediately turned into smoke.

In later dreams, it was very similar. No matter what dangers I was surrounded with, all I had to do was call out "Niguma Khyenno," and all sorts of evil scenes changed into auspicious signs.

Later on in life, when I encountered some dangerous situation in waking life, I would always invoke Niguma this way, and I was always able to have misfortune change into good fortune.

It was just these invocations that were repeatedly effective that made me never forget this bequest from my mother.

During the time when the fire on the death-dealing mandala was burning bright day after day, when all these evil signs kept appearing, as soon as I invoked "Niguma Khyenno," the oppressive feeling in my mind would immediately dissolve. Sometimes, as this oppressive feeling dissolved away, I was alone. But when I thought of Niguma, I realized that I was not alone. That's right, I was not only myself. I also had Niguma. Those two eyes of Niguma's, so full of compassion and mercy, were always silently gazing upon me. As my mother had told me, these eyes would send out waves of light. These waves that felt so powerful carried with them a kind of purity, a kind of peace, a kind of warm sweetness only mothers have, that would enter into the depths of my spirit.

In these times I would cry out with no restraint: Niguma, my mother lifetime after lifetime.

This power that comes from the depths of the spirit is present everywhere and always, and almost filled the years of childhood and my youth. Whenever the uproar before my eyes dissolved away, Niguma would appear before me. Later on, this became the indispensable atmosphere of my life.

I think that, even if those men had really had the capacity to slay people, Niguma would not have looked on and not saved me.

Therefore, when I heard that there were some people who wanted to slay me, I just gave a slight smile. Though I did visualize the defensive curtain of fire, still I thought, even without the defensive curtain of fire, Niguma would never abandon me.

13 The Adversarial Bodhisattva

Before I publically disclosed my decision to leave Bonpo, I first went to see my mother. My mother knew what was in my mind. My mother said she just hoped I would promise her one thing. First, not to go to India, because it was a long journey, and there were many robbers on the road, and this could put my life in danger. She just hoped that I would be able to find a way to practice austerities in Tibet. My mother said: "No matter if you believe in Bonpo or in Buddhism, you still are my son." She said: "If you can find someone in Tibet who can be your teacher, then first practice austerities in Tibet. If you cannot find such a person, then it will not be too late to go to India."

I made this promise to my mother.

One month later, I personally presided over the ritual for seating a teaching master, and I turned over my position as a Bonpo teacher to Yeshe. He had been my father's attendant, and later he had stayed on with me. Yeshe was a dependable, honest person, but he did not have the eloquence of Pema Nam. But I thought that no matter what religion, for a teaching master, the basic quality needed is goodness. Verbal cleverness is not important, as long as the teacher has a good heart.

They were feeling a lot of pain about me leaving Bonpo, so the atmosphere at the ceremony, which should have been joyous, was a bit suspicious and subdued. My leaving was seen as something that would cause a long-term loss of face for Bonpo.

At that time I basically did not know that Pema Nam, if he did not succeed me as teaching master, would bear me a deadly hatred. He vowed to become my lifelong enemy. Not much time had passed since I had left Bonpo, and Pema Nam was following me like a shadow. He became a shadow that I could not get rid of over the first half of my life. All the many adversities and troubles I had later were connected to him. After I founded my own religious group, Pema Nam still incited other groups to oppose me. Many years later, he died of a strange evil disease. His written works are still in circulation, however, and he has become a famous "Buddhist scholar."

In the second half of my life, whenever I remember Pema Nam, I always smile and call him "an adversarial bodhisattva."

If it were not for him, my life might have gone much more smoothly, but there would have been fewer of these uncanny events that seem like legends.

Chapter 2

On the Pilgrim's Road

The Secret History of Khyungpo says:

The ritual fire on these fire mandalas of the death-dealing methods is always ablaze. It mainly employs two kinds of evil spells. One kind is the death-dealing spell, one kind is the barrel of demons spell. The main purpose of the former is to cut off people's lives. Those who are cursed with it mostly have their lives ended, and not in a good way. The latter can make people plunge into a barrel of demons from which there is no way to escape. It is said that the latter kind of slaying is the most final kind of slaying. The former method can only be used on the physical body, while the latter can slay the spirit.

1 The Feeling of Weightlessness

Khyungpo Naljor left the Bonpo monastery, which was the biggest one in the area, and occupied the greater part of the mountain top.

His mental state was complex. I originally thought that he must certainly have had a sense of relaxation and relief. But in this *Secret Transmission* we do not see any record of this. Reading between the lines, I see on the contrary something extremely complicated.

I call that kind of feeling "weightlessness."

When he left the Bonpo monastery, Khyungpo Naljor suddenly had a feeling of being in suspended animation. He felt that he no longer had anything to rely on. In that instant he suddenly understood why all people need religion, why they need some kind of spiritual support, why people all must search so hard to find something beyond form. He said that religion certainly has its source in this kind of feeling of solitude, of having nothing to rely on. He felt that he himself has suddenly been "flung into" a strange unfamiliar state. Though he had made the choice himself, the feeling of being "thrown into something" was still very clear. More than nine hundred years later, a man named Heidegger interpreted this feeling, and people acclaimed him as the greatest philosopher of the twentieth century.

This feeling of being isolated and being flung into something unfamiliar stayed with Khyungpo Naljor for a long time. He felt as if he were wandering in an infinite space and a time without beginning or end, like a fallen leaf on a vast ocean. Sometimes he was like a yellow leaf blowing around in the autumn wind, flying from here to there in the sky, letting that autumn wind tear him apart. Originally he had thought that, when he had left Bonpo, he would be like a wild horse who had escaped being tied up and could happily run free. But he had not anticipated that he would suddenly have a kind of feeling of weightlessness.

Only when he thought of Niguma, did he feel there was something he could rely on.

But at this time Niguma was still only a symbol to him, and he was not able to merge her into this life so that she could become a spiritual support. Thus he often went into that feeling of weightlessness, and he could not master his mind.

He thought: How hard it is to seek true liberation!

He was right. Before he left Bonpo, he had so ardently wanted to leave it. He was so sick of those chattering people, and now he did not see them anymore. Though they were still busy chattering away, he didn't see them any more, he never saw their annoying eyes and faces any more. Who would have predicted that after these things were gone, he would end up with a feeling of facing the void. This too was unbearable to him.

He thought that this made it clear that all he had practiced before had not worked after all. As long as the mind needs something to rely on, this will not produce liberation.

But no matter what, Khyungpo Naljor had said goodbye to that illustrious Bonpo temple.

2 Past Lives Clearly Awakened To

Nine hundred years later, the author saw the ruins of this monastery. The religion that had had its temporary era of glory no longer showed the splendor of its early days. All this had been dispersed in the hurricane of time. The Bonpo monastery too, with its own life history, showed me the meaning of "all product are impermanent."

One time when we met, Khyungpo Naljor told me about the complicated psychology of his leaving the Bonpo monastery. On the one hand, he had a feeling of extraordinary relief. On the other hand, he couldn't help but have some worries for the future. This was the first choice of his life. Whether he would succeed or fail was all still unknown. He did not know where he would go, and he did not know what kind of transformations he would undergo. He saw the bluebirds circling high in the sky: they stretched out their wings, and flew carefree among the clouds. He saw how relaxed they looked, and felt their freedom and ease. This scene affected him, and banished the sense of loss he had after leaving the Bonpo monastery. All in all, he had spend more than twenty years in that splendid, imposing place. He had passed his growing-up years there, his childhood and his youth. The most formative period of his life had been lived there. Though he had doubts about the Bonpo religion, the formal instruction he had received in that monastery became a strong solid foundation for his whole life. The deep refinement and erudition of the Bonpo culture became for him another kind of spiritual nourishment.

I think that the reason for the great successes Khyungpo Naljor later achieved must be related to his absorbing the nourishment of many religions. Many times those who just understand one kind of religion cannot help but be limited by it. A true great teacher is formed by being nurtured by many cultures. That's why I often cannot help but laugh at those so-called great teachers who are complacent and set in their ways, and think they are right. Though they have been immersed in their own territory their whole lives, this immersion had become the greatest barrier for them. Someone sitting at the bottom of a well has a hard time seeing the whole sky.

Khyungpo Naljor saw a mountain range in the distance. The far-off mountains looked like the backbone of a wild animal running, rising and falling without end. That turbulent energy unfurled itself and flowed into his mind and spirit. I can understand his state of mind at this moment. Many times, I too have faced this kind of decision. Human life is made of decisions: countless decisions make up a rich complex human life. There are some people who are always able at the critical moments to understand their own fate clearly—because of this, they become the ones people call "great personages."

When Khyungpo Naljor left Bonpo and went toward Buddhism, he first chose the Nyingmapa school of Tibetan Buddhism. This is an ancient religion, with a culture of its own and great renown. For Khyungpo Naljor, it was already like thunder sounding in his ears. Khyungpo Naljor yearned for the Great Perfection of Nyingmapa. This teaching had the same kind of great reputation.

3 Encountering the Great Perfection

I have used the special mentality of a literary man to understand Khyungpo Naljor's state of mind at that time. At that time, having gone through many years of training in wisdom, I also could make contact with Khyungpo Naljor's mind. I often followed in his footsteps, and merged into that spirit of seeking.

In my view, Khyungpo Naljor had gone into that monastery with a face full of windblown dust from traveling. At that time he was twenty-eight years old, and his talent was in full flower.

He had come to pay a visit to an eminent teacher. He was called Losanger, and the story was that he had achieved the Dharma of Great Perfection.

The monastery was not large, and it was built in the Tibetan style.

Even now you can still see this kind of building in the mountain valleys of the Tibetan lands. Many times this has become a symbol, conveying the kind of spirit we long for.

Losanger was very pleased that Khyungpo Naljor had come. He praised Khyungpo Naljor for being a top-grade vessel for the Dharma. He did not speak in terms like "forsaking the darkness for the light" — on the contrary, he placed a very high value on the Bonpo culture.

Khyungpo Naljor was seeking the Dharma of Great Perfection from Losanger.

Losanger said:

"Son, this Dharma of Great Perfection is very excellent, it was taught by the original enlightened one, the Tathagata Samantabhadra. Its philosophy is that all phenomena are fundamentally pure, empty and without inherent nature.

"It is inherent wisdom, and it is the diamond body.

"Its worldview is that all phenomena are without inherent nature, are all equal, are the original reality, are one.

"Later on you will come to understand the encompassing profundity of this teaching."

4 The Original Enlightenment of Independent True Thusness

Not long after Khyungpo Naljor left Bonpo and came to study with Lama Losanger, Pema Nam also left Bonpo. He followed in the tracks of Khyungpo Naljor, and he also came to study the Dharma of Great Perfection. Khyungpo Naljor was very happy, and he thought Pema Nam's action was the same kind of awakening as his own. By nature Khyungpo Naljor was broadminded and tolerant, and he was always happy with any good deed. He even thought that Pema Nam's action was an expression of support for him. This was because, after Pema Nam left Bonpo, there was even more criticism within the religion, and gossip everywhere. There were many explanations for Pema Nam's leaving, but everyone said he had entered into delusion, that it was wrong to leave the post of Bonpo teaching master, and to go instead to be a novice in another religious group (Actually Khyungpo Naljor at this time was not even a novice Buddhist monk, and he had not even accepted the rules of discipline for novices.). There were also other explanations, and in general they were hard to listen to. That is why Khyungpo Naljor took Pema Nam's leaving Bonpo as an expression of support for what he had done.

Only later did he find out that the major reason for Pema Nam's leaving Bonpo was because he had not become a master of the teaching. His hatred for Khyungpo Naljor was deep in his bones. He had taken a vow before the guardian spirits of Bonpo that he would oppose Khyungpo Naljor for three lifetimes. I felt some doubt about this vow. I did not understand why Pema Nam's vow was known to the author of the *Secret History of Khyungpo*. This book considers those people who were to be opponents of Khyungpo in the future as the reincarnations of Pema Nam. The story goes that this was verified by someone who had achieved the power to know past lives. The records of Buddhism are filled with these kinds of wonder stories.

Khyungpo Naljor very quickly comprehended the teaching of great complete fundamental awakening, and not long after starting to study with Lama Losanger, he already stood out among his disciples. Sometimes the master called on him to give lectures on the teaching to newly arrived disciples.

If we look at the causal chain here, Khyungpo Naljor first came in contact with the Great Perfection. With this causal basis, after many years the Light of Great Perfection became one of the cores of the Shangpa Kagyu teaching. Together with the Great Mudra of Light, it was handed down as a torch through generations of teachers. In 1995, when the author was in Shangpa Kagyu, the master teacher first passed on to him the Great Perfection. After this, I gradually comprehended such essential teachings as the *Five Great Diamonds Teachings of Niguma* and the *Six Achievements Teachings of Niguma.*

At this point, in the light I had encountered, I asked Khyungpo Naljor to explain to me the inner core of the methods for cultivating the Great Perfection. The specific contents I have already written about in the chapter "Reaching Accord with the Inherent Nature of Mind" in the book *The Great Mudra of Light: Real Practice, Sudden Entry.*

Khyungpo Naljor said to me: "Son, after you come to know the fundamental enlightenment of things as they are, in your mind will appear the ultimate light of empty inherent nature. Once you have clearly understood inherent nature, then you can gradually detach from clinging and attachment, and always abide in empty inherent nature. You must leave behind ignorance and delusion and lack of perception. After you recognize fundamental enlightenment, you will understand clearly that everything in the world appears from inherent nature — this is the real door to liberation. You must experience this truly; you must not harbor doubts. After a long time, even your cultivation of practice will merge into inherent nature, and without the least bit of clinging or attachment, will dissolve into formlessness.

"As you make progress in cultivating practice, after you have had precious religious experiences, your life will be magnetized, and you will produce a mind of infinite faith. It will be as if you have the wish-granting gem, and all false thoughts will dissolve into inherent nature. Then other people, external objects, the world of emotions, the world in which we live, the whole universe, will revert to being illusory appearances, arising in the moment within your enlightened true nature. Then you will recognize clearly that all of this does not come from some external world, but originates from the inherent nature of your mind. Then you will have the confidence of a sage king who turns the Wheel of the Dharma, and you will be able to face the whole world as a sage king who turns the Wheel of the Dharma. At that time, because you have awakened to the fundamentally enlightened inherent nature, you will have the four great elements of transformation. Then, because of this ultimate liberation which you have attained through this rainbow transformation, you will no longer have to rely on this ordinary physical body, and you will have even more real experiences of liberation.

"Then your faith will be able to be as invulnerable as empty space, as immovable by the eight winds: prosperity, decline, honor, disgrace, praise, censure, pleasure and suffering as a great mountain, shining everywhere like the sun. You should know that this kind of complete inherent faith has its source in the perception and practice of the Great Perfection. You should understand clearly that you will be inherently liberated from the myriad things and events without cultivating practice, and all appearances in the end will dissolve into the light of the immaculate original reality. That state is like emptiness entering emptiness, like water dissolving in water, like clouds dispersing in the bright blue sky, like a light dissolving into infinity. You must understand that in an instant your own body may be dissolved into your own body, and you will be liberated from the myriad forms without relying on any external objects. This is like breaking a rock with a rock, like melting iron with iron, or like cleaning earth with earth. Within this ultimate immediate essence of inherent nature, the myriad forms are liberated in comprehension of the immediate original awareness. When you are like this, it is like pouring water into the ocean. The mother light of the fundamental essence and the child light of your own awakened mind come together and merge. Then, with what you rely on empty, and inherent nature empty, you can achieve liberation.

"If you can realize the rainbow transformation, then your body and mind and awareness will dissolve into the inherent body of perfect light at the rainbow transformation. Then you will awaken to the fact that the fundamental situation is fundamental enlightenment, and you will mesh with the root source of the myriad phenomena. Then you will understand that the light that appeared when you practice sudden awakening is just the appearance of inherent mind, its essential nature, like the images that appear when you are looking in the mirror. Because you have already meshed with the source of phenomena, the realization that happens at this time is like a mother and child meeting again after a long separation. Then you can attain ultimate liberation.

"Therefore, do not cling to that perfect light. Ultimately it will dissolve in the blink of an eye into your own body. All kinds of manifestations in the end return to the empty inherent nature. That which clearly understands is your immediate fundamental awareness. You will understand that all the many appearances since time without beginning are all ignorance, and beings revolving through the six planes of existence are all like illusory reflections in a mirror. Though so many things appear, they are still like dreams or illusions. At this time, your ignorance too will dissolve by itself, and you will no longer be troubled by the illusory forms of samsara. You will already have witnessed the real truth of existence — that is, fundamental enlightenment. False thoughts immediately dissolve by themselves, and there is no further need to oppose them. Then you will abide forever in the immediate reality that is right there, and so will no longer have any more doubt or confusion. You will always be in a state of stable concentration, but without leaving behind the necessities of everyday life like food, clothing, shelter. Whether you are walking or standing or sitting or lying down, you will not leave the empty inherent nature, and your actions will be like pouring water into water. Therefore, your deliberate cultivation will be like a snake uncoiling, and you will be able to spontaneously open up. From this point on, you will not have to rely on cultivating contrived efforts.

But if you cannot understand this level of perception, if you cannot recognize the true form of fundamental enlightenment, but instead you want to leave behind the true form and go off to seek in other places, or go beyond mind to seek the Dharma, then you will be going back into a blind alley and again be troubled by illusory forms."

Khyungpo Naljor said: "Remember, you must recognize the enlightenment that is right here right now, and you must always be in accord with the independent fundamental enlightenment of True Thusness."

"In the light I encountered on that occasion, Khyungpo Naljor told me to lie down on the earth, and fix my gaze on the sky. I just saw the silky blue sky, with no lines, no waves, a single expanse with no visible boundaries. That boundless expanse of blue filled my mind and gradually merged with me. The teacher told me to take my own mind and consciousness and merge with that endless blue sky, without getting attached to any forms, without thinking of good and evil, without pursuing the past, without thinking of the future — just to awaken into pure clarity here and now. I felt my mind and consciousness merging with emptiness. Gradually there was no me any more, and I just felt a grand clear light and empty spirit melting me.

Then from the sky there suddenly came the sounds of birds calling."

The teacher said: "Did you hear those birds calling? ... Right, that was it."

I suddenly understood what the teacher wanted to say.

In the utter stillness, I heard Khyungpo Naljor's hearty laugh.

His laughter was like a lily blooming in a deep valley.

5 The Bright Emptiness of Awakening

According to what is recorded in the *Secret History of Khyungpo*, for three months after Khyungpo Naljor had left Bonpo, the fire on the mandala in that mountain valley was still burning. Several Bonpo practitioners who deeply hated him were still at work on death-dealing magical methods. Once Khyungpo Naljor left, there were some people who also lost their faith in Bonpo and left it. This is why those Bonpo practitioners who were experts in death-dealing magical methods decided to make an example of them as a warning to others. They spread the word everywhere that the Bonpo guardian spirits were angry, and wanted to punish these "traitors." Every time someone else appeared who had left Bonpo, a new name would be added to the prayer paper on the death-dealing mandala.

What was written on this prayer paper were the intentions of those employing the death-dealing methods, and these were burned on the mandala of death-dealing magic. The names on the prayer paper of those they wanted to kill started with Khyungpo Naljor, and gradually came to include a lot of people. One day one of these people was riding a horse, when the horse bolted, and the rider was thrown off. His foot did not come out of the stirrup, and his head was smashed in by a rock on the ground. This event seemed to prove the story that was going around that the guardian spirits were angry. Some people whose minds had been wavering since Khyungpo Naljor's departure did not now dare to think of leaving anymore.

Whenever they saw the ritual fire on the fire mandala of death-dealing magical methods, there were some good people who were concerned for Khyungpo Naljor's safety.

After Khyungpo Naljor had studied at Lama Losanger's place for several months, he had already completely grasped the message of the Great Perfection. He practiced according to the teaching, but without any obvious sensations. This was because in Bonpo they also had a teaching they called the Great Perfection, with several stages of perception, which was very similar to the Buddhist teaching. Because the chain of causal conditions made it that way, whenever Khyungpo Naljor was practising meditation, Niguma always appeared before his eyes, and his spirit became entranced and would not stabilize.

When he saw that Khyungpo Naljor's spirit would not stabilize and focus, Pema Nam was secretly pleased. He took this symptom as a sign that the death-dealing methods of the Tashis were having an effect. Before his departure, Pema Nam used his own wealth to make offerings to these people who cultivated the death-dealing magical methods, so his name was not on their death list.

Khyungpo Naljor told Lama Losanger about the affair of some people using death-dealing magical methods against him. The Teacher said: "Do not be concerned. You are a person of great capacity, with an inherent ability to subdue demons. Ordinary worldly demons basically cannot get near you. If you have doubts, you can visualize a protective screen of fire. Visualize that on your five chakras there are five seed-words, and they can shoot out shafts of light like a wheel, which form a screen of fire of diamond shafts around your body on all sides like a cylinder. If you do this, the power of demonic spells cannot come near you. It's too bad that you have not yet illuminated mind and seen its inherent nature, but you have not. When you enter directly into the stable concentration of the Great Perfection, and your mind is like empty space, and you are not attached to any forms — when you are this way, these worldly demons will not be able to find you."

Khyungpo Naljor was following his teacher's instructions, but because the chain of causal conditions made it that way, he still could not achieve peace of mind.

Though, in theory, he understood clearly the special excellence of the Great Perfection, and he acknowledged that mental state as completely wondrous, and under his teacher's instruction he had tasted the flavor of the Dharma, still, he had no way to preserve that realization, and he could not become one with it. This was because there were concerns in his mind. He was always thinking of that prediction given to him by that great accomplished Indian teacher, and it was impossible to put his mind to rest. False thoughts were constantly assailing him, and dragging him out of that realization of the Great Perfection.

That awakening, that empty illumination, was like a thread blowing around in the wind — although it was always flashing in front of his eyes, he had no way to hold onto it. Even if sometimes he did catch hold of it, the realization changed into a wind, and slipped through his fingers.

But that concern for his destiny always troubled him. Khyungpo Naljor's kinsmen all knew that not long after he was born, a very accomplished teacher had come from India. The man was very special — he looked august and ancient, and his bearing was out of the ordinary. The story goes that he flew in like a sparrow. The people in the family became aware of a dark halo appearing in the sky, and that man descended to earth. He called himself Amoga, and this name became, from then on, something warm and sweet in Khyungpo Naljor's mind. That man consecrated Khyungpo Naljor with the Buddha of Eternal Life, and told his father, "This son of yours can be extraordinary. He will be the master on whom all sentient beings rely. You must bring him up well." Thanks to this scene, ever since he was born, Khyungpo Naljor's whole clan regarded him as a jewel among humans. Because of this, from an early age, Khyungpo Naljor was treated with incomparable respect."

Later, Khyungpo Naljor clearly remembered that when he was eight years old, he and his big sister were playing on the hillside. At that time, in the whole Khyungpo family, his big sister was the only one who did not treat him like some kind of future sage. His big sister was always teasing him by grabbing the roasted barley flour out of this hand, always wrestling him down and slapping his buttocks. Sometimes she would use so much force that his buttocks would turn red. He would cry out in pain, and his big sister would say: "Aren't you the future sage? How can you feel pain?" That particular day, his big sister got annoyed again, and took hold of Khyungpo Naljor and smashed him against the mountain. Khyungpo Naljor cried out in pain. As Khyungpo Naljor was crying out, he closed his eyes. He remembered that before he cried out, he had looked all around, and he thought he could not find anyone to rescue him; there was no sign of anyone around. When he closed his eyes and gave a loud cry, he heard a strange voice. Only later did he know that this was Amoga, the man who had given the prediction when he was born. Khyungpo Naljor saw a guy with long whiskers, how old he could not tell. All he could say was that he was between forty and sixty. Later, when Khyungpo Naljor went to India, he found out that even the people in India could not tell

Amoga's age. When his father saw him, he was like this, and a half century later, when his grandchildren saw him, he still had the same appearance. No one knows how long he ultimately lived. I've heard that he had been able to bring back the sweet dew of eternal life from the Buddha Land, and whenever he drank some, it could add another hundred years to his lifespan. Because such a thing is recorded, a thousand years later in China a bunch of charlatans have appeared who falsely claim that they can bring back the sweet dew from the Buddha Land, in order to swindle people out of large sums of money.

But Khyungpo Naljor knew that Amoga had really been able to bring back the sweet dew from the Buddha Land. One day many years later, he drank this sweet dew, which has a taste that cannot be described in human language. Because the sweet dew entered his body, his physiology underwent a great transformation. After that, he lived for one hundred and fifty years. Until he left the world, he was incomparably healthy.

After he cried out, Khyungpo Naljor saw Amoga. Amoga was already pulling him up. Amoga showed a look of anger, and said to Khyungpo Naljor's big sister, "Look!" The big sister then saw a strange sight: as Khyungpo Naljor was struggling, his feet were making many deep footprints in the rock, as if it were not rock, but soft mud. This rock later became a holy relic, and was visited by hundreds of thousands of believers. When I visited the Holy Shangpa Temple, I took a photo of the rock with deep footprints in it.

Amoga pointed out these footprints and said: "Look at this. You must not hit a bodhisattva. Hurry up and say you're sorry."

Although his big sister was surprised, she did not apologize. Although there were many people who recognized Khyungpo Naljor as the reincarnation of a holy sage, his big sister did not believe it. She did not believe that this little boy wiping his tears away could be a sage, and she did not believe that a little baby who wet the bed could be a sage, and most of all she did not believe that a cry baby who was always making her beat him till he cried could be a sage.

On this point, she is very like my wife — no matter how the world sees me, in her eyes, I am still a child who loves to make mistakes. From time to time she pulls me down, and beats me fiercely with the sole of her shoe. I don't know whether to laugh or cry, so I just say: "Careful! Careful! Don't sprain your back."

This is the reason why Rechungpa would not listen to what his master Milarepa said: in the eyes of their attendants, there are no holy sages. They treat them without respect because they have often seen the sages sneeze and cough, heard them fart, go to the toilet, and do many other ordinary things. They forget that, even when he is farting, a sage who has awakened to the empty inherent nature does not lose his wisdom because of this. A sage who likes to fart openly is still a sage, and a petty person who does not fart openly is still a petty person. The fundamental substance of the spirit cannot change because the sage does or does not fart. What a laugh.

Here let me say more. The light of enlightenment can often become an atmosphere in life that cannot be shaken off. It is impossible for true enlightenment to lose this light. No matter what mundane things the enlightened person does, whether walking, standing, sitting, or lying down, no matter whether or not the enlightened person has the outward appearance of someone who cultivates religious practice, the truly enlightened person can never, because of his or her actions, lose this light.

The story goes that Amoga looked at Khyungpo Naljor with a compassionate look. With every step he took, he made impressions in the rock on the mountain as if it were soft mud. His big sister was embarrassed, and she brushed the dirt off his body. But because she was on such close terms with him, she never felt any need to apologize. Many years later, she died. One day many years after that, when Khyungpo Naljor was already an accomplished man, he pointed to a little puppy who was always around him at his feet, that could not bear to leave him, and he told his disciples: This is the reincarnation of my big sister. Although she was my big sister, she hit a bodhisattva, and it was inevitable that she would get the corresponding reward.

Amoga said to Khyungpo Naljor:

"You must definitely remember what I tell you today. When you grow up, you must certainly go to India. There are many accomplished teachers there who are waiting for you. You have to receive the many lessons they will transmit to you. You will bring benefits to countless sentient beings. From this point on, no matter how many difficulties arise, you must seek the *Five Great Diamonds Teachings of Niguma*. This is the heart of Niguma, the dakini, the mother who moves through the void. After you have successfully cultivated them, the five chakras of your central channel will manifest the mandala of the Five Diamonds. Then your achievements of body, mouth, and mind will not be separate from the Diamond of the Secret Gathering, the Diamond of Mahamaya, the Diamond of Joy, the Diamond of Surpassing Bliss, and the Diamond of Great Virtue. Although in your life you will encounter many demonic barriers, do not fear. You are a bodhisattva riding on the bodhisattva vows who has come again, and there will be countless numbers of great nagas who support the Dharma and support you. No matter what demons rise up, they will not be able to do anything to you, just as the ravens, no matter how many of them there may be, cannot block off the sun. You will be in the world for one hundred and fifty years. During your life you will see innumerable people of great virtue in this later period of the propagation on Buddhism — they will shine as brightly as the constellations of stars in the sky. You will be one of the brightest stars among them. Your teaching may go on for a thousand years, and will be spread widely in the world after thirty-seven generations, to the benefit of countless sentient beings.

"Before you have been initiated by Niguma, you can recite 'Niguma Khyenno.' Every time you do this recitation sincerely, you will get Niguma's compassionate support. You can also tell all those who have faith in Niguma, no matter whether they have been initiated or not, as long as they beseech Niguma, they will all get the support of her wisdom. Right now, you and I will chant 'Niguma Khyenno' together."

That evening became a scene in the mind of Khyungpo Naljor that could not be erased. It planted the seeds in Khyungpo Naljor's mind that would control his fate, and become his reason for living. Thus, though the awe he felt for the Great Perfection increased, he was still concerned with that prediction by Amoga.

Niguma Khyenno!

Chapter 3

Niguma off in the Distance

Xuemo: "Master, at that time, what was the Niguma in your mind ultimately like?"

1 First Hearing of Niguma

At that time, in my impression of her, Niguma was a red-colored woman, her body was like a rainbow, bright as the rosy clouds.

True, she was a woman, but she was not an ordinary woman. She was a woman who had attained a rainbow body, visible but intangible, a body that could abide forever in the world, without being born and without dying, not ending and not decaying. Even now she still lives in peace in the Soshaling Pure Land, observing all sentient beings.

Son, in India at that time there were many people of great

accomplishment in yoga. They were resplendent as the stars, and they made the starry sky of India's culture brilliant. Those women who had achieved enlightenment we call dakinis: they are divided into dakinis in the world, and dakinis beyond the world. The dakinis in the world, though they cannot yet realize the empty true nature, have unlimited powers. They can be non-humans, and they can be yakshas. Although they have not yet realized the empty true nature, they have vowed to be guardians of the Buddhist teaching. Besides the many dakinis in the world, there are also many dakinis who transcend the world. They can be the mothers of the enlightened ones. For example, the consorts of many of the Sambhogakaya Buddhas can be women who have awakened to the empty inherent nature. Though you have heard the stories of the eighty-four great accomplished teaching masters, and stories of their spiritual wonders have been spread to every corner of India, this does not mean that India only had eighty-four great accomplished teaching masters. This is not so. Those great teaching masters who are famous are widely known to people only because of their unique deeds. But there are even more accomplished masters who did their work anonymously and are not known to people. They too, in their level of realization, were just as outstanding. Among them the most acclaimed are those dakinis who transcended the world. They did not necessarily have names, and some did not even have tangible form, and so they were referred to by people as dakinis without bodies. The essential nature of these dakinis without bodies in reality was the Great Mudra. That is to say, what they realized and experienced was in fact the ultimate enlightenment of the Great Mudra. We can also say that the basic substance of those dakinis without bodies is the Great Mudra.

The Vajravarahi (Thunderbolt sow) that you saw is the main enlightened one of the dakinis without bodies.

You can think of these dakinis as a kind of dark matter or dark force. Don't the scientists say that the universe only has four percent visible matter? That other ninety-six percent that cannot be seen is the dark matter. So how about we use that concept to explain this? Although all words and explanations may stray far from the real truth, people in the world need a kind of explanation they can recognize and accept.

Don't worry, I am going to talk about Niguma right now.

Niguma is not a dakini without body, but Niguma's realm of enlightenment is in no way inferior to those dakinis without bodies. On the contrary, at the gatherings of the dakinis, Niguma often sits at the head. In the eyes of those dakinis without bodies, Niguma is not separate from Vajravarahi. Vajravarahi is the chief enlightened one of the many dakinis. She commands something like hundreds of millions of dakinis. Do you understand Niguma's position? That's right, her essential nature is Vajravarahi.

But Niguma has a body.

Niguma's body has two parts.

The Niguma of the first part was born in Kashmir with a tangible physical body. You know that a human body is a great treasure for cultivating practice, and without the treasure of a human body, it is very difficult to achieve the true reward of enlightenment. Although Niguma was born in Kashmir with an ordinary woman's physical form, her essential nature was Vajravarahi. Thus, she did not have the ordinary woman's vanities and desires. She was pure. She never had the five poisons of ordinary worldly life, like craving, anger, ignorance and the rest. She did not like to dress up, and she did not like to pursue mundane pleasures. What she liked most was pure cultivation of Buddhist practice. She very much liked hearing the sutras, and whenever she heard the sutras, she would enter into meditative concentration. The sutra Niguma most liked to hear was the *Mahaprajna-paramita Sutra*. This is the ultimate wisdom scripture. Don't you like this sutra too? It is in fact the source of Mahamudra Yoga. Without the *Mahaprajna-paramita Sutra*, there would be no Mahamudra Yoga. The essential truth of Mahamudra is from the *Mahaprajna-paramita Sutra*.

My son, when I talk to you about this, you understand very easily. But your mission is to allow other people who are not the same as you to be able to understand this.

Now we will go on telling Niguma's story.

Your future teacher Niguma — in reality, the Vajravarahi you saw was Niguma — didn't she show you the true nature of mind? So she was the fundamental teacher. Whenever she heard the *Mahaprajna-paramita Sutra*, she would enter into meditative concentration — she had the capacity to go beyond ancient and modern. If someone asks you what capacity is, you can explain it as a natural endowment, though of course this is not natural endowment in the worldly sense.

Thus Niguma's understanding of truth came very early. A person of ordinary capacity might practice hard his whole life and still not necessarily reach the kind of enlightenment that Niguma experienced when she heard the *Mahaprajna-paramita Sutra*.

Niguma won the acclaim of many people of great religious merit with her ability to "hear one and understand ten" and her power of concentration and wisdom far beyond that of ordinary people. One after another they predicted enlightenment for her, and attested that this woman had extraordinary capacity, and that she was a genuine manifestation of a dakini of wisdom.

So they told this to Niguma's father and mother and told them definitely not to press her to get married. She was a person with superior capacity for cultivating practice and someone who would easily succeed with it.

2 Vajradhara in the Realm of Purity

In this way Niguma spent her youth listening to sutras. Day by day she was growing up, and she became a beauty heard of far and wide. Many princes thought it would be an honor to be able to see Niguma.

But Niguma's mind was like still water, and other than listen to the sutras, she liked to sit in solitude.

Don't ask if at this time she had already succeeded or not.

I wouldn't know what you mean by "succeed."

If you mean awakening to the true nature of mind, she had of course succeeded in that. As I said, she had already clearly understood the empty inherent nature in theory, she had understood the light of the ultimate truth. But her causal basis for understanding in practical affairs had still not arrived.

One day it finally came. That day her parents took Niguma to pay homage to the Diamond Seat. You're right, they went to visit the slab of stone under the Bodhi tree where the Buddha achieved enlightenment. But when the Buddha achieved enlightenment, there was no stone slab there, there was just the bodhi tree. Prince Siddhartha spread lucky grass under the tree; this was something a herdsman had offered to him. In the traditional Indian account, receiving the lucky grass was a very good circumstance.

This slab of stone was put there several hundred years later by King Ashoka. He ordered that it be called the "Diamond Seat." Later on a lot of people went so far as to consider this the navel of the world, meaning the center of the world. Of course the ones who accepted this account were only the Buddhists, and other religions had their own "navels."

The story goes that when Niguma visited the Diamond Seat, she saw Vajradhara (Thunderbolt-holder).

Naturally this was a change of substance, a qualitative change. Because Niguma had been listening all along to the *Mahaprajna-paramita Sutra* and was always pondering the true meaning of the *Mahaprajna-paramita Sutra*, and she was consistently guiding her own conduct according to the *Mahaprajna-paramita Sutra*, because, in other words, all along she was carrying on true genuine cultivation without the appearance of the names and forms of cultivation, therefore, when she went to the Diamond Seat, this was her moment of sudden enlightenment.

At this point, in this state of purity, Niguma saw Vajradhara. Of course, in the eyes of those who have truly attained, this was her seeing Vajradhara in her own inherent nature. Vajradhara is a realm of experience. We all have our own Vajradhara: it's just that, because we are covered over by ignorance and false thoughts, we cannot see it. You certainly understand this point. The fact is, you should not talk of this ultimate truth casually, or people will call you crazy.

You certainly can also recognize that Niguma saw Vajradhara in human form. Vajradhara is the source of all the esoteric teachings. Almost all the esoteric teachings come from Vajradhara. The Vajradhara that Niguma saw was sparkling with light, and very grand. He was like the sun filling up half the sky, with thirty-two auspicious marks, and eighty adornments. Vajradhara smiled at Niguma and said: "My child, I am very happy that you are able to have this kind of pure mind. Because of your focused effort to progress, all your karmic barriers have been purified, and thus you have seen me. In reality, at the level of the ultimate truth, I have never left you. Ever since you heard the *Mahaprajna-paramita Sutra* and had enough faith, I have been with you. Although at that time you did not yet see me, in reality you and I are not two, not separate."

Niguma joyously looked upon Vajradhara. You must realize that her joy was not the wild joy of the ordinary person who gets carried away. Her joy was the same as the absolute immovable joy. She felt that infinite golden light pouring into her heart, giving her endless purity.

Vajradhara said: "My child, do you want to ask me for some teaching? Do you want something to benefit you? Or to avoid some misfortune? Or to be soothed? Or to be subdued? Whatever you ask for, I can satisfy all your requests."

Niguma said: "I am not looking to gain benefits or to avoid misfortunes, and I do not hope to be soothed or subdued. In my eyes these things are all alike. I understand that all contrived phenomena are not the ultimate truth. All I seek is liberation, and I hope to enable countless sentient beings to attain liberation too."

Vajradhara said: "Very good, very good. I very much like this aspiration of yours. I can fulfill all your hopes. There are many honored teachings that all can enable you to reach what you aspire to. So I ask you: What kind of teaching do you want to study?"

Niguma said: "I want to learn the kind of supreme teaching that can encompass all the teachings. Since this is the sudden teaching, it has a level of perception which goes beyond the ordinary conventional thinking. It is also the gradual teaching, with procedures and practices that can be carried out at the practical level. It can contain all the Diamond teachings, and it can accommodate both the sharp and the dull, and apply to people of high, medium, and low capacities."

Vajradhara smiled and said: "Very good, very good. You have such a big heart, and so you have such big aspirations. Very well, then, you should go to that Soshaling cemetery. There, where people rarely go, I will transmit to you the Supreme Great Dharma which you seek."

3 Niguma Khyenno!

The story goes that the very instant that Niguma saw Vajradhara, her appearance changed. From this point on she had the third eye. My child, although this kind of story has become widespread, I would rather take it as a symbol. As I understand it, these three eyes are the wisdom that can see into the past, present, and future.

Of course, later Niguma really came to have the third eye, and in the future, you will be able to see what she looks like. The way I understand it, this was a manifestation that appeared after she attained the rainbow body.

The text which you have received, *Niguma's Teaching of the Combined Cultivation of the Five Great Diamonds*, or for short, the *Five Great Diamonds Teachings of Niguma*, was transmitted to Niguma by Vajradhara in the sky above Soshaling. My son, at that time, among all the Diamond Teachings circulating in India, the most famous were the Secret Collection Diamond, the Surpassing Joy Diamond, the Mahamaya Diamond, the Joy Diamond, and the Majestic Virtue Diamond. All the essentials of these five great Diamond Teachings were collected together in the *Five Great Diamonds Teachings of Niguma*. The Great Mudra of Light was the core of this teaching.

There is another story that Niguma became empowered with the *Five Great Diamonds Teachings of Niguma* in the Land of Secret

Adornment. This story has circulated very widely. In fact, in the eyes of those with true wisdom, Soshaling cemetery and the Land of Secret Adornment are not two separate things.

According to the story, Niguma was enlightened and had realization at the same time. That is to say, at the same time she opened up into enlightenment, she realized the ultimate. This is the most excellent place in the Great Mudra of Light. If you use these networked computers and data lines as a metaphor for the transmission of wisdom and realization, it comes near the original logic of this. But you must remember that, in fact, it is extremely difficult with any words to explain the original face of truth. Truth is far away from words. Many times, on the contrary, words and knowledge can block the light of the truth — this is what we call the barrier of what we think we know.

When Vajradhara empowered Niguma, Niguma experienced the three bodies of Buddha: the Body of Reality, the Body of Reward, and the Transformation Body. At the same time, she also was fully equipped with the Buddha's five kinds of wisdom: the Great Mirror Wisdom, the Equality Wisdom, the Wondrous Observing Wisdom, the Wisdom to Accomplish All Actions, and the Wisdom of the Essential Nature of the Realm of Reality.

Later, the unspoiled illumination in her mind was transformed into a Buddha Land no different than the Land of Secret Adornment. Its apparent position was up in the sky above Soshaling cemetery, but in reality it remains in the mind of everyone who has supreme faith in Niguma.

My son, Niguma's achievement was incomparably excellent, and what she realized was the rainbow body in which there is neither birth nor death, very similar to the state of realization achieved by the great teacher Padmasambhava. This means that she did not have to undergo death as the ordinary person experiences it. Her gross material body was directly transformed into a rainbow body. That rainbow body is not born and is not destroyed, it has no birth and no death. The mundane world can be destroyed, but that rainbow body is forever indestructible.

My son, your fundamental teacher is this great woman. You too may be an upholder and transmitter of her teaching line. Do not forget your own mission. You must always pray to her. Remember, when you sincerely invoke "Niguma Khyenno," she will appear before you and support you, so you can achieve your aspirations.

Of course, after you have cleared away all the karmic barriers, then you will constantly see her body of wisdom. Likewise, as long as you have faith and earnestly pray to her, you will be able to have her incomparable power supporting you. You will be able to achieve all you aspire to. To those who have a taste for science, you can use a kind of skillful expedient to tell them about it. Tell them you are utilizing something mobilized and deployed by a special methodology, which in fact is a kind of dark energy of the universe.

You must invoke "Niguma Khyenno" every day, and you will never get lost, and you will go straight to that esoteric pure land which she makes appear. No matter how many difficulties you face, you can never lose faith. This incomparable teaching which you have received can blaze up into the most beautiful scene in history.

My son, chant it with me: Niguma Khyenno! Niguma Khyenno!

4 Destroyed Faith

The days flew by like yellow leaves in the autumn wind.

Without realizing it, I had already been at Lama Losanger's place more than half a year. I still was unable to give up the concerns of a lifetime. Because of this, I was not able to fuse into one whole with the inherent nature I had recognized. I understood that the Teaching of Great Perfection did not suit me. This is not to say that the Teaching of Great Perfection was not good, but rather, since sentient beings have different capacities, there can be different teachings that they reach accord with.

Pema Nam also had his doubts about the Great Perfection. He was a clever talker, and he did not believe that the bright emptiness which could appear at any time could enable him to escape from revolving in birth and death. But Pema Nam was secretly telling me his doubts. In the beginning, I was not influenced by this very much, and I still kept faith in that bright emptiness which my teacher accepted. But with Pema Nam's repeated doubts, my faith was substantially undermined. Only many years later did I understand that this was a special method Pema Nam was using to hurt me. In this world, there is no damage deeper than damage to one's faith. Pema Nam used his talent with words again and again, and destroyed my faith in the Great Perfection.

I could still understand that which my teacher had made me recognize, but because my faith was damaged, false thoughts were flying around in profusion, and there was no fusing with that bright emptiness, and even that clear awareness of it became a forced effort.

Once my faith was damaged, Lama Losanger of course saw this, and even though I kept on cultivating practice, there could not be any great success. Lama Losanger sighed and said: "To cultivate the Path, you definitely need to get close to an enlightened teacher, and stay far away from evil friends. Those evil friends can ruin your faith, and this is even more to be feared than killing your physical body."

He said: "Go then, go to Master Namruwa's place to continue your studies. I do not know if the Great Mudra which he teaches will be a match for you or not."

All I could do was leave Lama Losanger. Because Pema Nam was always showing off his verbal cleverness, and always saying bad things about Lama Losanger, the teacher was afraid this evil influence in the group might influence other students, so he drove Pema Nam out.

Pema Nam of course followed me. But at that time, I did not realize that Pema Nam was an evil friend. Pema Nam was good at watching people's moods and getting into their good graces. Though to some extent I didn't like him, I thought: I don't care what they say, Pema Nam too is a sentient being, and maybe my cultivation of practice can start with tolerating and accepting Pema Nam. As we gradually got closer, my initial defensive attitude toward Pema Nam dissolved away. Just as when you spend a long time in a place where they make vinegar, you pick up a sour smell, my awareness of the bright emptiness which I had previously experienced began to recede.

At that time I even began to think that the Great Perfection transmitted to me by Lama Losanger was not the ultimate teaching I was looking for. So when I left Lama Losanger, I did not have the slightest sense of loss.

Although Pema Nam had maliciously destroyed my faith in the Great Perfection, if we look at history, in my own life, this was not necessarily a bad thing. If I had continued at Lama Losanger's place, energetically cultivating the Great Perfection, I would not have had my later travels seeking the teaching. That is why later I thought of Pema Nam as an "adversarial bodhisattva." Throughout my life there have been many adversarial bodhisattvas of this sort. Every one of these adversarial bodhisattvas became an adornment, a merit for me. When you first experienced enlightenment, in fact you also encountered adversarial bodhisattvas, and if not for the adverse circumstances they created, you definitely would not have merged with the Great Mudra of

Light within a few days of seeing your teacher.

That is why we must always salute all the people who criticize us, and say to them: "Thank you, my adversarial bodhisattva!"

5 Missing the Great Mudra

Like the clouds of smoke swirling around that fire mandala of death-dealing magic, like shadows following forms, Pema Nam and I took Master Namruwa as our teacher, and studied the Great Mudra.

Perhaps it was because of the long journey on foot, or maybe in my subconscious I still had some fear of those death-dealing methods: in those days I was in a bit of a trance. When I was studying the teaching of the Great Mudra with Master Namruwa, from time to time I fell into a daze. In this way, although I was encountering the teaching of the Great Mudra, I could not focus on it, and in the end it passed me by.

Although the Master explained for me the theory of the Great Mudra, due to causal conditions, I was always falling into a daze when I was meditating by stopping and observing. Though I managed to get the perception of the bright emptiness, it was often fleeting, and it was impossible for me to preserve it. Pema Nam was always maliciously destroying my faith in it, saying that he did not believe that what was called the Great Mudra of "the Mind of All the Buddhas" was so simple.

My mind of faith again began to waver.

The image of Niguma, on the other hand, was getting clearer and clearer.

At this point I thought: how about I go to India.

Many years later, when I had received the teaching of the Great Mudra from many great Indian teachers, I finally discovered that, although the form and the words were not the same, from the point of view of the basic essence, Master Namruwa had already expressed many of the essentials of the Great Mudra, but I had not comprehended them. Then I thought, without the basis of faith and blessing of wisdom, even if there are countless gold coins right in front of him, a blind man will not be able to see even a penny.

Because of this, even after Master Namruwa had shown me the essence of mind, my mind was still circling around the image of that woman, and in my mind, she was getting clearer and clearer. In that subtle smile of hers, I was always discovering an unexplainable mystic potential.

Chapter 4

Avalanches and Wolf Packs

Xuemo: "Master, when you left your home area and went to Nepal, what were the perils you encountered?"

1 A Small Boat Drifting on a Great Ocean

I remember, on my long journey to Nepal, that the most serious dangers were avalanches and wolf packs.

After I got the idea to go to Nepal, I first said goodbye to Master Namruwa, and then returned home. I sold off all the valuables that belonged to me, and exchanged them all for gold. According to the tradition at that time, if you went to India and Nepal to seek the teaching, you had to make offerings of gold, to show the precious value of the esoteric teaching. If you did not have gold, it was very hard to seek out the esoteric teaching. Because gold was rare in Tibet, the first time I went to Nepal, I did all I could and finally I accumulated several hundred gold pieces.

To have someone to help look after things, I set out together with Pema Nam. I bought thirty sheep from some herdsmen to use as pack animals. Although each pack animal could only carry twenty-plus pounds, with so many of them we had a great capacity, and basically the daily necessities for two travelers could be loaded on their backs. What's more, these thirty sheep themselves could be used for food. In this way we left our home village, driving the sheep along.

I felt like a small boat drifting on a large ocean, or like a feather flying through the sky, blown by a hurricane. I did not know whether or not I would find that smiling woman of my destiny. I did not know what kind of dangerous blizzards we would encounter on the journey. And I did not know whether or not these bones of mine would be able to return home all safe and sound.

My whole life I could never forget that feeling. This was the first time I had really taken a long journey. In my image of it, Nepal was as far away as the horizon. To mention nothing else, the Himalayas were a huge barrier blocking the Path. Who knew where they began and where they ended, this continuous line of snowy mountains rising and falling all the way to the horizon? Who knew if there were really ghosts and evil demons hidden in the deep mountain valleys? There were stories that many of those seeking the teaching had met untimely deaths in the repeated avalanches set off by these mountain ghosts. The flying dust kicked up by the pack animals spread out like a dreamy illusion, and without meaning to, I discovered myself walking in a gigantic dreamscape.

The sky was clear and blue, without a trace of clouds, as clean as if it had been washed with water a hundred times. It seemed as if it could send out countless clear waves, and blow into every pore, and penetrate right into a person's mind and spirit. Although I could not foretell the outcome of this journey, my mind was like the sky, pure and clean and without any defilements. This was the best I had felt since the sorcerers had set in motion their death-dealing magical methods. Later on, I realized that this set of circumstances symbolized that I would be able to achieve the ultimate realization of the Great Mudra.

At that time, I certainly did not know that Pema Nam, whom I had regarded all along as a close friend, would turn out to be the greatest adverse factor for me on this journey, and I did not know that my life would be in danger many times. Still less did I think that the greatest test of destiny was waiting for me far away in India.

The difficulties and dangers on the road to Nepal were very serious. On the way there were large expanses of uninhabited land, and the terrain was like a giant Gobi Desert. Who knows how many years ago, this had been an inland sea, and from time to time I could see black perlite rock with ripples. Often the sheep we were using as pack animals would graze on the grass, and this way we could save the green barley fodder they were carrying on their backs. The green barley fodder had been specially prepared for the sheep we were using as pack animals. What we had prepared for ourselves included butter and roasted barley flour, and there were also the sheep we slaughtered. After we had been travelling more than ten days, some of the sheep began to fall down dead. We would bleed the dead sheep, then skin them, then cut up the meat, then load it on the other pack animals, and when we stopped for the night we would cook the meat and eat it. Of all the times I have eaten mutton, the hardest to eat was the flesh of these sheep we were using for pack animals. This was because they were always carrying heavy loads on their backs, and even when they rested the packs stayed on, so half the sheep's backs were suppurated. Suppurated sheep back gives off a stench that assails the nose, and that stench is like the bad smell of the fluid seeping from a human corpse. It is the kind of evil stench that can make a person suffocate. Whenever we carved up a sheep, Pema Nam would cut off the suppurated flesh, and discard it somewhere far away. But the strange thing was, although he cut away that rotten flesh, every time we cooked the meat, I could still smell that uncanny stench.

Every time one of the sheep died, we would spend half a day cooking the meat. Because fresh meat cannot be stored for too long, we would have to pick an area where we would find some firewood, and gather some to cook the meat. This so-called cooking was just symbolic. Because of the high altitude, even if the water was boiling, its temperature was far below what it would have been in the flatlands. So the meat we had boiled was still very tough, and we could only manage to eat it by cutting it up with our knives. If a sheep died and we could not find any firewood, the best we could do was take the load that was on its back and put it onto another sheep. We would eat part of the meat of the dead sheep, and just throw the rest away. All in all I discarded five of the sheep. Later on, when we were in the mountains and starving to the point that our bellies were rumbling, Pema Nam was muttering complaints all the time, and he very much regretted that we had thrown away the mutton.

I remember how the wolf packs would appear when we were boiling the meat. Later, there were people who thought these wolf packs had been summoned by the death-dealing magic of the sorcerers. This is because in the Bonpo explanation, the mountain spirit fathers are the spirit guardians of Bonpo, and the wolves are the dogs of the mountain spirit fathers.

2 Avalanches with Wind and Lightning

The going got very tough for us.

You can imagine the hardships of this journey. In a period before there was any communications equipment, if you wanted to pass through an area where there were no people, and cross over the Himalayas at year's end in the deep snow, it was really not an easy thing to do.

We were on a rugged mountain Path. We had fewer and fewer pack animals. After we ascended into the snowy mountains, the sheep could not graze, and the supply of green barley loaded on their backs was soon eaten up. One by one the sheep dropped on the snowy ground. Because we could not find any firewood, we could not cook the meat, and the sheep just became frozen carcasses in the snow. Have you seen the dead body of a sheep frozen stiff? Their eyes stared out, wide open, and they stretched out their bodies lying in the snow; their fleece was covered with snow, and they were stiff as boards. Their bodies were so rigid we could not see any softness to their flesh. They were like bundles of wheat stretched out on the snow.

A line of foot prints ran over their bodies extending to the horizon. Can you picture me staggering along in the snow, there with Pema Nam, whom the general reader does not much like. You should have some sympathy for Pema Nam at this moment. Ultimately, in this most difficult and dangerous moment of my life, he was putting his own life on the line to accompany me. I even believe that the first time we went to Nepal, Pema Nam's intentions were pure. It is very hard for me to believe that someone whose intentions were not pure would leave his warm home, and go out into those snowy mountains with no idea where they might end, to reach a place people called "the Western

Heaven" (that is, the Indian subcontinent).

Great winds were always whipping up then, and these winds carried snow flakes, and people called them blizzards. Later on in a short verse, you used the metaphor of a blizzard. This is because you always saw me stumbling along in a blizzard. People from my homeland Liangzhou call blizzards "wind-blown snow." If you had gone through that blizzard, you would have seen my frostbitten face.

Because so much time has gone by, the mists of history have already covered over a lot of information about me. Later on, when you traveled through the many lands where I had once lived, you could not find any information about me. People had already forgotten me. All that was left were a few books, with pages yellowed by time, where it was still possible to find my name. But that name does not have the fresh life that you see now at this moment.

Of course my face was covered with windblown dust and showed the fatigue of the journey. If you had been traveling through snowy country for several months, you too would have this kind of wind-blown dust on you. You would have also seen frostbite on my face, and on Pema Nam's face too. This was where we were most alike. Because of this, I cannot ever hate Pema Nam. I even believe that Pema Nam was an adversarial bodhisattva given to me as a spiritual gift of fate. He appeared in order to help me attain my dignity.

The first time I went to Nepal, I encountered two disasters: one was the disaster of wolves, and the other one was the disaster of snow. People say that the snow disaster was conjured up by the Bonpo spirit guardians; they say that the spirits in those mountains are all Bonpo guardian spirits, and though they later were subdued by the Great Master Padmasambhava, they subsequently returned again, and renewed their defense and support of Bonpo. I am skeptical of this story, because the people of every religious group all claim the mountain spirits belong to their religious group, and think that in this way they will attract more believers.

When the avalanche happened, Pema Nam and I were resting. We were unbearably exhausted, and longed to go to sleep, but we were keeping each other awake. We both knew that if we fell asleep, we might never wake up again. We were eating some roasted barley flour, and I distinctly saw the blood in Pema Nam's mouth. You may not know it, but when you have been in snowy country freezing for a long time, and then you eat something, you bleed around your teeth. But he himself did not know this. Even though he had the pungent taste in his mouth, fatigue had blurred his sense of taste.

At this moment, that woman suddenly floated into my mind, and it was as if she were calling out. I was startled. Suddenly I knew what was happening. "Let's go," I said, and I pulled Pema Nam along and we got out of that mountain valley.

As soon as we got back to the foot of the hill, I discovered a place where there was a bit of mist flying at us where we could finally rest. This was a white flow, a silent whirl wind. This came from a patch of snow on the mountain top, and the story goes that there was a mountain spirit pushing it along. It was enveloped in wind and thunder, and in an instant it brought down that snow that was rumbling and about to move. At this point the snow let loose a great silent sound, and came hurtling down, wanting to bury us and make us corpses.

As we watched that snow slide, in an instant filling the valley where we had just set foot, I stared dumbstruck. I will never be able to forget this scene. When I am lecturing my disciples, I always use it as a classic example of the impermanence of all actions. I always say, life lasts from one breath to the next — if at that time I had not woken up,

I soon would have become a corpse buried in the snow. Then I would not have been seeking the Buddhist teaching later, and I would not have been able to have a hundred thousand disciples.

Many times a detail you look at casually could be something that changes history.

3 The Danger from Wolves

The story of Khyungpo Naljor's encounter with a wolf pack seems even more like a parable.

Khyungpo Naljor said that when he went into the great mountain range, he was like a fallen leaf being blown into the ocean. He was very fond of this metaphor. In our exchanges after we met, I heard him use this metaphor many times, and it was obvious that the feeling of being isolated and alone had penetrated to the depths of his spirit. Later on, when I left the remote area of Liangzhou and went to Shanghai and Beijing and other big cities, I also had this kind of feeling. So I said to Khyungpo Naljor, "Master, I can understand the feeling you had at that time." His profound gaze swept across my face—he of course knew that I could understand him. He said that many times in a person's life he will be faced with a great unknown. The ability to face the unknown is one of the important human abilities. In a certain sense, cultivating practice is cultivating the unknown. Because each one of us is going to die, for each one of us, death is really the greatest unknown. Nobody really dies twice. Of course, this refers to our current lives. If we take into account past lives, who knows how many times we have died.

At that time, Khyungpo Naljor would appear every night in my realm of light, and tell me his stories, transmitting to me wisdom and light. I also told him about my many encounters with Vajravarahi. He said: "Vajravarahi's essential nature is the Great Mudra, and she is also Niguma, and they are not separate entities. You must remember that you are inherently equipped with the Great Mudra, and it does not depend on external seeking — it is a manifestation of your inherent wisdom. This is not to say that your teacher gave it to you, and then you had the Great Mudra, and if your teacher had not transmitted it to you, then you would not have the Great Mudra. This is not so. The Great Mudra is there from birth — it is not added to or decreased, it is not defiled or purified. Careful practice does not increase it, laziness does not make it less. The function of the teacher is just to help you recognize that light. The teacher says, 'Look at that moon,' and then you see the moon. Do you understand or not?"

I nodded my head and spoke a verse:

> *The great wind blows on the white moon*
> *Pure light fills space*
> *Sweeping away things and enlightenment*
> *This is the Great Mudra*

"Right! Right!" He clapped his hands and laughed. Then we looked at each other and smiled, happy and content.

In those days, as soon as I entered into that realm of illumination, I could see that wise old man's serene, contented smile.

4 The Great Master Like a Child

In that peaceful state of bright emptiness, Khyungpo Naljor told me about his perilous encounter with the wolves. His smiling eyes were like a child's. That's right, like a child's. You must understand that a genuine great teaching master is sometimes very much like a child, so worldly people say a great master is like a child. Someone who is like a child is not necessarily a great teacher, but a great teacher is definitely like a child. This is because if he did not have a child's mind, he has surely not become a great teaching master. Thus when you see someone who is deliberately acting mysterious, you must know for sure that this person is definitely not a great teaching master. Of course, he is not necessarily a fraud.

In Khyungpo Naljor's simple unadorned narrative, I saw those wolves.

One great virtue has said that these attacking wolves may perhaps be a symbol, standing for those petty people who make insinuations and slander the true teaching. He says that in that period, Khyungpo Naljor encountered many petty people. These jealous ones attacked him like moths going at a flame, though in the end they were burned to ashes in the flames of history. In the long river of history, they were just a few bubbles who are all gone.

However, there are also those who say that the wolves were conjured up by the Bonpo guardian spirits, because Khyungpo Naljor had betrayed Bonpo. Some say the wolves were manifestations of the mountain spirits, because they did not want Khyungpo Naljor to go to India to get what were, in their eyes, "heretical teachings." There are others who say they were conjured up by spirits guarding India, because they knew that if Khyungpo Naljor went to India, he would get what they viewed as key secret teachings … There are many explanations, but I just considered them to be real wolves.

Through Khyungpo Naljor's eyes I saw these wolves charging up, like mosquitos swarming at dusk. I saw them sticking out their long tongues, tongues dripping with saliva. They seemed to be crying out:

"Onward, comrades, for the sake of our beloved bellies." Their voices shook heaven and earth, grabbing people's souls. But to me, this was as pleasing to the ear as the songs of the dakinis.

At that instant, the song I heard was this:

Oh feathers, how do you dwell? Fluttering in the ancient wind.

You do not respect the immortals in heaven, for a while you want to be a scholar.

Oh feathers, where will you dwell? The autumn waters are laughing and full.

I'd rather be a cypress, not like the dandelion.

Oh feathers, how will you manage? Don' t make the firefly lament.

Years and months rush by, at the village gate they have long awaited the lord.

I saw that Khyungpo Naljor's face had gotten pale. I believed he was scared—sages too can get frightened. If anyone thinks a sage is made of wood, I'll have to smack him. Sages are people too, and sages are the most sensitive people: they are always concerned with sentient beings. What's more, when Khyungpo Naljor encountered these wolves, he was not yet a sage. At that time he was just someone who wanted to become a sage.

Khyungpo Naljor asked me, "Do you know what kind of a feeling the wolves' howls had?"

I said, "Like the wind?"

He was surprised and said, "How did you know?"

I said, "At the time you realized that it really was the wind, and those waves of sound were like a great wind surging along, sweeping over your skin till it was numb, sweeping over your mind till it shuddered, sweeping over your scalp till it prickled. You felt the sound of the wind drumming; the wind entered your pores, rolled around like dust in your mind, tugged at your spirit, and pulled your brain waves. You certainly must have had the feeling you were going crazy, right?"

He said, "That's right. You are someone who knows me."

I said, "At that time, you still saw a twisted shapeless upside-down image spread across the sky, and you thought those were demons. At that time, you still did not understand that all of this was, in reality, the inherent nature of your own mind. Right?"

"That's right."

"At that time you discovered that all the sheep with you were trembling, like leaves in the wind."

"That's right, they were."

5 The Sheep as Pack Animals

As the frightening howls of those wolves swept toward us, I saw Pema Nam trembling. Though Pema Nam understood the Bonpo teaching, and had studied some of the Buddhist scriptures, his mind had not changed its basic substance. This is very normal—no matter how much a person has studied, when he must tremble, he will still tremble. As long as he is a person, fear can always master him. I saw a hopeless look from Pema Nam's eyes. He was definitely thinking, that's it, it's all over. I could see that his mind was blank, without any other thoughts, just a thick feeling enveloping him. I gave a loud shout and said, "Pema Nam, this is it!" I wanted very much to show him the inherent nature of mind, and let him find the inherent light. But there was no way for the sound of my voice to penetrate through the dense fog of history. So Pema Nam was still wrapped up in the old delusions.

The lead wolf came up to within ten or twelve meters of us. This wolf was very tall, and his shoulders were bulging with powerful muscles. I thought he must be the king of the wolves, because his body emanated a kind of kingly energy. The fur on the back of his neck was standing on end, and he radiated an incomparable menace. What appeared in Pema Nam's eyes was this wolf. Pema Nam also appeared in the wolf's eyes. They squared off, facing each other as opponents and looking right at each other.

That evening, after Khyungpo Naljor heard Pema Nam's cry of fear, he too discovered that the valley was full of wolves, as thick on the ground as if someone had scattered several handfuls of hemp seeds on the snowy ground. The sheep they were using as pack animals had huddled together, and could not stop shaking.

Pema Nam gave a long cry and said, "I didn't think we would end up filling the bellies of wolves."

But Khyungpo Naljor thought back to that prediction that had been made for him when he was young. In those days, the great accomplished teaching master called Amoga had predicted his future: Amoga said that after he grew up he would go to Nepal and to India to seek the Dharma; he would visit more than one hundred and fifty great accomplished teaching masters; he would meet someone called Niguma who had achieved the rainbow body; he would receive the *Five Great Diamonds Teachings of Niguma*; he would found the Shangpa Kagyu lineage, and have a hundred thousand disciples, and his teaching line would continue in Tibet for thirty-six generations; in the thirty-seventh generation the teaching would flourish greatly, and spread in the world like a prairie fire … Amoga had certainly not said that he would die in the mouth of a wolf. Khyungpo Naljor thought: "Amoga is a great accomplished teaching master, and he would not speak falsely." Amoga certainly had not predicted that he would become food for wolves. But in Khyungpo Naljor's past life, there had been some predictions that were not realized. For example, at a certain time, his father said that a disciple would live a long time, but unexpectedly, half a year later, that man had gotten a bad ulcer, and a great cavity opened in his breast, and you could even see his heart beating. His father explained that the man's grave illness was brought on by breaking the Samaya discipline between teacher and disciple, but his father had certainly not predicted that the man would violate the Samaya discipline. Then too, in his past life, predictions by several great worthy ones had not come true. Sometimes the people who they had predicted would succeed in their religious practice, ended up just betraying their teachers. Thus, even though Amoga had predicted that Khyungpo Naljor would be able to live for a hundred and fifty years, when the wolf pack appeared, it still frightened him.

As the wolves surrounded him, Khyungpo Naljor could see their bright eyes and their mouths watering. If it had been nighttime, those green eyes would have changed into green lights, and then there would have been countless green lights in the valley floating back and forth, giving off a ghostly smell. Pema Nam took the meat that the sheep were carrying on their backs and threw it toward the wolves, and every time he threw a piece, the wolf pack would howl and turn away. Compared to what the wolves were hungry for, these pieces of meat obviously would not do. Khyungpo Naljor was even afraid that this meat might stir up the wolves desire for food, and make them even more hungry, but he did not stop Pema Nam. He thought: if we are fated to end up in the mouths of wolves, no matter whether he tosses them meat or not, the outcome will be the same.

There were cries from the sheep. The sound was full of fear and hopelessness. The sound of these cries rolled around in Khyungpo Naljor's mind, like pebbles in the wind rolling around in an empty quiet mountain valley. The sheep seemed to understand their fate. Khyungpo Naljor thought: since you understand your fate, and you understand your cries are useless, why are still crying out?

Before long, all the meat the sheep had been carrying on their backs had been thrown to the wolves. The wolves began to stare steadily at the humans. The strange thing was, in the eyes of the wolves there was a certain relaxed presence; perhaps they had already made a meal of these two humans. Khyungpo Naljor looked up at the sky, thinking that if he was going to be thrown to the wolves, he would look at the sky one last time. He heard his father saying, "Three days after a person dies, he will enter the intermediate existence. In Buddhist terms, the intermediate existence is the time from when a person dies until the person is sent into a womb to return to the world reincarnated. The story goes that the intermediate existenced body has no eyes, and cannot see the sky or the sun or the moon. Everything the intermediate existenced body sees is pale bluish white. Khyungpo Naljor thought: if I'm going to die, I'm going to die. He wanted to get one last look at the sky.

The sun was no longer visible in the sky—it had gone behind the clouds. Due to this, the layer of clouds had reddened, and in the sky over the mountains to the west the clouds had formed a resplendent expanse. The scene was really very beautiful, and if it had not been for the pack of wolves casting baleful looks at the two men, Khyungpo

Naljor would have been moved by the scene. Khyungpo Naljor was a very emotional person—he was not like this father. He had a childlike natural innocence and simplicity, and a kind of poetic feeling was always welling up in his mind. His disciples all liked the guidelines for Bonpo practice he created, because the writing was full of the great beauty of those poetic feelings. They were not like the ones handed down by the ancestral teachers, which were just mechanical texts on meditation work.

Suddenly hearing a muffled thud, Khyungpo Naljor pulled back his gaze that had wandered toward the sky. He discovered Pema Nam had taken one of the sheep they were using as pack animals and thrown it to the wolves. When the sheep hit the ground, the pack of highland barley on its back burst open. The highland barley went in all directions with a whooshing sound. After the sheep hit the ground, it leaped right up, and wanted to flee. A wolf already had its mouth on the sheep's throat. The sheep bleated in a cry for help. Khyungpo Naljor's heart tightened, and he began to cry. He said to Pema Nam, "How could you do that?" Pema Nam said, "At that moment, if the sheep didn't die, then we would have died. I figured that there are twenty-five wolves, and after they have eaten the sheep, there will be no room in their stomachs for us." Khyungpo Naljor thought: "So haven't you been cultivating the bodhisattva Path?" But these words did not come out of his mouth. At this moment in time, the so-called bodhisattva Path was just an intention in his mind. He still had not generated the true mind of great enlightenment. But his mind was seized by anguish, and the sounds of the sheep struggling, and their hopeless tragic cries, poured into his ears.

The wolf pack pressed in on the sheep, and swarmed all over it. From the nostrils of the wolves came indistinct low sounds, as if they were savoring a fine flavor, and also as if they were warning their comrades they might bite them now and then. Khyungpo Naljor's brain filled up with these sounds, and then he had a thick dreamlike feeling. He was always like this: these dreamlike feelings were always wrapping around him. This is why he had no interest in the desires of the senses. For this reason Lama Losanger had said that his root intellect was very good, and he had the bright intellect. Khyungpo Naljor never understood that there was any relation between these empty illusions and his root intellect. Lama Losanger told him that many people cultivate practice for many years and never develop those kinds of sensations. If you have these kinds of sensations, then you will be able to correspondingly reduce clinging and attachment. The true meaning of cultivating practice lies in eliminating clinging and attachment. If you can eliminate the clinging to the self, you can become an arhat. If you can eliminate both the clinging to the self and the clinging to phenomena, you can become a bodhisattva.

Khyungpo Naljor clearly understood the danger surrounding them, but he had no great overwhelming fear; there was nothing to do about it. He always felt that he was in a dream: he was in a dream when he left Bonpo, in a dream when he studied the Mudra of Great Perfection, and in a dream when he left his hometown. At this moment, in a scene where a pack of wolves was tearing the sheep to pieces, this was also obviously a dream, wasn't it? Pema Nam was not this way: his face was contorted, and he picked up another sheep and threw it to the wolves. The sheep writhed as it flew through the air, but it could not change the fact that its body was flying on a trajectory toward a pack of wolves. Khyungpo Naljor felt the sheep's helplessness and thought, people too are really just as helpless. People have no way to change direction as they fly toward death. Though that movement is slower than this sheep flying toward the pack of wolves right now, in its basic essence, there is no difference.

The pack of wolves again surrounded this edible thing that had fallen on the ground. The sound of them gobbling it down was very loud—when wolves eat meat it is always very loud. But perhaps this was a mistaken perception on Khyungpo Naljor's part, because at this moment he also heard a thumping of a heartbeat filling the valley. That sound was like a great tide surging up, and it was also like the whistling of a gale wind sweeping through the trees. Later on, he always mentioned this detail to me. He said that, at that instant, he no longer had any miscellaneous feelings. This dreamlike illusion, this tension, or maybe this fear, had taken all his miscellaneous feelings and totally swept them away. Later on he told the dakini Sukhasiddhi of this perception. The dakini said, "Too bad. If there had been someone to show you the inherent nature of mind, at that time you would have become enlightened."

All in all, Pema Nam threw a dozen or so sheep to the wolves—this was something Khyungpo Naljor came to know only later. Khyungpo Naljor always felt bad about these dozen or so companions. After he got to Nepal, he went to a monastery and donated two gold pieces for the salvation of these dozen or so sheep that had perished on the journey in the mouths of wolves. In Khyungpo Naljor's eyes, they had saved Pema Nam and him.

In fact it was indeed like this. After they had devoured the flesh of those sheep, the wolves quieted down, and half a carcass of one sheep was still left over. The wolves stuck out their tongues and licked the drops of blood from their lips. Khyungpo Naljor even saw some gratitude in their eyes. Khyungpo Naljor was sorry about that highland barley that was scattered on the ground. He knew the wolves would not eat it. But Pema Nam gave him a tug, and they put on their backpacks, and drove the remaining sheep out of that valley filled with the smell of raw meat.

It was as if Khyungpo Naljor were wandering in a dream, as he kept touching the gold pieces in his backpack. He thought, "No matter what else may be lost, as long as we have the gold, then we can succeed in finding the teaching." He felt sorry about those sheep that Pema Nam had thrown to the wolves, because he himself had done nothing to stop it. But he understood that in that kind of situation, Pema Nam's choice may have been the best thing to do.

Khyungpo Naljor at this point made a vow that if he experienced true enlightenment, he would first bring salvation to these sheep.

In the *Secret History of Khyungpo* it says that later, after Khyungpo Naljor had experienced enlightenment and gathered together his first set of disciples, among them were the reincarnations of these dozen or so sheep.

Chapter 5

The Female Spirits of Nepal

Xuemo: "Master, after you got to Nepal, what spiritual experiences did you have?"

1 The Festival of The Female Spirits

Before the great snows sealed the mountain passes, we reached Nepal. Though we had picked the warmest season of the year for our journey, when we got up in the morning, the mountains that were covered with snow all year round let us taste the cold.

In that *Secret Transmission*, which you have read, the difficulties of our trip ahead on the road to Kantipur are recorded in detail, and in that I described the scenery of Nepal like this: "The mountains of Nepal are like a camel's back." As we traveled along, we saw a dense forest of mountain peaks, with ravines as numerous as wrinkles on an old lady's forehead. It was really "a thousand peaks without a bird in flight, ten thousand Paths without a human footprint." In those time the means of communication were donkeys and horses and people carrying things on their shoulders.

"Kantipur" means "city of light." Later it was changed to Kathmandu, and it became the capital city of Nepal. The Kantipur of olden times was a valley, with a great body of water in which there were flood dragons, so it was called the Dragon Pond. In the Nepali language it was called "Naga Daha." Following a change in the topography of the land, the water in the Dragon Pond ran dry, the valley dried out, and gradually humans gathered together there. Rulers through the ages have all looked with favor upon this holy ground of the Dragon Pond, and they have built a great many temples, so it is called "an open-air museum."

Kantipur is surrounded by mountains on all sides, and the climate is favorable to humans. It is like spring all year round, with green trees and fresh flowers in all four seasons without a break—the scenery is very beautiful. In a mountainous country like Nepal, Kantipur is a bright jewel, and almost all the religions which have flowed into Nepal have been able to find a place here in their time. Kantipur is not large in area, and the built-up city area is no more than seven square kilometers, but it is full of Buddhist stupas, shrines, sanctuaries, and temples. The story goes that there are more than two hundred and fifty of these, all very elegantly built, with a great atmosphere, each with its own special qualities and unique beauty. When you first enter the city, what first comes into view is a Hindu spirit temple towering up on a mountain peak, shining and magnificent, very eye-catching, dedicated to the chief Hindu god Brahma. Besides this, there is also the largest

Buddhist stupa built in the semicircular shape, and the famous Hindu temple Pashupati.

When we arrived in Nepal, we were just in time for Nepal's festival of the female spirits. This is probably the most lively of the local festivals. Wearing clothes that were strange to my eyes, the Nepalese came to pay homage to the female spirits. I took the fact that I was able to arrive in time to attend the festival of the female spirits as an important conjuncture of causes in my life. I was very happy. Later on, I made a mark in history as an heir to the Dharma lineage of the female teachers Niguma and Sukhasiddhi, and some people even think the Shangpa Kagyu teaching is the Dharma lineage of the dakinis of wisdom.

Only later did I come to know that there is a story about the provenance of the female spirits. It is told that a long time ago, Nepal had a king, and he invited a female spirit called Taleju to play cards. Because the female spirit was extraordinarily beautiful, the king was fantasizing about her. The female spirit got angry, shook out her sleeves and left. That night the king had a dream that the angry female spirit said to him, "Your wild lust is shameless, and your kingdom will face a great disaster. If you want to avoid this disaster, and protect your rivers and mountains, you have to worship Kumari, the living female spirit. She is my emanation body." The king resolved to repent, and he picked out the living female spirit, and worshipped her and made offerings to her. This story is a transformed spirit story, and there is no way to find out when it originated.

Those who are to fill the ritual position of female spirits are selected from among girls. The Nepalese worship girls; they consider girls to be the transformation bodies of the spirits. The position of girls in the family is very honorable, and even if they make mistakes, they cannot be scolded. On the day she gets married, the woman's position plummets, and all the arduous household labor is taken on by the women.

In order to commemorate Sakyamuni Buddha, the female spirits are all chosen from among the girls of the Sakya clan. The criteria for selection are very rigorous. There are more than thirty rules. They must have unusual beauty, good physiques, have no scars, be more courageous and insightful than average, and so on and so on. Whenever the female spirits are being selected, first they choose several dozen who meet the criteria, and then they shut them up in a spooky dark room, where the walls are covered with all kinds of pictures, mostly of demons with strange looks and green faces and long sharp teeth. When they first go into that dark room, the girls with less courage cry out, and those who make the selection "trim away" those who cry. Little by little, they weed them out, and the ones who are left at the very end then undergo an even more rigorous test. For example, the ones giving the test may imitate the howling of demons late at night when people are all quiet. If a girl can keep calm and self-possessed, and not get frightened, then she can be chosen to become a female spirit. She will be escorted to the temple of the female spirits, and receive offerings, and be worshipped, until she matures and begins to menstruate.

In that land, the female spirits are called dakinis. In reality this is an expedient teaching, and though it is not impossible, the issue is this: these female spirits are considered as such only for a certain period of time, whereas dakinis must be worshipped their whole lives. After these female spirits first menstruate, their life as female spirits is over. They then fall back from the spirit level and return to the human realm. Their status falls enormously, and they are even looked upon by the Nepalese as unlucky people.

Ordinarily, these female spirits are hidden away in their temples, and nobody can see them. They are uniquely honored as having incomparable spiritual powers. They have the power to speak out, and they can settle various kinds of disputes. Every year the king must obtain the blessing of the female spirits. Only if the female spirits put their auspicious mark on the forehead of the king, is the king reckoned to have the legal right to wield royal power for that year.

In the dense crowd of people at the festival, I saw a female spirit riding on a great elephant: she was about ten years old, and her bearing was very dignified. Her body was covered with various kinds of beautiful ornaments, ornaments for her head, for her neck, for her ears, for her breast, and for her arms — all bright and glittering, the epitome of splendor. On the female spirit's forehead there was a striking auspicious mark, as she appeared in all her glory. The people were cheering her, and singing songs praising the beauty of the female spirit, and they reached a wondrous resonance with the surrounding atmosphere. I felt myself being dissolved: the weariness of the journey, the hardships of our trek, and the spiritual quest, and the heaviness of the mundane efforts — this all was transformed into that beautiful melody, into a fragrant wind of pure clear spirit.

I simply sank into that melody. For many years after this, whenever I thought of Nepal, my mind would resound with the song of the female spirits. Many years later, when I saw the dakinis Niguma and Sukhasiddhi, I used this melody to convey to them my devotion.

The crowd madly surged toward the female spirit, but they were held off by the Gurkha soldiers. Gurkha is a district in Nepal where the people are very valiant, and this is Nepal's best source of soldiers. On this point, they are like the Cossacks in Russia. Though these soldiers are small in stature, they are very fierce, and sooner or later they always became the worst headache for anyone who invaded Nepal. They were faithful to their duty, and held back the flow of people that was crowding in around the female spirit. The female spirit showed her intent by giving a subtle smile to the crowd of people. All she had to do was glance their way, and every one of the believers felt that the female spirit was bestowing her blessing on them personally.

I felt that the causal chain between me and the people of Nepal was very good. The joyous atmosphere of the festival of the female spirits swept away all the worldly fatigue from my mind.

2 Sumadi's Daughter

Because I did not understand the language, I had no way of getting the information I wanted to get. Taking advantage of the opportunities of people being in the streets for three days before the festival of the female spirits, we asked around everywhere, wanting to find some scholars who knew Tibetan and Sanskrit, but basically people could not understand what we were saying.

But I did not believe that in this huge mass of people, it could be possible that there was no one who could understand Tibetan. I kept on asking till I was tired of talking, when on the third day I finally heard a refreshing voice say: "Have you come from Tibet?"

The person asking the question was a woman. She was unusually beautiful, and in her bearing there was the dignity of a female spirit. Later I found out that she really was a former female spirit who had retired from the role. She was called Sharwadi, which means female spirit of wisdom. Because she had often heard it spoken, Sharwadi understood some Tibetan. She told us that her father was a pandit who was an expert in Sanskrit and Tibetan texts: he was called Sumadi.

Sumadi was very famous in the area. He had many students studying with him, and besides the local students, there were several who had come from Tibet seeking the Dharma. At that time it had already become the custom for Tibetans to go to India and Nepal to seek the Dharma. The first thing those seeking the Dharma had to do was learn the language. Sumadi had taught many students, but unfortunately he has already fallen into oblivion and no one has heard of him.

Sumadi's tuition fees were very expensive because, not only was he a great scholar, but he was the holder of many esoteric methods as well. He was very strict in his selection of disciples, and he would not give a second glance to those he spurned, no matter how much money they would have paid him. He always said that the lion's milk cannot be dumped into a piss pot. He was very thin and tall, and at first glance, he seemed very acerbic. As for those students he painstakingly taught, their Sanskrit level was first class, and a good many of them became translators. Later on, I became expert in translating the Sanskrit Canon. Many years later, you would be able to discover in the Tibetan Bstang'gyur many works which I translated, like *Secret Methods of Cultivation of Special Excellence Tara* and others.

I made an offering to Sumadi of ten ounces of gold, to pay for Pema Nam and me to study Sanskrit. We rented a room not too far from Sumadi. Every week we went to the teacher's house twice, and began a serious study of Sanskrit. Sumadi liked me very much. The story was that the night before I arrived, Sumadi dreamed that there was a man on his roof blowing the conch shell, and the sound reverberated through heaven and earth. He thought I would be able to bring him great renown. Nine hundred years later, you can see that Sumadi's prediction came true. The reason the name "Sumadi" can still be seen in your books is just because he was my Sanskrit teacher. If not for this, then like other teachers of Sanskrit who were equally famous at that time, he would have sunk in the oblivion of time.

I stayed with Sumadi for more than a year, and he not only taught me Sanskrit and Nepali and other kinds of writing, he also gave me more than fifty initiations. He hoped I would be able to be his personal disciple, his "robe and bowl" disciple. He discovered that, among the Tibetans who were there with him to seek the Dharma and study, my natural talent level was a bit higher. No matter whether I was studying the scriptures or learning Sanskrit, it seemed I was exceptionally quick. He also discovered that I was never satisfied with my level of learning, and I was absorbing nutrition from him like a sponge takes in water. Then too, at that time, many of those seeking the Dharma had their eyes on attaining liberation, so they would seek methods that would enable them to achieve liberation, and then leave him. At that time I thought that for a truly faithful disciple who had received the genuine transmission, liberation was not difficult. But I had not come to Nepal for the sake of my own liberation. I wanted to absorb from that place all the elements that could nourish the spirit, and take them back to Tibet. Thus, even though by then I had received initiations in many teachings from Sumadi, I was still not satisfied.

From time to time I was still able to see Niguma's expectant gaze.

Then something happened that made me leave Sumadi.

Sumadi's daughter Sharwadi had been a female spirit, and was held in great esteem, and enjoyed wealth and rank. But according to the customs of Nepal, no one would dare marry a female spirit after she had withdrawn from the role. They thought that all sorts of ill fortune would befall anyone who married a former female spirit. Thus, despite her riches and incomparable beauty, a former female spirit would always pass the later part of her life confined in lonely isolation.

Sharwadi's future gave Sumadi great concern.

As for the reason why I left Sumadi, there are two stories in the histories. One story says that after I mastered Sanskrit, and my studies were completed, then I left. The other story says that Sumadi wanted to make me marry his daughter. Though no Nepalese would dare to marry a female spirit, Tibetans did not observe this taboo. In fact, I did not believe that marrying a female spirit would bring me bad luck. I thought that what can truly change one's fate is one's own mind, not external things, especially not a woman who happened to have been a female spirit. Because of the unique special qualities of the esoteric teaching, Sumadi hoped that I would be able to use the status of being a yoga master to save people. The Dharma name "Khyungpo Naljor" was picked by Sumadi: it means yoga master of the Khyungpo clan. Later on, although there were other teachers who picked names for me, like Tsultrim Kungpao, and so on, all these other names were washed away without a trace by the waves of time. The name that remains in the annals of history is still Khyungpo Naljor.

Sumadi nevertheless hoped that I would be able to continue his family tradition of learning. He said he was already old, and if it were said that he still had any worldly concern, it was that he could not abandon his daughter.

People have two stories for what happened then. One story says that Sharwadi fell in love with me, and one story says that Pema Nam fell in love with the beautiful Sharwadi.

Those who hunt for marvels see these kinds of stories as precious jewels. For those with true faith, they are beneath contempt. Your later-day drama series are filled with these kinds of stories.

Of course, you may think that those legends all come true.

Pema Nam's slander directed at me started in Sumadi's house. One day, Pema Nam said many bad things about me to Sharwadi. He said I was not a Buddhist with true faith. He said what I believed in was the heretical religion Bonpo, and that Bonpo powers included death-dealing spells, and he said that I had broken the precept against killing.

That evening Sharwadi told me what he had said. At this point I understood that I had already aroused Pema Nam's jealousy. For the next several years, though I did not publicly break with Pema Nam, I was already on guard against him.

At that moment I was facing the second great decision point in life. A beautiful female spirit, rich in material wealth, the glory of a pandit's family, sweet beautiful human love — all this created a huge temptation. I went through a complicated psychological struggle. But I knew that, although I had come to Nepal to seek a woman, what I sought was not the beauty of Sharwadi, but the wisdom of Niguma.

So at that time, what was always on my mind was still that smiling woman in my destiny.

3 Female Spirits

When I decided to leave Sumadi's house, Sharwadi was very hurt. This was quite natural. You can surely understand this kind of pain. Because Sharwadi was also a human being, as a human she had human nature, and love is the most basic true content of human nature.

Sharwadi had the dignity of a female spirit, and her demeanor was very much like the bodhisattva Guanyin. Of course, this was very natural too — the Nepalese would never choose a woman without dignity to be a female spirit. I had seen a red spot on Sharwadi's face over the bridge of her nose. The story was that the girls who had competed with

Sharwadi to be female spirits were all very outstanding, and all very beautiful and dignified, and did not become agitated when faced with danger. Sharwadi had said that, when she was left alone in that room with the walls covered with paintings of evil spirits, she was actually very frightened. But her father had warned her that if she cried out, her dream of being a female spirit would be ruined. Sharwadi's ideal was to be a female spirit. She had a kind of natural fear of ordinary conventional life. In Nepal, the ones who suffer most are the women — not only do they suffer from hard work, they are discriminated against as a separate kind of human being. Sharwadi did not want to live this way.

Sharwadi said that the experience of being abandoned in that room was the most fearful event in her memory. That night she did not dare open her eyes, because every time she did, those evil spirits with their fangs would spring at her eyes, and bite at her mind. She could really feel that biting. It was that night that she understood that fear is actually a feeling with energy and substance. But she still held out, because her father had told her that fear is the first barrier. There were many girls who wanted to be female spirits who could not get through this barrier.

The tests that came latter were not so hard after all. Because no matter whether it was in her learning or in her cultivation, Sharwadi was beyond compare. Later on, she and three other girls went into the final circle. In deciding victory in this final circle, Sharwadi's face played a major role, and the most important thing was that red spot on her face over the bridge of her nose. This was because all the Nepali female spirits have that lucky sign over the bridge of the nose, but on them that red spot is artificial, while Sharwadi's was natural. According to the account of a master of physiognomy, to have a red mark between the eyebrows is an incomparable sign of good fortune. The red spot between the eyebrows is like two dragons playing with a pearl, like two winds turning toward the sun, so even if there is temporary adversity, later on the person is bound to become a major vessel of the teaching. Later, it was on this point that Sharwadi came out the winner.

During the years that Sharwadi was a female spirit, Nepal enjoyed good weather, the nation was secure and the people were at peace, and people all attributed this to the female spirit's protection and blessing. Because of this, people made offerings to the female spirit of great quantities of wealth. According to the rules, this all belonged to the female spirit herself. Sharwadi was acclaimed as having wealth that rivalled the whole kingdom's. But she understood clearly that the day she left the position of female spirit, her isolation would begin.

And so it happened. When she first got her menstrual period, she was asked to leave the temple of the female spirits. From this point on, when people saw her, they would keep a respectful distance. Sharwadi felt that she was still that same self, but all she met with was the sky above and the earth below. It was having this kind of experience in life, that finally let her understand the impermanence of worldly things. Thus, she began to understand the Buddhist teaching. By her father's calculation, he had to find for her a practitioner of yoga who practiced the esoteric teaching, because if he had cultivated the esoteric teaching to a certain level, he would need an enlightened consort.

At this point Sharwadi thought, if I meet a man I am satisfied with, I will be his enlightened consort.

4 The Curse of the Barrel Full of Demons

In the *Secret History of Khyungpo* it is recorded: When Khyungpo Naljor met Sharwadi, this was the first effect of the curse of the barrel of demons from that mandala made by the enemy sorcerers. He was faced with another choice: Do you want to lead the conventional life of an ordinary person, or do you want to continue your quest?

After this, the powers of the spells of the death-dealing methods and the barrel of demons methods alternated with each other. For a very long time, Khyungpo Naljor could only feel the power of the spells of the former, and he had not felt the demonic power of the latter. Not until later, when he truly fell into that barrel of demons, did he realize that all along in his life, that barrel full of demons had been opening its big mouth to engulf him.

Later on, when Khyungpo Naljor spoke of Sharwadi, his eyes would fill with deep feeling. He said that when he went to Nepal to seek the Dharma, the gold that he had brought with him was soon used up. After that, Sharwadi helped out with all his expenses in Nepal. Not many people know this. Many people only know that Khyungpo Naljor was very prosperous, and they say he got help from Mahakala with six white arms (a deity protecting the Dharma). But a spirit or Buddha cannot directly give gold to a man in the world — all the help and support they give must always follow the rules of worldly phenomena. The help from Sharwadi was an external manifestation that followed the rules of worldly phenomena.

As for the story that Sharwadi became the consort of Khyungpo Naljor, there is definitely no proof of this. Later on, among Pema Nam's disciples, there were a lot of people who said this, and made this into something like gossip that spread all over. In the *Secret History of Khyungpo*, it says that Sharwadi treated Khyungpo Naljor very well, and her father considered Khyungpo Naljor as a disciple who was close to his heart, but between Sharwadi and Khyungpo Naljor there never developed any substantial emotional love. In the book, it says that it is hard for us to believe that a man who had vowed to journey to the West to seek the Dharma, without regard for his own life, could fall into ordinary worldly emotions and desires along the way. If he abandoned his search for the sake of a woman, he would not have had to traverse countless rivers and mountains to go to a strange land, because in his own home district there were countless women already. In the history of Buddhism, there are many stories of resisting temptation. For almost all those who found the Path, the first barrier before succeeding on the Path has been to resist temptation.

However, one time when Khyungpo Naljor and I met, he did tell me of his emotional state at the beginning…

Chapter 6

The Worries of a Female Spirit

Xuemo: "Master, I want to understand the real you. Even if that reality is hard for me to take, I must know the reality. Can you tell me something about your real worries at that time?"

1 Problems with a Woman

Son, to tell you the truth, Sharwadi was the first woman that I truly loved. I loved her very much. After I met her, I finally understood that such mysterious feelings exist in the ordinary human world. In those days the most beautiful sight in the world was Sharwadi's smile. Every time she looked at me and smiled, the whole world was bright. Even now, whenever I think of her smile, a spring breeze still wafts through my mind.

I really loved her very much.

When I discovered this, I was truly terrified. You should understand that, before this, in my eyes women were really just one kind of sentient beings. I loved sentient beings, but that kind of love was really compassion, and moreover, at the first stage compassion is only a kind of intent. I thought it had to be like this. What you said was correct: the mind of compassion is an ardent love for sentient beings, the mind of detachment is a distancing from human beings. I had always liked living in solitude. Thus, any women that were around me always seemed like pictures I was visualizing: in reality, they were illusory images.

It was only after Sharwadi appeared that a real live woman appeared in my life. I did not care if she was a female spirit or not. I just felt that if she were in my life, everything would have meaning. During that period there were many moments when I even thought like this: Doesn't a person just have one lifetime? And it goes by so fast. Why am I not cherishing the love that is right in front of me, and torturing myself instead? you thought there was a lot to be afraid of—at that time, I was finally going to seek out Niguma, and this also became a kind of torture. There was a lot to be afraid of.

I truly understood now why the ancestors called falling in love with a woman "a problem with a woman." It really was a problem with a woman. If you do not have sufficient power in stable concentration, that so-called love can turn into an incurable problem with a woman. Many men who could have become eminent monks and great worthies returned to lay life after meeting women whom they loved very much. Do you think the great teacher Xuanzang of the Tang Dynasty would have become Xuanzang if he had fallen in love with a woman?

Many days and nights in that period, Sharwadi's smiling face kept appearing before my eyes. She had already taken the place of the object of my visualization practice. No matter how I tried to practice visualization, it was always hard to visualize the image of my tulelary deity I was focusing on—what appeared before my eyes was always Sharwadi. What the Sixth Dalai Lama said several hundred years later was in fact what I was experiencing at that time: "We enter meditative concentration to work to open the eye of truth, and we pray that the Three Precious Jewels, Buddha, Dharma, and Sangha will descend to the sacred platform. In this contemplation, when have all the holy ones ever appeared? Yet my lover come by herself." That's right, it really is this way.

At that time there were two things in my mind always battling. One was my dream, one was my love. My dream told me: "You better leave her, you still have a longer road to travel." But the other voice said: "You love her, don't you? Where will you ever find such a good woman? In this world what is most worth cherishing is love. If you cultivate your practice and become greatly accomplished, without love, what does it mean?"

Sometimes I even thought, "I am not going to deliver sentient beings after all." Because with the onslaught of that kind of grand love, all I cared about was the woman in front of me, and even though Niguma was still in my mind smiling, this was something very far away. Think about it. No matter whether I was reading scriptures or practising meditation or contemplating and reciting mantras, in reality, I was always surrounded by Sharwadi. The situation was very much like a sandstorm in your hometown. That's right, love is a feeling like a sandstorm. It fills the sky with its sound. That was Sharwadi's breath. Her smiles, her sighs—at that time she would sigh unintentionally—her frowns—her look when she frowned tore at my heart. Everything she did was like pebbles hitting my mind.

For days on end I was always thinking: "I don't care about the world. What I care most about is really the smile of a woman."

One day Sharwadi gave me a notebook. This notebook was very ornate, it was something for the exclusive use of the female spirits, and inscribed in it were many words from her heart. I already recorded this in dakini script and hid it away in the deepest place in my life.

When you are in a clear state, you too will see that text —

2 The Female Spirit's Yearnings

At last the evening dusk has taken the sun, which has been flirting with us the whole day long, and driven it below the mountains. Suddenly a coolness spreads over the land. I'm standing on the Watching the Husband Cliff I know so well, looking out toward where you are living ...

For a long time I could not wait this patiently, but who am I waiting for? Am I expecting that happy wind to strike my feelings again and enter? Or am I waiting for the gentleness of that yellow dusk to draw out my shadow and make it longer and longer? I can only wait if my eyes have this liquid yellow dusk — I am waiting for you to appear. Sometimes you appear in the halo of the dusk, chanting those Sanskrit words. But more often I do not see what I want to see — you. Travelers from far-off places approach from afar, and drift by like silhouettes. I don't know if these two familiar eyes of mine are deceiving my mind, or if it is my mind that has left these familiar eyes desolate.

Bad luck? Good luck? Who in past lives arranged these billowing red dusts? Even if I'm standing in the wind, I have no regrets. Can it be that what I am waiting for is a dream? Will I have to wait in this loneliness my whole life? The evening colors are descending, and I am lonely, waiting.

The sky has darkened, the wind is up, and in the end you did not appear.

Khyung, my sun, apart from you, my heart is desolate. I have almost become a willow in the wind. As I look toward that familiar silhouette, gradually disappearing in the flow of people, I really want to cry out with deep emotion and with all my strength. I really cannot bear this indescribable misery and loneliness.

I do not know whether or not you, as you are today, still have that seeker's mind, whether or not you are still exhausted in your dream like that, whether or not you still sigh in the depths of the night, whether or not you can still see that woman who is waiting for you.

Every time I think of your search, your quest, I feel a loss. I think that the sun finally will leave me and go. The days when the sun was shining bright will certainly gradually depart.

For this lifetime, I have decided I must be alone, come and go alone, with no one to keep me company. I have woken up from a sweet fragrant dream journey, and in the end we must say goodbye—we must go our separate ways. This is something that feels unbearable.

I sit in a quiet room, shut the door, and suddenly there is another barrier. Your mind is there, busy, and my tears are here, flowing. My mind is in pain, and I cannot express clearly how I feel. I could not bear to see you again, I'm afraid that your familiar image would stab into me and fill my heart with pain.

My good fortune was too brief, and I already knew there would be this kind of parting. I think it would have been better if we had not met. At that point I had already accepted my fate, and I had decided to live alone my whole life. Who would call me to come out? You are a person who has decided you must seek. Falling in love with you was like falling in love with the wind. From then on, my sky darkened. All my yearnings are an overwhelming force, how can I clear away these ruinous emotions? It is always as if I am running through the clouds, always as if I am living in a dream. I do not know where I am going. Maybe a person who has lost love is like this, with a mind always lonely and cold.

Alas, just go! It would be best if you did not come back.

I waited the whole evening, shed tears the whole evening, but you never appeared. My mind was very depressed, very fatigued.

I don't know why, but suddenly there were many things that I had no way to describe. Perhaps I did something wrong, and it turned out unbearably muddied. Maybe, in your eyes, I am no more than a book you have read all the way through, and that has made you avoid me like this, and get fed up with me. I feel I have been greatly wronged, and the tears flow in my mind, rippling with a kind of unspeakable pain. I feel that my own life is very painful. My self-confidence has totally collapsed ...

Being lovesick makes people get old, it would have been better not to have met. Why wasn't I a genuine emotionless female spirit? Why was I always imagining living the same way as other people? Should I abandon the role of female spirit? Should I remain with it? Either way would bring sorrow. If I abandoned it, who could ever again play a wonderful song for me? If I remained with it, who could ever guarantee my love?

You have lived a life too painful and too difficult. For the sake of your seeking, you do not shrink from adversity, and adversity is rushing at you from all sides, but you never think you have many hardships. Why don't you think about how you should act to lead a better life for yourself?

Human feelings are very confusing, and the stage of human life, with its gatherings and scatterings, really makes people feel bored. If not for you, this little compound would make me lose hope, or make me feel strange. All that is left in my mind are the ripples of that warm feeling from when we were together. All that remains in the depths of time are those days of talking and laughing and noise ...

When you went out to study, and all that was left in this little compound was me, everything was very still. When it was lit by the rays of the bright sun, then I would always go to that temple of the female spirits. This was a very beautiful place, and there I passed the most beautiful period of my girlhood. There were many people there, some offering incense, some praying, some bowing down, a dense crowd of people. I would sit quietly under a tree. The leafy green shade was like a roof, and it faced a pond with blue waves, and I liked it very much. My feelings were very hard to bear, as I thought of your final departure—how could I not let myself feel dazed? At first I looked at the deep blue water moving with the wind, and my mind gradually sunk. Later I raised my eyes and looked at those graceful colorful afternoon clouds, and gradually I began to think of my childhood dream of becoming a spirit-immortal, and my mind went into a boundless reverie. At that time, my greatest hope was to call you, you who provoked both love and trouble, to come here and sit for a while with me, but I clearly recognized that all this was an pointless extravagant hope.

Recently, at dusk on these summer days, there is always a bit of rain. Whenever it gets to be dusk, the weather gradually cools off a little, and the footsteps of the raindrops come back, and at that point I slowly walk back home. As soon as I walk into the lane, a fine rain is falling. Before long, you people will return home too. You people are very noisy, but I am always quiet. Coming back to the house alone, I gently shut the door.

I wake up in the middle of the night, with my mind wound up in a thousand threads of longing. Suddenly I remember that today is the day you come to study with my father. Although you and your companion do not stay long, after three days have gone by, it seems to me that I have been suffering for a thousand years.

You are going to come back this afternoon. Although I cannot be alone with you, I already feel very lucky. When you come back, my eyes can see through all the walls, and see you smiling. When you come back, my ears can silence all the loud sounds, and my mind is clear and still as the water of a lake. When you come back, your familiar scent is floating in the air, and I no longer feel alone.

Soon I will sit down and become a melancholy nameless bird. You have just come back. You should know that every day I stand in the setting sun at dusk and let that spirit dove fly.

Although it cannot bring you a message, it can always look at you from up close. It thinks that it has a karmic connection with you, and no matter where you go, it will always be able to find you. In the life of a certain ancient hero in legend, there is always an eagle following him. In your life, what is following you is this spirit dove. Though I bought it from a Brahmin, still I think that spirit dove really belongs to you. You will discover that its karmic connection with you is deeper than its karmic connection with me. Every time I see it, a sweet misty feeling curls up in my heart.

But maybe you truly do not understand this flirtatious style. Maybe you basically did not think that I would stop here, in this waystation of youth, and look over this rarefied scenery of yours.

I think that when we are old, the sun will still be very red. That fresh pure wind we encountered when we were young will still be flowing briskly, but we will not be able to feel bad, because our own glory years have gone by. To walk hand in hand till old age with a beloved for whom our feelings never die—this is the most beautiful part of human life, don't you agree?

At that time, we were taking a walk on a little Path lit by the setting sun, feeling close to each other, loving each other, and you saw my face losing the rosy color of youth and getting covered with wrinkles, and I saw you with a headful of silver hair, with deep feeling in your eyes: a long long time went by, and the love inscribed in our hearts did not change. As I was about to close my eyes, at the very last instant as I was leaving the world, there in my heart, and flickering before my eyes, was still your warm smiling face ...

3 Moving Sharwadi

I understood Sharwadi, and I understood Khyungpo Naljor. I wrote a poem from Khyungpo Naljor's point of view, which he very much liked. He said that I had expressed what he was feeling at that time very poetically.

The title of the poem is "Moving Sharwadi."

They always think

That scene of meeting

Has already come to the season of yellowing

That atmosphere that dissolves the soul

That must make memories fade out

They always think it scrambled the code of fate

They always think it smashed the quest of a hundred generations

They always think it brought peace to a befuddled mind

They always think it disturbed a man's cozy death

They always think

That when the bamboo flowers open, that is the end of their lives

The lightning flash that dazzles the eye in the end becomes the dead black stillness

They always fear the story of "cooking the crane by burning the zither"
will be put on stage

They always fear the moon over the desert will be shattered into heavy
rain roiling the sky

They always think they will lock down those years and months that pass by

They always think they will pulverize the bright face of impermanence

They always think that chance encounters of fate can be made eternal

They always think that amazing beauty can be made into a permanent miracle

They always think that the wind over West Lake will flow with that
renowned beauty Su Xiaoxiao for a thousand years

They always think the eternal special name will die

They are always questioning the spirit

They are always wanting to sip poison

They are always thinking that at dusk in the wind and rain

They will go to a hassock where the shadows of people rarely go

They are always thinking of tramping through the dawn frost in the
waning moonlight

Making an image of wandering all over the world in solitude

Thus whenever I set forth a story

In a thousand episodes

There are a thousand versions of you

In the thousand versions of you

There are a thousand past events that will break a person's heart

Millions of events as changeable as the wind and clouds

Come together to form one word: "Break"

They always think that after a scorching July, there is sure to be a season of pure cool rain

They always think that after the fires of life burn, there must be ashen memories

They always think that after a sad turnaround, there will be a new path

They always think when they are newly born from the lotus womb, there will be no more lotus fibers to tie them up again

They always think the women of peach blossom island have already died

They always think the laughter beneath the snowy mountains has already faded away

They always think the wind that has flowed from ancient times in the end will cease

They always think the pure song of life will sink into silence

They always think the beautiful images in the mind have already turned to emptiness

They always think the meetings of the future have already become things of the past

All they fear is to present their feelings in a solitary lonely dream

All they fear is to divulge their secrets in the ripples of the ebb and flow they have sunken deeply into

All they fear is the solitary reflection in the dew left by the morning wind

All they fear is walking alone on a moonless night

All they fear is an inviting gaze in a chance encounter

All they fear is a sigh at the moment between dreaming and waking up

All they fear is the gentle strumming of a thousand-year-old lute in an empty valley

All they fear is that life will never again have meaning

All they fear is the heart's solitary grave

A talking laughing corpse

Often among fools, your face appears like crystal

Often on a moonless night, there you are

Often you take manly courage and change it into heartfelt grief

Often amid laughter you are crying

A million times you wave your hands

But you cannot break the bonds of grief

A million times you stamp your feet

But you cannot scare away the mass of distractions

A million times you curse

And a million more times you seek

Dispirited eyes without the will to try

Always divulging that

Within that soul are held a thousand layers of secrets ...

4 The Festival for Slaughtering Animals

Before I set out on my new journey of seeking, Sharwadi took me to attend the festival for slaughtering animals. This was almost the biggest festival day in the region. Thousands of chicken, cattle, sheep, and water buffalos were brought to the temples. These animals of course knew their fate, and they all were being dragged by the neck, and making all kinds of frightened noises, so that the town was filled with all sorts of shrill cries. The Nepalese never slaughtered animals at home, and they did not call upon professional butchers to do the work for them. They took their domestic animals and brought them to be slaughtered before the images of the spirits, so it would be tantamount to making offerings to the spirits — this originally was the sacrificial ritual of Brahmanism. This was very similar to your custom in Liangzhou. When people in Liangzhou finish putting the roof on a house, they too must slaughter an animal. Nominally, they must make an offering to the village god, but in reality this meat goes into the stomachs of the people. You said that when Liangzhou people offer up an animal, they first pour some cold wine into the animal's ears, and if the animal shivers, it means that the spirits have already accepted it, and this is called "accepting the sacrificial animal." Nepal and Liangzhou are thousands of miles apart, but this custom of killing living beings to offer to the spirits is surprisingly similar. Evidently this ugly custom is part of the "collective unconscious" of the human race. Ha, look at me, I am moving with the times—haven't I learned this expression from nine hundred years in the future?

Although the Nepalese believe that these domestic animals attain deliverance from rebirth because they are offered up to the spirits, the animals do not appreciate the favor. Their eyes are still full of hopelessness and dread, and the sound of their cries creates an end-of-the-world atmosphere, but this just brings a look of joyous celebration to the faces of the people. This world is definitely not a world for domestic animals—as long as the humans think it is a festive celebration, then the world celebrates.

The streets were filled with ox carts and donkey carts—these were then the main means of transportation in mountainous Nepal. The carts were hung with bright ribbons, and the shafts were wrapped in garlands. The offerings were placed in front of the carts, and included grain, red powder, fruit, and so on. In Nepal, carts also became vehicles for the spirits, and on this day of the festival for slaughtering animals, it was also necessary to offer sacrifices for the carts. People would take live sheep, roosters, and so on, pull them in front of the carts, and slaughter them one by one. Headless chickens would flop around on the ground, provoking all sorts of exclamations from the crowds.

At that time, I certainly did not know that, in the river of people flowing by at the festival for slaughtering animals, there was a pair of eyes secretly spying on me. The man's name was Kusang Dorje, and he was Sharwadi's cousin. His eyes were filled with poison as he stared at Sharwadi and me from afar. His appearance provided more color in my life. He too was an "adversarial bodhisattva."

When the people slaughtered the sheep, they poured the blood over the carts, to show they were offering sacrifices for the carts.

After this, the large-scale slaughter commenced. The sound of drums got louder, and the royal guards were drawn up in formation in the temple. They held up their swords, and let out with an oath that shook heaven and earth. After they pledged their oath, people drove the cattle and sheep into the temple. Again and again, the animals gave forth their plaintive cries, and although the animals that were to be slaughtered for the festival were going to become companions of the spirits, they still wanted to go on living like ordinary animals. On this point, they had the same insight as China's ancient philosopher Zhuangzi. He would rather be a little turtle dragging its tail in the mud, than be made into a specimen to be offered up in a temple. The sacrificial animals, like those soldiers in the honor guard who had proclaimed their oath, put out a sound that shook heaven and earth, a sound that was a plea. They were screaming: "We want to live! We want to live!" It was as if I understood their heartfelt cry, and tears welled up in my eyes. I thought, no matter what kind of spirits these are, they do not have the right to take away the lives of other living things. This aversion for killing living things prevented me in Nepal and in India from ever joining the religion of Brahmanism.

A water buffalo with a huge body was dragged to the stake to be slaughtered. A Brahmin chanted a spell and sprinkled water on the water buffalo's body. There was a guy holding onto the water buffalo's tail. The sound of the drums got louder, shaking heaven and earth. A military man with the look of a high official held a knife up in front of him, and struck a pose, displaying a very forceful look. He swung his arm, and the long knife came down in an arc, and like a flash of lightning slashed across the neck of the water buffalo. In the blink of an eye, the enormous water buffalo fell to the ground. Fresh blood gushed from the wound and spattered in all directions. I could not help but feel startled, and a numbness washed over my whole body. I hurriedly performed an expiation according to the Bonpo ritual forms I had learned. I had not anticipated that, although I had already left the Bonpo religion, when I was here in a different town in a different country, the easiest thing for me to think of would still be the Bonpo I had left. Obviously, the things a person learns when he is young will follow him throughout his whole life, just as a shadow follows a form.

The water buffalo's body crashed to the ground, stirring up some dust. One man had already moved the water buffalo's head to the side of a colorful banner, and some other men dragged its body around the banner. This was what was called sacrificing to the banner.

5 Nightmarish Memories

The slaughter was still going on, and blood was flowing everywhere.

The stench became a swirling wind. All in all, there were eight buffalo heads and one hundred and eight sheep heads offered up beneath the banner. The men carrying out the slaughter were all very excited, as if the goddess Durga who was receiving the offerings had already bestowed upon them matchless strength. The goddess Durga is the symbol of the spirits of war—he won eternal reverence because he defeated the evil demon Mahishasura. The festival for slaughtering animals was originally to commemorate and make sacrifices to the goddess Durga, but gradually it developed into a kind of ceremony for building up willpower. Military officers, when taking up their posts or retiring from their posts, all have to demonstrate their might and their prestige by killing living beings. The story was that by sacrificing to the banner by killing living things, they could attain the blessings of the spirits. But I was shuddering in horror. One of the reasons I had originally left Bonpo was that in Bonpo they are always killing living things in their sacrifices. But now here was a Brahmanist ritual of sacrifice killing even more living things. I thought: even if the result of killing living things would let me experience the rainbow body, I would not stoop so low as to do this.

As I looked at the animal heads that had tumbled to the ground, my heart hurt as if it were being twisted. I thought: over the course of time without beginning and without end, these animals have all been our mothers — how can we slaughter them?

Although all the animals were now dead, in my ears their plaintive cries were still resounding. These cries were like a dull saw blade cutting back and forth across my heart. My eyes were filled with the scarlet red color of blood, and the stench was still assailing my nostrils. I thought that if the spirits they are sacrificing to really like killing living beings, no matter what great all-pervading powers they might have, I will not venerate them. I thought that genuine great spirits must treat every living soul well.

This festival for slaughtering animals brought me nightmarish memories. The dead bodies of those animals are still thrashing around in my brain. In my dreams I still cannot get rid of the disturbance that this slaughter brought to me. I have had many dreams of the festival for slaughtering animals, and in every one of these dreams I feel terrified, and find myself covered in cold sweat.

For many years after that day, although I met many famous eminent masters of Brahmanism, I would never study with them. Many years later, Sukhasiddhi brought me to hear the *Bhagavad Gita*, and only then did I have a new appreciation of Brahmanism.

Chapter 7

Khyungpo Naljor's Dream Demons

Xuemo: "Master, I saw in the Secret History of Khyungpo that one time you were taken captive. Can you tell me in detail about what went on?"

1 Gift of Fate

The beginning of that incident had its origin in an engagement between Sharwadi and me.

At that time, I already felt that I would never leave Sharwadi. I found that our relationship was becoming closer and closer, and had gone far beyond the limits of the relationship between a mentor-older brother and a younger sister. I was like a rock rolling down a mountain, driven by the momentum of love, out of control, not knowing where I was going.

I decided to cut the thread of emotion with the sword of wisdom. I knew that if kept on vacillating, I would not be able to jump out of the well of emotional desire. Of course I did not anticipate that, to Kusang Dorje, my decision was a kind of betrayal of his cousin Sharwadi. So he kept an eye on me. He decided to give me a lecture.

That day I called the spirit dove to take a letter to Sharwadi, arranging to meet her in the forest behind the temple of the female spirits.

I wanted to have a serious talk with her. I wanted to tell her that although I was in love with her, I had decided I must leave her. I had already learned Sanskrit, Pali, and some local dialects, and I could communicate freely. I wanted to continue the search for truth that was my fate.

At that time, her father had all but publicly acknowledged me. Many people believed I would marry Sharwadi. Only Kusang Dorje knew what was on my mind, and whenever he saw me, the expression on his face was hard to bear. He thought I was trifling with his cousin. He had clearly told me many times: either I marry his cousin, or I should have no more contact with her. He said he had seen many women who had died from being lovesick, and he did not want his cousin to end up like this. He did not understand: since I loved Sharwadi so much, why would I go looking for another woman? Nor did he understand that if I had decided to go look for another woman, why did I still love his cousin?

He had asked the right question. Now when I think back on it, I really did have to get far away from Sharwadi. But you must know that many things in our fate cannot be planned. My love for Sharwadi was really a battle with my fate. I had been totally unprepared when I fell in love with her. When I discovered I was in love with her, her love for me was already incurable.

Still, when we look at this mutual love through the mist of a thousand years, I still feel grateful for the gift of fate. If not for Sharwadi, my life would have much worse. What I mean is not just in regard to emotions, I am also including my mission. During my thirty years of travelling in India, Sharwadi continued to be one of the poetic inspirations in my life. Though we did not become husband and wife in the ordinary worldly sense, if it were not for her, I am sure I would not have had my later glory. Later on, she took almost all the wealth she had received during her time as a female spirit, and used it for my work in seeking and spreading the Dharma. Think of it, just with the temples I built, there were a hundred and eight of them. Without Sharwadi, the line of Shangpa Kagyu that came later basically could not have existed.

Though I had decided to leave, there was a lot of excitement about that engagement. No matter whether a man was a monk or a holy man, as long as he was a male, there were certain to be women he was fond of. Later on when I achieved enlightenment, I discovered that I still could not get away from the law of attraction between the sexes. There is nothing to do about it. Although this can only be seen as a type of habit-energy, if not for the worldly discriminating mind, of itself it cannot create afflictions. But when it becomes the male habit-energy, it can be a controlling force for subtle good and evil. Even with the great master Padmasambhava, though he had already become an enlightened one, his feeling for his female disciple Yeshe Tsogyal certainly went beyond his feelings for his other disciples.

It was this way for me too. No matter before I achieved enlightenment or after, whenever I thought of Sharwadi, a warm current surged up in my mind. With her external appearanceas a worldly woman she gave me a feeling of poetic beauty I could never in my life forget. In my life there have been three women. Aside from the world-transcending Niguma and Sukhasiddhi, Sharwadi was a being I could not ignore. Though externally she was a phenomenon of the world, in her fundamental substance, she was like Guanyin Bodhisattva marrying that pirate she wanted to save and transform, a benefactor in another form.

Though in some written records considered to be correct, as in the *Secret History of Khyungpo*, they treat my meeting with Sharwadi as woman-trouble brought about by the Bonpo guardian spirits, I myself feel grateful that I met her.

That's right. I admit that not only at the time, but later on in my long search for truth, Sharwadi's love appeared outwardly to be a kind of temptation and something that caused difficulties. My feeling for her was a worry all along, and objectively was obstructing my search. But it was in these repeated struggles with myself that I became who I am.

2 Being Taken Captive

At that time nine hundred years ago, I got to the point that I saw Niguma as Sharwadi. Whenever I thought of her, my mind would always jump around crazily. This feeling would slowly soak in, like a drop of ink on a piece of paper. By the time I discovered this drop, it was already beyond fixing. At that time I was always filled with a poetic feeling as I awaited every meeting with her.

That day, I had gone to the forest behind the temple of the female spirits. It was relatively peaceful and quiet there. I remember the sky that day was blue, the wind was clear and pure, and everything was very beautiful. Several old people were circumambulating the stupa. Because they were Sharwadi's fellow-townsmen, as I looked at them, in my mind there was an unusual sweetness.

I did not wait for Sharwadi there.

I noticed that there were three guys following me. One of them was Sharwadi's cousin Kusang Dorje. Kusang Dorje was exasperated, and he had told me many times, either get married with his cousin, or do not bother her any more, give her some peace. He had told me not to meet with her alone again. When she and I went together to the festival of slaughtering animals, he said this brought shame to his family. If I did not do what he said, he and his family would intervene. He said, if necessary, he was willing to exchange a lamb skin for an old sheep skin, meaning that he would kill me and trade his life for mine.

Kusang Dorje perhaps did not know that emotional issues are not a matter of one plus one equals two. At that time in fact I was in the midst of a struggle. Suddenly I would want to marry Sharwadi and lead the life of an ordinary person; then suddenly I would want to go far away, and go searching for my own dream. My emotions and my rational nature were always clashing, ceaselessly bickering. This kind of emotional state is the same as that reflected in a poem from several hundred years later by the sixth Dalai Lama Tsangyang Gyatso:

If there are too many emotions, I fear it will hurt my religious practice

I go into the mountains, afraid to enter the town wrongly

In the world, how can I find the truth of double completeness?

Not to spurn the Tathagata, not to spurn the worldly lord.

The thing was, I did not understand how the men pursuing me knew of the engagement between Sharwadi and me. Even now, this is still a mystery. Some say it was Pema Nam who revealed the secret. Before this event, I had honestly discussed this matter with him, so he really had what was needed to tell the secret. This is just a guess, there has never been any proof.

From the ferocious look in the eyes of my adversaries, I naturally understood what it would mean if I went with them. I had heard that three years earlier the local men had beaten to death a Tibetan man who had tried to marry a female spirit. Perhaps to let a "crude fellow" — this is the way they saw it — who came from Tibet marry a female spirit was, to the local men, a dirty insult, a desecration. But even more possible is that it was jealousy. The local men might think: "If I cannot hope to get her, no one can." What's more, a female spirit had so much wealth that it made the local men red-eyed with envy. At the time, I thought that they just wanted to drive me away, so that that female spirit's great wealth would not fall into the hands of an outsider. But what I did not imagine is that, in fact, they would try to force me to marry the female spirit immediately.

When I discovered that I had fallen in love with Sharwadi, I had felt a lot of torment. Should I stay? Should I go far away? This question was haunting my mind all the time. On one side was my search for truth, on the other side was my beloved. I did not want to give up either one. I felt the pain of my soul being cut up. For a long time I had no way to break free of the chains of either side. I could not give up my attachment to seeking truth — that was my reason for living. Nor could I give up Sharwadi. She truly was a female spirit. After I met her, so many of my feelings were brought to life. I had never imagined that in the human world there ultimately was this kind of special wondrous feeling. At that time I even thought of the Land of Ultimate Bliss spoken of in the Buddhist sutras—is it like this? If it is like this, then the human world is the Pure Land. If it isn't like this, then what meaning is there to that Land of Ultimate Bliss?

The three men pulled me along. They took me to the back building of the spirit temple. I thought back to what had happened to my fellow countryman three years earlier, and I was scared. I thought: I still have not found the person I must find, and if I am beaten to death by these men, my life will have been lived in vain.

I clearly knew I could not avoid the physical suffering, but I had an unusual feeling of ease. I thought: if they ask me, I will truthfully tell them that I definitely do not want to marry your retired female spirit. With this thought, I felt I had shed the bonds that had been wrapped around me for so many years, and I had a kind of feeling of relief after being set free.

There were still the men waiting in the back building of the spirit temple. I could not flee, and I did not want to flee. I wanted to face it all.

Kusang Dorje looked ferocious as he had the men close the windows and lock the doors, and there was a guy holding a club guarding the door.

I felt no fear. I just wanted to tell them that I did not want to marry the female spirit. This thought was hard for me to bear, but it also made me relax. But the men did not ask me any questions, they just kept berating me in a fiendish way.

I decided to express clearly what was in my heart. Although I loved her very much, there was something more important in my life. I had not come in this lifetime to marry a female spirit.

I remembered that morning, as I was sitting in meditation, a mysterious voice said: "A woman, no matter how beautiful she may be, is always a problem. Do not harbor illusions about her."

I was facing a showdown with them, but those men did not ask me anything.

All I could do was wait in silence.

I had not thought that finally they would search my body. Ordinarily they had the look of very dignified men, religious men. But in the end they could abandon this façade and search my body. They found some gold pieces I was carrying. When they saw the gold pieces, a strange light flashed from their eyes.

Again I was surrounded by several men, and they found the Tibetan knife I always carried. One of the man cried out, "Aha, attempted murder. You have committed the crime of attempted murder." When they saw that Tibetan knife, it was as if they had found a treasure. Maybe they could find some justification in the local laws.

I laughed. Carrying a Tibetan knife was a habit of mine, but they were saying I wanted to kill the female spirit. This accusation was so clumsy, I began to look down on their intelligence.

3 Slaps in the Face Come Flying

Under Kusang Dorje's interrogation, I admitted that I liked Sharwadi. I did not say I loved her. Although by then I had already fallen in love with her, and this was a deep heartfelt love, I also loved that search for truth. As soon as they heard me say I liked Sharwadi, those men became infuriated. I did not understand why they were so angry. I thought that maybe they liked Sharwadi too.

Again I admitted it: "I really like her!"

One guy suddenly leaped up, and after saying "bah!" again and again, slapped me across the face several times.

Being beaten made me lose my bearings — this was the first time in my life I had been hit in the face. All at once I had the feeling of sudden awakening.

"Get ready, brothers." Kusang Dorje spat out a reproach. Four guys were clenching their fists, eager for a fight.

Kusang Dorje said, "He is still acting shamelessly. Beat him to death!"

Kusang Dorje was glaring at me in anger, and he hit me first. My brain was ringing, and I fell to the ground. I had not thought he would hit anyone, and I had thought of him as a fellow brethren. Our previous relationship had been very good. He knew that I loved his cousin, and he knew that she loved me. I had told him about my feelings for her, and about my search. I had said to him: "Though I love your cousin, I must go off on my search. I could not bear a life without the search." At that time he said, "Your thinking is wrong. You wanted to play with her, and then you found a reason to abandon her. No way!" I said that if I went away to search for truth, I would not be meeting with her, and in my mind the bright moon would be reflected.

When he heard this, he gave a cold laugh.

I had told him that, although it was very painful for me to leave Sharwadi, I knew this pain could not last forever. I knew that all suffering and good fortune in reality are only types of emotions. And all emotions are impermanent.

Sometimes I still sink into the pain of imagining her. In that place, no one would dare to marry a female spirit. She would pass her whole life in solitude and longing. Whenever I think about this, the thought of marrying her pops up again in my mind, but a thought is just a thought. When I do not follow them, all thoughts are like the autumn wind blowing in a donkey's ear.

But on a certain day, I discovered something very much to be feared. I discovered that when I thought of not having Sharwadi in my life, then I would not have any spirit anymore, any impetus, and that suddenly there was no happiness or meaning in human life. At that instant, I fearfully discovered that when I thought of leaving Sharwadi, my search for truth receded into the distance.

At that point, I finally decided to leave her, and set out on my search.

4 "Beat This Tibetan Dog to Death!"

Another fist came flying and hit me behind the ear.

I do not know whether or not I blacked out, but suddenly I found myself on the ground, with a sound like thunder in my ears. I remember that I groaned, and my brain went blank. I lost consciousness.

I don't know how much time went by before I came to. My head was bleeding, and it ached as if it would split apart.

I saw Kusang Dorje holding up an incense burner, howling and yelling, as if he was about to smash it down on me.

That one punch made my head ache for many years. Even though in later days I was on the road seeking Niguma, what stayed with me for the longest time was this head pain. Every time my head ached, I thought back to what happened in the temple of the female spirits.

There was a roaring sound in both my ears.

Another punch smashed me in the eye. A bloody welt appeared in the corner of my eye. Heaven and earth turned red. At that instant, I had even no thoughts.

Several other men were punching me. When I came to, I felt a sharp pain in my head.

I did not fight back. I knew what fighting back would provoke. My mind was empty and blank, and the roar in my brain did not let up.

After they beat me up, they came right to the point. Kusang Dorje spoke of three options and demanded I choose: One was to admit I had attempted to murder a female spirit, and to be immediately taken to court. The second option was to mutilate my body, to castrate myself. The third was for me to marry Sharwadi and live out a normal life, and never again mention that damn "search."

The female in charge of the temple of the female spirits raised another condition, demanding that I take all the money I had brought with me and donate it to the temple, to compensate for possible losses to the local area from damaging the sacred status of a female spirit.

That female in charge of the temple went on at length, reckoning up the account: one after another she brought up many historical cases where damaging the sacred status of a female spirit had brought harm to the local area. She said, "If we take you to court, your life will be over, and you will certainly be imprisoned. In this life, your mission, your faith, your position will all be finished. And your clan will be covered with shame because of you."

"Don't forget," that woman said, "even though Sharwadi loves you, it is Nepalese blood that flows in her veins."

"We already have all the proof." The female scoundrel triumphantly showed several pieces of paper on which were recorded all the sins I had supposedly confessed to. "Do you believe me?" she said. "I have the authority to imprison you immediately. You must believe it. Here, although the law does not explicitly forbid marriage with a female spirit, because of the influence of custom, it is impossible for anyone who marries a female spirit to lead a peaceful, prosperous life. By custom and by law, many kinds of forces bring 'bad luck' to anyone who marries a female spirit. I'm afraid that actually it's not that marrying a female spirit is 'bad luck,' but that it may delay more important things."

I said: "I do not know what the outcome will be if you are deliberately bringing false charges against me. I do not know."

"Bringing false charges? You dare speak of bringing false charges?" A man hit me again.

The other men shouted: "Beat him! Beat this Tibetan dog to death!"

The story was that the female in charge of the temple had been the wet nurse of the currently serving female spirit. She sat beside me, and grabbed me by the hair and said: "I am looking at this animal. Oh, he has a head and a face. Do you still want to slip away? I really do not understand, what does our female spirit ultimately see in you?"

That woman said: "You must know that what changes quickest in the world is a woman's mind. The thing to fear the most in the world is a woman who has changed her mind. If you really want to slip away, Sharwadi too will agree to take you to court. She surely will think: 'If I cannot get him, everyone else should also stop wanting to get him.'"

Sometimes they tried to entice me, sometimes they threatened me — this noisy drama went on for two days. It was as if I were experiencing hell. When I was having my beard pulled and being called an animal by this unbearably vulgar woman with her heavily made-up face, I really wanted to drop dead right on the table. But because I still had not found the person I had to find, I would die with eternal regret.

During those two days, I got a taste of many things in human nature that are called "evil," and felt a certain despair. I even suspected that Sharwadi had participated in this drama, and I felt very sickened by that. However, I soon repented my mistake of "using the mind of a petty person to measure the capacity of a noble person." I believe that Sharwadi definitely did not know about this business that Kusang Dorje was staging.

Seeing me stubbornly refusing again and again, Kusang Dorje lost his reason, and slapped me across the face many many times. Then I thought, "Right now the most important question is how to get out of the grasp of these thugs." With this thought, the light of the spirit's wisdom suddenly appeared. I realized that it was not necessary to be tangled up with these crude men, that I had to see Sharwadi, and get her help.

That night, I had a strange dream. I felt that I was in a giant mountain range, in total despair, and grey shadows were flashing before my eyes. The fearsome hopeless scene was making me suffocate, and all hope was gone. There was only hopelessness, only fear. I did not have a bit of energy. The meaning of life had vanished. I was like a lonely soul in the legends who wanders aimlessly all over. I could not find the way back. I could not see the light of the sky. I had no way to take control of my body, which was like a willow blowing in the wind. I seemed to have really reached the stage of the intermediate shadow body between death and rebirth. At this point I cried, and the sound of the cry appeared futile in the vast wilderness. At that moment, a woman appeared. I could not see her face clearly, but I knew she was Niguma. She encouraged me, and said she would be with me my whole life. I cried with great happiness, with great sadness—I had not cried like this for a long time. After that, like a mother giving me encouragement when I was little, she called my name again and again:

Khyungpo Ba—when you are cold, light the fire

Khyungpo Ba—when you are hungry, come eat

*Khyungpo Ba—when you are up high and get scared, come down to
someplace lower*

Khyungpo Ba—when you are in a hard place, come to where it's softer

Khyungpo Ba—your soul is coming to your body

As she was calling to me, I felt myself coming back to life. Then I made a vow: no matter what kind of adverse circumstances appeared, I would always seek her out.

I remembered that dream a long time. It contained many mystic secrets.

Although that dream was already imprinted deep in my soul, I still have no way to describe it clearly. You must understand that words are always pale and feeble, and many perceptions are very hard to describe. For example, I still have no way to describe to you the great bliss I felt after that woman took me into her arms.We held each other beside a small river, the sky was our cover, the earth was our bed, and except for some barking dogs, in all directions it was completely pure and bright and auspicious. I remember that in the dream the moonlight was very bright, and the river was very still in the moonlight, and the trees far away and the rocks nearby were all dissolved in the boundless moonlight. That was a very long, very beautiful dream.

Today when I relate it, I still feel very warm. Many vague faraway feelings come to me, and make me sigh. Though what I went through then did have much violence and blood, still, my mind ripples with a wondrous magical rhythm. All those people and events are all suffused with the beauty of the dusk and the hazy moonlight.

I feel grateful to life for having given me all this, and having made my human existence so very wonderful.

On the third day, I got out of the building behind the spirit temple. I promised to abide by the conditions that those people had set, and I signed the guarantee document that they told me to sign. I was really afraid they would cripple me. But my intent to leave was already settled.

Later on I understood Kusang Dorje. The story is that he had believed a provocation made by another man, who said that after I had toyed with Sharwadi, not caring whether a woman lived or died, I wanted to sneak away. Kusang Dorje felt that this had already brought shame on his family, so he incited other kinsman. These men then did their worst. Maybe they really did want to help a woman attain her hope. At the same time, they certainly also thought that they were acting for my own benefit. Unless I could marry such a beautiful woman for my wife, I would not be able to attain wealth that could rival the king's. Like a good doctor who forcefully takes measures on behalf of a stubborn and stupid sick man, they wanted to cure me of my failure to appreciate the favor I had been granted. At the beginning they were still a little bit reasonable, but later they got entirely into the role. They were carried away by the atmosphere they themselves had created. They did their utmost to play out the drama, and they left me with nightmarish memories.

To tell the truth, even now I still feel for Kusang Dorje very much. You must realize that Sharwadi's wealth could rivol the monarch's, and if Kusang Dorje had had any personal greed for it, he would have driven me away. That way, when Sharwadi and her father died, that wealth would have fallen into the hands of the extended family. But at that time what Kusang Dorje was worried about was, in the end, to make me marry the female spirit—he wanted to make me the owner of that wealth. Maybe, in his mind, the choice I made to abandon Sharwadi was the greatest insult to his cousin and to his family, as if a beggar looked at a throne that had been offered to him, and said he would have to think it over. If this could be tolerated, what could not be tolerated? I truly understood how he had lost his reason after getting utterly enraged with me.

As I left the spirit temple that day, the weather was really good, and everything seemed to be welcoming me with an overflowing spiritual energy. Because I had made my decision, I felt very relaxed. In my mind it was as if there was a happy fairy laughing, but it was a tearful laugh. My mind was agitated by a strange feeling. The heaviness I had been sunk in for so long had dissolved, and the layers of worry had been neutralized. How good it felt!

But because I had gone through this change, many beautiful feelings had gone far away, and there were many other things on my mind. I thought: the ocean of suffering is boundless, but turn around and the shore is right there.

The feeling of the ebb and flow of life flooded in like water, and submerged all my poetic feelings. My spirit had once more experienced a tortuous test of fate.

Sharwadi came to see me. During the three days I had been missing, she had aged ten years. On her lips there were two bloody scars. As soon as she saw me, she wept and wailed.

Sharwadi said that on that day she had not received my letter. Maybe the spirit dove lost the letter, or it was intercepted by someone — many people liked that spirit dove, and were very familiar with it.

She rubbed my wounds, and quietly cursed Kusang Dorje. She was cursing him and crying in distress.

After that, she again smiled brightly. I asked her the reason for her smile, and she said that in her dreams I had told her I would not leave her. She said that in the dream she had happily held me tight and jumped up. She smiled very brightly.

I felt as if my spirit had been stabbed by a knife, and suddenly my tears fell like rain.

After that day, whenever I thought of that pitiful dream of hers, I would always start crying.

This is because I knew that, no matter what kind of changes I experienced, I would never pass my days in peaceful private life with her—I would no longer forget my search.

5 For the Sake of That Dream

No matter what kind of spiritual torment Khyungpo Naljor went through, he told Sharwadi what he had decided to do. He told her his choice of fate, and said that even though he had signed an agreement promising to marry her, he had been forced into this. If she was willing, she would let him go on a long journey. If she wanted him to abide by that treaty signed under pressure in the temple of the female spirits, then he would marry her, but he would certainly suffer for it his whole life.

Sharwadi herself was suffering very much.

In the ebb and flow of my memory, Khyungpo Naljor and Sharwadi had a conversation like this:

"Do you really want to go?"

"Yes."

"Why do you want to go?"

"Because to go is my karmic fate. If I do not go now, then maybe I will never go."

"Why?"

"Because now I can remember my karmic fate from past lives. If I stay here for a year, the imprint of my past lives will have faded. If

I stay here two years, that imprint will fade even more. If I stay here three years, that imprint will be vague and barely discernible. As the waters of more time wash it away, I will not be able to remember my karmic fate from past lives anymore."

"Is that really so frightening?"

"It is. In the world there are many many people who potentially could be great, and they all have their karmic fate from past lives, but when this kind of awareness erodes away, they end up forgetting their own origins, and turn into nonentities."

"Maybe what you say is right. When I was serving as a female spirit, I felt that I really was a female spirit. Now I am just a lovesick woman. Barely five years have passed, and I have already forgotten so many things from when I was a female spirit."

"What you say is true. Right now, you have already begun to occupy my mind. If I continue to stay on, that woman called Niguma may gradually withdraw from my mind and spirit, and someone else will completely occupy me. She may be called Sharwadi, or she may have some other name—these are just names. But Niguma is not a name, she is my reason for living. Other women can only join in the process of my life. This is because what Niguma represents is a kind of search beyond form, whereas other women are beings living in the world of form."

"Why don't you take other women as that kind of search beyond form?"

"Because they carry a different spirit. Niguma represents the transcendental spirit of benefiting living beings. Other women represent certain rules of worldly phenomena."

"So then, are you about to leave?"

"That's right. While I am still awake and clear, I will force myself to leave this environment that is making me lose my memory. You understand more clearly than I do the influence which environments have on people. When you were in the temple of the female spirits, you were a female spirit. When you are together with me, you are just a lovesick woman. Whatever kind of environment you encounter, you might have that kind of mind."

"This is true, actually."

"You might not know the story of my father. When he was very young, he wanted to imitate those great worthy ones of ancient times and go to India to seek the Dharma. But later, he never did go there, because he kept on finding reasons not to go. This is because if anyone wants to find reasons, he will always be able to find any kind of reason. All the reasons in the world appear when you need them. Their intrinsic quality is to let you deceive yourself. My father was this way too: time and again he used those reasons to deceive himself. Day by day as he grew up, the reasons multiplied. Then one day he discovered that his initial way of thinking was too childish. So then he happily and willingly became a Bonpo teaching master. Later on, when I had the kind of urge to go seeking that he had had when he was young, in the end he wanted to stop me. This was because, in his eyes, the way I thought was just a sign of immaturity. In this way, the world to which my father became more and more accustomed, ended up killing his dreams."

"So he was never able to get out?"

"That's right. Early on, he felt that he did not have the strength to get out. So he thought: I'll wait till I have the strength, then I will go. In fact, he did not know that to really get out fundamentally did not require strength—all that was needed was the mental state to leave decisively. That mental state is the strongest power in the world. But my father kept on trying to accumulate the strength he considered necessary. Later on, he ended up having that kind of opportunity and strength, but he did not have the mind to leave. The day my father was about to die, he suddenly remembered his dream, and he quietly told me of his regrets. He told me that if he had another lifetime to come, he would realize his dream. I very much wanted to tell him, 'In your next lifetime, you will still have countless reasons holding you back. You will still not want to leave behind the life of comfort and ease you have at your fingertips. You will still fear the unfamiliar, and there will still be countless mediocrities to kill your dreams.' Though the wishes and regrets he had when he was about to die will appear in their reincarnated shapes in the substance of his life—in my father's next childhood, those dreams will still appear—nevertheless, the worldly environment will still erode his dreams from his former life, and seep into the youthful mind of his natural talent. Without that sword of wisdom that can cut this off, my father will still go on lifetime after lifetime with his regrets, and become another terrible case of revolving around birth and death. This is why I must guard my mind, and not let it become more and more worldly."

"When did you make up your mind?"

"It was when your father started treating me like his son. At that time, I suddenly discovered that all at once I would have a lot of things: position, property, a sister or a wife. And I also had so much unexpected warmth and sweetness. I suddenly discovered that fate had arranged everything, and I did not have to make so much effort any more. Because no matter how much I spent, I could not spend that much wealth. But at the same time, I discovered that I now had a kind of duty, and that limited many of my freedoms. Life was very just: when it gave me so many things, it also demanded things of equivalent value from my life — for example, my freedom, my search, my dream. At that point I thought: I have to leave."

"For the sake of your dream?"

"That's right. For the sake of that dream of mine."

"Alright. I understand you now. You should go then. I don't care anymore about your so-called contract. The so-called guarantee and agreement you were forced into signing — you don't have to abide by them. Don't worry about those men, I will go convince them. However, I know that Kusang Dorje's hatred and obsession are very strong. He certainly took the contract with you very seriously, and he will feel that you cheated them. He is sure to try to get revenge. Though I do not know what form his vengeance will take, you had better take precautions. I will do all I can to diffuse his anger and hatred, but you must realize that once a female spirit has left her ritual position, then she is not much different from all the women in this area, and she has no status. I don't know how effective my attempts to persuade him will be. I will also ask my father to try to mollify him. Let's try it and see. We will do all we can."

She also said: "After you go, I will always be waiting for you. You must promise me that after you find what you are searching for, you will definitely come find me. Take this agreement you made now, and put it off until you find your dream. Before, I too had my own dream. When I was very young, I wanted to be a female spirit. Later I got to be a female spirit. When I was a female spirit, I found that even though I had the appearance of a female spirit, I definitely was not a female spirit, because I had no clear understanding. Even when I was pointing out the right Path to so many lost people, I still had no clear understanding. At that time I thought: I must get to be a genuine female spirit. I must seek out the true characteristics of life, I must see into the secrets of birth and death. I must thoroughly understand the truth. I must build something of value that time cannot destroy."

"So this is your dream too."

"That's right, it is. When I left the temple of the female spirits, my mind was gray as ashes, because my dream of being a female spirit was smashed. From being an ordinary person, I became a female spirit, and now, from being a female spirit, I was going back to being an ordinary person. Though I possessed incalculable wealth, I was not blessed with good fortune. And I discovered that even when I was a female spirit, I still was not blessed with good fortune. Then I thought, does that sweet dew really exist in the world or not—that sweet dew that, when they drink it, can make people clearly understand, can make people forget their sorrows, and can make people attain ultimate good fortune?"

"When I seek Niguma, I too want to find this kind of thing."

"I do not know whether or not you will find this with Niguma. But the process of seeking is itself a blessing. Maybe that process of seeking is that sweet dew itself."

"What you say is right. So then, let each of us go off on our own search. When you find that kind of thing, you must tell me, and I will do the same."

Sharwadi said: "No, I cannot search any more. Searching was my dream before. Now my dream has changed. My dream is to wait for you. I have already found the sweet dew that can bless me with good fortune, and that is love for you. I will no longer go searching for any truth. I have discovered that when I think of you and love you, I am truly very blessed. That blessing, that good fortune, goes far beyond everything from when I served as a female spirit. I think there is no sweet dew that can do more than that to bless me with good fortune. I just want to wait for that. I believe that my waiting will be my good fortune. I will wait for you. I will wait for the rest of time for you to come back. I do not want to transcend, I do not want to break the attachment. I just want you. I just want that waiting and that promise. With that to accompany me, I do not need anything else."

"I understand you. Love has indeed become your dream."

"But I have a request. Let that spirit dove that you brought become the bridge between you and me. Let it always bring my letters to you, okay? You can answer those letters or not answer them. I just want to let you know what's in my heart."

"Good."

"My letters to you may not always contain things that you like. I may love you, I may scold you, I may complain to you, they might contain everything I want to say. Do not worry about the contents. Just consider them as the true feelings of a woman in love. I do not want to cover up what I feel. I just want to be like those people praying to Brahma, who say what they want to say."

"Good. I will be looking forward to your letters. Apart from my search, what I care about most is, in fact, the true mind of a certain woman."

"Why don't I release you from that agreement, and just postpone it until after you find what you are searching for? The reason is that I hope you will promise me that after you have truly found Niguma, and you have found that esoteric teaching, you will come find me—okay? I know that to cultivate the esoteric teaching one needs an enlightened consort. When your realization reaches the level of Tantric coupled practice, then allow me to be your enlightened consort, okay? I tell you, I am not a female spirit, I am just a woman. I yearn for love. Before you attain the realization where you can undertake the Tantric coupled practice, my practice will just be to wait for you. Do not worry about whether or not my love is holy and pure. I just want to tell you that my love is real, and I am willing to wait for this ordinary worldly love. I do not even want to make it into something spiritual. Please allow me to have this worldly love for you, allow me to smile at you fondly and scold you angrily, allow me to long for you and resent you, allow me to have all the feelings and thoughts that an ordinary woman has for the man she loves. Please do not laugh at me. I really do not want to get beyond this. I just want to be with the man I love, and quietly wait someplace that the world cannot find, and look at each other and smile, without wanting, without seeking. I hope I can realize this dream, I hope that this kind of love will truly appear in my life. If it cannot appear, then I will use my dreams to play out this kind of love."

"Good."

"You just have to remember that in your life, there is a woman waiting for you, waiting for your return. She will be experiencing the pain of longing day and night. This is something she is willing to do, and it will be her form of cultivating practice. Her entire aim in cultivating practice like this is to see you. What she most fears is that if she does not cultivate practice like this, she may, in a condition of extraordinary fatigue, abandon this love. Because of this love, I am even unwilling to engage in cultivating practice in the traditional sense—I am afraid that the transcendence I would achieve through cultivating practice might dissolve my love for you. No, I don't want it to be this way. All I want is this love. I just want to wait for this love. I want to wait to be your enlightened consort. What I need to tell you is that whether or not I am an enlightened consort in your eyes, all I wish for is to be your woman. It will be alright if you call me an enlightened consort, it will be alright if you call me a dakini, it will be alright if you call me your attendant or your daughter. I don't care, because in the depths of my inner mind, I am just your woman. Don't wreck my dream, okay?"

"Okay."

"I just hope you can keep your promise, and after you have found your destiny from past lives, you will come and find me. I will abandon everything, and go with you. I am willing to go with you to the far horizons, or stay in a mountain valley. I am willing to be your servant, your slave, or whatever role you need. I just hope I can stick with you in your life, and become your indispensable breath."

Khyungpo Naljor's whole face was covered with tears. He said that at this moment of parting, he even thought of giving up on his search, but Sharwadi shook her head. She said, "Even though your search makes me unhappy, what I love most is, in reality, this very intention of yours to search for truth. If you abandon the search, you won't be you. Though I have the mind of a woman, the basis of the female spirit still is there in my blood. You just have to keep your promise, and after you have found your objective, come back and find me. Then I will be happy."

The two of them touched hands and made a pledge.

Later Sharwadi kept writing letters to Khyungpo Naljor, and these moving letters were all preserved in the dakini script.

Every time I break out of dualism and enter into the realm of light, if I want to, I can always read this script.

In this utter silence, whenever I look at these writings, my heart is always swept by waves of pain.

Nevertheless, I do understand and appreciate Khyungpo Naljor. It is precisely because he made this choice that a thousand years later we have another scene. The flame of the wisdom he searched for and found started a prairie fire in the space and time of my life, and became a human cultural landscape that time cannot erase. If he had abandoned his search, ancient India would have just had one more ordinary man, and the world would have been deprived of countless adept teachers.

6 Saying Farewell to Sharwadi

The scene of Khyungpo Naljor saying farewell to Sharwadi was very moving. In my image of it, it was at dusk on an autumn day. The weather was a bit chilly. Of course this autumn day was not necessarily a natural autumn day—perhaps it was an autumn day of the spirit. Khyungpo Naljor actually felt a kind of awful atmosphere. This deadly atmosphere came from his awareness of impermanence. He felt that it had already been such a long time since he had left home, and although he had found some teachings, he still had not heard Niguma's message.

Apart from his own search for her, Khyungpo Naljor also asked other people, but Niguma remained at the level of just a story. Many people had heard of Niguma, but they had just heard of her, and that's all. No one could doubt the real existence of Niguma—they firmly believed that there was a Niguma in this world—but this being was far away, so far away she had become a dream.

According to the story, the thing about Khyungpo Naljor that moved Sharwadi most was his search for Niguma. These traditional accounts seem to worldly people to be no more than stories, and like all traditional tales, stories are just stories. But Khyungpo Naljor left his home because of that story, and that was like following one of his own dreams. What's more, for the sake of that dream, he had already given up a lot. He had given up his position as a Bonpo teaching master, he had given up the warmth of family feelings, he had given up his hometown, and now he was giving up Sharwadi, who loved him so deeply.

Although there were still a lot of expectations in giving up all this, from the point of view of ordinary worldly externals, he had really given up many tangible things.

Nine hundred years later, at a moment of extreme peace and quiet, a verse welled up in my mind:

Waving a hand,

Saying goodbye to that chance encounter,

Because there is a faraway road that must be traveled.

Deliberately taking it up,

It might be too deep,

Afraid of only one thing,

Traveling light as I am,

The sound so loud and clear will not be there anymore ...

7 The Sun Has Gone

The night that Khyungpo Naljor left, Sharwadi wrote a text like this:

The sun has gone without turning back, languishing shadows pull the eyes of the wind. Rain is floating in the sky and there is no way for an umbrella to block off the fine drizzle and the feelings in my heart.

In the misty rain I stand here at a loss in the rainy lane. The wind blows and makes my heart quiver. I know that the sun has gone.

The sun has finally gone, in this rainy dusk, and misty sorrow draws forth a reckless wind and fills my eyes with helplessness.

I dare not touch the things of the past.

I tell my heart to cool down again and again—the sun has gone.

Bit by bit, the boundless darkness of night submerges his long-gone figure. I stand in the entrance to the lane, not daring to look back on the road he came on. The greatest love has gone. My great love ebbs and flows like rain and snow—sadly it comes and sadly it goes, just leaving behind a feeling of love with no regrets that keeps me endlessly agitated. Many times I have wanted to turn into a black bolt of lightning, and pursue him as he rushed off so far away. We did not fix a time for the years and months to come—will the sun still rise in the days after we've parted?

My mind is blank, I have become a willow in the wind. I really want to use all my strength and deep feeling to cry out, but I will still endure this indescribable sadness ... I always feel that the sun has left me.

Those days when the sunshine was brilliant are getting farther and farther away ...

Chapter 8

The Pilgrimage

The Secret History of Khyungpo says: Those Bonpo sorcerers were using the method of the barrel of demons curse. That barrel of demons may be a symbol, but even more it is a reality and an objective technique of putting a curse on someone. The story goes that its origin lies in the most primeval Indian sorcery techniques, and it later was adopted by Bonpo. But according to the story, the barrel of demons curse that really caused so much trouble later for Khyungpo Naljor in fact came from India. Pema Nam learned it from an Indian Left Path sorcerer, and passed it on to a Bonpo master of the sacrificial mandala, and he continued to the end of his life to employ this method of putting curses on people.

1 Reflections of a Female Spirit

After leaving Sharwadi's father Sumadi, Khyungpo Naljor was formally ordained as a Buddhist monk at Dorje Dengba's place, and accepted the disciplinary code of a novice. According to the story in the *Secret History of Khyungpo*, when Khyungpo Naljor's hair was cut off, it all turned into Guanyin. On this point I am just passing along the story. In fact, it is not at all important whether or not his hair turned into Guanyin. What is important is mind. When your mind becomes Guanyin, then you have the merits of Guanyin. The hair on your head is only an external manifestation — whether or not it becomes Guanyin is meaningless.

In resolutely becoming a monk Khyungpo Naljor demonstrated a certain attitude. Sharwadi was absolutely heartbroken. Pema Nam had originally wanted to go on studying, and he wanted to go away with Khyungpo Naljor. He had grown close to Sharwadi, but Sharwadi drove him away. Sharwadi's attitude hurt Pema Nam, and he blamed this humiliation on Khyungpo Naljor. Later on, when Pema Nam was in charge of certain temple, he became the greatest creator of adverse circumstances for Khyungpo Naljor in the fragrant lands of Nepal.

Because Pema Nam had secretly tried to hurt Khyungpo Naljor, after he left Sumadi's house, he felt that he could not face Khyungpo Naljor again. So he went to a different teacher to study. However, compared to Esoteric Buddhism, Pema Nam felt even more interested in Buddhist theory. He began to study the works of Nagarjuna and Milarepa. He was very unhappy with Khyungpo Naljor's broader search into Esoteric Buddhism. He thought that to attain liberation, it was only necessary to cultivate one teaching, so why learn so many similar teachings? He had discovered that although there were many teachings circulating in Nepal with different names, their methods of cultivating practice were very similar, and the real beauty and variety lay in the theory. During the many years that Khyungpo Naljor went everywhere seeking the Dharma, Pema Nam studied a large quantity of scriptures. He went everywhere propounding theories and debating the scriptures, and before long his fame in Nepal was on the rise, and he was ranked as pandit, a man of consummate wisdom.

Sharwadi had served as a female spirit, and she was originally a believer in Brahmanism. At this period in Nepal, it was still the new Brahmanism that occupied the leading position. Though there was no lack of eminent teachers in Buddhism, because Buddhism at this time had become so complicated, there were some specialists who studied it their whole lives without necessarily being able to reach its inner secrets. The ordinary people usually took one look at it and backed away. But Brahmanism had advanced with the times, and was continuously adjusting itself, and was thereby able to win many believers. Later on, people attributed the disappearance of Buddhism in India to the Islamic invasions, but in fact, this was not all there was to it. When the Islamic armies invaded, they also struck mortal blows at Brahmanism, but later on, Brahmanism advanced with the times, and in the form of Hinduism passed on the fires of wisdom and, with the force to set a prairie ablaze, it reached the whole of the Indian subcontinent. We can see that advancing with the times is the secret to a religion flourishing.

Although Sharwadi had been a female spirit in Brahmanism, her respect for the Buddha had been increasing all along. Just as Buddhism had adopted the spirits of Brahmanism and made them into the spirit guardians protecting the Buddha Dharma, the Hindu religion also took the Buddha and make him into the teacher of enlightenment in their own religion. They definitely did not repudiate Sakyamuni Buddha. While Sharwadi was serving as a female spirit, and after she left that position, she had studied many Buddhist scriptures. At the beginning she was merely curious, but Khyungpo Naljor's interest in Esoteric Buddhism strongly moved her. She thought, if a young man born in some remote place in another country does not hesitate to risk his life and leave his home and family for the sake of this Esoteric Buddhist teaching, and he can look at all this wealth around him and turn a blind eye at it, then there must be something to it.

After Khyungpo Naljor became a Buddhist monk, Sharwadi began to think things over. Before long, she began studying the practices of Esoteric Buddhism.

Actually, she was too concerned with Khyungpo Naljor, and she never experienced the light. And for this reason, she left behind many writings about love.

2 Dorje Dengba

After Khyungpo Naljor became a Buddhist monk, he stayed with Dorje Dengba, and diligently practiced the esoteric teachings, and in time he received the one hundred and thirteen esoteric empowerments of the Five Honored Ones of Surpassing Bliss and others. At this time, Khyungpo Naljor had already mastered Sanskrit, and he could understand the fine points of Dorje Dengba's teachings. Dorje Dengba held Khyungpo Naljor in high esteem, and when he gave him the prediction of enlightenment, he said: "You are a master upon whom the sentient beings in the six planes of existence will rely. You will bring deliverance to countless sentient beings. You will experience the achievement of upholding the light through a long life. You will live in the world for one hundred and fifty years. After your complete nirvana when you die, you will become a bodhisattva in a place of honor in the presence of Amitabha Buddha in the Pure Land."

This prediction of enlightenment appears in many biographies and source materials on Khyungpo Naljor. Later, Khyungpo Naljor did indeed live in the world for one hundred and fifty years, and his disciples were numerous, and the lineage of his teaching was correspondingly long. But as for the story about him being reborn in Amitabha's Pure Land after his death, I think this was a provisional teaching, not the ultimate teaching. According to the teaching of Complete Truth, being reborn in the Pure Land is not final liberation, and if one goes to the Pure Land to be reborn, this must not be the ultimate stage. Many teachers of great virtue attested to his enlightenment, and all of them recognized that Khyungpo Naljor had realized the Three Bodies of Buddha, had reached the ultimate level, and had experienced the realm of nirvana of the Great Mudra, where there is no coming or going, no birth or death. Therefore this story of him being reborn in the Pure Land is actually just a case of holding up some yellow leaves to stop a child's crying.

At Dorje Dengba's place, a miraculous event happened. For the tenth day of a certain month, Khyungpo Naljor and his brethren conducted a gathering to make offerings to the Great Teacher Padmasambhava. Suddenly, rare flowers were falling from the sky, and there were sixteen fairies bringing rare and precious offerings who came forward to take part in making offerings. Many people saw this.

One day Khyungpo Naljor was talking to me about the teaching of the Great Mudra which he received at Dorje Dengba's place. He said:

"My son, you are a disciple with a karmic link to me, and your capacity and your merit are both very extraordinary. The lineage of my teaching will spread like wildfire because you will disseminate it widely. Right now it is as if I am pouring water into a pitcher. I am taking the teachings I received from each of my teachers and passing them on to you in all their fullness. You have the corresponding experience of enlightenment, but when the ice has frozen three feet thick, it is not from just one cold day. The young child needs time before he can become the powerful man — this takes patience. I understand your mind, and you are not seeking just your own personal liberation, but rather you have the Great Cause to work for universal enlightenment within you.

"My son, besides these esoteric teachings which you have studied, I also want to emphasize one point: there are myriad teachings in the world which cannot be separated from the everywhere-equal enlightened true nature. If you want to understand all the teachings in the world, they are born from the Realm of Reality, and they become extinct in the Realm of Reality; they arise from the Realm of Reality, and they end in the Realm of Reality; they gather in the Realm of Reality, and they disperse in the Realm of Reality. In what appears in that empty inherent nature, there is no right and wrong, no high and low, no beautiful and ugly, no good and bad, no center and periphery, no grasping and rejecting, no good and evil. In sum, there are no differences or distinctions. It is everywhere equal, complete and integrated. It is the same as empty space, clear within the everywhere equal light of the Great Mudra.

"My son, the enlightened true nature is like illimitable void, without barriers, without clinging. Although many things appear, they are all the wondrous functioning of the transformations of the enlightened true nature. They all return to the empty inherent nature, so their essence and function are everywhere equal, and there is no birth and no extinction. All those many manifestations appear, they are all contained in the true nature of inherent mind, and form a single great emptiness, apart from all one-sided clinging.

"My son, that enlightened true nature encompasses the myriad appearances — they all arise in that enlightened true nature, they all appear in that enlightened true nature, they all are liberated in that enlightened true nature. The myriad things and events are all included in the enlightened true nature, in the empty true nature. There is nothing else outside of this empty true nature. When we understand that this true nature and its forms are fundamentally one essence, then we achieve liberation, because the true nature of phenomena is everywhere equal.

"The same everywhere equal essence of the Great Mudra appears at the level of the causal basis, at the level of the Path, and at the level of the results. Being everywhere equal at the level of the causal basis is choosing the right views — we must understand that it does not fall into one-sided clinging, that it has no biases, that it is at peace in the Middle Path. When you use being everywhere equal at the level of the causal basis to guide your action, when you act so there is no longing and no grasping and no clinging or attachment, then this is being everywhere equal at the level of the Path. When you are on the Path that is everywhere equal, and you reach the goal of truly being everywhere equal, then you act so there is no seeking and no changing, this is being everywhere-equal at the level of the results.

"You must clearly understand that your mind that can grasp and the object that can be grasped both return to the empty inherent nature, both originate in a single essence. The mind which can grasp is the form and the objects which are grasped are the function — they are like the two sides of a single tapestry. Though outwardly they are different, their essential nature is the same. You must not grasp at one side, because they are equal. Therefore, from the point of view of the Ultimate Truth, samsara and nirvana are equal, enlightened beings and ordinary sentient beings are equal.

"In the same way, making efforts to work hard to cultivate practice and effortlessly going along with no contrived effort are equal. The one who cultivates practice and the practice which is cultivated are equal; the one who takes countermeasures and that to which countermeasures are applied are equal; the one who can rely upon something and that which is relied upon are equal. None of them are apart from the empty true nature, and the inherent nature's characteristic is to be everywhere equal.

"This idea of everywhere equal has the meaning of inherent original equality—this is the equality of the Great Mudra of the true nature of phenomena. In other words, the essence and the function of the Great Mudra are equal. The inherent essence is empty and still, and that light which it inherently manifests is also empty and still. Its inherent essence is pure and clear, its inherent nature is light, and its essence and function are inherent. The characteristic form of that pure clear mind is light, and that is a light that it inherently possesses. It is a light that appears spontaneously by itself, and it does not depend on any external objects to appear or rely on any other phenomena to arise. It is inherent, natural, not created or made—therefore, it is called inherent, original.

"This inherent original enlightened true nature is empty in its essence, but its external characteristic is light. Whatever is manifested, all comes from the essence of the enlightened true nature. This light and this empty true nature are originally a single essence—the emptiness is not apart from the light, and the light is not apart from the emptiness—thus, they are everywhere equal. The many manifestations of that light are the wondrous function that arises from the essence of enlightened true nature, and when we do not give rise to one-sided clinging, liberation appears along with it. Even if it is manifesting all sorts of false thoughts, these are like clouds floating by in the sky, appearing and disappearing as they will. If we look at them from the ultimate viewpoint of the reality of the inherent nature of phenomena, they all return to the fundamental essence that is empty and still.

"My son, in the eyes of the enlightened ones, all that appears in the world is that enlightened true nature and the wondrous functioning that arises from that enlightened true nature. The enlightened true nature is true emptiness; all forms are wondrous existence. True emptiness is not apart from wondrous existence, and wondrous existence is not apart from true emptiness. There is no divergence between the two—originally they are everywhere equal. The wondrous functioning of that clear enlightened true nature inherently appears in external manifestations, whether as all the various objects and forms of the six senses—colors in the eyes, sounds in the ears, smells in the nose, tastes on the tongue, touch on the body, thoughts in the conceptual mind—or as all the various adornments that are manifested by the interplay of causal factors, like mountains and rivers and lakes and seas, like the mandalas of Buddha-lands, like beings revolving in the six planes of existence, like pavilions and buildings. All of these are the play and the adornments engendered by that wondrous functioning. They are all like magical illusions, without any real meaning, like dew, like lightning, like dreams, like rainbows. Although they appear, they are not apart from the empty true nature, and if we look for their eternal unmoving basic essence, it cannot be found anywhere inside or outside. Therefore, all contrived phenomena are fundamentally equal.

"Therefore, what we call cultivating practice is taking this truth that everything is equal and making it permeate our behavior. Once there is no subject grasping, then there are no objects being grasped, no attachments at all, no biases, no dependencies, and we stay at peace in that great equanimity that is like void. Even though we see all kinds of realms, even if we are faced with a profusion of all kinds of beautiful colors, even if our ears are filled with all sorts of beautiful sounds, even if this world is like a kaleidoscope constantly changing every moment, we never leave that state of equanimity. Even if clouds appear by chance in that clear, bright mind, that everywhere equal mind will not be pulled away by them. Rather, it will maintain in all its clarity that bright, empty, naked enlightened inherent nature. Calmly putting them aside, we dwell at peace in equanimity. We do not engender states of mind toward objects, we do not grasp at objects — we do not grasp subject or object. Using this clear empty, naked, enlightened true nature, we take all objects and all states of mind, and fuse them into one whole. Body and mind are at peace without grasping, and we attain everywhere equal liberation.

"We must peacefully put aside our eyes, ears, nose, tongue, body, and conceptual mind and not give rise to any concerns. This is because none of these six sense organs and their associated types of consciousness can be separated from that vast bright emptiness of our enlightened inherent nature. Though our six forms of consciousness function in the world which they make appear, and though there are all kinds of things appearing, if we do not cling to them, and we are in a state of equanimity, they spontaneously manifest the light of emptiness, unfettered by subject and object, the natural light. When we are facing external objects, even if there is a complex multitude of objects before our eyes, we still must rest at peace in equanimity, and not go calculating and fussing over them and constructing pictures of them. Then the complex multitude of objects spontaneously returns to the empty, still purity. Our inner minds must detach from such functioning, detach from desiring and seeking, detach from covetous thoughts, detach from ignorance. Even if we have something to worry about, it is as if we are facing a falling leaf, and we let it fall to the ground naturally and decompose, without starting to grasp at it — then the mind that does the grasping will spontaneously become pure and clean. When the attraction that external objects have for you dissolves, when the grasping of your inner mind is removed, then you will be able to stay peacefully in that great equanimity.

"When you stay peacefully in that great equanimity, you will no longer have the separation between internal and external objects, or the distinction between emptiness and existence, or the distinction between cause and effect, or the distinction between samsara and nirvana.

"When you understand these truths, then you will clearly understand the essential meaning of the Great Mudra which Dorje Dengba showed to me.

"Dorje Dengba also said that he too had heard tell of Niguma, and her renown was greater than the blue sky, but he only knew her name, he had not met her. There were many legends about her. Some people said that she was the sister of the great adept Naropa. Some said she was the enlightened consort when Naropa cultivated the Esoteric Teaching. There were also some who said she had nothing to do with Naropa, that she was a true manifestation of Vajravarahi. Because Niguma had already achieved the rainbow body, people without excellent karmic connections could not see her. Dorje Dengba said to me: 'You are someone who does have the karmic connection. If only you seek her, you will definitely be able to meet her.'"

3 The Pilgrimage

There were two things Khyungpo Naljor most wanted to do after he got to India. One was to seek the Dharma, the true teaching. The other was to go on a pilgrimage, to visit holy places. The two endeavors could go hand in hand. Many times, the great teachers live in seclusion in holy places. Some might say that places where the great teachers live in seclusion are by their very nature holy places.

Besides seeking the true teaching with several clear goals, he very much wanted to go on a pilgrimage following in the footsteps of the Buddha over his lifetime. He wanted to go from where the Buddha was born, to where he cultivated the Path, to where he consummated the Path and achieved enlightenment, to the places where he spread the Dharma, and to go pay homage at the place where the Buddha achieved final nirvana. Obviously this would add some difficulty to his pilgrimage. Sometimes, to pay his respects to where the Buddha had traveled, he had to go back and forth many times along the same route, but because of this he witnessed the Buddha's whole life.

To fulfill our human lives, during our lifetimes we may travel again and again on countless pilgrimages. Every time we go on a pilgrimage, it is something that elevates our lives. Although the forms of pilgrimage are not the same, the content is: it is to offer our veneration and dedication to a sublime spirit.

In the same way, in my life I have gone on countless pilgrimages, and in a mystical fashion, I have even followed in the footsteps of Khyungpo Naljor's pilgrimage. Like putting into practice the Great Mudra of Light, it became an excellent causal factor pushing me higher. At this point as I write, the theme of Khyungpo Naljor's pilgrimage calls forth many deep feelings. I think that the reason that

Khyungpo Naljor was able to have such a high realm of attainment is to a great degree linked to his pilgrimage. On the surface, his journey to India and Nepal was to seek the Dharma, the true teaching, but if we look into his real substance, how was he ever not on a pilgrimage? Those great worthies were all the holy monks he went to see. Those wondrous teachings were the holy teachings he went to find. Wherever they lived were holy places in another sense. They all had the spirit that only the Buddha and bodhisattvas have. Every time Khyungpo Naljor went on a pilgrimage, he was always going toward and coming near this kind of spirit.

Thus I say that any people who pursue what is lofty and sublime are always on a pilgrimage their whole lives, if we look into the real substance of it. Sometimes they study a certain kind of spirit. Sometimes they go toward a certain kind of experiential realm. Sometimes they respect a certain kind of conduct. Sometimes they read a good book. No matter what form it takes, as long as the person's action can elevate the person's life, we can call this going on a pilgrimage.

My whole life has been a pilgrimage. Aside from practising those supreme yogic practices handed down by Khyungpo Naljor, I have also had many particular forms of pilgrimage. Many people have acclaimed my particular style of experiencing enlightenment and process of experiencing enlightenment, but they do not realize that not an hour, not a moment has gone by when I was not on a pilgrimage. My contemplation practice is a pilgrimage, my recitations are a pilgrimage, my reading books is a pilgrimage, my writing is a pilgrimage ... I am always venerating and going toward a certain kind of spiritual state — my going toward it and venerating it are also a pilgrimage.

More often, the sacred site we are headed for can be a person, can be some small thing, can be a good book, can be a piece of music ... In sum, anything at all can be called a "sacred site" as long as it can bring us wisdom and enlightenment. When we are facing these things for a casual moment, as long as we have an attitude of respect, this can be called "going on a pilgrimage." The Chinese term for "pilgrimage" reads literally as "going toward the holy." In my understanding, the "going toward" is the feeling respect and the going toward. The "holy" is the vehicle which can carry the spirit to benefit living beings. When your mind is full of reverence, and you look upon the myriad things in the world with the eye of wisdom and compassion, you will always be able to discover, within everything in the world of the senses, the cool refreshing purity that can make you empty out and awaken to enlightenment. Then you are really on a pilgrimage, going toward the holy. In many stories of the great Zen worthies attaining enlightenment, we discover many key moments that enabled them to open into enlightenment: sometimes it was a wisp of pure breeze; sometimes it was a peach blossom; sometimes it was a blow or a shout; sometimes it was a beating; sometimes it was a someone singing a song; sometimes it was the sound of bamboo breaking ... no two experiences were identical. Talking about those Zen masters, every key moment of enlightenment was a true pilgrimage.

It was the same way for me. My reading the scriptures has been a pilgrimage; my interchanges with Khyungpo Naljor have been a pilgrimage; my reading Tolstoy has been a pilgrimage; my studying Dostoyevsky has been a pilgrimage; my praising Mahatma Gandhi has been a pilgrimage; my transformative awakening has been a pilgrimage; my respecting my parents has been a pilgrimage; my making offering to great teachers has been a pilgrimage; my giving alms to beggars has been a pilgrimage; my loving my family members has been a pilgrimage; my caring about other people has been a pilgrimage; my founding the "Western Regions Cultural Appreciation Project" has been a pilgrimage; my helping the blind artists of Liangzhou has been a pilgrimage; my listening with respect to the traditional morality tales of Liangzhou has been a pilgrimage. All in all, in my life, every moment has been a pilgrimage. My pilgrimage has been under the contemplation of the light of the enlightened inherent nature, using the mind of reverence and respect to deal with everyone and everything in my life.

It was precisely this bit-by-bit "pilgrimage" that made it possible for me on a certain day later on to achieve sudden enlightenment.

Thus, I was able to become the person I am today because of the innumerable pilgrimages in my life.

4 Sharwadi Speaks

Khyungpo Naljor told me that in a place called Lumbini he received the first letter Sharwadi sent via the spirit dove.

Dear Khyung:

This is the first letter I have written to you. Originally I did not want to speak of any unhappy topics, but because I am always worrying about your safety, it should be alright to tell you a few things.

Kumari told me that Kusang Dorje has begun to put a curse on you. On the day of the festival of the raven, they lit the fire on the mandala of death-dealing magic. On that day, white-necked ravens filled the sky and covered the ground, calling chaotically on all sides. They kept circling in the sky over the mandala, and their cries never ceased. Before breakfast all the families took leaves from trees to cover the dishes, and covered them with millet fried in butter, to give as offerings to these emissaries from hell.

After the festival of the ravens was the festival of the dogs and the festival of the cattle. I fed the dogs and the cattle good food to eat, and I made auspicious marks on their foreheads. Following the custom, I prostrated myself and crawled under the bellies of the cattle. The content of my prayer was to hope that you are safe and sound, and that you will not be hit by their curse. But what made me feel strange was this: on the day of the festival where we pay our respects to the mountains, I had just made a little pile of cow dung, and stuck a tree branch into it, and placed on the branch a bit of cake and some green grass and some fruit. Just as I was about to light the incense and pray for you, I saw some ravens black as the night swoop down. Their flapping wings blew out the lamp, and they gobbled up the offerings, and they spattered the courtyard with their excrement.

According to what the sorcerers laying down the curse said, this meant that their curse had gotten a response.

I am very worried for you.

On the day of the festival of the elder sisters and younger brothers, Kusang Dorje came to my house. In the past, he had developed a grave illness, and Yama the King of the Dead had come in person to take him away. Of course, you can take this as a story, but on that day, I really did see a strange-looking man, very tall, like King Yama in the traditional stories. You must realize that when I was a female spirit, I could really

178

see things that other people could not see. On the one hand, I treated Yama hospitably, and on the other hand, following our customs, I performed the sending-off ritual for Kusang Dorje. On the one hand I prayed to Brahma, and on the other hand I sang hymns, and on behalf of Kusang Dorje I put on red powder, I wore a wreath of flowers, I lit lamps, I offered up green fruit. I was dragging out the time. You should know that when King Yama takes people, he has his own time in which to act, for demons cannot bear to see sunlight. In this way I helped Kusang Dorje get through that fearful time, and I saved his life.

Proceeding according to the customary norms of the festival of the elder sisters and younger brothers, I placed oil lamps around Kusang Dorje and sprinkled holy water. I put down walnuts, wanting him to be as strong as a walnut. I offered fresh flowers, wanting him to be as fair as fresh flowers. I made an auspicious mark on him, hoping he would give up on that curse against you. But he told me that, although he too had put a curse on you, he was not the one who most wanted to put a curse on you. Besides the men you saw that day in that incident at the temple of the female spirits, there were also several Tibetans who had come to find him, to join him in practising death-dealing magic together. Kumari told me that those Tibetans were very well acquainted with Pema Nam.

I know Kusang Dorje's nature, and he is very vengeful. I do not know if he will listen to me or not. Even if he can listen to me, those Tibetans will still continue laying curses on you.

So I want to alert you to this — you have to pay attention to keeping safe. I am even afraid that, apart from the curses, they may do something even more dastardly. You must be on guard.

You certainly must visualize the protective wheel. When I was a female spirit, this is what I taught those people who were afflicted by evil demons. No matter whether you are walking or standing or sitting or lying down, you must visualize diamond clubs spread out all around you on all sides, so close together no wind can get through, with a fierce fire spread out above you. Of course this is common knowledge, and you certainly already know about it, but I still wanted to emphasize it.

Beside this, I still want to tell you that I really love you very much.

Ever since I met you, I have wanted to clear out my whole life, and welcome you into it. Therefore, what I could dispense with, I have dispensed with. I also hope that you will be able to eliminate those things which make you feel weighed down, including this letter. After you have read it, just tear it up, and let it disappear forever in the wind. If I could be together with you, my whole heart would be filled with sweetness and joy, and naturally I would not be afraid of any gossip. But your shoulders already bear a duty that is so heavy. I always think that those scriptures on your back must be pressing on your heart. I really could not bear it, could not bear to add even the weight of a piece of paper onto your heart.

When I am face-to-face with you, then I will have so much I want to say. Those words all flow forth from my heart by themselves. If not for your love, it would not matter to me how long I live—I don't have any great objective. When I met you, I met the one person in the world who is most worthy of my love. I have no regrets, and I am not looking for anything. My so-called efforts are to pray to Brahma to grant me more time and more space to be together with you. Apart from praying, the thing I most want to do is to write you letters. Besides this, I have no wishes to express. Although my father still has several disciples who often come to the house, it is getting so I have nothing to say to them.

Last night I dreamed I saw you trudging along a road, and the pain in my heart was hard to hold back. Your words and actions and thoughts all live in dreams, and this is what makes me most happy. The food I prepared for you for the road you should finish soon, so it does not spoil. I'm sorry I did not cook more noodles, so you could sample them slowly, as if you were tasting me. Before, I mistook my plans as objectives, and I won't do that any more. In my plans, there is only waiting.

Before, I could never get rid of that heavy sense of drifting back and forth. Walking through the human world, there was no place for me to set foot. Now I have ended up having a true home to return to, and that is in the mind that is yours and mine. I hope that in the future when you think of me, in your mind there can be one more warm home to go back to. I am not a female spirit, I am just an ordinary woman, not as good as you expected.

Many changes can make people get old fast, and go on and on chattering.

When you have time, are you still thinking of that little woman in your life who is peacefully there waiting?

Keep going on your journey. It is not necessary to write back. I hear and understand your silence.

Put your mind at ease, I will take care of myself well for you. Sharwadi is yours, she is not mine.

Don' t laugh at me, I' m a good-for-nothing, okay?

Sharwadi

5 The Purity and Coolness of Lumbini

Khyungpo Naljor told me that Sharwadi's letter made a feeling of warmth surge up in his heart. He could always feel that pair of eyes silently looking at him, banishing all the solitude of his journey.

In those days, he was really often in a trance, and he did not know whether or not he was being hit by that curse. Overall, there was an odd fatigue. Every morning he woke up as if dragging himself out of a nightmare. All day long as he traveled, his feet felt as if they were walking on cotton, and the energy of his whole body was drained away. By the time night fell, he was dead tired. He had never been so fatigued. He felt as if he had lost his spirit. But the good thing was that his vow to Boddha could always conquer his physical fatigue, and he hoped that with his feet being so hard to move, this vow would gradually expand.

I can understand Khyungpo Naljor's state of mind on his pilgrimage, and I can understand why he wanted to go all over India and Nepal like a honeybee gathering nectar — to study, to seek the Dharma, to get experience, to enrich his own spirit. Without his pilgrimage in India, Khyungpo Naljor would definitely not have been the man he was later. Only by receiving much nourishment can a healthy child grow into a giant.

As for the Buddha's life story, because this was so long ago, there are quite a few stories scattered around in the world, and there are also some stories in the Buddhist scripture. In the seventeenth century, after the Great Powers of the West took control of India, they wanted to destroy the Buddhist faith in order to promote Christianity. They knew that armed force could not defeat the spirit, so they thought that through their cultural superiority, they could attain the goal that armed force could not attain. They said that Sakyamuni Buddha was not a historical personage, but rather came from myths that had been passed down. In order to destroy the basis of Buddhism, they sent many scholars to India to do research, wanting to find evidence that the Buddha had not existed. These scholars learned Pali, and they did archaeological excavations at historical sites. But what they had not anticipated was that all the evidence they found proved that the Buddha was a real historical personage. All their research verified that those holy places in the traditional account really were places where the Buddha had lived. The story goes that from that time onward, Buddhism began to be known of in the West, and began to be transmitted to the West.

Considering the causal connections of the Buddha's life, Khyungpo Naljor picked Lumbini as the first goal of his pilgrimage. Lumbini was originally part of India, but later was included in Nepal. In the history of Buddhist culture, this sacred site holds a unique position, with great fame and incomparable religious standing. Although it was not an important place where the Buddha set forth sutras and expounded the teaching, still, it was the birthplace of Sakyamuni Buddha. One day more than two thousand years ago, the Buddha was born here, fit to be the teacher of humans and gods. At that moment, heaven and earth came to a halt, and all living beings who could sense the spirit saw an incomparable light rise there. This light was not the milky light of the moon, or the bright light of the sun. It was a light soft as pure water that could bring sentient beings pure wisdom. This light has continued for more than two thousand years, bringing pure, refreshing coolness to countless spirits burning with affliction. We do not dare to imagine how many afflicted spirits there would be in the world, unable to attain liberation, if not for that dazzling moment in Lumbini more than two thousand years ago.

Khyungpo Naljor too felt that pure, refreshing coolness.

His mind was surging with warm waves that melted all the barriers in his mind. Warm tears welled up in his eyes, a warm feeling engulfed him that only thinking of a loving mother would bring. The warm light of the sun caressed Khyungpo Naljor. He wiped away his tears and looked eagerly at this place which appeared so often in the Buddhist sutras. He discovered that this eminently famous place was, in reality, an ordinary-looking village, without any special mountains, without lush forests, without vast expanses of water like the Ganges, and without any grand temples. It was as plain and simple as the Buddha smiling serenely. But it was precisely from this simplicity that Khyungpo Naljor felt a kind of peace suffusing his spirit. This peace was not something deliberately contrived—it seemed to be inherently like this.

Khyungpo Naljor stood there a long time, savoring this moment which had made heaven and earth pause so many years ago.

He saw a procession of horse-drawn carriages moving on the horizon: it was the Buddha's mother Queen Mahamaya going to her parents' home to give birth. For married women to return to their parents' home to give birth was a custom of the Sakya clan. There are many strange customs in the world. In my hometown Liangzhou, for example, a woman cannot give birth in her parents' home, and if she did give birth to a baby in her parents' home, then the parents' home, the story goes, would suffer misfortune. Thus, when a young man who plays around has not been able to get a wife, to make a young woman pregnant is the most effective method. The woman's family members are afraid that if their daughter gives birth to a baby at their house, it will always make their daughter be treated as cheap. For the Sakya clan, back more than two thousand years ago, it was exactly the opposite. If a woman did not go to her parent's house to give birth, for the woman this was the greatest disgrace. On the day when Queen Mahamaya was about to give birth, she was in a carriage with her attendants, hurrying to her parent's home.

Khyungpo Naljor saw that mother. He was surprised to discover that Queen Mahamaya's face looked very much like his own mother's. His mother's face was like a full moon, and she had the many special marks a noble person must have. Because of the jolts of the carriage, Queen Mahamaya's face was pale, and beads of sweat covered her forehead. Khyungpo Naljor knew she was about to give birth. Khyungpo Naljor had read many accounts of the Buddha's life, and he already knew this scene by heart.

A yellow curtain that only the royal family could use surrounded the mother, and the court ladies were in a flurry of activity amid the elegance. They, of course, had not thought that the queen would give birth outdoors, but, carefully trained as they were, they still did not lose their elegance and grace, and they used the curtain to enclose Queen Mahamaya. Khyungpo Naljor saw many trees bow their heads to Queen Mahamaya and offer their respects and bend down toward her. This detail is also recorded in many written accounts.

Khyungpo Naljor saw Queen Mahamaya writhing in pain, just like countless other mothers giving birth. But the records in the Buddhist scriptures say that she had no pain at all. In reality, whether or not she had pain is not important — even if there was pain, this would not influence the Buddha's greatness.

In the books it also says that the Buddha was born from Queen

Mahamaya's right side. But Khyungpo Naljor thought that it was not important where he was born from. A man's importance is not in his birth, but in his actions after he is born. The Buddha's eventual greatness was created by what he did later, and even if he was born like an ordinary baby from the birth canal, this cannot affect his greatness.

Khyungpo Naljor saw Queen Mahamaya holding tight to a branch with one hand, maybe to borrow from its strength, maybe because she could not stand the strain any longer. This place later became one of the holy sites.

Khyungpo Naljor saw the Buddha after he was delivered, shining with a golden light. This is also the story in the Buddhist sutras: this extraordinary baby was shining with a golden light as soon as he was born. He stood up and walked, a flower sprouting with his every step. With one hand he pointed to the sky and with the other hand he pointed to the earth, and he said: "In heaven and on earth, I alone am the honored one." Khyungpo Naljor really heard this sentence. He felt a huge tremor, and he understood that, in this statement, there was incomparable supporting strength. He immediately gave rise to the confidence in inherent enlightenment that a master teacher must seek.

The group of carriages moved off in a cloud of dust. Khyungpo Naljor discovered that he was alone in the forest. In the forest various plants grew in profusion. Because this was the place where the Buddha was born, there had been countless people here on pilgrimages. They had brought along fragrant flowers and various offerings. Bringing along their reverence and their expectations, they had come here from faraway places. Among them, the most famous was the man called King Ashoka. He too had come from a long distance, jolting along for many months, to come here to pay homage, with his immense cavalcade spattered with the dust of history. The story goes that he was a murderous demonic king, and wherever his sword turned, the skulls rolling on the ground were like fractured rocks overturned in a windstorm. Khyungpo Naljor saw King Ashoka bringing his great army like a whirlwind rolling across the lands of India, swirling the yellow leaves, raising the dust, and submerging countless kingdoms. Like Genghis Khan later on, King Ashoka also obliterated numberless kingdoms, and he unified the Indian subcontinent. Wherever he turned, people fled, and everywhere he went, there were mountains of corpses and oceans of blood. Because he appeared, there would be thousands more widows and orphans, and their tears flowed together to became another Ganges River.

Centuries later, a film called *King Ashoka* showed the life of this renowned monarch, and in it King Ashoka was presented as a hero to be praised. This gory film spectacle does condemn evil, but even more, with the laudatory viewpoint with which it is shot, it advocates an idea that I very much dislike. Like many texts in human history, it is subconsciously advocating violence.

6 King Ashoka's Stone Pillar

What must be explained is that the main reason King Ashoka became a hero, and has been revered by people for millennia, is not because of his warlike achievements, but because he felt remorse and repented. His life illustrates what is meant by the saying: "Put down the killing knife, and become enlightened then and there."

The story goes that one day King Ashoka suddenly understood that killing was evil, and completely repented. He took refuge in Buddhism, and used his military power to promote the spread of Buddhism. Before King Ashoka, in the Indian subcontinent there were countless small kingdoms, and this pattern of these so-called kingdoms that were really tribes had influenced the spread of Buddhism. Only after King Ashoka put an end to all these kingdoms and unified India did Buddhism truly spread widely across the Indian subcontinent. The story goes that King Ashoka with his great power in one night built, amid the red dusts of the mundane world, eighty-four thousand stupas containing the relics of Buddha. Centuries later, I myself saw one of these thousands of Buddhist stupas.

Khyungpo Naljor saw King Ashoka's troops coming to Lumbini to pay homage. There was a devout look on the faces of these soldiers, who had originally been as ferocious as wolves and tigers. They were pulling a stone pillar, on which were inscriptions and a carved horse head. The story goes that this was the only one of King Ashoka's stone pillars that had carved on it a horse's head. Later on, a thunderbolt summoned forth by evil spirits cracked the stone pillar, and there was a fissure in the body of the pillar, but it still stood upright for a thousand years, protecting a piece of true history.

There is another story that this stone pillar was not cracked by a thunderbolt called forth by evil spirits, but rather was destroyed by being blown up by non-Buddhists. There is some possibility of this. This is because both when the Buddha was alive, and also after his death, for centuries India was full of all sorts of non-Buddhists, and they carved up the cake of Indian religion: sometimes one sect prevailed, and sometimes another prevailed. Many times the religion that had the upper hand wanted to destroy all the images and symbols of its opponents, to show that they had triumphed.

At that time, religious conflict was very intense, and almost at the level of warfare. While Sakyamuni Buddha was in the world, many of his disciples were killed by non-Buddhists, including the one who was acclaimed as foremost in his supernatural power, the honored one Mahamaudgalyayana. On a journey to propagate the truth, he was seriously injured by rocks rolled down on him by non-Buddhists, and he perished.

There were many times when various religious sects all thought that seizing the throne would be the most effective route for propagating their religion, so that when a religion achieved recognition by the imperial power, that religion would spread relatively rapidly. But it was often the case that, within the royal palace, there would be different religious beliefs. While the famous King Ashoka believed in Buddhism, but his most beloved concubine believed in a non-Buddhist religion. Thus, an interesting story grew up around the bodhi tree: King Ashoka protected the tree, and the royal concubine secretly destroyed it. Because the non-Buddhists took the bodhi tree as a symbol, the tree at this time was no longer just a tree, and became a vehicle for the spirit of Buddhism. It was the same way with King Ashoka's stone pillar at Lumbini. That crack in the body of the pillar could have originated from non-Buddhists' artillery fire or explosives.

Similar stories appear here in the current twenty-first century. After the Taliban organization took political power in Afghanistan, they blew up those world-famous Buddha statues at Bamiyan. Their rationale was that Buddhism engages in idol worship. In many Arabic history books, they claim that Buddhism is idol worship. In fact, in Buddhism, all those many Buddha-images are just to enable believers to produce certain kinds of religious feelings — they are a kind of expedient means adapted to the world. Buddhism in fact is full of content that rejects forms. After my book the *Great Mudra of Light: Real Cultivation, Sudden Entry* was published, some people took what I proposed, the Great Mudra that advanced with the times and was of practical use for managing worldly affairs, and called it "Xuemo Zen" to demonstrate that it was distinct from the traditional teaching of the Great Mudra. "Xuemo Zen" also proposed rejecting formalism, and when answering questions raised by friends on the internet, I composed a poem on the spur of the moment:

What is Xuemo Zen?

Detaching from forms, emphasizing the spirit

Culture is the vehicle

Extending through ancient and modern

Following circumstance, gaining independence

Abiding peacefully in the mind of light

Wondrous functioning with the Great Mudra

Acting to benefit living beings

Breaking with formalism, refuting forms, is also the essence of the Buddhist ultimate meaning scriptures. As the Buddha says in the *Diamond Sutra*: "If one sees me in terms of form, if one seeks me by means of sound, this person is going on a misguided Path, and will not be able to see the Tathagata." It is obvious that Buddhism opposes idol worship. Buddhism strongly emphasizes the concept of no self and opposes the idea of a personal soul.

Those people who blew up King Ashoka's stone pillar and cracked it may have been misguided spirits who did not know that a stone pillar cannot represent Buddhism, because true Buddhism rejects forms and teaches there is no self. The spirit of Buddhism does not depend on external forms in order to exist. Even if they were to destroy all the material things which bear the Buddhist imprint, the spirit of Buddhism would pervade time and space as nourishment for the human spirit. This is because Buddhism did not invent the truth, but rather found the truth. Even before Sakyamuni appeared in the world, those truths already existed. The Buddha's greatness lay in cultivating practice and discovering those truths, and carrying out those truths. He was someone who discovered the truth, not someone who invented the truth.

That pillar that Khyungpo Naljor saw was very thick and very heavy, and was already partly buried in several meters of yellow earth. The many cracks on the body of the pillar were a most graphic comment on impermanence. The endless ripples on the body of the pillar washed like waves over Khyungpo Naljor's mind. The words inscribed on the pillar appeared blurred, and were not very clear, but Khyungpo Naljor nevertheless could understand the general sense:

In the twentieth year of his reign, the King by the grace of heaven came here in person to pay homage, because this is the birthplace of Sakyamuni Buddha. He had an image carved from stone, and set up a stone pillar, to show that the Buddha was born in this place. The village of Lumbini will be a tax-exempt religious area, and will only have to pay in taxes one-eighth of the harvest.

At that time Khyungpo Naljor did not know that this inconspicuous stone pillar would later be an important piece of material evidence that the Buddha was a genuine historical figure. Besides this, a great many cultural artifacts were unearthed in this place that proved the Buddha really existed. These cultural artifacts, which had been buried in the earth for millennia, told those scholars who had come to destroy

Buddhism, told them in their own language, that Sakyamuni was a real historical personage. Western missionaries who had been educated in the scientific spirit could not help but admit that Sakyamuni was a teacher who had really existed. When they returned to the West, the scholars wrote a great number of articles, and these were disseminated through books and journals. Thus, people in the West could see that there was another human cultural landscape very different from their own Christian culture. Though these writings were not enough to change their beliefs, overall they opened a window that let people discover a world with which they had never before had contact.

The real entry of Buddhism into the West, and its winning of a great number of believers there, were events that happened later. Through a gradual series of historical events, Buddhism came into the Western World by means of favorable causal conditions provided by history. Among these, the most important event was the great number of Tibetan lamas coming to the West in the past century. They brought meditation techniques that Westerners, too, could verify in practice. Many Westerners were won over by their experience of those special meditation practices, to the point that some Catholic priests even began to study Buddhist meditation. They took the cultivation of meditative concentration that originally belonged to religious practice, and made it into a science of life. Thus, in various places in the world, many organizations called meditation centers have continued to appear.

By this time, Buddhism has finally truly entered into the lives of the people of the West. And it was just the archaeological excavations of those scholars in Lumbini that finally caused Buddhism, this ancient Eastern culture, to appear everywhere in the field of vision of scholars in East and West.

7　Lumbini Sunk in Silence

Today's Lumbini is still sunk in silence, as it wordlessly receives pilgrims from all over the world. Previously, few people came here on pilgrimage, and basically could not be compared with the number of Muslim believers who make the pilgrimage to Mecca. And even now, Lumbini is still no more than an extremely inconspicuous little Nepalese village. Although history has painted it with an incomparable aura, the river of time has spared it. Like all the Buddhist holy places, it has faded out of the field of vision of the era. It is like a little flower that people overlook, set in a quiet corner, emitting its own unique pure fragrance.

In the time when Khyungpo Naljor made his pilgrimage there, Lumbini was very quiet and lonely. In fact, before the Buddha's birth, Lumbini was very inconspicuous. A thousand years after the Buddha's birth, its glory had gone, and it had returned to being plain and unadorned. From talking to some of the local people, Khyungpo Naljor found out that they did know that a great man had once been born here, but that was something in the remote past. That great man was already far, far away from their lives, and his appearing and his disappearing did not make the local people feel that anything very special had happened. Mostly, people had already forgotten about him. In their eyes, although many people came to this place on pilgrimage during the busy season for travel, for the local people there was nothing really special in their coming and going. At most, people could try some of the local products. But because the number of people who came on pilgrimage was not enough for forming a chain of enterprises, no one thought of making a business of providing goods for those travelers. In the life of the people of Nepal, Lumbini was really an inconspicuous place.

Khyungpo Naljor really felt the loneliness. He did not see any splendid buildings, just one little temple dedicated to Queen Mahamaya. The temple was very small, similar to the local temples in the Chinese lands, and very little incense was burned there. The temple was built in the Hindu style. Just from the architectural style, he could not see any of the special marks of Buddhism. He discovered that even when they made offerings to Queen Mahamaya, the local people thought of her as one of the Hindu goddesses.

Then Khyungpo Naljor understood that in this great miraculous place, the light of Buddhism was already growing weaker and weaker. The new Brahmanism was flourishing more and more, and it had absorbed the nutrition of Buddhism. Because it was in closer contact with the lower-class commoners, it had won a great number of believers. Hinduism, which developed from Brahmanism, had a very strong inclusive nature. It not only absorbed the nourishment of the doctrines of the religions that were close to it, it took the theories of the religions with doctrines that opposed its own, and remade them and put them to its own uses. It took Sakyamuni Buddha and absorbed him and made him into a deity that rubbed their heads. They said he was also a transformation of Visnu. They said that to destroy the faith of the rakshasi demons, he had deliberately propagated erroneous teachings, to make the rakshasi lose the true faith, and correspondingly lose their power, so that in the end they would be defeated. In the same way, Hinduism took Queen Mahamaya into the Hindu structure of deities, and made her the goddess in charge of giving birth. On the images of Queen Mahamaya they spread a blood red pigment — this was a special ritual form of the local people.

Khyungpo Naljor had very much wanted to find a teacher in

Lumbini, but he lost hope. He only saw the ruins of a monastery. Obviously, there had once been a monastery here, and monks, but that was many years ago. Now there was just the rustling wind blowing through the fallen leaves that covered the ground, blowing across the surface of the earth. Khyungpo Naljor felt that wind was also blowing into his mind. Khyungpo Naljor understood that no matter what glory Lumbini had had in the past, time had gone by, and just because it had welcomed the birth of Buddha, that would not let it avoid the cleansing ritual of impermanence.

Khyungpo Naljor was gripped in a kind of dense ebb and flow.

8 Fatal Curses

When Khyungpo Naljor left Lumbini, the spirit dove brought another letter from Sharwadi.

Khyung:

Are you well?

Kumari again told me some news. Besides the fire mandala, those men have also set in motion a kind of evil spell against you. They made a figurine of clay that very much resembles you, and they carved your name on it, and then they put it in the fire, at once firing it, and uttering curses. They have already gone on this way for seven days, firing the image and making curses. That clay figurine has already turned into a ceramic figurine. They took iron chains and bound the feet of the ceramic figurine, and on a black piece of cloth they wrote curses like "cut off his life," "shatter his heart," "fracture his body," and so on. They smeared the cloth with the curses written on it with a prostitute's menstrual blood. Really malicious, and really embarrassing for them. They also took clippings of your hair and finger nails — I don't know whether Pema Nam provided these — and included them in the ceramic figure, then tied it up in the cloth with the curses, and smeared on some more of the prostitute's menstrual blood, and chanted some curses.

To tell the truth, even though my father said you are a yoga master that a hundred poisons could not injure, I am still worried for you. I heard Kumari say that they requested the techniques they are using this time from a master of black curses. According to what people say, his curses have never failed to take effect.

From what that sorcerer said, the effectiveness of his curses generally lasts for three months, or thirteen months, or at most three years. All those whom he has cursed have died violent deaths, and he has never failed.

Have you been doing that visualization of the protective screen of fire that I spoke of in my last letter?

Before writing this letter, I had just finished sweeping the house, and I switched the positions of two mandalas, and I made an offering to Mahakala. Every day I will pray and ask him to protect you. Before this, I only made offerings there to Brahma, to Mahakala, and to Visnu, but now they have been shifted to the subordinate position. In my main hall, I make offerings to Sakyamuni and your Esoteric Buddhist tangka paintings. For a retired female spirit, this sort of change has a certain symbolic meaning, right?

I also moved out the corner at the side of the mandala,

and put it on that little table you used before for copying the scriptures. This way, my room looks at first glance like a workroom for two people—too bad you are not here then. Next month when I have a little free time, I will take those old clothes you left behind and give them a thorough washing and air them out, so that when you come back and put them on, you will be sure not to smell that odor of expensive incense.

There is nothing else, no words to say. But I always must write letters, just like everyday we must wash our faces, brush our teeth, and eat food.

My father is always going out, going to pass on his teaching, going to see his friends, and going to take his disciples somewhere. My mother's facial paralysis is still not better, and the corner of her mouth is slanted to one side. She probably feels ugly, and is afraid to lose face, so she has made arrangements for me to do certain things, and she herself has gone to the countryside. One month ago she took some medicine, but it had no effect, so she went to her hometown to find a traditional spirit healer. She came back the day before yesterday, and I saw that her crooked mouth is the way it was before, and more of her white hair had fallen out. I suspect that her nagging after you left may have angered the guardian spirits protecting the teaching. I have told her to repent, but she, of course, will not listen to what I say. The two of us speak to each other less and less, usually just a few words—we try and try but cannot find anything to say.

After you left, it was very hard for me to bear. My thoughts turned to ashes, and I had no interest in life at all. It was like this all the time. I could not keep writing, and I often cried without making a sound.

If there were no you, how would I understand? I could recite the Diamond Sutra ten thousand times, and pile up merit to the sky, but without you, how would it be?

Maybe it is really true that I am too greedy, and I want to keep the sun in my own pocket!

I know that the power of the word "feelings" made you become a wandering yogi, and for the time being, you will not be pulled away by the lamp in the ancient temple. As for me, the power of the word "feelings" — in truth, what does it mean?

Without asking for an answer, we are worrying in vain.

Without worrying about an answer, we are asking in vain.

However, do not worry about me, I will slowly get better. Day by day I will understand more and become more peaceful. But it is very hard to think of being happy, because you are not here.

I treasure the books you left behind, and I will be sure to read them diligently. How can I complain of the past? Things in the past were blessings, and they will accompany you for a long time. In my eyes they are more like antiques, they are priceless. I even envy them for having been silently at your side for so many years.

Do not worry, because I will make the tears of being in love and then in pain into sweet dew to swallow.

So let me sacrifice my life for Khyungpo Ba. I have sacrificed!

Sharwadi

With a hot flow surging up in his mind, Khyungpo Naljor's tears ran down his face.

He told me that at this time, although he was really wrapped up in a giant evil power—he suspected it was the power of those curses—his whole body was wracked with pain, and his spirit was in a daze, and it was always like a nightmare—but whenever he thought of Sharwadi, he felt a ray of light penetrating the thick fog of the nightmare.

Chapter 9

Long-gone Fallen Flowers

1 The Moment of Flowing Tears

I think that, at that moment in Lumbini when his tears were flowing, Khyungpo Naljor certainly felt impermanence. Certainly he did. Lumbini, which is mentioned so many times in the Buddhist scriptures, in the end had become no more than a very ordinary town. This is the best explanation of the impermanence of all things. It is true: no matter how famous a place may be, its fame is only a cloud passing before the eyes, its fame is like a bubble appearing and disappearing in the water. In the end it is just a fleeting chance event.

Later on, Khyungpo Naljor would see with his own eyes an even more direct demonstration of the laws of impermanence. He would see how so many holy places that had once been illustrious became faint traces a thousand years later. Time did not spare them because they were connected to Buddha. With their own histories, they explained that all things are impermanent and all things have no self, and they became the most direct evidence for the truth that the Buddha had discovered.

Over many years, I always used a special method to enter into Khyungpo Naljor's mind and spirit. What interested me the most was his spiritual progress in India. I wanted to know what kind of impressions his travels in India had left in his mind. I knew I had reached the goal. When I entered the realm of clear light, I could genuinely touch the excited beating of that great heart. Many times we had face-to-face exchanges, and we did not miss out on that joyous realm of clear emptiness where we merged into a single body. In Christianity some holy disciples also had this kind of experience, and they called the texts that flowed out under this kind of circumstance "divine revelations." Though he did not have a very high level of education, the founding teacher of Baha'i too, under this kind of circumstances, was also able to come out with texts that sounded like music from heaven. I have been moved more than once by these kinds of texts, just as I have been moved many time by texts that flowed from my own pen. Not believing in God, I naturally cannot take these sorts of texts as "divine revelations." I am more inclined to use another explanation for them: "not apart from, not separate from the tutelary deity." Though some people criticize the term "divine revelations," I can understand it. We must not expect that a chopstick can measure the depth of the ocean. What's more, in this mundane world of the senses, there are always nitpicking viewpoints: they might be ill-intentioned, or they might be motivated by good will. Toward the latter, I always feel respectful. Toward the former, I am still appreciative. I developed gradually in the midst of many nitpicking viewpoints. I can even predict the criticisms which people will make of certain chapters of this book. Thus, I have chosen a method which I call "symbolic." I took Khyungpo Naljor's story and wrote it into a novel called *Curses of Xixia*. Though the main character of the book cannot be said to be Khyungpo Naljor, when I was writing about him, what was moving in my mind were really images of Khyungpo Naljor. I even named the character "Khyung."

In that novel, I used a symbolic writing style and described the spiritual Path of a seeker. But you know, the reason I used symbolism was that I wanted to make that Path more ambiguous and have many meanings. I do not fear the criticisms of the noble people, but I do fear the slanders of the petty people. All I can do is use the word "novel" to ward off the vilifications of the slanderers. For the nitpicking critics, I can tell them that what I wrote is only a "novel," that's all. But anyone with wisdom will be able to see that in these fictions of mine, without a doubt, there is reality in the highest sense.

2 Nothing Can Be Done about It, the Flowers Have Fallen

When Khyungpo Naljor went to India to seek the Dharma, Buddhism in India was approaching its final stages. Khyungpo Naljor could only come in contact with Buddhism in a few temples and Buddhist universities, and it was mostly being preserved in the form of philosophy. Although there still were many accomplished teachers, they were mostly scattered around the various localities, living incognito. Like the other elite cultures that were already being ignored by that era, Buddhism had become just something that existed in a narrow circle. Its existence as a fresh and lively popular religion was already over in

India.

This state of affairs was already apparent over two hundred years before Khyungpo Naljor went to India. At that time, a great teacher from China called Xuanzang had discovered that many places that were famous in the history of Buddhism in India had already fallen into ruin. Only at Nalanda Monastery could he dimly see Buddhism as it had once flourished. Two hundred years after that, Khyungpo Naljor had the same lament in India: "Nothing can be done about it, the flowers have fallen."

Earlier I mentioned that at that time, Brahmanism, which was even more ancient than Buddhism, had attracted a lot of fresh new blood. Later, people called the new Brahmanism Hinduism, and with this demonstrated the difference from the old religion. Hinduism spread like wildfire over the great land of India, and a group of great Hindu teachers completed the rebuilding of the Hindu teaching. This resurgent religion demonstrated incomparable vitality. It drew nourishment from almost all the cultures current in India, including religious ideas that were similar to its own, and cultures that were contrary to its own. As I said before, even though Buddhism has certain areas that go against the religious theories of Hinduism, Hinduism still recognized Sakyamuni, and considered him one of the avatars of Visnu. Hinduism claimed that the reason Visnu appeared as Sakyamuni was that he wanted to have him spread fallacies, so that those sinful evil demons, the rakshasi, would go practice according to these fallacious doctrines, and then be unable to avoid their destiny to be defeated. So they accepted Sakyamuni, but they rejected the truth he transmitted.

This was a very clever trick.

There are scholars who propose some completely contradictory points of view on the demise of Buddhism in India. Some say that Buddhism gradually became more and more complicated and philosophical and academic, and this made it into a kind of learning studied by a small elite, and thus it lost the support of the masses. Some say that Buddhism in India went too far in following social customs, which caused it to gradually lose its own clear distinctiveness, and in the end be assimilated by Hinduism.

Khyungpo Naljor saw that the momentum of Hinduism was fierce, and there was already not much room for Buddhism. Some monasteries that had once been Buddhist monasteries had converted to Hinduism.

I believe that at that time Khyungpo Naljor developed a sense of mission. Like me, more than nine hundred years later, wanting to salvage the virtue and kindheartedness as well as filial obedience, and the Shangpa Kagyu Buddhism of Liangzhou, which was about to submerged by the wave of globalization, Khyungpo Naljor certainly also wanted to save that Buddhist culture that was on the verge of annihilation under the surge of Hinduism. During the several decades after this, he went to India and Nepal many times, and he studied with one hundred and fifty eminent teachers and learned Buddhist teachings as deep and broad as the ocean. Of course, he was not doing this for the sake of his own liberation. If it was just for his own liberation, just cultivating one of the esoteric teachings would have been sufficient. Because of Khyungpo Naljor's efforts, many of the esoteric teachings which were on the verge of being lost were transmitted from India and Nepal to Tibet.

A scholar called Khrom Tshemam (1928–2004) in *A Historical Outline of the Tibetan Transmission of the Buddhist Kagyu Sect* wrote:

The great master Khyungpo Naljor received the essence of wisdom from one hundred and fifty consummate adepts of

broad learning and virtuous conduct in the holy land of India.
Thus he became the teacher of the age who appeared in Tibet,
and his school was recognized as boundless and incomparable.

Later on, after I had entered deeply in Shangpa Kagyu, I truly discovered that its "school was boundless and incomparable."

The teachings and wisdom of Shangpa Kagyu are like a great ocean, and only those who dive deeply into it can discover its profundity, which few people know. Shangpa Kagyu is an even more wondrous place, and the higher your level of cultivation and realization, the more you can discover its incomparable grandeur and profundity. If you just practice to get a shallow taste of it and then stop, you basically will not be able to see into its innermost secrets.

3 Genes of Decay

Khyungpo Naljor discovered that Hindu culture had already permeated the daily life of the common people of India in that period. The scenes that had been criticized in the *Agama Sutra* had reappeared. Sacrificial rites were still widespread, and many animals were slaughtered, and the smell of their blood was everywhere. People worshipped Brahma and Shiva and Visnu. As opposed to the ultimate empty true nature sought in Buddhism, the Indian people hoped to have an eternal soul, a spiritual self.

From the point of view of the academic study of religion, Hinduism is without a doubt a great religion. Its lenience, its introspectiveness, and its way of moving with the times have enabled it to have an incomparable vitality. From the Vedic religion, to Brahmanism, and moving forward to become Hinduism, its life has shone with light again and again. It is a very mature religion, like Buddhism, and it has offered the human race much wisdom to refresh the spirit.

If we look at it objectively, during Khyungpo Naljor's life as a wandering student in Nepal, he held a critical attitude toward Hinduism. This is understandable. Looked upon from the viewpoint of an orthodox Buddhist believer, there are many points where religious rituals in Hinduism clash with Buddhism. When Sakyamuni Buddha was in the world, there were fierce clashes between Buddhism and Brahmanism, and both sides had their victories and defeats, but in the overall contest in the great land of India, Brahmanism ended up having the advantage, and we could even say it gained an overwhelming superiority.

According to some scholars, Hinduism finally gained the upper hand in the eighth century of the Common Era. At that time a great thinker was born in India called Sankara. According to the research, he was born on the west coast of South India in the small Cochin town Alvoi. He founded the nondualistic Advaita philosophy of the Vedanta school of philosophy; his teaching originated in the ancient *Upanishads* and some Brahmanist classics. Sankara propagated his own teaching in the form of a commentary on the *Bhagavad Gita*, from which he refined the essence of his nondualistic philosophy, which had a substantial link to the Madhyamika school of Buddhism and thus broke the barrier between Buddhism and Hinduism. Some go so far as to accuse Sankara of being a covert Buddhist. Whether or not Sankara was in fact a follower of Buddhism, by his external form, he was accepted as a Hindu thinker. His efforts enabled many believers to accept Hinduism, and some famous Buddhist temples changed their affiliation and converted to Hinduism. If we compare the territory of the believers in Hinduism to a cake, after Hinduism carved out a very big slice, the part belonging to Buddhism and other religions got smaller and smaller. From then on, it became more and more difficult to replenish the ranks of the monks at the Buddhist temples.

A noted historian of Buddhism called Charles Eliot (1862–1931) has written about it like this: "The dividing line between the followers of Buddhism and the ordinary followers of Hinduism became more and more unclear, and only in the Buddhist temples could they come into contact with a clear-cut Buddhist teaching. Recruitment for these temples was not good … But even the teaching that was taught in the Buddhist temples resembled Hinduism more than it resembled the teaching of Sakyamuni. Because of this lack of the will to resist, and this submissive way of adapting to each era's various types of thought, Indian Buddhism lost its individuality and its independent existence."

Shangpa Kagyu, founded later by Khyungpo Naljor, also faced this kind of situation. Although it had an incomparably excellent teaching, because its religious philosophy was not able to be widely disseminated in the world, a few centuries after he had founded the teaching, the lineage of the teaching disappeared and was heard of no more. It was truly to enable the distinctive religious philosophy of Shangpa Kagyu to be known to the people of the world, that I wrote such works as *The Great Mudra of Light: the Heart of Real Practice* and *The Great Mudra of Light: Real Practice, Sudden Entry.* The decline and disappearance of Buddhism in India tells us that a purely submissive response to the world, and a lack of the spirit to resist and object, could in the end cause us to be submerged by the noise and clamor of the era.

Some scholars claim that, even though Buddhist historians attribute the final demise of Buddhism in India to the invasion of the Islamic armies, in fact, even before this violence occurred, Buddhism in India had already lost the strength to live. Their evidence is that Hinduism also experienced bloody suppression by the great Islamic armies, but it rose again from the lake of blood, and immediately recovered its vigorous life force.

The regrettable thing is that when Khyungpo Naljor was in India, he mostly observed concrete religious teachings, and his cursory contact with the religion's philosophy was comparatively slight; this later became an important causal factor in the later decline of Shangpa Kagyu. Indian religion's millennia of effective experience did not bring Khyungpo Naljor a beneficial inspiration.

4 An Interesting Debate

According to the records in the *Secret History of Khyungpo*, Khyungpo Naljor, who had an expert knowledge of Sanskrit, had a debate with a Hindu.

I fictionalized it a little, and wrote about it in my novel *Curses of Xixia*:

> *The story goes that in a mountain valley, he happened to meet an old lady who was selling fried cakes. She picked up a fried cake and said, "If you can answer my question, then you can have a fried cake. I can also give you a pair of shoes."*
>
> *Then she asked: "Don't you say that all phenomena have no self? Then what do you liberate?"*
>
> *Khyung answered using the explanations of the Consciousness Only school.*
>
> *The old lady gave a sarcastic laugh.*
>
> *She also asked: "You say that all products are impermanent.*

So isn't that nirvana which you seek impermanent? If it is
impermanent, what meaning is there to your seeking? If it is
permanent, what about 'all phenomena are impermanent' ?"
    According to the account, Khyung had no answer.
    ... In a few days, he aged ten years.

There is another story in the *Secret History of Khyungpo*. In it, the
one debating with Khyungpo Naljor is not an old lady, but rather Pema
Nam. The story goes that at the time some followers of Hinduism were
debating with some followers of Buddhism. Again according to the
story, what Pema Nam wanted to do at the time was still to destroy
Khyungpo Naljor's basis of faith. Everyone knows that once the basis
of faith is destroyed, the palace of belief collapses.

Those questions which Sakyamuni Buddha paid no attention to
when he was in the world became the main issues for non-Buddhists
challenging Buddhism. For example: Is the world finite or infinite?
Does nirvana exist or is it nonexistent? And so on and so forth. They
put special emphasis on the question of existence or nonexistence after
nirvana, because this touches on the ultimate issue of belief, and the
result of not paying attention to this is always to call forth a hiss of
disapproval. The story goes that Pema Nam at least wavered for a time.
During the time of Khyungpo Naljor's pilgrimage, he made a serious
study of the *Bhagavad Gita* with an eminent Hindu teacher, and he was
always full of praise for the *Bhagavad Gita*.

5 Dog's Blood and Menstrual Blood

The spirit dove brought another letter.

Khyung:

Yesterday Kumari and I chatted for a long time. She is that woman I rescued from the funeral pyre of her late husband — you have seen her before. She is very pretty, and also very sad. She lived with a husband she did not love for three years, and during that time she fell in love with Kusang Dorje. After her husband got sick and died, according to custom, she had to immolate herself on his funeral pyre. People took her and placed her on the pyre, but I was able to save her using my status as a female spirit.

Maybe it was because Kusang Dorje also loved her, that I was able to find out what they were trying to do.

Those men were still chanting evil curses over that ceramic figure with your name written on it. Every day they chanted curses four times, for many hours each time. After each session of chanting, they would smear a prostitute's menstrual blood all over the ceramic figure. That menstrual blood they bought from the Hindu spirit temple — there were many temple prostitutes there selling sex. Kumari said that one day they made her go to buy the menstrual blood, but she got some dog's blood from a butcher. She thought by this method to protect you. But later they may have discovered what happened, so they would send a reliable man from their own group to go there to the temple prostitutes to procure the menstrual blood.

Kumari had already gradually been struggling to free herself from the fear of the past few years, and she was gradually moving toward independence. (Not only economic independence: obviously, ignorance and poverty can truly warp human nature.) She now could move into a broader world. I felt

*very gratified, and now there was one less woman who would
worry me during times when I was not mindful. My mind was
very tired, because I was constantly being moved by people
and events that seemed to have nothing to do with me, and for
a long time I could not forget my concerns. If you just look at
it from the point of view of our social positions, the distance
between Kumari and me was very great, but in her longing
for eternal true love, and her efforts to pursue her dreams,
she was like me—it was just that the roads we were traveling
were not the same. That is why I always felt a familiarity and
closeness to her. She seemed to be another me. In fact, from
this perspective, I myself, Kumari, my mother, and many many
other women with different names, are all the same.*

*I miss you very much. Yesterday evening, half dreaming
and half awake, I inadvertently leaned against her, mistakenly
thinking it was you. It was strange, I have never before done
this kind of thing. Obviously, the power of love is strong.*

*You changed me too much. You made real for me the most
powerful salvation in life. Earlier, my father and my family
used all their ingenuity so that I would be able to become a
female spirit. Later on, many of the experiences I had while
serving as a female spirit in fact contaminated me. In the end,
so much silver and gold and jewels were also a powerful force.
It got to the point where I was using the chains of the mundane
world to tie up my life. For example, I liked to bathe constantly.
I spent the whole day in the temple picking flowers and
grinding them into a fragrant paste, and I added vermillion
and rice flour. I gave all the women who came to have fun with
me auspicious marks on their foreheads. Another example: I*

always picked out the most beautiful earrings, and changed them several times a day; the precious stone set into the side of my nose was priceless ... These empty uncertain things were my life, and apart from them, I really could not live. I was like a walking corpse (I have written this far; my father is looking for me, another guest has come.) ...

6 Above All, Do Not Fall in Love with Me

This time Khyungpo Naljor summoned the spirit dove to take his reply back to Sharwadi.

When Khyungpo Naljor recounted this letter to me, I was shocked. In this letter, I saw the holy man I liked —

My Beloved Sharwadi:

When I saw your letter, I was very moved, and I felt very bad.

I am visualizing the protective circle. Recently though, I am really very fatigued, and my whole body hurts. I often have nightmares, and I am always in a trance seeing demons with long fangs and claws attacking me. Many times I feel that my life has become a fine thread, and it seems I am being pulled by two forces, and I always feel it is going to snap.

I wonder whether or not this is caused by those other people laying curses on me.

I cannot concern myself with other people's curses. Other people's curses are other people's business. All I can concern myself with is doing my own work. If they kill me with their curses, I will immediately return to the world and come again to seek Niguma. In my eyes, life and death is just an illusion, and my physical body is nothing more than the costume I put on to perform in that illusory drama.

I do not care about those curses. In my mind, what I care about most is still you.

I remember that when I was together with you, I made you unhappy many times. In those days I even hoped that you would leave me, and have your own life. Waiting is truly very painful, and I truly could not bear making you suffer the pain of longing any more. I wanted to make you angry so you would leave. I made you angry again and again. I thought that, after you left me, I would endure it for a time, and maybe then feel better. But these days I am still tormented by the pain of longing, and it is truly unbearable.

But I hadn't anticipated that when I had almost driven you away in anger, I would feel that everything had lost its meaning. As I walked beside the roaring river, I really had an impulse to jump in. I suddenly understood that if you chose to leave me, I would descend into even greater pain, and I would lose the joy of living. Then I finally understood clearly how stupid the idea of making you leave me was.

But you may not have known that over these days of being in contact with you, I already had no way to control my own mind anymore. Time and again it would escape from my control and get away into some fearful unknown state that I had never anticipated. This had its origin in the fact that I saw you like some sacred image I was obsessively visualizing, and it also had its origin in the emotion which your sincerity aroused in my mind. Before this, whenever I discovered concerns for the ordinary world were there in my mind, I immediately cut through the threads of emotion with the sword of wisdom. But unexpectedly, this time, fate ended up playing such a big joke. It finally took control of me, and forced me into territory where I had never been before. I felt a gigantic fear. At that time, when you smiled at one of the senior fellow apprentices, I of course felt jealous. For me, who had vowed to benefit sentient beings, this kind of attachment and selfishness was ridiculous, no? I really hated myself. I also understood that the most difficult barrier I still had to pass through in cultivating realization was the barrier of emotion. But I clearly knew that it was precisely the strength of "emotion" that had made me become a seeker, a yogi. Of course this "emotion" that I am speaking of is a great innate motivation to benefit living beings. It formed my mission, and my search exists because of its concerns, and in the end it could not be wrapped up in the quiet life of temple rituals.

You may not know that before this, I had a preconceived view of women. Whenever I met a woman, I would always think of "woman problems." Pema Nam was always talking about the content of the Tantric coupled practice, and I was very amazed by his deep knowledge, but I really thought it was not worth paying attention to. When it came to worldly matters, I always believed that less was better than more. When I began to associate with you, it seemed to prove that this was correct. I did not imagine that I would fall in love with you, and this would end up bringing me this great pain of longing. In the space of a few nights, I got a lot older.

Fate had really played a wondrous trick. All at once I was helpless.

You should know that, at the very start, I certainly did not love you. Although I liked you very much, it was far from the stage where it turned my spirit upside down. I was really very proficient at controlling my mind. One time I was arguing with Pema Nam, and I annoyed him, and after he had severely reproached me, I still lay down and fell asleep and snored heartily. I never cared about the world. When I was back home in Tibet, there was a woman who once took off her clothes to entice me, and even this did not break my mental calm.

So at the start I alerted you: above all, do not fall in love with me. You said you wouldn't, and I believed you. I thought that a woman who had served as a female spirit had the ability to rein in emotions more than other people did. And it was lucky you said what you said, or else I probably would have run away. Later, I would always comfort myself by saying, she will not fall in love with me. What I was afraid of was that, when I confirmed that you had fallen in love with me, I would discover in the end that I could not leave you. I liked you too much. Everything about you made me happy, made me intoxicated. I considered you as the most beautiful gift the fate had bestowed on me, and I was endlessly surprised. I let myself go and went after you. I was afraid that world-transcending wisdom would dissolve away my love, and I began the practice of visualizing you for two hours every day. I wanted to use the power of concentration I had developed to preserve that love.

There were many moments when I even took you for Niguma.

But I gradually discovered that there was no way for me to

*put aside the longing for you that was engraved in my heart.
I knew when you were thinking of me. I could always feel that
misty longing coming from where you were. Every time this
happened, in my breast, as in yours, there was a fierce strange
stone. It was always jabbing me with a dull pain.*

*I thought, if you are always like this, how will you live
through this long life? If I cannot be with you forever, it will be
very painful for you. I could understand your pain. I remember
that night I left your house, when I woke up crying, with that
longing gnawing at my whole heart. Even in that dream, I still
did not believe that you, whom I loved so deeply, would not in
the end accompany me on my search. In my dream I looked all
over, but I could not find you. I ended up crying out and waking
up from that dream. After I woke up, I discovered the people in
the house with me were looking at me in alarm. I believe that
your pain must have been like mine then. That fearful choking
was certainly a thousand times worse than having your breast
blocked up by a giant stone.*

I really cannot bear to make you live this way.

*I have intentionally or unintentionally reminded you to use
the sword of wisdom to cut through the threads of emotion, but
you always took this as a sign that I was about to run away.
No, although I could not abandon you, still, you must know:
how could I bear to make you experience such enormous pain?*

*Wisdom tells me that you are a good woman, that it would
be truly worth joining our lives together. There are many things
about you that delight me. In the unknowns of life, there really
are miracles. In our lives, there are truly things we cannot
explain.*

After I had you, I was very surprised that the life had brought such a great good fortune to me. But I had not thought that it would bring you such great suffering. And I also had not anticipated that, after I left you, waiting for your letters would become the greatest joy in my life these days. You could say that these days, in the whole time and space of my life, except for my search, all there is, is waiting for that spirit dove. I love you too much. Of course, when I read your letters, that great pain often makes it so I cannot draw a breath. All the pain that you are feeling—I suffer it all, too, at the same time.

At many moments, I am always resolving that I must not torment her any more. I am always reminding myself: once I made up my mind and left her, after she has endured it for several months, maybe it will be like she was used to before, didn' t you get used to the life of a female spirit the same way? If it were not that in my own mind I still cannot leave you, maybe I would have run away sooner. I truly cannot bear to make you suffer like this. I do not want to make you endure this hellish torment for my sake.

In my imagination I am always saying goodbye to you. Every time I think of us breaking off contact, I really feel relieved: she is finally free of me. My basic idea is that, if you really left me, then my pilgrimage journey would certainly eliminate my suffering.

But I did not anticipate that when I really reached a decision to leave you, I would end up enveloped by a deep melancholy. The whole world is gray as ashes. I walk alone through the mountains, thinking time and again of jumping off a cliff.

I do not know: is this the power of their curses, or is it the power of love?

I even wonder if what those men sent at me is the demon of emotion. This is because they would only be using the menstrual blood of those prostitutes if they were using sorcery techniques involving feelings.

If this is the way it is, they have already achieved their goal. I cannot leave you. You have already melded into my life in a fearful way. This feeling of losing our souls is really deadly!

Here it is later, and when I see that spirit dove again—I, the man who planned to leave you, cannot stop crying tears of joy.

I think that maybe one day you will discover the pain of my longing and not bear to make me suffer any more, and you may choose to leave me. I think that after I have really left you, you will suddenly discover that in the end I have melded into your life in a fearful way.

So then, once again we are no more saying goodbye to each other's lives, okay?

I promise you, when I am with you, I will treat you well. When you are not with me, I will do all I can to do the things I must do in my life. But after we parted, I have been hoping so much to hear your voice. Without your voice soothing me, I cannot endure such long nights! This is because after I see your letters, I can be sure that you still love me!

You should know that whenever I have been waiting a long time for the spirit dove to come, it always makes me start to think a fearful thought: "She has a new friend." Then suddenly there appear before my eyes images that are enough to drive me crazy.

Now you too may perhaps be able to understand the great impetus our parting gave me.

What is most frightening is that the sickness I have will only be cured when I do not love you.

But if I no longer loved you, would I still count as alive?

You may find this letter confused, but this confusion just expresses my confused emotions tonight. In my life such confusion is rare.

After you have finished reading this letter, you may be thinking, can it be that the person who wrote this letter is that dignified wise man Khyungpo Ba?

You tell me, is this or is this not the result of those curses they put on me?

Khyungpo Ba, written before dawn.

Chapter 10

Going Back

*The Secret History of Khyungpo says: Another result of
the curses from the fire mandala of Kusang Dorje and the
others was to put rumors into circulation. These rumors caused
trouble for Khyungpo Naljor all through his life, and even
affected the disciples to whom he transmitted the teaching. Due
to this, there were continuous disputes among his disciples.
Because spreading rumors was another weapon of those death-
dealing yogis, under the corrosive effect of these rumors, many
people lost their faith. Losing one's faith is tantamount to
losing one's soul, and this is even more cruel than killing the
physical body.*

1 Encountering Bandits

In Khyungpo Naljor's letters, I read of his inner struggle at that time. He was not a natural born holy man: he too had the emotional desires and concerns of an ordinary person, but what was different from the ordinary person was that he had self-awareness, and he had more self-discipline and direction. This let him end up leaving behind the narrow confines of ordinary life, and go toward greatness.

After he left Sharwadi, Khyungpo Naljor also met several great Buddhist teachers, and learned many forms of the esoteric teachings. These were teachers like Xiba Zasa Lianna, Gonpawa of Kashmir, Minian Dorje and others.

But Khyungpo Naljor was still not satisfied, and he traveled all over, as he continued to seek Niguma. But Niguma had already become a legend—everyone had heard tell of her, but no one had seen her.

Later on his steps turned toward India.

Maybe he was really suffering from the curses put on him. Khyungpo Naljor was always getting sick, and sometimes the sicknesses were very severe, time and again he was on the brink of death. Although he consistently practiced the visualization of the protective circle, he often felt that some of the demons could easily break through the protective curtain of fire and wield their sharp blades against him.

In that book which was never made public, an event is recorded: he encountered bandits. This was very common. More than nine hundred years ago, to meet up with brigands in wild areas was a very commonplace event.

People generally suppose that Khyungpo Naljor's encounter with bandits was also brought about by those sorcerers' curses. According to the explanations in the book, many events in the world that on the surface seem to be chance events and in reality have causes that people cannot necessarily understand clearly. The power of those sorcerers' curses would certainly have been able to alter the thinking of those bandits, and give them the idea to attack at the very moment Khyungpo Naljor was about to pass by.

In the book it also says that many of the adverse conditions in Khyungpo Naljor's life were all due to demons interfering with him. Those demons, using the power of that mandala of curses, always followed Khyungpo Naljor. Whenever there was an opportunity, they would appear.

One day, several big guys blocked the Path of Khyungpo Naljor and Pema Nam.

It should be explained that in those time, because it was such a long journey, people who traveled to India to seek the Dharma always had to travel together in groups. So Pema Nam again appears in that book. In that book, the relationship between Pema Nam and Khyungpo Naljor is similar to the relationship between Devadatta and Sakyamuni. Pema Nam was always there, playing the role of Khyungpo Naljor's opponent. This is very standard: many times, without evil, the value of goodness cannot be shown; without darkness, the rarity of light cannot be shown. Because of the contrast with Pema Nam and others, Khyungpo Naljor's light shows up as even more precious.

But, at times, many things are hard to explain. Although, in Buddhism, Devadatta is considered an unforgivable villain, still, there were many who believed in him. According to the records of Master Xuanzang, at the time when he traveled west to India to seek the Dharma, there were still many faithful followers of Devadatta in India. At that time, a thousand years had passed since Sakyamuni Buddha was in the world. Similarly, even now in many areas there are still those who believe in Pema Nam. They still employ their verbal skills to use the Buddhist teaching as something to profit from, and their words pour out like a waterfall, while in their minds evil thoughts fly around in confusion.

In the book it says that when Khyungpo Naljor and Pema Nam encountered the bandits, Pema Nam knelt down and begged for mercy. This story detail is indeed possible, because being quick to change is the mark of the petty person. When a petty person meets with mortal peril, it is indeed possible that he would go down on his knees. We can see this scenario in many novels, and what's more, they might also come out with something about their old mothers at home, begging for mercy.

According to what is recorded, at that time there were many robbers, because those who were traveling to Nepal and India in search of the Dharma were sure to be carrying gold. In those times, if you did not have gold, you could not find the Dharma. Khyungpo Naljor returned to Tibet many times, just because the gold he had brought had been used up, and he had to return to Tibet to again raise the resources needed to seek the Dharma. Of course, it was not that the great virtuous teachers in India and Nepal were greedy for wealth: rather, it was to show the precious value of the Dharma. If people got it too easily, they might abandon it too carelessly — that is why so many people at that time took precious esoteric teachings and casually tossed them aside.

With the pure wind stirring, as I see Khyungpo Naljor, on his face there is already a full beard. According to what it says in the *Secret History of Khyungpo*, at that time Khyungpo Naljor was only in his thirties, and although he was not old, due to his long years of traveling, with his face worn by the wind and frost, he looked older than his real age.

The bandits carried Tibetan knives, and they did not have the long spears and great cudgels that people imagine, because the bandits, too, were just common folk. They always acted opportunistically: when they saw an opportunity, they pulled out their knives and shouted out a threat. Unlike the robbers in China, they did not shout out to travelers to leave money to buy safe passage. They cried: "Put down the gold!"

Pema Nam was so frightened his face got pale.

Khyungpo Naljor said: "We are poor monks. How would we have money?"

The bandits did not believe him and said: "What is in those packs on your backs?"

Khyungpo Naljor said: "Scriptures in Sanskrit."

The bandits said: "Are they antiques?"

Khyungpo Naljor said: "How would we have antiques? We copied them out ourselves."

The bandits demanded: "Take them out so we can see!"

Khyungpo Naljor took out the scriptures, and the bandits looked through them. One of them said: "This is really damn bad luck. We wait here a few days, and in the end we get a pile of junk." He pulled out a volume, and ripped it up. The scraps of paper fluttered in the air like butterflies.

At that moment Khyungpo Naljor looked infuriated and pointed. This volume of scripture was to him more precious than life.

In the *Secret History of Khyungpo* it says: "He looked infuriated and pointed, and the robber spit up blood and died." If we use this as an explanation, Khyungpo Naljor at that time had already completed the procedure for generating enlightenment and had the power to increase good fortune, stop sickness and pain, reconcile enemies, and destroy anger. At the same time, in the book it is also written that Khyungpo Naljor took the spirits of the robbers and delivered them to the Buddha Land.

We do not know if it was one of the robbers who spit blood and died, or all the robbers.

We just know that Khyungpo Naljor had suddenly revealed a power he had cultivated and achieved, and this made Pema Nam jealous. He must have been thinking: "Everybody goes to India, but why are you the one who has this power?"

2 Rumors Following the Wind-blown Dust

Khyungpo Naljor had not been in India very long when the favorable causal conditions were fulfilled. Many people came to Khyungpo Naljor wanting to be his disciples.

Khyungpo Naljor's reputation was actually very widely known. No matter whether it was in Bonpo, or afterwards when he left Bonpo, or still later when he went to Nepal to seek the Dharma, he always became a topic of conversation locally, and there were always some who praised him and some who criticized him. But no matter whether they praised him or criticized him, they all recognized that he was a man of ability.

In those days, India and Nepal were like gold-plating for those who cultivated Buddhist practice. If they had gone from Tibet to India and Nepal, their value rose a thousand-fold. Although in Tibet gold was precious and rare, people were willing to take all their gold and use it for Buddhism. One year, a certain virtuous teacher was imprisoned, and he said to the person who brought gold to pay his ransom: "Save this gold, and go invite a great Buddhist teacher from Bengal." The story goes that, in order to invite a great teacher to come there, in Tibet they would put together the teacher's weight in gold. Later on, though, this gold was still used for Tibetan Buddhism, but this offering became a symbol of the deep reverence for the Buddha Dharma.

The disciples who swarmed around Khyungpo Naljor brought a lot of offerings, and they received the teachings they wanted. These teachings, along with his later work, the *Five Great Diamonds Teachings of Niguma*, became part of the riches of Buddhism. Even now, they are still precious gems in Tibetan culture that can nourish the soul.

Just as the stars spontaneously fade once the sun comes out, the appearance of Khyungpo Naljor made Pema Nam lose his glory. This time when he went to Nepal, Pema Nam had made many gains. But his gains were mainly at the level of Buddhist theory. While Khyungpo Naljor was broadly seeking esoteric teachings, Pema Nam was with a few learned men studying the *Yogacarabhumi Shastra*, an important text of the Yogacara school. Besides this, he was still studying some texts of the Hetu vidya philosophy (Buddhist Logic). Along the way, he had also collected a few disciples. But because of people's preference for Esoteric Buddhism, Pema Nam's disciples were few in number, and he did not receive many offerings. Though Khyungpo Naljor did all he could to recommend Pema Nam, people still gathered around Khyungpo Naljor like the stars around the moon.

Before long, a rumor began to circulate in the area that when Khyungpo Naljor was in Nepal, he had deceived a maiden and made her pregnant, using the pretext of the Tantric coupling practice, and that, having abused her, he abandoned her. This rumor spread rapidly, like a wind raising the dust, and quickly was circulating in all the

Buddhist circles in the area. Some people who had already been jealous of Khyungpo Naljor began to wink and nod to each other. They had originally been considered to be teaching masters, and they all had had a few disciples or a few dozen disciples, but once Khyungpo Naljor arrived, the disciples had all gone to take refuge with him. Even if their former students did not make offerings to them any more, the masters still had their pride. This rumor helped them.

As soon as he heard this rumor, Khyungpo Naljor just gave a faint smile. He never cared about such things that had no connection with liberation. But after certain initiation ceremonies, Khyungpo Naljor found a few of his disciples whispering.

Khyungpo Naljor questioned them, and, after being evasive for a moment, a disciple told him the rumor.

Khyungpo Naljor felt like laughing. He said: "How could such a thing be?"

The disciple spoke haltingly and said: "Somebody else gave all the details."

Khyungpo Naljor smiled and said: "A rumor that spreads everywhere certainly will have full details, or else who would believe it?"

"People are also saying what the girl's name is," said the disciple boldly.

"What is it?"

"Sharwadi."

Khyungpo Naljor was no longer smiling. He immediately understood the source of that rumor, because in all of India, except for Pema Nam, nobody knew of Sharwadi.

A deep sense of sorrow rose up in his mind. He had treated Pema Nam all along as a close friend. He had not anticipated that in the end he would act like this.

Khyungpo Naljor could not resolve this matter all at once. All he could do was go along with it. Luckily, the disciples with true faith did not take this matter as a terrible black mark, because when a yoga master's practice and realization had reached a certain level, to employ an enlightened consort to assist in the coupled practice was permitted.

But this rumor also brought a very great injury to Khyungpo Naljor. At this time he finally understood that not everyone was happy for his successes.

Some disciples whose faith had been damaged by the rumor left Khyungpo Naljor.

Khyungpo Naljor laughed and said: "Let them go. Those who believe the slanders of petty people and do not believe in the virtues of a master teacher are not fit to be my disciples."

In the *Secret History of Khyungpo*, this rumor is recognized as one of the results of those sorcerers making curses. From the time when people had set up an mandala for curses directed at Khyungpo Naljor, rumors became a shadow he had no way to escape. He was always being slandered by some people. However, it was precisely because of this slander that Khyungpo Naljor always became a topic of conversation for other people.

3 Religion's Shadow

All religions have light, but what has light at the same time also has a shadow.

Pema Nam and Devadatta are religion's shadow. Though the Buddhist sutras show Devadatta as a traitor, his power was very great. The story goes he had six groups of monks, which history terms "the Six Groups of Evil Bhikshus." While the Buddha was in the world, they created very serious adverse circumstances for him. Pema Nam was this way too. When I was writing this book, I encountered the curses of the disciples of Pema Nam's lineage.

In the first half of Khyungpo Naljor's life, Pema Nam was that shadow that accompanied the light.

Because Pema Nam was well versed in religious theory, and had an expert knowledge of many of the scriptures that were circulating in India at that time, he had many disciples who were famous for their learning. At the same time, because they were learned, they were well able to produce written works, and so they passed down many writings. Even now, in the works of some scholars, the view of Pema Nam and his disciples are often cited. For this reason, Pema Nam has entered history.

Whether or not Pema Nam achieved enlightenment has been a topic of unending debate. Some say he did achieve it, because among his disciples there are those who did achieve it. It's hard to say that a teacher who did not achieve enlightenment could turn out disciples who did. In the Esoteric Vehicle, the teacher is the source for achieving enlightenment. There is a traditional story in India that there was a pandit with a great reputation, but he had not really experienced enlightenment. He nevertheless produced many disciples who did achieve enlightenment, among whom were many arhats. Later on he asked one of his students who had become an arhat: "How did you achieve this?" The man said: "I cultivate practice according to the methods you taught." The teacher said: "What methods did I teach you? I have forgotten." So then the disciple took the teachings which the teacher had previously passed on to him, and passed them back to the teacher. The teacher cultivated realization according to the teachings, and he too experienced the result of becoming an arhat. Those who reject Pema Nam take this example to prove that, although he had disciples who achieved enlightenment, Pema Nam himself may not have achieved it. This kind of story may be accepted in the Lesser Vehicle, but in the Esoteric Vehicle, without an enlightened teacher, it is impossible to produce enlightened disciples. The Esoteric Vehicle emphasizes the sustaining power of the teacher and the transmission. Without the electric current of the teaching, the light bulb cannot light up.

In reality, whether or not Pema Nam achieved enlightenment is not important. What is important is whether or not he transmitted the truth. Even though when Pema Nam was in the world, he was always making things difficult for Khyungpo Naljor, I cannot reject all of his writings because of this. To tell the truth, before I came into contact with Shangpa Kagyu, I too was a fan of Pema Nam's writings. At least he was a learned man. He argued rigorously and presented clear theoretical discussions, and his knowledge was broad and deep. From his writings, I really could not see him as having made any great errors. But according to the accounts, when he was in the world, he really had too many battles with Khyungpo Naljor. Many times he took it to the point where there was a total clash.

Though the rumor Pema Nam concocted did not fundamentally injure Khyungpo Naljor, it made him come up with a new way of thinking. Rather than contend with people like Pema Nam for followers and offerings, it would be better to go do more important things in life.

Thus, he sent away his disciples and resumed his pilgrimage, to continue to search for Niguma.

4 Pyrotechnics from the Death-dealing Mandala in the Mountain Valley

According to the *Secret History of Khyungpo,* next to the Bonpo ancestral temple in the mountain valley, the pyrotechnics on the death-dealing mandala continued for a good many years. Some say it was more than ten years, some say it was several decades. The story goes that the dissension among Khyungpo Naljor's later disciples, who were always quarreling and could not get united, was an adverse circumstance created by the Bonpo guardian spirits.

According to another story, that rumor was also connected to the Bonpo guardian spirits. Although they very much wanted to get close to Khyungpo Naljor and take over his soul and invade his skin and eat his flesh, with his great innate strength Khyungpo Naljor was able to generate an extremely strong energy and keep them a hundred yards away every time. So they used Pema Nam as a vehicle, and launched a counterattack on Khyungpo Naljor. This, of course, is no more than a story. But people believe this type of story; they take this kind of symbol and call it one of the barriers of delusion.

Even so, uncountable numbers of people gathered around Khyungpo Naljor seeking the Dharma. Every day people came seeking the Dharma. Because he was planning to continue his search, Khyungpo Naljor had not built a teaching center, nor had he borrowed anyone else's teaching center in order to pass on the Buddha Dharma. He just stayed in the home of one of his local disciples. That disciple was from one of the area's illustrious wealthy families, and the house was very large and had a very stately Buddha hall. The disciple had spent a lot of money to have this built especially for his teacher. In this Buddha hall there were pictures and statues of almost all the tutelary deities that could be found in India at that time. Khyungpo Naljor performed initiatory rites in this Buddha hall for those who came seeking the Dharma. Some among them had come to seek the Dharma, other had come to study Sanskrit. Tibetans at that time were as enthusiastic to learn Sanskrit as people are now to learn English.

Because learning a language requires a lot of energy, Khyungpo Naljor was very rigorous in accepting students, and later he only kept two youngsters to learn Sanskrit. These two youngsters later became his attendants.

The rumor was still in circulation. In the Indian Buddhist world at that time, as in China now, sexual affairs were very sensitive. Gradually, in the process of passing the rumor along, it was added to and embellished, and eventually the story was that Khyungpo Naljor had made a whole group of Nepalese girls pregnant. This caused some of the so-called true believer disciples to fall away, because according to the local customs, people who broke the code of discipline were bad luck, and even those who broke the code of discipline in dreams were all very ill-omened. At this point, Khyungpo Naljor finally understood the evil of Pema Nam's intentions.

Some disciples with a sense of justice began to counterattack Pema Nam. At first there were disputes between the disciples. Although Pema Nam's disciples were not as numerous as Khyungpo Naljor's disciples, because Pema Nam had made studying Buddhist theory his main priority while in Nepal, and he had worked on the theory of causation, and his verbal talents were very good, there was a group of scholars who liked Buddhist studies who were all willing to have interchanges with him. Then too, in contrast to Khyungpo Naljor's rigorous precision, Pema Nam appeared to be very easygoing and approachable, and so a group of people soon gathered around him. These people later became a strong force in the Kadampa sect. They were best qualified to speak, and later they created many adverse situations for Khyungpo Naljor.

But Khyungpo Naljor's disciples were also become more and more numerous. People continued to approach him seeking the Dharma. This popularity had already gone beyond what it was when he was a Bonpo teaching master. Every day there was so much clamor, but amid all the noise, Khyungpo Naljor was always able to reflect. He was always concerned about that prediction of enlightenment.

5 A Woman in a Dream

One evening, Khyungpo Naljor once again dreamed clearly of that woman. He dreamed that he saw himself in a strange place, a place that was completely ordinary, but also incomparably resplendent. The ordinariness was the external appearance, the resplendent glory was a feeling. The woman towered up over the clouds. A light like a rainbow issued forth from her body, and a hundred lights entered his body like a downpour. He felt a completely wondrous, clear, refreshing coolness. That woman did not say a word, but Khyungpo Naljor felt she had said many things. He could never forget that pair of expectant eyes.

After he woke up, Khyungpo Naljor felt a kind of loneliness seeping into his heart. He went outside. The clear cold moon was hanging in the clear cold sky. The mountain valley was pitch black, and scattered through it was a kind of unexplainable spiritual sense. Although he still had some memories of rushing along on his journey, he understood clearly that if he did not constantly keep himself alert, before too long, he would never want to be stir himself to travel again. By nature he liked quiet, he liked pure practice, he did not like bustle and noise. But he understood that many times a man must have a trial of strength with himself. If he always went along with what he liked, then a man's animal nature, his character that likes a comfortable easy life, would cut off his initiative. Many people's dreams have been dissolved away by their own laziness.

Khyungpo Naljor discovered that he already had within himself the thought that he did not want to work hard and be on the go. This was very frightening. This of course was due to the length of the journeys he had made, and also because there were many ways in which he did not fit into these other countries. What was most unbearable was this feeling, when he was in foreign countries, that he had been thrown into an unfamiliar ocean. In Nepal, whenever he looked at anything, what he saw was always something strange striking his eye. Even if he stayed in one place, because he did not have any relatively enclosed space, he felt extremely exhausted.

Sometimes Khyungpo Naljor wanted very much to return to his home fown. The familiar scents of his hometown were always soothing to his tired mind. The mountains and rivers of home, that unique odor of the slow fires in his home town, the butter and roasted barley flour of his home town — all this was like a great force pouring into his body.

If he were to follow his own intentions, he would really not want to go traveling again to faraway places. But his rational nature told him that he still had to leave. He understood that if he did not leave, he would be nothing more than a Buddhist teacher. Of course, if it were just for the sake of individual liberation, what he had studied was already enough. If we compare liberation to a material thing, the liberation he sought was almost as easy as taking something out of his pocket. But there was always something he could not reconcile himself to. He always felt that in those faraway, strange places there was a kind of force pulling him. There was always a voice calling him. There was always some concern that could not be erased, inscribed on his bones and in his heart, that was always calling him to wake up, so that he could not sink into a sound sleep in that dream of home.

He thought: I am still going on the search.

When he made this decision, it was as if he saw a woman giving him a smile.

The next morning, he went ahead, as was his custom, with his pure practice. As soon as he went out the door, he discovered the spirit dove.

6 Forty-Nine Days of Black Magic

My beloved Khyungpo Ba, I've been busy for a long time — my father gave me a lot of things to take care of. Now I am writing you a letter again.

Today Kumari came again. She told me that those men have been chanting a text of black magic for forty-nine days. This is the first step of that black curse technique. They took that ceramic figure of you and dripped on it the blood of the black-faced butcher, the blood of a black-faced pregnant woman, the blood of a black mountain sheep, and the blood of a black dog. I have heard that black is the color of the god of death, and those who employ death-dealing methods must always use black. Besides this, they are looking everywhere for death-dealing objects, like the earth from a crossroads, the cinders from the iron filings on a blacksmith's floor, a rope that was used to hang a man, the knife that was used by someone who killed himself, a bowl that was used by a man who drank poison and died, an arrowhead that killed someone, or the bones, hair, and skin of a woman who died in childbirth. These are what people call "demons that smell of blood." They also took a widow's underwear or the paper she used to absorb her menstrual blood, dark spring water that has never seen the sunlight, live black spiders, live black scorpions, and so on and so forth. They took these death-dealing objects and shut them up together with that ceramic figure in a black yak's horn. They used the hair of a butcher who had died a violent death to close off the opening, and then they began to chant the text of black magic.

The reason I tell you about this content in detail, is because I hope you have the corresponding methods to neutralize evil. I have heard that to neutralize evil, it is best to know the content of the curses your enemies have laid down.

You must be sure to be careful, and do not forget to visualize that protective circle.

I too have begun to search for some lofty people. I think that in this world, if there are those who lay down curses, then there must be those who can neutralize them. The law of the world is that there is always something to conquer another thing. Do you think this is right?

I am still thinking of you.

Right now it is the middle of the night. I just looked at those books you left behind.Suddenly I had a very strong strange feeling. I felt strange, not only toward you, but also toward myself. I cannot explain the cause; maybe the environment has changed.

In reality, I no longer have anything to write about. My previous letters already told you everything about what I think and what I want. But I feel that I must keep my promise, and write you letters. You are always telling me not to write, to rest more, but I do not want to miss you. Though I am very tired, that doesn't matter, I still can persevere. If today I use being tired as a reason not to write, tomorrow I could also use being tired as a reason not to write, and after that I could use all kinds of fancy reasons as excuses, and abandon my own promises. In the same way, I could use all kinds of reasons and excuses and gradually abandon Khyungpo Ba, and finally let you become a faraway symbol.

But I am not willing to abandon Khyungpo Ba. I want to take the things I can do, do them to perfection, and make my greatest effort. If not, I would have no way to honor my promises, and I would not be able face you, the weary traveler. I cannot just deal with this feeling by taking it easy and being happy, and then when I have slept enough and slept soundly, casually flirt with someone else, and comfortably talk about love. Faced with Khyungpo Ba's promise, which was really a promise to his own mind and spirit—if I adopted this light playful attitude, probably I could not even face myself. I have to act this way, to be able to prove that I am not some empty, worthless diversion, just looking for fresh stimulation, casually attained and casually abandoned. I cannot act like this. I must use the mind of unselfish devotion to cherish this love.

I am determined: that is, I firmly believe we can go through this life. I am devoted: that is, I believe our love is the truest and most sincere and most beautiful love. True love must surely elevate people, not debase them.

I have slowly come to understand the importance of ritual. It must be firmly upheld as a cycle that runs its course and begins again, it must be strengthened, it must be solidified. Otherwise, I could very easily go numb and become oblivious. Once I go numb and become oblivious, evil thoughts and greedy thoughts could take advantage of the emptiness and come in, bit by bit invading the time and space of my thoughts, gradually expanding their territory, and making me turn back into the "female spirit" that I was.

Outside the window, all the sounds have quieted down. Between heaven and earth, there are just two hearts that will always be together, and they let nothing disturb them. As I finish writing this letter, I can escape into a warm broad embrace. Like a feather lightly floating in the earth's embrace — so empty and ethereal, so peaceful, so sure. The greatness of heaven and earth can contain the light spirit, the sweet beautiful dream this feather holds. As long as it is in the dreamer's mind, this attachment which cannot be wiped away will be there.

Here deep in the night, while it is so quiet, I still can think of your face as you slept soundly, calm and peaceful as a sleeping lotus. If we both fall deep asleep at this moment, who would go into whose dream? Tonight I am holding that dream as a mother holds her child.

When I am really thinking about Khyungpo Ba, I take the memories in my brain, and I replay them and replay them again and again ... On those wet rainy days, my shoes were already soaked through by the icy water, and I would pad them with many layers of cloth. Stepping on them, they were soft as cotton, but before long I felt the damp chill again, seeping up from the bottom of my feet. I remember at the time sitting in the back row, listening to my father's voice giving a dull lecture on the scriptures. I simply regretted being there — why had I come? Though my father was very learned, he was not stimulating, and I never liked his lectures on the scriptures...

I looked around the whole hall, and a yogi clad in dark red monastic robes was sitting quietly in another corner, his figure frozen, without a thread moving, like a statue. Who could have known that later on, by some strange coincidence, I would fall in love with this yogi ... life is really inconceivable.

I have written this far, and my eyelids are feeling heavy, and I really cannot lift them up. Probably it is already almost dawn, and I should just spare myself and get ready to take a rest. This letter really has no meaning, as you must see—I am just persisting with this ritual. You must remember: for all her faults and flaws, Sharwadi is the woman in the world who loves you the most.

Remember, you must always visualize that protective screen of fire.

Your Sharwadi

7 Khyungpo Ba's Mind

My female spirit:

Recently, I have still been exhausted. I am constantly having nightmares. In my dreams there is always a black scorpion as big as an ox biting me and sucking my blood. That black spider also stares at me with eyes big as bowls. I always see myself in dreams slogging through muck and mire, and when I wake up, I am exhausted.

According to the explanations handed down from the ancestors, I have really been put under a curse by someone.

Apart from the physical exhaustion, I am always encountering adverse circumstances, and I am constantly losing things. One day a book of scriptures just vanished. I remembered clearly putting it in a saddle bag, but now I cannot find it anywhere. This book was very ancient, and was made of human skin. There was an eminent monk who left instructions before his death to take his skin and make it into a book. The story goes that when this eminent monk was alive, he had begun to tattoo the text of a scripture onto his body. It contained an ancient spell which was used to remove evil curses. I really wanted to find in it methods to break up evil curses. I was reading through this scripture at night. Unexpectedly, I felt that on that man's skin there were prickly hairs. According to what it said in the text, this was inauspicious, and it meant there were evil demons concerned with me.

I had not thought that book would end up suddenly vanishing. Well, what's lost is lost — the thing that was lost was not mine.

Such a long time has passed in the blink of an eye. Human life is really too short. Again and again we go through life absent-minded, and then we get old, and then we will turn into two piles of bones without anything special about them.

But I am willing to take this life, which gold cannot buy, and spend it loving you, loving you with complete focus and no thought of gain, loving you with no regrets. This is also because I always take death as a reference point. I think that the value of a person's life is precisely what that person does, so I will use the timespan of my golden life to love a woman who is worth loving. I just wish that the life which is yours and mine will be raised to a higher level because of this.

I have told you that your conduct and your faith have

genuinely moved me. Though I love you very much, if I had not felt moved like that, my wisdom might have been able to dissolve this love. Because love requires a great deal of time and life energy, I am not willing to let external things disturb my focus and my tranquility. But ever since I have been reading your letters, I have been moved.

In your letters there is so much heartfelt expression that it can make me cry. Almost every day I look at them from the beginning; I use this ritual to carry out my cultivation of my love for you. This feeling of being moved will become one of the reasons for our love. Because it has appeared, we will be able to go on longer. If we can be moved for our whole lives, we can be together for our whole lives.

Khyungpo Ba at midnight

Chapter 11

On the Road to Enlightenment

Xuemo: Master, your letters to Sharwadi left me very surprised. I had always thought that her love for you had become a burden on your spirit, that it was something you thought about and wanted to break away from. I had not thought that you would end up having that spiritual feeling you express in your letters to her. Obviously, at the start, you really experienced the emotional complications that ordinary people experience.

Obviously, you were not a natural-born holy man, and although fate made you go on a search, and you were trying hard to realize this search, you still had no way to completely cut off the troubles caused by emotions.

In these texts of lingering tenderness, I get a sense of that tragic love howling in your soul.

1 Who Is Niguma?

You are right. I was still an ordinary man. I went through all the trials an ordinary man must go through to become a holy man.

That day at noon, after I had written back to Sharwadi, I took all the offerings I had received and exchanged them for gold, and I once again began my search. The dangers and difficulties of the journey go without saying. What was more frightening was that I was always sick: suddenly I would get cold, then suddenly I would be hot. This fatigue became a shadow I could not shake off. During the daytime, the pain was not too much, but the insomnia at night was really unbearable. As soon as I closed my eyes, many frightening scenes rushed at me. That black scorpion was always sucking in air. It would open its great bloody mouth like a siphon and suck all the colored lights from my body into its body. According to the ancestral stories, it was sucking out my vital energy. Later that black spider would also approach me, and put something like a sucking tube into my body. Although these were only dream scenes or illusory perceptions, my utter fatigue was very real.

But I kept on going, and as I was traveling, I kept doing the visualizations of the things I had to visualize. I thought, if worst comes to worst, I will die on the road. What is there to be afraid of?

I felt that those curses were taking effect. I often could not walk very long before I had to half recline and rest for a while. I began to harbor doubts about the earlier prediction that I would be able to live for a hundred and fifty years as a great accomplished master. I thought that if I go on like this, I will not be able to survive for even a few years.

But, I thought, however long I live, I will keep going that long. If I die, I still will come back and continue on the journey I have not completed.

I did not know how long I had been going. This is because sometimes, when you are in a certain state, you cannot keep track of time. When the tranquility of your mind reaches a certain level, time dissolves away. Thus, I never knew the time, and I was never clear about how many years had passed. What alerted me to the passage of time was my fingernails and my beard. They would get longer and longer, like a madman's, but when they reached a certain length, I would know that a long time had passed.

Along the pilgrimage road, as I walked peacefully on, there were silent mountains and rocks, and before me I saw unknown little paths going back and forth like silk strips. There was only the sound of my footsteps to accompany me, and in my mind I ceaselessly chanted mantras. Of course, I did not care how long I had been going. Time and space were both illusions. Though I lived a hundred and fifty years, to my surprise, it was not such a long time. Just put it into the long river of history, and it was not even a bubble. What is truly important is not how long we live, but what we do. What each one of us does creates the value of each of our lives.

At that time I was indeed like a fallen leaf thrown into the ocean, and I did not know how, in this vast expanse of other countries and other places, I would find what I was searching for. When I met people, I would inquire after Niguma. I asked several hundred people, but I heard only one answer: Who is Niguma?

There was only one man who knew a Niguma. He took me to where Niguma was, and I saw that the Niguma this man had been talking about was a boy. His mother had picked a girl's name for him.

At certain moments, I truly lost hope.

2 The Great God Shiva

One day as I came into a town, there was a crowd of people who were just then having a procession and holding up the image of a god. They were shouting wildly, and I could barely make out what they were shouting — they were praising a great god called Shiva.

This was a traditional festival of theirs.

I saw that the image of this god was not like anything I had ever seen before. What was most striking was its large phallus, and its fierce aggressive appearance. Male and female believers held this holy object in one hand, while in the other hand they held another totem shining with golden light. Looking at its shape, I saw that it was in the form of a phallus too. What was being carried on the shoulders of the priest presiding over the ceremony was also a phallus.

I felt this was interesting. I asked an old man, and he answered that this was a ceremony for the great deity Shiva. I asked who Shiva was, and the old man said that Shiva was a great god, the god of procreation, and also the god of destruction. He was in charge of life in the universe, and every few thousand eons, he would destroy the world. His destructive power was incomparable, and once he set in motion that destructive power, the sun, moon, and stars, and the humans and spirits, and all the beings in the six kinds of existence would be totally wiped out. The story was that even Brahma and Indra would not escape this catastrophe. One time, be witched by a woman, Shiva let loose his power and was wreaking havoc. Brahma created a ferocious tiger to attack Shiva, but instead this made Shiva crush the tiger to death and then skin it. Brahma then created a gnome, and the great god Visnu used a magic spell to provide a club that could subdue demons, and gave it to the gnome to go do battle with Shiva. The result was that the gnome was killed, and Shiva seized the club for defeating demons, and after this he made it into his own images.

I saw that, despite all this, the image of Shiva was not that fierce and evil-looking. He sat upright on the throne, and seemed to be immersed in contemplation. He had three eyes and four arms and held four kinds of weapons in his hands: a trident, a bow and arrow, a thunder hammer, and an axe. He wore a necklace made of skulls. The most striking thing about that statue was his phallus, which was standing upright, and looked extraordinarily fearsome. The story was that this was his most ferocious weapon. When he wanted to demonstrate his power, he would spray out a great fire from his phallus, which could incinerate cities, and burn up everything alive. If there was nobody to restrain him, even the realm of desire, the realm of form, and the formless realm would not escape the destruction.

The old man said that when Brahma subdued Shiva, first he cut away his power by castrating him, and only then did he break his magical powers. But Shiva's spirit was always like the grasses in the fields: the wild fires cannot completely burn them up, and they come to life again when the spring winds blow. Moreover, his lust was very strong, and he was always falling in love with the priests' women, and enticing them into having sex. In order to bring Shiva under control, the god Mahaishvara determined that, in the human world, the male genital organ should be used to symbolize Shiva, and the female genitalia should be used to symbolize Shiva's wife Durga, and these should be offered in all the temples in the country and be worshipped. The story goes that Brahma took Shiva's penis and divided it into thirty-nine pieces. Of these, nine were given to temples in the heavens, one was given to be worshipped in hell, and twenty-one were given to temples in this world so they could be used for ceremonies and worship services. The remaining eight pieces were given to other realms.

What I saw was a ceremony where people were worshipping Shiva. The dancing girls wore gold rings on their fingers and gold rings in their noses, and they were gorgeously dressed. They all had their arms and thighs bare, and they had silver ornaments on them. According to what I was told, they belonged to the temple, and all the money they took in from their clients was given as an offering to the temple. The dancing girls walked around and danced, and their dances were very elegant, and the ornamental bells on their clothes made sounds that pleased the ear.

The ceremony proceeded into the temple. Several sacred cows whose horns were inlaid with gold also went into the temple. In a loud voice a Brahmin priest cried out: "I am Brahma, I am the universe." The dancing girls were dancing to the ritual music, and they looked around radiantly, their beauty beyond compare, gently moving their waists and their hips, swaying flirtatiously. The whole scene was very lively, and had a powerful appeal.

The priest who was carrying the silver phallus on his shoulder took down the sacred object and extended it toward the believers, who were bowing down to pay homage. The believers poured sacred water from the Ganges over it, and kept kissing the sacred object. The women, too, rushed madly at the sacred object and offered up all kinds of flower garlands, and they too embraced it and kissed it. The story was that sincere believers could receive sexual spiritual power bestowed by Shiva.

I felt that the whole ritual had a great power, and there was really no way to resist that kind of appealing power. Though my rational nature was cautioning me, I still felt that I had been absorbed into that ritual, like a drop of water absorbed into the ocean.

The priest presiding over the ritual again began to chant, and the sound of his voice was long-drawn-out and devout. He said, "Let us in all sincerity cleanse the dirt from our souls." He rubbed his navel and he rubbed his penis, and he said: "The real fire is here! The sun is here! The moon is also here!" The priest's assistant took the dung that the sacred cow had just dropped and wiped a handful of it over the priest's body. According to the local customs, the dung of a sacred cow is itself something sacred.

The priest said: "Great Shiva is the god of creation. He created the whole world, and he created us, the human race. He created the sun and the moon and the stars. Without him, nothing would exist. Without him, there would be no earth, water, fire, and air. Oh Great God Shiva, we offer our praises to you. But you are also the god of destruction, and all things show impermanence because of you, the great mountains crumble because of you, the oceans dry up because of you, the stars fall out of the sky because of you, the fish and shrimp become extinct because of you. You are also the great god of sexual desire, and when you were fifteen your lust swept over all the milkmaids in the country and you made them ecstatic. That incomparable spiritual power of yours became a symbol of the life force."

The old man also gave me an introduction to Shiva. He told me that Shiva has many wives. His second wife was call Sati. This name has an interesting implication. It means "the great pleasure gotten from the female genitals." Sati had many worshippers, and they worship the female genital organs. Their method of cultivating practice was to face a very realistic image of a vulva and do a deep meditation. Later I was in a hidden place, and I saw the people worshipping Sati. They were in the midst of performing a ritual of making offerings. This form of practice was called meeting to bring down the spirit. At first the people were just meditating and imagining, but gradually a kind of spiritual power enveloped them, and then the worshippers embraced each other, and the whole scene showed signs of wild lust.

Although I did not totally understand their worship, I did understand them. I thought that in the eyes of these worshippers, this object of worship that looks like a male organ is the same kind of holy image as an image of Buddha is to me. I respected their belief.

3 The Old Man Manifested by the Dakini

Before I went to India, I had thought I would see a forest of temples and multitudes of Buddhist monks there. But when I traveled into India, I discovered that there, as in Nepal, it was a Brahmanist country. There were many Brahmanist sects, and they had already carved up the greater part of the cake of Indian religion, and what was left was mostly divided up among traditional religions like Jainism. I saw virtually no splendid Buddhist temples. I only heard that the monastery at Nalanda was a grand sight, but that was just hearsay.

One day I discovered an old man who did divination, and he looked very venerable and extraordinary. I asked him about Niguma, and the man asked in return: "Who is Niguma?"

I said: "Niguma is a great accomplished master."

When that man understood that Niguma was an accomplished Buddhist master, he said: "If you are seeking the great virtuous ones of Buddhism, you cannot go around aimlessly and haphazardly. I will teach you a method, and you can make contact directly with those historically Buddhist holy places and go search there. In those places there are always some Buddhist believers engaged in cultivating practice, or going back and forth on pilgrimages. No matter what, there is a higher probability you will meet them or find out some information that way, than if you go blindly blundering along."

I suddenly had a great awakening.

That man also said: "Look, the closest place to here is Bodh Gaya. This is the place where Buddha achieved enlightenment. If you are willing, you should go there first."

Thus, Bodh Gaya became the first holy place I visited on my pilgrimage in India.

Later on I thought that this old man was certainly manifested by the dakini.

4 The Atmosphere of Bodh Gaya

Do you know Bodh Gaya? If you have read the Buddhist sutras, you surely know Bodh Gaya. Because of differences in the translations, you may have seen another name, like Buddhagaya, or something else. This is the place where Buddha achieved enlightenment.

The Bodh Gaya I saw was very similar to the Bodh Gaya which Buddha saw a thousand years earlier. During that thousand years, it had welcomed a large number of pilgrims, and its land had certainly changed in ways not easy to detect. The trees there had lived and died again and again, and crop after crop of plants had lived and died, and the humans too had lived and died for countless generations. But in its external appearance, Bodh Gaya had not had any great changes over the flow of time. For example, what Buddha saw was a level plain, and what I saw was also a level plain. Buddha saw the forests, and I also saw the forests. Buddha saw a river, and I also saw a river. Of course, I did not suppose that what we saw was the same level plain, the same river, the same forests, because these material things, like all material things, all follow the law of impermanence and are changing every moment.

I felt the unique atmosphere of Bodh Gaya. It is very difficult for me to describe that atmosphere for you. Perhaps, at some moments when you were reading the sutras, you caught the scent of a delicate fragrance that seemed somehow intangible. This delicate fragrance would be hard for you to describe, but it would still affect you, and your mind would become very soft, and you would be very easily moved. In your mind a beautiful melody would surge up, and then you would feel that you were very pure and very peaceful. Gradually, you would have no more greed, no more hatred, no more ignorance. You would seem to feel you had raised your level of human dignity. Right, that's it. That kind of atmosphere, that kind of ambience, is just what I felt at this moment. Thus, you will say that I had gotten the support of the Buddha. This is right for you can understand it this way. Only after a certain enlightenment many years later, did I know that what was supporting me then was, in fact, my teacher Niguma and my own mind of faith. At that time, I had experienced the ultimate result of enlightenment. I clearly understood that the myriad things are not apart from the true nature of mind, and the true nature of mind is not apart from the myriad things, and the myriad things and the true nature of mind are in reality not apart from the ocean of wisdom of the fundamental teacher. This teacher and this mind of faith stimulated the inherent life force in my mind. Of course, this too is an expedient explanation using skill in means.

Bodh Gaya received me with a smile. So I saw the smiling earth, the smiling villages, the smiling river. There were many other things smiling too — I'll use the expression "the myriad things" to represent them. At this point I felt a kind of vastness and grandeur. That vastness

was a vastness that contained the myriad images. That grandeur was
the great beauty of a great image without form. I believe that Buddha
in those years also must have been moved by this great beauty to stay
here for a time. At that time, there were many ascetics living in the
forest—some swallowed cow dung, some lay down on beds of thorns,
some stared into the sun, some stood on one leg—in sum, there was
every kind of strange practice. Buddha was certainly attracted by
them. He thought: "This is a good place, with rivers, with forests, with
villages, with so many ascetics for companions." He thought: "So let
me stay here and cultivate the Path." So he stayed on. Do not laugh. If
you are a learned person, you will have seen this story in the Pali text
of the *Agama Sutra*.

I was genuinely moved. I felt waves of emotion. At that time,
though I had studied the Great Mudra, I had not yet awakened to
empty inherent nature, and that's why my mind was swept by waves of
emotion. At that time external things could still pull at my mind. You
must not think this strange—I was not born enlightened. I went through
ascetic practice and cultivation too, and it was just this ascetic practice
and cultivation that made me become your teacher.

A warm, pleasant breeze hit my face and blew into the depths of
my soul, and I felt an extraordinary pure, refreshing coolness. That
pure, refreshing coolness came from the depths of my mind, and it was
not necessary to seek it outside. Gradually it transformed and dissolved
away my clingings and attachments. Then I saw that ascetic prince
from a thousand years earlier. I saw him after he had been an ascetic for
many years, and he no longer had the look of a prince. His ribs were
protruding and his face had little more texture than a skeleton. When he
wanted to rub his belly, what he touched was his spine. At that time he
ate only one grain of linseed and one grain of wheat a day. There were

five other men with him, and in appearance and in spirit, they were all like skeletons. At that time I could not discern any of the Buddha's thirty-two auspicious marks. This, of course, is not important. What has made people revere him through the ages is not his appearance, but his character.

From time immemorial the wind and clouds have created a classic meaning, and I tasted this scenery as though I were savoring an ancient religious painting. I felt a kind of happiness and peace bathed in great virtue. The people who read this book of yours will certainly feel this way too. Of course, the prerequisite is that they must be devoted and reverent. I look at that king's son called Siddhartha, you look at me, people look at your book, your book looks at the distant future. In this way, we all go into an ancient story. What this story tells is how we go searching for enlightenment.

Tears flowed over my face, washing it in a cleansing ritual of great virtue and beauty. I was no longer that Tibetan novice I had been before. Bodh Gaya was like a mother holding me in her arms, giving me the warmth that could melt away the gloom in my mind.

I saw that Gautama had already been practising austerities for six years, and enlightenment still seemed far away in the indefinite future. He, of course, did not know that enlightenment had already begun to smile at him. This was because he suddenly discovered that all his ascetic practices seemed not to have brought him enlightenment.

One morning, as he was watching the ceaseless flow of the Niranjana River, a bamboo raft passed by, and on it sat a music teacher, who was telling his student: "If you make the strings too tight on this zither, they will break, and if you leave them too loose, when you pluck them they will not produce any sound." Gautama understood where his own issue was. He went into the Niranjana River, and washed the mud off his body, and he washed away his attachment to asceticism. He swam freely in the Niranjana River. He thought: "So I will choose the middle Path. This middle Path is in the middle of all extremes."

A little girl came from far away. Her name was Sujata. Because of the merit she won for giving an offering to Buddha, she won everlasting fame. Now people use her name to name villages, to name bridges, to name a mountain. The Tibetans even built a temple for her, called the Sujata Temple. On two sides of the temple are carved two girls — one is Sujata and one is her maid, who is said to have been called Poona.

As for where Sujata came from, there are many accounts. The traditional account which I heard said that she received the direction of a spirit, which told her that on this day she would give an offering to a bodhisattva. She got milk from a thousand dairy cows and fed five hundred cows; then she milked them to feed another hundred cows, and then milked them to feed fifty cows, and so on and on until she was feeding a single cow. This milk was not ordinary milk, but had become cream.

She took this cream and offered it to the bodhisattva who was just then swimming in the Niranjana River. I have some doubts about this story, because at the time Gautama's body was extremely weak, and it would seem that he would not have had the strength to go swimming. The real story must be that the bodhisattva was in the Niranjana River cleaning the dirt off his body.

The story goes that the bodhisattva took that cream and offered it to those men who had been pursuing ascetic practice with him. Those men angrily refused. They all thought: "Look at this spoiled princeling, falling to this level." They angrily shook their heads, and left Gautama. They thought the farther away they went, the better, and so they went to Sarnath (the Deer Park).

I saw Gautama, who had washed the dirt off his body, calmly drink the cream. Still hungry and thirsty from his ascetic practices, the cells of his body growled like mad, and they put out earth-shaking sounds. I clearly heard these sounds. The sounds represented the countless sentient beings seeking liberation. They called out, they sang, they knew that they would make a qualitative leap. After seven days, because of their master's enlightenment, they would achieve the bliss of quiet tranquility.

I saw Gautama under the bodhi tree. He was as still as an abyss, still as a lofty peak, and his eyes were like bright stars. He was not like the Buddha in the pictures, with his eyes closed, sunk in contemplation. No, his eyes were wide open. He made a great vow that has moved ancient and modern: "Unless I achieve true awakening, I will not get up from this seat."

This is an ancient story. But I still could taste the hot blood boiling up. I saw an army of those demons of delusion sweeping at him, and they were very frightening. They certainly did not come from outside, but from his own mind and spirit. They were another manifestation of the pollution of the mind and spirit. They were greed, they were hatred, they were ignorance, they were all the demons of the afflictions that had beset Gautama. They cried: "Do not cast me out, my master." Sometimes they were soft, sometimes they were hard, sometimes they were strong, sometimes they were mild, sometimes they enticed, sometimes they threatened. A rain of arrows was their hatred, a bouquet of fresh flowers was their seductiveness. They brandished all kinds of weapons and set up an endless clamor, like a carnival of birds. You can call them vexations — they are the defilements of the mind and spirit that much be cleared away before you can experience enlightenment.

We of course know the outcome: Gautama vanquished the army of demons.

We see a light like the full moon coming from his mind, spreading out like a wave, communicating to the realm of reality.

Later on, we would all be able to see this light from the images of Buddha. There is another way of describing this light — it is called the empty inherent nature.

I gave a long sigh of relief. I think that, if there had been no Buddha in the world, through the ages it would have been like an eternal night.

5 Seeking the One Who Cultivates the Path

I began to search for those who cultivated the Path. But the Bodh Gaya of a thousand years later was not the Bodh Gaya of a thousand years before. The flourishing asceticism no longer existed. There were only a few people who paid homage to the diamond seat. That was a thick red sandstone slab, covered over by the shadows of the huge bodhi tree. This tree was shaped like a giant umbrella, and it was incomparably cool under it. When they saw it, everyone would think of the Buddha's benevolence. I of course knew that, at first, when Gautama was cultivating the Path under the tree, this stone was not there. It had been placed there by King Ashoka to commemorate the Buddha, and with the passage of time, it had become a sacred object. The bodhi tree, too, had become a sacred object. Like Buddhism itself, this tree had gone through many vicissitudes, and had met with disaster many times, had been cut down and burned many times. But the dead branches had come back to life many times, and had grown back to give dense shade.

That slab of stone called the diamond seat was covered with flowers and offerings, and people came to visit and pay homage, among them both Buddhist monks and laypeople. I could not be sure that they were definitely believers in Buddhism, because Hinduism had also taken Sakyamuni into its scope of belief. Not far away, there were a few fire-worshippers performing a ritual. In their chants I heard the word "Brahma." They were definitely performing a ritual for Brahma. They thought that fire is the mouth of Brahma, and when they burned offerings, these all went into Brahma's stomach.

I picked an old man who looked very devout and ethereal—he was waiting in attendance on those fire-worshippers. I asked him: "Sir, have you heard of a woman called Niguma?" I deliberately emphasized the word "woman." The old man said: "I know three Nigumas. One is now the wife of one of the current officials in Bodh Gaya. One is an old woman who sells tea. One is a person who cultivates the Path. Which Niguma are you looking for?" I was delighted, and told him I was looking for the one who cultivates the Path. The old man said: "Is she Naropa's enlightened consort?" I had never heard the term "enlightened consort," but I did know that Niguma had a deep connection with Naropa, and it was said that she was his younger sister. At once I said: "That's her."

The old man said: "I have not seen Niguma, but I have heard quite a bit about her story. I've heard that when she was paying homage to the diamond seat, she saw Vajradhara, and some people say her transformation developed from this. Look, there she is ..." He pointed at a certain place and said: "She is there paying homage. Suddenly her body has turned red, and she is sending forth a golden light, coming out of her third eye ..." He kept talking like this.

I immediately said: "That's her. Please tell me, where is she now?"

The old man shook his head and said: "I don't know. You should not look for her. Nobody knows where she is. If you have a karmic connection with her, you do not need to search for her: she will appear right in front of you. If you do not have a karmic connection with her, then even if you search for her, it will be in vain. Surely you must have heard that she has already attained the rainbow body. Her body became a rainbow, and though when you look at her it appears to have form, when you touch it, there is nothing there. When she wants to show it, then it appears. When she wants to hide it, then it is hidden. You cannot find her by searching."

When I heard this, my mind suddenly went gray, but then I thought, I do have a karmic connection with her.

The old man said: "I have heard that the imperishable bright spot in her mind changes into a transformed realm, and it is very grand. However I have just heard of it; I have never heard of anyone who has reached that land."

The old man added: "But she is not a character in one of those spirit stories people make up. She really exists."

6 A Long Distance

I left Bodh Gaya, and set out on my journey in search of the truth. Though I had not heard where Niguma was, I had gotten some information, and my feelings were very complex. You should know that at that time I definitely had not experienced ultimate enlightenment. Though I had some worldly accomplishments, I was still a long distance from the ultimate accomplishment. As I was at that time, I still could not control the turmoil in my mind.

I decided to go to Sarnath: this is where the Buddha first turned the wheel of the Dharma. Maybe you have seen a sculpture on the roof of some temples of two deer facing each other, with a wheel between them. According to the story, this is to commemorate the Buddha first turning the wheel of the Dharma at Sarnath. I thought that since there was no way to get accurate information on Niguma, if I kept searching through the holy places, that would be a way of proceeding. Ultimately, the proportion of Buddhist followers and accomplished people in the holy places was bound to be much greater than in the ordinary towns.

The distance between Bodh Gaya and Sarnath, as it is spoken of in the Buddhist scriptures, does not seem to be too far, because after the Buddha achieved enlightenment, he went to Sarnath to teach the five bhikshus, Kaundinya and the others. Our impression is that the Buddha walked there, but, in fact, the two places are relatively far apart, so he must have been trekking for a good many days.

As I was walking along the road, a great love surged up in my mind. Without this great love, I would not have been able to walk the length of this strange land. It was just to search for a woman. Your whole life, in fact, you are searching for a woman. Of course, you can also understand this as a kind of vehicle for faith. You can take her as Niguma, or as the Vajravarahi—she is the same kind of pure, holy figure as the Niguma in my mind. To find her, you too have gone through a spiritual purgatory. So you have understood the poem by the Sixth Dalai Lama, Tsangyang Gyatso. At dusk on a certain day, a feeling so thick it could not be transformed engulfed you, and so you wrote the poem entitled "Traveling Together."

How much I want to travel with you together across the rivers and lakes

One hand holding a sword

One hand holding you tight in your white clothes

Leaning on the horse as the west wind howls

Drawing back the long bow

Shooting the arrow as you laugh and talk

The road through the rivers and lakes is long

So long it's like the string on a lute

This song I have been playing for a thousand years

You are the most beautiful musical note

You must know that a thousand years ago, I had that state of mind too: "People without great love cannot achieve enlightenment."

You certainly have understood me, and you use a very literary language to write of that feeling, so thick it could not be transformed. You will not desecrate that spiritual holiness in my mind, because when you write about it, you do not have any vulgar worldly thoughts at all.

7 The Solitude of the Lone Traveler

There is a lot of dust in India, but it is still India, and so there is a great beauty in that dust. The girls there had already spoiled my appetite. Their little faces are ill at ease, and as soon as they see you looking them over, they are shocked and close their eyes.

When the dusty wind is blowing, you certainly cannot find her. She only smiles in the spring. You have to mount a roan horse and go searching for a flock of sheep that has been scattered by the wind. That lamb that has just been born has already been carried off by wild wolves. After the sound of a deep sigh, you wipe away the tears, and you know you are just mourning a life long gone.

Heaven and earth are empty and vast, silent, without voices, without people to mull over the solitude of the lone traveler. So you are always worrying about that fated woman. Facing the timeless wilderness and the momentariness of life, you no longer care about the outcome.

Better the desert. There aren't so many rules. Because those rules are always killing you. All you want is to ride a roan horse and run wild in the wind. Your song is in the wind. Those people in city have eardrums that are too tender, and they always dislike those sounds of nature, they hurt themselves.

You always want to find a cozy harbor, and to call that sea breeze which does not mock you, and iron out the fatigue in your mind. But no one likes your body covered with windblown dust, and there is that burned spirit. You who do not want to burn anyone else, can only burn yourself.

You always want to look for a quiet out-of-the-way place, and your eyes quietly wipe away the turbulence of life. Though you speak of those tears, you are reflecting the world, and a good many people are cheering. Can you just be a solitary traveler? Can it be that you cannot lick the wounds that cover your body?

Think of yourself, on this solitary morning. A thick fog has seized me, and I do not know where it has enveloped me. The jackdaw in my mind has gone far away little by little, and what is near me is solitude, and your freshness. I move my hands, but I cannot erase you from my mind.

A great destruction has swept in, coming from afar, and has shattered all routines. The distant temple bell is still ringing, like your ghostly laugh. I intend to trudge on in the wind, but I fear that if I go far, I will lose my way.

I dare not look to you in this trance: I always fear that this burnt soul will burn you, who are so delicate. But you are also a bird, so can't you offer a pure refreshing song every lonely morning?

You in my mind are really a white feather tumbling in the wind, always stirring up a great wave rippling across the pond. I am always thinking of fleeing, fleeing into that light that cannot be named or described. But fate angrily says: Hey you! Why don't you dissolve yourself in that inferno of the bliss of emptiness?

I'm always thinking of that quiet solitary little temple in that mountain valley. Amidst the clamor of India, it has shrunk down to a vague dark blur. Your unexpected arrival was clearly the wind of fate. I look at that laurel in my mind, and it is slowly putting out pistils.

I don't want to go out, I just want to suffocate in this little room. I don't want to face false smiles. All I want is to change into a pure refreshing energy in your embrace.

I don't want to touch that long-gone twilight. The whistling of the wind is piercing my mind. I have become a flying dandelion. The great wind has become fascinated by the trees on the horizon, and I can no longer find the way home.

Where are the dreams you inhabit? Do they bewitch you like that, or not? Better to look at the vast empty firmament, but I cannot look at the shadow I want to look at.

I really want to reject all social gatherings, because at all social gatherings, you are not there. The guests are all at the table making a lot of noise, speaking with insincere cordiality. But I am eating alone, amid the infinite loneliness, waiting for the chopsticks you extend to me.

There is no yearning: yearning is a boiling swamp. Therein is the fire at the end of the age. I intend to melt into that fire, but I also fear losing myself.

My mind has become a great flowing wave. It is even more like an erupting volcano.The great love at the beginning turns into a literary text. In this moment of vertigo, I no longer dare encounter that name. You know that in this place, unexpected great winds arrive, and I am just a helpless child.

Earlier I could not see the root. The previous root was the rope binding my life, and your fierce mind cut it. All I could do was blow around in your wind. I forgot what place I should inhabit, and in my unconcerned eyes, my old home slowly slipped far away.

You are the biggest knife of fate, you are just now killing the immature me. But I am just an innocent child. Look, the rippling waves of that shadow are filled with the splendor of my spring flowers.

I have gone far away countless times. My dazed eyes are always flying around. I cannot find you, who missed our appointment. You inhabit the deepest place in the human stream. Fate says: look at her, she has gone far away.

Geese are flying past the window, and there a few more whistles, but I am waiting for your laugh. Though I say I know, every time I hear your charming laugh, it calls me to travel far.

You are a feather—where has it blown, and why are you so slow in coming? In that purple temple, I passed by my best self in vain. I'm just afraid that, arriving too late, I will never again dare to look to the eternal you.

The gray hair flies around in the wind, and no matter how long it goes, there is no resentment, just a gentle warmth. You came from the village that intoxicates the soul. I sleep soundly in your eyes, and the sense of spring is coming to an end.

No need to make promises. I am afraid of the confusion of words, which always give off some hypocritical sophistication. Though your laughter is pure and bright beyond compare, I want you to use your soft gentle eyes to intoxicate me.

In order to wait for you, I have refused all invitations. My thatched hut in the desert is blown by the wind into all kinds of colors. The vicissitudes of time wash through my little hut, but they cannot wash away the waiting and the expectations. Look, on that little bridge of fate, you are smiling tenderly again. Do not try to hide it, that sweet giddiness is flowing out on all sides. You, who cannot intoxicate the world, have first intoxicated yourself.

You always want to escape from that gigantic magnetic field, that collides so fiercely head-on. You are afraid to shatter your little hut. A great fog that fills the sky is sweeping in noisily, and no one knows how powerful it is.

To choose to bring back your tranquility, you should give yourself an order: Take her and turn her into amber! Don't call for her to look, bringing yourself pain. In this, you are contradicting yourself. Your heart says: Look for her, I want her. Wisdom says: It is precisely the distance and the regret that captures the beauty. Of course, there is also art that can capture the beauty. So you want to use the wisdom of Don Quixote to capture her beauty. Just think: when you are tilting at windmills, you will hear a charming laugh. Your sad world will then be lit up.

In your mind there must be something else — it's just that she has invaded and occupied your territory. In an instant of extreme cold, you want to go to sleep, and you fear that the cold will freeze your blood. Then, as your cry out, where will there be anyone to hear you?

8 A Boiling Soul

Khyungpo Naljor speaking to Xuemo:

From this, people can see the boiling soul of a seeker. Some people may say that you took the feelings in your own mind and shifted them to me. That's right, but they may or may not know that you and I are, in reality, two sides of a single tapestry. We are different shadows cast by a single moon, different transformations of a single essence, different fruits formed from a single root system, different cups filled with the same water. We both went through similar searches, similar awakenings, similar realizations of the Path. They must realize that the search before awakening is the nourishment for cultivating the Path. The "seeking" in the phrase "Wearing out iron shoes without any seeking" is precisely the "effort" in "attaining without expending any effort."

You perhaps have heard this story. A lady sent her maid to try to find a Zen monk whom she had been supporting for many years. The maid embraced him from behind and asked: "What do you feel?" The monk replied: "A dead tree on a cold cliff, three winters without warmth." The lady said: "I have supported an ordinary man for twenty years." Then she drove the monk out with a rain of blows. This monk's feeling was "dead tree Zen."

You might ask: "So then, what is true awakening?" I will tell you that true awakening is compassion for all, and great love filling every pore. That great love dissolves the ego, and that great compassion eliminates greedy clinging. When you are one body with sentient beings, and you are not apart from the Buddha, then you have realized true awakening.

Covered with windblown dust, my body bore the imprint of

the search, and also the imprint of future enlightenment. My future enlightenment had its origin in this period of searching. Without searching and seeking, there would have been nothing at all. My whole life was in seeking, seeking was my destiny from past lives. Otherwise, people will not understand why I visited one hundred and fifty teaching masters. They were one hundred and fifty burning torches, who could bring me the light of wisdom.

Their light merged into a great rushing river, and it has flowed on for a thousand years, and will flow on into your waking dreams.

You clearly feel the great love which is being passed on from me here.

Please continue to follow in my footsteps, and go see and experience my road to enlightenment.

Chapter 12

Reasons for Love

1 The Blood-drinking Yaksha

My beloved Khyungpo Ba:

I keep worrying about your physical safety.

Kumari is also very worried. This is because those men who are employing the curses are all very happy. They say that, judging from the omens, those evil curses have begun to take effect.

They have also begun to take the curses a step further.

Every night, the sorcerers are summoning those malevolent spirits and evil demons, and making offering to them with filthy blood. They are a band of blood-drinking yakshas. They like stinking flesh. Though quite a few people know about this, no one dares to reprimand them. One reason is that reprimands would not do any good. A second reason is that people are afraid that if they go near that mandala of curses, it will bring them misfortune. According to one story, a pregnant woman who carelessly approached that place actually hemorrhaged blood and died, and her body was bought by those sorcerers. I heard tell that her blood and flesh were the best sacrificial offerings. The sorcerers used a sharp knife to carve up that woman's flesh and, piece by piece, threw it onto the fire mandala. The sizzling sound of the fire burning up human flesh continued through the night, and even at a distance people could smell the odor stabbing into their nostrils.

That fire mandala was built of three large rocks that the sorcerers took from a graveyard and arranged in the shape of a triangle — this is a special arrangement for death-dealing methods. On the rocks, they placed the black yak horn with the ceramic figure representing you, and some bones from the butcher, and then they added some mud from the cemetery and the places where the evil demons appear and disappear.

Every night the sorcerers summon forth those malevolent spirits and angry guardian spirits, and offer them black sheep blood, black ox blood, and black chicken blood, and ask them to help the sorcerers slay the man called Khyungpo Naljor.

The sounds of the black curses of the sorcerers echo through the night, and terrify people to their bones. So I pray to Brahma and Mahakala, so I can protect my beloved.

Nevertheless, although worry for your safety fills my mind with anxieties, all I have to do is pick up one of your letters, and I feel that the sun has risen in my life.

Every day in the evening I always have to reread one of your letters. This has become my homework assignment.

In the morning I do my best not to read your letters. I want to do my best in front of people to uphold the duties of a retired female spirit. Sometimes I want to be alone for a bit of peace and quiet, to clear my thoughts and feelings, but ultimately I must face this world constantly, and I cannot fail to maintain the proper decorum. Before I knew you, I also often had to be alone to quiet my thoughts. I enjoy being alone. Being alone can make a person go to a higher level.

True love is not a sin. We cannot abandon it. If we abandon it, that only shows that our power of concentration was insufficient. I once knew a woman. She was pursuing a yogi, and the yogi at first refused, but later on he was moved by the love of the woman pursuing him, and so he abandoned his beliefs. But this woman produced doubts in the yogi's beliefs.

I think that no matter who we are, we all must keep in our minds a humble respect and reverence toward this unknown world. This could also dissolve away some of the unhappiness you feel after entering strange territory. You can be lenient with Sharwadi's ignorance, and so you can forgive other people's ignorance, because I have discovered that the collisions and conflicts in any religion all have their origins in ignorance or in problems that arise in communication.

You said: "Before, I really wanted to escape to a place where people rarely go, and quietly taste that great beauty. After I met you, I wanted to correctly understand everything about the time and place you were in. For a yogi, this is of course a good thing. Although that world might defile or destroy many of my things from before, I still want to take a look at it." I recognized that a good religion certainly cannot be defiled or destroyed. If your religious wisdom can be defiled that easily, maybe it shows that you had not really attained true wisdom, and that you still needed to search anew.

I also want to say that, if you want to, in the future you can settle down in India or Nepal.

I, Sharwadi, am willing to use the life I have received, and to use all I have accumulated in life, in order to feed this great lion of yours, but this is far from enough.

To feed a great lion requires high-quality food, requires even more resources. To feed a little mouse, to feed a sparrow, a few grains of rice are enough. The power of the environment to influence people is very great. Before, we brought up the topic of settling in India, and you were worried it might hurt the people who are waiting for you in Tibet. If this is the only reason, you do not have to tie yourself down. A great lion sooner or later must go to his world. We are now in a race against time, against life, against emptiness. It is not necessary to satisfy everyone. Only if we do not have any constraints in any form, can our mind and spirit be profound and great. In the Indian subcontinent, ultimately there are those eminent teachers for you, and there is also the woman Sharwadi, who is willing to give her life to you this way. Here, your sandalwood tree will never be cut down for firewood and burned up.

So think it over. In that festival for slaughtering animals, they spent thousands of gold, and there are too many of these kinds of affairs. You tell me: with this many resources, how many orphans could receive an education? How many valuable lives would not be swallowed up by disease? How many pure girls would not have to sell their bodies, and instead have the love and the life they want to have? How many swindlers' voices take possession of these resources, to spread even bigger lies?

Before I knew you, I too often sank into confusion and chaos. Being a woman, I felt there was nowhere for me to go. I had abandoned my brain and my ability to think, and was satisfied with the role of female spirit that the rulers need. I had already reached the ultimate point, and accumulated riches to rival the king's. If I had also abandoned my conscience and my self-awareness, and completely obeyed worldly customs, maybe I could have lived a life that worldly people would envy. But the problem was, once my mind and my thinking emerged from the surface of the water, then they would hit the ceiling. If I kept on beating my head against it, my head would be all bloody, and the one sacrificed would be me.

So I only had two choices: either I abandon my hopes to make progress and mature, or I become a housewife dependent on some man. But to abandon myself, my mind, and my spirit would be torture for me; it would be very painful. If I did not abandon them, there was still no way for me to go forward. So when I happened to meet you, Khyungpo Ba, it was so unexpected, like an ecstatic dream.

Sharwadi wants to spend her life for Khyungpo Ba, she is willing to go to her death smiling.

This is because everything is in the past, everything is dissolving away. As long as Khyungpo Ba is there, this heart will be listening, these two feet will be walking along, this pen will be recording it, and it will be more possible for those suffering people to detach from suffering and achieve bliss.

Finally, I also have a small request: if something unexpected happens to Sharwadi, please publish these letters at the appropriate time in the appropriate manner. My hope is not to cause embarrassment for my family members, or distort my original intent.

I hope that when children read these letters, they will be able to understand love better, and to believe that there is true love in the world. All children are angels from heaven, and we must let them understand that this kind of woman exists, and she wants to use love to influence others, and go on to influence the world. This is such a grand objective! But she actually was so silly, and so over-confident, that she went and did it.

Sharwadi, who loves you

2 Don't Give Up

Dearly beloved female spirit, I have really been feeling the evil force of those black spells—they have made my journey very difficult. I keep getting sick: suddenly cold, suddenly hot, suddenly confused, suddenly lucid, my whole body aching, very dispirited. But I have not stopped my search.During the day, I am walking along or studying. At night, I cultivate visualizations. But I can constantly feel malevolent spirits around my body. Now and then they act up and attack me. Sometimes I get a fearful feeling of wanting to retreat. Apart from this, unlucky things often appear beside me, and I am always losing things, and troublesome demons appear at my side from time to time

Sometimes I yell at them: "I am very afraid of you, but you cannot do anything to me!"

I am constantly feeling that I am going to die.

Every evening when I go to sleep, I do not know whether or not I will wake up the next day.

It is only when your letters come that I can feel warm and secure. As soon as I think of you, then I am wrapped up in a huge emotional feeling. Fate has truly given me an intimate friend who can cherish me and love me. I have not lived this life in vain.

I very much approve of much of what you say in your letters. You may not know that even now, those Bonpo men in my hometown have set up a sacrificial mandala, and want to kill me. I still encounter their attempts to block me and exclude me. An old man saw my predicament and said to me: "Khyungpo Ba, you should get out of here. There is a lot of territory outside. Don't let these petty people smother you."

He was right, life is too short, I have more important things I must do.

Therefore, although I very much want to live by your side, all I can do is follow causal conditions. There are a lot of things that you and I cannot control. If we try too hard to control them, we will bring ourselves trouble instead. If fate gives me the opportunity to settle in India, I will very gladly accept it. But my cultivation of practice in reality begins with resisting temptation. This is my most basic prerequisite for dealing with the world. Would you say this is right?

We must know that even after awakening, we must keep

our distance from evil companions and shut the door against them. During those days when I was in contact with you, I really was greedy. Obviously, once love encounters "material desire," it can become an inducement that forces people to fall down. Before, when I was a teaching master, many patrons really wanted to do things for me, but I did not know what I should require of them. I had no worries about food and clothing, I was healthy and happy, and I had a lot of time to use in cultivating practice. I did not know what else I needed. I understood very clearly that no matter how great the man is, he would not live forever. Why should I wreck the tranquility of mind and spirit by clinging to impermanent things?

But after I was in love with you, I really had "seeking." Obviously, when the mind has something to seek, then there is the possibility of defilement by "material desire." But where I am not the same as other people, is that I could immediately realize this, and understand clearly that this was material desire, and distance myself from it. That which understood the "wrong" of what I was doing was my mind of enlightenment. That is the light which illuminates me. All the realizations of enlightenment in the world are just so that we can realize that light of constant self-awareness.

Right now, I still have many faults. The defilements of my mind and spirit can still float up from my extreme quietude. For me, these are gifts given to me by fate. That is because it is only when these defilements float up in my mind, that I can discover them and cleanse them away. In my life, there are many faults, and most of them will appear just once. In my actions, after I understand them clearly, I seldom commit the same mistake twice. In my eyes, the true hero is not the person who conquers the world; it can only be the person who conquers his own mind.

However, do not take the fact that I am devoted to you and make it into a reason to fall down and abandon your faith. If you abandon me, I will honor your choice. You must know that my wisdom and compassion will not permit me tocling to a woman, unless she loves me. This is because she belongs to me only if she truly loves me.

If you abandon me, then after my search, I will return to the Qinghai-Tibet Plateau. I will spread the light in my own world. When I again wake up from a trance, everything will be different, my beard and hair will be white, and your temples are going gray too.

So we should not speak lightly of abandoning. Abandoning is the deadliest way to kill love and faith. Really, if you abandon me, I will have to put something else in my mind to be able to push the pain out. Right now, I take your love for me as the greatest blessing in my life, which came unexpectedly. I am very grateful for the gift that life has given me, and I can feel a kind of poetic quality of life that can engulf everything. This will certainly become an inexhaustible source of the water of life for my wisdom. I recognize without the slightest doubt that you are the best gift that fate has presented to me.

I think that the true dakini is the woman whom I deeply love and who makes me go upward. As long as I genuinely love her, and take this love and elevate it to faith, then I will be able to reach complete beauty in the true sense.

Around your body there is an aura of very pure light, which fills you with an incomparable great beauty. You have a heart like gold. In your body you carry what a woman must have, but what already has been lost in this world: that woman's heart with simplicity, genuineness, purity, generosity, goodness. Your conduct itself offers a kind of wholly new value. If everyone could love this way, the human world would become a Pure Land.

All the love and faith in the world is in fact destroyed in certain bad causal conditions. This can be something very small that happens, or that is said. We must protect love and faith as carefully as we protect our own eyes. When love and faith grow into a mighty spirit tree, then even a sharp blade cannot cut them down.

Always remember, whatever kind of person you want to become, as long as you have sufficient faith, then you will surely be able to become that kind of person. Human life is a choice: your choices structure your actions, and your actions determine your value.

Now I must go to Sarnath. That is truly a wondrous place.

Khyungpo Ba

Chapter 13

The Light of Sarnath

1 Hurrying to Sarnath

There are very many accounts of when Khyungpo Naljor met Sukhasiddhi. Some say he saw her the first time he went to India. Some say he saw her later. There are also different accounts of where they met. Among these is the story that they met in Sarnath. I like this story very much. As for when and where they actually met, this is not at all important; what is important is that I recognize that they met sometime, somewhere. In other words, it is not important how this world ultimately is; what is important is how this world ultimately is in my mind. In the view of some people, the world is painful. In the eyes of another group of people, the world is perfect and flawless, and this perfection is displayed everywhere. Thus, the Buddha used a verse to express a truth: "If people want to fully know all the Buddhas of the past, present, and future, they must see that in the inherent nature of the Realm of Reality, all is made by mind."

So then, let us choose Sarnath.

Thus, we see a man covered with the windblown dust, hurrying toward the Sarnath. In this book, there are two men covered with the windblown dust, hurrying toward Sarnath. The two men are separated by more than a thousand years: one is the Buddha, one is Khyungpo Naljor. The former wants to save those five practitioners who left him. The latter is searching for a woman. The former is acting to spread the Dharma. The latter is acting to seek the Dharma. Though the two are different on the outside, their minds have one objective: to give the world pure, cool refreshment.

Some people may not know that when the Buddha achieved Enlightenment in Bodh Gaya and understood the truth, he wanted to enter directly into the final extinction of nirvana. The good spirits got flustered and said: "Don't do it, don't do it. O Blessed One, sentient beings need this light. You must do a good job spreading it to them." At this, the Buddha began to think it over.

Although it is impossible for us to fathom the Buddha's deliberations, luckily he left an account of his thinking in the human world, and in the Pali Canon, there are many texts of this sort. Buddha knew that if what he said was too lofty, it would be hard to find people who would know what he meant. In India at that time, it would be hard for there to be people who would thoroughly know and understand the truth which he had awakened to. He thought: "Who should I tell the truth to first?" He first thought of the two old teachers who had taught him meditative concentration. Their wisdom was extraordinary, and certainly they would be able to awaken to the truth. But people told him that those two men had already died.

So then he thought of those five men who later would become the first set of Buddhist monks. He thought: "Though these five men turned their backs on me, that was because they liked me. They are naturally very intelligent, they focus their energy without slacking off, and they have attended me as I cultivated the Path. I should deliver them first."

The road to Sarnath was long, but the Buddha was not tired. You perhaps do not know that a person who has experienced the empty inherent nature, no matter what he is doing, never leaves the empty true nature. For him, all forms are unified, motion and stillness are one suchness, and there are no concerns. Even the words "tired out" cannot reach him. As he was on the road to Sarnath, Khyungpo Naljor seemed to feel the sense of ease and calm that the Buddha had felt more than a thousand years earlier.

2 The Sun in a Blind Man's Eyes

Khyungpo Naljor discovered something interesting that had happened in that time and place more than a thousand years earlier. On the road to Sarnath, Buddha met a follower of another Path. This man was naked; he was not wearing a stitch of clothing. He at once saw the Buddha's extraordinary light and sense of ease. So he asked: "Venerable One, all your faculties are harmonized, and your light is bright and clear, and your bearing is not that of an ordinary person. You seem to have had some experience of realization. May I ask who your benevolent teacher might be?"

Khyungpo Naljor knew that in India at that time, this was a typical question that was asked when people cultivating the Path met: the man was inquiring about the Buddha's lineage. So then the Buddha answered: "I have experienced the myriad things, and I no longer have any doubts. I am not subject to defilement by the various things: I have detached from the myriad things. Greed and desire cannot corrupt me, I have found all wisdom. How could there be a teacher in the world that I would have to follow and study with? There is no one in the world who could be my teacher, nor is there anyone who can compare with me. Even the devas cannot match me. I have already realized the holy Path. It is really no lie: I am the teacher of devas and humans, and in the whole world no one can rival me. I am the only one with true enlightenment, the supremely honored one. The flames of desire have already stopped, and I have already personally experienced nirvana. In order to set the wheel of the true teaching turning, I am going to Varanasi, the capital of the kingdom of Kashi. The eyes of the people of the world are as blind, and so I am going to let them encounter the voice of the true teaching."

Khyungpo Naljor read this story in the Pali Canon in the *Majjhima-nikaya.*

In that scripture, he also saw a very funny scene. A disdainful smile appeared on the face of this stark-naked religious man. He was surely thinking: "What crazy believers there are in the world." He, of course, did not know that he was missing an opportunity that would be hard to come across once in a thousand years.

On the road to Sarnath, Khyungpo Naljor thought of that scene the Buddha had encountered more than a thousand years earlier, and he could not help heaving a long sigh of regret. He thought: "The eyes of the blind cannot see the sun."

Kashi (now known as Varanasi, or Benares) is a holy city for Indian religion. It is situated on the west bank of the Ganges. The Ganges River was like a great clear mirror, reflecting the sky. Khyungpo Naljor was in a small boat, and the wind from the Ganges was blowing like a mother's kiss. On the surface of the water, beneath the scorching sun, floated countless golden lights: this was a good conjunction of karmic conditions. As you know, people at that time always loved to talk about karmic conditions. At this point, Khyungpo Naljor felt a great interest.

In Sarnath there was a lush forest, and many grassy fields and marshes. In those days there were wild deer—hence the name "sarnath" means deer park. When Khyungpo Naljor arrived there, one could still see herds of deer. In the eyes of the Indian people, deer, like cows, were one of the auspicious things, and could not be indiscriminately killed.

A variety of religious practitioners mingled with the deer. They believed in different religions, and made offerings to different gods. There were fire-worshipping Brahmins, naked followers of other Paths, and those who practiced various kinds of asceticism. When Khyungpo Naljor arrived, there was smoke everywhere, as the fire-worshippers were in the midst of carrying out their ceremonies of making offerings to the fire. They would set fire to cow dung, and scatter the five grains on it, so the air was full of the special clear odor of the five grains.

3 The Dhamekh Stupa

When Khyungpo Naljor first saw Dhamekh Stupa, it was a special stupa, more than a hundred feet high, divided into two sections. The upper part was built of red bricks, while the lower part was built of stone. On the stone portion were carved very beautiful decorative designs: there were people, flowering plants, flying birds, and other kinds of patterns. This was the structure in Sarnath which moved people the most. The story was that it had been first built by King

Ashoka, and enlarged later by generations of kings who believed in Buddhism. It differed from other Buddhist stupas in having a solid core. The lower part of the stupa had an octagonal shape, and above it there was a Buddha shrine with a life-size image of the Buddha.

Khyungpo Naljor discovered that there were many signs of damage on the stupa, which may have been caused by believers from other religions. But because the quality of the stone building material was very good, this damage had not been able to spoil the great beauty of the stupa. The stupa was strong and beautiful, but two hundred years later, it would meet with a great catastrophe. At that time, the artillery fire of the Islamic army would destroy those beautiful carved reliefs. Group after group of fiery dragons would attack Dhamekh Stupa, exploding with endless dense smoke. What surprised people was that after the smoke cleared, the stupa was still its old self, and though many beautiful decorative designs had been effaced, the stupa itself appeared even stronger and more beautiful. Eight hundred years later, the ruler of Kashi planned to do an even more thorough job of wiping it off the earth — he was called Babu Jagat. He wanted to use the stone from the lower part of the stupa to build a marketplace. He, of course, did not anticipate that despite all their efforts, his underlings would not be able to cut through that stone. This was because the builders of the stupa had used an extremely hard metallic material combined with the stone. I saw Khyungpo Naljor smiled. He certainly understood that impermanence is an immutable truth. No matter how solid a stupa is, it would be destroyed in the end by the passage of time — just as the great mountains made of stone, even if they were not eroded away by the wind and rain, will be turned into countless grains of dust at the instant when the empty eon arrives, in the universal catastrophe.

The other great building in Sarnath is the Stupa of the Dharma

King, which is shaped like an inverted bowl. According to tradition, this was built by King Ashoka—the famous man I spoke of before, who unified India through great carnage. He used military force to spread Buddhism more widely. To promote the Buddha Dharma, he collected eight sets of relics of the Buddha that were scattered in various parts of India, and divided them further into several thousand sets, and built stupas in various areas as an offering, and he also erected stone pillars. Sarnath once had one of King Ashoka's stone pillars, and on the pillar were four lions, facing the four directions, and roaring. By now, all these stone pillars have been destroyed. The story goes that they were shattered by evil dragons, but it is more probable that they were destroyed in warfare.

The Stupa of the Dharma King was built to commemorate the Buddha's initial turning of the Wheel of the Dharma. Beneath it, the story goes, are buried relics of the Buddha. Six hundred years after Khyungpo Naljor, sure enough, some people discovered in the ruins a stone box containing the relics.

The Stupa of the Dharma King that Khyungpo Naljor saw was still very majestic. Though he understood that, however majestic a building was, it still could not avoid impermanence, he was still affected by this grandeur. This is the charm of art. Some people who do not understand that art, but also can be a vehicle for the spirit are always denouncing Buddhism as idol worship. Maybe they do not realize that in the eyes of the worshippers, all these images are in reality a kind of spirit.

Because it has various kinds of buildings, Sarnath has lost some of the peace and quiet it ought to have. It is right the group of buildings are togather relatively, the open country beyond the group of buildings is very much like the Sarnath which in Khyungpo Naljor's mind. He wandered into the open country, and here there were still marshes and grassy fields and streams, and sometimes he saw wild deer at play. He could always see some people cultivating the Path. More than a thousand years earlier, when the Buddha was here turning the Wheel of the Dharma, the landscape may well have looked like this. At that time, when the Buddha arrived here after a long journey on foot, those five men who were cultivating practice caught sight of him far in the distance, and agreed among themselves not to pay attention to him anymore. But as Buddha approached with firm footsteps, those five men saw that the Buddha looked like a calm, dignified holy man, and they involuntarily started to believe in him, and one by one they got up and bowed to him.

The Buddha told them he had already achieved true awakening. Later, he set forth the Four Noble Truths of suffering, the formation of suffering, extinction of suffering, and Path to the extinction of suffering. This was the initial turning of the Wheel of the Dharma. Starting from that moment over two thousand years ago, the Three Jewels of the Buddha, Dharma, and Sangha have been in this world.

The Pali Canon, in the *Majjhima-nikaya*, gives a detailed account of the Buddha's teaching process at that time. While three of the five men went out to go begging, Buddha taught the remaining two; and when these two went out begging, he instructed the first three. In this way, Buddha diligently taught the first group of Buddhist monks in the world. Finally one day, the man called Kaundinya became the first arhat after Buddha had achieved enlightenment. He expressed what he had awakened to in a verse:

> *When I first heard the wondrous teaching,*
>
> *Joy arose in my mind;*

Hearing the teaching, I cut off grasping.

And extinguishing greedy desires.

The enlightened one has no greed

And dispels all false views;

In this human world,

Correct purpose is unusual.

Like the wind removing the ashes and dust,

The bhikshu leaves behind false thoughts;

Correct contemplation gives rise to wisdom,

Wisdom gives rise to correct perception.

All actions are impermanent,

With real contemplation we can awaken;

Amid suffering we give rise to detachment,

This is the supreme pure Path.

All actions bring suffering,

With wisdom we can awaken;

Amid suffering we give rise to detachment,

This is the supreme pure Path.

To respect the Buddha and know the Buddha Dharma,

Bhikshu Kaundinya,

Advance diligently and extinguish birth and death;

Purify your practice and attain the Holy Path.

This means that it was in Sarnath that the first arhat was produced from among the Buddha's disciples.

4 The Woman Selling Wine

Khyungpo Naljor had not expected that in Sarnath he would run into a woman.

He always thought that she was a manifestation of the dakini of wisdom.

That woman was with several other women at the fire ceremony. The fire ceremony is a kind of ritual of making offerings. First they build a fire mandala, and the participants chant mantras beside it, and throw items of food into the fire mandala. These food items will go into the mouths of the deities and spirits to whom the offerings are made. As I have said, in the teachings of Brahmanism, fire is the mouth of Brahma. This kind of story entered deeply into the minds and spirits of the people of India, and because of this, fire ceremonies where offerings were made had become an important ritual form in many religions there.

The woman looked at Khyungpo Naljor. The two people looked at each other for a while, and both of them felt a kind of strange sense of familiarity.

Khyungpo Naljor told her that he was on a search for a teaching master called Niguma.

The woman said: "I have heard of Niguma, but she has already realized the rainbow body, and so it is very hard for anyone without merit to see her. Why don't you worship Sukhasiddhi as the teacher?"

"Who is Sukhasiddhi?" asked Khyungpo Naljor.

"She is a great enlightened one."

The woman told Khyungpo Naljor the story of Sukhasiddhi. She had a great natural talent with language, and through it, Khyungpo Naljor was seeing an old woman who had been driven out by her husband and children. She was Sukhasiddhi before she experienced enlightenment.

Amid the voices of many men reproaching her, that woman cried out that she was leaving the house. This happened because she had taken the last bit of vital grain in the house, and offered it to a monk as alms.

That year, she was fifty-nine years old. Too much hard labor had already destroyed her health, and she was already elderly in appearance. In Khyungpo Naljor's image of this, the feet of that woman as she fled the house gradually raised a cloud of dust that filled the sky, and the road behind her turned into a gray dragon. One of her sons was so exasperated that he picked up a mud brick and threw it at his mother. When that brick hit the ground, it shattered into countless fragments. Although the brick did not hit the mother, it did break her heart. Later, every time she thought of her son, the mother would always think of this scene. It told Sukhasiddhi in the most intuitive way what suffering and impermanence are. At that time, she of course did not know that, if it had not been for her being driven from home this way, there would have just been one more old person in the human world at the end of her days, ready to die, and one less great woman whose glory would shine through the ages. She used her life's journey to tell the people of the world not to fear getting old, not to fear misfortune. All you need is to have the mind of faith, and you definitely can achieve immortal merit.

The woman telling the story to Khyungpo Naljor said: "In this way, that great teacher was driven out of her home. She drifted around and lived as a beggar." We always see beggars in certain places, but our physical eyes naturally cannot distinguish if a beggar is the manifestation of Sukhasiddhi. So whenever I see those people reaching out their hands to me, I consider them to be her, and I approach them and give them alms, never trying to distinguish if they are swindlers or not.

Just because there were many good Indians who, like me, think this way, Sukhasiddhi did not starve to death. Her aged face became fuller by the day, and she finally managed to rent an old house. In the house was a broken box which contained a bit of leftover grain. She began to make wine. Through this, she ended up encountering the great teacher of her destiny.

One day, a woman came to buy wine, and Sukhasiddhi did not ask for money. This was because that woman told her that she was buying the wine for a teaching master called Birwapa. This name was very famous in India at that time. In the eyes of the people of India, Birwapa was almost equal to a heavenly spirit. Of course, this story actually devalues that great teacher. That is because heavenly spirits still have faults, while Birwapa had already attained a faultless state.

Sukhasiddhi was thinking: "Why do I need money? If I can make an offering to such a great person, this is my good fortune."

So in this way she happily made offerings to Birwapa for two years.

After two years she was then sixty-two years old—that great teacher said to his maidservant: "Bring that woman who sells wine here."

That night, Birwapa initiated Sukhasiddhi and transmitted the teaching to her.

That night, she experienced enlightenment.

In the traditional stories of the worldly people, Sukhasiddhi attained realization of the rainbow body in a single night. But this story is not right. The true story is that Sukhasiddhi attained enlightenment in one night. In fact, after she had attained enlightenment, Sukhasiddhi still went through a rigorous practice of austerities. The story goes that she worked at this practice of austerities for six months, or eight months. She used six methods to bring to full maturity the wisdom she had awakened to. People call those methods "the Six Methods of Sukhasiddhi."

According to the story, Sukhasiddhi's rainbow body was realized after practising austerities. To explain it another way, to go from being an ordinary person to the first stage of being a bodhisattva took Sukhasiddhi a single night, but the cultivation for reaching all ten stages of being a bodhisattva was something that came later. It is from this that we have the "Six Methods of Sukhasiddhi." Later still, those six methods passed beyond the time of a thousand years, and entered into my mind, and I became an important inheritor of the "Six Methods of Sukhasiddhi."

That woman told Khyungpo Naljor that Sukhasiddhi had already achieved the deathless rainbow body. Her body is like a colorful rainbow. If we look at it, it has form, but if we touch it, there is nothing—it is not born and does not die, it has no coming or going.

From this, Khyungpo Naljor developed a great mind of faith. He said to the woman: "Please take me to see that great teacher."

5 The Girl of Sixteen

According to the account in the *Secret History of Khyungpo*, before he saw Sukhasiddhi, Khyungpo Naljor had participated in one dakini ritual gathering. In that era, India had many great women who used their lives to put into practice the teachings of the Buddha. We call them dakinis. Some of them awakened to the empty inherent nature and became dakinis in the world. Some of them had still not experienced the empty inherent nature. But whether or not they had experienced enlightenment, they all could conduct ritual gatherings, just as we in the ordinary human world like to have dinner parties. Many times these dinner parties are also a form of religious ritual.

I have some doubts about the story in the *Secret History of Khyungpo*. I do not know what kind of dakini party Khyungpo Naljor attended: were these dakinis without bodies, or dakinis in the human world? I have these doubts because, at that time, Khyungpo Naljor had not yet reached the ultimate attainment. Though he had achieved some power with mantras, and he was sometimes able to achieve what he wished for, his ultimate enlightenment still lay in the future. That is to say, although he had seen many teachers, his two most important teachers were Niguma and Sukhasiddhi. One publicly acknowledged fact is that Khyungpo Naljor's fundamental teacher was Niguma: that is, the one who showed Khyungpo Naljor the inherent nature of mind and enabled him to understand the empty inherent nature was Niguma.

There is more than one explanation of "fundamental teacher," but the explanation that most people can accept is that your fundamental teacher is the one who can allow you to clearly understand mind and see its inherent nature, to awaken and become enlightened. Of course, if you are not able to clearly understand mind and see its inherent nature, there will be a different standard.

Thus, I have doubts. The first time Khyungpo Naljor saw Sukhasiddhi, they were just forming a karmic connection. His causal connection with Sukhasiddhi was something that came later.

In his later years, Khyungpo Naljor told his disciples that, although on the surface he did not get any great benefit from that dakini gathering, it was already storing up immeasurable resources for his later experience of enlightenment.

At that gathering Khyungpo Naljor saw a sixteen-year-old adolescent girl. Many people believe this story, but he did not see any rainbow light body. He did not know that the story of the rainbow light body is just a symbol.

That girl did not say much. She had a pure, cool appearance. Khyungpo Naljor felt the light of her eyes penetrate his mind, like a pure wind blowing in. In the blazing heat of India, he suddenly felt cool.

The girl smiled. She looked like a skinny little girl, and seemed a bit shy.

The dakini gathering was very splendid, because Khyungpo Naljor had donated ten ounces of gold, and bought all the good things to eat that could be bought around there. During the whole event, he felt as if he were dreaming.

After the gathering came to an end, the dakinis who had participated left.

That girl said to Khyungpo Naljor: "Right, it does feel like we're dreaming."

After that, she flashed a smile at Khyungpo Naljor and said: "You really have good fortune about you."

She also said: "Though I could show you the inherent nature of mind, that is not my task. The one who will do this for you is Niguma."

As soon as he heard the name "Niguma," Khyungpo Naljor burst into tears, sank to his knees, and asked: "Where is she?"

The girl said: "You should ask yourself this question."

Several years later Khyungpo Naljor finally understood what this girl had said. At that time, Niguma would tell him: "I have been with you all along, but your karmic barriers were heavy, and you could not see me."

She also said: "I will be with all those who chant 'Niguma Khyenno.' Although their karmic barriers are heavy, and they cannot see me, they still must understand that in the light of sincere faith, I am with them like a shadow following a form."

6 India's Sandalwood Forest

The scent from the incense of the dakini gathering spread like a misty cloud, and the feeling of dreamy illusion in Khyungpo Naljor's mind was still developing.

Another woman complained to Khyungpo Naljor: "Why aren't you seeking the Dharma? That woman who was just talking to you was Sukhasiddhi."

Seeing Khyungpo Naljor's look of regret, she also said: "It's not important. You can go to the Sandalwood Forest. Her mandala is there."

The woman also said: "That mandala is not a solid object—it is impossible for those without a karmic connection to see it. If you have a karmic connection, you just have to pray sincerely, and you will definitely be able to see it. There, you can receive the core of the great yoga teaching."

Khyungpo Naljor then hastened toward the Sandalwood Forest. I do not know which sandalwood forest this ultimately refers to. In the view of historians, places and times are both important, but in the view of people of spiritual accomplishment, time and space are one flavor, and there are no distinctions. Because human life is short, it is not at all important where we experience enlightenment, or when we experience enlightenment. What is important is whether or not we experience enlightenment. If we experience enlightenment in the morning, and die in the evening, it is still something to be happy about. There is an ancient saying that attests to this: "If we hear of the Path in the morning, it is alright to die that evening." Thus, people in India were lazy about recording times, and so in the Buddhist scriptures there are many cases where they designate the time by saying "at one time." In the eyes of those who cultivate the Path, it is not important whether this "one time" was a hundred years ago, or a thousand years ago, or ten thousand years ago. Because in the cycle of lifetime after lifetime, they have gone through who knows how many "at one times." Whether it was this "one time" or that "one time," can be ignored.

India has many sandalwood forests, and in them there are many people cultivating the Path. The story goes that sandalwood has an inherent natural power to drive away demons. When those who cultivate the Path reach a certain realm of experience, they may attract many demons, and these are always attacking them with their teeth and claws. But when they encounter the scent of sandalwood, the demons crash and scatter. This has been the experience of many people who cultivate the Path. But they do not realize that what can drive away the army of demons is in fact their own mind of faith. So it is not actually the scent of sandalwood that is sure to dispel the demons; in fact, it is building up your mind of faith. From the viewpoint of the ultimate truth, those demonic forces attacking you in fact come from your mind's inherent nature.

At that time, many people who came from Tibet to seek the Path received the teaching in sandalwood forests. My other teacher Tendon Lama also received the medicine of immortality and the esoteric teaching of the fruit of the Path from Master Virupa in a sandalwood forest. Do not be confused by the phrase "sandalwood forest," and assume that it is a holy place with beautiful scenery. You have to understand that in ancient India, the sandalwood forest was often the place where the local people left corpses. It was precisely because of that intuitive sense of impermanence there, that many of those who were cultivating the Path carried on their practice in the sandalwood forests.

When that woman pointed out the way, Khyungpo Naljor knew where Sukhasiddhi was. He took a pack full of gold and hurried off to the sandalwood forest.

The story goes that Khyungpo Naljor brought five hundred ounces of gold for Sukhasiddhi. He always had a lot of gold, and always made big offerings. Of course, we can switch the story and say that, because he was always making offerings, therefore he was always well off. Those countless offerings allowed Khyungpo Naljor to have countless blessings. In the West now, a thousand years later, many rich people become philanthropists. Some say that it precisely because of their philanthropy that they get richer and richer. Being able to give back to society unselfishly is the secret to gaining immeasurable wealth.

The urgency showed in Khyungpo Naljor's pace as he moved on. In my image, Khyungpo Naljor's pace is always very urgent. Even though he lived for a hundred and fifty years, it was as if he was running his whole life. He had an intuitive feeling for the impermanence of life. He always saw his own life flowing away like water in a spillway. In every moment, Khyungpo Naljor died, and in every moment, he was reborn. Before the god of death caught up with him, he would finish all the work he had to do. He already was understanding his mission more and more clearly: his goal in this life was to take the spark of the fire that was facing extinction in India back to Tibet, and make it set the plains alight. When he was in Nepal, when he went to where a man of great attainment had lived, that man had already died. The story was that this man had received many esoteric teachings, but, after his mortal illness, these esoteric teachings became only as symbols.

I can certainly understand Khyungpo Naljor's sense of urgency. Right now, a wave of globalization is sweeping over us, and the cultures of many peoples are being submerged. Often, this process of being submerged may mean that they are lost forever. What many of these weak, small peoples are losing is not only their languages and cultures: even their physical existence is being absorbed into that vast uniformity. I clearly see this transformation. The martial arts of Liangzhou, the family values of Liangzhou, and so on, the culture that has been passed down for a thousand years, is at this very moment being swallowed up in the sweeping tide of the era. And agricultural civilization, even more so, has become like the sun setting over the western mountains, and will soon be swallowed by the eternal darkness. It is precisely because I understand this point that I used twenty years of time that money cannot buy to write *Desert Rites, Desert Hunters,* and *White Tiger Gate.* I wanted to define the pattern of that existence which is about to be lost.

What Khyungpo Naljor faced then was also this kind of situation. At the time, Hinduism and other religions were pervading India with a momentum that was sweeping all before it, and Buddhism seemed to have become a candle flickering in the wind.

Khyungpo Naljor clearly felt this change, and therefore he went to India and Nepal many times. His footsteps were always hurried, and the dust he stirred up obscured the backdrop of his long journeys.

In the *Secret History of Khyungpo*, it seems that very little is written of his austerities. In fact, his practice of austerities was mostly completed during his seeking. When you are traveling in the uninhabited wilderness, above you is the bright cloudless sky, and all that accompanies you is your own footsteps. When your mind is sunk in the peace and joy of solitary travel, in reality you are cultivating practice. I think Khyungpo Naljor's search was one of the components in his cultivation of austerities.

All the same, we cannot forget the first two times Khyungpo Naljor sought the Buddhist teaching after he left the Bonpo religion. Those two teachers do not seem to be that important in his life, but in fact that experience planted very important seeds for him. That was the stage of first seeing the Path. After we have eaten the sixth dumpling and feel full, we definitely cannot deny the first dumpling and think it was useless. Human life is lived bit by bit. It's just that those little bits, which may not seem remarkable in themselves, make up the trajectory of a glorious human life.

Can we say it like this? The process of Khyungpo Naljor's search was exactly the process of awakening to and digesting the wisdom which those teachers transmitted to him. That long, lonesome journey of his searching can in fact be seen, as a whole, to have been his road of cultivating practice. It's like that for me: my writing and reading books was in fact my form of cultivating practice. After I took myself and merged into the bright emptiness, all my actions can be seen as a form of preserving it.

Therefore, high-level cultivation is in fact completed in the midst of everyday activities like walking, standing, sitting, and lying down. Genuine cultivation is taking that enlightenment and merging it into every time and place in life.

7 Thirty Silver Coins

Khyungpo Naljor arrived at the sandalwood forest where Sukhasiddhi was. We do not know how long this took, and Khyungpo Naljor himself did not know how long he had been walking, because he was still enveloped in that immense feeling of dreamlike illusion. Since he had attended that festive gathering of the dakinis, it was like this, as if he had fallen into a dream. The feeling was very strange. Before, although he also had the feeling of dreamlike illusion, that had mostly been brought about by visualization. But this time, he was actually not using any visualizations, and everything was like a dream or an illusion. What made him feel even stranger was that his body ended up feeling light as a bubble. In this way, the hardships of traveling were correspondingly greatly reduced.

The sandalwood forest was not as beautiful as the name suggests. Though there were sandalwood trees, there was the lingering odor of the corpses. The bones of the dead were scattered everywhere. The older skeletons had already faded to an ashen white, but the newer skeletons still gave off an evil stench. Sometimes packs of wolves wandered the forest, but they did not attack the people. They just fed on the newer corpses, and they did not even dare to think of attacking the people who were not yet dead. In the stories of the Indian people, these wolves were manifestations of the dakinis, and when they at someone's flesh, that person would go to be reborn in a Buddha Land. Later, this kind of story was also transmitted to Tibet. They then considered the spirit eagles at the "sky burials" also to be manifestations of the dakinis.

Apart from the skeletons, Khyungpo Naljor also saw pieces of cloth scattered all around—these were the cloths that had been used to wrap the corpses. They were worn by the ascetic monks who were practising as mendicants. They would pick up those scraps of cloth and sew them together, then go to the riverbank to wash them, then wear them on their bodies. This way they did not have to give any thought to getting clothes to wear, and could use all their time for cultivating the Path.

When Khyungpo Naljor arrived there, the sandalwood forest seemed very pure and clean. He did not see anyone cultivating the Path, and he did not see anyone abandoning corpses. All around it was very quiet, and though there was the slight sound of the wind moving through the trees, that sound was filled with peaceful silence. Khyungpo Naljor still was immersed in that feeling of dreamlike illusion. He saw the sky above the forest, clear and bright without a trace of clouds. He happened to hear a strange bird call. He did not know what kind of bird it was, and he did not bother to go find out its name.

He looked all around, but he did not see the mandala that woman had spoken of. But he remembered that she had said, if he wanted to see Sukhasiddhi the dakini, he must sincerely pay homage to her. He put down the sack he was carrying on his back, and quieted his mind for a moment, waiting for that great feeling to pervade his mind again. He began to pray reverently and sincerely.

Khyungpo Naljor's prayer dissolved away his self. He was like a lost child longing for a mother, like a blind man turning toward the light, like a hungry ghost craving food. He began to pray in earnest. Gradually, heaven and earth dissolved away, his self dissolved away, and even the sandalwood forest dissolved away, and there was only the seeking, like a wave of reverent, sincere contemplation.

On a certain night a thousand years later, I too merged into

Khyungpo Naljor's reverence at that time. At that, a great rhythm took hold of me. The following text then flowed out from my mind:

How wondrous the dakini is —

Sukhasiddhi the virtuous one, the revered one.

Her journey is rare in a thousand years,

Her achievement spans ancient and modern.

Without hard work or bravery,

She rapidly achieved the rainbow body.

Without cultivation and without realization,

She reverently serves as a master teacher.

As master teacher she is equipped with great virtue,

As mother she also is equipped with the mind of compassion.

Once with vital grain,

She gave alms to a wandering monk.

Her giving had merit and wisdom,

She was full of infinite virtue.

She begged for food in the bustling city,

Without losing the mind of enlightenment.

After she realized the rainbow body,

She still was equipped with the ordinary mind.

She served time and again as the Mudra Mother

Bestowing virtue and wisdom on sentient beings.

I pray to the dakini:

Let your great benevolence descend on me.

Inspire me with great wisdom,

Bestow upon me great ability;

Develop me with your great power,

Have compassion for me with your great heart;

Let what touches my eyes become a Buddha Land,

Let what fills my ears be the sound of mantras;

Let greed and anger blow away like smoke,

Let ignorance and arrogance not be born;

Let envy be like the frost on the grass,

Which leaves no trace when the sun is blazing down;

Nurture the expansiveness of my mind,

Purify the contents of my mouth;

Let empty wisdom arise with the mind,

Let the joy of meditation never leave my body;

I pray to you, mother, to protect me and help me,

Like a shadow follows a form.

I pray to you, the dakini:

May the ship of your compassion arrive.

May your light cover my disciples,

And protect all sentient beings.

May the Five Great Diamonds Teachings of Niguma

Follow the wind raising the dust of the Dharma,

Like the sun shining in all directions,

Like the moon illuminating myriad homes;

Like the waters filling the earth,

Like the thunder shaking the sky;

I pray to you, mother, to receive your children,

So the eight winds do not move their minds.

The mother is the sunshine of three springtime's,

We are minds like blades of grass;

The mother is the vast ocean tide,

We are born from the spray;

The mother is the great universe,

We are the scattered stars;

The mother sings the song of the great wind,

We are dandelions.

Our intent is to carry out the mother's teaching,

To serve the honored mother with body and mind;

The great sun may wither away,

But this intent will not change.

First, we pray that her light will shine in all directions,

So our minds can contact the honored mother.

Second, we pray that the mother will smile,

So her blessings and compassion are bestowed on us.

Third, we pray that as the mother looks to the void,

The bliss of meditation will fall like rain.

Uproot suffering and leave the ground of defilement,

Attain bliss and cool purity is born.

The gentle wind blows a fragrant air,

Eliminating the sounds of the worldly dusts.

Cleansing away all delusion and confusion,

Waking up the person in the dream.

Later after this verse was widely distributed, countless people read it and received the cool purity.

I believe that, at that moment a thousand years ago, Khyungpo Naljor certainly prayed the way I did. Though the content of his prayer was not the same as the body of my verse, the sincere reverence was surely similar. At that time the great beauty dissolved away the ugliness, the great goodness melted the discontent, the great truth penetrated the falsity. Great love pulled in the great power, and the myriad things were transformed into a warm, fragrant wind which dispersed the age-old dark clouds of clinging.

He did not know how much time had gone by.

Suddenly, Khyungpo Naljor felt an infinite light, a colorful light pouring down like rain. He saw a mandala.

There are many different accounts of what this mandala looked like. Some said it was as beautiful as a heavenly palace, with jade towers and houses, splendid and magnificent, too beautiful to take in. Some say its large structures were built of a pile of human heads, and its smaller buildings were made of human bones, and it had many layers of protective circles: one ring of skulls, one ring of diamond rods, one ring of lotus flowers, one ring that was a screen of fire ... In sum, there are many many stories about it.

There also seem to be many accounts of what Sukhasiddhi looked like. In my book *The Great Mudra of Light: The Heart of Real Practice* I wrote: "Around the dakini was a circle of valorous warriors. The mandala was solemn, and beautiful beyond compare. In the middle was a woman who looked twenty-eight, dignified as a celestial being, with an elegant manner. All in all, she was extremely beautiful."

Khyungpo Naljor begged her to impart the teaching to him.

Sukhasiddhi smiled coolly and said: "The teaching you ask for I of course have, but this is lion's milk, and cannot be poured into a chamber pot. I ask you, you want to seek my teaching, but do you have the resources to seek the Dharma?"

Khyungpo Naljor took out his gold and gave it to the dakini.

Sukhasiddhi took a handful of gold and tossed them aside, and those bits of gold scattered all around her. The dakini smiled coldly and said: "Can this kind of vulgar thing serve as a resource? In your eyes it is certainly a valuable thing, but do you know where its value lies?"

This was the first time Khyungpo Naljor had ever encountered a teacher who had been offered gold and not accepted it, and his face filled with shame, and he did not know how to answer.

The dakini again smiled and said: "In my eyes, gold has as much value as dung. I do not know where its value lies. If I make it into a chamber pot, then it is a chamber pot; if I make it into a Buddha-image, then it is a Buddha-image; if I use it as a Buddha-crown, then it is valuable beyond compare; if I make it into the sole of a shoe, then it is just good for me to walk on. I do not know where its value lies. Do you have something more valuable to offer me?"

Khyungpo Naljor took out his agate jewels, but as soon as he offered them, they were thrown down.

Khyungpo Naljor did feel depressed, but he was also very happy. He was depressed because the dakini had ended up discarding his offerings like worn-out shoes. He was happy because he had finally encountered a teacher who looked upon gold as dung. With some of the teachers he had met before, as soon as they saw gold, the greed would light up in their eyes. He believed that this dakini was a genuine master of great accomplishment.

But did he or did he not have something more valuable?

Khyungpo Naljor was depressed to say he did not.

The dakini smiled coldly and said: "So what teaching were you seeking when you came to India? In your eyes, are only gold and jewels valuable?"

Khyungpo Naljor roused himself and said: "I also have the Dharma I sought and received from other teachers. In my eyes, these are a hundred times more valuable than gold."

The dakini smiled coldly and said: "In your eyes they are certainly valuable beyond compare. In my eyes, they are just like a broken boat. You must realize that all the Buddhist scriptures are just to guide you to illuminate mind and see its inherent nature. Once you illuminate mind and see its inherent nature and realize the ultimate, then, for you, they will become a pile of useless words. Do you think I still need this old furniture?"

Khyungpo Naljor's face turned red. He had not thought that the wondrous teachings, which he saw as precious jewels, would be a pile of useless old furniture in the eyes of the dakini. Nevertheless, if we can really reach a realm of experience like Sukhasiddhi's, all the teaching methods in the world really are of no use. The Buddha said: "The teaching is like a boat—if even the teaching must be left behind, how much the more so that which is not the teaching." Suddenly Khyungpo Naljor realized that what was more valuable than gold was his life, so he said to Sukhasiddhi: "I want to making an offering of my body, mouth, and mind to you, Teacher."

At this, the dakini showed a smiling face and said: "This is finally reasonable. However, let me ask you, do you know how to offer body, mouth, and mind?"

Khyungpo Naljor said: "From now on, my body, mouth, and mind no longer belong to me. They are entirely yours, Teacher."

The dakini said: "If I slaughter you this minute and sell your flesh, would you have regrets?"

Khyungpo Naljor said: "I would have no regrets."

The dakini smiled and said: "That's good. Now you have become my man, and everything of yours is up to me to manage."

After she finished saying this, she brought Khyungpo Naljor into the town, and found a large temple, and sold him for thirty silver coins.

Khyungpo Naljor thought: "I offered her so much gold, and she was not greedy for it, so why did she want these thirty silver coins?" Though there were doubts in his mind, he did not dare let his thoughts run wild again. Since he had already offered the teacher his body, mouth, and mind, whatever the teacher wanted him to do, he would go along with it.

But then he thought:since I have offered my body, mouth, and mind, does this count as a kind of betrayal of the messages that come via the spirit dove?

8 The Fish King Spirit

Khyung:

How is your current situation?

Today Kumari and I attended the Great Chariot Festival. I heard her say that the night before the Great Chariot Festival, the sorcerers completed the second phase of their curses.

The Great Chariot Festival is a sacrifice to the Fish King Spirit. His spiritual powers are vast, and he is very intent on justice. Before, I did not like to appear in public. This time, I very reverently took part in the Great Chariot Festival. In the customary manner of the local people, I prayed to the Fish King Spirit to protect you, and not let you come to any harm from those evil curses.

As for the Fish King Spirit, the traditional story goes like this. Many years ago, a mother gave birth to a baby. Because he looked very dangerous when he was born, the family members took him and threw him into the river. Later on, a great fish rescued him, and let him grow up inside its own belly.

One day the goddess Uma prayed to Mahadeva seeking an esoteric teaching, and Mahadeva said: "My teaching cannot be passed on lightly. If you want to obtain an esoteric teaching, you must build a house in the ocean. I will transmit the teaching to you in that house." The goddess built a nice house, and invited Mahadeva to come there. When he was transmitting the teaching, the great fish was just passing by, and the child in the fish's belly heard the contents of the esoteric teaching. Uma, on the other hand, was so exhausted she fell asleep. After he had transmitted the teaching, Mahadeva asked, "Did you understand?" The child answered that he had understood. Before long, Uma woke up from her sleep, and again asked Mahadeva for the teaching. Mahadeva said: "I have already given it to you." The goddess said: "I just heard half of it, and then I fell asleep."

Mahadeva used his spiritual powers to look into it, and he saw the child in the belly of the great fish, and he accepted him as a disciple. Thus the child practiced meditation inside the fish's belly, and after twelve years, he was fully equipped with countless spiritual powers. He was in charge of the rainfall and the harvest, and people called him the Fish King Spirit.

Four hundred years before, there had been a great drought such as is not encountered once in a hundred years. For twelve years there was not a drop of rain, and the earth was cracked and parched, and countless people and animals died of thirst. Actually, what happened was that the Fish King Spirit's disciples were displeased with the local people for not respecting the Fish King Spirit, so they captured the nine spirit snakes who were in charge of rainfall. The common people prayed to the Fish King Spirit to release these spirit snakes, and that finally ended the drought. From that time onward, the people of Nepal had to have an observance every year to express their respect for the Fish King Spirit.

The Fish King Spirit who received the offerings sat in a

small wooden shrine. A great ancient chariot with wooden wheels pulled that small shrine along. On the top of the shrine was a round pillar, pointed at the sky, and pine branches were stuck on top of it. That chariot went along a route determined by astrologers, stopping now and then, and then proceeding again. Sometimes in a whole day it could not go even a few hundred paces. Wherever the chariot went, the people crowded around. That day, I changed my clothes and dressed up as a man, and followed along with that chariot, praying for you. I believe the prayers had power, because I clearly felt the spiritual energy coming from the Fish King Spirit. Besides this, I also prayed to the daughter of the Fish King Spirit, who is called Chakuwa Dyah, who sits in a little shrine on another chariot.

That day I also saw a shirt of jewels. It was originally from the Snake Spirit. At a certain time, a peasant successfully treated the Snake Spirit's wife for an eye disease, and so the Snake Spirit gave him a garment of jewels. Later, the shirt of jewels was stolen by a demon. During one Great Chariot Festival, an enlightened person had captured the demon, and taken back the garment of jewels. People then took this and offered it to the Fish King Spirit. Ordinarily it is kept in a box sealed with melted wax, but on the day of the Great Chariot Festival, it is taken out and displayed.

Though the jeweled shirt was a black sleeveless jacket, it gave off an uncanny jewel light. One of the officiants held it up, and shook it and swung it north, south, east, and west. After he had displayed in all four directions, he put it back into the box. In the instant that I saw the jewel light, what I was visualizing was dissolving away for you the adverse circumstances and difficulties which those evil curses have brought.

After I returned from taking part in the Great Chariot Festival, I saw the spirit dove.

I read the letter from you which the spirit dove had brought, and it put a stop to my worries about you. The festivities of the Great Chariot Festival were suddenly over, and I was very happy to have gone from the atmosphere of the Great Chariot Festival, and entered into the world linked to you.

In communicating with you, there is real sincerity, good will, promises, true faith, love ... so many, many of the words which are so beautiful to experience, which have always supported the human mind and spirit. Again and again I come back to life, I wake up. Like the princess asleep for a hundred years who is awakened by the prince's kiss, life shows me one corner of the frozen mountain of her genuineness, her spiritual wonder, her grandeur, her delusion, her sympathy and compassion, just because I begin to deal with her carefully.

With your strength and your search, this world shows her greatness. Even if the world still has so much filth, from you I still get back my faith in this world. As you expressed with that sigh you let out on the day of the Festival of Slaughtering Animals, this world really is fickle and self-indulgent, and morality is going to ruin. I am sick of those spiritual methods too which take pleasure from killing living beings. In fact, placed in its midst, everyone finds it hard to escape responsibilities, everyone wants to shirk duties. As with rotten fruit, the rot is just an external sign. Inwardly, every person secretly condones his own gradual deterioration, and this creates the moral decline of this world. It is us who abandon ourselves. It is also ourselves who allow the unbearable corruption of the world.

I still will go on writing letters to you. For me to redeem myself, this is a necessity. This is necessary for me to redeem myself, necessary for my mind and spirit to breathe. If I give up this practice, it will be no different than suicide. Taking love and elevating it to faith, taking my love of Khyungpo Ba and making it into a faith—this may seem like crazy, mixed-up behavior, but in fact it is the most clear, lucid, rational decision I have made in many years.

In my psychological time and space, I am always together with Khyungpo Ba, and we rely on each other to live, and we are always looking after each other. Every person has his or her own life and world. Only when I am with Khyungpo Ba do I belong to my own world. This love is the top luxury in the world, and it is also the necessary ingredient for Sharwadi to survive.

Maybe I have decided that, while I am alive, I will pass the time waiting. We are like two trees whose roots are joined beneath the ground, while above ground we look to each other from far away. Without their own direct experience of it, who would be able to comprehend the bitterness and pain and sense of being wronged that this word "faraway" contains? But at least there is no enmity and no regret. If I could be together with Khyungpo Ba, I truly would not want to ask for anything or do anything. Nothing in the world is worth my leaving Khyungpo Ba and going to search for him. Sometimes I prefer to be stupid like this, loving him and going with him.

One day Khyungpo Ba may grow tired of me, or, on his search, he may encounter a woman who suits him better. So what would that mean for me?

On the day of the Festival for Slaughtering Animals, when I saw you in the streets barely looking at a woman — of course that sight was a bit unbearable for me — all day long that simple detail was like a knife piercing my heart, enough to kill me. But it was not a quick death from being stabbed with a knife, rather, it drilled into a soft tender heart, exerting its force bit by bit, turning around and around, penetrating inch by inch. This process was much harder to bear than death.

In all this muddle, I feel myself going along very painfully, going along a road with an unknown goal.

Well then, I have to get up. I have to erase the scars of longing, and go laugh at human life. It is really a bit tiring.

Shawardi, who loves you.

9 The Cursed Black Yak Horn

Khyung:

I slipped away from my father's house to write you a follow-up letter. I may not be able to write you a letter for a good many days.

Kumari told me some new things. She said that those sorcerers took the black yak horn on which they had laid the curse and buried it at a crossroads. Originally, they had wanted to bury this black yak horn in the house where you had lived. But the owner of the house had strongly opposed this. He had sufficient reason: he was afraid that the evil power of that sorcery curse would affect his own family.

So the best they could do was to bury that accursed object at a crossroads, saying that those blood-drinking yakshas would naturally meet up with you there and bring a great disaster upon you.

According to what Kumari said, the real power of this sorcery is after six months. This was the first step in their series of curses. They are going to continue employing their evil curses and death-dealing methods. In sum, you still must not forget to visualize that protective ring around you.

I too have found a spiritually elevated person. She is an accomplished dakini called Bandi. I have heard that she has expert knowledge of methods for removing evil. But recently she has not been home. She went to another town and is working to dispel evil for a family who buried a family members without being cautious about angering the spirits of the land. I've heard that four young people in this family have already died.

When she comes back, I will invite her to come neutralize the black curse the sorcerers aimed at you. If she is willing, I will pay homage to her as a teacher, and learn these methods of hers. This way, I will be able to employ these methods for you at any time and any place, and help you attain all your wishes.

I always want to call you husband, but I am always a little ashamed to, because it is too intimate. Later on, will you please permit me to address you like this?

I have said to you, we depend on each other to live. If you want to, then you can always keep to your original rules for living. At this time, I am facing the world as a substitute for you, and dealing with life's "diamond of activities." You do not have to have any worries or concerns, all you have to do is call on your servant Sharwadi. I must go from a limited life, go from the impermanence of changing illusions, and do all I can to get more time and more food to feed and nurture this "lion" of yours. I am very willing to become another set of eyes for you, another mind. I will go even deeper into the culture you want to understand. Given the precondition that "you preserve your health, you are not with me, I only love Khyungpo Ba," I will be able to help people who need help.

I think you have to do everything possible to broaden your studies. India after all is an ancient land, with a very deep accumulation of wisdom. It is a magical land that will give you a very good starting point and opportunity. When you have traveled the world and have gotten tired of traveling, then come here to me. I hope that your first stop when you return will be here with me.

Kumari has built a new Buddha hall. This is also the result of my efforts, and today I have been called to give it my support. She is also a piece of history, watching me all along in silence as I go. I have made a promise to her. I think, because of my efforts, there will be more people in the world who have the same faith as you—this too is a form of loving you.

I won't say anymore. I'll eat quickly and then go out. It is in the outskirts, quite far.

Do not feel isolated, Sharwadi is always by your side.

Yours truly, Sharwadi

10 You Really Fell in Love with Her

Female Spirit:

After I received your letter, what most struck me were the words "not with me." This pierced my mind, and the cold hit me. Because that phrase was there, all your promises became meaningless. I do not know: do I, I who am "not with you," still need anything from you? I have taken knowing you as a summons to me from fate. I truly had no way to resist that poetic feeling coming from you. I was always conflicted: I did not want to abandon my dream, and I did not want to abandon your true love. Just as I am constantly being pulled back and forth by this, your phrase "not with me" has woken me up. I suddenly understand: in reality you did not hope that I would stay with you.

I finally understand that, in fact, fate really did not want me to leave off my search. No matter what kind of plans you make, in the light of that "not with me" of yours, they all change into illusions.

The moment I finished reading your letter, my mind all at once became lethargic. I could not keep going at all. I did not know whether my lethargic footsteps would be able to keep up with your ever-changing plans. I even began to doubt myself: in the precious length of time I am alive, do I or do I not really need to enjoy another kind of happy life, which basically does not belong to me? I really have to quiet down. Though I have a child's mind, I do understand that I have already come to my middle years, and if I am the least bit absent-minded, the second half of my life will pass by in vain.

Though I treasure having met you, I clearly recognize that intoxicating romantic feeling made me pay the price of longing. But I am still rushing toward it, pleasantly surprised. This is because I understand that, after many years, after my physical body is on the wane, even if I want to be in love, I will no longer have the physical basis for love. So while I am still able to love and be loved, I have fully accepted this love.

Although in your letter there were many plans and promises, those words "not with me" really did pierce my heart with pain. This is because I understood certain things that were hidden in your subconscious mind when you wrote this. At the time, you may not have paid attention to this.

You may even be unaware of it, but since you did write this, it makes it clear that, in your mind, there is surely a reason for writing this. In my sensitive mind, I recognized that you were certainly hinting at something, and this hint is what I very much don't like.

Did you really not know that this "not with me" is an unfavorable causal condition?

It is already past midnight, but I don't want to go to sleep at all. I am thinking: does everything I have done recently ultimately have meaning in my life, or not? Should I still continue like before, being solitary, or not?

Khyungpo Ba

11 A Causal Condition That Is Not Good

I said to Khyungpo Naljor: "Though I like the letters between you and Sharwadi very much, when my son Chen Yixin read them, he said they have already very much influenced the reading of the novel, and influenced the structure of the novel, and influenced the quality of the novel. Chen Yixin said that, except for speaking of emotions and love, they show almost nothing of the hardships of the search and the increase of wisdom. He said that, as for the content that must be written, you have passed over it in the letters, and in them, there is no content that people have to know."

Khyungpo Naljor laughed and said: "How would he know that all the content in my letter is my search. You must realize that, in the process of my search, the most important thing was my spiritual process. This is all embodied in my letters. You must know that in a long search, what is hardest for me to forget is in fact not the difficulties of the journey, but rather the spiritual struggles. These are all reflected in my letters. It is only in these letters that you can feel the intense struggles of these two living hearts."

I said: "That's right. Every time I read them, my heart feels the pain."

Khyungpo Naljor also said: "For all the people in the world who want to go on a search for truth, what is hardest to give up is really 'emotions.' Thus, some people even think that Sharwadi's emotions were demons sent by those sorcerers — the demons of emotion."

I asked: "Do you think of them this way too?"

Khyungpo Naljor said: "Hard to say. Although her emotions objectively did influence my mind, without that experience, would I still be Khyungpo Naljor? What people really needed was not a Khyungpo Naljor who was a born holy man. What they needed was a Khyungpo Naljor with emotions and ideas, with desires and clingings, who could nevertheless get stronger and stronger until in the end, he could realize transcendence and liberation. Do you think this is correct?"

I said: "It is correct. And it is in your letters that I read of you as a living, breathing man … You really fell in love with her."

Khyungpo Naljor first laughed, and then let out a long sigh.

He said: "Maybe those words 'not with me' really were an unfavorable causal condition."

When he said that, there was a sense of suffocation in my heart.

Then I asked: "Later on, did you return to be at her side or not?"

He said: "Later on you will find out."

Chapter 14

Experience for the Soul

Xuemo: Master, in the Secret History it says that you served a spirit slave girl in a spirit temple in India, and this became an important experience in your life. Can say something about this experience?

1 A Hard Laborer in a Spirit Temple in India

Xuemo, child of my heart, in this world, if you want to build up a major accomplishment, first there must be major destruction.

If there is no smashing, how will there be transcendence?

Son, for me the most important smashing was completed in a spirit temple.

At that time, the demons of sickness were following me. Though, to look at me, I was like an ordinary person, no one knew I was undergoing tremendous pain. Apart from the pain of longing, I also was experiencing physical pain. Besides the fatigue and absent-mindedness, I often felt that my internal organs were burning. I believe that this was the result of the curses aimed at me by those sorcerers. Sometime I could also see those evil demons with their fangs and claws. Do not think this was a delusion. You should realize that, for me at that time, they were absolutely real.

The place where I was sold into bondage by the dakini was a Hindu spirit temple. When I first realized all this, I felt that I had been wronged. I thought: "Even if you have really sold me, you should have sold me to do hard labor in a Buddhist temple; you should not have sold me to a non-Buddhist spirit temple."

The spirit temples at that time had two kinds of slaves. One category was the temple prostitutes: these were women who had either been forced into it by debt, or had voluntarily gone into spirit temples to sell their bodies. The other category was the men who specialized in serving these women. All the income of the former went to the spirit temples and was used for daily expenses. In the Indian tradition at that time, those women who sold their bodies were not despised, because all that they did was considered to be the will of the gods. They received many men, and the money they earned went to support the temples.

When I went into the spirit temple, my feelings were very complex. Ever since I had been born, I had been favored by fate, no matter whether in Bonpo, or in the later course of seeking the Dharma. In Bonpo, I was the son of a teaching master, and ever since I was little, I had always been looked after by people with great respect and been the center of attention. Later, when I was seeking the Dharma, everywhere I went, I quickly became the teaching master's favorite. This was because, no matter whether in terms of worldly blessings or world-transcending enlightened nature, I always surpassed most people. I was quick to understand where the essence was of the teaching the master was passing on. Therefore, when I entered the spirit temple, I most definitely felt a sense of being treated unjustly. But at the same time, I understood that this sense of being wronged was in fact my discriminating mind making trouble. I thought that perhaps the dakini had done this precisely to apply a corrective to my discriminating mind.

The atmosphere of the spirit temple was very dignified. Images of Visnu, Brahma, Shiva, and other gods seemed to display a kind of great world-transcending spiritual power. In the traditions of Hinduism, they are seen as eternal divine spirits. But I knew that in this world there is no such thing as lasting forever, and everything would in the end go back to the empty inherent nature. In many aspects, Hinduism had religious rituals that where similar to the Esoteric Teaching of Buddhism at that time, like the fire offering, and many others. The two religions had both absorbed nourishment from each other. Sometimes, in descriptions of religious experience, it is said that the Hindu unity of Brahman and Atman is completely similar to Esoteric Buddhism's awakening to the empty inherent nature, but if we investigate the reality of it, there is still a major difference. If we weigh the differences between the two, there are the three seals of the Buddha Dharma: all phenomena are empty and selfless, all products are impermanent, and silent nirvana. That kind of eternal spirits that Hinduism recognizes is in fact, in my eyes, also impermanent. But I still give the appropriate respect to those solemn or frightening Hindu deities, because in the Esoteric Teaching of Buddhism, they are made into the deities protecting the Dharma.

The work that was assigned to me was to serve those temple

prostitutes. Working with me was a middle-aged man called Bapu. This name was in common use among the peasants in that area, but the strange thing was, his look was very aristocratic. The story was that he, too, had been sold to the temple by his teacher: the objective was to break down his overweening pride. Our duties we shared. I was in charge of the temple prostitutes' clothing and food and shelter and transportation, while Bapu was specifically in charge of getting them their sexual partners. Every day, Bapu stood by the temple gate, looking for those men who wanted a temple prostitute.

Those days left a deep impression on me. Nevertheless, some accounts conceal the record of this period of time, or they only speak in general terms about Sukhasiddhi refining my mind's nature, and are very vague about the process. It is only in the secret history written in dakini script, which you have read, that this period is recorded in detail. Although other teachers also passed on to me the supreme esoteric teachings, Sukhasiddhi became one of my fundamental teacher, as important as Niguma. The reason is that Sukhasiddhi carried out this special refining of my mind's nature for me.

I can say that, if not for Sukhasiddhi carrying out this special tempering of my mind's nature, I would have been unable to have my subsequent achievements.

This period of time at the Hindu temple became the most important learning environment in my life, just like the work the Sixth Patriarch of Zen Huineng did husking rice.

2 The Bearing and Voices of the Temple Prostitutes

Every morning I got up before daybreak. The first thing I did was sit in meditation. Suffering the physical pain brought on by the malevolent curses, I threw off the covers and got out of bed, and worked at the several Buddhist techniques I had to cultivate. Because of time constraints, I could not practice all the methods my teachers had taught me: all I could do was pick the important ones and cultivate them. At that time, my principal visualization was the Diamond of Surpassing Bliss, which was said to have come from the holy sage Luipa.

After meditating, I would begin the day's work. My work was menial: it included sweeping up the rooms of the temple prostitutes, carrying water, splitting firewood, arranging for the water to wash their faces, and so on — the many chores done by a servant. What was different from the typical servant was that, while I was performing these activities, I was working according to my teacher's instructions. I took all these mundane activities and transformed them into a visualization of helping sentient beings. For example, when I was carrying water, I always visualized myself walking on the great Path of enlightenment, with countless fathers and mothers from all six planes of existence behind me. When I was washing the temple prostitutes' faces, I visualized myself removing the karmic barriers for sentient beings. When I was splitting firewood, I visualized myself cutting off my own selfish clingings. When I brought those temple prostitutes broth or water, I visualized myself making offerings to Buddha and the many dakinis. In this way I used my own daily work for cultivating visualization. Nobody knew that this servant who had come from Tibet was carrying on these secret visualizations in what seemed to be ordinary daily life.

No matter how painful the activity is, I could always take it on. But there was no way for me to endure the bearing of the temple prostitutes as they came and went. The story was that those temple prostitutes had all undergone specialized training and understood all the arts of seduction. But the technique that people on the ordinary Path could not necessarily accept was their ability to be taken as proud. This was called by the local believers "the wisdom of the female spirits." When the ultra-feminine voice of this wisdom came to my ears, what I felt was a kind of torment.

Inspired by the wisdom of the temple prostitutes, many men came to the temple, appreciating the charms of the temple prostitutes. For Bapu and me, our workload was very heavy, and we would be busy very late before we could rest. Sometimes, late at night, when everyone was quiet, I would feel like quitting. I would think: "I came to India to seek the Dharma, not to be a servant doing chores." It got to the point that I doubted whether or not I should stay on here. Because I had already found many teachings which accomplished teaching masters called "teachings of special excellence," all I had to do was to enter deeply into one of them, and liberation would be as easy as reaching into my pocket and taking something out. Though when I was doing my work, I also made every effort to cultivate visualization according to my teacher's instructions, more often the strenuous labor drove out that kind of special feeling. I often lost my concentration. Later on, many people assumed that my accomplishments were not like Milarepa going through that process of completely remolding himself, but in fact, for me, that experience was completed in the process of seeking the Dharma in India.

No matter whether in Bonpo or at the places of other teachers, what I perceived was always a purity. What those ascetics and pandits brought to me was even more a kind of cool purity. But once I entered the spirit temple, that purity melted away like frost. For a long time previously, I thought I could control my mind. Only when I entered the spirit temple did I discover that my mind would not obey. When I heard the voices of those temple prostitutes, my mind would keep on shaking.

You must realize that at that time, I was still a young man.

3　A Disciple of Luipa

Before long, I discovered that the man called Bapu had an unusual ability to control his mind. Even when he was leading those men into the rooms of the temple prostitutes, and he was taking money from their hands, he still had the same look as when he was sitting in meditation. He was always calm and mild. Many times, when the temple prostitutes lost their tempers, he would still be smiling the same as always. One time, he ended up washing the feet of one of the temple prostitutes. Even then, the look on his face still had that same kind of peace and tranquility he showed when on the meditation seat.

During a conversation with him, I found out that Bapu's teacher was Luipa. Luipa had been born into a very high-ranking aristocratic family: like Sakyamuni, Luipa was also a prince. Because he had extraordinary personality and charm, almost everyone liked him. He was appointed by his father, the king, to be his lawful successor. One day an ascetic came to the palace. The king received him and offered him a lot of gold and silver. But that man would only accept a few meals and a bolt of cloth, and he politely declined everything else. This greatly surprised Luipa. Most of the people around him were obsessively scheming to acquire gold and silver, and they paid no attention to this religious man who had drifted in. That was the first time Luipa experienced any spiritual stirring. Later, Luipa's wisdom developed, and he got a glimpse of impermanence, and he resolutely left home.

Bapu said, at that time, the whole country knew that Luipa was a virtuous and able man, and everyone was hoping he would be able to succeed to the kingship. In this way, when one man is blessed, he brings along the whole crowd: because of Luipa's blessings and merit, the people of the kingdom would be able to lead comparatively fortunate lives. The king and Luipa's brothers hoped even more that he would be able to succeed to the throne. In the kingdom at that time, because all the royal brothers were virtuous and able, there was no struggle for power and advantage: on the contrary, everyone revered Luipa very much. So they followed after Luipa when he had left home and brought him back, and locked him up inside the palace with chains made of gold. But on one dark, moonless stormy night, Luipa took the gold chains and presented them to the guards, changed into the clothes of a poor man, and fled into a forest graveyard.

In that forest graveyard at that time, there were many accomplished mystics. On the outside they looked crazy, but their inner attainments were of the highest order. So Luipa found the most excellent teaching of the Diamond of Surpassing Bliss, and began his own career of cultivating ascetic practice.

Bapu was always talking with me about Luipa. The two of us lived in the same house. Later, I also found a small house in the back flower garden filled with all sorts of things, and I cleaned it up a bit and used it for sitting in meditation. But more often, I was very willing to listen to Bapu tell stories about those great accomplished teachers. It was from those wondrous stories that I learned many things.

When Bapu spoke, he spoke very slowly, as slowly as sipping rice water. When he was slowly telling those stories, I always felt a kind of peace, making me forget both myself and other things, so subject and object were both empty. Later, Bapu told me this was the normal mind. At that time, I still did not know that this kind of normal mind is in fact a very special, excellent feeling.

When visitors to the spirit temple were few, we could relax a bit. At these times, Bapu's chatterbox opened up. In Bapu's narratives, I saw Luipa. He was a lean practitioner, with a high nose and deep eyes; his whole face was thin. He had the classic look of an Indian ascetic monk. All he wore was a single piece of ragged cloth which people called a dung sweeper's cloth. Bapu said that Luipa took cultivating the Teaching of Surpassing Bliss as his main purpose, and that he was very dedicated, and that he had already attained many realizations that must be sought for in the two processes of generating and completing enlightenment. But for his final enlightenment, he had made use of an ascetic practice that had nothing to do with Buddhist methods: eating fish guts. The meaning of the name "Luipa" is "the man who eats fish guts."

4　Luipa's Show

Bapu was always talking about the afternoon Luipa encountered the dakini. It was an ordinary afternoon. We see Luipa walk into our field of vision. Because of his restricted diet and his austere practices, Luipa looked very emaciated, and his ragged garment looked as if it were hanging on a tree branch. There was a look of empty desolation.

The rustling autumn wind was blowing across the yellow leaves on the ground, and there was a strong flavor of fall in the air. Luipa's garment put out a rustling sound. His long hair was blowing in the wind. But his external shabbiness still could not conceal the nobility that flowed forth from every pore of Luipa's body. The story goes that, because Luipa was so handsome, all the local women wanted to use their best food to make offerings to him. To avoid these offerings, Luipa fled from the towns where people knew the details of his life, but he could not survive on wind and dew, so he went out begging for food. We see him walking toward a woman as extremely emaciated as himself; she was a beggar woman. All around her was a big pile of what could be called trash. In India at the time, there were such women everywhere. In China later on, there were also women like this everywhere. From her external appearance, we cannot see that there is anything about her different from the other beggar women. But if you understood them, then you would understand that they are the holy ones who are most deserving of people's offerings. Because they have awakened to the empty inherent nature, we call them dakinis.

Luipa did not know that this woman in the wind, watching him gradually approach, was a dakini. He just thought: hopefully, through her making an offering to him, it will transform her fate. The Buddhist scriptures are full of stories like this: because she makes an offering to a holy man, a beggar woman after she dies becomes a devi, a celestial woman.

Luipa walked toward that woman.

He held out his begging bowl to that woman.The woman did not take his bowl; she just passed him her own earthenware jar that was filled with food. Luipa looked at the food in it. It was some sour-smelling mess, with some bubbles floating in it. On the sides of the jar some black hairs were growing. We always see this kind of rotting food in the hot summer weather. We also know that if we eat this kind of food, it will upset our stomachs. So of course we can understand why Luipa had a furrowed brow.

At this point, the woman laughed. We can hear her voice saying: "If you like good food, why didn't you stay in the palace?"

Luipa got red in the face. He wanted to eat that food very much, but every time he looked at it, he was about to vomit.

Then the woman took back the food, and gulped down a few mouthfuls. Luipa suddenly understood something. He thought: "Can it be that she is a dakini?"

She took the rest of the food and gave it to a little dog. Having woken up, Luipa was just in time to snatch a bit of gravy from the dog's mouth. In this little bit of gravy, Luipa discovered a flavor of the Dharma that he had never had before. Some people say that this food, which to look at was so nauseating, in reality came from a far-off Buddha Land, and we call it sweet dew. Other people say that if Luipa had eaten it without the least hesitation, he would not have needed his subsequent austerities, and he would have immediately experienced the ultimate accomplishment. Still other people say that it was just because he tasted that bit of gravy, that he was able to become the chief of eighty-four teaching masters of great accomplishment later on. Others say that the little dog who ate the sweet dew later achieved the great accomplishment, and came to be called the "great master of the dogs."

We can see on Luipa's face that he was blaming himself. Dissatisfaction with Luipa was also written on the face of the dakini. She said: "The karmic barriers in your other chakras have all been purified, but there is still a bit of defilement in your heart chakra. This is created by your discriminating mind. You have to apply the antidote to your discriminating mind." She also said: "In reality, all the goals of cultivating practice are to counteract the discriminating mind. This is because the root of all afflictions is the discriminating mind. Without the discriminating mind, there would be no afflictions."

The dakini said: "I really do not understand. You have cultivated practice for many years, but ultimately what have you attained? Can it be that what you have cultivated is the appearance of an ascetic monk? If so, then you are just putting on an act."

She also said: "Haven't you realized that you are putting on a show? When you go through the motions of reciting scriptures, you are really just putting on a show. When you go through the motions of sitting in meditation, you are really just putting on a show, too. When you refused the enticements of being the king of the country, you still did not get away from putting on a show. When you cultivate all these austerities, you still have the mentality of putting on a show. When people are there, you put on a show of looking at them. When you are alone, you put on a show of observing yourself. Although you often make yourself feel moved, you have certainly never subdued your own mind, because you still have your discriminating mind. If you have the discriminating mind, then you have clinging and attachments. But the true goal of cultivating practice is in fact to remove your own clinging and attachments. When you get rid of your clinging to the self, then you will be an arhat. When you get rid of your clinging to the Dharma, then you will be a bodhisattva. It doesn't matter that you chant those ritual forms which you see as so vital. All you have to do is clear away your clinging and attachments: this is the best way to cultivate practice."

5 The Shock of Being Enlightened

Luipa felt a shock, as though he had been enlightened.

The dakini also said: "You remember, no matter how you go through the motions of practising according to those teachings, no matter what you chant or visualize, no matter how much other people praise your accomplishments, no matter what austerities you practice, as long as your mind has not been transformed because of them, you are just putting on a show. To cultivate practice genuinely is to transform your own mind. And the sign that you are transforming your mind is that those conventional worldly things in your mind are decreasing day by day, and are not being added to. Don't pay attention to what feelings you are giving rise to or adding to, because all feelings are just feelings, and all contrived feelings are impermanent. They are like everything in the world, as evanescent as dew, as lightning, like dreams and illusions, like bubbles and shadows. Don't go clinging to those contrived feelings. You must see whether or not the things in your mind are always decreasing: for example, decreasing greed, decreasing anger, decreasing ignorance, decreasing vexation. You must see whether or not your mind is returning day by day to the uncontrived, returning to purity, returning to peace, returning to tranquility. You must see whether or not your mind is really its own master: whether it has truly become your own mind, and is no longer subject to control by external things, no longer troubled by external appearances, no longer a slave to outside worlds. When you see that there is ultimately no distinction between this delicious food and that rotten stuff, then, as it always says in the scriptures, 'when gold and dung are equal in value, when there is no difference between empty space and the palm of the hand' — only then will your cultivation of practice have meaning. That's because it is only when you reach this point, that your mind really belongs to you."

Bapu said: "Later Luipa always said that his fundamental teacher was really that dakini. Although the earlier teachers had given him many teachings, the one who enabled him to really achieve the ultimate benefit of the teaching was that dakini."

Bapu said: "The reason I tell this story is because I have read your mind. When you see those temple prostitutes and your teacher as the same, when you can be just as pure serving here in this spirit temple as you are serving at your teacher's place, only then will your past cultivation of practice have meaning."

I was drenched with sweat.

6 Bapu Takes Refuge with a Teacher

From this we have seen that practitioner called Luipa. It is just because of that dakini whose name we still do not know, that we have seen the real Luipa.

When that practitioner, who was as noble as a king's son, died, amid the clamor of people's voices in the town, there was another person who looked like a madman. The reason he was called a madman by other people was because he often chose for his food the fish guts that people had thrown away. When people saw him pick up this mushy stuff and swallow it, they all covered their noses and furrowed their brows. They did not know that, even when he was eating filthy fish guts, the man who appeared to be crazy had not lost his holy man's mind, and the light of empty inherent nature made him truly achieve the state where unclean and clean are one suchness.

Bapu said that Luipa went through many stages in this practice of eating fish guts. At the beginning, as soon as he saw the fish guts, he would feel nauseous and vomit. There was no question of eating them: all he had to do was think of them, and that would be enough to make him vomit out bile. In the second stage, he began to swallow the fish guts. As soon as he began to eat the fish guts, he would vomit out as much as he ate, but he did not care, and after vomiting, he would eat more. In the third stage, after a year of using fish guts for food, in his eyes fish guts were the same as the five grains, and he never relied on any other food to satisfy his hunger. In the fourth stage, for him there was no longer any dividing line between the five grains and fish guts, unclean and clean were one suchness, and he did not make distinctions. In the fifth stage, he got to the point where there was no food and not food, no doing and not doing, and he had absolutely no worries. At this point he had finally transcended dualism, and the pure light of the Great Mudra had become the inescapable atmosphere of his life.

Later on, although he was a master of the Diamond of Surpassing Bliss, people still called him Luipa, "the one who eats fish guts."

One day, Luipa encountered Bapu. At that time Bapu was not called Bapu, he was called Surya, which means Sun God. At that time Surya was still the king of a country: every day there was singing and dancing and celebration, and he was living a life of intoxication and dreams. Although he was surrounded by mountains of gold and silver and a multitude of beautiful women, still, he was always unhappy, because he could not find the meaning of life. At that time he was always liable to start thinking of death, and as soon as he took death as the reference point, all his happiness melted away like frost in the blazing sun. It was midday when he met Luipa. Surya was out on the road amusing himself with his favorite concobine. He saw the shadow of that lean body. A slight breeze was blowing through that man's hair, but it could not blow away the holiness from his face. Bapu said: "At that time, I suddenly felt a unique faith in him, because I saw an aura of holiness, which gave that lean face an inexplicable charisma. Looking at his appearance, it seemed that even if the sky shattered and the earth collapsed, nothing could break his peace and tranquility. And so I walked up to him."

Bapu said: "I asked him: 'Honored One, why is it that you have this kind of holy light on your face?' The man said: 'The light on my face has its origin in the light in my mind.' I also asked: 'Where does the light in your mind originate?' The man said: 'It is fundamentally inherent, it does not depend on external seeking.' "

Bapu also asked him: "Is it also inherent in me?"

The man said: "It is, it is also inherent in you. It is just that the precious jewel is covered by dirt, the black clouds are hiding the sun, so the light has no way to shine forth."

Bapu said: "At that moment I suddenly developed the greatest faith. I said: 'Honored One, can you accept an offering from me?' "

The man said: "Yes I can. What do you want to offer me?"

I said: "All the delicacies of the lands and seas."

The man said: "In my eyes, fish guts are no different from the delicacies of the lands and seas. I do not need your things."

I said: "So how about if I offer you gold and silver and pearls and jewels?"

The man said: "In my eyes there is no place that is not pearls and jewels, and everywhere I look is gold and silver. That bit you have there won't seem special to me."

I said: "So how about if I offer you my kingdom. My kingdom has a vast territory and it is extremely powerful. I can divide it in two—would you accept it?"

The man said: "I look upon a royal throne as something worthless. What in your eyes is a royal throne, in my eyes is a cage to imprison people. How could I see it as some special attraction?"

I said: "Honored One, so do you need anything?"

The man said: "Do you have the immortal sweet dew? If you have it, please bestow it on me."

I said: "I do not have it. In this world whatever is born must die.

How can there be an immortal sweet dew?"

The man said: "When you have understood this point, that is the immortal sweet dew. Why do you keep to this cage and not let it go?"

Bapu said to Khyungpo Naljor: "At that instant, a strong electric current flowed into the top of my head. I said to the man: 'Master, I have something else I can offer to you.' "

"The man said: 'What?'

"I said: 'My body, mouth, and mind.' "

Bapu told Khyungpo Naljor: "This is how I left home. I abandoned the throne, and shed the royal robes which were precious as gold, and I changed into the clothes of a mendicant. I also got rid of that name Surya, which is the same as the Sun God's name, and changed my name to Bapu, which is a name commonly used by the peasants. I went with Luipa and we left the city. On the second day, he gave me an initiation, and communicated to me the visualization method of the Diamond of Surpassing Bliss. Later, he took me and sold me to this spirit temple. At first my daily task was to wash the feet of those temple prostitutes. Nobody knew that this Bapu washing their feet for them had been a king.

"Similarly, nobody knew that you, this servant waiting on the temple prostitutes, were once a religious teaching master."

I said: "I understand," and I felt grateful to Sukhasiddhi.

7 The Longing They Most Want to Record

The spirit dove brought another letter.

To Khyung whom I miss so much:

When I read your letter, my emotions were so complicated

it is impossible to explain them all in a few words.

You misunderstood me. When I said "you are not with me," what I meant was when you went off on your search. I have discovered that you really care very much about me. This makes me very happy.

In the middle of the night I was frightened by a nightmare and woke up, and it was hard to go back to sleep. I wanted to write a letter, but there was no oil in the lamp. All around me everything was pitch black, as if a nameless monster was about to strike at any time and bite through my throat. I was terrified. I just lay there quietly, and gradually I faded out, and when I awoke it was already morning. In a trance, I really believed that after twenty years, I would be living for Khyungpo Ba. I had a strong desire to remove the fetters binding me. These days, as I have been helping my father do things, I have been thinking, this might be my last time to be with my father, so I wanted to be very serious about it. I thought, no matter when Khyungpo Ba returns, I will go off with him and travel all over the world.

In the afternoon, Kumari again brought news of the sorcerers. She said that after they buried that black yak horn of curses, they started a new cycle of curses. They went to the primeval forest, found a poisonous tree, collected the poison sap, combined it with the earth from a gravesite, and made an image, and then they used sandalwood sap to write your name on the image. This thing is a symbol of your life. They took it and put it on the fire mandala and burned black animal grease. Once that grease went into the fire, a cloud of smoke rose up and covered the image. While the sorcerers were chanting curses, they took their demon swords and stabbed the head of the image. They went on like this, burning grease, chanting curses, and stabbing. The story is that if they do this for forty-nine days, they will be able to make you go mad.

They are really intent on this. This time Kumari heard clearly that it is really Pema Nam who is furnishing them with all your information, and also clippings of your fingernails and hair. He even told the sorcerers about your family tree. They say that, this way, they will be more effective. Kumari says that those men are putting an extraordinary amount of effort into this just because Pema Nam is inciting them. Of course, my cousin Kusang Dorje's enmity is the most important cooperating cause in this process of placing curses on you. I do not know why they are so evil.

I have discovered that he has really changed. Before, he wanted to do his utmost to bring us together. Now his goal has changed to getting revenge. Is this change in him related to something I said? I remember one day I said that if I die, all my wealth should be given to Khyungpo Naljor, to enable him to go spread the Dharma. I remember Kusang Dorje giving a couple of cold laughs. Of course, if my father died, and I died, according to the local custom, everything would be his. Do you think that I can let this wealth become a cooperating cause for him to do evil?

I have already thought of a good way to deal with it.

But if I cannot wait till I finally see you, I am not willing to die.

I have discovered that I am getting old fast.

As soon as I think of you, I become lost in thought. When

I wash my feet, I knock over the basin for washing my hands and face on the ground, and the water goes all over me and all over the floor. For the first instant I get angry, but then I turn and think, Khyungpo Ba said he will take his own heart and shatter it, and merge into one body with the myriad things of the world. Suddenly I think religion is a tool for interpreting the world, or a language for communicating with the world. Whatever kind of mind you have, then you will have that kind of interpretation. If you think the world is hell, then it is hell. If in your eyes the world is heaven, then it is heaven. It's like when I met Khyungpo Ba, I felt the world as I saw it had changed.

No matter how bad this world is, at least it gave me a Khyungpo Ba, so how can I still say that it is not benevolent enough?

And finally, I have a proposal. After you have completed cultivating your practice at the temple, you are supposed to make a pilgrimage to the royal city Rajgir.

Sharwadi

8 I Really Feel Those Demonic Curses

My female spirit, I have discovered that I am really feeling those demonic curses, and I have gone mad.

I regretted that last letter of mine as soon as I had the spirit dove take it. I knew that it might hurt you. But I still had the spirit dove take the letter. I wanted to preserve the tracks of my soul. In the future, if there are karmic connections, this may let the world see a real Khyungpo Ba. He was not a natural-born holy man; he still had private desires and the energies of his habits. He was dreadfully sensitive, but it was precisely this sensitivity that formed him. If not for that sensitivity, he would have been like a million other guys from Tibet, and, under life's heavy pressures, he would have already lost that sense of direction.

Compared to the yoga masters, I am really more like a wandering poet. The poets I like can make the common people praise them and not fear being sent into exile by the lords; they can sympathize with everyone and everything, with great impressive energy. The effect I want to achieve in life is no more than this.

I just hope that after experiencing being exiled by fate, in the concerns of the woman my heart loves, I can cry in pain or sing a song. Having written this much, I suddenly just understood why I picked you. In your eyes, I truly found that feeling that I am just a man, not a yoga master or a holy man.

Please don't make me have the face of a holy man. I don't want to. When you are together with me, you can open up your mind and be happy. Become more energetic and clearer day by day, and then it will be achieved. All you have to do, when you are in contact with me, is to wake up to the here and now, be happy and without worries, and be filled with great love. Then you will be the one receiving the greatest benefit in the world. In this world there is no religious idea that is greater than love, no thought that is more important than being good, no trait that is more worthy of praise than true sincerity. When you have these, then you are the most accomplished kind of person. Will you still go looking for some great teacher with a solemn face?

In the harbor of your spirit, I am like a ship after a long journey, unfettered, enjoying the happiness of being human. I have never before experienced this kind of freedom and joy. It is this that makes you become the woman in the human world I love the most. But this is not a world-transcending dakini.

In the future, when I am on a journey that is too long, and enduring too much wind and rain, and carrying out a mission that is too heavy, I will just think of the woman I love in my heart, let go of all my cares, and enter a fragrant sweet dream, like a baby in his mother's arms after nursing.

I just want to make my woman happy. I just want it to be like that day of the Festival of Slaughtering Animals when I went all covered in sweat to buy her some water; no matter whether I lost my money because of this, I could not refuse. I just want to be in her life and hold her in an intoxicating romance, and make her happily become a fool. I just want to use these strong arms to embrace her, and make her sleep peacefully and sweetly and soundly. I just want to make her understand that no matter where she is, a pair of eyes will always be gazing at her with true deep emotion, worried for her, happy for her, singing for her, crying for her.

You do not need a great teacher. A great teacher belongs to the world, not to you. All I want is that after I am finished being the "great teacher" I have to be in the face of society, I will again be quietly facing my woman, being a man who makes her feel pity, makes her heart ache, makes her worry.

9 Water for Washing Sukhasiddhi's Feet

Xuemo, don't look at me like that. That is the most real me. Don't worry about what your son Chen Yixin said, he is still young. He likes stories, he hopes this book of yours will be like a bestseller, that it will be able to draw in those already impulsive eyes, or it will describe some sort of miracle, or it will show some artistic quality. But you are more willing to describe my spiritual journey in a plain, unpretentious way.

I know that in your eyes, this is the meaning of your writings.

When your son has lived a few more decades, maybe he will appreciate your current way of writing more.

That's right. Though I experienced countless miracles, the most miraculous was the fact that I went from being a person with desires and expectations, hemmed in by emotional desires, and ended up becoming a holy man.

In all the searches I went through, the thing that was the hardest for me to bear was my longing for Sharwadi. In my whole life, that was the thing that was the most difficult to conquer, but in the end I did conquer it.

Thinking about it now, there are really some lingering fears. Think about it. At that time, all I had to do was start thinking of turning back, and then I would have grown old and died in Nepal, and turned into a pile of ordinary bones. I would not have had the everlasting attainment I achieved later. Although Buddhism considers all products impermanent, this is just said in reference to worldly phenomena. As for people who have genuinely experienced nirvana, they realize the everlasting attainment. This is because, in contrast to the impermanence, suffering, lack of fixed identity, and impurity of the worldly, nirvana has the four qualities of permanence, bliss, identity, and purity.

Only those people who hold the misguided view of nirvana as annihilation think that nirvana is nihilistic, empty nothingness. In fact, nirvana transcends being and nothingness. Only those who realize nirvana understand what nirvana is.

In those days, I was really hit by the curses the sorcerers had directed at me, and I was seriously ill for more than a month, always hovering between life and death. Your son Chen Yixin hopes you will exaggerate this being on the brink of death as much as you want, but hovering between life and death is hovering between life and death. Whether I was "dying" or "coming back to life" is not important. In my eyes, these are really not separate things. At that time, in reality, I had already abandoned life and death. For me at that time, giving up life and death was a lot easier than giving up Sharwadi.

Let me tell you, in that period of time, what I most could not give up was Sharwadi. That emotional desire is truly the one thing in the world most to be feared.

Thus, in the letters below, you will still be able to read much that is connected with this. You must not casually delete them.

You will discover that, even after those dakinis showed me the inherent nature of mind, I would still often be controlled by emotional desires. You shouldn't be surprised, because even after I clearly understood the inherent nature of mind, those emotional desires were still the things that were hardest for me to counteract. Besides their basis in physiology, emotional desires are to be feared because they are given the label of love, and, among human emotions, they are the closest thing to faith. They can often produce a lofty feeling, and dilute true faith with this lofty feeling.

But at that time, besides the demons of emotion, I was really encountering the external demons brought to me by those sorcerers' curses. You can think of those external demons as a kind of negative dark energy. Though you could not see it or touch it, it really had a kind of effective existence.

Bapu said that there was an evil force surrounding me. Even the slave girls whom I served said I was very unlucky. Sometimes I obviously gave them clean water, but they said it was filthy-smelling bloody pus. Whatever I touched was, in their eyes, utterly nauseating.

Bapu said that in this lifetime, those demons would follow me like maggots sticking to a bone. Later as it turned out, aside from the mortal perils I would encounter from time to time, I was always in disputes. In the years of my life, there were also incidents of "adversarial bodhisattvas" from other religions and from among my own disciples doing bad things to me. These all originated in demons being concerned with me.

Of course, looking back on it now, what I did later actually benefited from those demons. They were like gadflies on an ox: whenever I, the old ox, wanted to slack off, they would sting me, and make me wake up and move forward energetically.

Later, Bapu did a fire offering to Shiva on my behalf, and then my body gradually recovered.

One particular day, Sukhasiddhi came looking for me. She still had a frosty look, and I could not see a bit of warmth on her face. I suspected that she knew about the letters going back and forth between Sharwadi and me. I thought of confessing, but I was also afraid to provoke her displeasure. According to the teachings of the Esoteric Vehicle, we must do all we can to make the teacher happy: we must not say or do anything that makes the teacher unhappy. Since she did not ask, I did not want to disappoint her.

I knelt on the ground, touching my head to the dakini's feet.

Sukhasiddhi said coldly: "Go make some hot water, and wash my feet."

I happily heated some water, then knelt on the ground and washed Sukhasiddhi's feet. When I had finished washing them, I used the hair on my head to wipe the water off her feet. Then I asked: "Teacher, do you need me to do something else?"

Sukhasiddhi pointed to the dirty water in the wash basin and said: "Drink it."

If Bapu had not told me the story of Luipa, I wouldn't have drunk that water. But by now, I was not the person I was before. Without the least hesitation, I picked up the wash basin and drank the water. But there was too much water, and some was left over. I immediately took a bowl and poured the water into it, and said: "I'll drink this in a moment."

Sukhasiddhi looked amused, and said: "Because of this causal condition, you will be able to live in the world for one hundred and fifty years. Also because of this causal condition, I will communicate to you a teaching of the bodiless dakinis, which may be able to eliminate your current difficulties in life … Come, pick up that bowl."

I picked up that bowl, and the water in the bowl was shaking. Sukhasiddhi took out a hairpin and stirred the water. Ripples appeared in the water where the hairpin passed through it, but when the hairpin was taken out, the surface of the water became peaceful and still.

Sukhasiddhi said: "Look, this water is your mind. This hairpin represents a sword. All external appearances in the world are, for you, a sword stabbing you. They can all stab into your mind. That also means that your mind can always feel the movements of that sword. If you could not feel the movements of that sword, then you would fall into oblivion and numb emptiness. But although that sword is moving, although it can make waves, still, all it needs to do is stop, and the surface of the water returns to a state of being peaceful and still. Do you understand?"

I murmured: "Is what you mean that we must give rise to mind without abiding anywhere?"

Sukhasiddhi looked amused, and said: "That's right. Remember, the secret to cultivating practice is to be like the sword cutting into the surface of the water. When you are face-to-face with those temple prostitutes and their clients, though your mind must look at them, still, you must not cling to them. Your mind should be like that still water, responding without responding, paying attention without paying attention, being aware without being aware. Although all outer appearances and actions leave a mark on your mind, when the sword has swept past, the surface of the water returns to a state of being peaceful and still. It pierces without piercing, it cuts without cutting, it does not give rise to clinging, it does not give rise to concerns. If you are like this, then nothing in the world can harm you."

10 The Original Substance of Life

Sukhasiddhi said: "You must realize that demons, too, are a product of the false mind. When your true mind can magnetize your false mind, the demons will become spirits protecting the Dharma. To truly conquer the demons of delusion, you need the wisdom of the Great Mudra.

"The Great Mudra is original and inherent, and fundamentally present: it is something we are born with, not something achieved later through contrived practice. Therefore, if you clearly understand this point, then you clearly understand that the real cultivation of practice is something that proceeds spontaneously, without artificial action. Like the air that fills the space in which we live, the truth is everywhere in the realm of reality. The truth is omnipresent. As a great teacher in

China once said, 'The Path is there in shitting and pissing.' That is to say, even in the lowest, most filthy places, the truth exists, because it is fundamentally inherently present.

"The truth is a kind of fundamental order, not something created by human effort. For example, mind and things are not apart from the truth, though there is a distinction between mind and things. Mind is the essence, things are the function: essence and function are originally one body. Though they have all kinds of manifestations, they all go back to the empty inherent nature.

"The nature of void is the enlightened inherent nature. All the beings revolving in the six planes of existence, and peaceful nirvana too, are nothing but the wondrous function of the enlightened inherent nature. The world of feelings, the multitudes of sentient beings, impure and pure, high and low, right and wrong, good and evil, the interplay of cause and effect, all the many natural phenomena and psychological manifestations, et cetera, et cetera: all this is the wondrous function of the enlightened inherent nature. Although when we look at all this, it appears to be complex and multitudinous, its essential inherent nature is not apart from the empty inherent nature. Thus, the apparent is not different from emptiness, and emptiness is not different from the apparent. The apparent is like the moon reflected in the water, like flowers reflected in a mirror. The essence is empty and clear and pure. These two were not made by heaven and earth, and not made by humans: they are inherently originally complete. The enlightened inherent nature appears and gives rise to wondrous function; although it appears, its essential nature is empty and still. Though essential nature is empty, it will become manifest in external things, which can function only because of the essence. It is like the wish-granting jewel; if we seek its ultimate, it cannot be attained, but its wondrous function can manifest all things. All phenomena are not apart from empty inherent nature, it can manifest all phenomena. There is no distinction of the same or different between the original enlightened nature and all the phenomena which it manifests. The two are not apart from each other, not separate, without duality, without difference. From this original enlightened inherent nature are born the three bodies of Buddha. The empty clear purity of enlightened inherent nature is distinguished as the Dharmakaya, the Body of Reality. Its illumination is the Sambhogakaya, the Body of Reward. Its various manifestations are the Nirmanakaya, the Transformation Body. The three bodies are one essence, and this is also inherent.

"The enlightened inherent nature in its essence is fundamentally pure, and unattainable. Although illusory feelings appear, they are born from the functioning of the original essence too. The enlightened inherent nature is fundamentally without ignorance, but when the discriminating mind arises, ignorance is born, and manifests the realms of experience.

"All the complex things and events of the world are all different manifestations of that original enlightened inherent nature. Some of them are defiled, some are pure, spontaneously illumined, spontaneously appearing. This is the process of all the phenomena in the world originating through the interplay of cause and effect. The light of mind is the root of all the many external manifestations, as it explains in the *Huayan Sutra*: 'If people want to fully know all the Buddhas of the past, present, and future, they must observe the inherent nature of the realm of reality: everything is created by mind alone.' If there is defilement or purity in the mind, then there will be defilement or purity in the external manifestation. The mind of compassion, the wisdom, the light, that crude physical body, that discriminating mind, that wisdom without discrimination, all those defiled states of mind, all those various kinds of pure virtues: they all are born from that inherent mind.

"Both deluded clinging and enlightenment originate in the inherent mind. But all the many wondrous functions, all the many manifestations, in the end will return to the basic essence, like bubbles returning to the ocean, like clouds scattering in the sky, like a rainbow dissolving in the heavens, like smoke vanishing without a trace. Those seven lights which appear under the bright sun will ultimately merge into the three-cornered crystal. The samsara and nirvana which appear with the three realms of existence (realm of desire, realm of form and formless realm) will also merge back into the inherent ground of fundamental purity, into the everywhere-equal liberation in the original realm.

"Apart from mind there is no teaching. Apart from mind there is no cultivation. Apart from mind there is no achievement. Apart from mind there is no failure. The three bodies and five wisdoms of the Buddhas, the afflictions of the three forms of karma of sentient beings (the actions of body, mouth, and conceptual mind), all originated in inherent mind: outside mind, there is nothing else. Those who seek the truth outside of mind are not Buddhists.

"Therefore, when we are cultivating practice, we must fully know that bright enlightened nature of void. We are inherently equipped with it, and we do not rely on external seeking. It is as brilliant as a crystal sphere, and is inherently equipped with the five lights of earth, water, fire, air, and space. It can manifest all realms. Though it is very hard at the level of sentient beings in the karmic power of ignorance to go beyond sensory consciousness, nevertheless, that knowing light is the inherent function of the enlightened inherent nature. It knows clearly without giving rise to false distinctions; it does not use concepts to think things over; its sensory consciousness and thoughts are inherently empty; it pulls its functioning back to the essence: thus it can spontaneously dwell in peace in the clear essence.

"Though the six sense organs and the six associated forms of consciousness manifest all things, this is not apart from the bright, empty enlightened inherent nature. The essential body of that enlightened inherent nature is like the inherent purity of empty space. Thus we must put aside everything, without cultivating, without controlling. Let go of the six forms of consciousness, without cultivating, without doing. Let it go its own way freely, and rest peacefully in the enlightened inherent nature. This is the great samadhi of abiding in inherent nature.

"In our daily activities, we must recognize clearly that all those manifestations in the world are all fundamentally there in that enlightened inherent nature. They are like scenes in a dream, they are inherent in the inherent true nature. The world of feelings, the material world, the samsara and nirvana which appear with the three planes of existence—these are all nothing but the play of the illusory transformations of the enlightened inherent nature. They are like all the images that appear in a kaleidoscope, like all the light rays refracted in a crystal. They all come from the inherent essence. There are not more of them if we work hard, nor fewer of them if we slack off. They form in the natural course of things, and do not depend on being deliberately created.

"That original essential empty inherent nature is changeless. The essential enlightened inherent nature is bright and empty and inherently pure, and its functioning makes everything appear. The realm of form, the realm of desire, the formless realm, birth and death, samsara, nirvana — these are all the playful manifestations of that inherent essence. They are like the apparitions that a magician conjures up: empty and illusory and without reality. If we seek their basic substance, it cannot be found. The apparent and the empty are not two. Those who understand this truth understand the realm of Vajradhara. It cuts off thinking and departs from words. It has no gain and no loss, no transformation, no up or down, no good or bad, no inside or outside, none of the external manifestations projected by the discriminating mind. Everything that appears goes beyond thinking and talking. It leaves far behind the four positions of nihilism and eternalism and being and nothingness. Even this talk of being inherent is just setting up a provisional term; it is not really existent.

"If you understand the truths explained above, then you must wake up here and now: preserve it in the original enlightened inherent nature, preserve it in the original fundamental purity, preserve it apart from words and thoughts, preserve it in the original ultimate, and in the end you will find liberation."

Sukhasiddhi also said: "You should just cultivate this kind of visualization, and when you realize that there is no duality between this spirit temple and the Buddha Land, I will come and seek you out."

Having finished speaking, she went away.

11 The Genuine Tutelary Deity

I had been at the spirit temple working as an attendant for nearly a year. Only a few people knew this experience of mine. From that servant called Bapu, I learned what patience is, what the true mind without discrimination is, what it means to offer up body, mouth, and mind, and what genuine esoteric practice is. No one knew Bapu's original social status. Bapu himself had even forgotten that he used to be a king. He was able to smile courteously through all the loud insistent orders from the women who were his bosses, and he was able to introduce the special points of each of the temple prostitutes in a very natural manner to the clients. Many times he even washed out the chamber pots for the temple prostitutes, washed their feet, and even washed out their menstrual cloths. While doing this work, Bapu showed the same sincerity and engagement as when he was practising meditation in the middle of the night. In his eyes, there was no longer any high or low, no longer any coming out of meditative concentration or going into meditative concentration. Toward everything, his attention was that focused. With his real behavior, he was telling me what genuinely cultivating practice is.

Speaking in the strict sense of the word, Bapu had become my tutelary deity for my practice. In daily life, Bapu was my model. When I took all forms, without clinging to them and without rejecting them, and fused them into the empty inherent nature, I no longer had clingings or attachments. Gradually I discovered that many pains and vexations were, in fact, the discriminating mind making trouble. Because the discriminating mind was there, there was greed, there was hatred, there was ignorance, there was vexation. However, although I clearly understood this in theory, in actual fact, I still was not able to control my own mind freely. Whenever I heard the soft voices and lewd talk of those temple prostitutes, my mind would lose its tranquility.

In my long life, my experience in the spirit temple was only one short year, but that year was the year I gained the most, because Bapu through his real actions told me how to cultivate practice. The business of the temple prostitutes was mostly in the evening, and Bapu and I went to sleep very late. The next morning, while the temple prostitutes were still in dreamland, the people who came to worship at the spirit temple would arrive: some for early lessons, and some to make offerings. Therefore, it was very hard for me to spend great stretches of time sitting in meditation, as I had done before. I could only cultivate contemplation at the same time as I was doing various chores. In this way, I developed the good habit of cultivating contemplation in the midst of ordinary activities. I preserved this habit my whole life long. Some people are always praising me for my great accomplishments. But they do not know that I benefited from this cultivation in the midst of ordinary activities, because no matter what I was doing, whether walking, standing, sitting, or lying down, in reality I would never depart from contemplating this empty inherent nature that I had witnessed. In my lifetime, beginning from when I was thirty years old and first met Sukhasiddhi, I have had a least a hundred years of dedicated practice time. On the other hand, even if he meets an enlightened teacher and awakens to empty inherent nature, the average person will have, apart from sleeping and eating and work and so on, no more than twenty or thirty years of time that is really used for dedicated practice.

Bapu's departure was something that occurred half a year after I arrived at the spirit temple. The story of his leaving has been disseminated very widely. The sequence of events was approximately like this. One night, a certain high official who had come to the spirit temple and was staying the night, got up in the night and discovered that there was a red light behind the building, shining up into the sky. He was amazed and went to take a look. He saw his former monarch there, and he also saw twelve beautiful dakinis surrounding him. He told the woman who was in charge of the spirit temple about this, and she realized, at last, that this servant she had been making use of was the former king. What surprised her even more was that this king had actually experienced the achievement of the Great Mudra.

The next day Bapu left without saying goodbye. No one knew where he had gone. Later on, when I held a ceremonial offering on an unprecedented scale, Bapu and Luipa came to give offerings. We just looked at each other and smiled. The situation was very much like what happened at the meeting on Spirit Peak, when Sakyamuni and Kashyapa smiled at each other.

Half a year later, Sukhasiddhi took me out of the temple. She had just sold me for one year. By that time I had taken the spirit temple's liberating intent as the tutelary deity's mandala. My discriminating mind was much lighter than before, but compared to Bapu, I still had a long way to go, because Bapu no longer needed deliberate intent. In Bapu's eyes, the tutelary deity's mandala and the brothel were truly not two different things.

12 Genuine Provisions

After Sukhasiddhi took me out of the temple, she transmitted the teaching to me.

As for the content of the teaching Sukhasiddhi transmitted to me, there are also many various stories. Some say she empowered me with the two procedures for giving rise to enlightenment and for completing enlightenment, and she passed these on to me with her physical presence. With the wisdom of the bliss of emptiness, she helped her disciple achieve the Path. This is the story that is cited in your book *The Great Mudra: The Heart of Real Cultivation*.

In fact, this time in the Sandalwood Forest, Sukhasiddhi just empowered me with the two procedures for giving rise to enlightenment and for completing enlightenment with the Diamond of Joy. Her acting as the Mudra Mother to me was something that happened later. This is because the first time I went to India, if Sukhasiddhi had helped me with her physical presence, then I certainly would have been able to awaken to the Path, and the process of my subsequent search might not have been so difficult. But because of my own special causal conditions, I still had to keep on developing.

According to the story that has been in circulation for the past thousand years, Sukhasiddhi acted as the Mudra Mother for me for more than ten years. But during the time I was seeking my teacher Niguma, and during the time I was seeking the Dharma after meeting Niguma, it seems I was definitely not accompanied by Sukhasiddhi. The reason is that, when Sukhasiddhi first transmitted the teaching to me, she only gave me the empowerment of the Diamond of Joy. Her acting as Mudra Mother for me and teaching me Sukhasiddhi's Six Methods were events that happened after I met Niguma.

Sukhasiddhi said to me: "Of course I could also show you the inherent nature of mind, but looking at this from the point of view of the chain of causal conditions, that is something that will be accomplished by another teacher. She is call Niguma. After you meet that great teacher, I will be able to add support for you with the wisdom of the bliss of emptiness, and help you attain enlightenment."

As soon as I heard the name Niguma, I burst into tears. I cried and fell to my knees and asked: "Where is she?"

Sukhasiddhi said: "Though I know where she is, now you two still do not have the causal conditions to meet each other. You have to store up provisions first."

I asked: "Teacher, what do you mean when you say 'provisions' ?"

Sukhasiddhi said: "The mind of faith!"

Not understanding, I asked: "Can it be that my present mind of faith is not yet sufficient?"

Sukhasiddhi said: "Your present mind of faith can only receive the general esoteric teaching. If you want to comprehend a teaching like the *Five Great Diamonds Teachings of Niguma*, I suspect it is still not sufficient. To receive the milk of the lion you must be a superior vessel. Although you have a great enough causal connection, you still have to polish your mind's inherent nature. Now you can go on to Rajgir. Go to find a virtuous teacher called Maitripa and seek from him the thirteen Mahakalas (protectors of the Dharma). After you complete this teaching, you will have unlimited wealth and power, and it will benefit your work."

Sukhasiddhi took the gold I had previously donated to her and gave it back to me, saying she could not longer use such things, and if I took it, I could offer it to those teachers who valued it. Later, she laughed at herself and said: "If those people really still care about gold, are they fit to be your teacher? However, sometimes the gold can show your sincerity, so go ahead and take it with you. Remember, you must consistently pray to me, because the karmic link between us is very deep."

She also said: "You already made an offering to me of your body, mouth, and mind. Your life is mine. I am relatively pleased with this journey of yours to the spirit temple. Though it did not enable you to experience ultimate enlightenment, for yourself, it is wealth that you will not be able to use up in this life. Later on, when I have no money to spend, I still might sell you."

I said a tearful goodbye to Sukhasiddhi, and headed off for Rajgir.

Chapter 15

Tasting Rajgir

1 Causal Conditions of Rajgir

Rajgir is ninety kilometers from Bodh Gaya. It is surrounded by hills and has a pleasant natural landscape. Khyungpo Naljor knew that Rajgir held a highly honored place in Buddhist history. The first place the Buddha went to cultivate the Path after he left the royal palace was in Rajgir. At that time, he was learning meditative concentration with two old teachers. One was called Alara Kalama, and one was called Uddaka Ramaputta. Both men were famous at the time as meditation teachers. When Sakyamuni was first cultivating the Path, he practiced meditative concentration with these two men for many years. Although he entered into deep concentration, joyous and peaceful, there were still vexations in his mind, and he had no way to dispel his doubts, so he was thinking of leaving. In the Pali Canon, in the twenty-sixth text of the *Majjhima Nikaya (Collection of Medium-Length Discourses)*, it vividly relates the Buddha's thought process: "O Bhikshus, my mind suddenly gave rise to the following thought: 'This teaching can only reach the state that is neither consciousness nor unconsciousness, but it cannot lead to detachment, to the state without desire, to stopping and resting, to quietude, to the power of wisdom, to supreme wisdom, or to nirvana.' Thus, O Bhikshus, I cannot keep believing in this teaching, and I am not willing to serve this teaching, and so I am leaving here to continue my journey."

When Buddha was in Rajgir, he discovered something that influenced the progress of Buddhism. One day when he was begging in the city, he met the king of Magadha, King Bimbisara. The king saw the impressive dignity of the young Siddhartha, and developed the highest faith in him. He wanted Siddhartha to stop cultivating practice, and to rule the kingdom with him. He was willing to donate half the land in the kingdom to him. Siddhartha refused. The king then hoped that, after Siddhartha experienced enlightenment, he would come to Rajgir to spread the teaching. Several years later, the Buddha brought his followers, who by then numbered over a thousand, to Rajgir, and King Bimbisara became the greatest patron of the Buddhist community. At that time all the offerings that the monastic community received throughout the year were furnished by the king. With his protection and support, Buddhism became the most powerful of the newly arisen religions.

It was mostly flat land as he journeyed along, but when he came to the hills surrounding Rajgir, Khyungpo Naljor's feelings were changed. He saw that this royal city, Rajgir, was truly an excellent place for spreading the Dharma. Just from the point of view of its geomantic

356 *Chapter 15 Tasting Rajgir*

quality, Rajgir had an unusual topography. Outside the city was the Spirit Vulture Hill, and it was here that Buddha set forth the *Lotus Sutra* and the *Surangama Sutra* and other famous Mahayana sutras. On the mountain there were many caves used by those cultivating the Path: holy men like Mahakashyapa and Shariputra and Mahamaudgalyayana and others all practiced meditative concentration in the mountain caves.

The story goes that while Buddha was in the world, almost all of the famous religions of India at that time gathered in Rajgir, like Brahmanism and Jainism and so on. In Rajgir they had a suitably large territory.

According to what is recorded in the sutras, after Buddha first set the wheel of the Dharma turning in sarnath (the Deer Park), he accepted as followers the three Kashyapa brothers, who together had a thousand disciples. Later Buddha brought these thousand or more disciples to Rajgir, where they received King Bimbisara's warm welcome and support. The Buddhist monks then began to spread the teaching in Rajgir. One day a man called Shariputra discover an honored one called Assaji. The honored one was exceptionally dignified, and his six senses were tamed, so that for him movement and stillness were one. Shariputra felt joy in his heart, and asked Assaji who his teacher was. The honored one Assaji told Shariputra what teacher he had relied on, and he chanted a verse:

All phenomena arise from causal conditions

All phenomena perish through causal conditions

My teacher the great Shramana

Always said this

When Shariputra heard this, his eye for the truth was cleansed, and he detached from all sensory defilements, and joy arose in his mind. Together with his good friend Mahamaudgalyayana, they took refuge with the Buddha, and became the Buddha's right-hand men.

With this causal basis, Maitripa thought Khyungpo Naljor's arrival was an especially excellent causal condition, and he gave him a prediction of enlightenment, saying that, among his disciples, Khyungpo Naljor would become a person like Shariputra, and that he was certain to take his teaching and spread it. Khyungpo Naljor presented Maitripa with two gold ritual objects: one weighed thirteen ounces, and one weighed seven ounces. Maitripa was very happy and asked Khyungpo Naljor what teaching he was seeking. Khyungpo Naljor said: "I have sought many teachings on the tutelary deity, but not many in the category of methods to protect the Dharma. This time I am seeking a method to protect the Dharma, but not a worldly one. It should enable me to attain the ultimate benefit that is both worldly and world-transcending: while I am alive, I will be able to get its protection, and have limitless wealth and power to aid my mission. When I am reborn, it will be able to accompany me, so we can go to the Buddha Land together."

Maitripa said: "So then, I will teach you the thirteen Mahakalas who protect the Dharma."

After Maitripa passed on the teaching to Khyungpo Naljor, Maitripa spent thirteen days to practise self-confinement with him, and Khyungpo Naljor achieved accord and saw the tutelary deities. After this, the Mahakalas were like a shadow that never left him and helped him achieve countless meritorious deeds.

2 The Bamboo Forest Monastery and the Murderous Demon King

After they came out from the self-confinement, Maitripa assigned one of his disciples to accompany Khyungpo Naljor around Rajgir for several days. Khyungpo Naljor discovered that this city is very strange: there are two cities. When he asked the reason for this, someone gave him an introduction, telling him that originally there was just a single one. In the city they produced lemon grass that was used for cushions at ceremonial sacrifices, and so the city was called Kusagrapura. Because it was surrounded by hills on all sides, in the basin where the city was located, the grass easily caught fire, and there were frequent fires in the city. Often when a house caught fire, it spread through the whole neighborhood. King Bimbisara issued an order that henceforth, if anyone's house caught fire, then the family would have to move to the forest on the outskirts of the city that was used for laying the dead to rest. No one anticipated that not long after this edict was issued, the palace itself would be the first building to catch fire. King Bimbisara then moved out of the palace, built another city in the cold forests on the outskirts of the city, and settled there. This was how there came to be two cities.

Khyungpo Naljor also took a tour of the Bamboo Forest Monastery that is famous in Buddhist history. Here the Buddha expounded many truths. The Bamboo Forest Monastery (Venuvana) was built through the patronage of a rich and powerful man called Karanda, and so it was also called Karanda Monastery. The Bamboo Forest Monastery was built in the dense forest and was very peaceful and still, which was good for practising meditative concentration. India has a rainy season of several months, and when the rainy season arrives, life is very inconvenient for those cultivating practice outside in the wilderness.

First, the roads are mired in mud, so it is not easy to go begging. Second, there are many insects on the roads, and it is easy to step on them and kill them. So after the Bamboo Forest Monastery came into being, the community of monks had a place to settle for the summer retreat.

In Buddhist history the Bamboo Forest Monastery is very famous, not only because the Buddha passed more than ten rainy seasons here, but also because at the time it created a controversy. In the Indian tradition, those cultivating the Path had to practice austerities, and those practising austerities had to live outdoors and could not live in houses. Practitioners mostly lived under big trees. To prevent practitioners from developing concerns about the trees, some religious sects went so far as to make it a rule that they could not spend three nights under the same tree. Thus, when the Buddha accepted the Bamboo Forest Monastery, it provoked attacks from some non-Buddhist ascetics, and he was bitterly reviled, and it was as if a black cloud hung over the city. Even more inconceivable, the Bamboo Forest Monastery not only provoked attacks from non-Buddhists, it also brought about a split in the community of Buddhist monks. The first split in the community of monks in Buddhist history had a definite connection to the Bamboo Forest Monastery. The origin of this event was that Devadatta wanted to seize the leadership of Buddhism, and he met with the Buddha's rebuke. The artful character of the Buddha's rebuke is recorded in the *Samyuktagama Sutra* in the Buddhist Canon. This is what it says: "The fruit of the banana trees died, and so did the reeds. The donkeys got pregnant and died, the gentlemen lost themselves in greed. Their normal actions were not righteous actions, they knew a lot but did not avoid being foolish. Good things decreased by the day, the stems dried up and the roots also perished." The Buddha meant that usually there is no good way out for self-satisfied and greedy people.

After being rebuked by the Buddha, Devadatta began to split the community of monks. He and his followers were determined not to stay in the Bamboo Forest Monastery. Instead, they practiced five austerities. Throughout their lives, they wore filthy clothes. Throughout their lives, they always begged for their food. Throughout their lives, they made it their practice to eat only once a day. Throughout their lives, they lived outdoors. Throughout their lives, they did not eat fish or meat or salt or vinegar or milk and so on. Many followed Devadatta, and according to the accounts there were six groups of monks. In the traditional Buddhist account, Devadatta met with an evil payback, and he was reborn in hell. But in real life, for a thousand years there continued to be people who believed in him. When the great Master Xuanzang went to India to seek the Dharma in the seventh century, he still saw people who believed in Devadatta. We can see the tenacity of his life force.

Devadatta's great power originated when King Ajatasattu took power. He was originally King Bimbisara's crown prince. Before Ajatasattu came into the world, King Bimbisara has received a prediction that he would die at the hands of one of his own sons. Later on Prince Ajatasattu did indeed collude with Devadatta, and imprisoned King Bimbisara in a stone cell. After starving his father to death, King Ajatasattu supported Devadatta, and the first great split appeared in the community of Buddhist monks.

When he was visiting the Spirit Vulture Hill, Khyungpo Naljor saw that stone cell where King Bimbisara had been imprisoned. The stone cell was not very big, and iron rings which had been used to shackle King Bimbisara were embedded in the walls. Outside the cell, there was a fair-sized ball field. Around the sides of the field was a stone wall foundation, and the wall was quite thick, about four or five feet. It was obvious that in those days it had been unusually solid and strong. When King Bimbisara, who had been so powerful, was imprisoned in that small stone cell, his son was determined to starve him to death. Luckily, Bimbisara's wife would always rub cream on her body after she bathed (to feed to Bimbisara when she visited him), to enable him to survive for a few more days.

Amid the endless vicissitudes of life, I see King Bimbisara in the stone cell. He is as thin as a stick, his face is as yellow as wax, and tears are flowing down his few wisps of beard. He could not have anticipated that the son whom he loved so deeply could have become the greatest adverse factor in his fate. He could not have thought that, despite all the charitable offerings he had made on such a wide scale, he would still be unable to escape that fearful prediction. But he was still very content, because he could look through the window in the stone cell and see the Buddha coming down from the Spirit Vulture Hill to go begging for food. Seen from afar, the Buddha's body, which was actually big and strong, appeared very small. When King Bimbisara caught sight of that figure, a wave of cool purity would wash across his mind. During his final period of imprisonment in the stone cell, it was the Buddha's words of wisdom that gave tranquility to King Bimbisara's spirit. He understood clearly that no matter how perilous the external scene before his eyes, in the end this would become the past. He did not even hate his son. He only hoped that at some point his son would wake up and support Buddha, as Bimbisara himself had done before.

The story goes that the one who suffered more than King Bimbisara himself was his queen. She was caught between her husband and her son, and death seemed preferable to life. Later on, in order to free her from her suffering, Buddha communicated to her the *Sutra of the Visualizations of the Buddha of Infinite Life* and the *Nirvana Sutra*.

"Ajatasattu" means "unborn enemy, the one without enemies." From the time Ajatasattu was born onward, he seemed to be opposed to his father. His father believed in Buddhism; he believed in Jainism. Later, out of political considerations, he collaborated with Devadatta. After starving his father to death, King Ajatasattu supported Devadatta and provided him with a large quantity of offerings. Some monks turned their backs on the Buddha, for the sake of material gain, and turned toward Devadatta.

Perhaps that was the first great crisis the Buddhist teaching faced after its founding. At the time, the Buddha pacified his disciples, telling them that not to dispute right and wrong is liberation, and telling them to cultivate their practice well.

In the cave on the Hill, absorbed in meditative concentration, the Buddha was solid as a mountain. The story goes that one day Devadatta discovered where the Buddha was meditating, and he pushed down a huge rock (intending to kill him), which made an abrasion on the Buddha's foot. This action, like the evil deed he committed when he beat the nun Uppalavannā to death, became one of the reasons that Devadatta fell into uninterrupted hell.

Even a man as great as the Buddha could ultimately encounter such great adverse circumstances: we can see the dangerous evil of the human mind. But at the same time, it was precisely the existence of an evil follower like Devadatta that highlights the greatness of the Buddha's character.

After Khyungpo Naljor's visit was over, as he was going down from the Spirit Vulture Hill, the spirit dove again caught up with him.

3 Curses from Far in the Past

Dearly beloved Khyungpo Ba, please allow me to keep this ceremony of deeply loving you and respecting you. When you are not by my side, I must write letters to you.

One evening Kumari took me to that sorcery mandala. The sorcery mandala is in a mountain valley, and is very well hidden. There is a dark wind blowing there, and strange jagged rock — it is very frightening. When I say frightening, I do not only mean the place, but even more, the atmosphere. Amid the smoke and flames, the sorcerers took that image with symbolizes your life and placed it in the fire to burn. They threw animal fat into the fire, and the fire sizzled and gave out puffs of dense smoke. Kumari says that this animal fat was taken from the body of a black dog, and the story goes that this can increase the power of the curses.

After they burn the fat from the black dog, the sorcerers also throw black plant materials into the fire. They use poisoned needles to pierce that image, and chant evil spells.

Kumari says that when the laying down of the curses is completed, on a moonless night the sorcerers will take the image and send it to where the female demon called Mamu lives. This will symbolize that from this point on your soul will belong to that female demon, and that in the human world you will go mad.

I am very worried.

That dakini called Bandi has not come back. I sought out several yoga masters, and when they heard of those curses from your opponents, none of them would dare to attempt to avert them. This is because if their strength cannot prevail over the other side, the power of those curses would fall entirely on them. They are very fearful, and they said that the kind of curses which your opponents are using are come from the distant past.

To remove these evil curses, I went to Pashupatinath Temple. This temple was built by the water, and it goes higher and higher and is very magnificent. It is dedicated to the god Shiva. There are three eyes on Shiva's head, and in his hand he holds a steel trident, and a poisonous cobra is wrapped around his neck. In one body he combines creation, preservation, and destruction; his spiritual powers are vast, and there is nothing he cannot do. Representing you, I entered the sacred river and performed a sacred ablution, and on your behalf I washed away all the karmic barriers from past lives. I think that no matter what kind of power your opponents' evil curses have, if you yourself have no karmic barriers, they won't be able to do anything to you. Do you think this is right?

In Pashupatinath Temple, the thing that will be the most impossible for me to forget is the platform for burning corpses on the west bank of the river. Many people bring corpses and give them their final sacred washing there. Then they proceed with the transformation by fire. I got washed in the water of the sacred river along with those dead people. I fell into a reverie of random thoughts and kept sighing and sighing. I don't know whether or not, before I was waiting for you, I would have become one of those dead people being washed.

Besides worrying about you, there is something else that is depressing me: the wisdom and the freedom that I have been seeking all along are ultimately so vulnerable when I am in front of you. If I still had a bit of intelligence, a little spiritual beauty, it has already been shattered into a self-justifying, stupidly ridiculous detail. My independence has already been taken away "emotionally" by you, because when I am facing you, I no longer have a choice. Ultimately, what is this? I do not understand it.

My feeling for you, when I am writing these letters, is even more respectful. I am writing to an imaginary lover, and I can quietly and calmly love you. But the moment I think of your image, then I lose my self-control, and my heart leaps up and my ears burn. At that instant a burning force hits me, and I have no way to save myself, and I almost suffocate.

Starting now, I no longer need to think, I no longer need to be independent, I want you to decide everything. Even if I sink down and become a beggar, I still will not care, because I am your woman.

Starting tomorrow, I must do my lessons, look at all kinds of books, books I never thought were worth reading before. I will read about how to take care of my skin, how to cook, how to put on make up, and so on and so forth. I will have to learn from those dance masters how to act more elegant and refined. For me, this is simply a matter of completely reshaping myself, of remaking how I act as a person. This is being a woman. But if this were known to my female friends, they would surely fall down laughing! Is this still Sharwadi, the female spirit?

I am not clear about what is happening after all. Since I met Khyungpo Ba, my world is being torn down and rebuilt, rebuilt as a world that belongs only to two people, Khyungpo

Ba and Sharwadi.

　　Now sleeping has become my big task. I must do all I can to get more rest. After you come back, I cannot have you seeing a sallow-faced old lady. I just hope that at that time Sharwadi will still be a honeymoon bride, bashful and pretty.

　　Over the past year my heart has been overflowing with a longing so thick it cannot be relieved. One day in heaven, a thousand years in the human realm. I've been in a trance thinking back on you and me in the red dusts of the senses. Those companions of the spirit immortals have encountered the jealousy of the heavenly spirits and been demoted to the ordinary world, and have already become an ordinary couple. As they look at each other and smile, it is that ordinary, worldly, compassionate feeling warming their hearts. Khyungpo Ba, promise me, promise this intimate friend who really loves you so much and aches for you, that you will no longer be a monk practising austerities, that you will no longer stand in the snow at the Buddha's door practising in solitude with a single lamp, that you will not go off for such a long time on your search. It will be much better to stay home. When you come back, you will have a beautiful wife by your side tending to you, you will have intelligent sons and daughters happily playing around you. What else is there to seek in this life? If you want to cultivate practice, then cultivate practice. If you don't want to cultivate practice, then keep your family company. Whether or not you are a great accomplished teacher, whether or not you spread the teaching — what importance does this have? Simple food and clothing is best for being clear-eyed and nurturing the mind. As long as the whole family is harmonious and happy and peaceful all year round—this is better than anything. When the Buddha and ancestral teachers see this, they will bless us and they will say: Khyungpo Ba, go back to your family!

Does what Sharwadi says sound sweet? While you are happy, you quickly misunderstand. Be sure not to get angry, be sure to forgive me. That day I was thinking of you too much, and my feelings were out of control, and on the back of the image of Shiva where nobody would notice, I inscribed the words "Sharwadi loves Khyungpo Ba." After I wrote this, I felt guilty. But it was alright: around there, people in general would not care. But if anyone saw this, they would know that this was a trace left by me. This would add to your troubles. My good husband, forgive Sharwadi, she loves you to the point of acting silly.

Husband, are you angry? Don't get angry, okay? Sharwadi apologizes to you. Laugh it off, okay? You're not laughing? So how would you say I should be punished? In fact, Sharwadi has already laid down her arms and surrendered. Though we ourselves are pure as jade, actually in my mind, I have already offered up all the lands and cities, and even my body and mind are Khyungpo Ba's. So what could I receive the punishment with? Really, do not get angry. For women to love you is something very ordinary. If you think it over, you will not get very annoyed. It would be best to let them look at you, to let them to rise together and follow you—that might be interesting. Look at yourself, look at yourself—are you really looking so unhappy? Sharwadi will first slip away, and then come back after your anger has dissipated.

Finally, I want to tell you one more thing. Those sorcerers are still working on the fire god magic. The story goes that they are using an evil ritual to send at you a great evil demon who can control fire. You must keep alert, and when you go to sleep at night, do not sleep too deeply. Do not close the doors and windows too tight. It would be best to always keep a bucket of water in your room. Before you go to sleep, be sure to put out any open flames, because no matter how evil the fire god is, it must depend on open flames in the human realm as the seed or the causal basis. Only then can it exercise its own evil magical power.

Ah, ever since she was with you, Sharwadi's heart has been choking her with anxiety.

4 Noisy Feelings

My dear Sharwadi, your feelings are unrestrained and reveal the mysteries of love. I am happy, but I still cannot come to you. How could I blame you? Let those words go forever: they are evidence of our love for each other.

After I did meditation practice in the morning, when I read your letter, I could not repress my feelings. I want to write you a letter. There is nothing to be done about it: at this moment, this letter must flow out. I tried to block it several times, but I could not suppress its surging force, and all I can do is go along with it. There is nothing I can do about it. You see how, at certain times, fate takes control of me and compels me to do things that were not determined by my life plan.

From the time I met you until now, I have been immersed in the poetic sense of life and I have become completely intoxicated. Indeed, following my own expressed desires, I have said some things I had to say. Because I have set out on the journey of seeking, I have little time to record my own actions. If I were not writing these things when I want to talk with you, there would really be almost no one in this world who could understand me.

In my memory, it seems I have undergone very few hardships, really. Except for the great impetus that my father's death gave me, and the austerities I had to practice before I was a Bonpo teaching master, in reality I have experienced the joys of cultivating practice and seeking truth. Thus, even though your heart aches for me, what in the eyes of people in general are painful troubles, are to me things to enjoy. Do you understand?

Loneliness is really there. There is nothing to do about it. When you climb a high peak alone, and there is nobody to be seen in any direction, and you discover a black cloud covering the moon, you are sure to feel the vastness of the universe and the smallness of humankind. Truly, I feel a loneliness that penetrates to the marrow. This is an extraordinarily lucid loneliness, or an extraordinarily lonely lucidity. Though I do not want to be lonely, this is something I cannot do anything about. It is as if, after I open my eyes, I can never again make that light of the mind and spirit vanish. My clear understanding makes me have a different kind of viewpoint when I look at the world. Everything in the human realm has become a dreamlike illusion, and I myself am always dissolved in the light of that dreamlike illusion. That silence and solitude gives me a unique wisdom. In the many years I have experienced human life, for me the wisdom of mind has never been covered by the trash of temporary fashions.

But I did not anticipate that, after I met you, I would in the end still be controlled by these insistent emotional feelings. Although I always use contemplation and reciting mantras to drive them away, in my mind there is always a kind of dark surging passion sweeping through. Many times I even welcome it with surprise and joy. This is because I understand that, when I take this passion and extend it to all humankind or all sentient beings, my cultivation of practice will then take on another coloration. Perhaps this is another benevolent gift to me from fate. Even more likely, you are sent from heaven above. Heaven sent you to provide me with a different kind of redemption.

I never could think through why I could fall in love with you. From the ordinary worldly point of view, this is really difficult to understand. At this moment, as I am thinking of you, it is still passion surging, and it cannot stop itself. I am not clear about how, ultimately, this female spirit, more holy than any sacred image, can move me. All I can do is trace it back to a karmic connection, or to fate controlling me. Other than this, I truly cannot explain it. This is because I have met so many beautiful women, but I was always able to restrain myself. But after I met you, unexpectedly my spirit was turned upside down. I think I was struck by the true sincerity and goodness and genuineness on your face. Your person has a life force and a pervasive goodness which cannot be artificially simulated. In this world filled with desires and hope, it is very rare to see a woman with such radiance. Of course, this is not to say that you are not of this world. Before you met me, you could have done these things very successfully. But I believe that, at least in the time and place in life that we met each other, you have given me complete sincerity and love. This is enough. It is not important how far you and I go after this. Often, what can affect us, and affect the world, is in fact just a few details, nothing more.

I also want to tell you: you are a world, you are a world that can nourish my spirit this way. You must not lose yourself. You must not let that Sharwadi with such great energy dissolve into an ordinary Nepalese woman. You must understand that what you brought to me, besides that intoxicating poetic feeling, was all the information about that world you inhabit. Your appearance and your contact with me may become a key opportunity that turned me toward another world. This is because the people of Nepal and the people of India are humans and, like all humans, they face afflictions and ignorance, they need cool clarity, they need to be tolerant, they need to feel universal love, they need clear understanding and transcendence.

My Sharwadi, would you say this is correct?

I have truly been pleasantly surprised to be in love with you. You must understand that falling in love with a woman means truly developing a connection with her time and place and community, having concern and understanding, so that you can truly feel their spirit. Without you, in people's eyes I might have really become just the yoga master "Khyungpo." My love for you assures that it will be possible for me to go beyond that territory.

Would you say this is right?

I said to Khyungpo Naljor: "This letter of yours does not seem to match your religious practice. Before this, when you were working at the spirit temple, you already had a measure of meditative power. In this letter, how can you still have this emotional longing?"

Khyungpo Naljor gave a long sigh and said: "Son, this shows concretely the difficulty of cultivating practice. Cultivating practice is like heading upstream in a boat. If you do not go forward, then you fall back, or sometimes you go forward and sometimes you fall back. Even if you have reached the stages of the bodhisattvas, before you truly reach the eighth stage, the unmoving state, it is still possible to regress. The habit-energy of the ordinary world can always start operating. Clearing away that habit-energy is like peeling an onion: you peel away one layer, and there will still be another layer. Only if you keep on peeling layer after layer, will you be able to realize the final clearing away. In this world, there has never been an enlightened person who realized the final result from a single awakening. Awakening is just going in the door, just discovering the direction. The road after awakening is still very long. The genuine sages are the people who kept on following the true road. Do you understand? Do not dislike my letter for going on too long, and do not dislike it for not having that kind of ferocious wisdom that you were expecting.

"You must understand that, even if a person clearly understands, that person must truly put that 'understanding' into practice, and this still requires a process of hard work and refinement. Those people addicted to smoking who have understood the danger of smoking, all still find it very difficult to stop smoking. It is not that they do not want to stop, it's that their bodies will not obey them. In the same way, even though I had been through that process of refinement in the spirit temple, I still had not penetrated through that word 'emotion.' In this world, the hardest thing to break through is the 'barrier of emotion.' That's why the ancients said, it is hard for a hero to pass through the barrier of beautiful women."

5 Mahakashyapa's Pipphali Cave

Khyungpo Naljor met with another great teaching master on a mountain called Pipphali.

At the foot of the mountain, there was a famous warm spring. The water from the spring was rich in minerals and could cure rheumatoid arthritis. According to the story, the Buddha had cured the inflammation in his joints in this warm spring. The historical Buddha did get sick: besides inflammation of the joints, he was troubled by back pain throughout his life. The story goes that these two ailments were brought about by sitting in meditation. That back pain, like sickness of the cervical vertebra or the thoracic vertebra, arises from long periods of sitting quietly. In the *Agama Sutra* we can see Buddha saying, "Ananda, my back hurts." Whenever I read this material, my eyes fill with tears. In my eyes, the Buddha is the enlightened one. Whether or not he had back pain, he could never turn back from enlightenment to delusion. What we respect and honor is precisely that enlightenment of his.

Even now there are some deluded people who lose faith whenever they read or hear that people of great virtue get sick. They do not know that the reason people of great virtue are called "great" is because of their superior human character and their enlightened minds. Although they have realized wisdom, their physical bodies are still made of the physical elements, and the physical elements can still get out of order, and the physical body can get sick. But the enlightenment which they have realized does not turn back to illusion and chaos just because they get sick. Thus, we cannot lose faith just because the Buddha once cured his arthritis in this warm spring.

Khyungpo Naljoralso bathed in the warm spring. As the warm spring water washed over him, it dissolved away the fatigue of the journey. When he thought that the Buddha had once washed in this same pond, Khyungpo Naljor felt an immense joy.

All through his journey, whenever he talked of Rajgir, what the Indians brought up was not that it was a place where the Buddha taught, but rather that it had this warm spring. The Buddha's achievements at Rajgir had been erased from the memory of the people of India. For Khyungpo Naljor, this was very hard to bear. But he understood that any particular time always gets blurred in the flood of the passing ages, and it is not because so many people muddle along that they are enshrined in history. Though the number of wise people is not necessarily great, their names are the most glorious in history.

After he bathed, Khyungpo Naljor went up the mountain. He wanted to go to a mountain cave called Pipphali, to pay his respects to a great virtuous one who practiced there in secret. He was called Bäpä Naljor.

He was the inheritor and preserver of the teachings of the five Venerable Ones of Mercy and the teachings of the red dakinis and white dakinis. According to accounts, the mountain cave was the place where Mahakashyapa had practised meditation when he was young. Mahakashyapa was one of the Buddha's ten great disciples. His original name was Pipphali, so the mountain cave had been given this name. Mahakashyapa had been born into a wealthy, high-ranking family. From his early years onward, he was determined to leave home and wholeheartedly seek liberation. He obeyed his parents' command and got married, but afterwards both he and his wife were intent on pure cultivation and did not engage in the ordinary pleasures. Later, they made an agreement to leave home. So Mahakashyapa engaged in pure practice in this mountain cave for many years. Later, he encountered the Buddha and awakened to the correct Path. He brought the woman who had been his wife when they were in lay life into the community of monastics, and they realized the results of becoming arhats.

Khyungpo Naljor had always had great respect for Mahakashyapa. Mahakashyapa was acclaimed as the number one ascetic. All through his life, he upheld the practice of being a mendicant monk: he lived outdoors among the burial mounds, he wore rags, he only ate once a day. Because of his long years of practising austerities, Mahakashyapa looked shabby, and he often met with mockery from the younger monks. Whenever the Buddha heard such talk, he would always praise Mahakashyapa. Mahakashyapa was someone who quietly put Buddhism into practice. He was not good at socializing, and his whole life he lived simply, apart from the crowd, specializing in pure practice, and winning reverence that has lasted down through the ages.

Bäpä Naljor also liked to live simply apart from society, but he still showed great joy when Khyungpo Naljor arrived. He said that Khyungpo Naljor was his disciple because of the karmic connection between them, and that he had been waiting for him all along. Khyungpo Naljor made him an offering of seven ounces of gold, and Bäpä Naljor then passed on to him the teaching of the five Venerable Ones of Mercy and the teachings of the red and white dakinis. These teachings later merged into the great ocean of wisdom of the Shangpa Kagyu school, and I myself became someone who received the benefit.

Later on Bäpä Naljor said to Khyungpo Naljor: "You have developed your mind very well, and you have studied widely in the holy teachings. But remember, pure cultivation is required for realizing enlightenment. From the perspective of the ultimate truth, the mind of enlightenment means loving sentient beings, the mind of detachment means detaching from human society, and the two do not contradict each other."

At the end, Bäpä Naljor recited a verse for Khyungpo Naljor:

Mahakashyapa comes back, carrying his begging bowl

He ascends the mountain alone

His body and mind are without fear

He cultivates meditative contemplation in all its purity.

Deep in the mountains there are no traces of people

The wild animals always gather

The flocks of birds soar in the sky

My mind is always joyous.

A person must live in solitude

And not become part of the crowd.

If we live in the crowd, our minds become vexed and confused

And it is hard to achieve pure wisdom.

Socializing with the worldly

We wear ourselves out in vain.

Once we know this intent

We take no joy in living with people.

Bäpä Naljor said: "This verse was composed by Mahakashyapa.

It was only because Mahakashyapa engaged in pure practice his whole life long, and accumulated real power, that he had the ability to complete the first assembly of Buddhist scriptures."

After teacher and disciple came out of Pipphali cave, they continued up the mountain. There were many small temples on the mountain, colored grey and white, and built very simply. Most of the practitioners in them went naked: they were believers in Jainism. In the Jain religion there was a sect called the sky-clad sect, which thought that they must abandon all worldly things, and that only after they truly arrived at a state with no concerns, would they be able to reach ultimate liberation. Clothing was, of course, among the things they abandoned. The Jain religion has a long history. The founder, Nirgrantha, lived in the same era as the Buddha, and once received the Buddha's praise. But in Rajgir, Jainism was the most important opponent of Buddhism and was respected by worldly people because it advocated asceticism. At that time the struggle between religions was very brutal, and the Buddha's great disciple Mahamaudgalyayana was stoned to death by naked Jains. The influence of Jainism continued through the centuries, and even today it still has a very great influence. When, during the Tang Dynasty, Master Xuanzang went to India to acquire Buddhist scriptures, he too made a pilgrimage to this mountain. At that time he also discovered that there were many small Jain temples on the mountain, and this is accordingly noted in his book *The Great Tang Record of the Western Regions*.

Khyungpo Naljor was always very respectful to the various religions. He thought that as long as they were good teachings, they were all worth respecting. When he entered those small Jain temples, he joined his palms together to convey his respect to the holy images in the shrines to which offerings were made.

6　The Vicissitudes of the Cave of the Chestnut Tree

Bäpä Naljor and Khyungpo Naljor again went up and then went down some stone steps, and they came to a level platform behind the mountain wall. The platform had a rectangular shape, and from it they could see the whole vast panorama of the scenery below the mountain.

Bäpä Naljor pointed out several caves on the right and said: "Can you guess what place this is?"

Khyungpo Naljor said: "Isn't this the Cave of the Chestnut Tree?"

He had already heard tell of the Cave of the Chestnut Tree. This was a renowned place: the first collection of Buddhist scriptures was put together in the Cave of the Chestnut Tree. But he hadn't dared to believe that the Cave of the Chestnut Tree would be this run-down. There was an evil stench of wet rot coming from the cave, and he could detect the faint smell of bat excrement.

Bäpä Naljor smiled with disappointment and said: "That's right, this is the Cave of the Chestnut Tree. See — worldly things truly are impermanent. This is the place that once was so famous. At that time, a thousand years ago, this place was filled with arhats. Now even the chestnut tree is gone, and bats are all that is left in the cave." His voice was filled with a thick sense of the vicissitudes of life.

Khyungpo Naljor seemed to have gone into a dream. He had read the *Agama Sutra*, and he knew that it was in the Cave of the Chestnut Tree that what would later be the *Agama Sutra* was put together. Although the *Agama Sutra* is considered a Hinayana scripture, Khyungpo Naljor had always liked its plainness. He knew that those who believed in the Hinayana teaching only accepted the *Agama Sutra*.

Bäpä Naljor said: "After the Buddha's death, some evil bhikshus, rejoicing in the tragedy, spitefully said: 'Before, we were rigorously controlled by this great monk. From now on, no one will control us anymore.' When Mahakashyapa heard them say this, he realized that the situation was very serious, and that if he continued to live alone, apart from the group, the Buddha's teaching would be ruined in the hands of these evil bhikshus. So he called together five hundred great arhats and, in the Cave of the Chestnut Tree, undertook the process of creating the first assembly of the sutras."

The first time the scriptures were assembled together, Ananda recited the sutras, Upali recited the disciplinary precepts, and they went through a process of being verified by the great arhats until there were no more doubtful points. Only then did they take a set form. The scriptures at that time were not in the form of written texts; they were just committed to memory by various great arhats, and then passed on to disciples via oral transmission.

The process of first assembling the scriptures took three months, and the expenses were covered by King Ajatasattu, the patricide who had changed his evil ways and returned to the correct Path.

As he stood in front of Cave of the Chestnut Tree, Khyungpo Naljor felt waves of emotion: he seemed to hear the sound of the arhats chanting the sutras. It seemed like a group of frogs croaking after a rainstorm. That was the clear cool sound of the true teaching, penetrating through the mists of history, resounding across several thousand years.

7 Bright Empty Naked Enlightened Inherent Nature

Bäpä Naljor concentrated on showing Khyungpo Naljor the enlightened inherent nature. He said:

"Though the treasury of Buddhist scriptures is as vast as the open sea, and comprises an immense number of books, if we get to its fundamental basis, it cannot be separated from empty inherent nature and enlightened wisdom.

"That enlightened inherent nature, as well as that empty inherent nature, is spontaneous wisdom, and is the basis of all phenomena.

"What is called enlightenment is just completely awakening to that clear enlightened inherent nature, revealed naked here and now. What is called revolving in birth and death is not understanding that clear empty enlightened inherent nature, generating ignorance with discriminating thought, so that when you miss the road it is hard to go back.

"All the images that appear in the ordinary world are not apart from the empty inherent nature: that empty stillness of objects and forms is the ultimate inner truth of the realm of reality. The essence of the enlightened inherent nature is like void. The four premises—nihilism, eternalism, being, nothingness—are all just wordplay, just sophistry, and we must detach from them. There is no difference between all forms and the enlightened inherent nature: they are fundamentally a single flavor, perfectly fused without obstruction. Even amid the tumult of the play of the myriad things and the myriad appearances, that unique enlightened inherent nature does not fluctuate in its great everywhere-equal presence. All the phenomena displayed by external objects are all the light of inherent enlightenment. You must clearly understand that in their basic substance they are unborn and undying. You must detach from the discriminating mind that diverges from it, and abandon the clinging mind that tries to grasp it. If there is no external seeking, and no internal ignorance, the enlightened true nature stands naked, and then there is no mind that can grasp it. You must understand that the enlightened true nature has no body, and is apart from words and thoughts. Although everything appears, it never wavers. You must understand that external objects are the essential body of mind, and the function of mind is external objects, and fundamentally the two are not separate. This is the only absolute meaning.

"Once we know that objects and mind are one flavor, and everything is the manifestation of spontaneous wisdom, then liberation and delusion are like waves on the water. When the waves are still, it's the water; when the water moves, it's the waves; waves and water are not one. Then we understand that liberation, in fact, is the play of inherent wisdom. All that is necessary is that motion and stillness not be two, that they do not depart from the empty inherent nature, that they do not depart from the realm of enlightenment, that objects and mind are not two, that there is no grasping and rejecting. Then we are spontaneously liberated.

"Twenty-four hours a day, whether you are walking or standing or sitting or lying down, you definitely must understand clearly that all phenomena are not apart from the enlightened inherent nature, that all appearances are the manifestations of the basic essence of the enlightened inherent nature. The enlightened inherent nature is like the ocean, and what appears is like the waves. From the essence arises the function: essence and function are not different. Whatever appears, it is all the manifestation of the basic essence of the enlightened inherent nature. The realm of desire, the realm of form, the formless realm, samsara, and nirvana are nothing but reflections projected by the enlightened inherent nature. Except for this enlightened inherent nature, there is nothing else to be found.

"The enlightened inherent nature has no beginning and no end, no arising and no extinction. Even when the cycle of birth and death has not yet been emptied, enlightened inherent nature is not changed in the least and has no birth or extinction. All you have to do is preserve that clear empty naked enlightened inherent nature; detach from clinging to subject and object; understand that the essential nature of the external objects you grasp at is basically empty and is just the manifestation of the enlightened inherent nature. You also have to understand clearly that the mind which can grasp is also empty; that so-called awakening of enlightened inherent nature is also ultimately unattainable. This way, you will detach from one-sided clinging and reach the point where subject and object are both empty: the differentiating mind dissolves along with them, and you are pure and clear as empty space. That kind of perception is very hard to describe in words; it goes beyond explanations and is far removed from verbalism; it has no birth and no extinction. Though we speak of enlightenment, even after so-called enlightenment, that enlightened inherent nature will not be increased by a person becoming enlightened or reduced by a person being deluded; it will not be increased by joy or decreased by sorrow. There is no difference in that enlightened inherent nature after the experience of enlightenment and before the experience of enlightenment; it is not increased in holy people or diminished in ordinary people.

"All in all, the enlightened inherent nature of the Great Mudra has no birth and no extinction. There is no reifying its forms, and no cultivating its inherent results. It is fundamentally pure, without defilement, not born and not destroyed, not increased and not decreased, fundamentally inherently present, not created by people. Though it has no inherent nature, it can create all kinds of wondrous qualities as necessary and create all kinds of realms as needed. It is perfectly merged with no obstructions, neither annihilated nor eternal. Its inherent quality is like void, vast and clear, totally boundless. Its essential nature is clear and empty and naked, like the great heart of

Vajradhara. It is very hard to describe it in words."

When Khyungpo Naljor was about to depart, Bäpä Naljor also said: "Nalanda Monastery is not far from here. If you are interested, you can go there. My friend Devi Dorje is there, and he is very wise. You won't be disappointed."

8 The Glory of Nalanda Monastery

Khyungpo Naljor left Rajgir, traveled north for one day, and arrived at Nalanda Monastery. Nalanda Monastery was at that time the most famous Buddhist university in India. It was a magnificent structure, very brilliant. When Khyungpo Naljor arrived at Nalanda Monastery, it had about two thousand teachers and over ten thousand monks. There were many schools of thought which coexisted and flourished together, and although there were debates, most were peaceful.

According to accounts, the basic intent of Nalanda was the notion of "giving lotuses," here the lotuses represent wisdom. Another story is that the meaning of the transliteration of "Nalanda" is "tireless generosity." It was the name of a king who liked to provide charity, and the monastery was named for this.

Kings through the ages had been very supportive of Nalanda Monastery, and had endowed it with a territory containing more than a hundred farming villages, from which it received the land revenue. Besides this, the kings had also ordered over two hundred of the surrounding villagers to provide for its daily needs. With this generous support, its monks did not need to go out begging, so they had time to do intensive study of Buddhist texts. Its scholarly atmosphere was famous far and near.

At that time, debate was still flourishing in India, and there were frequent debates among the various religious sects. Nalanda became a target for a lot of arrows. Even the monks who kept watch at the gates were good at debate, and those who came as challengers often could not get in the gate, and just fled.

In Nalanda Monastery there were many learned pandits, but Devi Dorje was very famous. Because he was both a learned pandit and an accomplished master, there were many who came to him to seek the Dharma.

Devi Dorje lived in the eastern area of the monastery. In the western area there was a forest with many stupas. Among them was the stupa of the Buddha's great disciple Shariputra. This was very close to Shariputra's home town, the village of Upatissa. The Venerable Mudgalyaya's home town Kolitha is also close to Nalanda Monastery. Some scholars think that Nalanda Monastery was gradually built up around the stupa of Shariputra.

Devi Dorje's dwelling place was very grand. Besides receiving large quantities of offerings from those seeking the Dharma, the monastery provided him every day with three measures of "rice for the great." This was a kind of large-grained rice that was specially offered to the king and the great virtuous ones. A grain of this rice was as large as a black bean, and it was very fragrant. All the teaching masters in the monastery received this kind of rice. This was provided specially by the king.

Khyungpo Naljor made an offering to Devi Dorje of thirteen ounces of gold and received in return magical techniques to oppose the gods of death like "Yamantaka" and others.

After initiating him, Devi Dorje brought Khyungpo Naljor to see the scriptural depositories of Nalanda Monastery. In the monastery there were three scriptural depositories, which were distinguished by different names: "The Luster of Jewels," "The Sea of Jewels," and "The Ocean of Jewels." Together these libraries contained more than nine million volumes of Buddhist scriptures. The Ocean of Jewels was a tower nine stories high, and when people went into it, they suddenly felt tiny. Khyungpo Naljor thought: "Even if I work hard my whole life, how much of the fire of wisdom can I bring back from India?"

Khyungpo Naljor took part in the studies in the monastery. He was feeling a kind of atmosphere rather than studying. He discovered that the vogue for debate was even flourishing in the classrooms. The monastery welcomed many challengers, great and small, and most of them ended victoriously for the Nalanda scholars. But over a hundred years earlier, when two great Brahmanist masters had swept away the Buddhists of India, Nalanda Monastery had not been able to gain victory. The monks of Nalanda Monastery could not forget those two names: the Mimamsa school's Kumarila and the Vedanta school's Sankara. From an objective point of view, they revitalized Brahmanism, because from then on, Buddhism withdrew from its place among the people, and went back into the temples. What was alive and active among the people was the new Brahmanism.

After listening to lessons for a time, Khyungpo Naljor gradually got sick of it. He discovered that the monastery's monks' learning had already diverged from the original simplicity of the Buddhist teaching and had entered into abstruse intellectualism. This degree of abstruseness would be impossible to master even with a lifetime of mental effort. Even more difficult for him to understand was the fact that those pandits, who were experts in this intellectualistic learning, had definitely not detached from desires. Their deep learning had not caused them to attain the pure cool bliss of nirvana. At times they used all their thinking to win themselves relatively higher positions in the monastery.

One day Khyungpo Naljor told Devi Dorje that he did not understand this. Devi Dorje laughed and said: "This is a paradox. Ultimately, it is not a good thing to become a religious sect without one's own profound theories. But if you sink deeply into theories, you may distance yourself from the original spirit of the religion."

He sighed and said: "One of the primary causes for why Buddhism has reached the stage it is at today, if we explain it from the point of view of the greater process, is that it has descended into obscure intellectualism. How can ordinary people find time to study the theory of logic? The true goal of religion is liberation; it is not to research learned theories."

Devi Dorje said: "As of now, the lamp of Buddhism is only still burning at places like Nalanda Monastery. But ultimately, how long can it keep burning?"

9 The Mischievous Novices

One day, Khyungpo Naljor went out from the monastery. He had already completely understood the esoteric teachings which Devi Dorje had taught him. His goal was to learn the esoteric teachings, and he did not feel interested in those abstruse theories. He thought: "Human life is painful and short. If I sink into complex theorizing and do not do genuine cultivation, then it will be impossible to detach from suffering and find bliss."

He saw two Brahmans who had previously come begging for food. In this period, Brahmanism had already achieved its own revival and had become a living religion. The common people were very respectful toward Brahmanism, and Brahmanist teachings and standards of behavior had already penetrated the lives of the common folk.

These two elderly Brahmans appeared to be upholders of asceticism. Their clothing was in tatters, and they were skinny as sticks. Several peasants had put food into their begging bowls. Suddenly several mischievous Buddhist novices ran by and overturned their bowls. The food spilled out on the ground.

Khyungpo Naljor knew that this was the result of what they had been taught by their teachers. In the monastery there were some extremist Buddhist teachers who always spoke of Brahmanism in an insulting way. They were always urging their disciples to study diligently, so that they could launch a deadly competition with Brahmanism.

Those two elderly Brahmans got very angry, and each grabbed hold of two of the Buddhist novices. They wanted to go into Nalanda Monastery and find their teachers and talk things out with them. The gatekeepers would not let them go in. Both sides started to argue. The men watching the gate were clever talkers, and out argued the Brahmans till they had nothing to say. Seeing their opponents losing the argument, the novices took some dirty water and doused the Brahmans with it.

One of the Brahmans said angrily: "We cannot out argue you, but we will ask Brahma to punish you."

They gathered a lot of firewood, and lit a ritual fire on the periphery of the monastery.

Looked at superficially, what these two Brahmans built was just an ordinary ritual fire. They built a fire mandala, and burned some firewood, and stood beside it chanting and throwing some grain into the flames. Khyungpo Naljor himself had often made this kind of ritual fire. A ritual fire was a kind of *homa* ceremony, and for those cultivating the Path, it was a very ordinary thing. So the novices kept laughing as they watched it for a while, then they all went back into the monastery.

Though Khyungpo Naljor sympathized with those two Brahmans, ultimately he was a guest at the monastery, and he did not want to say anything, so he returned to the monastery. He told Devi Dorje about this incident. Devi Dorje said: "If they do not find the original cause in themselves, what's the use of blaming others? Even if you wipe out all the Brahmans, the common people still will not be able to understand your theories."

Devi Dorje was very worried. He said: "If they go on like this, sooner or later they will cause trouble."

Khyungpo Naljor suddenly thought of a letter Sharwadi had sent, in which she mentioned that those sorcerers were in the process of cultivating the methods of the fire gods, and that they were going to send the great demon who controlled fire to make mischief.

He told this to Devi Dorje.

Devi Dorje entered into meditative concentration and, after a long time contemplating, just gave a long sigh.

10 The Great Fire Comes Flying

Khyungpo Naljor did not think that the great fire would come so quickly. In the middle of the night, he suddenly heard a shout. He opened his eyes and discovered the light of a fire was already shining on the wall. He called to wake up Devi Dorje, and the two men rushed out of the house. They discovered that fires had already broken out in many places, and the light of the fires soared up toward the sky. The monks were in a state of chaos. Some were throwing water on the flames, some were crying out in confusion, some were running helter-skelter in all directions. There were still torches flying in from outside the monastery, and there was a voice shouting: "O Brahma, we will burn up these people who do not believe in the gods."

Khyungpo Naljor did not know whether this fire was set by those two Brahmans, or whether it was caused by the power of the curses of those sorcerers who were cultivating the methods of the fire gods. From external appearances, it must be the former, but many times, behind the external appearances, there also could be a kind of mysterious power. Though he could not be sure it was the latter, he still had a bad feeling.

Sparks flew out from the monastery, and many palaces and houses caught fire. Most of the monastery buildings were made of wood, and when one of them caught fire, the fire spread in all directions.

The great fire flared up into the sky, and the light of the fire cast a red glow on the nine-story tower that housed the depository of scriptures. Khyungpo Naljor thought: "Above all, do not let that tower catch fire." Remember, stored within it were many rare and precious volumes. Some were still preserved in manuscript form, and once these were destroyed, they would be irrecoverably lost. At Khyungpo's prompting, Devi Dorje dispatched a group of his disciples to go protect the Ocean of Jewels tower with its depository of scriptures. Khyungpo Naljor too picked up a water bucket, but the problem was he did not know the layout of the complex well enough, and there was no place to get water.

Inside the monastery there was a lot of yelling and shouting, and some of the monks had already taken up wooden clubs and left the monastery to go looking for those two Brahmans who set the fire. They thought those two men had decided to go to their deaths. The story goes that when the monks caught up with them, they were still going to the monastery to throw torches on the buildings in the monastery. When the monks overtook them, they did not want to flee. After screaming out, the two men were beaten bloody.

But the great fire was already very difficult to control. Organized by their teachers, the monks kept throwing water on the flames, but the great fire hurtled with unstoppable momentum toward those wooden sculptures that were trembling in the light of the fire.

In the light of the fire, the cries shook the heavens.

The great fire burned for several days, and many great palaces were turned to ashes. Quite a few monks also lost their lives in the sea of flames, and the whole of Nalanda Monastery was a mess.

What most filled Khyungpo Naljor with regret was that the nine-story tower with the scriptural depository, and millions of volumes of precious texts, had all gone up in smoke in the flames of the fire.

At that point in time, Khyungpo Naljor did not know that more than two hundred years later, there would be an even bigger fire that would burn Nalanda Monastery to the ground. After that, in the great land of India, it would be very difficult to hear the authentic voice of the Buddhist scriptures. But at that time, along with Nalanda Monastery itself, thousands and thousands of Hindu temples were also reduced to ashes. Even the god Brahma, who was worshipped in Hinduism, did not save the temples where offerings were made to him. Where Hinduism differed from Buddhism was that, because Hinduism had already become an indispensable part of the life of the people of India, after the great fire was extinguished, Hinduism could put forth new green shoots from the blackened ruins and, with its strong vitality, could extend to the whole of the Indian subcontinent. But Buddhism, after these lofty and profound scriptures were burned, withdrew from the life of the people of India.

Just as Khyungpo Naljor was pondering that scorched earth, the spirit dove again found him.

Chapter 16

Sukhasiddhi's Test

1 A Salve for Long Life Made from a Baby

Beloved Khyung, it is noon and I originally did not plan to write a letter, but I am really feeling very nervous.

This morning I was very happy, as I imagined getting together with you, but then I heard something: those sorcerers are saying that according to their standards for observation, that fire god magic has already taken effect. I am very worried about you. Please, you must write back to me.

Besides working their spells, so that they can live long lives, the sorcerers ended up buying a baby and cooking it down into a soup. They are going to refine this into a kind of salve for long life. I had an unbearable feeling, so I locked the door, and I cannot stop crying.

I am just a woman, and when I hear about something like this, I feel so bad there is no way to describe it. Kumari said that even though she thinks the human mind is very bad, she never thought that in the end it could be as bad as this. Having gone down the long river of history for many thousand years, human nature seems not really to have changed. I truly do not know what meaning this practice of theirs has. You have said that the human mind does not change, it is an unalterable fate. So-called history is nothing but a recurring tragedy that happens over and over again. I cannot help crying for the human race. I am even tired of those jewels which have left me with dreams of unlimited beauty. If I could trade them for that baby's life, I would very happily abandon them. I am atoning for my sins. I too am a human being, I too am a woman.

I am always troubled by my own numbness, but today I have been shaken up again. The only thing that is worth doing with our lives is to wake up people's minds, but this is also the hardest thing to do. Moreover, just as you previously pointed out my feral child nature, I know that all changes must first start with oneself. Genuine action is more important than anything.

From now on, except for what I need to support my father and mother in their old age, I am going to use all my own personal wealth for your activities to redeem people's minds. I have already begun to put this into action. I have already entrusted it to two people. One is the current female spirit, who looks upon me as a big sister. The other is Kumari. If by some chance something unexpected happens to me, you should go find them. I will arrange everything properly.

I think that now that I have understood, I must go act. And I am not complaining or blaming anybody else. The world has no shortage of people complaining. What is most lacking are those who are continually trying to correct their own conduct. If we want to change other people, we have to start first by changing ourselves.

I am not saying that I must become a female bodhisattva. There is nothing I seek. I have no ideal of everlasting fame; I have just seen this phenomenon that is extremely unbearable. It brutally destroyed my feeling of being blessed with good fortune, my feeling of happiness, and added to my feeling of unease, my feeling of guilt, my feeling of destruction. I must seek to recover my happiness, my good fortune, my peace.

And I still worry about whether our love will let me sink down into a private sense of being blessed, so I become even more insensitive.

You must always help me preserve my wakefulness. Otherwise I will regret it later.

After this, I am always going to eat a simple vegetarian diet. Before, when my grandmother died, I ate vegetarian food, but that was just a ritual. But now I really will not swallow any meat. I think of those babies who died, and I feel they are all my mothers, they are all my children, they are all me myself.

This evening after I bathe I will recite the Diamond Sutra, and I will wish them peace and rest and that their rebirths will be blessed with good fortune.

2 The Ultimate Meaning

Sharwadi, whom I long for:

Maybe the curses of those sorcerers have taken effect. I did really encounter a great fire, and it burned up many worldly treasures, though I myself was left safe and sound.

Right now it is hard for me to bear!

As soon as you say that, I feel even more regret. I think I am truly a person who brings bad luck. If I had not gone to Nalanda Monastery, maybe there wouldn't have been this disastrous fire.

You once said that you wanted to inquire into the ultimate meaning of women's existence, for example wisdom and freedom. True, you need wisdom; that is, you need to understand clearly how to genuinely love a man who is worthy of your love. You also need freedom: that is, to the greatest extent possible, to live and die with your beloved and share mutual intimacy and mutual love. Apart from this, there is no so-called ultimate meaning. This is because no matter how you try, there is no way to compete with death and impermanence. Because what you said when you were a female spirit was filled with false words and clichés, as soon as they came out of your mouth, they had already turned into trash. The temple of the female spirits you served has also been swallowed up the same way by impermanence.

Think about it: even the library of Buddhist scriptures at Nalanda Monastery was burned to ashes by a fierce fire—is there anything in the world that does not change?

A hundred year or so from now, all those buildings that

bear your father's seal, including your own house, may all be torn down and rebuilt. At that time, your family may not exist any more, you may not exist any more, and everything might be gone. The wealth of yours hare been already squandered completely by people. On those ruins there may be some people cursing, there may be some people singing, there may be some other people beating their breasts and stamping their feet. Many who once thought they were people will have changed into heaps of bones, will have become names buried in the end by the passage of time.

At that time, the wisdom passed down by Khyungpo Ba will definitely remain in the world and continue to nourish later generations of people.

3 A Beggar Who Only Wanted Gold

After the great fire, I was sick for a good many months. I did not know if that sickness came from sorrow over the destruction of that depository, or if I had really been affected by the curses of those sorcerers. Whatever it was, for a few months I kept on getting fevers, and the fevers were very severe. That frightful fire was always appearing before my eyes, and in the fire were countless demonic faces. They were truly sucking my blood. I heard a little monk say that I was always crying out deep in the night, and my face would often get flushed, and I would keep screaming wildly like a madman. People in the monastery thought of many methods to cure my sickness: they recited *Niguma's Auspicious Scripture* on my behalf for seven days, and they did many fire offerings to subdue demons.

After this, my spirit gradually became lucid again, and my physical health improved some.

One day when I was out in the sun outside the monastery, Sukhasiddhi found me. At first I did not know it was Sukhasiddhi, because what I saw was an old beggar woman who was extremely ugly. Her body was covered with lumps, and she wore ragged clothes and cotton batting, and there were more weird things about her that I could not give a name to. Because her face had not been washed for a long time, the dirt had covered her original features, but it was still possible to see vaguely that she was a woman.

I was in the habit of giving alms to all beggars, so I gave her a little piece of silver. Unexpectedly she took the bit of silver and threw it on the ground, and in an enraged voice said: "Can you spare this bit of silver?"

Several monks laughed out loud. My face got all red. I had never before encountered this kind of beggar woman. So I took out a few silver coins and gave them to her. How could I know? She again took the silver and threw it away, and harshly said: "I do not want silver, I want gold."

"Ha! A beggar who only wants gold," said a little monk laughingly.

The spirit light flashed in my brain, and I finally noticed that on this beggar woman's person was something I was very familiar with. I carefully sized her up, and I discovered that, apart from those eyes that were as clear as black and white, in fact I had not discerned that there was something about her that was different from the usual beggars. This was a very old woman, at least sixty years old, emaciated, dirty, with hair withered and yellow like autumn grass in the wind, and stained with all sorts of indescribable filth. Her face was covered with a layer of dirt, and you could not see her skin color. The tattered clothes on her body had merged with her shape, to form the classic distinguishing marks of a beggar. So I thought: "Maybe she is a madwoman. Am I not following the bodhisattva oath? Some bodhisattvas would give their eyes when people asked for them, so how could I not be able to part with a little gold?"

I took out a piece of gold and gave it to the beggar woman. I heard the beggar woman mutter, "This at last is reasonable."

I was about to turn around and leave, when I also heard her say, "Come with me." After she said this, she started off.

In that sentence, "Come with me," I clearly discerned the presence of Sukhasiddhi, and my heart leaped wildly. But I was in doubt: why had a woman as beautiful as a heavenly being taken on this kind of appearance? Just as I was having doubts, her reproach came at me: "Why are you acting stupid? Do you want to make me not be able to sell you?"

This time, I had no more doubts. I just gave a word of instruction to the little monk I knew well, telling him to take word to our teacher to tell him that I would be gone for a while, in order to get some scriptural texts and other things.

The little monk did not understand and asked: "What? You are going off with that old beggar woman?"

I smiled and said: "Her? She is my teacher."

4 Ultimately, Am I Beautiful or Am I Ugly?

Having sought after her for so long, I finally had found Sukhasiddhi. The woman angrily said: "Aren't you totally unconcerned? Why are you talking so much nonsense? If you were to go be reborn at this instant, wouldn't being this way not work? This time, you will understand clearly what it means to be tired of material things. All the wealth in the world is something that blocks liberation.

If you cannot even give up that little thing, what practice are you cultivating?"

I explained: "What I cannot give up are those scriptures. I want to bring them back to Tibet."

The woman smiled coldly and said: "Isn't the purpose of those scriptures to make you give them up? If you cannot even give them up, won't they become encumbrances for you? What do you need them for?"

I did not dare explain further. I was very afraid of her. Before, when she was so beautiful, I still feared her. I looked away, then stole a glance at her, and I saw that, except for her voice, she did not have any of the beauty which Sukhasiddhi had had. I thought: "This is really strange. Did I see her wrongly before?"

As I thought this, Sukhasiddhi smiled coldly. "That's right—before you clung to an illusion as real, and now even more, you are accepting the false as true. My previous beautiful appearance covered over the mucus in my nose, the excrement in my intestines, the blood under my skin, and you accepted it as beauty. The dirt now covers over the physical beauty, covers over the great vows in my mind, covers over my wisdom and compassion, and you feel that I am unbearably ugly. So you tell me: ultimately, am I beautiful or am I ugly?"

I immediately said: "Beautiful, beautiful of course."

The woman said: "Truly beautiful?"

"Of course. Of course."

"Good. So I want you to marry me. Will you?"

When I heard this, I got scared. I said: "I won't, I won't, I have accepted the monastic code of discipline."

Sukhasiddhi smiled coldly and said: "Didn't you just accept the code of discipline for novices? You have offered your body, mouth, and mind to me. What code can you not abandon?"

I felt my tongue instantly go dry, and I did not know how to answer.

Sukhasiddhi said: "Don't you dislike me being old and ugly and dirty?"

I immediately shook my head: "No, no."

"That is your answer?"

"No! No!"

"Did you not offer me your body, mouth, and mind? Are you going back on your word?"

My forehead broke out in a sweat. A strange buzzing noise sounded in my brain. I thought: how can I marry her? But I also thought: didn't I offer her my body, mouth, and mind? If she orders me to die, I must die.

Sukhasiddhi said: "Look carefully at me."

I wiped the sweat off mybrow, raised my head, and looked up at Sukhasiddhi. With this look, my heart grew colder. How could this be that beautiful dakini I had first seen? Obviously, this was a filthy old beggar woman. From her eyes two poisonous rays of light flashed out, as if my hesitation had constituted an enormous insult to her.

The woman said: "As a person who has taken the bodhisattva vows, even if I ask you for your eyes, you would have to give them to me. How much the more so, when all I have done is to ask you to marry me. If you are this type of person, to take these vows — what meaning does it have?"

I thought: she's right; the Buddha gave his body to feed tiger. I was ashamed of my own hesitation, so I said: "Alright then. I'll marry you."

That beggar woman smiled coldly and said: "Too late. You missed your karmic opportunity."

5 Happy Salamanders

When we reached the Sandalwood Forest, Sukhasiddhi hid among the trees. I discovered that the Sandalwood Forest had also changed. I discovered that the Sandalwood Forest was always changing. I thought: "Maybe it is my mind that has changed." When I thought about it in detail, in recent days I had certainly gone through too many things. The experience at the spirit temple in particular had tempered my mind, and it was no different from being reborn. But when I thought of the hesitation I had just gone through, I still blamed myself a bit. I thought: "The dakini was correct in scolding me. My hesitations, in fact, are still the work of the discriminating mind making trouble. If she still had an external appearance as beautiful as before, would I have hesitated or not?"

Just as I was blaming myself, Sukhasiddhi emerged from the forest. Before my eyes there was brightness. The Sukhasiddhi I saw now was still as beautiful as before, and when she turned and smiled, the forest shone. There was some wavering in my mind. I thought: "Will she ask me to marry her or not?"

How could I have known that as soon as I had a thought, the dakini was already aware of it. She smiled coldly and said: "Still that same person, but when the outer appearance changes, then your mind also changes. Isn't your mind completely controlled by my external appearance? That year in the spirit temple — did you spend it in vain?"

I was ashamed and said nothing.

Sukhasiddhi said: "Cultivating practice is, in reality, a matter of cultivating the mind. If your mind does not change, then all your cultivation is meaningless. Even if you chant a mantra ten million times and cultivate contemplation thousands of times, if the nature of your mind does not change, your cultivation is no more than self-deception."

She also said: "If just now you had said with no hesitation that you would marry me, I could have made you experience enlightenment in a single night. But you spoiled the karmic opportunity, and indeed you should regret it."

I got extremely upset. I thought: "I am really a fool. I clearly knew she is a dakini. Why was my mind thrown into confusion by that nauseating external appearance?"

Sukhasiddhi said: "Like Luipa, you have excellent potential and top-level merit, but because your discriminating mind makes mischief, your mind chakra still has defilements. Even though you made great progress during the year in the spirit temple, you still have a lot of habit-energy that is waiting to be cleared away."

"Let's go," she said.

"Go where?" I asked.

"Wherever we want to go, we will go there."

When the dakini had finished speaking, she went off without any further consultation. I followed behind. Nothing was said during the entire journey. We came to another quiet place, and saw several people at a fire mandala. They were chanting spells and were holding five kinds of grain, which they threw into the fire handful by handful. Sukhasiddhi stopped and looked at me with a faint smile. After a long time she finally asked: "I asked you to marry me, but you wouldn't. Right now, if I have you jump into the fire mandala, would you dare to do it or not?"

I was regretting my earlier hesitation. As soon as I saw that the dakini wanted to test me, I said: "Why not dare?"

"So then, jump in." Sukhasiddhi still had that faint smile.

I walked toward the fire mandala. Those few practitioners there looked at me, not understanding what I was doing.

As soon as I got close to the fire mandala, I felt a kind of hot wave hit my face. I carefully looked at the fire mandala, and saw that it was just some clay bricks piled on the ground, and supported with firewood. If I jumped in, there would be no mortal danger, but I certainly would suffer burns. I was deliberating, when I heard Sukhasiddhi again speak: "So? Are you going to decide to retreat again?"

I turned my head and smiled. "How could I?" I was thinking that even if I got burned to death, that was nothing. It could be considered for now as making an offering to the teacher. I steeled my mind, and jumped into the fire mandala. I felt a bunch of hot ashes hit my nose, and then the smoke. At first, I did not feel the heat, because that fire mandala was not large, and my body was heavy, and I crushed out the flames. Thick smoke rose all around. One man cried out in surprise: "What are you doing? How can you extinguish our fire mandala?" Another man said: "Don't you want to make offerings to Brahma?"

The thick smoke rushed by along with the ashes, and made me choke and cough, and tears blurred my eyes. I just felt an irritation in my nasal cavities, but unexpectedly I did not feel the heat. However, though the flames of the fire were extinguished, the embers of the fire still continued to emit heat, and quickly burned through my clothing. Several salamanders bored into my body, and happily played, gnawing at me until my whole body was burning with pain.

One of the practitioners came by and angrily called to me: "Come out of there. Come out. If you want to die, go die somewhere else." As he was speaking, two other men came up, and without saying anything, lifted me up and threw me out of there as far as they could.

I was battered to the point that I felt dizzy and there was a constant ringing in my ears. There still was a burning pain in my back, and I assumed my clothes were still on fire, so I might as well roll over a few times. On the ground there was mud everywhere, and my whole body got covered with it, but I assumed that the fire was out.

As soon as I crawled up, I again heard Sukhasiddhi's voice:

"Why did you pick a small fire mandala to jump into? Isn't this like choosing a small bowl to go draw water?"

As I stood up, I thought I was certainly in a difficult position. My nasal passages were still acidic, and my eyes were still watering, but in my mind I was very happy, because I had finally conquered myself. I thought: "That fire mandala may have been small, but not just anyone would want to jump into it, and then dare to jump in." I also heard a bit of satisfaction in Sukhasiddhi's tone of voice. But when I lifted my eyes to look at her, I saw she still had a look of scorn on her face.

That practitioner was still berating me. I listened to what he was saying: they had just been performing a fire offering to improve their karma in order to seek eternal life, and this disturbance which I had caused had spoiled the karmic conditions. According to the explanation of the taboo, there might be troubles for them in the future.

Sukhasiddhi also said: "You succeeded, you succeeded. Even though you chose a small fire mandala, at least you did not go against my intent. Ha-ha. This time, you are not much better than that beggar woman."

I of course understood where my own embarrassment lay: the hair on my head had been burned off, and there were many holes burnt on the back of my clothes, and my trousers were covered with mud and black ashes, and mucus and tears were flowing over my face ... When I thought of how bedraggled I looked, I could not help laughing.

6 Brahma's Big Mouth

We continued forward. Sukhasiddhi still kept going on at me: "Though you jumped onto the fire mandala, that doesn't mean that you have the mind of faith. Because that fire mandala was too small, you extinguished it as soon as you lay on it. I've discovered that you are tricky: you clearly knew there was no danger. But you wear that look of awe-inspiring righteousness. You are quite a schemer."

I knew she was engaged in taming my mind, and I did not give rise to any anger in my mind from what she said.

Sukhasiddhi said: "Hmm, you think I do not know those little calculations going on in your mind? You look very honest, but in fact you are not a bit honest. Look at that man Naropa: when his teacher told him to leap off a mountain, he knew that he could be smashed to pieces, but he still jumped off. He did not pick a lesser height to jump from. But you, you took a look and saw that there were three fire mandalas there, so why didn't you jump into the large fire mandala, why did you pick that small one instead? As soon as you jumped in, the fire was put out. I originally wanted to make you burn into a burnt stick: how could I know that you would not even burn a piece of skin?"

I said: "Look here. Who says I have no burns? Look." I pulled up my sleeve and pointed to a burn and said: "This is all burned here."

Sukhasiddhi smiled coldly and said: "How can you count that as a burn? If you could attain the supreme esoteric teaching by burning that little bit of skin, would Naropa have had to die the great death twelve times?"

I said: "There are also burns on my back."

Sukhasiddhi smiled coldly and said: "Even if you were burned in a hundred places, there is still a world of difference between your leap and Naropa's leap. That man was willing to risk inevitable death, and he knew full well that he would smashed to pieces. But it was his duty, so there was no looking back. But you, hmm, all you did was to take the opportunity to be tricky."

I said, "So I'll pick a bigger one to jump into." I looked all around and saw that not far away there were several dozen people around a large fire mandala performing a ritual sacrifice to Brahma, so I ran over there. Sukhasiddhi did not stop me.

Because fire is the mouth of Brahma, there were a lot of things among the sacrificial items. There were a lot of things, and the fire was large, with flames blazing up to the sky. I thought, if I jump in this time, there is not much hope of surviving. Inevitably, I felt anxious and upset. I felt that if I died without achieving supreme enlightenment, it would be tantamount to having lived this life in vain. The Buddha said: "Once we lose the human body, we might not get it back for ten thousand ages." If I really were to die, it would not be a good thing. I turned my head and looked back at Sukhasiddhi, hoping she would urge me to stop, and I would take the easy way out. Because there are thousands of ways to show sincere dedication, I didn't necessarily have to burn myself to death. How could I have known that, as soon as she saw me look back, Sukhasiddhi would raise her voice and cry out, "Jump!" and so I would jump. I was beyond crying or laughing, and I thought: "This look of hers is not like a holy dakini, she's obviously a cunning and capricious girl."

So I'll jump into the fire then. Don't let her think I am a sly opportunist.

How could I know, the closer I came to the fire, the more I saw how huge that fire was. Because some people were offering sandalwood to Brahma, once that fire got burning, it was very strong, and the firelight was extremely fierce, and the roar of the flames went beyond heaven and earth. Though some people had thrown things like mutton into the fire, the sizzling sound could not be heard, and it was as if the flesh had instantly become flames of fire. I thought: "If I jumped in, there would really be no saving me."

I was frightened, but once the arrow is shot, there's no getting it back, so all I could do was approach the fire.

The fire was truly huge. My face was already getting scorched. Though I was some distance away from the fire, the waves of heat radiating from it were unbearable. Those waves of heat surged on and on. The fire in the fire mandala was already showing a white light, and to all appearances the temperature was extremely high. The people making offerings were throwing things like silk cloth into the fire, and the offerings were being engulfed by the tongues of flame even before they went into the mandala.

I was thinking, "I' m afraid I will not dare jump in." I was also thinking, "This time, even if someone comes to save me, my flesh will be totally burned off."

Again I looked to Sukhasiddhi, thinking: "Probably she will give some tacit signal, and I will still have a way out." But Sukhasiddhi was still smiling coldly.

"So jump in," I thought. "What that man Naropa can do, I too can do."

Reaching the edge of the mandala, I gathered my strength to jump. As soon as I flexed by legs, I felt a great force sweep me along, and my body flew up like a whirlwind, and by the time I came to and knew what was happening, I was already lying on a slope.

As I struggled to get up, I saw a man pointing to me and rebuking me: "If you want to die, go do it somewhere else. Our place here is a sacred mandala for sacrificing to Brahma, not a crematorium."

Someone else said: "If you wash yourself completely clean, that might do. I could take you as a sacrificial offering like a pig or a sheep, and throw you into the fire to offer to Brahma. But right now, look at you, you look like a beggar. As soon as I see you I get nauseous. Needless to say, so would Brahma."

Another man said: "That's right. If you had not just now put out the fire mandala of those other people, we would not have been on guard against you. I saw you come here sneaking around like a mad dog, and I knew then you are not of sound mind. If you want to make an offering to Brahma, okay then, go away and fast for a few days, then get washed a few dozen times in hot water. Then pick an auspicious day and come look for me, and I will help you achieve your goal."

I unexpectedly fell down, and lost my bearings, and this made the other men rebuke me in all sorts of ways, and I did not know how to answer. I thought that if I jumped into the fire mandala again, the men would beat me a second time. So I went back to Sukhasiddhi. I was thinking: "Anyway, I did jump. If I hadn't jumped, the causal conditions would not have been complete. Let's see what you will say."

I saw that Sukhasiddhi would deliberately get angry at me. Again she smiled coldly and said: "If you really jumped, why so sluggish? You deliberately waited for other people to come to throw you. How can you be like that? Look at that other man, Naropa. He knew that down below in the pit there were sharp bamboo stakes, but when his teacher told him to jump, did he not immediately jump? Although the bamboo stakes pierced his body, he had no regrets. But when you do things, you always leave yourself some leeway."

What the dakini said was certainly true. On the road to the fire mandala, I truly had hesitated, and so my mind felt ashamed: I did not dare make excuses. All I felt was my face burning.

Sukhasiddhi kept smiling sardonically.

7 Do You Understand the Secret Truth of the Esoteric Teaching?

We left the cold forest and kept on going forward. I was still ashamed. I kept comparing myself with Naropa, and every time I did, I felt secretly ashamed.

Sukhasiddhi said: "Look at that man Naropa. He was a great learned man at Nalanda Monastery, and he refuted clinging and attachment, and then he broke his clingings and attachments. He abandoned his earth-shaking reputation. He abandoned his status that was lofty as royalty. He abandoned the mountains of offerings that had been bestowed on him. He abandoned his comfortable surroundings and then took as his teacher a man who did the hard labor of grinding sesame seeds. But you? Even though you were a Bonpo teaching master, you could be so haughty and arrogant?"

Though I did not have a haughty and arrogant mind, I did not dare talk back.

Sukhasiddhi said: "At first, Naropa was famous over a wide area. He had an expert knowledge of the Buddhist Canon, and he was the abbot of Nalanda Monastery. Every day he gave lessons to scholars and monks. One day he went out from the monastery, and he saw a beggar woman. That person asked: 'Naropa, do you understand the scriptures or not?' Naropa said: 'I do understand them.' The beggar woman then laughed and danced for joy and was very delighted. Then she asked: 'Naropa, do you understand the secret truth after the scriptures?' Naropa said: 'Of course I understand it.' The beggar woman then started to cry. She said: 'I didn't think the world-famous Naropa would deceive people.' Naropa realized she was the manifestation of a dakini, so he immediately knelt down and asked her: 'In the world today, who can understand the secret truth after the scriptures?' The beggar woman said: 'Tilopa.' Naropa asked: 'Who is Tilopa?' The beggar woman said: 'He is a workman who grinds sesame seeds to extract the oil in a certain corner of a certain village in a certain area, and specializes in grinding sesame seeds to make a living. Do you want to go to find him?'

"In this way, Naropa abandoned his illustrious position and grand reputation and went to look for an unknown man who made his living grinding sesame seeds. Can you guess what Tilopa told him? He said: 'My teaching is lion's milk, and cannot be poured into a chamber pot like you.' And he refused to pass on the teaching to Naropa. Later on, after Naropa had experienced twelve great deaths and twelve minor deaths and had been through countless trials and hardships, Tilopa finally transmitted the Great Mudra to him on the banks of the Ganges. So people call this the Great Mudra of the Ganges River."

Sukhasiddhi asked: "Now I am asking you, do you understand the secret truth of the scriptures?"

I did not dare answer.

Sukhasiddhi also asked: "You have followed so many teachers, and you have sought so many esoteric teachings, so I ask you, do you understand the secret truth of the esoteric teachings?"

I thought for a moment and said: "I do not dare say that I do understand, but I also do not dare say that I do not understand. If I say I understand, that is not correct, and if I say I do not understand, that is not correct either. However, I think that in the end, I have received so many transmissions of the teaching, that I think I may know these secret truths to some degree."

Sukhasiddhi asked: "So then, please tell me, what is the secret truth of the esoteric teachings?"

I felt that the question was not difficult, but as I waited to give an answer, there was nowhere to start.

Again Sukhasiddhi gave a cold smile. She gave a snort and said: "If you think that getting formulas is getting the secret truth of the esoteric teachings, then you are mistaken. All those formulas are just a route to get to that secret truth. Always remember, the road is the road, the road is not the destination."

"So then, what is the destination?"

Sukhasiddhi just gave a subtle smile.

8 A Frightening Mad Elephant

Just as Sukhasiddhi and I were talking, I suddenly heard some people screaming, and the sound was horrifying. I raised my head and saw a mad elephant, charging wildly at us. India has a multitude of elephants, and sometimes you can see mad elephants. There are two kinds of mad elephants. One kind are mad elephants with genuine nervous disorders. These elephants are often killed. The other kind are the rutting bull elephants. Ordinarily, they are tame and docile, but when they are rutting, their wild nature breaks loose, and they look all over for female elephants. If they cannot find a female elephant, they wildly pursue humans, and sometimes they will crush or trample them. Every year, there are some people who perish under the feet of mad elephants.

The fearsome trumpeting of a mad elephant resounded through the air. People were fleeing in all directions.

As soon as I saw that mad elephant, I too fled in panic. I looked all around me, hoping to find a safe place, but I heard Sukhasiddhi laughing and saying: "Look, now the time has come. You don't have to jump into that fire mandala. Go ahead, go play with that mad elephant."

When I heard this, I felt faint. I said: "Auntie, do not torment me. Use any other method to teach me, but this game now could cost me my life."

Sukhasiddhi said sternly: "How can you say this is a game? When Naropa jumped off the cliff, did he bargain with Tilopa?"

I rubbed the skin on my head and there was a pained look on my face. It was as if I already saw the white foam in that mad elephant's mouth.

Sukhasiddhi said in a stern voice: "Are you going or not?"

I thought: "Haven't I made a vow to follow my teacher in life and death, and not turn back even from death? How could I let a mad elephant scare me?" So I said: "I'm going, I'm going."

A very sacred emotion rose up in my mind. I thought: "That's it then, I am obeying the command of heaven. Since I have taken refuge with the dakini, whatever she tells me to do, I will do. My life is hers. What's more, I have also offered her my body, mouth, and mind."

Suddenly Sukhasiddhi laughed gently, and when that mad elephant heard the sound of her laugh, it became terrified, and charged at me, running and trumpeting.

I felt my heart beating in my chest in mortal fear, and my mouth was totally dry, and my tongue had become like a dry piece of leather. I did not dare look at the mad elephant, but my eyes would not obey me. I saw the eyes of the mad elephant were staring directly at me, and the feeling in them was very much like the eyes of a pig, but brimming with red light. The elephant's saliva sprayed out with the sounds it made, and made the ground all wet.

I thought this time I would certainly die. I had heard that there are several ways a mad elephant injures people. One way is to trample the person in anger, crushing the person to a bloody pulp. Another way if for the mad bull elephant to treat the person as a female elephant, and press down on top of the person; the result is the same as being trampled. There is another form where the elephant wraps its trunk around the person, throws him up into the air, and then after that tramples him to death ... In sum, the person dies a gruesome death. But I was also thinking: "When that man Naropa was seeking the Dharma, he put aside all concerns of life and death." Although I was thinking this way, my heart was pounding even more terribly, and my feet seemed to be as powerless as if I were walking on cotton.

The mad elephant gradually got closer, and the people who had originally been fleeing in all directions stood still. They all held their breath and looked on: they did not dare make a sound, thinking that the sounds of their fear would provoke the mad elephant.

I realized I could not escape the inevitable disaster. I lifted my head and looked up at the sky. On the one hand, my powers of concentration scattered, and on the other hand, I wanted to take a last look at the sky. I saw several pure white clouds just as they were changing shape, like a bunch of lotus flowers opening. I thought: "If I really die, I have no other regrets — just that I was not able to transmit the esoteric teachings of my many teachers widely in Tibet." I also wanted to take one last look at Sukhasiddhi, but I discovered that Sukhasiddhi was still looking at me with a faint shadow of a smile. I thought: "Isn't she hard-hearted?" But then I was also ashamed of this thought.

The mad elephant got closer and closer, and the sound of his feet hitting the ground was very loud, deep and heavy, as if he were walking on my chest.

I gave a long sigh and thought: "I'd better go along with circumstances." I visualized that mad elephant as a mother. I thought: "Many lifetimes ago in the past, this elephant was my own mother. Right now, even if the mother demands my life, I will give it to her without the least hesitation." With this visualization, in my mind the mad elephant was not as frightening as it had just been.

As the mad elephant got closer and closer, I could already hear it breathing in and out. This was a big noise like a bellows being pumped. I suspected this was an illusion, but I really felt a great current of air on my face. I thought: "Here, at this moment, mother is giving me a bath."

I discovered mother extending a hand to me, this was the elephant's long trunk. I felt that mother was holding me, and when I opened my eyes, I discovered that the elephant's trunk was already wrapped around me. Suddenly it took me and with great force, tossed me into the air.

9 I No Longer See Myself

At this time I finally realized that no matter how I myself visualized it, a mad elephant is still a mad elephant. At that moment, as I was in a trance, the mad elephant wrapped its trunk around me and threw me into the air. I was flying, as light as a leaf. I felt myself being thrown very high, almost halfway to the sky. When I saw the people far away, they were all looking at me in astonishment. Further away in the river there were a lot of people — I don't know if they were washing or performing a ceremony. Opposite the river there was also a large fire — I don't know if the people there were doing a fire ritual or cremating corpses. I heard the sound of the wind filling my breast. I did not have any random thoughts. My mind had become a clear mirror. I felt a kind of pure clarity and ethereal spirit the likes of which I had never had before.

I began to come back down. The ground rushed up at me. The elephant was still there. He had opened his mouth toward the sky, but I did not know whether or not he was trumpeting — in any case, I could not hear any sound. I wanted to warn the mad elephant very much: "When I fall, please do not meet me with your tusks." I was thinking that the feeling of having my body pierced by the elephant's tusks would certainly be hard to bear.

I wanted to catch sight of Sukhasiddhi very much. I was wondering whether or not she was still looking at me with that faint smile. Surely she was. I remembered that ever since I met her, she was always cold as ice. The strange thing was, I had always had the greatest faith in her. There was no way around it—maybe this is what they call a karmic connection. But I could not see Sukhasiddhi, because I had no way to control my falling body.

I felt myself being held tight again by the elephant's soft trunk. The elephant's trunk was like a great boa constrictor, soft and flexible, yet also moving with a kind of incomparable power. It is said that an elephant's trunk can uproot a large tree. If it squeezed hard, it could certainly crush my bones. But the mad elephant did not curl up its trunk—it tossed me up again, and I again flew through the air. This time, I did see Sukhasiddhi. Sukhasiddhi seemed to be looking at me, but I couldn't make out what expression she had on her face. But her expression clearly was as carefree as if she were watching a circus act: there was not a bit of tension. I felt aggrieved, thinking: "Look at her. If I get trampled by this elephant, she won't feel sad."

After the elephant had thrown me up in the air several times, I did not get frightened anymore. On the contrary, that sensation of going up and down was very stimulating. For a moment I even forgot that it was a mad elephant throwing me, because there was a sort of empty clarity that kept coming at me, submerging all my false thoughts. This was an empty clarity like the sky, an empty clarity like ten thousand miles of space all taken in at a glance. In this bright emptiness, I no longer had fear, I no longer had false thoughts, I no longer had any concerns, I no longer worried about gain and loss, I no longer had the discriminating mind. At that time, although I could still hear the elephant's trumpeting, that sound seemed to have nothing to do with me. My mind had become a mirror: it could reflect the myriad things, but unchanged and did not move.

Suddenly I felt the elephant take me and throw me onto the ground. A dull pain flooded through my body, and the dust was flying, and it irritated my nasal cavity. It was clear to me that the mad elephant did not feel like throwing me around any more. What next? Would he do as other mad elephants do and trample me? I did not know. It was as if this had already become someone else's concern—it seemed to have nothing to do with me. I saw the legs of the great elephant like pillars moving back and forth. I realized I should feel afraid, but again I felt that this had nothing to do with me. The mad elephant, being thrown around, falling, even the elephant's legs moving back and forth, and Sukhasiddhi's face with that faint smile—none of this had anything to do with me. Because in that empty clarity, I genuinely discovered I no longer saw myself.

This was a feeling I had never had before. Previously, no matter how I cultivated the contemplation of having no self, this was only a theoretical intent, and I had never in my life truly felt anything that could be called having no self. Never. In this moment today, I truly felt what it is to have no self, what the bright emptiness is, what it is for the mind to be like a clear mirror reflecting the myriad things, what it is to be thus and unmoving. I thought: "Even if I die right now, I will not have the least bit of clinging or regret.

I seriously tried to examine the fear I had felt, and I discovered that I could no longer find any fear. I knew clearly that the mad elephant was still by my side, and still could threaten my life, but amazingly enough, I was no longer afraid. I discovered that fear is a strange thing: when you recognize it, you discover that it has no inherent nature. I went on to examine many other things, like my regrets, like my concerns, like all my clingings and attachments. I discovered that when I looked at them from within that clear emptiness, they would melt away like frost in the blazing sun.

10 Marry Me with the Marriage of the Supreme Truth

When that mad elephant could no longer really constitute a threat for me — that is, when there was no longer any fear of the mad elephant in my mind, and even if the mad elephant could trample me, my mind said to me, "There is no threat" — I heard Sukhasiddhi's voice.

"Get up!"

At last I saw Sukhasiddhi. I don't know when, but she had already seated herself upon that elephant. Actually, this elephant was not a mad elephant in the true sense, but after Sukhasiddhi had tamed him, was ready to be ridden. In India, elephants were a common sight as a means of transportation, and they were as widespread as horses were in China. Elephants were used for transport, often using carrying frames and passenger seats and so on. In ancient times, elephants were also used in warfare. In those times, a large elephant was the equivalent of a war chariot, and could carry several soldiers who carried bows and arrows and long lances to do battle with the enemy. The most serious and great defeat suffered by the world-renowned king Alexander the Great was inflicted by the Indian military forces made up of the elephant "war chariots." Elephants are without a doubt one of the most intelligent species of all animals.

Sukhasiddhi was still looking at me with that faint smile. But I discovered that the implication in it seemed to have changed. I understood that she was very satisfied with me, but strangely enough, I did not care whether or not she was satisfied. I discovered that I had already clearly distinguished two people: me before encountering the elephant, and me after encountering the elephant.

Sukhasiddhi gave a whistle, and the elephant knelt down. She said: "Get on." I brushed the dirt off my body. Taking hold of the hand Sukhasiddhi extended, I stepped onto the elephant's trunk and got up onto its back.

I felt Sukhasiddhi holding me, and she seemed to be exerting a lot of strength. I heard Sukhasiddhi laugh and say: "You passed the first-level test. Now I will ask you again: do you want to marry me?"

Without the slightest hesitation I said: "I do want to."

Sukhasiddhi said with a smile: "Do you know that these tests you have gone through are all caused by your karmic barriers? I'll tell you, when you were tossed up into the air by that elephant, the light of your mind and spirit shone forth. If you remember that feeling, and through it awaken to enlightenment, then you will be able to understand clearly what true mind is. Always remember, the 'mind' in the saying 'what is mind *is* Buddha' is the true mind. This is why only people who understand clearly what true mind is are qualified to say 'what is mind *is* Buddha.' Those people for whom false mind covers over true mind are not qualified to say 'what is mind *is* Buddha.'"

She also said: "When I talk about getting married, this is not ordinary conventional marriage; this is the marriage of the supreme truth. I will tell you what it means to 'take greed as the Path.' You must know, you cannot achieve Buddhahood if you just have wisdom, and you cannot achieve Buddhahood if you just have skill in means. Only when you have both wisdom and skill in means will you be able to experience the ultimate accomplishment."

The elephant was moving along slowly, and its back was undulating. Many people looked at the two of us on the elephant's back with wonderment. They were certainly surprised that this mad elephants had suddenly become so tame. Sukhasiddhi was accustomed to riding elephants, but I kept feeling that I would slip off. The elephant's back was very broad, and it was not like a horse's back which can be gripped tightly with your legs. Ordinarily, people who ride elephants use a kind of platform or seat; not many people rode as we were doing, on the elephant's bare back.

Although I kept feeling that I would slip off the elephant's back, my mind was still overflowing with that intoxicating joy. I was woozy, as though I were drunk. Although I could hear Sukhasiddhi's voice, in my perceptions, I felt her like a pure wind, like a rainbow, like a dream lingering in my mind. She seemed to have no coarse physical body: she was always this graceful, always this dreamlike. She was always bringing me a poetic feeling that could not be erased.

Sukhasiddhi said: "Now you have already illuminated the mind, but you have not seen inherent nature yet. Illuminating the mind is clearly understanding what the true mind is. You can clearly distinguish what is the true mind and what is the false mind, and thus you are qualified to say 'what is mind *is* Buddha.' But for you to see the Path truly and correctly in concrete events — probably you will only be able to accomplish this someday in the future. Son, you must know that even though I jokingly told you to marry me, joking like that was ultimately just joking. You must remember that, in revolving through birth and death lifetime after lifetime, I don't know how many times I have been your mother, and you don't know how many times you have been my mother. Revolving through birth and death is a giant game, and when you clearly understand that it is a game, you will genuinely have the possibility of liberation. Many times cultivating practice is not to dissolve away doubt and confusion, but rather is to make you understand clearly that fundamentally you do not have doubt and confusion. When you use the supreme viewpoint to look at the supreme meaning, you will then discover that supreme meaning. When you truly discover that supreme meaning, then you will have reached liberation."

11 Is This Enlightenment?

I felt myself washed in a fragrant wind, and the fragrance entered into every pore. My mind was totally lucid and clear. A perception like a cloudless clear sky appeared in my mind. I suddenly realized that Sukhasiddhi was actually my own self. Though she and I differed in name and form, ultimately, in fact, we were not two, not separate.

Sukhasiddhi smiled. She said: "It truly is like this. Only when you produce this perception can you be counted as having truly entered into accord with the Esoteric Vehicle. In the future there will be a day when you tell other people about this supreme liberation, and they will laugh at you, and they will say you are crazy. They may bring out some harsh reasons to deride you. Those people will not understand that they themselves are in fact not different from the teacher's tutelary deity. They are not even people outside the gate, because people outside the gate can still see the gate. They are just a bunch of headless flies flying around at random in the wilderness. Cycle of birth and death is prepared just for them.

"You must realize that the true power of liberation is to give rise to correct views. And the true correct view is that all external appearances are empty illusions and impermanent. You must clearly understand those empty illusions, and only then will you be able to talk about liberation. Speaking at the level of the ultimate truth, in reality, there is nothing for you to liberate.

"Son, do you understand what I am saying?"

Tears were running down my face, and choking back a sob I said: "I understand, my mother."

Sukhasiddhi smiled and said: "Remember, since I am your mother, I am also your enlightened consort. Since I am your teacher, I am also your servant. Since I am teaching you to clearly understand the inherent nature of mind, I am also receiving the wisdom that comes from you. You must not be constrained by these names and forms. In this world, what binds you is always your own mind. When you eliminate the final bit of clinging and attachment from your mind, then you will discover that, in reality, basically nothing exists that is worth liberating."

Something like rolling thunder surged up in my mind, bombarding every channel in my body. I even heard a lot of entanglements breaking up. I was both listening to Sukhasiddhi's instructions, and reflecting on the memory of that strange feeling of being thrown into the air by that elephant. Previously, although I had heard who knows how many esoteric teachings, and studied who knows how many scriptures, these things always existed in my mind in the form of intellectual knowledge. No matter whether I was lecturing on the Bonpo teachings or lecturing on the Buddhist esoteric teachings, I recognized that I was at best just parroting learned words. Although I had a better memory than most people, and I could remember anything I heard or read, and I could do and think about many things at once, nevertheless, everything that I had studied had not enabled me to produce this perception that Sukhasiddhi had bestowed on me. I realized that I had genuinely understood the scriptures, and the esoteric truth behind the scriptures, and where the gist of everything that the Buddha said lay.

I asked Sukhasiddhi: "Mother, is this enlightenment?"

Sukhasiddhi smiled and said: "This is still just the level of illuminating mind. It is not yet true enlightenment. True enlightenment is you seeing reality. At that time, the sky shatters and the earth collapses, and you will discover that all your clingings and attachments have been blown up and turned to smoke. At last, even this smoke is gone. At that time, sea and sky are one color, there are no hang-ups and no obstructions, no Buddha and no self, no birth and no death, no coming and no going, no clinging and no relinquishing. Only then can you be reckoned to have truly entered into seeing the Path. That is to say, only when you reach that moment, can you be counted as having begun to genuinely cultivate practice. All the efforts you made before this are just you seeking a way into cultivating the Path. That means, the true objective of these esoteric teachings which you have sought is to let you be able to enter into the Path that will enable you to reach ultimate enlightenment.

"Son, although you have visited more than a hundred teachers, and have sought hundreds of wondrous teachings, your goal in all of this has just been to enable you and the sentient beings who have a karmic connection to you to find the road that leads to enlightenment. This is like crossing a river. Though you may have a million boats, your goal is just to cross that river. After you have crossed the river, you will discover that all those boats, for you, have just become an encumbrance.

"Son, you have now illuminated mind. You are already not the person you were before. Although you have still not arrived at the final accomplishment, you now know the road to enlightenment. You cannot take the wrong road.

"But because of the sediment of the habit-energy of past lifetimes, you still will have a lot of habit-energy which you must clear away. You might regress at times from your enlightened state, just like dark clouds may at times cover the sun. But do not worry: those dark clouds will in the end disperse, and you will see the light of that sun.

"Indeed, from this point on, there is still a relatively long road that you must travel."

Chapter 17

The Light of the Great Mudra

1 The Myriad Forms So Numerous and Complex

Sukhasiddhi told Khyungpo Naljor that the special excellence of the Great Mudra lies principally in the level of perception. She had to point out directly that the original face is the real inherent nature of the suchness of phenomena, and this inherent nature has no birth and no defilement, but is revealed naked, right here and now.

Sukhasiddhi said: "The essence of the mind of sentient beings is fundamentally enlightened, fundamentally pure and clean, spiritually bright and empty, apart from all false thoughts, equal to the realm of the void, omnipresent. When the Buddhas awaken to it, it is not elevated, and when the sentient beings are deluded about it, it is not lowered. It is the everywhere-equal Dharmakaya of the Tathagatas, the

Body of Reality of Those Who Have Come from Thusness."

Sukhasiddhi said: "My child, the myriad events and things of the world are all manifestations of the inherent nature of mind. Seen from the surface, they are numerous and complex, maybe regular and orderly, maybe diverse and dynamic. But seen by the enlightened person, they do not really exist, because they are phenomena brought about by the interplay of causes and conditions, and none of them have an eternal unchanging inherent nature, so they have no real existence and are ultimately unattainable. When you understand this truth, then the myriad appearances spontaneously dissolve into the inherent body, and there is no need to take countermeasures."

Sukhasiddhi taught: "How can we be inherently liberated from those myriad appearances which are so numerous and complex? When worldly external appearances appear in your consciousness, you must immediately mesh directly with the clear empty inherent nature. Because external appearances are also manifestations of the inherent nature, the mind of inherent nature can spontaneously recognize this. It's like when two people who speak the same language meet in a foreign country: they can recognize each other when they hear each other's voices. In the same way, your five poisons — greed, anger, ignorance, pride, envy and so on — are manifestations of inherent nature, and when they appear in your mind, you only have to mesh with the empty inherent nature, and the five poisons will dissolve themselves. When the illusory external objects of the world and your illusory mind meet, you only have to mesh with the empty inherent nature, and it will be like cream dissolving in cream: all illusory forms will dissolve themselves based on their being illusory. When your conscious mind, the child of the light, seeks for itself, it directly meshes with the inherent body, and enlightenment spontaneously liberates itself based on its being enlightened, like water can certainly dissolve in water. When you are seeking the nondual real inherent nature, real inherent nature directly meshes with itself, and the truth of this goes beyond all verbal explanations, as the sky can definitely join with the sky."

Sukhasiddhi said: "This fundamental enlightenment of phenomena as they are is one, and has no duality. All it can do is spontaneously realize itself. When you understand inherent nature, and see through the falsity of the myriad appearances which are so numerous and complex, then right there you will experience the ultimate enlightenment. It is like when a man and woman in love meet. That ultimate meeting can only be completed by you yourself: the worldly externals cannot 'meet' for you.

"Though, from the superficial point of view, externally manifested objects are numerous and complex and diverse, you just have to penetrate through those numerous complex appearances and directly penetrate to the essence of their empty inherent nature, and then everything will spontaneously dissolve into the empty inherent nature. To make a comparison, all you have to do is cut the knot in the mind, and then the hundred knots of false thoughts and consciousness will also be untied. Therefore, the one and only ultimate liberation can only come from your mind of inherent enlightenment."

2 Mamu, the Female Demon

Beloved Khyungpo Ba, today as soon as Kumari arrived at my house, she threw into confusion the purity I had cultivated this morning reading the Diamond Sutra . This is because my power of meditative concentration is insufficient.

She had again heard some information about those men

who are directing curses at you. Their main deity is that female demon Mamu. The curses they did last time were a kind of preliminary method. This time is the true effort. First they drew a mandala. On the four sides of the mandala are four arrows, four hammers, four nets of illusion, and there are also some peacock feathers. Overall, it is some unheard-of strange trick. The offerings they are making are also very strange: the blood of various kinds of black animals, like last time, and they are also going to burn some grease from various kinds of black animals. Kusang Dorje told Kumari that the whole scene was shrouded in smoke, and dark and gloomy.

Kumari said that female demon Mamu—they of course call her a goddess—lives in the north. That is a red world: the mountains are red, the rivers are red, the rocks are red, the sky is red. In the very center of that red-colored world, there is an immense castle, made of ox hide, with sharp horns pointing up piercing the sky. This is the palace of this female demon. This palace is filled with the dead bodies of people and horses, stinks to high heaven, and has a murderous air to it. Under the command of the female demon Mamu are ten thousand flesh-eating yaksha demons. Their bodies are jet black, and they go forth like a raging fire. Their mouths are dripping with human blood and fat, and around their waists are tied the skins of newly slain people. They also have terrifying headdresses, and prayer beads made of fresh human heads, and necklaces made of fresh human hearts. These prayer beads and necklaces are strung together with writhing cobras.

The sorcerers invited Mamu and her female demons to come, and they presented them with various offerings to make them happy.

After this, the sorcerers began to pray:

"Goddess Mamu, please devour Khyungpo Ba's heart, please drink Khyungpo Ba's blood. Please use your soul-catching iron hook to pull out his heart, please use your noose to strangle him ..."

See, this is what they are up to. I don't know where the compassion they cultivated went. No matter whether it is Bonpo or Brahmanism, they both say that sentient beings are our fathers and mothers. But when they meet this Khyungpo Ba who does not satisfy them, why do they want to cause his death?

This is truly frightening!

I have discovered that people with a religious background are even more to be feared than ordinary people. This is because what that religious background brings to them can be a kind of noble-seeming fanaticism. Under their noble banner, they can always engage in very shameless maneuvers.

Look at this point of view of mine: how is it like a retired female spirit?

My father came and had a talk with me. He could see my anxiety, and he told me frankly that what I am seeking is the moonlight reflected in the water.

I cannot tell: between you and my faith, which do I love more? Did I go toward faith because I love you, or do I love you because I went toward faith? The two are cause and effect for each other. But right now I am tired of looking for the ultimate, and everything is all mixed together, so I'll just let it go, it doesn't have to be clear. It's just that I have a slight regret, that I cannot enjoy the singing and dancing at the temple of the female spirits with you. Probably, after this, it will be hard to get together, and even harder to find the time and place. It's like being a famous actor whose song is over and who has grown old: the stage is empty except for some lingering melody, how can I bear this feeling?

In the evening I read for a long time. Those books you left behind are very good. I just browse through them, and I feel my face perspiring. No wonder you always said that I just saw the most superficial things about you. You always regretted that I did not come up to your expectations.

Over doing it in love, clinging to illusion and not awakening — I know this is where my problems lie. This has already become the greatest barrier keeping me from entering the world of light which you praised, and which I want to enter deeply into. The aspect of you that acts like an "ordinary person" in words and deeds and every detail makes people deluded. Only when I stubbornly take you and put you on the holy man's seat, do the false thoughts in my mind gradually quiet down and clear away. Only then can I use my mind to read and understand the fine books you recommended. To read at a deep level, one must deliberately come into accord with the author: only then will there be spiritual interchange. Otherwise, it is just skimming over the surface. As for the true value of good books, just as with real people, it is always impossible to get to the real truth by only looking at the surface, because their outer appearance is not different from ordinary people. Just like with you.

Now I am diligently reciting and reading, and living a

peaceful life, so you should not worry about me.

If I think forward to ten years from now, if you and I can be cultivating practice in a quiet mountain valley, eating simply, living simply, calmly listening to the sutras, how free we will be, excellent as spirit immortals — this graceful fantasy has already become the most important reason that supports me as I go on waiting soexuberantly. Being your student in Buddhist studies, I respect the teacher like a Buddha, and what I regret is that I am comparatively ignorant and always make you feel there is nothing that can be done about it. I hope I can make up for my ineptitude by diligence and, after following you, become the clumsy bird who is not left behind by the flock. Then my heart will be satisfied.

Has it already been four years since you left me? I miss you very much.

As long as I recite the Diamond Sutra, I will have the spiritual strength to dissolve away my longings.

When I look at this old book you left behind, I hold it lovingly, and I almost want to cry. I stroke the object and think of the person, and sadness and joy intermingle.

Because I am an old friend, I am surprised to feel the years flowing by. Because I am an old friend, I see more that the feeling is deep and the intent is far-reaching.

We have only known each other for a few years, and, as if in a trance, we have already formed a pact for three lifetimes.

You better not write. If you write again, I will cry again.

When will your Sharwadi finally be able to achieve the spiritual power to travel a thousand miles in a night?

With this thought, suddenly my mind goes sour. Obviously

you are still on my mind, heavy, impossible to move.
So that remains.

3 The Key to Conquering Demons

Sukhasiddhi said to Khyungpo Naljor:

"Son, do not be afraid of that female demon, and do not be afraid of those sorcerers' curses.

"This is because all you have to do is recognize the pure light of the Great Mudra, and those evil demons will not be able to do anything to you. Whether that female demon Mamu or the other flesh-eating yakshas, they are all located in dualism. When your mind is also located in dualism, their evil techniques may be able to take effect. This is because the basis of their demonic methods is hatred and the false mind. When their false mind makes trouble for your false mind, then you might be subject to their control.

"But the pure light of the Great Mudra is the manifestation of the true mind.

"There are two basic principles for conquering demons. The one which is not the ultimate is to use violence to control violence, to use evil to control evil, to use force to control force. Only when your power is greater than the demons' power will you be able to succeed in conquering demons like this. The other one is the ultimate principal for conquering demons. That is to use your own true mind to subdue the demons' false mind.

"The Great Mudra is the latter method.

"Those who practice the Great Mudra have a natural ability to conquer demons, and when you are genuinely and permanently in the true mind, you are empty space, and the demons cannot find you.

And not just demons, even Yama the King of Death will not be able to find you. The rope of the god of death can tie up heroes who can uproot mountains, can tie up beauties who can overthrow kingdoms, but can it tie up empty space? Those who achieve the Great Mudra are like empty space, without clinging, without abandoning, unmoving and unshakable as mountains. When you experience this pure light, no matter what demons you meet, manifesting any form whatsoever, they will have no way to shake your mind. On the contrary, your mind of compassion and your wisdom will be able to magnetize your opponents. Only this is the real conquering of demons.

"The Great Mudra is divided into three: the Great Mudra of Reality, the Great Mudra of Composition, and the Great Mudra of Light. The Great Mudra of Reality belongs to the Great Mudra of the exoteric schools. You awaken to it and enter into it by taking the cultivation and realization of the reality of all phenomena as the principle thing, and by studying such scriptures as the *Treatise of the Middce Way*. The Great Mudra of the esoteric schools is divided into the Great Mudra of Composition and the Great Mudra of Light. The Great Mudra of Composition relies on the mudra to engender the bliss of emptiness, and realize fundamental enlightenment, and experience the light of great bliss. The Great Mudra of Light is the Great Mudra method of sudden entry. If an enlightened virtuous teacher encounters a student of superior potential, and if the karmic situation is ripe, the teacher has the student undergo the process of visualizing the wondrous characteristic of the teacher's tutelary deity, so the student can experience enlightenment then and there."

Sukhasiddhi said: "The level of perception of Great Perfection is lofty and transcendent, but it is only appropriate for people of superior potential. If one does not set about it from a basis in reality, it is very easy to drift into crazy wisdom. The Great Mudra is not this way. It is a level of perception, and it is also a teaching method. It is not a simple name and form; it is a teaching method that can lead the person who is cultivating practice to experience enlightenment. My teacher said: 'The only road to enlightenment is real cultivation. Just hearing of the Great Mudra is no way to get enlightened.' However, the Great Mudra is the light at the level of results. As long as there is pure faith, as long as there is real cultivation according to the teaching, realizing enlightenment is sure to happen. It is like being born a prince in a royal family — you don't have to work hard ploughing and weaving, but you will naturally have a rich life. In the same way, people who cultivate and uphold the Great Mudra, will naturally be able to obtain the support for the enlightened inherent nature growing within them."

Sukhasiddhi taught Khyungpo Naljor to put aside all the knowledge he had studied in the past. She said: "Knowledge and intelligence have nothing to do with enlightenment. Enlightenment cannot be separated from receiving the bequest of the teaching and really cultivating it. Even if you learn the five kinds of knowledge: phonology, logic, medicine, arts and technology, Buddhism, and you read through all the scriptures, if you do not have the genuine bequest of the teaching and you do not cultivate practice according to the teaching, you will not be able to succeed."

Sukhasiddhi said: "The 'greatness' of the Great Mudra contains all sentient beings, no matter whether poor or rich, high-ranking or low-ranking, no matter whether male or female or old or young. All sentient beings have the latent potential for enlightenment. The word 'mudra' means a symbol; it represents the mind seal of the Buddha. If you cultivate and uphold the Great Mudra, you do not have to cultivate any other method. This is because the Great Mudra already contains the essence of all teaching methods. It is as complete as the full moon, as omnipresent as the air. It is like the sky covering everything, like a great mountain which cannot be moved.

"The Great Mudra can be divided into three sections: 'the Root,' 'the Path,' and 'the Result.'

"What is called the Root Great Mudra means that all sentient beings have buddha-nature. This buddha-nature means the enlightened inherent nature concealed in every sentient being. This enlightened inherent nature is fundamentally complete of itself, originally so, without defilements or flaws, fundamentally pristine and pure. But people's greed and desires can always build up delusions and doubts in the mind, like dark clouds covering the sky; ignorance can always obstruct the pure, clear, enlightened nature that people originally have. The revolving in birth and death in the six planes of existence is the product of ignorance. When you understand the Root Great Mudra, then you will have three kinds of faith. One is the 'bright clear faith' that has faith that you, like your teacher, and like all the Buddhas and bodhisattvas, have the seed for becoming enlightened. This faith is solid and clear and immovable as a mountain. Second is the 'faith in looking forward.' Since you have the same buddha-nature and characteristics as all the Buddhas, you will long to realize ultimate wisdom, just as they do. Third is 'pure clear faith,' firmly believing that innumerable practitioners relying on the practice of the Great Mudra have already realized the supreme result of Buddhahood.

"What is called the Path Great Mudra means the methods of genuinely cultivating the Great Mudra. You must follow the proper order and gradually progress. First you cultivate the detachment of the Lesser Vehicle, then the mind of enlightenment of the Greater Vehicle, and then you mesh with the Esoteric Vehicle."

Sukhasiddhi said: "The theoretical foundation of the Great Mudra of Reality is the *Prajna Sutra*, which includes the extended version, the medium version, and the abbreviated version of the *Prajna Sutra*; these are also known as the *Million Commentaries on Prajna*, the *Twenty-four Thousand Commentaries on Prajna*, and the *Eight Thousand Commentaries on Prajna*, and so on. The principle set forth in these scriptures, that the inherent nature of all phenomena is true emptiness, is the theoretical foundation of the Great Mudra of Reality. The holy bodhisattva Nagarjuna said that we cannot find true liberation if we depart from the theory that the inherent nature of prajna is empty. No matter whether it is the Greater Vehicle or the Lesser Vehicle, no matter whether it is Yogacara or Madhyamika, and no matter whether it is the Exoteric School or the Esoteric School, if we want to reach real liberation, we must direct our contemplation practice according to the core content of the *Prajna Sutra*—only then will we be able to understand the original face of mind and, in the end, achieve true liberation.

"The Great Mudra has different names in the different schools of Buddhism. Some call it 'joining cultivation with life.' Some call it 'the great seal.' some call it 'the ability to cut off phenomena.' some call it 'the great contemplation of the mean.' Some call it 'the box of jewels.' And so on and so on. Though there are many bottles, each with a different shape, the wine in the bottles never diverges from that true perception of prajna."

Sukhasiddhi said: "There are very many methods of cultivation in the world, but if we explore their real substance and sum it up, there are only twotypes:

"The first type starts from the level of perception, and from perception seeks to cultivate practice. This means starting first from the inherent nature of mind, and first attaining the true perception of empty inherent nature, and then going on to cultivate meditative concentration.

"The other type seeks perception from cultivation. This means to start first by cultivating meditative concentration, to cultivate methods of stabilizing the mind, to dissolve away random scattering, to dissolve away sinking into confusion, so you pacify the restless wavering mind, and reach the state where body and mind are at peace. After you achieve meditative concentration, then from *stopping* you generate *observing*, and you observe the reality of all phenomena and achieve enlightenment."

Before this, the Great Perfection cultivated by Khyungpo Naljor was an example of starting from the level of perception and understanding the inherent nature of mind. But because his power of *stopping* was insufficient, it was also hard to preserve that *observing*. Thus, Sukhasiddhi drew on the past instructions, and first taught him meditative concentration (*stopping*), and had him cultivate his power of concentration; then, after he achieved concentration, she taught him to observe the basic substance of the myriad phenomena, and progress to removing the clinging to self and the clinging to phenomena.

Sukhasiddhi first taught Khyungpo Naljor how to harmonize the different parts of his body during sitting meditation and how to adjust his breathing to purify his karmic barriers. Because Khyungpo Naljor had an appropriate basis for meditation practice when he was in Bonpo, he was able to easily enter into these forms of meditation. Sukhasiddhi first taught him to rely on generating the aspiration for enlightenment, to visualize a field of provisions, the generations of teachers, the four continuing Buddhas, the hundred protective methods, and so on. After he took refuge in generating the aspiration for enlightenment, and visualizing the offerings, that field of provisions gradually fused with the basic teacher in the very center of the mirror of taking refuge. The teacher changed from being large to being small, and became the size of a grain of rice, and from the chakra on top of his head, flowed down along the central channel into the top of his head, and fused into an indestructible point of light in his mind.

Sukhasiddhi said: "Son, at this time, at this moment, you are the teacher, and the teacher is you, and you are not separate from your teacher's tutelary deity.

"Now that you are in this kind of quiet concentration, do not waver. Don't let your body waver, and don't let your mind waver. Do not think of the past. Do not think of the future. Stay at peace in the here and now. Do not worry about gain or loss. Do not let the imprint of the conventional world stay in your mind. Do not start discriminating thoughts toward anything. Do not have any expectations or any doubts. Even more, do not have any desires or hopes. You should visualize the teacher in your mind and your own inherent nature as not two, not separate. You are me and I am you. Apart from this, do not have any other random thoughts. But you must remember, this state you are in at this moment is not a daze, is not oblivion, is not anything at all. Remember, if the state of having no thoughts were the Great Mudra, then the grass and trees and mountains and rocks would already have become Buddhas.

"You must not fall into dull emptiness: that kind of inert emptiness, which is like soaking a rock in cold water, is meaningless. That correct meditative concentration is not a trance, is not hibernation, is not oblivious, unthinking, dull emptiness. You must not suppress thoughts. Your concentrated mind should extend through your central channel with the body of your teacher that is not separate from your inherent nature. You visualize that mantra in your teacher's mind: it is bright as the burning wick in a lamp. Link your thoughts to this, and do not waver. But at the same time, you must engender another kind of wisdom. This other kind of wisdom of yours must observe whether or not you are following the method, whether or not you are sinking into oblivion, whether or not you are scattering in confusion, whether or not there are random thoughts, whether or not your mind is beginning to waver. Your mind that observes must be like an eagle in the sky spotting its prey. You must not let any alteration in your mind go, you must pursue it, oversee it, observe it.

"Son, you must use the eye of wisdom and focus on that process of observation. That means your observing eye should not be too strong, and should not hurt your mind that is quiet and still. When your observing eye is too strong, your quiet and still mind might waver. The relationship between these two is very subtle — going too far is as bad as not going far enough. It is like the strings on a musical instrument: if the strings are too tight, they may break; if they are too loose, when you pluck them they produce no sound. You have to keep up the correct mindfulness of that wisdom observing at all times. It's like this: your power of *stopping* and your power of *observing* must approximately match each other. To concentrate on your teacher's body in your mind is a very clear condition for entering into meditative concentration. Of course sometimes, that power of *observing* will be less than that power of *stopping*. What you have to do time and again is to keep up that correct mindfulness of *observing*. Then it will be alright. At such times, you certainly must not forget how you are cultivating contemplation at this moment: it really is a very clear and bright state. That is, do not let your teacher get blurred in your mind, do not fade out — you must be very clear. At the same time, you must observe whether or not you are getting numb, and whether or not you are giving rise to the discriminating mind."

4 Do Not Fear That Demon Woman

Sukhasiddhi is speaking to Khyungpo Naljor:

"From the viewpoint of the people of wisdom, the discriminating mind is the demon. Look at those sorcerers who are cultivating the female demon Mamu. All they are doing is using the discriminating mind that draws distinctions between dirty and clean in the worldly sense to implement their curses. Of course, when the sorcerers' intent can mobilize the latent power of the world to resonate with their curses, then their curses can function. I even think that those sorcerers deliberately let that woman Kumari know the techniques they were using for these curses, knowing that they would have more power than if you did not know about them. Because, if you are still in a dualistic position, the demon of your discriminating mind and the demon of the power of their curses may resonate together and create an effect.

"Therefore, the key to conquering demons is to eliminate the discriminating mind.

"If you observe that you are already giving rise to the discriminating mind, then you must use two methods to counteract it. One is the method of suggestion: you suggest to yourself that this is the discriminating mind. And the discriminating mind is the greatest barrier to cultivating the Path, so you should not give rise to it. In this lucid state, you observe that discriminating mind which you have given rise to. When you observe it, and think about it, and suggest to yourself that you must not give rise to it, then that discriminating mind will melt away like frost in the hot sun. This is because, no matter what kind of discriminating mind it is, its fundamental substance is still impermanent, and still goes back to the nature of void. You must realize that the world is empty and false, and that the discriminating mind is even more empty and false. When you observe it with wisdom, then you discover that it is ultimately unattainable.

"Of course, in contrast to *stopping*, *observing* is a kind of discriminating state of mind. But when you begin to practice meditation, you cannot be without this discriminating mind. This is what people call correct mindfulness. It is like a watchman guarding a building: the purpose is to stop thieves from entering. You must become good at using this correct mindfulness, and use it to wipe out the other uninvited guests: whenever one appears, it gets wiped out. After practising and perfecting this for a long time, that storm of subtle discriminating states of mind gradually lessens. Just as a stormy ocean will ultimately settle down, your false thoughts will become fewer and fewer. Finally, the observing subject and the object being observed merge into one, and you reach the point where *stopping* and *observing* are moving together. Then you will have *stopping* within *observing* and *observing* within *stopping*: both *observing* and *stopping*, both *stopping* and *observing*. In the end, you will not even cling to that correct mindfulness any more."

5 A Moving Tadpole

Sukhasiddhi is speaking to Khyungpo Naljor:

"At this point, worldly spirits like the female demon Mamu will no longer be able do anything to you.

"When you reach that state of empty stillness, you will discover that you no longer distinguish among colors and sounds and odors and tastes and textures, and you will no longer have so many ordinary worldly discriminating states of mind. In this state, you will have been transformed so that there are no marks of self, no marks of others, no marks of sentient beings, no marks of life. Your mind will be like a wall, absolutely unwavering. As you go on visualizing, in your teacher's mind there will be a lake. It will be very bright, like a bright mirror, and the water will be flat as a mirror, without any waves or ripples. Although the water has no waves or ripples, in the water they will be a tadpole moving. That tadpole will be the size of a mosquito, like a light, like a rainbow, seeming to be there, seeming not to be there, but clearly in focus. That water will be very bright, radiating light like a bright mirror. You concentrate and observe that tadpole. The tadpole's movements are very graceful, graceful to the point that you cannot see any ripples in the water. That tadpole is really your previous observing wisdom, and you are in a state of *stopping* that is like still water. You are using the little tadpole of wisdom to observe yourself, to observe your own basic substance. At the same time, you are also observing that mind where you and your teacher are not two and not separate, and of course you are also observing your teacher's basic substance in your own mind. Pay attention to the scale of the observing: it is a very small tadpole in a giant body of still water. Do not make that tadpole get big, do not stir up big waves.

"First you observe yourself. You observe where that 'self' of yours ultimately is, and what ultimately it is composed of. Is it a solid? Is it a liquid? Is it heat? Is it air? You will end up discovering that your physical body is no more than a combination of material causes and conditions. It came from emptiness, and in the end it will return to emptiness. While you are alive, it seems to have physical form, and once you are dead, the material elements separate, and then you will no longer be able to find that 'self.' You will discover that so-called 'self' is in reality a big hoax. It is just a false name placed on a temporary form made up of a combination of causes and conditions. When you think it through and analyze it step by step, you truly cannot find the existence of a 'self.' You end up discovering that you have entered into a state where nothing is there. Your meditation practice, in reality ultimately returns to the empty inherent nature, and then you eliminate all the clinging and attachment. When you go on cultivating contemplation like this, you will discover that no matter whether 'the self' or 'phenomena,' none of it has an ultimately unchanging, true, inherent nature, and all of it is nothing but the manifestation of illusory transformations, and it has no real essence that exists independently.

"Remember, in their basic substance, all the myriad forms in the world are your discriminating mind. It is empty and illusory and not real. Its basic substance is impermanent, and has no eternal unchanging basic essence. As you observe it again and again, you will discover that it falls into emptiness again and again, and you will slowly lose your clingings and attachments and enter into a state of meditative concentration. And in this state of meditative concentration, the myriad things will reveal even more their fundamental state of empty inherent nature. No matter whether worldly phenomena or world-transcending phenomena, nothing is not like this. Though they have the process of interdependent origination manifested by cause and effect, though cause and effect are not empty, those causes and effects in reality also have no inherent nature. When you keep on pursuing this, you will discover that there is nothing that does not go back to the empty inherent nature. When you observe this way, when you constantly observe, you will fuse the empty inherent nature and your own cultivation of meditation into a single whole. After a long time, you will get to the point that you do not have to deliberately observe, and then that awareness and correct perception will always arise, and observe your human life. Whatever situations you are faced with, you will always be able to directly recognize the inherent emptiness of the myriad phenomena, and in a state where subject and object are both empty, you will spontaneously enter a state of stable meditative concentration. Then you will be able to get to the point where *stopping* and *observing* are working together, and you can move forward and eliminate clinging to self and clinging to phenomena.

"You should know that people's habit-energy is formed by a long process of influences. The surrounding environment can change a person's habit-energy. When you are always with an enlightened teacher, after a long time, you will be imbued with good habit-energy, and you will become a good person. If you are always with bad associates, after a long time, you will be imbued with bad habit-energy, and you will become a bad person. A standard example is when a child is carried off by a wolf into a wolf's den. After living there for a few years, the child will turn into a wolf-child. Even if you take the child back to the human world, it will be very hard for him to get rid of the habit-energy of a wolf-child. However, hard to get rid of does not mean impossible to get rid of. If someone can change from a person into a wolf, by the same token, as long as there is a good environment, there is the possibility of changing a bad person into a good person. The goal of contemplation practice is to exert a good influence on a person. When you enter into wisdom and contemplation practice over a long time, and you discover that there is nothing in the world worth clinging to, all your clingings and attachments are accordingly removed. One day, when you truly discover your original face, and see the light of the empty inherent nature, even if just for a brief moment, because you have already experienced the flavor of this perception, and you have already recognized it, then it will be possible for you to preserve this correct mindfulness. Then, after a long period of practice, you will be able to fuse into one with it.

"When you have removed all attachments to apparent phenomena, you will then be able to feel the basic substance of the myriad things, and that realm of the empty inherent nature will spontaneously manifest itself. When you enter in stable concentration in the midst of this kind of manifestation, you will be able to enter into very excellent states of concentration.

"You will discover that, at the same time the myriad things are in the process of interdependent origination, they are not apart from the inherent emptiness, and the inherent emptiness at the same time manifests the process of interdependent origination. It is not that the myriad things only have interdependent origination or only have inherent emptiness. It's that the two are one essence, and run in parallel without interfering with each other. This way you can leave behind the two extremes of nihilism and eternalism.

"When you observe seriously like this, no matter what kind of appearances are manifested by the six sense organs (eyes, ears, nose, tongue, body, conceptual mind) and the six sense objects (form, sound, scent, flavor, touch, conceptualized things), you will understand clearly that they have no inherent nature and are empty and false. This way, you will not cling to them, and then you will notice that you are observing their original face, and mesh with the empty inherent nature. You will discover that everything in the world is like this, and no matter what its manifest form from the process of interdependent origination, its basic substance is that it returns to the empty inherent nature. When, on the meditation seat, you have eliminated the nihilist view and the eternalist view and sophistries, and you have imprinted your life with the wisdom of correct perception, then even when you come out of meditative concentration, that wisdom will still observe your human life, and you will discover that everything before your eyes is illusory and impermanent. These things are as illusory as the moon reflected in the water or flowers reflected in a mirror, as unattainable as a mirage, as illusory as a rainbow. Then you will discover that, although all sorts of things and events manifest differently, their fundamental nature still returns to the empty inherent nature and has no real substance. The manifestations of interdependent causal origination are not apart from the emptiness of inherent nature, and the basic substance of the emptiness of inherent nature does not obstruct interdependent causal origination."

6 Resting at Peace in the Here and Now

Sukhasiddhi said: "If we summarize it, *stopping* is cultivating stable meditative concentration. *stopping* can enable us to awake to the ultimate inherent nature of our own mind. Strong solid *stopping* is the foundation for any cultivation of practice. Success in cultivating *stopping* can enable you to completely fulfill any teaching method. Only when you have a strong power of meditative concentration will you be able to enter the realm of *observing*, and be able to receive the essentials of mind of the Great Mudra, and be able to achieve the results of the Great Mudra. *observing* is cultivating wisdom. When we have gone through the cultivation of *stopping*, we will then be able to awaken to the inherent nature of all apparent phenomena, which is neither born nor destroyed — this is *observing*. We must realize that, for all the myriad things in the world, as well as the 'self' which every person clings to, their basic substance is the empty inherent nature. But sentient beings cling to the illusory as real and consider the false as true. Because the greatest ignorance is clinging to the self, since time without beginning, the fact that sentient beings cling to the existence of the 'self' has produced clinging and attachment, and the habit-energy of the five poisons is born from this. If practitioners observe according to the true teaching, they will discover that the 'self' does not exist: it is not outside the body, not inside the body, not in the cells, not in illusory thoughts. The 'self' is just an assembly of all kinds of causal conditions: its inherent nature is fundamentally empty, and there is ultimately nothing there. This is also so for the 'selves' of phenomena: all phenomena are born from causal conditions, and all phenomena perish from causal conditions."

Sukhasiddhi said: "The realm of using inherent mind to directly observe inherent mind goes beyond everything. If we can stay in this kind of realm, that is *observing*, and it is also staying in the inherent nature of the Great Mudra. Then we do not worry about the past, and we are not hung up on the future, and we stay at peace in a state of equilibrium in the here and now, far removed from all false thoughts, directly observing the fundamental nature of inherent mind. This transcends dualism, and all paired concepts like subject and object. This then is the 'ultimate wisdom'sought by the Great Mudra."

Sukhasiddhi said: "When you are directly observing inherent mind, sometimes there may be false thoughts flying around, but you must not cling to them, and you must not distinguish them. Let the ones that come, come by themselves, and let the ones that go, go by themselves. Do not be happy about the good ones or sad about the bad ones. Do not suppress them, do not push them away. All you have to do is observe their basic substance, and that will do. This way, in an instant, we can directly mesh with the pure inherent nature that has been fundamentally so from the beginning. If you understand how to stay at peace in the fundamental nature of inherent mind, and you can hold onto it from moment to moment, this is the highest most profound method."

Sukhasiddhi said: "Staying at peace in meditative concentration without thoughts and without clingings is definitely not the oblivion of being unconscious. Rather, we must stay in the fundamental nature of inherent mind. This inherent nature is far removed from idle theorizing, it is pure and unified, one flavor, this is the realm of the Dharmakaya, the Body of Reality of the Buddhas. The purity and clarity of inherent nature is the realm of the Sambhogakaya, the Reward Body of the Buddhas. This clarity and purity has no real essence but does have all kinds of manifestations; though it is the empty inherent nature, it has so much arising from interdependent causal origination — this is the realm of the Nirmanakaya, the Body of Transformation of the Buddhas. In other words, the oneness of the mind detached from argument is the Body of Reality, the clarity and purity of the mind is the Body of Reward, and the endlessness of the mind is the Body of Transformation."

Sukhasiddhi said: "Staying at peace in inherent nature is the essential meaning of all the teaching methods.When this one teaching is comprehended, there is complete liberation. If we can stay at peace in this, there is no need to study any other teachings. After a long time, afflictions gradually dissolve, wisdom gradually increases, compassion and wisdom expand. All ignorance and greed and anger and stupidity spontaneously let go like a snake uncoiling.

"Son, in order to take a step forward in maturing the inherent nature of your mind, I will bring you to that sacred land of the dakinis and let you go forward in receiving the undefiled teachings of many dakinis."

7 The Spell of the Female Demon Mamu

Sharwadi went to look for the dakini Bandi.

Bandi was very famous in Nepal;from the king on down to the ordinary people, almost everyone knew of her. She had successfully cultivated the teaching of the White Vajravarahi, and she was good at removing obstacles and stopping disasters, and she had eliminated troubles for many people. Bandi was a dakini living at the lower levels of society. She had won wide respect with her real accomplishments. At that time, there were many dakinis in Nepal cultivating the esoteric teachings. They were not the same as the female spirits. The female spirits were recognized and supported by the monarch. The worship of the female spirits was like a national religion, whereas the dakinis just won the belief of the lower orders. The royal house gave a lot of support to the female spirits, but it was not the same for dakinis like Bandi. The royal family did not dare to offend dakinis of this kind, but they were not willing to openly support them or aid them. They were very fearful of the social influence of the dakinis, and feared that their political power might challenge the power of the king. The social status of the dakinis was a bit like that of the spirit women in my home area of Liangzhou: though they were widely believed in, they never had any great social status. What was different from the spirit women of Liangzhou was that the dakinis were holy women who had experienced realization of the empty inherent nature, while the spirit women were still just ordinary people.

Bandi lived in a cave in the mountains far from the city. The cave was open all year long. Inside there were some religious vessels and some offerings, but besides this, nothing else. No one would dare to steal Bandi's things, and besides, in Bandi's cave there was nothing that would interest the common person. It was said that Bandi was as rich as the king, but she was penniless. She did not love wealth. There had been countless people who donated countless precious jewels to her, but she turned around and gave them away to other people. She knew the location of a lot of buried treasures, but she never thought of going to dig them up.

Sharwadi cut off her own hair, and tied it to an iron ring at the entrance to the dakini Bandi's cave. By this means she showed her sincerity, and this was the equivalent of making an appointment. The dakini would help other people resolve problems based on their appointments.

Sharwadi was thinking: "When will Bandi finally come back?"

After she went home, Sharwadi wrote another letter to Khyungpo Naljor:

My dear husband:

I heard tell you got sick, and I am very worried. I went again to find that dakini Bandi, who can avert the curses, and I hear that she will return soon. Once she comes back, I will go find her. I believe she will help me. Of course, I will offer her a very sumptuous present.

I inquired around and found out that the mandala set out by those men is called the net of illusion. They used the power of a strange spell to take some empty space and weave it into a strange net. After that, they used a special method to draw those demons into the net. They may have made offerings to them, or they may have used witchcraft, but then they let them go, and had them pursue you to go to do the things the sorcerers ordered them to do.

Kumari said that those sorcerers took the female demon Mamu's spell and wrote it on a piece of paper and drew a picture of the female demon, and placed it inside the net of illusion to symbolize the foundation of Mount Sumeru. On the four sides of the picture of the female demon there are four black men, and they are pulling handles dripping fresh blood. There are also four men holding the medicinal herb mahuang. Besides this there are also many other things, like a hundred and eight effigies, arrows, twenty-four shin bones drenched in fresh blood, and so on and so forth. In all, it is very frightening.

Every day these men take poisonous sand, which has been cursed, and throw it toward the direction of your search, and they release those evil demons. According to their explanation, these demonic children and grandchildren will pursue you, deploy their demonic powers to make you sick, and cause you to face afflictions and karmic barriers and so on.

I do not know: is your illness related to this or not?

I am always very worried for you.

Lately, I am always in a daze, and my throat is very sore. When I am awake, I think about you and miss you a lot, and I remember little bits and pieces from when we were together.

Really I am very tired, but I will persevere and carry on. You said that love needs a kind of ritual form. Persevering is a kind of ritual form. Because I love you, I cannot lose you.

As I have said, as long as I am alone, I must write you letters. I must keep my own promise. This is my choice. If I leave you with the bad impression that I am fickle and do not do my duty, then one day you will meet another woman you can love and trust, and that could shake your love for me. As long as that woman has not yet appeared, I must work hard to clear away that residual habit-energy; I cannot create the opportunity for another woman. I am actually a person who has no conflict with the world; I just want to win my lover's heart.

Khyung, you do not know how much I have suffered to find you, how many tears I have cried, how many twisting and turning roads I have traveled. I am not much different from that little girl begging in the street, with her straw sandals all worn out. This is because I am foolish, and I have not yet developed the two eyes of wisdom. In this vast ocean of people, I cannot tell who will be my husband in this lifetime. It was I who carelessly lost you. How anxious I am. I am always seeking you. Finally, one day, I will meet you.

Under your fiery look, I suddenly get alarmed: I have found him. Our meeting each other may have happened with the help of the spirits. Up until today, I still feel as if I were dreaming, as if I were stupid and drunk; my mind is in a daze, and I am unwilling to wake up. I clearly know that loving you is very painful and very difficult, but I still do not know how long a road I must travel, I still do not know what kind of wind and rain I will meet with on the road. But I can happily accept it all. Do not trouble yourself about this. This is my affair.

In my mind there is a feeling of gratitude, of thankfulness to heaven for allowing us to recognize each other in the years when we can still love each other. If not, my mind would still be hanging, without a branch to perch on. Think of how many people in this world who muddle along in ignorance and do not realize it, who let the people they are closest to, the people they love the most, just brush by them and go. So is there still anything I should seek? Is there anything else to be greedy for? How can I abandon this?

I saw you in a dream last night. How happy I was, jumping for joy like a little bird, flapping my wings and flying away, stopping on your knee, intently looking at you, chirping and pecking at your hand (the chirping was me gently saying "I ... love ... you"). At the end I saw your head of hair like a dense forest, and on it I made a nest and roosted. Every day at dawn I will be at the window still singing a song for you to hear.

I'm tired and drowsy, and do not know what I am saying. Please do not laugh at me.

Thank you for loving me.

Your Sharwadi

Also:

Let me write another letter to you. The spirit dove has gone once and is very tired, and I will tell it to bring a bit more of my love.

When I finished the work that my father assigned me, and I returned to my room, it was already very late. I stood on the balcony and looked for a moment at the night sky, and the full moon seemed to be hidden and then seemed to appear. I thought of you. The thing that is most necessary to do, for a woman, is maybe to look far up into the starry sky—this way she can keep herself from being too wrapped up in the trivial things of life.

I was thinking that by this time, you would already be fast asleep. Sleeping deeply, sleeping peacefully, with your mind especially steady. I thought of the way you peacefully fall asleep, and then it was as if I had turned back into a young person, peaceful and without worries.

I again began to feel heartache. I know that what you bear on your shoulders, what you bear in your mind, are too many responsibilities, duties, missions — and all of this was not forced on you by anybody. A person who has clearly understood must take on responsibilities, but you must not get too exhausted. When you get tired, then put it down. I am more willing to be an ordinary woman.

I am not used to the status of female spirit any more, and I do not worry any more about what happens after this life, and I do not think about things like the meaning of life. What does it matter whether or not people remember me after I die — I don't care. As I wrote to you in a letter, what I care about are my needs while I am alive, like breathing, and not about leaving behind a famous name after I die. I am just an ordinary woman, and I like a good man, and liking is liking, not for any purpose. I like seeing you happy, and if some day you get tired of being a yoga master, than don't be one. If your search makes you unhappy, then do not search anymore. Whether you are a Buddhist monk or a herdsman, whatever makes you content, then do that. Why do you always have to take on a mission? If you are not happy, then slow down a bit. After you have slowed down, then talk about it again.

Loving you is like climbing a mountain. The higher I climb, the thinner the air is. Human footprints are very rare and the challenges are very dangerous. It gets harder and harder to go forward or go up. Don't you see? What is so hard about being a plain ordinary person, moving along the streets, walking on level ground?

If you feel it is hard, if you feel exhausted, it is still the same, you are certainly climbing—you must be happy, then it is right. But you also must slow down at the appropriate times, relax and take it easy. Do not push yourself too much.

Searching and trekking is too hard. If you do not want to go on again, then why not slow down for a while? No one except you is forcing you to take on this mission. You could be a free, sincere, wayward, wild child, barefoot and running free, singing out loud the whole way ... Ah, I'm thinking, then my house would have no space to let you sing, and would suffocate you.

I am like you. I am very unwilling to go up to the spirit altar. You should lower your expectations, I am definitely no female spirit. I just like you, and I do the things a woman must do, just this and no more.

The longer I write my letter, the longer I can be with you.

Sharwadi, who loves you.

8　I Don't Regret Knowing You

My female spirit:

After hearing my teacher Sukhasiddhi's exposition on the Great Mudra, a lot dropped from my mind, and my body got very much better.

Although my body still gets sick from time to time, I do not consider this to be caused by the female demon Mamu. In fact, in my eyes Mamu, the female demon, is a mother, and if she were to need my life, I would give it to her.

I still often see those demons with their fangs and claws, and I even believe that they are really sent by those sorcerers. I basically do not have to have them take action to eat me— I will kill myself and make an offering to them. I think that, by giving charity to those demons, I will complete my own bodhi-mind. The strange thing is, at the beginning, no matter how I visualized the protective circle—I could clearly visualize the protective curtain of rods, and the defensive canopy of fierce flames, I had no way to block the evil demons attacking me. But when I simply took my physical body and life and gave it to them, contrary to expectations, my body became much better.

When I've read your letters, I am always intoxicated, and a deep lovesick feeling pours out. When I am traveling, the feeling changes. The person I was before was a sinner exiled by Heaven to live among humans. The person I am now is a man in the grip of great good fortune. After my teacher Sukhasiddhi taught me the inherent nature of mind, my mind was clear and wide as the sky, without a wisp of clouds. I did not anticipate that all I have been working to cultivate would be smashed to pieces by your letter.

Last night I dreamed of you. I was embracing you, lying there blessedly intoxicated. In the light of the dream, a dakini told me: "Sharwadi is your woman. You must calmly accept everything from her."

Your perfect genuineness and purity has moved me. If it had been before, I would have fled. I feared I would hurt you, because for a woman who fell in love with me, it might be that once she had crossed the sea, no other body of water would compare. This is what Bapu said when I was talking about you with him. He said that even if you meet someone else in life, that person might lose his color in contrast to me, and then you will painfully search your whole life long, but you will never again find someone like me. I don't know whether or not what Bapu said had some truth in it.

But I still do not regret knowing you. Though the heartache I feel toward you has become an element disturbing my tranquility, at the same time, I feel engulfed in a great poetic feeling. This will accompany me throughout my whole life, and has merged into my life.

Khyungpo Naljor, who loves you

9　Was She Really a Demon Bewitching You with Emotions?

Xuemo's voice:

When I read Khyungpo Naljor's letter, I smiled and said: "If I just read this letter, you hardly seem like an accomplished teacher who has sought liberation — it's simply emotion running free. Could it be that those previous instructions from Sukhasiddhi had no effect on you at all?"

The old man laughed. "Son, I'll tell you a story. Some years ago, in a certain incarnation I appeared as a fish. What was different about me from the other fish was that I could think like a human. I had a wisdom that the ordinary fish does not have. One day, as I was swimming somewhere, suddenly I sensed a fine flavor. I looked, and it was some bait. I knew this was dangerous, and I knew that if I got caught, I would end up as food in the fisherman's bowl. So I swam away. But that fragrant flavor was like a rope tied to me. Again and again I swam away from it, and again and again I was pulled back by it. My rational nature told me I could not swallow the bait, but my body would not listen. Later I couldn't help myself, and I swallowed the bait, and that ended that particular lifetime.

"Son, this is what the ancestors said: 'You see through it with your eyes, but your stomach cannot bear to let it go.' To understand the inherent nature of mind is not the same thing as being about to rest peacefully in the inherent nature of mind. Theoretically understanding it cannot take the place of resting there peacefully in fact.

"Although I understood the empty illusory nature of emotions, many times my mind would not necessarily obey me.

"You certainly must remember, in the process of my long search, the most difficult thing was not crossing myriad mountains and rivers; rather, it was breaking away from Sharwadi's feelings. In the same way, in my eyes, those sorcerers' curses were in fact not to be feared, but Sharwadi's letters could always make me begin to think of turning back. Though I understood that the search was my reason for living, whenever I thought of Sharwadi, I would feel an enormous attraction that would pull me back to the place that would let me be content with happiness and enjoy the pleasures of family life.

"For this reason, some people even consider Sharwadi as a demon bewitching me with emotions."

I asked: "In your eyes, was she really a demon bewitching you with emotions?"

Khyungpo Naljor did not say anything. He just let out a long sigh.

Chapter 18

Teaching the Sweet Dew of the Dakinis

Xuemo: "Master, can you tell us something of those wondrous journeys of the dakinis?"

1 Could It Be That You Forgot Your True Mind?

Sukhasiddhi said to me: "There are textual teachings that are certainly of special excellence, but even more excellent are the transmissions of mind that come like droplets from the mind of the dakinis. This is because true enlightenment is difficult to explain in words. Those great wordless teachings are still present in the inherent nature of the enlightened mind of the dakinis, waiting for people with karmic connections to come receive them. Son, I feel that your karmic connection has arrived. You and I will go meet with those great enlightened females. I just hope you can become an important link in the chain of transmission of those dakini teachings."

So we mounted a great elephant and went together to that famous sacred ground of the dakinis. As to where this sacred ground of the dakinis is ultimately located, there are many accounts.

Sukhasiddhi said: "Son, although you will be able to receive pure stainless teachings from me here, and you will not have to travel far, nevertheless you must know that sometimes I would rather that you meet with those great enlightened females. Though at the level of the ultimate truth, I am not separate from them, from the point of view of interdependent causal origination, it would undoubtedly be an excellent causal condition for you to meet with them. Because of this causal condition, all the successors in your teaching line will get the direct support of the dakinis. A thousand years in the future, these dakinis will come in the form of ordinary women to protect and support your line of transmission of the teaching, and enable it to start a prairie fire of wisdom that will fill the world."

The sacred ground of the dakinis that I saw was a wild mountain valley with no human tracks. Because I had not yet experienced ultimate enlightenment, the sacred ground of the dakinis which I traveled through was made in the form of a dream realm of light. I saw that hill flooded with red light; that red was like rust. I understood that what I was seeing was only an apparent realm, and that what Sukhasiddhi had brought me to visit was a secret realm. So then, at Sukhasiddhi's request, I entered into a dream realm of light and immediately I saw a very majestic mandala. It appeared in the bright clear sky like a dark color spreading out on paper. At first I saw the outer layer of the mandala, composed of countless skulls linked together, expressing the selflessness of all phenomena and the impermanence of all actions. Then I saw the second layer: it was a protective circle made of lotus flowers strung together, expressing purity without defilement. Then there were curtains of fire woven of diamond rods — I recognized that those many curtains of fire also existed at the same time within the inherent nature of my mind. I also saw boundless infinite grandeur, and in the same way I recognized that all this grandeur also existed within the inherent nature of my mind.

I felt the immense added support of the mandala, and my mind suddenly became very pure, very supple, without afflictions. I saw the dakinis traveling through the sky like a flock of birds. Among them were diamond dakinis, lotus dakinis, dakinis with Buddhas, jewel-born dakinis, dakinis with work to do. They were all world-transcending dakinis. Around each world-transcending dakini countless this-worldly dakinis were circling. Although the this-worldly dakinis had not yet achieved ultimate enlightenment, they had all generated the mind of enlightenment, and made vows to protect and uphold the True Dharma, and to undertake the various tasks of those who practice according to the Dharma.

At the entrance to the mandala, those I met first were this category of this-worldly dakinis. They were as frightening as yakshas, opening their huge mouths, as though they had infinite hatred for me as this dirty thing who wanted to enter the sacred precincts. Since their duty was to protect the sacred precincts, they would absolutely not permit those who had not yet experienced empty inherent nature to come in and disturb the purity of the sacred ground. So they opened their huge mouths, which were like mountain caves, and spewed out a current of air like a black wind; in this current of air there were all sorts of poisonous insects, like scorpions, spiders, centipedes, and so on. Now and then they also came out with huge claps of thunder. The thunder sounded terrifying, and spread a sulfurous odor that assaulted the nostrils. After this, there was a downpour of rain, not an ordinary downpour, but one that held the stench of blood in the rain and wind, as if countless streams of purulent blood were pouring down along with the rain. Wriggling in the purulent blood, there were all sorts of toads and lizards and other scary, poisonous things. Those poisonous creatures were also letting forth ear-splitting noises, like saws rasping. All this pulled back and forth at my nerves and made me feel like killing myself. After this, this great thunder finally rolled out into spherical bolts of lightning, like giant wheels rolling at me.

I could not help shrieking.

Then the voice of Sukhasiddhi sounded in my ears: "Could it be that you have forgotten your true mind?"

At this, I remembered Sukhasiddhi's teaching, and I immediately entered into an enlightened state. The strange thing was, as soon as I entered into the enlightened state, all those evil dangerous apparitions instantly changed into cool refreshing purity. That rolling thunder became a heavenly woman scattering flowers, and all those poisonous things turned into lotus flowers covering the ground.

The worldly dakinis became even more enraged. They bared their sharp fangs, and glared angrily at Sukhasiddhi. Sukhasiddhi smiled and said: "O dakinis who have made vows, do not waste your mental energy. All your effort is, in my eyes, only child's play. Look, I have not even moved a single hair." As she said this, Sukhasiddhi looked at them with intense focus. Her "body" became as solid as a mountain, immovable, unshakeable. Her "speech" was like a deep abyss, without wave, without ripples. Her "mind" was like a diamond, with no sense of danger or fear. Her whole body emitted the sacred pure light which only the truth has, and that light instantly magnetized those worldly dakinis. They started to cry, and knelt down on the ground. They said: "O Great Mother, please forgive our crude behavior. Your light is like the sun, and we are just moths flying into the fire. Please receive us. We want to offer you our life force and our mind mantras and to follow your orders lifetime after lifetime."

Sukhasiddhi smiled and said: "Chopsticks cannot reach the bottom of the ocean. I understand your behavior. You should cultivate yourselves well. You should not look down on this son of mine. He is like the young offspring of the giant roc. Though his wings are still weak, and he cannot soar about the nine heavens, a big sparrow is still a sparrow, and a giant roc, though still small, will still be a giant roc. All it will take is some time, and the fire of his wisdom will surely be able to start a prairie fire."

Saying this, Sukhasiddhi took me and continued forward.

2 The Guests Who Arrive Unexpected

We had not gone ahead very far when I discovered a river. The river water was pure and clear, and there was a gurgling sound. We were just about to cross the river, but we saw a spark flying forward like a shooting star. After it hit the water, the river water burst into flames. At first the flame was not large, but gradually it spread out, and after a while, the whole surface of the river was burning. That gurgling water sound changed into the sound of a crackling fire. It was as if what was burning was not a liquid, but rather an endless supply of firewood.

The light of the fire hit the sky, and the clouds in half the sky also burst into flames. The river had already become a ferocious writhing fire dragon. Sparks shot out in every direction, and gradually the sparks turned into a mass of flying dakinis. They were dancing and singing in the flames. We heard the words of their song clearly:

The forms of the world of phenomena are all made by mind,

The guests that arrive unexpected;

The fire of the world of phenomena is wisdom,

The guest that arrives unexpected;

Those burning afflictions originate in your mind,

The guests that arrive unexpected;

Completely realizing that all things are dreamlike illusions,

The guests that arrive unexpected.

Sukhasiddhi smiled and said: "Did you hear that clearly, son?"

I said: "I heard it clearly."

Sukhasiddhi smiled and said: "Then you already know what you have to do."

I said: "That's right. I already know that all those great fires, in reality, have no inherent nature, are all created by mind, and there should be no worry or fear. But the strange thing is, although theoretically I understand that the fire is an illusory form, I still feel the hot waves hitting my face, to the point that they are singeing my hair." I took a step back, and then I heard Sukhasiddhi call out: "Son, in reality that heat is not the fire, it is your discriminating mind. Do not forget what I taught you. Take all those forms and merge them into inherent nature."

I was secretly ashamed, thinking, "How did I again lose the

enlightened state?" So I brought up correct mindfulness, and I waded into the river. But I discovered that what I had entered into was a real river, and all kinds of cool refreshing feelings came over me. The water was making a gurgling sound, and there were innumerable waves on the surface, and still there were fish swimming freely in the water. I lifted my head, and I saw Sukhasiddhi was already on the other bank, I don't know for how long, looking right at me with a clear smile.

"Do you understand yet? Everything which has form is all empty illusion," she said, smiling.

Again we went on, and we came to a huge deep valley. It stretched to the horizon and was deep beyond measure. In the valley a great mushroom cloud rose up. When I first looked at it, the mushroom cloud was still small, about the size of a skull, but it expanded with alarming speed, and in a instant, it extended out to the horizon. It was as if it were a mushroom-shaped giant mouth that was devouring the sky. And the blue sky really turned into a liquid, and was flowing into that giant mouth.

I saw a flock of small birds flying toward it, and once they were seized by that mushroom cloud, they all fell to earth, burned black. I thought, "What kind of cloud is this anyway?" I looked up at Sukhasiddhi, but she smiled without answering.

I thought: "I understand that is a poison cloud." Previously, I had heard that it was very difficult on the road to the sacred land of the dakinis, and sometimes you would encounter poisonous air. And there were some dakinis whose holy lands were the islands of poisonous dragons. Because there was a poisonous atmosphere, people rarely went there, and it was advantageous for cultivating practice.

I saw that that poisonous mushroom cloud had already expanded to the sky and was moving toward me. Judging by the speed with which it was engulfing the sky, I would not be able to stop it getting me. I did not know what kind of feeling I would have from being pulled into a poisonous atmosphere, and I thought it would be harder to take than being put into a chimney. If that poisonous air had a very strong corrosive power, my physical body would surely be obliterated. Buddha said, once we lose our human body, we might not get it back in ten thousand eons. I had already sought and found so many teachings, it would not be worth risking such a danger in order to get any teaching.

I wanted very much to tell Sukhasiddhi that we should go back. I turned my head and saw Sukhasiddhi with a cold smile on her face.

I thought that if my teacher is this unhappy, it must be because the way I have just been thinking is not correct. I thought: "So then, I will go into the poisonous air and, for the sake of the Dharma, forget about my physical body. Though I might die, I will still be reborn, and besides, this is how my teacher has told me to act. I have already offered her my body, mouth, and mind, and whatever she tells me to do, I surely cannot hold back."

I looked at Sukhasiddhi again with an inquiring look, and I saw she still was smiling coldly.

I thought: "I don't care whether or not she is pleased, I have to take this body and offer it up for her."

But as soon as I took a step forward, I felt that the gas would really choke a person. It seemed like the smell of sulfur, but a hundred times more as phyxiating than sulfur. I thought that if there were a single spark, that gas would explode. As I thought this, I saw a little man appear in that gas, wearing red clothes, with his hair in a bun, looking very cunning. He took a flint and struck it again and again. I thought, with such a thick sulfur smell, if this little guy strikes a spark, this place will explode into a sea of flames.

As I was worrying, I saw that the flint in that little one's hand had already produced several sparks, and then I heard a terrifying roar, and several great fireballs exploded before my eyes. What's more, after the sound of these explosions, there were the sounds of explosions on all sides. It's all over, I thought. I closed my eyes, and I felt great explosive waves pressing in on me from the front and the back. The sulfurous smell became even more asphyxiating.

I struggled to open my eyes, and saw smoke spreading out on all sides. I could not see anyone, and I did not even know where Sukhasiddhi had gone. In the faint light, I could still see flames blazing in the thick smoke, and I saw that the explosions were still going on. I thought, that's it then: no matter whether it explodes or not, it is still going on, and I will probably die, but it is for the Dharma that I am dying.

I called out in a loud voice: "Teacher, Teacher …"

Faintly, from far away in the thick smoke, came a weak voice: "I am here." But the place where this voice came from was blazing with huge flames. Though I knew there were still explosions going on there, I moved toward the place.

As I moved forward, I seemed to catch sight of Sukhasiddhi. She was wearing a garment of a glowing red color, which stood out in the smoke and haze. I calmed down and thought: "As long as the Teacher is safe, then all is well." How could I have known that, as we continued with our journey, I would end up seeing Sukhasiddhi hanging from a cliff over a void, clinging to a delicate branch, crying out for me to save her life?

I felt the blood surging in my head. I thought: "I can't let my teacher fall off a cliff." I did not pay any more attention to which was solid ground and which was the cliff, and I rushed over. I felt myself walking on air, and my body plummeted down like a stone. I discovered that as I was falling, my teacher was also falling and that glowing red was shining in front of my eyes all the way. I thought: "It's not important. Even if I die, I will be together with my teacher."

I felt I was descending fast, and before long I would overtake my teacher. I grabbed her hand, and her hand was very soft and warm. I let out a long sigh.

I felt I had come down on solid ground, and only then did I finally see my teacher smiling graciously. Gradually, the smoke around my teacher dispersed, and there was a pure light all around her. I discovered that fundamentally there was no cliff where we were, and in the sky there was no mushroom cloud of poisonous air. I thought: "Actually, this was another illusion of these dakinis. I am still recognizing the false as true and clinging to illusion as reality." I thought: "My teacher is definitely going to scold me."

But Sukhasiddhi was just smiling graciously. She said: "Don't blame yourself. Although this time you again made a mistake, your sincerity toward your teacher has offset your mistake. So I am very satisfied."

3 As Long As You Have Feet, There Will Be a Road

We continued going forward. The strange thing was that the mandala I had just seen had disappeared. I suspected that it had been my own deluded perception. This was because, after I entered the gate of the mandala, I no longer saw anything grand, and in the end it seemed more and more deserted, and even the worldly dakinis were seldom seen.

I asked Sukhasiddhi: "Teacher, can it be that we have taken the wrong road?"

Sukhasiddhi said: "I don't know. Because you cannot distinguish clearly between what is wrong and what is right, sometimes what's wrong is right and what's right is wrong."

So we continued on our way. Although this place appeared strange, I nevertheless had the feeling I had been here before, because in this strangeness, there was always a kind of familiarity seeping through.

Suddenly I discovered that there was no road beneath my feet. A cliff like a giant gaping mouth appeared before me. I called out: "Teacher, there is no road any more." Sukhasiddhi smiled and said: "How can there be no road? As long as you have feet, there will be a road. Any place you can put your feet is a road."

I pointed to the cliff that went down so far you could not see the bottom of it and asked: "Is your idea to have me go down there?"

Sukhasiddhi said: "I do not have any such idea. You have to have your own idea. See for yourself: do you have to go down there or not?"

I said: "If that is the road I must travel, then I will go down."

Sukhasiddhi gave no indication if I should go or not.

So I descended the cliff. At first glance the cliff was steep and sheer, but as I made my way down there were footholds. I said: "I have decided. I am going down it."

Sukhasiddhi smiled and said nothing.

I did not pay attention to her: I focused on making my way down. I gradually descended a long way. I thought: "This route is in fact not that difficult." I raised my head and looked up, and I saw I had covered a long distance, and I could no longer see Sukhasiddhi's form. The strange thing was, none of those footholds I used when I was coming down were still visible, and the cliff seemed as sheer as if it had been cut with a knife, like tofu that had been sliced with a sharp blade. I felt alarmed and frightened, but when I looked down, there were still places where I could put my feet. So I used my hands and feet and slowly went down.

After I had descended for a while, I discovered that those footholds were becoming more and more shallow, and finally there were no hollows at all. I don't know when I saw that I had already reached the midpoint of the cliff. No matter whether I looked upward or downward, the cliff face was all as smooth as tofu that had been cut with a knife. And the bottom of the cliff was still an immeasurable distance down. I felt scared and nervous. I thought: "It's over, this time it's over." If I let go, I would inevitably be smashed to a bloody pulp.

I raised my head, and what I saw was a sheer cliff. I thought: "A cliff like this would be very hard to climb up. So I cannot go down and I cannot go up — I am truly in mortal peril." I thought: "Why don't I see my teacher? Can it be that this cliff is also manifested by her?" But I was harboring doubts, because I had discovered little birds nesting on the cliff face.

A wind blew from the dark valley, blowing on my sweaty body, and it was very cold, and very gloomy. It seemed there was still that stench of blood that I had just been smelling. I thought: "No matter what I say, I still have to keep going. Though the road is hard to travel, a road that is even harder to travel is still a road." So then I tried to climb down. I found that even though I was wrapped up in a very thick feeling of dreamlike illusion, the rocks on the cliff under my hands were very real, and did not seem like empty illusory apparitions at all. My fingers also felt the pain of being ground against the stone.

I continued to descend, and gradually it got so there was no place to put my feet or my hands, and my body got heavier and heavier.

The wind also became more severe, buffeting me more forcibly, and it seemed that it would take me and hurl me off the cliff. I thought: "It doesn't matter if I fall to my death. Humans live for a hundred years, and end up dying. But it is really too bad about those esoteric teachings I have found. It would be much better if the people of Tibet could get those esoteric teachings."

I felt the drumming of the wind getting stronger and stronger, as if there were someone pulling my jacket, trying to pull me off the cliff. At this moment there was no question of continuing to descend. All I could do was keep my body steady and not let the wind blow me off, and this made me exert all my physical strength. As I struggled, my whole body was covered with sweat, and some of the sweat flowed into my shoes, and they got slippery, and it was hard to endure. I struggled to look down, and I still could not see the bottom. Though there was no mist and nothing in the way, I still could not see the bottom — obviously, this abyss was truly deep.

At this moment a voice came to me gently: "Jump, jump."

It seemed to be Sukhasiddhi's voice.

I looked to see where the voice was coming from, but I could not see any human form.

My fingers hurt a lot, and the pads of my fingers had already been rubbed raw, and my whole body was in severe pain. But I thought: "Isn't this an illusion?"

I heard that voice come to me again: "Jump, jump."

I could tell that the voice was clearly Sukhasiddhi's.

But again I thought: "If I cannot see your bodily form, I will die. I will not jump." I thought: "If that voice is my own illusory perception, won't I have died in vain?"

Then I saw that the bottom of the valley seemed to have come closer, and I could not say for sure if I had descended some, or that valley floor had risen some. One way or the other, I could see things on the valley floor. I discovered that there was a shallow stream on the valley floor, and in the water were many crocodiles opening their mouths, greedily looking at me. I saw Sukhasiddhi standing on a rock in the valley stream, with many crocodiles surrounding her on all sides. I felt this was strange, and I thought: "Wasn't she just up at the top of the cliff? How did she get to the bottom?" Though I felt this was strange, I was still worried. I thought: "Look at that, it's extremely dangerous."

Then I again heard Sukhasiddhi calling out in a loud voice: "Jump, jump. If again you do not jump, it may be too late."

I heard that this voice truly was coming from Sukhasiddhi. I even saw her worried look. I discovered several crocodiles had already crawled up onto the rock, and their mouths could already reach Sukhasiddhi's feet.

I very much wanted to say: "Wait, wait. I'll jump right away." I thought: "If I really jump off, I will certainly be smashed into a bloody pulp, but no matter whether or not I become a mangled mass of flesh, I'll be food in the mouths of those crocodiles. I'm not afraid of falling to my death, it's just that I feel the very fact of jumping from such a high cliff is itself frightening."

I very much wanted to hear Sukhasiddhi's voice again. I thought: "If you just call to me again, then I will jump." But Sukhasiddhi did not call to me again. I even saw her lips making that cold smile again.

I thought: "If I hesitate again, I will certainly lose my teacher."

I thought: "If I die or if I live, so be it. I'll jump." Then I let go and jumped.

I felt that the distance of the fall was also very strange. I could say that it was far, but I could see the expression on Sukhasiddhi's face, for example, the cold smile that had just floated across her lips. I could say that it was close, but the time it took to fall was apparently very long. I felt that I was descending into a giant black cave: the wind was blowing in my ears, and my body felt weightless. Every time I remembered this experience later, I was continually amazed. My impression was that this was not an ordinary fall, but rather a long-drawn-out life-journey.

I was still falling. I opened my eyes, and what I saw was not the cliff face flying up, but a myriad colored light rays. This scene was like the stars you see after a blow to the head. Lights exploded in my brain like a million sparks, wave after wave of them, disappearing into the distance.

I thought: "Will I get to the bottom soon?"

I thought: "No matter what shape I'm in from the fall, if my teacher told me to jump, there was a reason to tell me to jump."

In this way I kept on falling for a very long time. I cannot say for sure how long, ultimately, I was falling, maybe an hour, maybe several moments. I just remembered that if I truly had no discriminating mind, that sensation was the same as the feeling of being thrown up and down by that great elephant's trunk.

4 Entering the Mandala of the Dakini

I felt myself descending like the colored clouds, because after descending, I went from descending to floating, and I gently floated and floated. When I opened my eyes, I discovered that I was already on the ground, and all around me were many women. Some of the women were still looking at me angrily, but I was no longer afraid of them. If I did not even fear that high cliff, how could I fear a few little women?

What a laugh! So at this point I looked at them with that feeling from when I was falling. In that feeling I had no worries or fears. At this point those women laughed. One of them said: "Look at him, what nerve!"

Sukhasiddhi smiled and said: "You should not underestimate him. Don't look at him now as just the light of a candle. That fire of wisdom will in the end be a fire that burns across the prairie. All that is necessary is to skillfully add compassion and to add the fuel of accomplished virtue, and the light of the candle will ultimately have the brilliance of the sun. He has already received many wondrous teachings. Originally, he came here unable to use them, but because of the completeness and special excellence of the causal conditions, he finally came here to ask for instruction."

Using the mind without discrimination, I looked at the woman who was still angrily glaring at me, and I saw her lower her head in embarrassment. Sukhasiddhi smiled and said: "Good, good. You have already undergone many tests, and you have come to the genuine sacred place of the dakinis."

The sound of her voice dropped away. In the sky there appeared many rainbows, and countless numbers of dakinis of wisdom appeared. Sanskrit mantras filled the emptiness, and I heard that what they were reciting was the mantra of the Vajravarahi.

Sukhasiddhi smiled and asked: "What do you hear, son?"

I said: "It's the mantra of the Vajravarahi."

Sukhasiddhi smiled and said: "Wrong, wrong. Above all you must not descend into the swamp of names and forms. I will tell you what I hear:

"Son, I hear mute people chanting. They are sending forth a sound that is hard to express in words. I hear deaf people listening. They are hearing a wondrous meaning which there is no way to explain with words. I hear shapes and colors which blind people are looking at, and all those shapes and colors are like wondrous flavors which people who cannot speak have tasted but have no way to communicate. Son, can you understand what I am saying?"

I felt an indescribable joy, and said: "My teacher, it is so, it is so. You hear that wondrous voice that has no sound. You see that great image which has no shape. You taste that indescribable wondrous flavor of the bliss of the Dharma. Although I, your son, am stupid, I still taste a bit of the flavor of the Dharma."

"What flavor of the Dharma?" Sukhasiddhi asked, smiling.

I said: "My desire without eyes does not know what I should look at. My seeking without sound or form does not know what I should listen to. My desire without the ability to communicate does not know what I should say."

I said: "Teacher, I have no ability to taste with the tongue, and that wondrous flavor is even more unattainable. What would you have me say?

"My teacher, that bright sky is the gate to wondrous form, that great ocean without waves is the voice for all ears. Though all flavors are there in that mind which shines like a jewel mirror on the myriad things, in reality there is nothing to taste."

Sukhasiddhi smiled and said: "Son, at the level of theoretical truth you already understand, and although your enlightenment at the level of practical things and events still needs time to develop, the direction you are going in cannot be wrong. Come, son, come enter into the mandala of the dakinis."

5 The Teaching of the Pure Body

Sukhasiddhi asked: "Son, you have come to this holy place of the dakinis. What kind of ocean of teaching do you want to attain?"

I said: "I want to attain the teaching on the utmost purity of body, speech, and thought, in order to achieve infinite merits and virtues."

Sukhasiddhi praised me, saying: "Good, I am not ashamed that you are my son." She turned toward the chief of the dakinis and smiled and asked: "O my sister, you who have realized supreme wisdom, please plant the best causal conditions for my son."

Then the chief dakini held up a bowl of pure water. Evening was approaching, and the full moon was hanging in the sky, and the disk of the moon was reflected in the pure water.

Sukhasiddhi smiled and said: "Son, this is the pure body. Although it displays in many forms, it has no inherent nature. At the same time it is giving rise to many kinds of wondrous forms, it is still empty and pale, like the moon in the water. Son, this is the teaching of the most excellent body."

I said: "Mother, this is truly the supreme pure teaching. Though it is simple, its implications are very profound and far-reaching. I will always remember this excellent wondrous teaching, and I will no longer cling to the empty, illusory, unreal body of the moon in the water."

The dakinis sang:

Khyungpo Ba, the guest who arrived unexpectedly, you must not cling to that empty illusory body.

This body is a temporary assemblage, utterly without inherent identity, empty and faint as the reflection of the moon in the water.

No matter whether it is your own body or the body of theBuddha, they are all like illusory images and have no real substance.

Though they may be magnificent beyond compare, they are like rainbows, like light and shadows.

Worldly people cling to the physical body, which is a temporary assembly, but they do not know that it is a combination of the four elements.

Because they accept the false as true and cling to the illusory as real, they give rise to all sorts of greed and clinging.

From a hundred kinds of love they give rise to afflictions, and the afflictions cover the light of fundamental being.

Where the light arises is just that fundamental enlightenment, and fundamental enlightenment must observe the body of illusory transformations.

Clinging to the body is the greatest ignorance in human life, it directly brings on so much confusion and conflict.

The actions of war and killing and wrongdoing and evil are all poisonous mushrooms produced by clinging to the body.

From the eye craving beautiful forms arises the mind of rapacity, to seize beautiful women and seize palaces and plunder the beautiful possessions of other people.

When the ear hears beautiful sounds, it dissolves away wisdom in the same way; no matter whether they are seductive voices or tremulous speech, they are still the sounds of heaven.

All those deceptive enticements enter through the doors of the six senses, like six thieves sneaking into to rob the master of the house.

The mirror of the light is obscured by this, and then has no way to shine through to the clear emptiness.

Clinging to the body is the greatest affliction of sentient beings. They get greedy for enjoyment and it makes them lazy and wastes their energy.

Those who cultivate the Path must make austerity their work. They intend to break through and eliminate clinging to the body and rise to a higher level.

In reality, this wanting to break through the clinging to the body is the same kind of clinging to the illusory as real—this body is fundamentally empty and illusory as the reflections in the water.

After originating in the four elements, we disperse back into the four elements; when earth, water, fire, and air disperse, there is no trace of us.

This is actually a plain, easy-to-understand truth: people understand it in theory but act falsely in practice.

Our hundred kinds of cravings are reflections in this realm of experience and, because of affliction, the illusory images of the six planes of existence appear.

The supreme teaching on the body is not just in this—even the bodies of the Buddhas are like rainbows, like images.

You must understand this truth: only then can you be reckoned to have understood the ultimate illusory body.

You must see the mountains, rivers, and the great earth all as illusory transformations — they are also all manifestations of the inherent Buddha.

Whatever appears by transformation is all like flowers reflected in a mirror, like the moon reflected in the water. When there are no clingings, you will clearly comprehend the true within the false.

Nothing in your garden and your house is not like this — your city and your village are all like illusory reflections.

Your family name and your nationality all return to theBuddha's Body of Reality — that mind and those external objects are all dreamlike reflections of illusory transformations.

In the same way, you should not cling to the body of thatBuddha as real; as soon as you cling to it as real, the barrier of demonic delusions is suddenly born.

Countless people who have clung to it as real have made themselves into fierce demons by their cultivation and have sunk into delusion for ten thousand eons without return, so it is impossible for them to rise above it.

The Buddha's Body of Reality of ultimate truth is all an illusory transformation, and all those illusory transformations are not apart from true mind.

That true mind is yourBuddha, my unexpected guest.

You must know that everything in the world is a manifestation of the inherent Buddha, and this inherent Buddha is not apart from your true mind.

So the true is also illusory, and the illusory is also true: one flavor, without distinctions; you still must awaken to this dreamlike illusion here and now.

Your understanding of this truth is still far from sufficient: it is like an illusory sword that cannot cut the enemy.

You must still take the appropriate countermeasures at the level of things and events, and while walking, standing, sitting, and lying down, go on living strong and solid.

When you are in that Body of Reality of illusory transformation, when you completely comprehend those empty illusory reflections in the mirror,

When you do not cling to all those false forms, then you will attain the complete Buddha Body.

6 Words of Ultimate Completeness

The second dakini held out a large gong inlaid with a mantra. Sukhasiddhi took it, and struck it, and the great gong gave forth a loud sound, and the sound reverberated over a long distance, and gradually became silent again.

Sukhasiddhi said: "Son, remember, all the sounds in the world are like the sound of this gong. Though for a while they may be loud, they have no real substance, and at that same time they go forth, they are returning to the empty inherent nature and cannot be grasped. The most complete, most pure words are far removed from all the useless talk and discussion in the world: they are always reciting the mantras of the Buddhas. Those useless discussions ruin our lives, wrangling futilely about right and wrong, without the least benefit. Therefore, fill your time for talking with those pure mantras: this is the teaching about the most complete words."

I said: "Mother, I understand.Words are the most useless thing in the world. They no sooner come out of our mouths than they return to the boundless nothingness. The most valuable and precious things are also words, because the heart and marrow of the teachers and the Buddhas use words as a vehicle. Without words, we would not have the treasures of the teachings that have been passed on. I will detach from the capacity for useless clever talk and use words to pass on the light of the truth. Only if we change words into jewels of wisdom will they be words of ultimate completeness."

The dakinis sang:

That great gong sends out a great sound which stirs heaven and earth; seen from the surface, it truly shatters the rocks and shakes the sky.

But when you look quietly at where that sound is, you cannot find a bit of imperishable basic essence.

That great fame which impresses the world is like the sound of this gong: if you look, it seems to have form, but it is like an echo in an empty valley.

Fame gradually fades away like smoke and ends up dissolving in the distant blue sky.

Though insults make people feel it is hard to bear, in fact their real substance is like the illusory sound of the gong.

As soon as the sound of criticism arises, it dissolves in the trackless emptiness, and the wise will not let it worry their minds.

All blame and praise are like bird calls in the sky, like the leftover sound of a great wind whistling by.

Why should you care about it disturbing the purity? With unmoving clarity, we look upon this as illusory images in a mirror.

Idle talk likewise does you no good, and you must detach from it; what good is your lofty talk and your wide-ranging discussions for cultivating practice?

Wrangling over right and wrong is also not the least bit effective: you are adding to your afflictions in vain and wasting your life.

The pure teaching of words is far removed from the conventional meaning: it just takes the heart-mantra of the inherent Buddha and puts it in your mind.

Your body is like hollow bamboo and your mind doesn't have a speck of dust: you use the sound of the mantra to fill the time and space of life.

In your eyes, all sounds are empty inherent identity, and empty inherent identity is the pure voice of the inherent Buddha.

No matter what kind of sound it may be in the ordinary world, you look at them all as the careful offering of the heart-mantra.

You look at the sky and a bird calls as it goes by: the sound is sad, the sound is lonely.

When I hear it though, it is the eternal sacred song, coming softly from the mandala of the inherent Buddha.

Though the sound of those birdcalls in the wind has another meaning, in my eyes they are no different from the inherent Buddha.

You must cultivate contemplation of all the sounds in the world like this: only this is the pure cultivation of sound.

Your ears hear those sounds, your eyes view those forms, your nose smells the meaning of that mantra and your tongue tastes that sound,

Your body touches those sound waves, your mind thinks of the meaning of that mantra—only when you take charge of the six sense organs do you approach that fundamental truth.

You must observe that everything in the world is the sound of the mantra, so that the whole sensory world is transformed into that sound.

The whole universe is utterly empty, without any real substance, and there is nothing that is not the inherent nature of the sound of the mantra.

You also take yourself and merge into that empty intent, but that emptiness is carrying the abilities of all the Buddhas.

Though all sounds are impermanent, they can still carry things: they are what continues the transmission of wisdom.

We take all sounds and see them as the secret intent of the Buddha, we take all sounds and see them as transformation of the holy truth.

*They manifest the clear empty stillness without inherent nature: in the
pure clarity you experience the wondrous ability of sounds.*

7 The Teaching of the Most Complete Mind

The third dakini held out a crystal. In the moonlight, the crystal
sent forth myriad rays of light. Sukhasiddhi said: "Son, this is the
teaching of the most complete mind. The enlightened mind, like the
crystal, has no defilements at all, and it is utterly exquisite. But it still
is always able to generate wondrous functioning. The enlightened mind
is not a dead, quiescent sea; rather, it is bright and resplendent, like a
crystal. Son, have you understood the implication in this or not?"

I said: "I have, Mother. Though the enlightened mind is empty and
still, its light is clear and distinct. It is far removed from dead stillness,
far removed from blank emptiness. From the stillness it sends forth
infinite light."

The dakinis sang:

*The mind of enlightenment is not a dried-up river bed, though there is
that empty valley without the sound of water.*

*The mind of enlightenment is not a dark empty room, though there is
that empty shell without a master.*

*The mind of enlightenmentis that clear crystal, and though there is
nothing else mixed in, it sends forth infinite light.*

*Bright as crystal, it illuminates everything in the world, but its fundamental
essence does not change or alter, and it is as it is and does not move.*

Perhaps you have seen the surface of the water with no waves; when the waves have stopped, it can illuminate empty space.

If we view the water moving when the wind blows as false mind appearing, the mirror-like water is the true mind after false thoughts have ceased.

The true mind is like a crystal shining brightly on all forms; the true mind is like a crystal with no waves or ripples.

The true mind is like a crystal with nothing at all mixed in; the true mind is like a crystal with no discriminating mind.

The facets of the crystal are a metaphor for all the forms of mind; though there are all kinds of manifestations, the fundamental essence is pure and clear.

All those manifestations are relative to all the forms of the sensory world, and all the lights radiate out endless illusory objects.

All the illusory forms originated from the bright crystal; the basic essence of the light radiating in all directions does not waver.

The basic substance of true mind also must be like this, a clear light without ripples, without waves.

Some people consider emptiness without light as the realm of realization, but in fact this is another name for blank emptiness and oblivious ignorance.

Being cold and inertwill never have any meaning, and if we are cold and still as a dead tree, it will be impossible to go to a higher level.

There is also that sinking into a nebulous state, and this too always blocks us from achieving the light.

It is like when you cover a bright mirror with dust and ashes, it is very hard to radiate out all the scenes of the realm of reality.

The true light shines on heaven and earth, and it is as it is and does not move, clear as crystal.

It is exquisite and fine, but emptyand without a single thing—this is the teaching of the pure mind.

You take this crystalline mind and generate wondrous functioning, and all the forms in that world of sensory dusts are transformed into crystal.

They are like reflections, like rainbows, without any real substance, translucent and sparkling, but still like illusory reflections.

Even if by chance there are clouds that rush across the sky, the colors of those clouds cannot stain the pure light of the sky.

Even if waves happen to appear on that great ocean, when the waves cease, the surface of the water is still like a bright mirror.

In the ultimate mind there are no obstacles whatsoever, just like there is not a speck of dust in the bright clean sky.

That eternal skyis without a wisp of clouds for ten thousand miles, that great ocean is without a wave or ripple for ten thousand square miles.

Khyungpo Ba, our unexpected guest, this is the teaching of the intent of the dakinis.

Inscribe this in your mind and do not get lazy, rejoice in pure faith, and preserve your dedication to practising it.

8 The Sweet Dew of the Three Gates of the Diamond Vehicle

The fourth dakini held out a diamond. Sukhasiddhi said: "Son, this diamond symbolizes the merits and virtues of the Buddhas. It is not born and it is not extinguished, it is not cut off and it is not eternal. As long as you can purify your body, speech, and thoughts, you will be able to have the supreme merits and virtues of all the Buddhas. That bright moon in the pure water symbolizes the Transformation Body of the Buddha, which appears but without inherent nature. That mantra symbolizes the Reward Body of the Buddhas, and that crystal symbolizes the Reality Body of the Buddha. This diamond symbolizes the Buddha's Body of Inherent Nature.

"Son, although you have not attained an extension of the scriptures in verbal form, what you have attained is the sweet dew of the Diamond Vehicle's three gates of body, mouth, and mind. From this, you have the genuine pure transmission of the dakinis. Son, remember this sea of teachings, and you will get the supreme wish-granting jewel.

"If you understand the teaching of the Transformation Body, then you understand empty inherent nature. If you understand the teaching of the Reward Body, then you have the pact of samadhi. If you understand the teaching of the Reality Body, then you fully understand the basic substance of the nature of mind. This will produce results in your Great Mudra yoga that has no cultivation. Son, these three teachings are in fact three keys to enter the gate of real truth.

"When that teaching for the body lies in establishing your level of perception: from now on, in all the contemplations you cultivate, you must never forget that moon in the water. Without its guidance, you might cling to the illusory as real and accept the false as true. You must use that level of perception to observe all your experiences cultivating meditation. You will understand that genuine awakening does not come from outside inherent mind, but rather comes from the inner mind. You must use that correct perception to observe your whole human life. Without this level of perception, it will be very difficult for you to enter the gate of genuine meditative concentration.

"For cultivating that teaching of the Reward Body, what you rely upon is the pure transmission of your fundamental teacher, which has never been interrupted. If you have no teacher, you will not achieve anything. Son, although you have had many teachers, like the teachers who initiated you, the teachers who passed on the teachings to you, the teachers who bestowed the rules of discipline on you, the teachers who bestowed the transmission on you, the teachers who taught you the scriptures—nevertheless, among all these teachers, the most important is your fundamental teacher, that is, the teacher who showed you the inherent nature of mind. Strictly speaking, in a person's life there is only one fundamental teacher. This is because your truly illuminating mind and seeing its inherent nature only happens once. Whoever can enable you to illuminate mind and see its inherent nature, that person is your fundamental teacher. No matter whether or not I have the name and form of a teacher, no matter whether my external appearance it that of a beggar or a whoremonger, no matter what style I use, as long as I can enable you to illuminate mind and see its inherent nature, then I am your fundamental teacher. You can have countless teachers who initiate you and teachers who teach the scriptures, and you can have countless teachers who show you secrets and teachers who pass on the teachings to you, but there is only one teacher who shows you the inherent nature of mind and lets you illuminate mind and see its inherent nature. That one is your fundamental teacher.

"In the traditions of the Esoteric Teaching, showing someone the inherent nature of mind is also called the initiation of the great light, and it is the most excellent of all initiations. It is also called the verbal initiation of the power of truth, or the verbal initiation. It is also called the initiation of the Great Mudra. When your teacher shows you the inherent nature of mind, when the light of your mind begins to shine, then you form the pact of samadhi with your teacher. This is the guarantee that from then on, continuously from the source, you will get the support of the light of all the Buddhas and bodhisattvas in the realm of reality. When you have this, the candle of your wisdom will be able to set the prairie ablaze and become the great fire of wisdom. If you do not have this, then your understanding of the inherent nature of mind will just remain at the level of theory. This is because the support of all the power of the realm of reality can only be channeled through your faith in your fundamental teacher. Without such accord, there will be no support. If you cannot get the nourishment of the power of the realm of reality, your merely theoretical awakening will easily degenerate into crazy wisdom. Therefore, you must clear away all names and forms, and accurately recognize who is your fundamental teacher, and understand with whom you will ultimately form the pact of samadhi. Above all, you must not be controlled by intellectual knowledge and concepts and make a mistake in calculating this.

"You must know that the fundamental teacher, who shows you the inherent nature of mind, represents the Sambhogakaya Buddha, the Buddha's Body of Reward.

"You must accurately put into practice the instructions of your fundamental teacher. You must guard your pact of samadhi as you would protect your eyes. You certainly must be fully equipped with a pure mind, a strong mind of faith, and disinterested compassion. Compassion and faith must run through all your actions. Compassion and wisdom can arise only when you are accurately putting into practice the teaching on the inherent nature of mind which you received from your fundamental teacher, and remembering and preserving the light that was transmitted from your fundamental teacher.

"Remember, the purity of the transmission and faith in the fundamental teacher are the secret keys to success in Mantrayana. If you depart from them, it is basically impossible to succeed.

"Let that pure and constant faith run through every time and place in your life. It is the source and protector of all achievements. If you are without it, there is fundamentally no way for you to enter the gate of liberation.

"What is bright as a crystal is that other jewel of yours, your basic inherent nature. This is the key to open up the mind's spirit. I call it fundamental enlightenment: it is the essential subtle characteristic of the wisdom of prajna.

"If you do not know to open up the complete awakening of fundamental enlightenment, you will have no way to penetrate through the illusory forms that appear externally, and you will have no way to understand the genuine truth contained in the teachings. And as for your true wish-granting gem, you will have no way to open up the treasure room of inherent nature.

"You must know that in the Path of correct cultivation of practice, first you must have the direction of wisdom's correct perception. That is to say, you must first light the lamp in your mind. Only if the candle of wisdom is shining can you become enlightened and be able to fully know the original face of the myriad phenomena—that is, their real characteristic.

"Our cultivation of practice is often called cultivating the Path. The Path is the road that was traveled by people before us; it is a set of guidelines, a standard for action that must be followed when we are enlightened. Only when you go forward following 'the Path,' will your enlightened inherent nature slowly become manifest; only then will you be able to recognize clearly the secret meaning of all your actions; only then will the fundamental enlightenment of the wisdom within you be uncovered; only then will you understand that inner experiences are the light of inherent wisdom, and that they are fundamentally like this, and do not need to be sought externally. When you recognize the light of inherent enlightenment, we call this opening up into enlightenment. This will make your wisdom's fundamental enlightenment appear in your life and become totally pure and clear, clear as a beacon on a dark night. You will discover that beacon is in fact also the light of your inherent nature. It is not something you develop, it is something you discover. It is the light in your inherent nature, with which you are fully equipped from the beginning.

"Therefore, in your process of realizing enlightenment, those three kinds of teaching have a definite function. Under the direction of correct perception, you must choose the methods of cultivating practice which are appropriate for you, nurture the compassion in your mind's spirit, recognize your inherent wisdom, and thereby arrive at genuine complete enlightenment.

"After you are truly enlightened, the candle of your wisdom will have three kinds of adornment. We call these the Three Bodies. The Three Bodies are in fact three manifestations of realizing enlightenment.

"The Transformation Body is the light manifested externally by the candle of wisdom. It appears in all sorts of externally manifested material shapes. It can be predictive directions, or people and things bearing wisdom so they can give direction to practitioners who need help entering experiences at deeper levels. Son, all the many dakinis, with their clever flapping tongues, are showing you the inherent nature of mind. They are lighting the candle of your inherent enlightenment, and driving away the age-old darkness, in order to enable the light of your inherent nature to spontaneously appear. Son, the secret of liberation is an inherent secret, and in the same way it is inherent and complete. But only people whose mind and spirit have awakened can fully awaken to it and control it. When your inherent enlightenment emits its light, it will spontaneously drive out ignorance. You must realize that inherent enlightenment transcends the discriminating mind. In the light of inherent enlightenment, there is no dualism. It is fundamentally pure and clear, and sparkles with the energy of wisdom. It is the wisdom of direct enlightenment and, without depending on thinking and discriminating, it completely understands the myriad forms.

"The Reward Body is the inherent body of the lamp of wisdom. The source of achieving enlightenment comes from the Reward Body; the teachings and guidance given by the Reward Body often accompany achieving and passing on enlightenment. It is magnificent, profound, and vast: it symbolizes the key to the wish-granting jewel of samadhi. The truth we transmit in the form of sounds through these mantras and teachings we call the wondrous functioning of the Reward Body. It has nothing artificial; it does not rely on causes and conditions; it needs no liberation; it needs no change. The basic nature of the inherent nature of mind is self-liberating. Therefore, the spontaneous light and manifestations of liberation can only arise in the body of a person who has completely awakened to the original inherent nature of mind.

"Son, you must preserve the pact of samadhi you have with your teacher and protect your complete undefiled enlightened inherent nature as if you were protecting your eyes. You must let it grow uninterruptedly in the light of the teaching, as if you were nurturing a seed. After a long time, its light will truly become manifest and go on to produce merits and virtues of special excellence. You must know that the fundamental body of that enlightened nature is the highest-level discipline of samadhi. The special substance of enlightened inherent nature is original liberation, original freedom. That is to say, we are certainly not leading that enlightened inherent nature toward liberation; rather, that enlightened inherent nature fundamentally *is* liberation. If we want to enter the realm of true thusness, all we can do is let the original body of true thusness come through. Therefore, fully awakening to the enlightened nature of the Reality Body of true thusness is the highest pact among all the pacts. It is not a method, it is not a route to reach some objective. It itself *is* the objective, it itself *is* liberation.

"The term 'Reality Body' is another way of expressing the fundamental essence of the wisdom of the light. It is originated from the subtle wondrous inherent nature. It is linked to the mind and spirit, and its essence manifests supreme enlightenment and the profound, wondrous, enlightened inherent nature. It is the secret key to the real inherent nature. Son, you must not artificially counteract the experiential realm of the mind and spirit, you must not artificially counteract the memories in your mind. The inherent nature's basic substance is the Reality Body. The basic substance of all things is the Reality Body. This is the perception on the Reality Body without discrimination, and it is also the original face of the mind's inherent nature. When you are in the state of enlightened inherent nature, and you go forward into contemplation without cultivation, then you will no longer fabricate those conceptualized actions, and you will no longer need to counteract these states of mind.

"Son, even though the substance of the inherent nature of mind is liberation, you still should not forget to make energetic progress. If you want to realize the perfect Buddha body, you must certainly work hard cultivating the contemplation of the form of the inherent Buddha. This is because the body of the Buddha is the most perfect body, and it symbolizes all the merits and virtues of the inherent Buddha, and it symbolizes the special achievements of the inherent Buddha. It has reached the highest degree of perfection in what material things can make manifest. You must constantly contemplate it, until you and the tutelary deity are not two separate things.

"Son, if you want to realize the ultimate accomplishment of words, you must energetically ask your teachers, or recite the mantras of the tutelary deity. This is because that asking and those mantras convey the most complete supporting power, and it represents the highest form of understanding words and can directly convey the ultimate substance of the Reward Body.

"Son, if you want to reach ultimate enlightenment, you must diligently cultivate the Great Mudra. The inherent nature of mind does not change: it is holy and wondrous. It is the inherently enlightened Reality Body of the Buddhas. It has no shape or form. It is apart from concepts, and apart from striving. It can give rise to the myriad phenomena, and it can spontaneously accomplish the deeds of body, mouth, and mind. To reach the mind's ultimate pure clarity, you cannot depart from the Great Mudra's realm of awakening.

"Son, be sure to remember that these three secret keys together sum up three methods of cultivation: with material things, with sounds, and with the mind and spirit. All three are very important, and you cannot neglect any of them.

"Son, though you have come to the pure land of the dakinis, and received the teachings related above, you must realize that speaking from the perspective of ultimate truth, the pure land of the dakinis is everywhere in the realm of reality. Similarly, those dakinis do not come from outside your mind, but rather are another aspect of your own mind of enlightenment. They are present throughout time and space: they are one of the many manifestations of omnipresent enlightenment. When you understand this, then you will truly be able to mesh with the realm where there is no cultivation, and enter into the realm of the Reality Body where the inherent nature of mind is completely pure and clear. Then you will be able to attain ultimate liberation in the midst of the impurity of all that is empty, illusory, temporary.

"Son, you must remember that the inherent nature of mind is originally pure — it cannot be changed. It is always pure and clean. After you have gotten rid of all the kinds of defilement engendered by the discriminating mind, then you will see the changeless, fundamentally pure inherent nature of mind. Then child light and the mother light will meet: the mother light and the child light will recognize each other and fuse into one. When you have truly transcended subject and object, there will be no more difference between subject and object, because the distinction you make between subject and object will be fused into the true realm where both are born and both appear in inherent nature.

"Son, because at first you rejected me, this time we spend together now will end here. You can return to Nalanda Monastery and take back your scriptures and books, and go to Tibet. The meeting where we make further progress will happen later.

"Do not take it hard. The karmic connection between us is very deep, and it is not the typical karmic connection. This time, you have already gained a lot. You will come again—I'll be waiting for you. Remember, no matter when you pray to me, I will always immediately return to your side. Tell all your disciples and all those who have faith in me, that all they have to do is pray to me, and I will come to them at once, like a mother who hears her sick child crying. Of course, because they are covered by karmic barriers, they will not necessarily be able to see my physical form. But the Buddha said: 'If they see me in terms of form, if they seek me in terms of sound, these people are following a false Path, and cannot see the Tathagata, the one who has come from Thusness.'

"As for the many yoga teachings like kundalini, dream contemplation, the illusory body, the light, directed rebirth, intermediate existence in bardo between death and rebirth, and so on, after Niguma has initiated you, I will provide you with explanations.

"Go then. Your tree has already started to get healthy and strong."

I was very happy.

9 The Grease of a Simpleton

Honored husband:

I just bought some things to use in the fire ceremony. I want to make offerings to Brahma and those spirits that protect the teaching, to let them give you some help, to let you have fewer adverse circumstances, and to be able to find Niguma soon.

Kumari again brought me news from there. Those sorcerers

have again started working on an even more evil curse. They want to make you turn into an idiot—when I think of this word, my heart trembles.

A simple-minded man who was a street beggar died—you had seen him, that guy who was always picking up and eating filthy food. The sorcerers got hold of his corpse and used his brain-matter to write your name and put it on the fire mandala and burned it. The offering for the fire mandala was the grease rendered from that simpleton's corpse. The sorcerers were chanting spells and at the same time holding that piece of paper on which they had written your name in the rising smoke.

Think of it, what a repulsive thing to do. As soon as Kumari told me about it, I vomited.

Let's talk about our own things. You are probably really tired out. Look at that letter you wrote a few days ago, what content you wrote. I still do not dare to re-read that letter. It's laughable. The Khyungpo Ba who was originally jealous will also be confused.

I am your woman whose energy does not run away or die out. I am not ashamed about you, I have no regrets. After you came, I thought you would not go. When you left, I thought you had never come.

However, I strongly believe that we can go on for a lifetime. This is because, in this world, I love you most of all.

Soon the lamp will be out of oil. When you come back, Sharwadi will make amends and wrap you in warmth ... Do you miss me?

Your Sharwadi

10 Hoping Their Curse Works

To Sharwadi, whom I miss:

Contrary to what you might expect, I truly hope their curse works and makes me get more foolish. The ancestors said: "A fool has a fool's good fortune." Therefore, since I am not a fool in the eyes of the people of the world, all I can do is live this kind of busy life running around.

Every time I finish writing a letter to you, I can peacefully go to sleep. As soon as my head touches the pillow, I am snoring heartily. Apparently I am a mindless person, but I have already done what I had to do. Every time, after I have done something I had to do, I can always calmly go to sleep. Besides, in reality it is the scope of the power of fate. I do not want to seize the power of fate. And I understand even more that any clinging or attachment just tortures our own minds.

Of course I understand your mind. You are really very contradictory. If you part from me, your life loses some brilliance. If you do not part from me, you cannot bear that pain of longing. Perhaps at some moment you truly want very much to abandon me. At that moment, my heart will ache for you, but I will think: "That's okay, let's go along with circumstances."

I understand that many times, all the plans a person has made can come to naught because the person's mind has changed. If we have expectations, there is bound to be loss, and then we can lose our peace of mind and spirit. Many times, there is truly nothing I am seeking from this world. All I can do is to go along with circumstances. If I can return to you there,

I will be very happy. If you abandon me, I will also be very happy.

Thinking about it calmly and coolly, in my whole life I have truly never produced an emotional feeling as strong as this one. Maybe it was repressed for too long, maybe it is that you are truly worthy of my loving you. Even more likely, I took you as the true love that I had been searching for all along in my life. Without it, I would not have cultivated practice. My spirit has been torn apart all along by poetic feelings and by religion. When that powerful intense poetic feeling got the upper hand, I wanted to be a poetic seeker and a practitioner. When religious faith got the upper hand, I wanted to go behind closed doors and cultivate practice. I used to think that there is no shortage of people cultivating religious practice in the world, and no shortage of yogis, but there is a lack of good poets — you may not have thought of it, but I even wanted to be a poet.

After I met you, I was truly very amazed and happy. Your intimacy, your goodness, your warmth and sincerity made me intoxicated. There was also that spiritual refinement and holy purity which developed from your experience as a female spirit — that was always delighting me. I was carried off by something. Although my wisdom was always trying to alert me, nevertheless I was willing to sink down into it and did not want to pull myself out. I understood that it could become the most important passion in my life. In those days my religious search was blown away by your love.

But, last night, I truly wanted to let you go. I feel that I am too cruel. You are really too exhausted. As soon as I thought of letting you go, I felt a sense of loss, and at the same time

I also felt a kind of relief. The loss was that I could lose you, whom I love so deeply, but there was also relief in the fact that you would no longer have the pain of longing. I truly love you dearly. To make it easier for you to bear, I can respect your letting me go.

But I clearly know where the sorrow in your mind is: you are afraid that after your old world of sweetness and warmth is shattered, there will be no way for you to build a new beautiful world. You are even more afraid that the fate of other female spirits will be played out again in your own life.

Maybe you are right. But you definitely do not know my wisdom. I understand the impermanence of life too well to value it in an unprincipled way. It is just like this.

Thank you for having given me that poetic sense and brilliance. I discovered that you truly put in your full sincerity. We really must treasure it. When this feeling is not in life, people become animals. Before long, all that you have will leave you. You only have one life, and in the end it dissolves. What can be more worth treasuring than being in love when you are young and healthy? I think that if we calm down a little, or we wait for time to dissolve away that troublesome longing, we may go forth on a very long road. Our lives may burst forth with flames of extraordinary radiance.

Many years ago, on many nights before I "understood clearly" or "awakened to enlightenment," I often wandered late at night in the mountain valley behind the Bonpo temple, shouting like a madman. I could not get rid of the sense of isolation. I often thought of killing myself, and I often wanted to take a knife and plunge it into my heart. But in the end I survived, and of course it was cultivating practice that saved me. At that time, nobody could rescue me. All that could rescue me was clear understanding of the mind, or that true love which I sought.

Luckily, after cultivating austerities, I finally understood a bit. I very much wanted to take this understanding of mine and pass it on to the people who were feeling the same kind of pain as me.

My wisdom also told me: All seeking for worldly things is ultimately without meaning. Many years later, when the world is destroyed, everything will be obliterated along with it. I want to search for something that is more meaningful and can last forever. The search then becomes the eternity that I choose. From time to time it takes me from the peaceful high plains of snowy regions, and pulls me toward the holy land of India.

I think, after burning so long, and loving you with my whole heart and mind, I must make a firm decision, and do what I must do in my life.

I have decided to accept the precepts and become a Buddhist monk.

Khyungpo Ba, who loves you.

11 Spiritual Truth

Khyungpo Naljor returned to Tibet. He managed to get together a lot of gold, and he went to India again, to search for more esoteric teachings.

All in all, he visited more than one hundred and forty teachers, and found almost all the esoteric teachings that were circulating in India at that time. At the same time, according to circumstances, he made offerings to the teachers whom he met on the road of his search, and sought those esoteric teachings which he had not found before. But none of these teachers knew any information about Niguma. Some people said they had seen Niguma at gatherings of dakinis, but they did not know where she was now. Some people even said: "You cannot find Niguma, she is only a legend." Other people said that Niguma has already achieved the perfect peace of nirvana and died. But Khyungpo Naljor thought: "Even if she has truly achieved perfect peace and died, the Reality Body is not extinguished." He had heard that Marpa had seen Naropa after he had achieved perfect peace. In this way Marpa got from Naropa "the six methods of Naropa" and other esoteric methods. What's more, he heard that Niguma had already achieved the immortal rainbow body.

The road he traveled in his search was so long, and the disciples who traveled with him were not adapted to the Indian climate, and many were struck down by illness. Khyungpo Naljor arranged for them to rest and recuperate, and he took the load of gold on his own back and searched all over for Niguma.

Impatient readers may be annoyed that the pace of my narrative is too slow: we are already more than halfway through the book, and Khyungpo Naljor is still on his search. Of course, a slow pace is one of the special marks of my novels. The problem is that, many times, the process of searching in fact is also the goal. The destination of everyone's life is death, but the most colorful aspect is the process of moving toward death. Khyungpo Naljor elevated himself to the sublime precisely in the process of his search.

I had thought of taking Khyungpo Naljor's travels in Nepal and India in search of the Dharma and recording them one by one, but I discovered that it was easy to descend into trivia. This is more because the process of seeking the Dharma is much the same, with minor differences — in most cases, it is nothing but a difficult, arduous search. After using the same kind of descriptions many times, it may happen that reading gets tiresome. Let me also say, the sharp-eyed reader may discover that the writing of this book is not the same as the average biographical novel. It tends much more toward the spiritual reality, and is not seeking the so-called realism of concrete descriptions.

In the same way, I do not want to use the typical documentary style for Khyungpo Naljor's experiences while seek the Dharma; I prefer to use a symbolic writing style. This way of writing I used amply in *Curses of Xixia* and *The Grey Wolf of Xixia*. I have said that the original model for "Khyung" in *Curses of Xixia* was in fact the Khyungpo Naljor in my mind. When I wrote of him, I was likewise emphasizing the spiritual reality, and not the reality of appearances.

The fundamental reason why I use a great deal of symbolism is that I have truly received much wisdom from Khyungpo Naljor's era. Using symbolism is one of the special characteristics of Buddhism. *Curses of Xixia* employed a great deal of symbolism in order to write about the process of a dakini and an accomplished teacher experiencing enlightenment. But because, ultimately, it is a novel, many friends do not necessarily take it seriously.

It can be said of any of the times Khyungpo Naljor went seeking the Dharma, that it was never a smooth journey, that they were all filled with difficulties and dangers. But to present those difficulties again is almost impossible, because I cannot go on and on describing each and every one of those sequences of events like an old lady chattering to her daughter-in-law. Even if I truly described those concrete sequences of events, the result would not necessarily be any better than my using symbolism.

The course of Khyungpo Naljor's search was like the process of Marpa seeking Kukuripa. Though there is some color of demonic illusion, it is truth at a higher level of meaning. It is like the 16th century Chinese classic novel *The Journey to the West*: it has a truth that goes beyond the written word and the surface of the story, and contains almost all the possibilities of the search for wisdom.

Because of the limitations of the written word, I cannot take the course of Khyungpo Naljor's search for the Dharma and lay it out piece by piece, because that way it would be easy for it to become a day-by-day journal. But I also cannot ignore the many difficulties Khyungpo Naljor encountered, because those difficulties objectively existed. Moreover, in the process of humans seeking the eternal, they must face all the difficulties and dilemmas. Khyungpo Naljor's search for wisdom was no exception.

Therefore, although you may not necessarily approve of my way of writing, it will definitely bring you a different kind of feeling for reading and aesthetic experience. This was the factor that won out for choosing a symbolic writing style when I was writing this book. Clear-eyed people will be able to see at once its truth at the level of spiritual meaning. Spiritual truth is real truth. This is because any apparent truth can lose its truthfulness when the appearances change. Only spiritual truth is substantive truth. Thus, from the works of my *Great Mudra of Light* series, you will always be able to read out the kind of wisdom that can make you open through to enlightenment. If you can really awaken to enlightenment, you will even be able to feel the cool purity transmitted from the mind of light that is still leaping with life.

If we speak of the people who truly have faith, what they read is not just the written word. Though some people will think that the related information I got from the dakini texts is just a symbol, in actual fact, I do not think that those texts only exist in my imagination. Naturally, I recognize that the dakini texts do in fact objectively exist; they are like dark matter and dark energy, a type of existence that goes beyond the vision of the human race, but definitely exists in the universe. In history, there have been many accomplished adepts who have gotten from the dakini texts much wisdom that has benefitted the human race. A work we know well, *The Songs of Milarepa*, was translated by a Tibetan adept from the dakini text. It was just that later, some careless publishers overlooked that great adept.

12 Explanations of Possession and Nonduality

For an explanation of the transcription of the dakini texts, some scholars use another explanation — "being possessed." This explanation also accepts that there is a kind of existence greater than the human race. It sometimes can attach to human bodies and transmit a kind of truth.

After my novel *Curses of Xixia* was published, the famous critic Chen Xiaoming, who is a professor in the Chinese Language and Literature Department of Peking University, wrote an essay *How Can Literature Be Free: From Culture to Religion — From a Talk on Xuemo's Curses of Xixia"* (*Journal of the Humanities*, 2011, no. 4). In the essay there is a discussion of *being possessed.* He writes about it like this:

> It can almost be said that the novel *Curses of Xixia* is
> something entirely new ... In it there is a kind of continuously

flowing religious feeling secretly exerting its strength, which appears in the textual narrative. It is like being possessed by a spirit, which makes it so that the narrative of the novel can approach the limits of existence without any misgivings ... Xuemo himself is playing with boundaries and going beyond them. If he wants to go beyond those boundaries, he is daring and bold. Under the attitude that there are no standards, he finds his own standards—he seems to be possessed by some spirit. Otherwise, how would he have this courage, how would he write like this, how would he have such poise?

...

It can be said that Xuemo is one of the very small number of contemporary Chinese writers who have engaged in a religious search. He has more than twenty years experience cultivating religious practice and has studied many of the world's religions. He has especially applied his energies to studying the Great Mudra. Xuemo's work The Great Mudra: The Heart of Real Practice has been an especially influential book, and even though he states that he cannot become a religious follower, still in fact he truly has correspondingly deep religious feelings.

...

Xuemo's Curses of Xixia is a richly challenging work, as few others are. Contemporary literature again must create unfamiliar experiences, and this is already extremely difficult. But religious feelings make it possible for authors to open up their own unique individual Paths. With his sincere devotion to religion, with his experience approaching the ultimate limits of life, Xuemo goes beyond the boundaries and reaches the ultimate limits. Making use of religious emotions, Xuemo's writing is like being possessed by a spirit, and just this possessed writing can let him escape from the contemporary bonds and fly free, penetrate through them, leave them behind, and present a unique body of work for the contemporary novel.

Madame Chen Yanjin, M.A. in contemporary literature from Peking University, senior editor of the People's Literary Publishing House, took part in a colloquium at Peking University, and she wrote this:

May 6, 2011, at Room 316, Building 2, Peking University, Professor Chen Xiaoming is again presenting his new and fascinating course in which the teacher and students together read The Curses of Xixia. Hu Xingzhou, a student in the class, said that The Curses of Xixia is really a superb work. Doctoral student Cong Zhicheng said that he simply was not qualified to discuss this book, because it already went beyond the scope of a novel, and there was something about it he could not understand. The text of the novel is more like a spirit medium talking, and it would be like blasphemy to try to dissect it according to any novelistic standards. This book blends scriptures, poetry, historical accounts, legends, myths, and the novel, and opens up history, politics, and religion. In his view, Xuemo as a writer is not simply a novelist, but is more of a believer, and the part that is a believer extends in a vast unrestrained way. This leaves him with no way to understand, and leaves him with big blind spots when it comes to grasping the novel. Professor Chen Xiaoming also pointed out that it is an extremely unique work: using a very vivid style and attitude, it offers a new narrative experience, and raises challenges and stimulates contemporary theory and criticism. As a researcher, he tried to find a raison d' être for its narrative in the realm of contemporary literary history, and this is "writing by being possessed." He said, if we say that, in the case of many authors, we can always construct their self-image from their literary works, in the case of Curses of Xixia, it is very difficult based on the text to build a clear image of the author, and through the text there is almost no way to imagine or get a feel for the author. The voice of the author in the text seems not to be his voice, but rather another voice, and the text itself does not seem to have been written by the author, but rather by another force attached to the author making him write. So he feels that the author and the text were both possessed.

Professor Chen Xiaoming considers that writing by being possessed is in fact a religious question. Looked at from the context of contemporary literary history, Chinese literature— from history to culture—has already reached it limits, so if religion becomes a source for writing, it may be offering a way out for twenty-first century authors. When authors rely on strong religious feelings, and write in the manner of being possessed by spirits, they can go beyond the aesthetic scope of history and literature, and enable their works to show a kind of freedom. In his view, Curses of Xixia offers a possibility for contemporary literature to move forward from history and culture towards religion. Seen from the whole history of contemporary literature, this experience of writing is extremely rare, and therefore is very much worth taking seriously and investigating.

From this, Chen Xiaoming points out, religion, like literature and music and the other forms of art, may be a way for the human race to enable itself to survive. Xuemo uses a religious narrative to express a cultural narrative, and entering a dreamlike realm, writes of an evil world, like the sunlight on a winter day in the wild plateaus of the west, shining on the soil, all pale. It is real but has no strength; it is false but also real;it reveals an experience that goes beyond apparent reality. He calls it "China's magical realism." This magic is not the same as the magic of Latin America's Garcia Marquez, but gets its source directly from religion. Using Michel Leiris's description of Georges Bataille: "After he turned into an inconceivable person, he got lost in all that he could discover in the reality which he could not accept ... He expanded his field of vision ... and recognized that, only if people can find their own standard in this situation where there are no standards, can they truly become human. Only when he reached this kind of realm, when, in the madness of Dionysus, he allowed high and low to merge into one, and eliminated the separation between wholeness and emptiness, could he then become an inconceivable person." Chen Xiaoming points out that Chinese literature up until now has already accumulated too much literary experience, and must go beyond this experience; authors themselves must first become "inconceivable people" and write inconceivable works, extreme works like The Curses of Xixia. Xuemo spontaneously has changed into an "inconceivable person" who has reached the realm where "he allowed high and low

to merge into one, and eliminated the separation between
wholeness and emptiness." With this kind of writing, Xuemo
has also "found his own standard in this situation where there
are no standards" and "only then can truly become human."

Xuemo's voice:

I discovered that, for the expression we are accustomed to using
in the Buddhist realm: "no duality, no separation," Professor Chen
Xiaoming's essay has another description, which arrives at the same
destination by another route: "Only when he reached this kind of
realm, when, in the madness of Dionysus, he allowed high and low to
merge into one, and eliminated the separation between wholeness and
emptiness, could he then become an inconceivable person."

Without a doubt, Mr. Chen Xiaoming has acute vision, and he
has revealed a certain truth about what happens when I write: my
works in fact pass on the light emitted by the fire of wisdom over
millennia. In the text later on in this book, no matter whether its
external appearance is beautiful or plain, in the same way, I am
transmitting a kind of wisdom that can enable us to open through to
clear understanding.

It must be added that when I was writing this book, I was controlled
by a great mystical power, and there was no dualism, and no artificial
contrivance. My mind was clear and empty as the sky, without a single
word, but when I began to write, endless scenes poured out. I invited
a great adept to verify this. He said: "This time, there is no duality, no
separation between you and all the Buddhas or tutelary deities." When
I dissolved away all clinging and attachment and merged into one great
existence, a spiritual force took control of me, and the text burst forth
like a volcano erupting. It was as if it was not me writing this book, but

I was just a way for it to come out. I just entered into the realm of clear light, and it made the text flow out from my mind that had no clinging or attachment. Of course, some times I savored the words with surprise and delight, like a vintner tasting the excellent wine he had unwittingly produced.

Chapter 19

The Soul of the Search

1 There is Also Marriage of Supreme Truth

Out of consideration for impatient readers, I will omit some of the things that Khyungpo Naljor encountered on his search, and I will also skip over the events of his seeking of the Dharma again and again from many eminent teachers during his three trips to India. Instead, I will write mostly about the process by which Khyungpo Naljor realized enlightenment and about his life experiences.

After a journey made up of countless treks, one day Khyungpo Naljor heard a group of people talking about stories of Niguma changing form. As soon as he heard her name, Khyungpo Naljor's hair stood on end and he started to cry. Readers who are familiar with the stories of the esoteric teaching will all know that when a disciple with a karmic connection meets a teacher with virtue, this kind of thing may always happen. I have had this kind of experience many times myself.

Khyungpo Naljor saw that it was a group of women who were talking about Niguma. Can we know from this that they were dakinis pointing the way for Khyungpo Naljor? At least Khyungpo Naljor himself thought it was really like this. He put down his backpack and joined his palms to offer his respects to those women. The women covered their mouths and laughed.

One asked: "Do you know Niguma?"

Khyungpo Naljor said: "Not only do I know her, I have been looking for her for several years."

Another one of the women asked: "Which Niguma are you looking for?"

Khyungpo Naljor said: "The one you were just talking about, the woman who changes form."

The first woman smiled and said: "Well, your ears are certainly sharp enough. We were talking quietly, yet you heard clearly. I see how you look—aren't you a man in love? Are you looking for Niguma because you want to marry her and make her your wife?"

Khyungpo Naljor quickly said: "I wouldn't dare say such a crazy thing. The Niguma in my mind is not separate from Buddha."

The women doubled over with laughter. One of them said: "Look at your appearance. To save a robber, didn't the Bodhisattva Guanyin marry the robber? Why then couldn't Niguma marry you? Could it be that you are worse than a robber?"

Khyungpo Naljor's forehead was dripping with sweat, and he was at a loss. He said: "I would not dare to say this. Really, this should not be spoken of irresponsibly. It would create karma of the mouth, and I would fall into hell."

The women laughed gaily for a while. One of them said: "We won't tease you any more. We don't know where Niguma ultimately is either. But we hear that she is in the void above Soshaling cemetery. This may be so, but we often go there, and we have not seen anything of Niguma. Some people say that she changed into the secret realm of the dakinis, but this is just a story we've heard, that's all. No one has ever seen that secret realm. If you truly have the mind of faith, you might as well go there and look for her. Whether or not you have a karmic link to her depends on your good fortune."

The women went away laughing merrily. He heard one of them saying: "Look at that fool. One word about marriage, and he gets that scared. Ha-ha. He does not know that in that marriage, there is also marriage with supreme truth."

When Khyungpo Naljor heard this, he was still completely confused.

2 The Mandala of the Red Master of Life

Beloved Khyungpo Ba:

Let me tell you about something.

Among those sorcerers, there is a magician who does divination. They say he can figure out everything about you. He says that the reason their curses are failing time after time is because a woman in red is protecting you. I do not know if this is the Sukhasiddhi you have spoken about, or the Niguma you have been seeking. She is your protective spirit. Therefore, the sorcerers have decided to first trap that woman, and imprison her in a secret mandala, and then launch their curses at you. Right now they are building a mandala called the Red Master of Life. This mandala can trap the spirit protecting the person who is to be slain.

Under the guidance of Kumari, I secretly went and looked at that mandala. The mandala is set up in a mountain valley. There is a tree there that looks very much like a walking stick. They first drew a black triangular shape, and as I have said, this is the pattern for their death-dealing mandala.

That was really a frightening place. I felt that there was a chilly wind secretly surging up, a dark coldness that could penetrate to the marrow. I felt that my own spirit was being pulled into the mandala by them, and my body was curling up against the cold. At that moment I made a vow. I thought that if their curses really took effect, I would be willing to have them pull me into the mandala. That way, we could be together forever. As for me, whether I live or die is something I don't feel like thinking about. All I want is to be with you forever. I think that if I can be together with you, maybe the Land of Ultimate Bliss you all talk about is no more than this.

Kumari said that they killed a black owl, cut off its skin, and on it wrote your name and what they want. They want to cripple you. See how what they want changes from day to day. Before, they hoped to kill you. Then they hoped to turn you into an idiot. Now, after that, they want to cripple you. I wonder whether or not they are bargaining with your protective spirit. They have kept on lowering their expectations for their curses, but they have one goal, to make it so you do not go on your search again. They seem to be very afraid that you will succeed. I cannot figure out the reason in all this. In the past, the demon king Mara most feared that Buddha would become enlightened, because if there were one more person cultivating the Path, he would have fewer children and grandchildren. Are these sorcerers now like Mara?

I have discovered that there are many people who truly want you dead. One group is comprised of your religious rivals: they see Tibet as a cake, and they just want to slice it up among themselves: they do not want to have another powerful rival. No matter whether it is the Bonpo people, or Pema Nam, it seems they are all like this. Kusang Dorje seems to have something else in mind. Before, he still really hoped you would marry me. But later I discovered he had changed. Under the tutelage of those sorcerers, he began to get greedy. Maybe he hoped I would not give my wealth to you to use to spread the teaching. Maybe he thought that if I died, he would be the natural inheritor of my riches ... However, I have already thought of a good way to deal with this.

When they wrote your name and their wishes on the skin of the black owl, they used the blood of a bald eagle. They danced around brandishing the stake of Vajrakilaya, and chanting an evil spell. After that they took the cursed object and a short sword and put it into a bag and hung it on a tree in a graveyard. Unexpectedly, before they had turned around to leave, a very strong wind tore down the bag. The stake of Vajrakilaya poked through the bag and pierced the shoulder of one of the sorcerers. It was really very amusing. When this happened, the sorcerers were all embarrassed. Ha-ha! The sorcerers did not succeed, and instead one of them was wounded by the stake.

As Kumari was telling me this, she smiled with joy. I too

was very joyful.

As I write this letter, the night has already grown dark. I really miss you.

As I was about to put my pen down, I could not hold back my feelings, and without my mind being aware of it, my hand had already written the word "husband," and I hurriedly erased it. I stared at it for a moment, then added it back, but later I thought about it more, and again erased it. Just now, hot tears were about to flow from my eyes, but I tried hard and managed to hold them back. I was about to say something, but I won't. My mind has turned sour.

You are a person who must take a long journey. It's better for me to leave out the word "husband".

The other day, as soon as I saw the words "I have decided to become a monk" in your letter, I was struck dumb. I had not anticipated that you would make this kind of decision, and I returned to my room in a daze. I ended up limp, with no strength, and showed my true colors. I became what you spoke of once as a drunken snake immortal. You are not the same as the immortal, you have found a home to return to. So the tears welling up in my mind in the end cannot become a vast ocean reaching to the sky. My enemy is not Fahai Monk—all I can do is submerge myself.

... In the end I was crying. Originally, my mind was full of joy: I thought I had found a man who would be my companion and travel together with me. Whatever I look at makes me think of you, and even when I dream, you are always smiling. I do not want to dream this happily and then wake up. This is a road one must travel oneself. Before, you said you felt sorry

that I was so isolated. Before, I did not feel that I was isolated, because I always carried you around in my mind. Now I finally do feel isolated, and so I cry for myself.

Do you want to use this cruel coldness and explain that "all things are impermanent"? When you told me to recite the Diamond Sutra, did you want to help me clear away clinging and attachment and ignorance and delusion?

If so, I have definitely not been a good student. If, to cultivate practice, I must in exchange completely cut off my feelings for you, then I am definitely not taking refuge with the teaching. I do not seek future lives, I do not seek Buddha lands. When I chant the sutras and pray, I am just hoping to spend this lifetime with you. Now you are all gone, and I have nothing to seek. My heart is all gone, and I cannot feel heartache. Do not be concerned, you can go on with no worries or concerns.

I am very stupid, and I let you suffer in vain. You have decided to accept the precepts and become a Buddhist monk, and perhaps I should be happy.

No more writing. Take good care of yourself.

Sharwadi

3 The Dakini in the Sound of the Wolves Howling

Xuemo: Master, what I most want to know about is really the process of your search. I hope you can emphasize the key points and talk about those spiritual experiences. This is because the truths of the teaching are all there in the Buddhist Canon, but your own seeking and search belong just to you.

Khyungpo Naljor:

Good. What delighted me most in my life was indeed this.

I remember that day. Those women gradually got farther away. It was as if I were in a dream — I was very happy. I had finally gotten some information on Niguma. I had heard that Soshaling cemetery was a famous mortuary forest in India, and many traditional stories had originated there. Among the eighty-four great masters of the Great Mudra, there was a lethargic lazy fellow. According to the story, his laziness reached such an extreme point that his family members could not bear it, so they took him and abandoned him in the Soshaling forest cemetery. Later he met a master teacher, who told him to visualize a bright spot on the top of his head, and to visualize all the worlds in the cosmos entering into it. After a long time, his thoughts ceased, and he awakened to empty inherent nature.

I easily found out the location of the Soshaling forest cemetery, and I went there carrying my gold. Because I was so overjoyed, I had no sense of fatigue. I went along the road and saw a bend in the river. There were many trees there, but the leaves were dried out and the branches pointed up into the sky waving back and forth. At the bend of the river there was a woman crying out in pain; the sound of her cries was sad and shrill and filled the river bend with a desolate feeling. I looked all around, and I did not see anything else that caught my eye. I wanted to ask that women whether or not she had seen Niguma, but I saw the tears swirling in her eyes, and she kept on sobbing. I knew that asking her would be useless, so I gave a lonesome sigh.

Unexpectedly that woman cried a while more and finally stopped. I took the opportunity to ask her: "Do you know Niguma?"

The woman said: "Niguma, Niguma — my son too was always asking about Niguma. He asked and asked, but he did not escape the god of death."

I got more interested and asked: "Did your son know Niguma?"

The woman said: "Who comes here without knowing Niguma? You may be thinking of Niguma, but that Niguma may not be thinking of you. Everyone says there is some Pure Land here, but why can't I see any Pure Land?"

The woman talked on at length, and I heard that her son had been stricken with a serious illness. She heard that if she found Niguma, she could cure her son's illness, and she came here looking for her. She looked all over, looked until her heart was filled with grief, and then cried out in pain.

The woman said: "Everyone says Niguma's secret realm is here, but there is no one who can really see it. I have heard that only those with a karmic connection would be able to see her. But what is a karmic connection? I have also heard that only those with the mind of faith can see her. But what is the mind of faith?"

The woman went away crying her eyes out. The wind began blowing and blew away the marks on the ground of where the woman had been kneeling. It got quiet all around, and when the woman's image disappeared at the end of the cemetery forest, I began to suspect it had been a dream.

I thought: "If only our effort is deep enough, we can grind an iron pestle down to a needle." So I thought this bend in the river must be Soshaling forest cemetery, and I would first do a hundred thousand prostrations. So then, thinking this bend in the river was the forest cemetery, I started doing prostrations and praying to Niguma. When I had done the full hundred thousand prostrations, the earth trembled, and a rosy cloud appeared in the sky. Suddenly a voice came from the colored light:

Niguma's secret realm is to the east, a magnificent pure wondrous realm beyond compare.

She is the lord who rescues people from suffering; you must travel east with sincere faith.

I thought: "Actually, this place is not the Soshaling forest cemetery. Although this is not the forest cemetery, still, I at least got the direction to the forest cemetery." So then I happily traveled toward the east. After traveling for several days, the road ended up in the mountains, and there were fewer and fewer signs of human habitation. Along the route the scenery was wild and desolate, and there were human skeletons, and it was very frightening. But I was thinking, since there are skeletons, I think this is the forest cemetery. I also saw the wolves getting more numerous, making noise here and there in the mountain valley. In my mind I said: "O wolves, I have not come looking for you, I am looking for Master Niguma. If you know any information about her, then tell me. If you don't know anything, then do not come bother me. When I achieve true enlightenment, if you are still interested in me, I will offer up my body to you. Okay?"

A wolf let out a long howl, as if to say, "Okay, okay."

But although this wolf was saying "Okay, okay," there were several wolves circling me. Their mouths were open wide, dripping with saliva, and some of them were also clacking their teeth together, and that sound was very horrible. I thought: "Could it be that they are really going to eat me?" I also said: "I must not fear death. That other man Buddha offered his body to feed a tiger. But right now, I still have not found Master Niguma, and I have not received her teaching line, and if I die now, I will not really be resigned to it. It would be better if you wolves got farther away from me."

The wolves heard this, and they did not advance, but neither did they move farther away. They just followed me at a distance.

The wind blew from where the wolves were, and I smelled a thick stench: it was surely the odor from within the mouths of the wolves. I thought: "Didn't that voice direct me to go east? How is it that I have encountered wolves?" But I also thought: "These wolves must be manifestations of those accomplished masters and dakinis, mustn't they?" I had heard it said that many dakinis transform themselves into wolves, to deliver those dead people.

They eat those dead bodies, and the dead then arrive at the dakini's Buddha Land. So then I said to those wolves: "If you are really dakinis, come toward me again clacking your teeth together." But the wolves did not move a bit. I had a good laugh and thought: "My nerves are really getting too sensitive."

Those wolves were just following me at a distance, and they did not attack, but they were still clacking their teeth. I was used to hearing that sound, but I had never been scared before.

That red glow on the horizon gradually disappeared, and night descended. I felt very cold, and I knew this was psychological. I could still see the wolves eyes like lights off in the distance, but I was too afraid to look. I thought: "Probably dying on the road to seek the Dharma is still worth it."

Suddenly, one wolf let out a long howl, and the whole pack of wolves joined in howling, with a sound that shook heaven and earth. I was frightened, and in my mind I thought: "If they attack, don't be too clever." I saw a tree nearby, so I hurriedly climbed up into it. Not a minute later, I saw all those lights surrounding the base of the tree. I drew a cold breath and thought: "If I had been a few steps slower, probably they would have eaten me." But it was strange, when those wolves had followed me on the road, why hadn't they attacked? I thought again: "Maybe they were afraid that I was armed."

The night was very dark, and I could not see anything clearly. Apart from those wolves' eyes that looked like a mass of lights, everything else was hidden in the darkness. The night air was very cold. Although this was not the season of the coldest weather, I still felt a bit chilly, and I suspected that this was caused by fear. So then I blamed myself some: "I have cultivated practice for such a long time, but I cannot even conquer fear." With this thought, I finally truly discovered my own fear. I thought: "When I was on the road just now, if these wolves had attacked me all together, where would I be right now at this instant?" I pursued this further, and discovered that this "I" in fact was always deceiving me.

Fundamentally, there is no I, so what would those wolves have been eating? Although in theory I understood that there was no self, that lingering fear was still coming on in waves. I thought: "If I was this afraid then, maybe I will not be able to complete such a long journey."

I climbed higher in the tree, and found a place to sit where three branches joined. I took off my backpack frame. This I had brought with me from Tibet—some people called it a human saddle. If you carry things on your back without using a backpack frame, it is easy to wear out your back. I hung this backpack frame on a forked branch that had been broken off. I closed my eyes and reviewed the things that had happened recently—it was truly like having a dream. At this moment, I thought that many things were like dreams. In a dream I studied Sanskrit. In a dream I met Sharwadi and Sukhasiddhi. In a dream I visited so many accomplished masters. In a dream I went though so many scenes ... All this was like dreaming. In my impressions, Sharwadi and Sukhasiddhi very much seemed to be the same person, especially when Sukhasiddhi appeared as a young woman. I even suspected that Sharwadi might be a transformation body of Sukhasiddhi.

I discovered that no matter what kind of master teacher I encountered, the concern in my mind was still Niguma, and maybe this was a karmic connection from past lives. My yearning for this teacher, whom I had never met before, had become a concern in my life that I could not break free from.

As soon as I thought of Niguma, I always felt a kind of thick feeling controlling me. I could not help but pray to her:

Niguma, my mother

Please consider me.

You are the master Buddha of the dakinis of the ten directions

You are the Mahakala, the protector of the Dharma, upon whom humans and devas rely

You are the sun in the depths of winter

You are the lamp that lights the eternal night

Niguma Khyenno!

I kept on chanting "Niguma Khyenno" without stopping. Gradually the wolf pack melted away, and all I felt was a pure light surrounding me. Tears ran down over my face, and in my mind I thought: "Even if I really end up buried in the belly of a wolf, I will take that as a Pure Land."

When I opened my eyes, I saw that bunch of lights was still gathered at the base of the tree, and the wolves seemed to be waiting for me to come down. I thought of Buddha giving up his body to feed the tiger, and I felt very ashamed. I thought: "To save a hungry tiger, Buddha gave himself into the tiger's mouth, but I really do not have the mind of compassion." Often after encountering some event, I would think of the distance that separated me from Buddha. But even though I felt ashamed, if someone had really told me to give up my body to feed the wolves, I still would have been unwilling to do so.

I thought: "I still have things I must do that are more important than feeding wolves." With this thought, my mind calmed down.

But very quickly I again felt shame about this calming down.

Suddenly I heard a voice coming from far away, saying "Help, save me." In the very quiet night, this voice calling for help was extraordinarily clear in my ears. Once they heard that human voice, the green-eyed ones at the base of the tree charged off like a swarm of bees. I thought: "That person who cried out has probably lost his life." I very much wanted to go help, but again I thought of how many wolves there were. Even if I gave my own life, I still would not necessarily be able to save another person.

From not far away came the sounds of tearing and biting and a woman shrieking and calling out. A point of bright light penetrated the dark night, and gradually it moved. After some time, I finally could make out a flaming torch. The woman who was crying out was holding up the torch and staggering toward me. The pack of wolves was growling as it kept pursuing her.

I called out: "Come here!"

When that woman heard a human voice, she kept crying out "Save me, save me!"

I said: "Quick! Come here, up the tree!"

But the wolves were faster than the woman, and before she had reached the base of the tree, they already had her surrounded. This was only two or three meters away from the tree where I was perched, pitying her.

The wolves surrounded the torch and were howling wildly, and the woman burst out screaming. She swung the torch, and the wolves who were about to come up to her were forced to retreat a few steps.

I called out: "Try to move closer to the tree."

The woman cried: "I cannot move, there is not a bit of strength left in my legs. You must help me."

I tried to climb down the tree, but as soon as I had come down a few steps, I saw that several wolves were already waiting for me at the base of the tree, looking at me and howling. I quickly climbed back up.

The woman was already in great danger, because the torch was about to burn out. Once the torch went out, the woman would surely be torn to pieces by those wolves. But if I went down, I probably would not be able to save her.

The woman shouted right at me: "Save me, save me!"

I shouted out: "Swing the torch and come over here to the tree."

The woman said: "If I had the strength, I would have already climbed a tree. Would I have waited till now?"

I said: "In this situation, even if I come down, I would just be risking death in vain."

The woman wept and said: "Are you really going to watch me die and not help?"

I hurriedly rubbed my hands together and tried to break off a branch of the tree. I thought that if I could get something like a club in my hands, then I would climb down from the tree and rescue her. But I felt around for a while, and discovered that the branches near me were too thick, and even if I used an axe, it would probably be impossible to cut them in time.

The woman cried and said: "If you still won't try to save me, I will surely die."

As we were talking, the torch in the woman's hand went out. She let out a fearful scream, and the wolves retreated a few steps in fright.

But very quickly, without waiting for the sparks on the end of the torch to be fully extinguished, the wolves rushed at her. The woman screamed bitterly and seemed to be struggling. But the sounds of the wolves tearing and biting came through and gradually silenced the woman's cries.

At one moment, between the sounds of tearing and biting, that woman's voice came through: "So this is the way you cultivate the mind of enlightenment?"

My face was running with sweat, but I still did not dare come down from the tree. An enormous sense of shame arose in me, but I still did not have the courage to come down from the tree and save the person.

From far away came a voice. It seemed to be a woman singing:

Empty talk about compassion is not good for much; it's not as good as saving someone right before your eyes from birth and death.

When you seek the supreme teaching, if you do not put it into real practice, what use is it?

You want to find the supreme teacher, but in your mind there are still selfish elements.

Though you say sentient beings are your mothers and fathers, why don't you save the person who is right in front of you?

*I am the dakini Niguma, and in my hands is the boat to take human
beings across.*

*Too bad the incomparable milk of the lion does not want to be poured
into a piss-pot.*

*If you want to get to see the dakini, resolve to repent and seek, and seek
some more.*

*Wait for the day that the light of mind shines forth, and wait some more
for the supreme causal basis for being my child.*

The voice gradually moved farther and farther away. I was stunned.
I thought: "When I listen to that woman's tone of voice, it surely is my
teacher Niguma." I wanted to climb down from the tree and go after
her, but I was worried about the wolf pack. Unexpectedly, just as I was
hesitating, the sounds of the wolves biting and tearing ceased, and there
was a peaceful stillness on all sides. I did not hear the wolves howling,
and there was nobody calling out, and even the sound of the wind was
gone.

There came the faint sounds of sardonic laughter. A woman said:
"With this kind of mind, do you still think you will see Niguma?"

When I heard the voice, I started to cry bitterly. I quickly climbed
down from the tree and rushed toward the place the voice was coming
from. I tripped and fell many times along the way. But all I saw
was blackness on all sides, and everything had returned to peaceful
stillness.

I was full of regret, thinking: "I have trekked several thousand
miles and spent many years searching for Niguma. I did not anticipate
that at the key moment, I would not be able to generate the necessary

mind of compassion, that I would come so close and miss my chance."

I sat dumbstruck in the tree, as if I had been struck by lightning—
my brain was blank. After a long while I revived, and I thought: "Even
though I always generate the mind of compassion every time I cultivate
contemplation, all that directed attention seems not to have changed
my intrinsic quality. Compared to Buddha cutting off pieces of his flesh
to feed the eagles, or giving up his body to feed the tigers, I have truly
fallen far short."

I was blaming myself and crying bitterly and feeling regret. The
sky gradually brightened. With nothing else I could do, I picked up my
backpack frame and came down from the tree. I saw that there were
no wolf tracks on the ground, and then I realized that all of last night's
scenes were all manifestations of the dakini. My mind was even more
full of regrets, and I thought: "I am truly useless. Even if I had fed
myself to the wolves then, so what? A bodhisattva who has been fed
to the wolves is still a bodhisattva. An ordinary man who is greedy for
life is still an ordinary man."

4 Self-Posed Paradoxes

Beloved Khyungpo Ba, they are still laying curses on you.

*You keep searching without stopping, and they keep laying
curses without stopping. This situation is like light and dark:
two brothers who cannot be separated.*

*I have been praying to Brahma all along, hoping that I
can bear the power of their curses. To tell the truth, I am a bit
scared. They have invited various sorcerers. That Pema Nam
who came with you knows a lot of sorcerers. I do not know why
he hates you so much—didn't you grow up in the same area?*

You treated him so well before ... I really cannot understand it.

Ever since I entered that mandala, I am always trembling, as if my soul has really been captured by them.

Maybe I am really withstanding the power of their curses on your behalf; yesterday afternoon my whole body got cold. When I was washing my head, some water ran down my back, and it was like being stuck with a piece of ice. Later my body ached all over and I had no strength. My head felt heavy and I was unsteady on my feet, and I got a fever. Suddenly I'd be hot, then suddenly I'd be cold: it was going back and forth. In the morning at the house, another person came seeking the Dharma and needed me to talk on and on. I was not free to keep quiet and not be smiling.

My father insists that I must talk without stopping, chattering on and on, and I am tired of talking. In fact, what I most want to say is what is here in these letters. The surprising happiness I felt when I had just met you let me forget why I had been talking for so long. But now, gradually, I have gotten tired of talking. Maybe this is not a good sign. Now that we are thousands of miles apart, if we do not maintain the necessary sincere conversation, the beautiful memories we share might get more distant and more tenuous, and finally will be like a bit of light sand scattered in a great desert, vanishing without a trace. Even the two of us will vanish in the sea of people.

I am constantly sinking into self-posed paradoxes. With feelings of ignorance and delusion, I feel pain I cannot bear, and it would be better to die than to live. But if I abandon you (you verbally acknowledge that I must free myself), there would be no way to maintain our feelings, and they would quickly dissolve away. The key to all this depends on how I treat you. This is because you are definitely not going to abandon everything for a woman—I am very clear on this point. So then, in order to preserve your pride, I am always trying to talk about forgetting the sharp pain of that indescribable ridicule you directed at me. For example, from the tone of what you say, I seem to be especially, unbearably lonely. But could a woman who is unbearably lonely heedlessly pursue you and wait for you? In order to protect your solitude, she innocently, and without counting the effort, wants to block off the intrusions of the noise of the mundane world.

We both have a multifaceted nature that is extremely complex and contradictory. This contradictory quality comes from the strength and independence of both our inner minds: we do not depend on each other, we do not rely on each other, we definitely will not compromise. We both live in our own individual worlds. Maybe this similar individuality will clash in the future with this tender feeling between us. Will it hurt or not? How much will it hurt? Only we ourselves will experience the feeling. You are a holy man, without anything to impede you, but I am an ordinary person, looking for ways to suffer. But I hope that by passing through this ordeal, I will welcome a new breakthrough and a new maturity.

Because your time seems to be more valuable, and your life seems to be more precious and rare, because I think I am still your beloved, every time I am the one who comes to patch things up. I am the one who works hard to make this feeling more complete and stronger, and not let it get eroded by time, so it will grow into a towering tree that reaches up to heaven.

I don't know whether or not this ice-cold seriousness and persistence of mine will make you feel estranged.

Solid and strong Sharwadi

5 The Frightening Marshland

Khyungpo Naljor:

After I watched the spirit dove fly away into the distance, and merge with the sky, I ate a little of the food from my backpack and sat under the tree and began to repent. I had concentrated on reciting the "Hundred Word Illumination" mantra a hundred thousand times, and only then did I feel that I could face Niguma and pray to her again. So I cleared my mind and silenced my thoughts and began to pray:

Niguma, my mother,

Please care about me.

You are my reason for living,

You are the meaning of my life,

You are the bright lamp in the perpetual night,

You are the boat in the ocean of suffering.

Niguma Khyenno!

I do not know how long I chanted this, but suddenly, I don't know from where, quietly there came a voice:

When you know your faults, change your faults, my Dharma son.

Let bygones be bygones, and have no regrets.

If you want to find your fundamental teacher,

Get up and go quickly toward the south to seek her.

I thought: "Yesterday she told me to go east to search, so today why has it become south?" Though I had doubts, I did not dare spoil the causal circumstances again. So I again put my pack on my back, and I went south. After I had been going for a while, I discovered that there was a zone of marshland ahead of me, and I thought: "This place is truly strange. Just now it was still high mountains, but at this moment it has become a marsh."

That marshland had an incomparably strange stench. It was emitting a bad smell that would make people vomit, as if a pile of dung had been fermenting here for a thousand years.

I covered my nose and went on, but my head felt dizzy and my vision blurred.

After traveling for several days, I discovered that there was no road anymore, and what appeared before my eyes was a boundless expanse of muddy ground. The mud was bubbling, and every time the bubbles appeared, I was hit with an evil stench. I endured it for a time, but in the end my whole body showed signs of weakening.

I thought: "Isn't this atmosphere poisonous?" I had heard that in India there was a place called the Poison Dragon Island, which was filled with poisonous vapor, and it was very hard for the people who went there to come back alive. I thought I might not keep going forward, but then I recalled what had happened that other night, and

I thought: "No matter what, even if I die, I will go on. This time my mind is like iron, and I cannot spoil the causal circumstances."

I continued to go forward. I went on for another few days, until I discovered that there was really no place to put my feet.

I saw the marsh putting forth countless gas bubbles. Whenever one of these bubbles burst, it emitted a stench that could make a person suffocate. But the strange thing was, in the marshland ahead of me, there was a line of tracks that looked a lot like footprints. I thought: "Who could go into this?" I also thought: "If other people can, why can't I? Maybe Niguma is in there."

With this thought, my mood improved, and I went forward following those footprints. Though I felt again and again that I was in danger of sinking into the swamp, in the end I did not sink in.

After proceeding on for a while, I discovered that the ground under my feet had obviously begun to sink down. If I slowed down a bit, the mud would cover the tops of my feet. My shoes were all muddy. I thought: "As long as I do not sink in, it will be alright." But I was always afraid that if I really did sink into the mud, probably there would not be anyone to call to for help.

The line of tracks still extended forward, and I did not know where it would end. Gradually I could make out that these were human footprints, and later I also discovered a torn shoe. I was very happy and thought: "As long as other people could go here, then I can go here." Thus, even though from time to time my feet sank into the mud, I kept moving forward with increased confidence.

I walked for another day, and I saw that all around me was swampland, and without those footprints, I might not even be able to get my bearings. I could see the horizon of the sky in all directions. The sky was like an enormous bowl, fastened on top of the earth. I vaguely remembered that there had been mountains, but at this moment I could not see any, just swamp and more swamp. Except for that line of footprints, I could not see any sign of human habitation, and there were not even any birdcalls—it was truly strange. It was as if I were walking in a dreamlike illusion. Although there was the constant plopping sound of my footsteps, for me it was always like traveling in a dream.

Gradually, I felt that it was getting harder and harder to walk, and my feet were sinking into the mud more and more frequently. If it had not been for the footprints which were still stretching out into the distance, I would have absolutely never dared to keep on walking forward. The further I walked, the more I trembled with fear. If I had not firmly believed that Niguma was up ahead, I definitely would not have kept on going forward.

Suddenly, the sound of a voice calling for help came from up ahead. I was startled, but then very quickly I felt happy—this was the first time I had heard a human voice since I had entered into the marshland. I sped up my pace, without thinking that as soon as I had taken a few steps, I would feel my feet slipping. By the time I reacted, I was already knee-deep in the mud. Going through the marshland, I had gained some experience, so I immediately adjusted to the situation and sat down, and then lay down facing the sky. I saw a huge cloud in the sky above me, with a sinister shape very much like a Mahakala, a great protector of the Dharma, so I prayed: "O Mahakala, surely you will protect me and not let my body be buried in the swamp." I said this for a while, and I began to slowly pull my feet out of the mud. Though there was a lot of suction, I kept trying for a time, and finally succeeded in pulling my feet out of the mud.

I wiped the sweat off my brow. I discovered that the suction power of this mud was very great. Though I had only sunk in up to my calves, that was all I could take. If I had sunk in up to my thighs, probably it would have been very hard for me to escape. I had heard that, of the many people who get mired in swamps, apart from those whose whole bodies are submerged and suffocate to death, many of those who sink in halfway starve to death if there is no one around to pull them out. If I had sunk in, probably there wouldn't have been anyone to save me.

Then I saw that the person crying for help was up ahead of me. I dimly saw an old man, who appeared to be very skinny. If so thin a man had sunk into the mud, how much the more so would a hale and hearty guy like me. That man again let out a call for help. He was speaking Pali. I had studied Pali, because Pali was among the three great language families used in the transmission of the Buddhist teaching. The other two were Chinese and Tibetan.

The old man was calling out to be rescued in Pali.

I asked: "Why did you come into this swampland?"

The old man said: "My son is sick, and he needs a medicinal herb which comes from this swampland. Look, this is it." He shook his hand, and I saw that in his hand he had some wild plants that looked like a bunch of flowers. But I could not say what they were called, so I asked: "What herb is that?" The man said: "They are called bodhisattva flowers." I said: "I have never heard that there are bodhisattva flowers." The man said: "They are called by different names in various places. I do not know what you call them where you're from … To cure my son's illness, what I will use is the heart of the bodhisattva flower."

"What sickness does he have?" I asked.

The old man said: "Don't ask. While you keep asking questions, I'll be totally submerged here."

Sure enough, I saw that he had already sunk in up to his buttocks, and even if he did not sink down anymore, it would be very hard for him to save himself. So I quickly said: "Don't worry, I'll be right there."

The old man said: "Be careful."

I took a few steps forward, and even though I did all I could to pick spots with a lot of grass to step onto, my feet still often sank in.

I advanced another few steps. I clearly saw a place with a bunch of grass to step onto, but unexpectedly, as soon as I put my foot down, I ended up sinking into the mud up to my calves. I was alarmed, and I sank in deeper, and even my knees had sunk into the mud.

The old man said: "Be careful! Be careful! If you die, it won't just be one man who dies — six people will die."

I was afraid if I kept standing up any longer I would sink in deeper, so I lay down on my back in the mud. I heard the old man talking strangely, so I asked: "How will it become six people?"

The old man said: "Once you die, there will me no one to save me, and I will die too. If I die, my son will not be able to get the medicine to cure him, and he will surely die too. Once my son dies, my daughter-in-law will have to be burned on his funeral pyre, and she too will die. Once we are dead, there will be no way for my wife to live, and she will surely hang herself or throw herself into the river. When she is dead, won't our grandson starve to death? Just count it up — won't this be six people?"

I felt that was funny, and I thought: "How can he do this kind of accounting?" But I saw that old guy had already sunk in up to his waist, and I quickly called out to him: "Don't talk anymore. Lie down flat, and you won't sink in any further."

The old man said: "I know that, of course, but don't you see that behind my back there is a nest of little quails? If I lie flat, won't I crush them?"

Though I had not seen any quails' nest, I lifted my head and looked. I saw that not far away there really were two quails calling, and I thought: "He's right after all."

I had laid my body down flat, and when I tried to pull my legs out of the mud, I used all my strength, but I could only pull them out a few inches. I struggled till I was covered with sweat, and I finally saw my knees. I thought: "This is really deadly. Against a force like this, if I had not known the secret of lying down, by now I probably would have sunk down without a trace."

But I also thought: "If I had really sunk down and vanished without a trace, where would this moment's 'I' have gone?"

The old man called out again: "Hurry up. This is not the time for you to study meditation. What 'I' or 'not I' are you concerned about?"

I was secretly surprised. I thought: "How does he know the thoughts in my mind?"

I saw that the old man had sunk in a lot further, and the mud was already above his waist. I hurriedly said: "You should lie down flat." The old man said: "Didn't I tell you about the quail's nest?" He also said: "Now I have sunk in more than waist-deep—how can you tell me to lie down flat? The only way is for you to come over here fast. You lie down flat, and I will pull on your hand. It might still be possible to save me. But if you save me, it will be equivalent to saving four other people."

I thought, alright then. I lay my body out flat, and at the same time tried to pull my legs out. After quite a while, sweating all over, I finally managed to pull my legs out.

I saw that the old man had already sunk in up to his chest. I moved as fast as I could over to his side to pull him out, but how could I know that with every step I took, I would sink into the mud. Every time I noticed signs that I was sinking down, I would adapt to the situation and lie flat and pull out my legs. This way, although I was soon covered in sweat, I was still a few meters away from the old man.

With some difficulty, the old man said: "Never mind, forget it. You do not have any sincerity. I see that, for you, the desire to save your own life comes ahead of the thought of rescuing another person. How could there be someone cultivating the bodhisattva Path like this?"

I felt very ashamed, but I thought: "Even if I had rushed ahead with no thought for my own safety, I might not have been able to save you. You have sunk in up to your neck, and even if you pulled my hand, maybe you still would have dragged me in."

The old man cried: "Hey you! Why don't you roll over here? If I were you, I would lie down flat, and roll my body over here. What's the use of putting on a show like this? Forget it, never mind. Just go away. It's okay if you let me die. Even if all five people in my family die, it has nothing to do with you."

I thought: "He is really right. Lie down and roll over there — maybe that really is the thing to do." But I also thought: "Even if I really lie down and roll over there, I still may not be able to save the old man. Since he has already sunk into the mud up to his neck, if I pull his arms, it won't have much effect."

The old man sunk in a bit deeper, and the mud seemed about to flow into his mouth. I heard him say: "I'm telling you, the heart of this bodhisattva flower is also called the mind of enlightenment, and it can cure many sicknesses. I think that maybe you need it." As he said this, he took the bunch of flowers and threw it over.

I sensed a pungent odor in my nose, and suddenly I laid my body down flat and rolled over toward him. But the old man could no longer be seen: all I saw was some bubbles gurgling on the surface of the mud.

I heard a voice laughing derisively and saying: "A man who watches somebody die without trying to save him, and he still wants to see Niguma? Bah!"

Now I discovered that in this swamp, there were in fact nobody else's footprints, only the footprints I made when I came here, extending clearly into the distance. It was silent and still all around, and I could not say for sure that it was really that the marsh had swallowed up the old man, or that actually there had not been any old man, but only my own illusory perception.

I thought: "Surely this is Master Niguma testing me." I thought: "I have truly failed to be worthy of her, and I was wrong." Having thought this, I couldn't help crying bitterly.

The strange thing was, the bodhisattva flowers that the old man had thrown were still lying on the mud in front of me, and were just then smiling at me. As I was crying, I took hold of the heart of one of the flowers and stuffed it into my mouth. I tasted an extraordinary bitterness.

I thought: "Strange, how can this mind of enlightenment end up being so bitter?"

6 An Ancient Art of Evil Curses

When Khyungpo Naljor was entering into the marshland, Sharwadi was secretly going with Kumari to see a new mandala of death-dealing methods.

A small path led from the dark mountains through the mountainside above the death-dealing mandala. There was a tree on the mountainside, and Sharwadi and Kumari climbed up into it. They could clearly see the death-dealing mandala, while their opponents could not see them.

Those sorcerers were again beginning a new, even more frightening, curse.

Recently Sharwadi had discovered that Kusang Dorje's physiognomy had completely changed. Because of his hatred, there was a sinister look on his face. If a person is always full of hatred and anger, this will form an inertial force in his life, and after a long time, this hatred will permeate his mind and become its basic substance. It was this way with Kusang Dorje. Sharwadi very much missed the simple innocent man he had been before.

The mandala of curses was set up in a graveyard, and it was very secluded and quiet. It was at the intersection of three mountains and three rivers. It was a tradition among Nepalese who cultivated religious practice to go into retreat in graveyards, because there they could symbolically see impermanence. But Sharwadi could not understand why these men, who considered themselves to have seen through impermanence, could never see through their own hatred. How could they not know that this feeling of hatred was in fact also impermanent?

They had already begun on those curses called the curses of the Red Master of Life. This was a technique of placing curses on people which been handed down from ancient times, and it was unusually effective. Earlier on, some famous sorcerers in Nepal relied on this to make their living. When she was serving as female spirit, Sharwadi had managed a dispute which had some connection to these evil curses. The person concerned had laid a curse so that more than two hundred people from a single clan had died; they all died from a mysterious plague. But this plague was very strange, and just circulated within this clan, and never affected anyone else. It was as if the plague could recognize people. This was where the mystery of that evil curse lay.

Among the cultivators of esoteric practices in Nepal, there were many frightening stories going around about this evil curse.

The sorcerers, with their hair disheveled and sinister looks on their faces, spat out angry curses from their mouths. This technique was not like the other techniques that they cultivated; it demanded that the sorcerers truly had to display signs of anger, and their minds truly had to be filled with hatred. The words of the curses were secretly assembled like hailstones and written on the effigy and the life-stone of the one who was to be slain in the mandala. The story was that if the hatred in the minds of the sorcerers was aided by the death-dealing mandala, so that it managed to resonate with the destructive force in the phenomenal realm, the one to be slain would then die an unnatural death.

The fire on the death-dealing altar was dark and secretive and put forth a faint blue light. The sorcerers chanted their spells, and at the same time scattered black offerings on the altar. The black rapeseed split and crackled in the fire, and the fat from black animals put out a foul smell. Black smoke swirled around, covering the death-dealing altar. In the smoke there seemed to be countless demons dancing.

Kumari said: "I have heard that those who are hit by this evil curse are sure to die an unnatural death, within three months if it is fast, within three years if it is slow."

Sharwadi was horror-stricken.

When she was serving as a female spirit, she had studied certain kinds of techniques and taken in the power of those evil spells. She realized that countless dark energies had entered into her body. Her whole body went numb.

But she did not know if her own acceptance of the power of spells would really enable her to lessen the harm the evil spells could do to

Khyungpo Naljor.

For Sharwadi, the power of spells was not frightening. What was hardest for her to bear was still her longing ...

Sharwadi writes:

> *I am always worrying for you, life has no rest, worries never cease.*
>
> *Perhaps this is my fate from a previous life.*
>
> *In the evenings, I lounge lazily in my chair, not doing anything, thinking of you. In the whole day, this is the only time I am not disturbed.*
>
> *I am very tired of my current life where I am too busy with work, but there is nothing to be done about it — it is always very lively at home. If father did not take on so many disciples, or if I had not been a female spirit, maybe it would have been another kind of life. Life is this way: if there are gains, then there will be losses.*
>
> *Mother has been back home these two days, and she and father have been quarreling nonstop the whole time. This kind of antagonistic, estranged atmosphere makes me tired, and almost hopeless. If I did not have my longing for you, this family that has no love but only recrimination would just be a set of shackles that would make anyone suffocate. It's good there is the Diamond Sutra which you left with me. I always have it with me, and if I get any free time, I go through it. I think of opening it, but nothing happens; just as mother says, maybe I can be surrounded by good fortune and not know it. Even more likely, I think about being with you, and this really is a kind of major greed.*

It's just that I am too far away from you, and we have been apart for too long, and I am always missing you and crying. It is very clear to me that the present situation seems unchangeable. You cannot abandon your search, and there is no way for me to abandon my parents ... Of course, this is only my rationale; in fact, if you would just beckon to me, I surely would go with you to the ends of the earth. But this is truly up to heaven to decide.

There is nothing more, just that I miss you very much, and so I've written this nonsense.

I truly cannot say anything; it's just that I am thinking of you all the time wherever I go. I have not studied the Diamond Sutra properly—I still cannot let go of you. I do not dare imagine: if it were not for those days with you, would I be able endure a single day?

I think it over and it is still truly strange. Once you appeared in my life, you turned my world upside down, and it became a total mess, the wreckage of a broken wall, and I can't do anything about it. I did not think that my mind, which had been content and tranquil while I lived the life of a female spirit for several years, would fall into the hell of lovelorn longing.

I miss you very much—there is no way to describe it. If I happen to be reading a book, if I even see the word "search," I want to cry. So I am doing all I can to help myself, and I am careful as can be to steer clear of the word "emotion" and the word "love," like a boat steers clear of a reef. I am afraid I will sink. If it were just me, I could face any kind of situation, but we do not belong entirely to ourselves—my father demands that I do all I can to maintain the decorum of a female spirit. Maybe all that belongs totally to me is the one or two hours a day when I can let myself talk with you. This talk is more like talking to myself. Whether you hear it or not is not important. I am talking with myself.

There are many things which I don't dare think about, which I cannot bear to think about, so I do not think about them.

I am like a leaf drifting with the current. Originally, I considered myself comparatively strong, being able to go through life according to my own ideas. But after I met you, I discovered that I am powerless and helpless like this.

You may think that I am demoralized, but you do not know how much strength I require just to force myself to be able to control that giant longing that seems to be about to gush forth. My energy is all used to deal with my own false thoughts.

What kind of love is this? Enough to make me self-destruct.

Maybe the one waving this banner of love is only my own greed and selfish desire.

As you said, my whole life will pass by very quickly.

7 A Herd of Deer in a Trap

In those days, I would still often think of Sharwadi, but she was like an image in the fog, and the image had already started to appear indistinct.

After I tasted the very bitter heart of the bodhisattva flower, I again repented for a long time.

Because there was no road anymore through the marshland, all I could do was go back by the original route. The good thing was that my footprints from when I had come were still there, and after I had walked a few days, I ended up back at the place where I had been doing prostrations to Niguma. I thought: "Look, I thought before that I had the mind of enlightenment, but in fact it was no more than an intention, and I really never had the genuine, sincere mind of enlightenment." Everything I had gone through in the past few days was like a dream, like an illusion. I firmly believed that the old man was an illusory manifestation of my teacher, so I regretted that I had not been able to stand up to the test. As for whether an old man had really sunk down into the mud, I no longer worried about that. I thought he was certainly not real.

But the self-criticism came at me like a tide. I thought of the story of how a bodhisattva, when his woman servant came to him demanding his eyes, plucked them out without the least hesitation and gave them to her. Compared with that bodhisattva, I felt so far short. I thought: "What that old man said was right. In fact, I am a person who very much needs to take that 'mind of enlightenment' medicine."

I was worshipping and praying:

Niguma, my mother,

Please take heed of me.

You save the fragile egg in this world,

You rescue the one who is about to fall into the raging waves,

You save the multitudes who are deluded in the present,

You spread the Great Work in annals of history.

Niguma Khyenno!

When I had completed the full hundred thousand great prostrations, I heard the quiet sound of a woman's voice:

When you know your error, change your error, son of my heart

Repentance has dissolved away a hundred kinds of karma

If you wish to seek Niguma

With a clear sincere mind, go toward the west.

I thought: "Last time I went east, and then I went south. Although I have not seen Niguma, although I did not pass the dakini's test, in the end I did get to see transformation bodies of the dakini. That woman, that old man, certainly were manifestations of the dakini. This time I will go toward the west, and no matter what kind of situation I encounter, I will offer my body without hesitation."

So I put my pack on my back, and started to travel west. After several days, I had gone into the mountains. I thought: "This is truly strange. Last time when I went into the marshland, all I saw on all sides was marshland going on forever; I did not see any mountains. Where did these mountains come from?" Though there were doubts in my mind, I did not stop walking. When I met other travelers, I would ask about Niguma, but unfortunately no one knew who Niguma was.

When I first went into the mountains, the mountains were not too high, but after walking for several days, I discovered that the mountains were getting higher by the day, and in the end it felt like being in Nepal. Nepal is a famous mountainous country, and many of the most famous high mountains in the whole world are in Nepal. I had not thought that India, which was known for its plains, would have such high mountains. I traveled for several days, thinking the entire time that if I discovered someone in difficulty, no matter what kind of situation he was in, I would make every effort to save him without a thought for my own physical safety. Even if it meant sacrificing my own life, I would not hesitate. A great strength was surging through my body. But there was not even the shadow of the person in danger I was hoping to discover.

I thought: "This is really too bad. I want to meet someone who needs help, and in the end I haven't met one."

The farther west I went, the higher the mountains got. Sometimes it took a good many days to cross over a single mountain. I constantly felt that I was traveling in a dream, because according to my reasoning, there were no mountains here. So how could I be having this strange experience of traveling across a great mountain range? Though I felt doubtful, still, I did not dare turn back, because doing that might spoil the interplay of causal conditions.

Gradually the mountains got higher, and the people got fewer and fewer. Gradually there were not even any birds to be seen. As I traveled along, I ended up feeling very cold. I felt this was strange, and I thought: "I remember India being very hot. How can there be a place this cold?" But I also thought: "There are a lot of things in the world that cannot be explained. Don't worry about it. If my teacher told me to go west, I will go west."

I walked along for several more days. I met a few people, and I hoped they would turn out to be in trouble, and they would ask me for help. How could I have known that not only did they not ask me for help, but instead they helped me, giving me food and water. I was happy, but I was also dismayed. Other people did not seek help from me, did not lack for anything, and in fact needed no help.

I went on for a few more days, and I saw no more signs of human habitation at all. The food and water in my backpack was dwindling. Nothing had appeared that would test me like the last two times, and there was no way to inquire about where Niguma was. I did not know how long I would still have to keep going. Although I was worried, I planned to keep on going, since compared to my previous searches that stretched on and on with no goal, knowing which direction to go already counted as seeing some hope, so I planned to keep on going.

One night I stayed with a family. This family were hunters, and the walls of their house were hung with animal skins. I had always felt very opposed to hunters who kill living things, but because there were really no other people living in the area, I thought: "It's not important. I'll stay one night, then go on."

In the night I heard the sound of a gong coming from outside. This seemed strange, and just as I was feeling doubt, the hunter pushed open the door and said to me: "Let's go. Hurry up. I have driven a herd of deer into a net, and I cannot kill them all by myself, so you can help me."

I went out the door with him, and in the ravine in front of us, I saw a hidden net extended across the opening. Many deer had been caught in the mesh of the net. I knew that hunters in Tibet too often use this method in the mountains. They use all kinds of methods to make animals run into nets that have already been set out. The animals do not know they should pull back, and when they discover something holding them by the neck, they struggle to go forward. The result is that the more they press forward, the more firmly they are stuck in the net. The hunter first caught a few of the young deer and placed them in a pen he had set up. The cries for help from the young deer drew in many larger deer coming to save them. The hunter picked a good angle and beat the gong. The frightened deer charged forward, and they were all entrapped in the net.

The herd of deer were giving out plaintive whining sounds, and when they saw humans coming, they struggled even harder to go forward; they surged into the net and made it sway, but the necks of the deer were trapped even tighter.

The hunter gave me a sharp knife and said: "Come, honored guest, help me. I cannot slaughter all these deer by myself."

I said: "Don't tell me you did not notice that I am a Buddhist monk. I have accepted the monastic code."

The man said: "There is no one else here. Who cares whether you break the rules or not?"

I said: "That won't do. When I accepted the monastic discipline, I did not do it for someone else. I cannot violate the rules. Killing living beings would be a major violation."

The man said: "It is not important. You help me, and I will help you. This afternoon you asked me where Niguma lives, and I did not tell you. In fact, I do know. If you help me kill these deer, I will help you go to see Niguma."

But I thought: "When he says this, he is deceiving me. How could a hunter who kills living things know Niguma? Then again, even if he really knows Niguma, if he tells me to kill living beings, I still will not do it. I am searching for Niguma in order to seek the Dharma. If I am a butcher who breaks the discipline, what's the use of seeking the Dharma?" So I said: "I cannot help you kill living beings. Even if you really know Niguma, I still cannot kill living beings."

The man said: "But you took the bodhisattva vows. Didn't you take a vow that you must help other people?"

I said: "I took a vow to benefit sentient beings, not to kill or injure sentient beings."

The man asked: "So won't you really help?"

I said: "I won't help!"

The man laughed coldly for a while. He went up and killed one of the deer. He was very skillful, and with a few strokes skinned the deer and threw its guts on the ground. After this he asked another question: "If you won't help me kill them, that is alright, but won't you help me clean up the guts?"

I said no.

The man asked: "You haven't eaten anything yet. So if I give you some deer meat, won't you certainly refuse then?"

I said: "Although I do eat meat, what I eat is meat that is pure in three ways: I do not see the animal being killed, I do not hear the animal being killed, and it was not killed for me. I cannot ask for your deer meat."

The man laughed coldly and said: "That's okay then. I hunt deer intending to use it for food. Since you do not want to ask for any, then I will simply release them." As he said this, he took those deer one by one out of the net, and set them free.

I said: "Good. I can help you do this."

The man laughed coldly and said: "That's not necessary." He was fast with his hands, and the deer scattered and fled in all directions.

Finally the only one that remained was the deer he had already killed. The man took the innards and the skin and everything and put it in a pile, and said as if to scold it, "What are you waiting for?" He clapped his hands, and the deer which had been slaughtered came back to life and ran off.

I stared, dumbfounded.

The man turned around and went back up the ridge. Faintly, there came the sound of a song:

I am the fearless dakini, already gone beyond dualism.

In my realm there is no birth and death: death is birth, and birth is death.

My net is the illusory body without desire, my knife is the great bliss without greed.

My killing is the light of inherent nature, these deer are the five aggregates of the false self.

I kill, but there is no killing; there is no killing, but I kill. You cling to the illusory as real, and accept the false as true.

You cling to the empty and false so-called precepts of discipline, but you prefer to abandon the fundamental teacher.

This kind of foolish ignorant person — how is he fit to see the honored Niguma?

When I heard this, it was like being hit by a bolt of lightning. I called out: "O Teacher, forgive my foolish ignorance." But all that answered me was the sound of the wind. I cried out in pain several times, and fainted dead away.

When I came to, the sky was already light, and I discovered that there was nobody else in the mountain valley. I realized that this too had been an illusion created by the dakini. Then I stamped my foot and gave out a long sigh and said: "How can I be so stupid? During this whole journey, I have been hoping that people will ask me for help, but when a person really asked me for help, I refused that person." In my mind, though I felt ashamed, I also thought: "If in the future there is someone else who asks me to break the precepts and kill a living being, will I agree to or not?" I asked myself this several times, but I still could not be sure.

Having told the story to this point, Khyungpo Naljor asked me: "Xuemo, if you were put in my place, would you have killed a living being or not?"

I said: "I would not have."

He asked again: "If killing a living being would let you have infinite wisdom, would you kill it or not?"

I answered: "I would not!"

He also asked: "If killing a living being could let you experience the achievement of the rainbow body, would you kill a living being or not?"

I said: "I would not! No matter if killing a living being could let me live forever without growing old, I still would not kill a living being. Do you know that some people, in order to live forever, will even drink broth made by cooking a baby? What would be the meaning of such eternal life? How is this any different from those demons who wanted to eat the flesh of the Tang Monk in order to live forever without growing old?"

Khyungpo Naljor sighed deeply and said: "Then you can understand me as I was then."

8 Frightening Curses

Beloved Khyungpo Ba, I went with Kumari again to that mandala of the Red Master of Life. According to the tradition of the Esoteric Religion in Nepal, a death-dealing mandala cannot be viewed, because sometimes evil spirits and the force of the curses can flow out of it and do harm to those who are viewing it.

That place was truly howling with the sound of an ill wind, with evil energy soaring up to the sky. As before, as soon as I arrived at such a place, I got a splitting headache. Maybe the reason is that I cannot stand the foul odor of the surroundings.

In the mandala of the Red Master of Life, the firelight is dark and dim, the thick smoke overflows on all sides, and the posture of the sorcerers is like the swaying shadows of demons. Some of them blow musical instruments, some dance around, some carry black dog skins that have been cut off whole. They shake the skins and chant frightening curses. The story goes that the reason they shake the dog skins is to disturb your Dharma protectors and make them forget to guard you. If not for the protection of those spirits protecting the Dharma, many terrifying illusory perceptions would appear in your life, thereby influencing your true karmic fate. I heard Kumari say that they have cursed many people this way. Those people all had the potential capacity to be great teachers, but later they become ordinary people. They were deluded by the illusory forms of daily life and they forgot what they most had to do.

The sound from shaking the dog skins was horrifying, and as soon as I heard that sound, my mind would get flustered. The sensation was like having a bunch of maggots rolling around chaotically in my heart and blood vessels.

If you are deluded by them, then this life of mine will truly be in vain. Although what I need is a husband, nevertheless, I still hope that you will become a great teacher.

However, I have discovered that you have begun to change. This is what your silence tells me.

I thought that you would praise me for studying the Diamond Sutra and having a great awakening, and that I would not have the purity and empty illusion of my mind confused again by the likes of Kumari. But your silence tells me that maybe you are not thinking this way.

When I hear you mention beings like Sukhasiddhi, it is like a million tiny poisonous snakes drilling into my mind. But this time, I was in extreme pain, recalling the pain, suffering such pain that I did not want to live, and in that state I finally figured it out. If I cling to the private passions of a girl, if I look upon Khyungpo Ba as the lover I possess for myself, I will certainly bring myself torment that makes it better to die than to go on living. If I act like this, how can we go through our lives? I would soon get carried away, die of pain, kill myself. Therefore, I have decided to abandon myself and go along with you.

Because of this, I have understood even more the Diamond Sutra's theory of refuting forms and its concept of "emptiness."

It is because I deeply agree with the perspective of "emptiness" that I wanted to write this letter. Because then I realized that you and I still must preserve a fully sufficient, truly sincere and frank communication. If not, we will not be able to escape from the cycling in birth and death and the curses that we wrongly go through because we misunderstand these emotions — though they are as genuine and deep as can be. This is because the rivals we have in common are time and space, are differences in gender and culture, and so on. I wonder whether or not you too recognize this?

In this world it is very rare to be able to find frank and open friends who treat each other sincerely, and are completely honest with each other — how much the more so with lovers? I very much value the fact that you appeared. I have never treasured a person like this.

I still think that actions are better than promises.

I love you.

Solid and strong Sharwadi

9 The Dry and Thirsty Desert

Khyungpo Naljor's voice:

Xuemo, my son, you are looking at me so seriously.

You do not have to suffer for her. It was precisely having that longing that made Sharwadi be Sharwadi. If there were no longing, there would have been no her. All of her actions constituted her value.

Although I had again gone wrong in my causal conditions because I was unwilling to kill living beings, this time was not the same as the previous times, and I did not feel too much regret. Even in appearance, I was still not willing to kill living beings. You said you would have acted this way too. But you must know that according to the rules of the Esoteric Teaching, I should have obeyed my teacher's command. In many biographies from the Esoteric Vehicle, if your teacher demands that you kill a living being, you must kill the living being. You must realize that for accomplished adepts who have transcended dualism, in fact there is no one killing living beings, and no living beings that can be killed, and furthermore, there is no such thing as the act of killing itself.

When I left the mountains, I was suffering from a strange illness.

I was always parched and thirsty, and no matter how much water I drank, I could not relieve that burning thirst. Red flames were always appearing before my eyes, and in the flames were all kinds of strange-looking evil demons. They were gnashing their teeth and waving their claws, rolling around wildly like maggots in my brain. You must know that these were not delusions produced by my sensitivity; they had real power. In moments of extreme agitation, I would begin to think of turning back, and I would see the meaninglessness of life, and I would feel that I had already seen through the world of the senses and did not want to do anything more. One day I even thought of killing myself. When Buddha was in the world, many arhats also had this kind of feeling. Some monks went so far as to actually ask people to kill them. Later, the Buddha finally made it part of the code of monastic discipline that you could not kill yourself.

Maybe you can understand me.

The good thing was, my wisdom still could let me preserve my vigilance. So I started to make a big effort to dissolve away my karma, and after I had recited the Hundred Word Illumination mantra a hundred thousand times, I finally struggled out of these delusions. They still pursued me, and were always entangled with me, but I still continued to travel on the road of the search.

I went back via the original route, and after I had traveled for many days, I finally returned to the place where I had done the worship. I began to do worship and pray at the same time:

Niguma, my mother,

Please take heed of me.

The sacred pillar you erected stands for a thousand years,

Your light is illustrious for ten thousand generations,

Your compassion flows into eternity,

Your brilliance fills heaven and earth.

Niguma Khyenno!

When I had completed the full hundred thousand worship, I again heard the quiet sound of a woman singing:

When you know your error, change your error, Khyungpo Ba,

All karmic barriers have already been repented and cleansed.

If you want to seek Niguma,

With a clear sincere mind, go toward the north.

As soon as I heard this, I was wildly happy. I thought: "Though I did not find Niguma those previous times, I did encounter miracles manifested by the dakini, and this was who knows how many times as powerful as my previous vague seeking. This time I will be sure to be alert. I must not again mistake the causal conditions that will enable me to meet my teacher." So I arranged for some food and water, put my pack on my back, and set off toward the north.

After traveling many days, I discovered to the north it was finally a giant Gobi. Like that marshland, this Gobi looked boundless, and it was spread with a dark mass of stones. Maybe because of the blazing sunlight, these stones appeared black and shiny. Before, I had never seen the black Gobi, and as I first entered into it, I unexpectedly felt a bit happy. I looked east and looked west, and it was like falling into a dream. But as the sun climbed into the sky, it became as hard to take as entering into an oven. At this point, I finally discovered that I had made a mistake: I had brought too little water. Because on the last two journeys there had always been people on the road, and it was not difficult to find water, I had not thought that this time, after all, it would be the Gobi. There was no one around anywhere, and the hot sun was beating down, and traveling on the road was like being a frog on a hot stove. That little bit of water I had brought along was half gone after I had drunk from it a few times. I no longer dared to drink water as I pleased.

I continued on for several days, and I discovered that gradually there were more plants in the Gobi, and even though they were desert needle grasses hardly worth noticing, I was still very happy. When I stopped to rest, I used the grass to weave together a sun shade, and even though it did not block very much sunlight, psychologically it made me feel a bit more comfortable. I thought: "This place is not good. Suddenly there is this terrain, then suddenly there is that terrain. Suddenly it is cold, and suddenly it is hot. It is like a world of demonic illusions." The feeling of dreamlike illusion in my mind got thicker, and overall I felt that I was traveling in a dream.

Originally I had thought that when I saw plants like the needle grasses, I would be able to see some signs of human habitation. If I saw some people's dwellings, then I could ask about Niguma. I did not think, as I kept going forward, that the Gobi would turn into a desert, with wave after wave of sand twisting and turning off into the unknown. I thought: "Look at this landscape. I don't know how much farther I can go. If I keep going into the desert, this little bit of water will definitely not be able to sustain my life." I thought: "It's strange alright. I never heard that this region has a desert, and in the books it was never mentioned that there was a desert here. But I have finally really encountered a desert. Can it be that what I have entered into is really a dream landscape?" I pinched myself, but I felt the pain.

I shook my water bag, and discovered that there was not much water left, so I thought: "I cannot go into the desert. With this little water, it would be easy on the way in, but difficult on the way out. If I cannot replenish this water, I will die of thirst on the road. But if I do not go into the desert, I might miss the causal connection with Niguma. I have already gone east, gone south, and gone west. After this trip north, will my teacher give me another chance?"

Suddenly I thought: "Maybe this desert is an apparition that my teacher or the dakinis made appear, to test my faith again." At this thought, I laughed. This was definitely possible. Though I had never heard of there being a desert here, the dakinis could make rivers and mountains appear, so certainly they could make a desert appear. So I strengthened my spirit, and thought: "No matter what happens, I am still going to go forward."

How could I have known? I went on for half a day, but I saw that the desert was more and more real, not a bit like an illusory apparition. The burning sun was beating down on my head, and the ground was pulsing with waves of heat. My mouth was burning and my tongue was dry, my body was weak and my legs were sore. Though I had brought food, because I did not dare use much water, there was no way to swallow the food, and I might as well not eat. But by not eating I became faint with hunger. There was no alternative, and as my head was spinning and I was about to collapse, I chewed a bit of a bun and drank half a mouthful of water. I thought: "If this desert is not an apparition conjured up by the dakinis, this will be deadly for me. Even if I do not go on, and just go back, it is possible that I will die of thirst on the journey."

After walking for two days, I still could not see the end of the desert. I felt discouraged, because I had at most two or three mouthfuls of water left, and with this sun shining down, a person could soon turn into a dry corpse. I thought: "Many times it is easy to make a vow, but hard to put it into practice. To say, theoretically, 'I will not turn back even from death' is easy, but once you are truly faced with death, no one can guarantee that they won't start to think of retreating."

Just at this moment, I saw in a depression in the sand that unexpectedly there was something wriggling.

10 Encountering the Woman With Leprosy

It seemed to be a woman. I say seemed to be, because she barely looked like a woman. On her body she carried many things that seemed like bunches of cloth. Previously, in Tibet. I was always meeting this kind of woman vagabond. They carried their homes on their backs, and wandered all around. I thought: "Presumably this woman is the manifestation of a dakini."

But after assessing her more carefully, I had my doubts, because she was really too far from the dakinis in my imagination. I suspected she had contracted the dragon sickness. The dragon sickness also has another name: "leprosy." In Tibet there are many people who suffer from leprosy. Because they fear contagion, people make the people afflicted with leprosy live in the wilderness, and let them live and die on their own. Of course, among the people afflicted with leprosy, some recovered. The story goes that the most effective means of curing leprosy is to cultivate religious practice, because leprosy is the dragon sickness, and the natural enemy of dragons is the giant golden-winged garuda. According to the story, when the golden-winged garuda eats a dragon, it only has to flap its wings once and it can part the oceans, and reveal the ocean bed. The damnable dragon, then has no way to hide, and the golden-winged garuda takes the dragon in its mouth, then raises its neck, and swallows the dragon. According to the story, the golden-winged garuda would eat tens of thousands of dragons every year. Afterwards, the dragons went to seek the Buddha. So the Buddha took the golden-winged garuda in to be a protector of the Dharma. The golden-winged garuda said: "By nature I eat dragons. If I do not eat dragons, I will starve to death." The Buddha agreed and said: "I will tell my disciples to offer you a meal every day." So among those to whom offerings were made, there were many golden-winged garudas. The ritual formula said: "Great golden-winged garuda, in the wilderness the demons and spirits are legion. Mother of the raksha demons, the sweet dew fills everything." They then recite a mantra seven times: Om Mani Svaha.

Because the great golden-winged garuda is the natural enemy of dragons, to treat leprosy, the dragon disease, the most effective practice is the method of the golden-winged garuda. Milarepa's disciple Rechungpa suffered from leprosy. Later, when he went to India, he found the method of the golden-winged garuda, and only then was his leprosy cured. Besides this, there is said to be another method, which is to use the urine of a great virtuous one who is an accomplished adept to wash the afflicted places on the body of the person afflicted with leprosy, and this too can cure leprosy.

When I got closer to the woman and looked her over, I discovered that it was in fact leprosy that she was suffering from. Because her nose had totally deteriorated, all that was left on her face was a big hole. Apart from this, there were many other sores, and they were oozing pus.

Although I felt nauseated, I suppressed the feeling and asked her: "Why did you come to this place?"

The woman said: "Don't you see how I look? If I wanted to live where there are many people, would the people let me live there?" Because her nose had deteriorated, her voice was very difficult to listen to. She also said: "I do not want to live in a place where there are no people, but the other people insisted I be brought here."

"How do you live?"

"Every two weeks, people come with some food and water. But this time, I don't know why, they are three days late, and I have no more water. Do you have any water or not?"

I thought: "I just have a little bit of water left." But even though I was unbearably thirsty, I reached out with my water bag and put its opening in the iron bowl in front of that woman.

The woman said: "Don't pour it, lest you spill some. I will drink out of the water bag."

I felt nauseated, but because I had had the previous few experiences, I thought: "Probably this again is a dakini testing me." So I took the water bag and gave it to her. The woman took the water bag, and drank up all the water with a few gulps. I saw that her pus had run down onto the opening of the water bag, and I felt disgusted.

The woman said: "Don't worry about this water. I figure that today or tomorrow they will surely come to give me some food, and when they arrive, I will pay you back with interest, and give you back a bag full of water."

I said: "It's not important. Go ahead and drink, drink."

The woman gave the water bag back to me and said: "You gave me water, so you are my benefactor. Shall I invite you into my home to sit a while?"

The woman put something that looked like a bundle of trash on her back and tottered off, heading north. I followed the woman, and after we had walked a couple of kilometers, I saw that there was a mound in a depression in the sand, and in the mound there was a cave. The woman said: "Well, this is my home."

I went into the cave, and discovered that the interior was unexpectedly very large, but it was full of what looked like piles of trash, something like pieces of cloth. The woman said: "Look at my possessions — quite a lot, aren't there? ... Don't look down on them. The world only has useless people — there are no useless things. Don't look down on these pieces of cloth. When winter comes, they can be used to keep warm, they can be burned for warmth, and they have many other uses. I can also use them for a mat for my little dog. Ah, where is my little dog then?" She called out several times, and from far away a small dog came running. I saw that this little dog also turned out to be mangy and covered with sores, as if the dog too was suffering from leprosy. I thought: "No wonder. Living with a person sick with leprosy, it would more likely than not get sick too." I had heard if a person touched this pus, he could also get leprosy.

When the little dog saw me, he rubbed up against me very affectionately, and I was afraid I would touch the pus from his body, so I tried to dodge him. But the little dog paid no attention to this and kept rubbing against me. All I could do was gently push him away with my foot.

The woman was not happy with this. She said: "There are a good many false people in the world. With their lips they say sentient beings are their fathers and mothers, but they do not have the least bit of compassion, and they always treat sentient beings with a disdainful attitude. Though people like this might cultivate practice for thousands of eons, what can their cultivation achieve?"

My face got red. I thought: "Listen to her tone of voice — it seems she has her reasons for saying this."

The woman said: "But I am not talking about you. I am talking about my former kinfolk. Don't look at me as I am now, so ugly. Before, I was very pretty and charming. I am not that old, only twenty-three. Five years ago, because my father is a wealthy merchant and I had grown up to be pretty, I was the bright pearl in my father's hand, and men seeking to marry me were lined up at the door. But we did not anticipate that I would end up getting this disease. Toward this disease, the world shows its true face. Not only did all those suitors disappear, even my own father began to avoid me, fearing that I would pass the disease on to him. Later on, they finally sent me here, intending that I should live and die by myself. Fortunately, my mother could not bear to have me starve to death, so twice a month she sends someone to bring me food and water, and thus I have survived until now."

She held the dog in her arms. The woman and the dog held each other, stuck out their tongues and licked each other. The woman said: "Do not underestimate this dog. He was good to me before, when I was not sick. After I got sick, other people all treated me badly, but this little dog was still good to me. He is much better than people are. I discovered that the best animal in the world is the dog. No matter if you are poor or rich, no matter if you are healthy or sick, as long as you treat a dog well, the dog will treat you well. If you gave him a bone ten years ago, ten years later he will still remember. But those people who received favors from me — today I don't see a trace of them."

As I listened, I felt choked up and I was about to cry. I thought: "What this woman has experienced is truly tragic." I regretted that feeling of nausea I had gotten as soon as I saw her. But there was nothing to say. No matter what advice I offered, it wouldn't seem right. So I just listened earnestly.

The woman said: "Now, despite it all, I am grateful to this disease. If it weren't for this disease, I would not be cultivating practice. It was just this disease that made me see the impermanence of the world, and only then did I begin to read Buddhist books ... Well these are the ones, look." She took out several books from under the pillow and passed them to me. I looked them over. Actually, they were some books of very commonplace popular literature. So I said: "These are only intellectual knowledge. If you want to genuinely cultivate practice, go find a teacher, seek the Esoteric Teaching, and cultivate it well. Even though this place of yours is a bit remote, it is a good place for cultivating practice."

The woman said: "How would I have the good fortune to go visit a teacher? See how I look—people take one look at me then flee far away."

I said: "If you truly want to cultivate practice, I could teach you."

When the woman heard this, she smiled happily. Because her nose had deteriorated, the smiling face, which originally must have been pretty, appeared very scary. I felt a great sense of compassion, and then I explained to the woman the mind of detachment and the mind of compassion. I set forth some basic common knowledge about cultivating practice, and I also gave her the empowerment of Green Tara. Because I did not have a picture of Green Tara at hand, I gave her a detailed description of Green Tara's image. Although the woman was ugly, her mind had not been dulled by the leprosy, and in less than half a day, she had learned how to recite the mantra of Green Tara and cultivate the visualization.

To express her thanks for my kindness in instructing her, the woman took a pot filled with food and offered me food she was reluctant to eat. I took a look and saw something strange that looked like a New Year's cake, but because the weather was hot, the top of it was covered by a green layer of mold. I knew that this thing had already become inedible, but I saw the sincerity on that woman's face, and I accepted it. The woman was looking up at me, and that hideous face was filled with expectation, hoping that the teacher could accept her offering and would eat this beautiful food. Thought I was very moved by her sincerity, there was no way I would put that poisonous stuff in my mouth. I thought: "Even without mentioning this green mold, who knows how much of her saliva had soaked into it. If I eat it, I think I will get leprosy."

The woman waited for quite a while, but in the end lost hope. She took that piece of New Year's cake from my hand, and tossed it to the little dog. The dog gladly ate it, and sounded happy.

"I won't trouble you," the woman said. "I know that some people will not dare to touch anything I have been eating, but I don't understand—weren't you just talking about eliminating the discriminating mind? I don't know—don't you consider this the discriminating mind?"

My face flushed. Hadn't I just been telling her about many of the secrets for how to eliminate the discriminating mind? But why then, as soon as I encountered something, was I still unable to control my mind and spirit? But I thought: "Even those great virtuous adepts of true achievement probably would not eat food soaked in the saliva of a person with leprosy, right?"

The woman said: "The proverb says 'A lord does not stand under a dangerous wall.' I certainly cannot blame you. It's okay. Ultimately I have this disease, and it's okay for you to be careful."

11 The Absurd Request of the Woman Afflicted with Leprosy

That afternoon, the woman's mother sent someone to deliver the food and water. There was a lot of food, but because the weather was hot, I thought it could not be kept for several days or it would get moldy. The water could be stored for longer. The woman told the man who had come that he should wash out the opening of my water bag carefully, and fill it for me.

After the man who had come left, the woman invited me to eat my fill. Because it was food that had just been brought to us, I did not refuse. After we had eaten, the woman again asked me to explain some things about cultivating practice. So I seriously explained many secrets of cultivating practice, and I said that if she cultivated practice according to the methods I had taught her, liberation would be as easy as taking something out of a bag.

At night, the woman knew I might feel an aversion to the things she had used, so she did not spread out any bedding for me. I went along like a donkey going downhill and found a convenient place and lay down. Because it had been a long hard journey, I quickly fell asleep.

In a dream I saw Sharwadi, and she said she was a manifestation of Sukhasiddhi. She looked right at me and smiled. Suddenly I became aware of someone pushing me, and I immediately woke up. I heard the sound of coarse panting, and when I realized where my body was, I got a shock. Good heavens! It was that woman with leprosy. I felt a hand groping my body. I remembered I had seen her hand that day, and the back of that hand was disfigured by leprosy. I was alarmed and sat up. Fearing that I might touch one of the sores and get wet with the pus, I backed away.

"What are you doing?" I cried out.

The moonlight was coming in from outside the cave, shining on the frightening face of the woman afflicted with leprosy, and her deteriorated nose seemed even bigger than it did in the daylight, and her whole face had become a skull. An odor like a rotting corpse assailed me, and I did not know if the odor came from those suppurating sores or from inside the woman's mouth.

She was panting heavily as she said: "Teacher, save me. I do not seek anything else, I just ask you to give me a baby. I am too lonely staying here all by myself. I want a baby."

When I heard this, I almost vomited, but I held back the nausea and said: "Do not come any closer! Do not come any closer!"

Her voice again burst forth with that rotten corpse stench: "Really, I do not seek anything else, I just want to have a baby. Look at me here on my own. The whole world has abandoned me, including my father and mother. I do not have anyone close to me. I just want a son. I think that if I bring up a son, he will not shun his mother for being ugly, and I will then have someone close to me. And when I get old, I will also have someone to depend on. Think about it. Here I am, one woman, waiting in this wilderness. If I do not have a son, how can I live through those long years of old age? I'm begging you, show some compassion."

I was so tense I could not breath. I quickly said: "This won't do, this is impossible. I am a monk, and I have accepted the code of monastic discipline."

The woman said: "Although you have accepted the code of monastic discipline, you have also vowed to travel the bodhisattva Path. Bodhisattvas go along with sentient beings. I have not heard of any bodhisattva who would not fulfill the wishes of sentient beings. Help me with this one thing." As she was talking, the woman burrowed into my chest, and ran her hands freely over my body. I could not see if there were suppurating sores on the woman's body, so I pushed her away a few times.

The woman started to cry. As she was crying she said: "O bodhisattva, I'm begging you. Don't I just want a son? I am not asking for your life. When someone asked that bodhisattva Nagarjuna for his life, didn't he give it as he was asked to? When someone asked that bodhisattva Shantideva for his eyes, didn't he give them as he was asked to? What about you? Didn't I ask you to make me pregnant with a child? What are you afraid of? You are not lacking anything." As she spoke, her hand started touching me again.

I was so tense my whole body was covered with sweat. As I pushed her hand away I kept telling her it would not happen.

She also said: "Teacher, my bodhisattva, two hours ago you were teaching me about generating the mind of enlightenment. Now I am looking at you to see whether or not you have the mind of enlightenment. For you, what I ask for is not too much, just a moment's work. If we succeed, then you will go back a bit sooner. If we do not succeed this time, you will stay a few months more, until you have made me pregnant. Then you will leave here again."

My head was covered with sweat, and I could neither cry nor laugh. I noticed that rotten corpse smell getting thicker and thicker, and an unbearable nausea was rising in my gorge. I said: "Do not try to force me. If you try to force me again, I might get angry."

The sound of the woman's crying stopped, and she began again to beseech me in a gentle way: "O bodhisattva, my bodhisattva, you must know that as a woman suffering from leprosy, perhaps my request is a bit too much, but you are not like other people. My father and mother are ordinary people—they have not generated the mind of enlightenment. When they abandoned me that way, though it was hard for me to bear, I could still understand—in the end, they were afraid of my sickness. If I were not sick, they would still love me. But you are a great bodhisattva, and a great bodhisattva does not have the discriminating mind. Compared to those bodhisattvas who gave their lives or their eyes, what I am asking for really does not amount to much. So why can't satisfy me on this little point?"

I said: "Although I have generated the mind of enlightenment, I also accepted the monastic precepts of discipline. I love preserving the precepts as I love my eyes."

The woman said: "If you agree to do what I ask, you will realize the rainbow body. Do you agree or not?"

I said: "No!"

The woman spoke again: "If you promise to do what I ask, you will immediately see the teacher you are seeking. Do you promise or not?"

I thought: "If I get leprosy, even if I truly attained the supreme teaching, it still would be very difficult to benefit sentient beings." So I said: "No!"

The woman said: "If you promise me, in the future you will fly to the Pure Land with your physical body. Do you promise or not?"

I felt the stinking vapor from the woman's mouth getting thicker and thicker, and I was afraid I would not be able to endure the nausea, so I said: "No!"

The woman did not ask again. She was quiet for a time, and in the end gave a cold laugh. She said: "Let me ask you this. If I were not suffering from leprosy, if I were as beautiful as a heavenly goddess, if I had a face that could overthrow countries and cities, if I used the form of a beautiful woman to cultivate the coupled practice with you, would you still be this adamant?"

I stared, dumbstruck, and did not know how to reply.

That woman lit a pine branch, and called her little dog to come. She held the little dog affectionately in her arms, and coldly said: "Little dog, this man despises me as this woman with leprosy. What a fine bodhisattva, without the discriminating mind! Instead this little dog gets all the benefits. Can it be that you did not know that that moldy New Year's cake in fact came from the sweet dew of the Buddha Land? If you had eaten it, at the very least you would have achieved the great transfer body and achieved deathlessness. Look, at this little dog's appearance."

I was astonished to discover that the little dog's body had turned into the form of a rainbow, visible but intangible. Though I felt regret, I was not too regretful, because I had truly seen the insignificance of birth and death.

That woman rubbed her hand over her face, finally rubbed off her mask, and revealed an extremely beautiful face. She shed the rags she was wearing, and covering her body was a dress like fine muslin. In the twinkling of an eye, that hideous woman afflicted with leprosy had changed into an matchless beauty.

She looked at me there, staring dumbfounded, and walked away, merging into the moonlight.

12 The Sound of the Dakini's Song

Under the moonlight there came the pure clear sound of a song.

No one knows, that song is the song of the dakini, or it also comes from Xuemo's inherent nature a thousand years later:

Khyungpo Ba, you who come from the land of Tibet,

Though you have a mind of faith that goes beyond most people,

Still, in your dualistic mind, the mind of faith will forever only be an aspiration.

You must know, Khyungpo Ba, in the ultimate truth,

There is no duality and no difference between the leper and the rainbow body,

The myriad things in the world are fused in one flavor, without distinction.

Because the power of your past habits limits your thinking, your mind is imprisoned in the shackles of discriminating thought,

All afflictions are born from this, and they go on blocking the possibility of liberation.

Although great compassion is not lacking in your mind, it is shut up in the bottle of selfish clinging.

Only if you use the hammer of the empty inherent nature will you be able to smash the skull of selfish clinging.

Although, in theory, you have understood the inherent nature of mind,
that is a case of it being hard to satisfy hunger with a picture of a cake.

Only when you realize the ultimate unborn inherent nature will you be
able to break the bonds of revolving in birth and death.

Though you have sought and found many wondrous teachings, other
people's money will not make you rich.

Only if you always use the pure water of those wondrous teachings will
you be able to wash away the dust of ongoing habits.

You keep on encountering the deceptions of illusory forms,

Because of dualism, it is hard to be liberated from them.

You do not counteract the habit-energy of clinging and attachment in
your mind,

But instead, in a fragmented way, pursue the joys of selfish clinging
perceptions.

Dualistic discrimination nourishes greed and anger and ignorance,

The habit-energy of the three poisons is deep-rooted and hard to
eliminate.

If you seek to merge with the ultimate inherent nature of all sentient beings,

You must constantly counteract your karmic habits.

Though you do not surrender to the delusive demon of laziness,

You keep on energetically seeking the Teacher.

Your mind of faith is sufficient and your sincerity is genuine and solid,

So you are sure to become a valuable vessel of the Dharma.

It's just that your eyes are too sharp, you can always understand the small subtle ties and comprehend the fine points.

You must develop the ability to look without seeing.

Only then will you be able not to be deceived by false images and not to mistake the false for the real.

Your ears are even more incomparably intelligent, and all sounds provoke ripples in your mind.

When will you finally be able to hear without hearing, and stop all the sounds from opening the door to your mind's inherent nature?

Your mouth is more able to relate good arguments, and in your way of explaining the sutras your mouth is like a whirlwind.

When will you finally be able to speak without speaking: in fact, it is only that great silence that is the great voice.

Your seeking a hundred teachings is certainly an occasion for joy, but when will it not be a type of clinging and attachment for you?

Because your discriminating mind haunts you all along, you do not realize that one equals a hundred, and a hundred equal one.

Do not forget that one teaching is equipped with the wondrous virtues of a hundred teachings,

Do not forget that one eye has the wondrous abilities of a hundred eyes,

Do not forget that one ear has the effectiveness of a hundred ears,

Do not forget that one teacher is the transformation body of ten thousand Buddhas.

Because your causal connection lies in much learning, all the dakinis rejoice in your good actions.

But if being very learned does not counteract your habit-energy, you will become another name for a shelf of scriptures.

Although you seek the Dharma again and again a hundred times, you must awaken to the empty inherent nature by entering deeply through a single gate.

A hundred teachers and a thousand teachings have a single purpose: you must find that ultimate basic essence.

That ultimate basic essence is also called the empty inherent nature, the basic emptiness behind all the colored clouds and illusory transformations.

If you are busy seeking the illusory characteristics of the colored clouds, you will be reversing the root and the branch and wasting your life.

You are returning to the starting point of your search: do not rush around in all directions like a kite without a string.

In reality Niguma has never left you: why do you have to seek Buddha outside mind and be in a constant state of anxiety?

Though in name and form Soshaling is in India, though in name and form Niguma is in the cemetery forest there,

Though in name and form there also is a Buddha Land there, nevertheless at the same time they are complete in the inherent nature of your mind.

When you have cleaned away afflictions and dissolved away habit energies, the Soshaling Pure Land will put forth its light,

In this light there will be the Niguma of light, and Niguma will smile and look upon you with favor.

If you rush around in all directions and the inherent nature of your mind is not stabilized, you will go on as usual clinging to the illusory as real and recognizing the false as true.

Although you knew that the leper woman could be a dakini, your habit-energy was still the habit-energy that controls you.

When the mind is pure, the Buddha Land is also pure: that Pure Land originates from your pure clear mind.

If you donot understand this truth, you are no different from those fools.

The great Niguma is even more yourself: all theBuddhas have their origin in your inherent mind.

Those who seek the Dharma outside of mind are surely fools, and those who seek a teacher outside of mind are even more stupid.

Though in terms of external forms there is the teacher and there is you, when we look at it from the ultimate viewpoint, in fact there is one essence.

Though in terms of external forms there is India and there is Tibet, when we look at it from the ultimate viewpoint, in fact there is no difference.

This is because all those forms return to the empty inherent nature; this is because that clear emptiness is all a single essence.

What need is there for you to discriminate among the various forms of the one essence? If there is discrimination, then there will be revolving in birth and death and the six planes of existence.

When the illusory forms of the six planes of existence take hold of you, you cannot help being born and dying over and over again.

When you understand that this is all a play, then liberation is simultaneous with your understanding.

It is not the case that outside understanding there is something else, liberation; it is not the case that outside the inherent nature of mind there is something else, the basic essence.

When you comprehend that basic substance of the myriad phenomena and the myriad forms, this fact can liberate yourself.

But because of the habit-energy formed by your continuous habits, you always make those straw ropes into poisonous snakes.

You cry out in confusion, but in fact what is scaring you is yourself.

When you understand that this poisonous snake is in fact a straw rope, you get to the point where there is no need to cultivate practice, and you will not be frightened anymore.

When you understand that revolving in birth and death is like a dream, in the same way there is no need to cultivate practice, and then you can be liberated.

The problem is that the mind does not necessarily hear what is said, and theoretical understanding still needs to be brought to bear to deal with practical affairs.

Only when you achieve the state of spontaneously being thus in practical affairs and in theoretical truth, can you be counted as having independent mind energy.

Those whose mind energy is independent are teachers, and at the same time they are Buddhas.

They comprehend that the myriad things are thusness as it is, unmoving, like a mirror bright with light.

Though that mind mirror can reflect the myriad things, the essence of the mirror cannot be disturbed, no matter what happens.

It will not see beautiful forms and be happy, or encounter evil scenes and be afraid.

That shining bright mirror is the essence of your mind — though all forms are there, it is crystal clear, empty, and still.

All those forms are reflections of the essence of your mind, and even though all kinds of things appear, they are all empty and illusory and without reality.

Even if you are a person without knowledge, you still will not be able tocling to the reflections in the mirror.

When you understand this truth, at the same time you understand, you will be able to have no clingings.

Ah, Khyungpo Ba, disciple of my heart, though you have studied with so many teachers,

The ultimate real substance of all that activity is still to get to the essence of your own mind.

This is because other people's greatness cannot make you great, this is because other people's understanding cannot save your from your own ignorance,

This is because other people's legs cannot walk your journey, this is because other people's throats cannot take in food to fill your belly.

All your teachers have only pointed out the road for you,

There is only one ultimate aim, and no matter how many people you ask, they cannot change the basic substance of the aim.

So I urge you not to go rushing around anymore. All you have to do is wait for the bright countenance of Niguma.

I say "wait for," I don't say "search for," because the genuine teacher cannot be found by searching.

When you truly are equipped with the mind of faith, when you truly have compassion,

When you truly end affliction, when you truly clear away habit-energy,

Your teacher will come looking for you.

It does not matter whether or not you come to India, it does not matter whether or not you are still in Tibet,

It does not matter whether or not you rush off on long journeys, it does not matter whether or not you bring enough gold.

That teacher comes from your own pure mind, that teacher in the same way is a manifestation of the inherent nature of your mind.

Though our forms are all different and our natures are not the same, our real substance still comes from one and the same basic essence.

That ultimate truth is forever the ultimate: the empty inherent nature, the enlightened inherent nature, and the true thusness of the enlightened essence —

Though names and forms differ, the basic substance is still only one, and teachers and religious lineages are just different manifestations.

Thus you know all the winding roads: they are the daughters of the discriminating mind.

Because they abandon the basic substance and go off pursuing the branches, it is hard for the deluded ones to escape the bondage of revolving in birth and death.

No matter whether they recite mantras a hundred million times, no matter whether they give mountains of offerings,

If they do not understand the basic essence they are cultivating, success will forever be far off in the future.

I often see those foolish practitioners, their faces flushed with sincerity,

Or their whole bodies covered with the dust of ascetic practices,

But since they have always abandoned the root to pursue the branches,

*Even on the brink of death, they still have not understood the
fundamental essence.*

*Even if they really go to the Western Paradise to be reborn, even if they
really go to the Buddha's Pure Land,*

*Even if they pile up merit to the sky, for liberation they still must truly
rely on cultivating that fundamental essence.*

*The cultivation of the fundamental essence is removing clingings and
attachments, and these clingings and attachments include those to
liberation itself.*

*Genuine liberation has no going to be reborn in the Pure Land: if there
is going to be reborn in the Pure Land, there will be the final clinging
and attachment.*

*Clinging and attachment to liberation is still clinging and attachment;
clinging and attachment is the big enemy of cultivating practice;*

*Though all the bits of gold glitter, if they get into our eyes they will
pierce our eyeballs.*

*The secret of cultivation lies in abandoning: abandoning clingings and
attachments, abandoning hopes and expectations,*

*Abandoning afflictions and abandoning liberation: genuine
abandoning is liberation.*

Go then, Khyungpo Ba. Though you rejected the leper woman's final plea,

Still, because you still had compassion for her, I could say to you what I have just said,

Confident that it will mature your mind's nature.

Return again to the starting point of that search, and use the wondrous teachings to cleanse away the barriers of your karmic energy.

When you have truly purified your mind, then you will be able to see the true teacher ...

As I heard the sound of this song, I felt as if I had been initiated, I felt incomparably refreshed. The tears covered my face, and I lay flat on the ground performing the great prostration until the sky brightened.

Xuemo, my son, in that bright clear light which you have experienced, you too heard the sound of this song. The Vajravarahi used her angelic voice to sing this song for you. Your face was covered with tears and you couldn't stop trembling. You must know that she too is Niguma. The essential nature of Niguma is the Vajravarahi, and the essential nature of the Vajravarahi is the Great Mudra of Light. In the sound of the song, you were filled with great bliss, empty stillness beyond compare, clear bright light, unmoving thusness. That's right, that is the Great Mudra of Light.

Only later did I understand that the woman with leprosy was a manifestation of the Vajravarahi. She is the chief Buddha of the billions of dakinis.

I repented for many days, but I did not hear that song again directing me to search. All I could do was leave the land where I was searching and go look for Sukhasiddhi. When she saw me, she still had that expression on her face, like smiling but not smiling, aloof, as if there and not there.

She asked: "You went riding a camel to go search for a camel — how did you do, did you gain anything?"

I related many of the wondrous events I had encountered on the journey. She listened, and just kept giving a cold smile.

Chapter 20

The Bloody Light of Kapilavastu

The Secret History of Khyungpo says: Another power of the barrel of demons spell was to make the itinerant monk think of skrinking back. Countless evil demons sent out a huge thought wave calling on Khyungpo Naljor to abandon his search. Once he abandoned the search, it would be like shutting the door on his intention to go toward the light. Once the light was gone, the darkness would come. Then, Khyungpo Naljor would not yet know it, but in this world there would really be a barrel of demons. He did not think anymore that in the end he would really be trapped in that barrel of demons.

1 Black Dog's Blood Splashed in the Mandala

Sharwadi again went with Kumari secretly to look at that death-dealing mandala. Those sorcerers had already completed the "preliminary practices" and had prepared the ritual objects. After the "preliminary practices," the "true practices" began.

The sorcerers took the blood of a black dog and splashed it into the mandala. There was a patch of red on the ground, and outside of this they also spread a red powder and drew a strange-looking mandala. The sorcerers took their own tutelary deities' picture and a thangka of the Red Master of Life and hung them in the mandala. They made many rich offerings, and most of the things offered up were red in color: a red sheep, a red horse, a red dog, a red yak, and so on. If the thing was not naturally red, they colored it. Actually these things could be made of flour, but to express their sincere veneration, they were using the actual animals.

The sorcerers used gold powder to write the Red Master of Life's curse on a piece of paper. Around the curse, they also wrote what they were praying for, and they wrote many wishes which they hoped to achieve.

A sorcerer with wild unkempt hair was chanting in a mystifying way:

"O Incomparably Great Red Master of Life, we ask you to apply your supreme magical power, and punish that barbarian Khyungpo Ba, who has treated the female spirit with contempt. Use your soul-catching hooks to hook his soul, use your diamond knife to cut his lifeline. Suck out his five great essences, and bleed out his wisdom and enlightenment. Let his physical body scatter like flour in the wind. Let his spiritual knowledge be dirtied like the dust of the earth. Let him fall into greed and anger and ignorance so he cannot pull himself out ..."

Sharwadi was very frightened. She saw that in the atmosphere that reeked of blood, there really were many red-colored demons. They were showing their fangs and claws and spewing out a red-colored poisonous vapor at Khyungpo Naljor's life-stone. That life-stone was trembling and shaking in the poisonous red vapor.

A strange heaviness and melancholy enveloped her.

After she returned home, Sharwadi used a technique she had learned before, when she was serving as a female spirit, and she performed a ritual for Khyungpo Naljor to stop any misfortune. At the same time, as she had done all along, she continued to take on the power of those curses. She discovered that the power of those curses was truly a kind of dark force. Every time she took it on, it would lead to a serious illness.

Nevertheless, even when she was sick, she still felt fortunate. She thought: "In this world, is there anything more fortunate than to get sick for the sake of the one I love?" The longing and the pain were able to open up her hard outer shell layer by layer, until her most tender inner heart was exposed.

For many years in the past, in order to adapt to the present reality, Sharwadi had made herself into an iconic female spirit, and whether consciously or not, she had abandoned many things of her human nature. Only when she met Khyungpo Naljor did she understand that those things which she had discarded or all but discarded were in fact very precious. She wanted to pick this up again, but maybe it was trash. She discovered that many points of view in this world are in fact upside down and erroneous. The good thing was that she ended up having the good fortune to hear Khyungpo Naljor's voice, and she recognized that he was right.

In fact, sometimes this longing she felt for him was too intense. It would make her unable to control herself, and make it hard for her to resist its demonic power. To eliminate this longing, Sharwadi would take her father's place and lecture on the scriptures. Their message of liberation and her feelings of love became intertwined and were often in contradiction to each other, often entangled with each other like flesh and blood, and inseparable from each other. She needed to proceed to dissect them and split them apart, but the world-transcending and the worldly often flavored each other, and she could not distinguish them clearly. Sometimes she thought of going far away from her present life situation, leaving it behind to devote herself to pure cultivation, but what her father needed was the worldly conventional Sharwadi. There was nothing she could do about it—all she could do was accept it and wait for Khyungpo Naljor to return. But the problem was, she did not know when he would return. Even more frightening, she suddenly noticed that she was getting much older. She knew that while someone is focused on the search, it is as if there is no such thing as time, whereas for the person waiting, that time spent waiting gets endlessly longer.

All she could do was to keep on writing letters. This was the only way for her to try to save herself. In her eyes, nothing was more important or more worth doing than writing these letters.

So in this way, she was writing letters that were like prayers, and going on as before, waiting for Khyungpo Naljor.

2 Khyungpo Naljor Says

Child, in those days I was always getting sick, always producing illusory perceptions, always tiredout, as if drained of energy.

I felt I was really going to die.

From time to time I sank into a huge red cloud, and I was always dizzy and confused. These symptoms were already there before Sharwadi told me about the death-dealing mandala of the Red Master of Life. I believe that this was truly a kind of evil negative force. When there are people who can carry out certain kinds of rituals, the evil will obey their command.

When that red cloud flooded in, it was more like a nightmare that often left me dazed, and I lost my clarity. It went so far that I was always thinking of turn back—how frightening!

When I fell into that red cloud, some thoughts would often pop up … I would think: "That's it, that's enough. A person is a thing that does not last more than a few decades—why should I work so hard?" Sometimes I would also think: "I' ll go back and marry her, that's it … See, this is how it will be." When these thoughts arose, I was too exhausted to move any more, and all I could do was stay inside for a few days and concentrate on praying to Niguma.

If it had not been for Niguma calling to me and supporting me, I might have really abandoned the search.

It was truly difficult.

Obviously, a person's success is not an easy thing.

When, unexpectedly, my mind was calm, I would also think of her, but these occasional thoughts were as faint as if they were a world away.

Human life is truly like a dream.

Every night when it was quiet, I would think of Sharwadi, and there was always a warm feeling in my mind. I thought how there was still someone in the world waiting for me that way, and I felt speechless. The mental isolation would then truly melt away. Finally, there would be an image in my mind, a beautiful image. Knowing her was really a great gain in my life.

Child, on that monotonous lonely journey, if there had not been that pair of eyes looking at my back, how dull it would have been!

In the same way, if in the book of yours there were no Sharwadi, it too would have been so colorless!

3 A Great Demon Who Swallows the Sky

Though he was always getting sick, Khyungpo Naljor was still searching for Niguma.

He had already visited many holy places, but he had not had any more fortuitous encounters like the one in the desert. His journeys in India seeking the Dharma gradually became plain and ordinary.

In his mind, it was as if Niguma had really become a legend.

At this juncture, Sukhasiddhi passed on to him six techniques for accomplishing enlightenment—these are called "Sukhasiddhi's Six Teachings." But what Khyungpo Naljor recited constantly was still "Niguma Khyenno." There was nothing to do about it; the great karmic force from previous lifetimes left him unable to forget that prediction of enlightenment in his own life. His search for Niguma had become his reason for living.

Khyungpo Naljor said that although those evil spirits created many adverse causal conditions, at the same time, they were even more a helpful causal condition. It was precisely because he was hardened by those adverse causal conditions that, day by day, he shrank from trivial concerns.

During that period, from time to time, he would discover in the sky inverted images of evil spirits twisting and turning. They were holding up all kinds of weapons, like diamond scimitars, tridents, lassos, soul hooks, and so on, waiting for the opportunity to set about taking his life. This was the period when Khyungpo Naljor was starting to think of shrinking back.

Khyungpo Naljor told me, if only he had not been thinking of shrinking back, then he would have been communicating with the Path of light in the great existence, and then he would have received a great supporting power. Then the plot of those evil demons would not have been able to succeed.

I asked: "What plot?"

He said: "The plot of those evil demons in fact can be summed up in the words 'thoughts of shrinking back' ."

They were waiting for him to abandon his search. Once Khyungpo Naljor abandoned his search, he could become part of the demons' family. The downfall of many people has begun when they gave up their search.

This giving up amounts to shutting the door on the mind that goes toward the light. Once the light is gone, the darkness arises.

At the same time, the evil spirits were still creating a lot of sinister danger. They wanted to use adverse causal conditions to wear down Khyungpo Naljor's sharp, seeking mind.

On this particular day, Khyungpo Naljor had a very sinister, dangerous dream. In the dream, muddy slime was seething and turbid waves were draining, and from the mud a giant crocodile rose up and bit off half his body. When he woke up, he discovered that the lower half of his body actually showed signs of numbness.

For a long time after this, he seemed to be in a trance, and there was no strength in his body. From time to time he saw rushing toward him a huge demon devouring the sky. Before long, he developed a bad fever that was very prevalent in India. Even today, nine hundred years later, every year hundreds of Indians die of this bad fever.

One time in the mirror of light, Khyungpo Naljor related to me what he encountered at that time ...

4 A Lamp on a Dark Night

My child, you should know that in the past thousand years, there have been very few who have understood me as you do. If I am the sun, you are the light of the sun. Through this light, countless people will understand the value of the sun.

Child, for a very long period of time, I was always in a trance. My spirit would wander off, and I had no strength in my whole body. During that period I did know that this was due to the power of the curses. Child, though the basic substance of the power of curses does indeed return to the empty inherent nature, in terms of interdependent causation and external forms, it still does exist. For a person who has not yet truly awakened to empty inherent nature, the power of curses is something that objectively exists.

At that point in time, although in theory I understood that the myriad things are like illusions, in my mind I had not really broken through clinging.

Thus, I was always seeing those great demons of Bonpo and beings like the Red Master of Life, and they were angrily staring at me with their fearsome eyes, opening their great mouths and spewing out poisonous vapors at me. They had in fact become a kind of atmosphere. Within that atmosphere, I was always coming up with thoughts like this: "Maybe Niguma is only a legend. I have already wasted too much of my life in searching. I should go back."

What a horrifying thought!

Every time this thought arose, I would think of leaving India sooner and returning to Tibet. Of the few disciples who had followed me to India, some had died, some had gone back. I was always alone.

You might ask: "Wasn't Sukhasiddhi accompanying you?"

She was. Sukhasiddhi was accompanying me. But this kind of accompanying is not the kind of accompanying you imagine. She was not a woman who came when she was called and left when she was dismissed. In reality she was more like a wind that comes unexpectedly. I very much like your poem in *Curses of Xixia*:

> *The frosty wind has swept your black hair white*
>
> *But it cannot sweep your search and make it old*
>
> *Bit by bit the plum blossoms*
>
> *Night after night shooting toward the horizon*
>
> *Your husband is not there on the road at the horizon*
>
> *Your husband is the ebb and flow of rain and snow*
>
> *He always comes quietly*
>
> *And quietly he goes ...*

Sukhasiddhi was also rain and snow that ebbed and flowed. I had no way to call her to come, and no way to control her leaving. She always arrived unexpectedly. Moreover, during those days, she appeared more and more cunning and weird. I knew she was adjusting my mind and nature. Sometimes she seemed more like a blacksmith: she would take my mind and put in on the anvil and lift her hammer and pound again and again. Through this repeated pounding, the miscellaneous material in my mind and spirit turned into sparks that splashed out on all sides ... Time and again she took my mind and pounded it into a thin sheet of iron, then rolled it up and put it back into the hearth to smelt it again ... It was always like this. When I sank into isolation and needed her, she would not show her face for a long time. I could not even hear her breathing.

That kind of isolation is really hard for an ordinary person to endure.

During that period a voice was always calling out: "Go back, go back. Niguma is just a legend."

I had already been searching for a very long time, and in the course of the search I had experienced many wonders, but by that time I had begun to suspect that everything I had experienced was perhaps just a dream. Amid so many trances, I even began to have doubts about whether or not I had really encountered so many dakinis.

Besides this, the many esoteric methods I had found also began to trouble me. Sometimes I felt this method was good, sometimes I felt that method was good. So today I would cultivate this method, and tomorrow I would cultivate that method. But I did not want to discard any of these methods, because every one of them had cost me a lot of time and gold ... Of course, I had never had any feeling for gold. In my eyes, it was just a tool for seeking the Dharma. In fact, you now can appreciate my feeling for gold at that time. Now when you mention my offering that gold, this is without any feeling, right? You can say the number, like five hundred ounces or a thousand ounces and so on, but these are just numbers. What you care about is those teachings I found. They reach through a thousand years of time and space, and keep flowing into your great sea of wisdom ... That's right, the great sea of wisdom. I understand what you have said: you have said that the Shangpa Kagyu teaching lineage is just one stream that has flowed into your great ocean of wisdom. I understand this statement you made. Because at that time, my great ocean of wisdom was formed in the same way, by the confluence of many streams. The ocean does not shun streams, and thus it can be called great. Only the shallow ones think that what fills their own cup is the whole great ocean.

But in fact you do understand that, among the streams that flowed into your ocean of wisdom, the undefiled wisdom coming from Niguma was without a doubt the most important one. Thus you can never give up Shangpa Kagyu. It is the same way for me. The way I was at that time, if I had not undertaken the final search, there would have been a gap in my wisdom that would have been extremely difficult to make whole.

So it was precisely because I had the warning from the wisdom of previous lives, that I did not abandon the search for the ultimate goal.

At countless moments, those Bonpo guardian spirits and those other evil spirits sent out thought waves to make me start thinking of shrinking back. They wanted to disrupt my mind.

In my thoughts at that time, other than suspecting that Niguma was only a legend, the one that appeared most often was telling me "to be satisfied." A voice was always telling me: You have already attained the mind marrow of more than a hundred and forty great adepts. That's enough, that's enough. You are already the great teacher in Tibet who has found the most teachings. Like Marpa, who only got the transmission of mind from Naropa, or like Naropa, who only got the transmission of mind from Tilopa—they still became great teachers. You got the mind marrow from so many great teachers—how is it that you are still not satisfied?"

At that time there was another voice calling to me: "Why don't you go back, transmit the teaching, save sentient beings. How many people are there like you in Tibet? You do not need to search any more. If you delay, who knows how many people will lose the precious jewel of a human incarnation in the meantime?"

This was truly an incomparably great reason. I nearly abandoned the search.

You can think about it now. If I had abandoned the search at that time, what a regrettable thing that would have been. Even if I had become a great teacher, that would have been a great teacher in another sense. I would not have been Niguma's successor. And if Khyungpo Naljor had not developed a relationship with Niguma, how regrettable that would have been! It would be like Shangpa Kagyu not having you, or you not having Shangpa Kagyu—there would certainly have been less brilliance in this world.

You must realize that, many times, what is most to be feared is the laziness that comes with the external appearance of benefitting people. I almost really gave up my search. But every time I thought of giving it up, suddenly I would develop a feeling of weightlessness. I would think: "If I do not search for Niguma, then is there any meaning to my being alive?"

This unwillingness to give up was like a lamp on a dark night, and it accompanied me through my long journey in search of Niguma.

5 A Demon's Stone

Beloved Khyungpo Ba, I am getting more and more frightened.

I am still taking on the force of that curse for you—it has made me develop the feeling that the sickness has entered the area below my heart, and my throat is always choking, and the pain has begun to attack. I am afraid I will not be able to bear the power of this evil curse that is spread over heaven and earth. I am always seeing the grit of those evil curses still spreading toward you as you go on searching.

The sorcerers found another piece of demon's stone in the mountains, and they will take your soul and pull it onto the demon's stone. The story goes that this is your life-stone, which represents your spirit. They have already taken three of your life-stones. These represent "red bodhi," "white bodhi," and the "immortal point of light" (bindu). They distinguish the souls (karmic spirits) that come from your father, your mother, and your past lives.

They have already completed the prescribed chants, and they have taken that piece of paper with their prayers and their mantras, and various jewels, and wrapped them up in a piece of red cloth, and together with your three life-stones, packed them into the hearts of a red mountain sheep and a black sheep.

They want to make you enter into a fearful demonic realm. That demonic realm will delude your clear mind of wisdom.

I am to the point that I hope you will tell me whether or not, to you, my infatuation with you is also a kind of demonic realm.

I read your letter. I am very worried about you, and my heart aches, but there is nothing else I can do but go on as before and take on the force of those curses for you.

Every person is seeking for a kind of ultimate meaning. How can everything go as we wish—I just want to have a clear conscience with nothing to be ashamed of. The wisdom and enlightenment that you are trading your life for and spending all your mental energy on — in the view of many people, this is perhaps not necessary, and may even bring you adversity. That is the fate of those who are willing to be rogue this way. When you call to them to wake up, as long as a few minds hear it, that will be enough. I know that you are already using all your strength.

You don't know how great your are: you have brought me so much goodness! I am such an aloof and proud person, but toward you I am docile and obedient and willing to be your servant. I may be ignorant and uninformed, and I am not clear about what other women need, but in my eyes, all those men with ostentatious wealth and power cannot be compared with the wisdom and purity and understanding which you have brought to me. For this I have countless times felt grateful to fate, felt thankful to life, and felt even more thankful to you.

Do not be influenced by worldly values: hold firmly to yourself, hold firmly to your enlightenment, hold firmly to your direction, hold firmly to your Path. I am very confident that you are right.

You have already reached a very lofty realm. With every step you advance higher, and it is all extraordinarily difficult, even more difficult than it was originally. But do not worry about this. This is surely the most difficult thing — how can a great achievement be that easy? So do not feel downhearted, just take your time.

Khyungpo Ba is Khyungpo Ba. In reality, living by doing whatever you please is not living for anything.

I love you.

I am very tired now, and I have to stop writing.

My throat is still very sore. I don't knew whether I can keep going till you return.

6 Khyungpo Naljor Says

Sharwadi, my dear one:

My heart aches for you.

You must go see a doctor, and also do some fire offerings to stop disasters.

Do not keep on taking on the power of those curses for me. For people who have not yet experienced the empty inherent nature, the power of those curses is something that really exists. They can damage your physical well-being.

I also miss you vey much. In my mind there is still a feeling so strong I cannot transform it. You are a good woman, and my life has more color only because I have you.

Even if I have realized a bit of wisdom, you are still the greatest inspiration in my mind, and this has become the reason I still stay in the world of mortals. Whenever I think of you, then I feel that life is truly very wonderful.

For the past many years, I have only been an ascetic monk exiled by fate. Only after I met you did I think that I had lived for a few days. After I have completed this journey, then the time will come to see you. I am very happy. I hope you can read aloud those scriptures I left you — this will amount to giving me another gift. When you have been able to read out the cool refreshing purity from those scriptures, then you will have truly encountered me.

How I hope that you will be able to be happy and to

clearly understand. If you will be able to live better than before
because you met me, that I will not have brought you heartache
in vain.

Khyungpo Naljor

I told Khyungpo Naljor that when my son Chen Yixin read this, he
commented: "He was still an ordinary monk."

Khyungpo Naljor laughed out loud. He said: "Your son thinks
that a Buddhist monk does not partake of the ordinary human world.
How would he know that after I had realized the great achievement, I
would still have endless tender feelings. After achieving enlightenment
I had even more boundless tender feelings than before I achieved
enlightenment. Before I achieved it, what concerned me was mostly
my mother. After I achieved it, I had countless mothers. What is
achieving enlightenment? Achieving enlightenment is the release
after experiencing empty inherent nature, it is the joy of being filled
with great compassion, it is the transcendent state of having countless
concerns but not a bit of affliction. It is like the poetic feeling of a
person in love, loving all sentient beings that way.

"Do you understand?"

7 The Essential Nature of the Bodiless Dakini

Child, do not give me that look.

There is nothing wrong with you feeling sorry for Sharwadi, but
you must realize that this life of mine was not for seeking her.

I had come to seek Niguma.

Though there would be many choices in my fate, only what I most had
to do at each moment could be the most important thing in my mind.

Only after I had found the most important thing, could I pay attention to the other things.

In my life, Sharwadi was even more like a female spirit. Countless times on my journey of searching, when I was very isolated, I would think of her. In my memories of the past, everything connected to her became a wave of warmth filling my mind.

However, Sharwadi could only represent the beauty and goodness of worldly phenomena; she could not represent world-transcending wisdom. You must realize that it was the latter that was most important to me.

In order to bring the nature of my mind to maturity, those bodiless dakinis also would open up for me the secrets of cultivating Supreme Yoga. These included all the secrets of the Vajrayana yoga for cultivating realization — these are called the mind marrow of the dakinis.

Before I realized enlightenment, my interactions with the bodiless dakinis all depended on Sukhasiddhi. She could see many realms of experience that ordinary people cannot see, and she could thoroughly comprehend many secrets which are impossible for many people to understand.

Look: Sukhasiddhi is still dancing, dancing and singing, and the sound of her song is very beautiful:

The wisdom of theRealm of Reality inherently exists and is perfectly complete: it does not depend on external power; it is naturally fully complete.

Its light is bright, exquisite, limpid, like a glittering clear crystal: though it has no form, it is like the herbs of the immortals, exuding all kinds of beautiful fragrances.

Since time without beginning, it has never been lost: it is stored in the dakinis' infinite storehouse of consciousness.

Now, when circumstances are ripe, the treasure chest opens and it flows into the jewel pitcher of your mind's inherent nature.

Sukhasiddhi said: "Son, your merit and wisdom are rarely seen in any era, ancient or modern. This is the secret that is the same as the mind marrow of the dakinis. It is transmitted from the mouths and ears of the bodiless dakinis — outside of their realm it is very difficult to understand. It comes from Gandhara in the country of Uddiyana. This is a sacred ground where the dakinis meet."

At that time, the dakinis all lived in the dakini land. On the surface, they are very ordinary. Some are very lowly in the social order, but in the depths of their inner minds they always preserve that enlightenment in the mind. One day I went to visit this place, and it was my good fortune to win the joy of the dakinis and receive the special transmission of the dakinis:

When you have fully matured the nature of your mind, then you will have the Dharma treasure of liberation.

That liberation comes from that fully matured inherent nature mind, and it will surely cut through what entangles your mind.

The entanglements of your mind originate in the discriminating mind, and the discriminating mind comes from your delusions.

Because you are deluded and confused, you take the illusory as real, and because you take the illusory as real, you fall into the trap.

All the things you cling to are without inherent nature; they are like the moon reflected in the water, like reflections in a mirror.

These empty reflection, this moon reflected in the water, are fundamentally illusory forms in your mind; in reality they have no real essence that is worth your deluded obsessions.

When you clearly understand the foregoing truth, then finally your mind's nature can be considered fully mature.

When your mind's nature is fully mature, this is called liberation: it comes from your own mind and does not depend on external seeking.

If you think that liberation comes from the Buddha, then you are still revolving in birth and death.

Revolving in birth and death is in reality the functioning of illusory forms; when you have clearly understood illusory forms, you will be far removed from clingings and attachments.

Son, do you smell that special fragrance? It comes from your mind's nature the same way, and you are inherently provided with it.

Although the dakinis' song carries it, this song is all coming forth from your own mind ground.

Sukhasiddhi said: "Son, you should not underestimate this teaching. All the practices and observances of the Vajrayana are contained in it. You should certainly apply your understanding to it well. No matter whether you ponder it or silently recite it, it will have an incomparable supporting power for you. Son, you must remember, the essential nature of the bodiless dakinis is the Great Mudra. Without the guidance of the level of perception of the Great Mudra, it will be very hard for you to realize enlightenment.

"Son, your mind and spirit are fundamentally pure and clean, and the inherent nature of mind is fundamentally inherently fully mature. It has an ultimate enlightened nature that has never been defiled, just as the bright pure sky has never been defiled by the dust. But because the dark clouds of false thoughts cover it up, you cannot see the nature of mind that is fundamentally there. If you undergo genuine cultivation of practice, then you will clear away the confusion which is obstructing the fundamental merit of your inherent mind, and fully awaken to the enlightened nature of your own inherent mind. Son, that great net which is obstructing and covering your pure inherent nature is entirely created by the discriminating mind. Those dualistic thoughts and habits become bonds tying up your inherent enlightened nature — those are what you must cut through."

The dakinis all joined in and voiced their agreement. One of them said: "That is correct. All you have to do is not be deceived by those false thoughts, then you will succeed. We do not know that there is anything else you should work on." Another dakini said: "That's it. All your afflictions are the mental bondage imposed on you by false mind, and it's just because of this that you cannot see the original face of true mind." Another dakini said: "Didn't the Great Teacher Tilopa say it? In sesame seeds there is sesame oil — in the same way, our buddha-nature exists within the inherent nature of our minds." Another dakini said: "When you throw off these ridiculous bonds, the original face of true mind will spontaneously appear."

8 Kapilavastu

Child, though the dakinis taught me time and again about the inherent nature of mind, I discovered that there was still a great distance between theoretical understanding and independence in action. No matter what kind of awakening I had in theory, whenever I encountered different external circumstances, delusion and confusion would still interfere with my true mind.

In Kapilavastu I undertook to carry out some ceremonial offerings, and so I hurried to accumulate some supplies. I made offerings to all my teachers: first, to thank them for instructing me; and second, I wanted to make use of the power of making offerings to holy men to clear away the barriers to my mind and spirit as quickly as possible. I also thought of inviting those great adepts that I could invite to come. I even had the extravagant hope that Niguma could also come along with those adepts and take part in my offerings ceremony.

For the location of the gathering, I chose Kapilavastu. This was the capital of the Sakya clan, and it was located on a plain at the foot of the Himalaya mountains.

The Buddha had lived for twenty-nine years in Kapilavastu. For us to hold a ceremonial gathering here would be very good from the point of view of interdependent causation. All those teachers of mine wanted to come visit Kapilavastu. In our minds, this place, like Rajgir and Sravasti, was a holy place we had looked forward to visiting for a long time.

But only when I arrived in Kapilavastu did I discover that Kapilavastu had already turned into a ruin, and there were no signs of its former glory to be seen. In fact, the Sakya kingdom, which was so famous in history, was just a rustic city-state. That so-called kingdom was only a confederation of small city-states—it was much like one of today's republics. Before the time of the Buddha's father King Suddhodana, it chose its king by democratic means. Starting with King Suddhodana, a system of hereditary succession appeared in Kapilavastu. In order to be able to continue to exist under pressure from stronger powers, the villages that were scattered around Kapilavastu united together in the form of a confederation, to become a comparatively large state. King Suddhodana was the chief of this confederation.

The Sakya clan lived mainly by agriculture, and its clan name was "Gotama," and it was also called "Gautama." In the Buddhist scriptures we often see non-Buddhists call the Buddha this: it's often "Gautama, Gautama." This is originally the name of an ancient hero, which means "the finest bull." It was indeed this hero called "the finest bull" who founded the city of the Sakya clan. To commemorate him, the Sakya clan took "Gautama" as its clan name.

In the culture of the Sakya clan, the air of agriculture and husbandry is very strong. Its historical leaders are all named after foodstuffs, like King Suddhodana, King Suklodana, King Amrodana, and King Dronodana; these names are all redolent of agriculture. More than two thousand years ago, the most splendid festival of the Sakya clan was the festival of plowing and planting. On that day the whole country rejoiced, and it was a very lively celebration. On that day, the king would take part in plowing and planting, in order to show veneration and respect for agriculture.

History always displays marvels: here, in this rustic agricultural area, was born a great personage whose light has shone down through the ages.

Many times, in an ordinary little pond, a lotus flower may grow whose brilliance overflows in all directions. So while there is no way for us to pick our social origins, we do pick our actions.

In those times the Sakya clan was surrounded on all sides by powerful enemies. Hemmed in by these strong powers, this small kingdom of city states was in a precarious position. It's situation was like an egg with a giant rock above it, tottering and about to fall. Everyone in the whole Sakya clan was hoping that a great man would be born, and they wanted to use the great man's abilities to transform the dangerous situation in which they existed. Thus, they were expecting a "wheel-turning sage king." The Buddhist scriptures are full of descriptions of the Wheel-Turning Sage King. This king would have seven jewels: the wheel jewel, elephant jewel, horse jewel, pearl jewel, woman jewel, treasurer jewel, military commander jewel; these all would be great jewels not seen in the realm of the senses, along with great virtue, and the power of the Great Dharma, and the capacity for great achievement. These could help the Sage King and unify the whole country. In the *Longer Agama Spoken by Buddha* it says that when the kings of the nations see the Sage King arrive, then "with gold bowls filled with silver grains and with silver bowls filled with gold grains, they will come to visit the king's abode, bow down and say: 'Excellent, Oh Great King. Now these eastern lands are prosperous and happy, with all kinds of precious jewels, and the people are flourishing, and their temperament is humane and harmonious, and they are compassionate and filial and loyal and obedient, and they only hope that the Sage King will establish his rule here! We will serve you and take on whatever duties are needed.' " Only after the appearance of this legendary Wheel-Turning Sage King, would the Sakya clan be able to be genuinely revitalized.

Amid this endless waiting, the great man finally came. When the royal consort was thirty years old, one night she dreamed that a white elephant entered her womb. In ancient India in that period, this was an extremely auspicious dream, predicting that she would give birth to a great and noble person.

Before long, the king's son was born. The king invited someone to create a lucky name: Siddhartha, which means "all wishes can be attained."

King Suddhodana invited a famous holy man to examine the physiognomy of the prince. That holy man, called Ashita, had been cultivating practice in the Himalayas his whole life, and his conduct was noble and profound. When he saw the young prince, he first laughed, and then cried. When asked why, the holy man said: "I laughed because this child will be a great and noble person. If he enters the conventional world and becomes king, he will be able to become a Wheel-Turning Sage King and rule the world. If he leaves home to cultivate the Path, he will be able to achieve supreme true equanimity and true enlightenment. I cried because I am already old, and I do not have much time left, and I will not be able to be there in person to receive the teachings of the prince after he realizes the Path to enlightenment."

In this place called Kapilavastu, Siddhartha passed the first twenty-nine years of his life. He had no material worries, and he was highly respected and honored. In order to guard against him developing an aversion to the world, King Suddhodana provided him the best material conditions and let his son enjoy the wondrous joys of the five desires. But the prince would always quickly become unhappy. This was because his wisdom could always let him discover the suffering hidden in the flowing pleasure.

In the clear mirror of the light, I see Prince Siddhartha at that time. In those days, though he was surrounded by wondrous pleasures on all sides, a look of weariness and boredom came from the prince's eyes. By that time, he had already studied almost all the branches of learning that were flourishing in the area, but there was no way to dispel the boredom and sense of emptiness in his mind. No matter whether the classics of literary culture or the techniques of warfare, the prince quickly picked the best of them. In the world at that time, there were very few people who could serve as teachers for him.

So at a moment when heaven and earth had paused for it, as the prince was going out through the east gate of the palace, taking with him the charioteer called Chandaka, he caught sight of an old man. The old man's face was all wrinkled, and he was as emaciated as a stick of wood, and his beard was dripping with mucus, and his body was trembling like a leaf in the wind. The prince asked: "Chandaka, why does this man look like this?" Chandaka said: "Prince, it is because he has gotten old." The prince asked: "Will I get old too?" Chandaka said: "Of course. All human beings get old." So, deep in thought, the prince returned to the citadel. The dark clouds brought on by his discovery of old age began to cover the sky of his life.

In the clear light of my mind's spirit, the prince goes out again, through the south gate of the palace. He heard a sick man groaning, and the sound was tragic — his pain and suffering were intense. The sick man's face was covered with black spots, and there was a bad smell coming from his decomposing body. The prince asked: "Chandaka, why is this man crying out so tragically?" Chandaka said: "Prince, it is because he is sick. An unexpected sickness has damaged his health." Again the prince asked: "Will I get sick too?" Chandaka said: "Yes. In this world, all human beings get sick. Sickness shadows human beings. If you have a body, then it can happen that the four great elements get out of harmony, and then there is sickness. Sickness is something inevitable in human life." At that point the prince looked up to the sky and sighed and silently pondered this.

In the clear mirror of the light, the prince appears in the west gate of the palace. Outside the west gate there was a dead man: the warmth had already left his body, and he was a rigid as a dead tree lying flat. His relatives were by his side, wailing as they lifted him onto the funeral pyre. When the funeral pyre was set alight, black smoke and flames covered the corpse. The prince was startled, and he again questioned Chandaka. Chandaka said: "Prince, that man has already died." The prince asked: "Will I die too?" Chandaka said: "Death is something inevitable in every human life. If there is birth, there is bound to be death. No matter whether strong or weak, king or commoner, no one can escape being overtaken by the god of death."

Thus did this prince, who had grown up in depths of the palace, end up discovering birth, old age, sickness, and death. These four bonds that have tied up sentient beings for countless ages finally came into his field of vision.

Sukhasiddhi said: "The situations which the prince saw at those four gates were in fact manifestations of the world-transcending guardian spirits who protect the Dharma. They used a direct illustration style to awaken the prince's intention to leave." She said: "Many times, the wondrous pleasures of the five desires can allow a wise man to sink into delusion. That old man, that sick man, that dead man — all of them were alarm bells sounding. The alarm bell rang out dramatically several times, and woke up the prince who had been sunk into the wondrous pleasures of the five desires."

Because of this, the first of the later Four Noble Truths began to become visible in the prince's life. That is the word "suffering."

Soon after this, in Siddhartha's life there appeared another different kind of light. He walked out through the north gate of the palace and saw a monk. That monk was very dignified, and his face was like the full moon. He was very composed and aloof, indifferent to how people treated him. The prince asked Chandaka: "What kind of person is this?" Chandaka said: "This is someone who cultivates the Path." The prince asked: "Why does he cultivate the Path?" Chandaka said: "In order to go beyond the ocean of suffering of birth, old age, sickness, and death."

Sukhasiddhi said: "From then on, the prince developed the intention to leave."

I became extremely interested in Chandaka. In my eyes, this charioteer called Chandaka could almost be put on a par with the dakini that Luipa encountered. Though he did not explain the inherent nature of mind for the Buddha, he did enable him to develop the intention to leave the palace. And developing the desire to leave, directly brought about the Buddha's leaving home later.

So, on a certain night, Siddhartha looked with compassion on his wife, who was sleeping soundly, and look at the beloved child to whom she had just given birth, and left the city of Kapilavastu, accompanied by Chandaka. He went to a cemetery forest where people cultivated the Path, and began the ascetic practices which would go on for six years.

What is described above is seen in the Buddhist scriptures.

But when I look at it, the story above is not without its symbolism. I think that a prince who had studied all sorts of worldly learning could not have not known about the rules of birth and death. The ancient Indian classic texts of that period are filled with that kind of knowledge. The prince's wisdom, it seems, did not necessarily be started with the charioteer. More likely, at that moment in history, the Buddha was just playing a scene. He used the method of direct illustration to tell people they must see through birth, old age, sickness, and death.

I seem to have discovered a clue in the name Siddhartha gave his son. Buddha named the son he had before he left home "Rahula," which means "barrier" and "lunar eclipse." In fact this appellation is not auspicious. In the teachings which circulated later in Tibet, they consider the appearance of a lunar eclipse or solar eclipse to be due to the star Rahu blocking the light of the sun or moon. When I was cultivating the evocation stage of Kalachakra, I had to visualize the Rahu chakra. At specially defined times, it always creates a barrier to the light flowing from the sun and the moon toward the human world. Why did the Buddha give his son this kind of name? Maybe this name represents Siddhartha's psychology before he left home. At that time, what was hardest for him to part with was his newly born son. He certainly hesitated and went back and forth. The name "Rahula" represented his most genuine mixed feelings. Just as we are always concerned about our spouses and children, before he left Kapilavastu, the Buddha also certainly experienced a painful choice. Before he had truly conquered himself, the birth of his son became a very great barrier to his leaving home to cultivate the Path.

But in the end, he cut through the love for his family members, went beyond the barriers, and left the city.

At that time, all the barriers in the world could not stop Siddhartha as he went toward truth.

He escaped from Kapilavastu, and went to the cemetery forest, which was suffused with the odor of rotting corpses.

9 Deadly Energy Rushing at Kinfolk

From this point on, there would be more possibility of being saved for the sentient beings living among the world of mortals of sensory experience.

But the Buddha, who is always considered all-powerful by people, in fact could not change seven things: birth, old age, sickness, death, wrongdoing, merit, and the process of cause and effect.

The Buddha used wisdom to rescue countless sentient beings sunk in the sea of suffering, but he could not save Kapilavastu, the city that had brought him up. Many years later, King Virudhaka's great army would destroy this city in which the great man was born.

By means of his own unique methods, three times the Buddha blocked deadly energy rushing at his kinfolk. But the destruction of the Sakya clan was still destined because of the set rules of cause and effect.

According to the story that has circulated rather widely, the demise of the Sakya clan came about because in earlier generations they had been fishermen. In order to survive, they had killed millions of living things. In the infinite river of life, although they had changed appearances countless times, the reactive force created by those evil deeds followed them like a shadow following a form. Those seeds of evil ripened not long after the Buddha became enlightened, and resulted in evil fruit.

When King Virudhaka's great army drew near to Kapilavastu in a cloud of dust kicked up by their cavalry, in the pure light I saw the Buddha sitting peacefully under a dead tree. King Virudhaka asked him: "World Honored One, there are many trees in this forest, and there is a lot of shade. Why then are you sitting under a dead tree?" The Buddha said: "How can the shelter offered by these trees compare with the shelter offered by family?" At this, King Virudhaka could not bear to proceed with the attack, and ordered his army to withdraw. But although the army withdrew, King Virudhaka's murderous intent was hard to pacify, and before long, he sent his soldiers again. It happened like this three times. Each time they saw the Buddha on the road, and the Buddha answered them with the idea of the family giving shelter.

The fourth time King Virudhaka dispatched his forces, the Buddha understood that the past evil deeds of the Sakya clan had ripened. He told his disciples: "You should not be concerned. The evil causal factors from the past lives of the Sakya clan today have already ripened, and the time has come when that debt for taking so many lives must be repaid." Then the pall of dust kicked up by the thousands of horses of King Virudhaka's cavalry covered the sky over Kapilavastu. Coming through that dust I saw that the Sakya clan had a young hero riding out with his bow in hand, valorous beyond compare. He shot arrows to defend his side, and every arrow hit an enemy warrior, and he almost shot and killed King Virudhaka. Then an old man of the Sakya clan rebuked the young man: "How can you kill living beings as you please, and spoil the good name of our Sakyas, and bring disgrace to our Sakya family? Didn't the Buddha teach us to treat sentient beings well? We do not want to harm even insects, so how can you shoot arrows and wound people? Surely you know that if you kill sentient beings, you will have to suffer in hell." Then the Sakya people drove out that sharpshooter and calmly accepted the karmic retribution.

In the clear light of my mind and spirit, there also appeared the Venerable Maudgalyayana. The venerable one could not bear having harm done to the people of the Sakya clan, so he said to the Buddha: "World Honored One, I want to save the Sakya clan, maybe take them and put them into empty space, or put them in the middle of the ocean, or put them between two surrounding iron mountains, or move them to another country so King Virudhaka cannot find them." The Buddha said: "Though you have spiritual powers, you cannot change seven things: birth, old age, sickness, death, wrongdoing, merit, the process of cause and effect. There is no way for your spiritual powers to remove their evil karma from past lifetimes."

But Maudgalyayana still could not bear it, so he secretly deployed his spiritual powers. He flew up carrying a giant bowl that could swallow and spit out heaven and earth. He took the brave hero of the Sakya clan facing bloody disaster, and put him into the bowl, and brought it back to his abode. But he was horrified to discover that the man had already turned into bloody water. This story became the best commentary on the idea that "spiritual powers cannot oppose the force of karma."

In Kapilavastu I discovered an old historic site called "the place where the Sakyas were exterminated." In that place there was an old stone tablet with an inscription on it: "When King Virudhaka conquered the Sakyas, he captured their clansmen, nine thousand nine hundred and ninety myriads of people, and he slaughtered them all. He piled up their corpses in a huge mound, and the blood flowed out and made a pond, as a warning from heaven to human hearts, and he collected the bones and buried them ..." This inscription offers historical testimony for the destruction of the Sakya clan.

At the same time, in the Buddhist scriptures a historical fact is recorded, that after the Buddha's death, his relics were divided among eight nations, one of which was the Sakya clan. This makes it clear that the Sakya clan was still in existence after Buddha's death.

So this become a historical riddle.

There is another story that says that the Sakya clan was definitely not totally annihilated. It says that after King Virudhaka entered the city of Kapilavastu, he didn't want the trouble of killing people, so he ordered them to be buried in the ground, and he wanted to have elephants trample them. At this time the Sakya King Mahanama said to King Virudhaka: "Though you and I are now enemies, according to the rules, I am still your maternal grandfather. I cannot bear to have the common people killed, but I ask for one thing. Please take me and submerge me in the water, and let the common people flee. Those who have not had time to flee before I float to the surface, I will let you go ahead and kill. What about that?" King Virudhaka felt this was interesting, and so he agreed. When King Mahanama was submerged in the water, King Virudhaka permitted the Sakyans to escape. But after many of them had escaped, he still did not see King Mahanama come up to the surface, and he sent men to go pull him out. They saw that King Mahanama had tied his hair to a tree root under the water, to guarantee that more people would be able to get away.

In my eyes, this was the manifestation of a great bodhisattva.

10 The Red Master of Life Riding on a Mountain Sheep

Beloved Khyungpo Ba, please hold my hand.

I have not written a letter for a long time. Lately I am always exhausted. It seems that someone is draining away my energy. First, I miss you too much; second, I have definitely been hit by those sorcerers' curses. That pain has become even more of a nightmare for me.

I am always falling into a kind of delusional state involuntarily: I can always see those sorcerers and the mandala of the Red Master of Life. I do not know whether or not they have hooked my consciousness. I have seen a giant triangular offering made out of blood wine and flour—this is the sort of thing you called flower agate. I still see the blood of the black dog and other offerings. The most striking is the garland strung on an animal's windpipe. I still see those things that you often used— that diamond bell and diamond club and human-headed drum.

Those sorcerers are all doing visualizations and chanting as they meditate.

Because you are a male, the sorcerers are visualizing themselves a male version of the Red Master of Life. If you were a woman, they would have to visualize themselves as the red-faced female demon. Come to think of it, the sorcerers are afraid of alien influences. I see those Red Masters of Life all riding on male mountain sheep.

At the beginning, I thought that this was a delusion of mine. Later, Kumari told me that what I was seeing is a real scene.

There are two possibilities for this kind of scene to appear: either I have realized the power of the heavenly eye to see things at a distance, or my soul is being pulled into that mandala.

I think it is the latter, because if I had realized the heavenly eye, I would be able to see what I most want to see: you, and it would not be the danger of this mandala.

However, I am not a bit afraid. If I can truly die in your place, this is what I most want to do.

Forgive me, I still love you very much, and it has become more and more incurable. My body is obviously not as it was before. I even suspect that I have gotten an incurable disease. My throat is always sore, and I feel that there is something strange there. According to what one Brahman said, this was created by my karma of speaking.

Of course, if the sickness of longing is also an incurable disease, the disease is already beyond remedy.

I have discovered that if I try to give you up, and not care about you, then I have no way to do anything. Then, for me, it is as if a rushing spring of passion is pumped out and suddenly becomes a pool of stagnant water, sluggish, dirty, totally bereft of the joy of living. My madly loving your breath is like the atmosphere that I cannot leave. Without you, I would stop breathing.

Now I understand more and more that, at first, you perhaps did not really plan to go with me for very long. In your mind, I was only a hard-to-forget chance encounter, and that's all. You were an ordinary person going along with circumstances — it was myself who decided I wanted to spend my life with you. Therefore, every hour and every minute, I am always using all my mental energy to keep you. I know that the distance between us is too great, and if I do not diligently try to keep you, and make you occasionally look back, you might already be long gone. Other than making this effort, what other advantage do I have? You have even seen through birth and death, so how can you be drawn in by a little woman?

If heaven does not let me keep going, then I do not understand why it has to be so cruel to me. It let me get to know you, but it let you leave me! I don't know whether or not I will become a burden for you — throw me off, and maybe you will be able to go faster!

Just like this — a person sitting depressed, thinking random thoughts.

I don't want to talk more to you about what, in your eyes, may be things in the category of scheming. But I know that if you want to have major accomplishments in your future, in your work of spreading the teaching, you will need some helpful causal conditions. If the Buddha had not had his patrons and his disciples, he would not have been able to have the brilliance that came later. I understand very clearly how I must proceed. I understand you, and I know what resources and what friends will be helpful causal conditions for you, and what praise and acclaim can be a burden and a trap. In religious competitions, the cunning, the mixed motives, the traps go far beyond what we imagine. We must be unchanged as we respond to myriad changes, to do our work well with a calm mind. I am looking for talented people who genuinely are far-seeing, who have a mission, who have good accomplishments. If I can find them, it is everyone's good fortune. If I cannot find any, I still have not wasted my time. Everything I do now is making efforts to let your voice get bigger, in order to attract the attention of those people we must find. My reasoning is that the most important thing is to disseminate the message to people with a high cultural level, and let them hear your voice. With them affirming and promoting your teaching, it will spread widely in various forms — as the saying goes, "climb up to a high place and call out." If we proceed this way, we will guarantee the freedom and independence and purity you need, and accomplish the task much more effectively. If not, then it will be like the situation you encountered before in your home area: though you picked people in order to benefit them, they preferred to believe lies. They preferred the false talk of deceivers, and even became the accomplices of the deceivers, to help them encircle and annihilate you. Before you had completed saving them, you would have worked yourself to death.

I am already using my father's resources, and I have created a lot of momentum for you. Right now, in my father's and my circle, there is almost no one who does not know of Khyungpo Naljor.

I have never deified you. I have a deep knowledge of your direction in this life and your seeking. Therefore, heedless of everything else, I protect your purity, your calm, your clarity: this is the bright lamp of salvation that so many people hope to see when they are in despair, depressed, and sick of the world. I am working hard to protect this, so it will not be blown out by the crazy winds of the mundane world and its ways—I do not know whether or not I am overestimating myself, but I think this is my most important duty. If I do not do it, then I am unworthy of heaven arranging for us to be together.

Let us just prepare ourselves well. Everything else, let fate decide.

Sharwadi

11 The Samadhi of Mind and Spirit

Khyungpo Naljor speaks:

I had spent a thousand ounces of gold and had ordered many precious things from various places to use as offerings, and told people to deliver them to Kapilavastu in twenty-five days. On the vast ruins I had erected a giant tent and spread out a large red carpet.

The setting for the ceremony was very magnificent, and all my teachers, more than eighty great Indian adepts, and all the brave dakinis of the twenty-four realms of surpassing excellence and the ultimate heaven of form, attended the ceremonial gathering.

At that ceremonial gathering all the adept teachers showed their spiritual powers. Some of them demonstrated playing with spiritual power, emitting fire above their bodies and water below their bodies. Some demonstrated levitation, sitting cross-legged in the air. Some changed form into wild beasts. Some changed form into mountains ... There were all kinds of mystical displays, too many to tell.

All the great holy ones gave me a prediction of enlightenment, saying: "Khyungpo Ba, you will get supreme accomplished merits and achieve the ultimate spiritual power (*siddhi*). There will be no duality between your body and Guhyasamaja, no duality between your speech and Mahamaya, no duality between your mind and Hevajra, no duality between your merits and Chakrasamvara, no duality between your actions and Vajrabhairava."

Sukhasiddhi was very happy, and she too gave me a prediction of enlightenment, saying: "Son, your resources of merit and virtue surpass ancient and modern, and you will have a hundred thousand disciples. They will be born in the birthplace of Mahadeva, in the birthplace of the Vajra of Surpassing Excellence, and in the birthplace of Savannah Avalokiteshvara. They will all receive my support and protection. After this, as long as they develop pure faith in the teacher they are inheriting the teaching from, and constantly recite 'Niguma Khyenno,' all the disciples in your line of succession will be reborn in the Pure Land of the dakinis. A thousand years later, the fire of the wisdom you have inherited and passed on will be transmitted to the world, and it will bring supreme refreshing purity to sentient beings."

Sukhasiddhi sang:

Do not forget the samadhi of your inherent nature; it is not the three refuges or the five precepts or the many rules and principles.

Though the rules and precepts are the protectors of attainment, they are like walls that keep the evil winds from invading.

This is because, although the fire of the mind and spirit has sprung up, it still cannot set the prairie alight.

If at this time the evil winds sweep in, the flame of the candle will be extinguished.

Therefore, you must have the walls of the rules and precepts; only then can you protect the candle of wisdom.

Wait till the flame of the candle becomes a great fire; after it sets the prairie a light, then you need not fear wind and rain.

But the samadhi of which I speak does not mean rules and precepts; in reality, it has always been the fundamental essence of the inherent nature of mind.

When the dakinis polish the bright mirror of your mind, you must certainly constantly observe it and not let it get lost.

You can take what I am telling you as a guarantee, but this statement is not the final truth.

The true clear mirror of the inherent nature of mind is fundamentally sufficient: it shines through heaven and earth and has never been lost.

It is just because you have the dust and ashes of false thoughts, that you have no way to see this bright light.

After you wipe them away, you will see the true reality, and then you must perceive that clear essence at all times.

That clear mirror shines brightly with the myriad things, and thusness does not move: your mind too must be crystal clear like this.

O wise Khyungpo Ba, you must always observe the clear mirror of your inherent mind.

Sukhasiddhi said: "Son, the samadhi of your mind and spirit is fundamentally inherent and sufficient. It does not change, and it exists within the undefiled inherent nature of mind. It is only because of the delusion and confusion of your mind and spirit that you are not able to recognize it. That deluded mind of yours is always accepting the false as true and taking all sorts of empty illusory experiences as really existing. In your confused and chaotic mind, you have a deep faith without doubts toward these false perceptions. For this reason, you need various kinds of deliberate purification to polish the promise inherent in that objective essence. This way, you will eliminate dualistic false clinging, and your mind will finally become a clear mirror. Son, when your mind is able to shine brightly with the myriad things, and as it is without moving, then you will finally understand the reality of all phenomena. At that time, you will clearly understand the nature of the inherent mind you are fundamentally equipped with: it is spontaneously sufficient and detached from effort and striving.

"When you have seen the ultimate reality of the myriad phenomena, then you will enter the first stage of being a bodhisattva.

The ultimate joy in your life will start from this. You will constantly enjoy the light of the empty inherent nature and continuously improve your concentration and advancement in meditative concentration.

"Of course, because of the barriers of subtle ignorance, there will still be some separation between your observing mind and the objects that are observed. Only when you transcend duality will the light of reality completely and spontaneously appear.

"Son, there are many methods for dealing with the mind. First you must understand what true mind is. True mind and false mind are fundamentally a single essence. When false mind ceases, true mind will appear: it is like when the dark clouds disperse, the clear sky suddenly appears. You must be good at observing your own mind and attracting the good and dispelling the evil. When false thoughts arise, you use the true mind to observe them; after a long time, you will fully comprehend your own mind. When you understand how to observe mind, then you go on to advance in correct mindfulness and enlightened nature. At this time, you must build a high wall of discipline to block rogue winds from blowing out your candle of enlightenment. After your enlightenment sets the prairie ablaze and becomes a great fire of wisdom, then you will enjoy the bliss of perpetual purity."

Sukhasiddhi said: "With the question of the inherent nature of mind, it is not that you discover a question and then take it and kill it; rather, it is that fundamentally there is no question. All you have to do is peacefully abide in the essential nature of false thoughts, and then you will be spontaneously liberated from false thoughts.

"Son, the teachings of the dakinis have already entered into your mind and spirit, and you have experienced some awakening to bright empty wisdom. Although you are still not able to make it fully your own, you just need time, and you will certainly experience the ultimate.

"Son, although your liberation is not a problem, your mission still is to seek Niguma's teaching. The *Five Great Diamonds Teachings of Niguma* contains the jewel among all jewels of the esoteric teachings. You certainly must find it, and take it back to Tibet. A thousand years from now, it will benefit countless sentient beings. The people who practice it and achieve attainment will be as many as the stars in the sky. Do not be satisfied with the esoteric teachings you have gotten up till now. You must cultivate pure practice and at the same time continue to seek Niguma. Go on pilgrimages and keep searching. Those holy places will bring you added support you cannot imagine."

Chapter 21

The Light of the Bliss of Emptiness

1 The Dakini of Wisdom

After that great ceremonial gathering, Khyungpo Naljor cultivated practice in seclusion and kept praying to the dakinis who protect the Dharma, hoping they could help him find Niguma.

After finishing up the first period of seclusion, Sukhasiddhi brought Khyungpo Naljor on a pilgrimage to the city of Sravasti. Sravasti holds an extremely important place in the history of Buddhism: the Buddha did his summer retreat here twenty-four times. That is to say, during the years when the Buddha was propagating the teaching, he spent twenty-four rainy seasons in Sravasti. Except for Shariputra, Mahakashyapa, and Mahamaudgalyayana and the others from Rajgir, many of the Buddha's disciples were people from Sravasti. The Buddha spent a lot of effort to teach the sentient beings of Sravasti and was able to achieve great success. Many famous scriptures were set forth by the Buddha in Sravasti.

Sukhasiddhi was always traveling all over, teaching sentient beings who had karmic connections to her according to circumstances. She never built a teaching center in any particular place. In this, she was very much in accord with the special mark of the original Buddhism. The Buddha and his disciples were the same. Except during the rainy seasons, when they settled in a given place for the summer for the sentient beings who were not traveling on the road, at other times they were always traveling around, teaching according to circumstances. One day an elder called Sudatta discovered Buddha meditating among the tombs, so he approached him, bowed and asked: "O World Honored One, are your body and mind at peace?" The Buddha answered: "O Brahman, nirvana is eternal peace and bliss. Undefiled by desires, liberated with nothing left over. Ending all hopes, tempering the mind's fire. The mind finds peace and cessation, cessation rests secure at peace." Later, what the Buddha had said to him enabled Sudatta to find pure bliss. Sudatta invited the Buddha to go on to the city of Sravasti, so that the sentient beings in the city could also receive the Buddha's teaching. The Buddha silently accepted. This is a story told in the Buddhist scriptures of the causal conditions for the famous Jetavana Monastery.

Sukhasiddhi said: "Sudatta's family was powerful and very wealthy, and he was always providing support for solitary poor people, so people called him 'the elder who gives to the solitary ones.' After he returned to Sravasti, he began to look for a good location. After looking for a long time, he discovered that the flower garden of Prince Jeta of Sravasti was extremely elegant, so he went to inquire about it, wanting to buy it and build a monastery. He did not know that the prince loved this garden, and he could not bear parting with it. The prince did not explain this, but asked a high price, telling Sudatta: 'If you can take gold and spread it out to cover this garden, then I will sell it.' The prince wanted to let Sudatta know that it would be impossible to buy, and to give up. He did not expect that, when Sudatta heard what he said, he would be very happy. Sudatta returned home, sold off his precious things, and converted them to gold. Several elephants carried the gold on their backs to the garden. Unexpectedly, when the gold had all been used, there was still a little patch of ground that was not covered. Sudatta wanted to return home and trade for some more gold, but the heart of the prince was moved, so he took the space and the trees in the garden and donated them all to the Buddha. This monastery was the Jetavana Monastery that appears so often in the Buddhist scriptures."

Thanks to the aspirations and virtues of the Elder Sudatta and Prince Jeta, the people of Sravasti received the nurturing rain of the Buddha's teachings for a long time. The city of Sravasti became one of the important strongholds of Buddhism in India during that time.

Sukhasiddhi said: "Sravasti at that time was the capital of the kingdom of Kosala. Because it was at the junction of three important trade routes, it was extremely prosperous and bustling. Various religions all wanted to occupy some space in this city. The Jains called it the city of the bright moon, because two of their holy figures, the Honorably Born Lord and the Moonlight Lord, had been born in this city. The Brahmanists also made painstaking efforts in this city, and they had made it into an important place for studying Vedic thought.

"Not long after the Buddha entered Sravasti, he achieved a great success: the king and the ministers were all moved by the plain, authentic unadorned truth of Buddhism, and flocked to become disciples of the Buddha. When this happened, it disrupted the religious pattern of Sravasti at that time. Before the Buddha appeared, the

Brahmanists in the city were able to enjoy a lot of support, but now, the king and the wealthy and powerful people turned and supported the Buddha. Since the Brahmanists could not use official power to fight against the Buddha and suppress him, and they could not win in their debates with the Buddha, they used all their ingenuity thinking to damage Buddhism by some secret plots. One day, while the Buddha was teaching, there suddenly came a woman called Cinca Manavika. She put a wooden bowl under her clothing and cried in a loud voice: 'Look, that great monk who is just now explaining his teaching may look holy enough, but he is a fraud. Look at my belly — it was he who made it this big." The Buddha's attitude was calm and composed, and he did not argue with her. The woman got more and more agitated, and finally took the wooden bowl from under her clothes and threw it down, which provoked a big laugh that filled the hall."

Sukhasiddhi said: "At that time, many religious factions all wanted to expel the Buddha from Sravasti, and they employed various strategies. One time they sent a prostitute called Sundari to where the Buddha was to hear him teach, and after a few days they killed the prostitute and buried her corpse in the Jetavana Monastery. Later, like a thief shouting 'Stop thief!' they created a big storm. For a time, the public sentiment of Shravasti was aroused and directed against the Buddha. But not long afterwards, an internal conflict started among the true evildoers because they could not share the spoils equally, and the truth finally emerged."

Sukhasiddhi said: "Spreading the truth has never been smooth sailing. It was in these conflicts with those misguided teachings that Buddhism won respect through the ages. At that time, it was not only attacks from outside parties that the Buddha faced; even more serious was the betrayal by the six groups of monks led by Devadatta and others." She pointed to the three large lakes and said: "Look, that is the place where Devadatta and his disciple Goshala and Cinca Manavika were trapped in hell. But ignorance always accompanies sentient beings, so after Devadatta was trapped in hell, he still had many people who followed him, and even now there are many ascetics who believe in the teachings of Devadatta. They call themselves Buddhists, but they only venerate the three Buddhas of the past, they do not venerate Sakyamuni Buddha."

Sukhasiddhi said: "Later on, disputes may arise among your disciples and within your lineage. You must not be upset by this. Error will always exist alongside truth, just as dark clouds will always float across the blue sky."

Sukhasiddhi again sang:

Above all do not forget your clear wisdom; that clear wisdom is the light of fundamental enlightenment.

That fundamental enlightenment is the empty inherent nature you see; there are also some people who call that empty inherent nature "true thusness."

The basic substance of true thusness is your true mind; though it is called "true mind," it is suchness that is as it is and does not move.

When your false mind stops, true mind appears, and then you merge into the empty sky of that fundamental enlightenment.

The light of that fundamental enlightenment has shapes and forms; the light of that fundamental enlightenment has no shape and no form.

The light of that fundamental enlightenment is impossible to express in words; the light of that fundamental enlightenment is born everywhere.

The myriad things come from the light of that fundamental enlightenment; the myriad things also end in the light of that fundamental enlightenment.

The myriad things are not apart from the inherent nature of that fundamental enlightenment; the myriad things do not abandon the illumination of that fundamental enlightenment.

That fundamental enlightenment is there in all times and all places; that fundamental enlightenment exists eternally, although few people know it.

This is because the dark clouds of ignorance cover the empty sky; this is because the age-old dark night covers the clear mirror.

When you light the candle of wisdom, there is no shadow and no trace of that age-old dark night.

When you dispel the clouds of affliction, that vast eternal empty sky is a single great expanse of blue.

When you see that all-encompassing heavenly light, that fundamental enlightenment becomes your bright lamp.

You observe its form at all times, and it illuminates your Path at all times.

Then you can be spontaneously liberated, then you merge with the Great Mudra of Light.

The basic substance of the Great Mudra is liberation, and that Great

Mudra likewise has its source in the inherent nature of mind.

It is not that, outside the inherent nature of mind, there is some other Great Mudra; it is not that, outside the inherent nature of mind, there is some other light.

It is not that, outside the inherent nature of mind, there is some other liberation; all the many myriad forms are all the offspring of the inherent nature of mind.

The basic substance of that inherent nature of mind is the light; the basic substance of the light is liberation.

The day when the light appears is the time when liberation is born.

The process of liberation does not depend on external seeking, nor is it a pair of hands untying the bonds for you.

That situation is very much like a snake at play: its body coils up and can also release itself.

When the light of your mind's inherent nature shines through and dispels the dark night, in the pure light of the Great Mudra, discriminating thought is obliterated.

When your eye of wisdom sees through empty falsity, that liberation is born then and there.

Though you give rise to thoughts, you do not follow them; though you see illusory forms, you do not cling to them.

Though you carry out all actions, there are absolutely no worries: you do them without doing, and nothing hangs you up.

Just like that colorful brush drawing shapes in empty space, you spontaneously manage to concentrate and control the six sense organs.

Although you have awakened to pure clarity in the here and now, in your mind, in the emptiness, there are no shadows or traces.

O child of wisdom, the light of the Great Mudra is shining brightly in your mind;

The flavor of fundamental enlightenment is boiling in your mind; they fill every pore, but without clinging to them and without abandoning them, you are happily intoxicated.

This, then, is the supreme flavor of the truth of liberation; its source is in the inherent light of your mind.

When you are like a mute who tastes the flavor and cannot describe it in words, this is clear wisdom and the Great Mudra.

Sukhasiddhi instructed me, saying: "Son, do you know what clear wisdom is? I'll tell you: what is called clear wisdom is the inherent nature of the light of the mind. The mind's basic substance is empty, and it has no independently existing fundamental essence. The basic substance of all the apparent forms experienced by the mind is also empty: they are there based on various kinds of causes and conditions. But this emptiness we speak of is not a dead and blind emptiness, or a nihilistic emptiness. It is a pure light, like crystal, shining like glass, fragrant as the mountain flowers, clear and pure as the sky. It has an inherent nature of endless infinite light, and contains within it surpassing wisdom, and it is overflowing with boundless clear wisdom. Under the observation of this clear wisdom, we can understand that originally there is no one-sided clinging or confusion, nor have there ever been all the afflictions we experienced before we realized enlightenment. Son, the mind I speak of is that true mind: it is not born and does not perish; it has no defilement or purity; it is not increased or diminished. It is the lamp of fundamental enlightenment.

"Son, above all you must remember that your level of perception is much more important than particular techniques. All religions have their own theoretical bases, and to establish them, there must be scriptural texts that they depend on. Do not 'trim the foot to fit the shoe,' and use the viewpoint of other sects to guide how you cultivate practice. We cannot say whether they are right or wrong, but remember, the compass that guides our actions is the level of perception of the Great Mudra. All your expedient methods must take the level of perception of the Great Mudra as the guide. As for the aspect of liberation, the level of perception has elements of a definitive character, and practitioners must be equipped with a mature level of perception, and must use this to match with the states of enlightenment obtained in cultivating meditation. I have pointed out to you the teaching of the Great Mudra, with a theory of mental states like this, and you certainly must apply it well and cultivate and uphold it. Your perception of the Great Mudra will merge into your life in a deeper way. When your theoretical knowledge and real cultivation of the Great Mudra combine together, you will be spontaneously liberated from those things that were originally seen by you as barriers, and they will dissolve themselves.

"Son, be sure to remember that all phenomena are nurtured by the inherent nature of your mind, and cannot become fetters for your soul. In the days to come, among the disciples to whom you transmit this bequest, there will be some who always put on the shoes of other sects and confine the feet of your teaching. All the conflicts will start from this. Even more to be feared is that, under the guidance of other theories, your disciples may lose the mind of faith. But this will not be important. When you genuinely bring the inherent nature of their minds to maturity, and they come to rely upon the light of the Great Mudra, only then will they be counted as having genuinely entered into accord with the Esoteric Vehicle. Then at last, their enlightened state will be as unshakable as the snowy mountains.

"Son, the knots in a rope need a person to untie them, but the coils of a snake can be released spontaneously and smoothly and skillfully. Right now, the majority of sentient beings are tied up by their dualistic discriminating minds, and all their bonds are created by their dualistic views. When they can enter into accord with the Great Mudra, then they can awaken to the fact that there is no difference between this dualism and the fundamental substance of their minds. At that point they will discover that their own minds have the same ability as the snake, and they will be able to liberate themselves from all that binds them. As long as you go along with the pure light here and now, and bathe in the light of the Great Mudra, your mind will not be deluded any more.

"The fully mature inherent nature of mind does not need any hardworking heroism — it is like the snake opening up its coils, so without expending any effort it can spontaneously be liberated.

"This is because, when you have transcended dualism, everywhere in the world is auspicious."

2 The Body of Truth That Is Never Extinguished

Under Sukhasiddhi's guidance, Khyungpo Naljor went on a pilgrimage to that famous monastery that is mentioned so often in the

Buddhist scriptures. The wilderness had already reclaimed that place, and it was very hard to make out its former brilliance. A deep sense of loss and listlessness filled Khyungpo Naljor's mind.

According to the accounts, at first the Jetavana Monastery was very majestic and had seven stories. The eminent Chinese monk Faxian in his *Record of the Buddhist Kingdoms* (c 400 CE) recorded this: "The Jetavana Monastery originally had seven stories, and kings and commoners joyously made offering there. It was hung with silk banners and strewn with flowers, and incense was burning and lamps were always shining bright, day after day without interruption." It was in this flourishing monastery that the Buddha related many famous sutras. But what happened to the monastery also testifies to a truth put forward by the Buddha: all compounded thing are impermanent. The monastery that was so glorious for a period of time ended up one day being burned to a ruin by a great fire. The cause was a stubborn little rat: it took a burning candle wick in its mouth to play with and ended up setting fire to a cloth banner in a shrine, and that developed into a great fire.

When Sukhasiddhi took Khyungpo Naljor on a pilgrimage there, there was nothing to be seen of the monastery's former glory. Only King Ashoka's stone pillars were still there. The stone pillar on the right displayed the shape of an ox head, and the pillar on the left showed a circular shape. Everything that had been donated by the Elder Sudatta had been washed away without a trace by the river of time. All that remained in the human realm was that ever-remembered, ever-new truth, still there to nourish the minds and spirits burning with affliction.

Sukhasiddhi said to Khyungpo Naljor: "People call the Buddha's teaching words 'the body of truth that is never extinguished,' and there is truth in this. Everything that is built in the world is eroded away by the hurricane of time, and will become a dim memory: only the truth exists forever. In the future, you may rely on wealth and power to build many teaching centers. Like this monastery, they may be brilliant for a time, but what will be left at the end will still be the wisdom of the teaching."

Khyungpo Naljor said: "I too know that all contrived things are ultimately impermanent, but without buildings to rely on, it will also be very hard for the teaching itself to survive for a long time. In Tibet there are many great adepts who live in the mountain caves and practice austerities their whole lives, and they may achieve the ultimate realization, but because their detachment goes too far, and they cut off contact with the world, they become people practising only for themselves. So sometimes religious forms are necessary. Sometimes, without forms, there is no content."

Sukhasiddhi said: "That's right. Sometimes the form is the content."

In its early period, Jetavana was very large, and within it there were many monastery buildings, like Kosambakuti Monastery. Because the Buddha often stayed here, it became a sacred site. The story goes that the Buddha traveled on the Path, so they built a platform as a memorial. On one side there was a stone room, and inside it there was an ancient statue: this was the only precious image of the Buddha left after that great fire. After the great fire, people were surprised and delighted to discover that the statue had survived intact, so they built a two-story tower for it. Several hundred years passed, and there was nothing left of the tower either, and there was only the statue still being venerated by people.

Sukhasiddhi said: "At that time Sakyamuni's teaching was able to win over people's minds very quickly, primarily because of its humanistic nature.There are many accounts like this left from

Shravasti. The king at that time, Prasenajit, loved to eat and suffered from morbid obesity, and so he was always in pain that was unbearable. The Buddha told him to restrain his eating and spoke a verse to him:

A person must be mindful of himself,
And every time he eats, know how to regulate the amount.
If he does this and always eats sparingly,
He will digest his food in peace and preserve his life.

"King Prasenajit instructed his attendant to constantly recite this verse, to admonish himself, and later he cured his obesity."

Sukhasiddhi said: "The goal of all the Buddha's teachings was to tell people to leave behind suffering and attain happiness, to put a stop to afflictions. The basic intent of Buddhism is Buddhism in human life, Buddhism in the human world. The later decline of Buddhism was because it became too abstruse and got away from the life of the common people."

3 The Enlightenment of a Devilish Murderer

After leaving the monastery, Khyungpo Naljor saw a stupa shaped like a grave mound, made of red brick. At the bottom there was a tunnel which led into the stupa. Sukhasiddhi said: "Look, this is the stupa of Angulimala." Khyungpo Naljor said: "Wasn't he that devilish murderer? Sukhasiddhi said: "That's right."

Angulimala is a famous devilish murderer in the Buddhist scriptures. This tunnel was where he hid out in those years. His whole life presents the story behind the saying "put down the killing knife and immediately become enlightened."

Sukhasiddhi said: "The name 'Angulimala' means 'good.' His father was a court official in the kingdom of Kosala. When he was twelve years old, he took a Brahman as his teacher and cultivated pure practices. One day his teacher went out, and the teacher's wife was the only one home. Seeing that the disciple was charming and handsome, she began to think lustful thoughts, and she approached him to entice him. The disciple looked upon his teacher as a father, and so of course he refused. The teacher's wife was so embarrassed she got angry. When the Brahman returned home, she said that the disciple had wanted to rape her. Burning with anger, the teacher thought of a poisonous plan. He said to the disciple: 'Don't you still want to complete the Path to enlightenment? I will tell you a secret method. You go kill people, and every time you kill a person, cut off his thumb and string it on a chain. When you have killed a thousand people, take this chain with the severed thumbs and hang it around your neck — then you can complete the Path.' With his deep belief in his teacher, the disciple did not doubt him. So day after day he went out and committed acts of violence, and at night he hid in the tunnel. He easily killed nine hundred and ninety-nine people. His mother could not bear to see this and admonished him to stop the killing and to do good. Instead, he brandished his knife at her. The mother fled outside, and the son pursued her. On the Path they encountered the Buddha. The Buddha showed him the true teaching, and Angulimala suddenly saw the error of his ways and awakened. He followed the Buddha and left home, and before long realized the Path and became an arhat."

"In the Buddhist Canon it is recorded that the Buddha spoke a verse to admonish Angulimala:

"Angulimala! A constant in my teachings is to stop using violence toward all sentient beings. If you fear sentient beings, the evil karma will not cease. I abide in the teaching of ceasing. Do not be lax in anything. You have not seen the Four Noble Truths, so you do not see yourself being lax.' By contemplating the Four Noble Truths, Angulimala finally experienced enlightenment.

"The story of Angulimala is rich in symbolic meaning. Not only is it the inspiration for the saying 'put down the killing knife and immediately become enlightened.' It also leads us to other considerations. Who knows how many teachers there are in life like that Brahman, who either deliberately or unwittingly pass along errors. Who knows how many good disciples they wrongly send down deviant Paths."

Sukhasiddhi also said: "In this world who knows how many blind men there are leading blind horses, who fall into deep pits and do not know how to save themselves." She pointed to the stupa and said: "Angulimala committed acts of violence here, he cultivated the Path here, he found enlightenment here, he became extinct here. The same man, the same place — but because his mind changed, his fate was totally and utterly transformed. Obviously, it all has its source in the inherent nature of mind. The practices of all the teachings emphasize the inherent nature of mind — remember this, remember this!"

Sukhasiddhi said: "It's just that in cultivating the inherent nature of mind, we cannot leave behind physical cultivation." She sang:

Though the bright mirror of your mind illuminates heaven and earth,
the mind's understanding still needs the body's help.

If you only understand mind, your body may become a barrier for you.

Haven't you seen that there are many people who, although they understand mind, get frightened and lose control when things happen to them.

This is because, although the body is a great treasure for cultivating the Path, great suffering can also come from this body.

If you cultivate only the mind, it is very hard to reach the ultimate—you also certainly must cultivate the energy channels and the points of light

You must constantly visualize those three channels and six chakras, and rely on the power of mantras to open up those chakra knots.

Those entangled knots in the channels are in fact afflictions; only when the mind is liberated and the channels are open can the light shine clearly.

If your channels have no life force, if they are like a tangled strands,

They will obstruct the light of the mind, and your mind's enlightenment will not be complete.

This is why the true practitioner cultivates both mind and body; only when the mind and the energy are independent is considered ultimate enlightenment.

O wise Khyungpo Ba, though you have the level of perception of the Great Mudra,

You still need to provide your energy channels with life force.

If you rely on the wondrous teaching of the bliss of emptiness, above all do not forget to preserve your enlightenment.

That enlightenment has two kinds: this-worldly and transcendent; you must not casually lose either of these.

When your mind has realized enlightenment, when you have truly cleansed away the barriers,

Then you will enter the secret sky, and there will be dakinis to help you consummate the Path.

You must chant "Niguma Khyenno" often: she is the source adding power to your wisdom.

Her merits and virtues are beyond compare, and her essential nature is itself enlightenment.

Sukhasiddhi said: "Son, in the future you must continue to search for Niguma and find the *Five Great Diamonds Teachings of Niguma*. In it there are many expedient skillful methods to train the practitioner's energy channels. Many times the mind's enlightenment still requires the help of the energy channels. When your channels are filled with entanglements, your body can block the bright emptiness of your mind. Son, make use of these expedient methods—they can enable you to make better use of those internal subtle bodies and purify the negative energy channels. All of this will increase your clear emptiness.

"Your precious jewel in the gate of language is the essence of the energy, and it is also called the chakra of wisdom. When the chakras in the energy channels are stimulated, the great bliss of fundamental enlightenment will arise. Son, remember well, that no matter what the cost, you must certainly do all you can to preserve your mind of enlightenment.

"You must be like a king and, from a calm and relaxed mind,

spontaneously manifest the virtues of your line. You must be like a warrior, relying on movement and posture to regulate your energy channels."

Sukhasiddhi also said: "When great bliss dissolves away the various bonds in your mind, for some it will depend on people, for some it will be achieved with the help of the secret wondrous teachings.

"In the future, I will help you consummate the Path of enlightenment."

4 Sharwadi Speaks

Khyung, my love, you should go with me!

Recently, a demon always appears in my dreams with all sorts of chicken feathers and ox horns stuck in its head, and I am very exhausted.

The demons of sickness and pain are also constantly wreaking havoc, making it impossible for me to sleep through the night.

If I could control the clouds, I would make them turn into likenesses of you and float in the sky in the most conspicuous places, so I could see them at a glance.

Husband, at this moment, where are you going? You are like a breeze whispering to me to go to sleep. Are you hidden?

Just come back, won't you, and give me your knowing eyes, and your lively smile, and the sound of those heavy footsteps.

Autumn has gotten chilly. I have truly become a longing plant that is always indoors, and day by day I am getting more haggard. Won't you come visit me, my beloved? Surely you can bear to let me grow old for you in the autumn wind?

At home it is so busy and noisy, but I am annoyed to death.

Those faces full of warm feelings make me feel strange and weary. There are always people being so polite and attentive, but I dislike it very much. I don't even want to go to my father's room, for fear I will see all those eyes I cannot stand.

I am still depressed, so depressed it makes me nervous. When will that refreshing shadow finally be able to return?

There are many things I don't know how to say: it's just that on such a gloomy night, I truly miss you!

I often think of drinking with you a cup of turbid wine infused with chrysanthemum and archaic swords, and to lie down drunk in the wind and rain and listen to a wondrous tune. I want to walk hand in hand with you, carefree in the dusty world, happy faces laughing and talking, looking at each other fondly as we grow old. But, my sunshine, do I dare throw everything to the autumn wind and go off toward you? Let them turn any way, I don't care, but I do care about your eyes flying in the wind. In the end, whose dream is it in?

The sky is bleak, cloudy and cold, with no moon to be seen. In my mind I add layers of autumn clouds and gloomy mists. I wait for the sun I can love to rise, but there is still something of a distance. This night without moon and sun—won't there have to be a continuous autumn rain?

It is like having a perpetual dream I cannot wake up from. I drag my mind into the dream, and so I am perpetually the prisoner of the dream.

The sun approaches in the colored clouds; heaven and earth become cool and pure; the wind cannot bear to stay in isolation, and ends up crying.

The wind is not the charming woman. It cannot be endlessly fascinating just because it can influence the nerves of myriad beings.

... My love, the weather this afternoon is still gloomy, and when I woke up from my midday nap, what I saw when I raised my eyes to look were the dense leaden clouds pressing down on the window. My feelings are even more distraught and unbearable. During these listless days, how should I go on? How should I repair these ruined feelings? Everything is so agitated, like the stink from a sewer, like wandering in a nightmare.

Opening the door, I leave this suffocating place, and I slowly walk along that none-too-clean horse path. I want to go into the depths of the backstreets and release these gloomy feelings. But I don't know what for, my mind aches, I am very sad. This is a feeling of hopelessness, with no way to pull back. I don't know how to be candid to the wind by my side ...

When will the fortunate female spirit finally visit me? Every minute, every second, I am waiting for her to show her appreciation. I discover that I am quickly getting old. The pinkness has already disappeared from my face.

The rain is beginning to fall from the gloomy sky, and the tears are pouring down my face in a torrent. My hands have no strength, and they cannot grasp the wind and rain. In this lonely season, the sun will not lift up a sad woman.

... I just took some medicine, and I lay down on a little bed in the alcove to close my eyes and nurture my spirit.

Suddenly I felt a completely new pure wakefulness rush at me. I understood clearly the many feelings of this wind. So then I pulled open the window screen, and leaned out the window, and bathed this spiritual nature given to me by Nature. A wind slowly arrived and carefully wrapped around me and took firm hold of me. At this, I took the melancholy tune played by the sickness and the longing, pulled my distant eyes away, and banished it far away ...

In the small courtyard, the colored flowers were being pulled with the vines swaying in the wind. My father with his white hair was there in the courtyard, now standing still, now moving. Later, he would turn around from time to time and look at me and smile and call out, "Sharwadi! Sharwadi!" I smiled at my father, and I felt very grief-stricken. My father has gotten old. He is already doddering, but for the sake of his so-called mission, he still hurries around in all directions in the wind and the rain.

Yesterday was my father's rejuvenation day, and at our home a lively celebration went on. Many people came: some officials, some disciples. Nepalese think that seventy-seven is the maximum age for a person, and when a person lives until the seventh hour of the seventh day of the seventh month of his seventy-seventh year, the first lifetime is over. What begins after this is another new life. Then the family members not only must treat the old person as an old person, they must also cherish him or her like a baby. On this day, I ought to have been happy, but I was crying. You of course do not know this, but a Nepali woman's average lifespan is less than forty years. Though my father has lived to an advanced age, this does not guarantee that his daughter will be able to wait for her far-off husband.

You certainly have the look of someone who will live a long life, but I have discovered that many illnesses have begun to attack me.

I thought again of how I am waiting, and it is still like the sadness of me being in exile and not knowing where to go. What security will I be able to give to my aged parents? I feel a bit of selfishness, or maybe sadness. Why must I be like that lotus flower growing in a quiet place with nobody to appreciate it, wasted in its glorious springtime, silent and unknown?

The sounds of the sorcerers chanting their spells and shaking their dog skins are still ringing in my ears. These evil sounds are everywhere all the time. I am already saturated with them.

I sent someone to look for that dakini Bandi who is skilled in removing evils, but she has not yet returned from abroad.

I lie in my sickbed writing you a letter — I don't know whether or not this counts as a letter. Maybe it is just me talking to myself, like those helpless old ladies praying to the god Brahma, no longer caring whether or not Brahma can really hear them.

I do not know where my spirit dove lost its way. Maybe, like you, it already forgot that on the far horizon, there is a woman whose hopeful eyes wish they could see all the way to you, a woman who is suffering in expectation.

5 The Power of Correct Faith and Wisdom

Khyungpo Naljor said that he was always hearing that sound of the dog skins being shaken. He was often getting sick, and from time to time he would fall seriously ill. He would feel faint, and a mass of red energy would rush at him: in it there would be a female demon, opening her great mouth, sucking away his energy.

That journey seemed exceptionally difficult.

However, his trip to Sravasti had left a very deep impression on Khyungpo Naljor's mind. Here was recorded the Buddha's initial glory and difficulties. Besides the great contributions of King Prasenajit and the Elder Sudatta, there is also a record left of the ups and downs experienced in the course of spreading the true teaching. The Buddha's opponents thought of all sorts of strategies to seize territory. They waited for an opportunity, and one day when King Prasenajit was meeting with the Buddha, they incited Prince Virudhaka to launch a coup. King Prasenajit left the palace to rally the troops and died on the road.

Sukhasiddhi said by way of introduction: "Prince Virudhaka was originally a nephew of the royal family of the Sakya kingdom. After the death of the Buddha's father, King Suddhodana, the Sakya royal family hoped that Sakyamuni Buddha would choose to assume the throne and become his successor, but the Buddha told them: "A person who has left home to become a monk does not take charge of worldly affairs, and it's all up to you to decide." The chief ministers then chose Mahanama to become the king.

"Mahanama had a daughter, a princess who was extremely beautiful. The princess had a maid servant who came from the lowly Shudra people, and she was as beautiful as the princess. When the two women put on the same finery, it was very hard for people who did not know them well to distinguish their status. Mahanama would often have the two women dress alike. He would call upon guests to distinguish which one was the princess and afterwards have a big laugh.

"One day the king of the Kosamila kingdom came to seek a marriage alliance with the Sakya clan. He hoped to be able to take the princess as his wife. Mahanama could not part with this daughter, so he passed the maid servant off as the princess and married her to the king. The king of Kosamila did not know the true state of affairs, and thought he had married the princess. He was very much in love with her, and later they had a child: this was Prince Virudhaka.

"One day Prince Virudhaka went to the Sakya kingdom for a visit and happened upon a ceremony in the hall where the Buddha expounded the scriptures. Prince Virudhaka went in and was fooling around, and when one of the high officials saw this, he got angry and rebuked him saying: 'Get out of here, you son of a low-caste mother. How dare you come here!' Many noblemen also scolded the prince. Thus the prince came to know the true circumstances of his birth. He was infuriated, and vowed that if he became king in the future, he would wipe out the Sakya clan.

"After Prince Virudhaka rose to the position of king, in order to wipe clean the shame of his birth, he sent an army to invade the realm of the Sakya clan. Three times the Buddha blocked them on the road, but because the force of karma is hard to turn back, the Sakya clan was finally drowned in blood."

Sukhasiddhi said: "During the period when the Buddha was traveling around teaching, King Prasenajit and King Bimbisara both came to tragic ends because of coups. Later on, some short-sighted scholars used these incidents as classic examples to slander Buddhism. In their opinion, since those who protected Buddhism met with a bad fate, talk of the merit of Buddhism is false."

Just as noble people in the world will often be judged by petty people, a religion of true faith can sometimes fall to a low ebb, and great practitioners with correct views will often be squeezed out by petty people. This is very typical. There is a rule in economics: bad coin drives out good coin. When bad coins that contain only ten percent gold enter the marketplace, people will all take their good coins, store them away in their homes, and use the bad coins at hand to put into circulation. After a time, the market will be captured by the bad coins. When many truly noble people preserve their integrity and keep a low profile and cultivate pure practices, the space left open will be occupied by petty people. As time goes by, the petty people will put their Path into widespread practice, and it will be hard for the noble people to carry on.

This is even more true because noble people have a baseline for human conduct, and they understand there are things to do and things not to do; whereas there is nothing petty people will not do. Petty people often unscrupulously frame noble people. Therefore, many times noble people are pushed aside by petty people, and may even suffer temporary defeat or disgrace. But time is just, and ultimately the true is itself true and the false is itself false. Great beauty does not have to be spoken of, and great ugliness reveals itself. When the snow melts, the corpse buried in the snow will come to light.

Thus, during the time when Sakyamuni Buddha was teaching, his opponents used all their ingenuity to monopolize the religious marketplace: some made false accusations, some secretly plotted to kill him, some concocted slanderous rumors … They employed all the dirty tricks they could think of, but the Buddhism of true faith preserved its integrity and strictly regulated itself, and in the end, the light of truth was still transmitted to the world.

There were many times when the petty people could prevail for a while, because of the contemptible baseness of the base ones and the perverse evil of the evil ones. But with the dissolving of their physical bodies, with the great waves of time sweeping away the sand, true faith and wisdom in the end produced an incomparable power. This point is matched by the lines in a famous poem by the poet Bei Dao: "Baseness is the passport of the base ones. Nobility is the epitaph of the noble ones."

King Prasenajit and King Bimbisara still live on in this world because of the Buddhist scriptures, and because their good deeds have won them respect down through the ages, whereas those who relied on violence and plotting were prominent for a time, but have already become a pile of dog crap that nobody mentions.

Chapter 22

A Distant Holy Song

1　The Dharma Rules for Positive Action

To enable me to draw nourishment from Indian religion, Sukhasiddhi brought me to a temple. All year round at that temple there were people singing an ancient ballad that was in circulation in India at that time. That song had an enormous influence on my later life, and I hope it will also be able to influence you.

In that temple, an old man sang like this:

If you do not join in certain kinds of work, it will be hard to achieve the merit of uncontrived action.

If you only rely on renunciation, it will be very hard to achieve success.

No matter who you are, if you completely stop, then you will not be able to maintain uncontrived action for an instant.

The reason why people act and cannot be autonomous is that they are still being driven by the three qualities of inherent nature.

Although the karmic results of your conduct is under control, your mind is still revolving around in the sense organs and sense objects.

Thus you become a basically ignorant person who can only be called a hypocrite.

When I heard the words of this song, I was very surprised. This was because, in the religious truth as I had understood it, they mostly advocate no action, whereas the song was encouraging people to go actively do things. Sukhasiddhi gave me this introduction: "What that old man was singing is the *Bhagavad Gita*, and it comes from a famous Indian historical poem, the *Mahabharata* . Later on many scholars annotated and interpreted this book, and this book became an important scripture for Brahmanism. What the man is singing is the yoga of action, among the four yogas mentioned in the *Bhagavad Gita*. Brahmanism considers that in society, every social individual must fulfill a corresponding social duty, and follow the corresponding guidelines for living. This is the 'Dharma.' Some people translate this as 'action' or 'law' —the word 'Dharma' has many implications. It can be understood as the ultimate rules and as the truth, as the laws for a country and its people, as the mission or destiny of an individual person, and so on. Brahmanism requires that every person must fulfill the mission which that person has to fulfill, and must do things in complete accordance with the demands of the rules. They must go beyond utilitarian notions, and not calculate the later results, not calculate gain and loss. Only if you truly realize your own human life and complete the mission you must complete — only then does your life have meaning, only then, after you die, can you attain true liberation."

The old man sang:

If you understand the mission of your own Dharma, then you must not hesitate indecisively and have misgivings.

Because this war accords with the rules of the Dharma, there is no better action for a warrior.

These warriors are truly fortunate; warfare is the great gate to heaven.

If you do not take part in this great war, if you abandon this war which is in accord with the rules of the Dharma,

Sin and evil will be born from this, and then, because you have failed in your duty, you will lose your good name.

Sukhasiddhi said: "Listen, in this song they are actually urging people to take part in a war, because that war is in accord with the rules of the Dharma. That religious doctrine considers that the rules of the Dharma are higher than anything else, and definitely must be actively carried out. Comparing this to the traditional religious ideas, this kind of teaching marks an epoch. This is because traditional Indian religion holds that what blocks human liberation is the power of karma, and the power of karma is the force reacting to actions; if there is action, then there will be the power of karma. If there is good karma, there will be good results, and if there is bad karma, there will be bad results. Good results mean ascending to heaven; bad results mean going to hell. But even with the best karmic results, going to heaven, the person is still revolving in birth and death in the six ways of existence, and there is no liberation. Thus, the traditional religions of India require people to eliminate the karmic results of past lifetimes and, at the same time, require them to get to the level where there is no action, so they do not create new karma. People must continually renounce the life of the self and the external world, and only then can they reach final liberation. This is why in India there appeared many ascetic monks who left ordinary life and lived in solitude. They abandoned knowledge and desires, mortified the flesh and extinguished the intellect, expecting to find liberation.

"But the *Bhagavad Gita* took a clear stand in opposing passive inaction and advocating positive action. It demanded that people must realize the value of their own human lives to the fullest extent possible, under the direction of the Dharma. Thus, in later Indian religion, there appeared many great teachers who opposed the traditional avoidance of the world and advocated positive engagement in the world, so in the end, they would become great personages who influenced the forward progress of human civilization."

The old man was still singing:

If there are people who use the true inherent nature to control their sense organs, and rely on their karmic roots to really practice yoga,

But they have not a trace of clinging or attachment or concerns, they, Arjuna, are the holy sages.

You must know that action is better than non-action, so you certainly must work hard and act.

Your mission is to do the things you ought to do, but do not be concerned with the results of your deeds.

You must not let the concern for gain become your motive force, and you must not cling to non-action and become passive.

If you practice yoga with pure faith, and also clear away clinging and attachment, then you must fulfill your duty.

You must regard success and defeat as one; when you look at success and defeat with equanimity, this finally is what you call yoga.

Therefore, do not have any clingings or attachments, and never lose the strength of your actions.

A person who focuses on action and has no clingings or attachments finally can reach the highest realm.

Sukhasiddhisaid: "The words of this song were an encouragement to Arjuna by the god Krishna. Their meaning was to call on him to leap out of the discriminating mind of good and evil, and to go fulfill his destiny without calculations of glory or later results. In other words, they were telling him to use the mind that transcends the world to carry out tasks in the world."

The old man continued singing:

If you work hard in action, and your mind has no concerns or obstructions, when you have no self and objects and no self-conceit,

Then all desires will leave you, and you can attain equanimity and peace.

This is the world of the Brahma heaven, and when you reach this world there is no darkness.

If you can rest peacefully in this realm, when your life ends you can have pure nirvana.

I was very surprised by this teaching. I thought: "Brahmanism was truly a great religion, and no wonder it has flourished for centuries without declining." Later, I investigated its teachings and theories seriously, and discovered that it really had something special. Buddhist philosophy takes transcending the world as a basic principle. Though there is something especially excellent in this, hasn't this also been a limitation on its development? In Indian religion, the worldly and the world-transcending are both emphasized, and one is not emphasized at the expense of the other. It takes religion and human life and joins them together, and has influenced the lives of the people of India. When the *Bhagavad Gita* appeared, it made Brahmanism flourish again and revealed a revolutionary new page.

Sukhasiddhi told me: "In the *Bhagavad Gita* they divide yoga into four categories: the yoga of karma, the yoga of wisdom, the yoga of faith, and the royal yoga. Each kind of yoga has its own particular emphasis. For the yoga of karma, working hard to do things; for the yoga of wisdom, becoming knowledgeable and seeking the Path; for the yoga of faith, sincere devotion without doubts; for the royal yoga, concentrating on sincerity and making spiritual progress. Among the four kinds of yoga, the yoga of karma has a ground-breaking significance. In the traditional religious teachings of India, whenever there is 'karma,' there must be the results of karma. Thus, for liberation, first one must clear away the results of karma from previous lifetimes, and second, one must not create any new karma. In the course of life one should continuously abandon the self and abandon external objects, and with the mind of non-action, realize the final unity with Brahma. But in the *Bhagavad Gita,* it changes from the idea of 'non-action' in the traditional religious teaching, and emphasizes action, working hard to do things. Thus the yoga of karma is also called the yoga of conduct or the yoga of action."

Still, if we look at it from the point of view of reality, the most ultimate truth is still Buddhism.

The fact that, later on, I did not retreat from the world to practice, and had more than a hundred thousand disciples, perhaps has its origin in the inspiration given to me by this kind of wisdom.

2 The Wisdom that Awakens to the Fundamental Source

More and more people came to visit the temple, and they all came to hear the *Gita*, and it was clear that people all greatly respected the man who chanted the *Bhagavad Gita* . The many voices all faded away, and there was just the pure holy sound floating in the air:

Those wise people had great wisdom, and entirely abandoned the results of karma.

They cut the bonds of life, and acted so there were no disasters or difficulties.

Compared to those evildoers, your evil deeds truly tower to the heavens.

Because of this, only if you rely on the ship of wisdom, can you cross over that great ocean of evil deeds.

Arjuna, just as those blazing flames can burn up a pile of firewood,

You must rely on the flame of wisdom: only then will you burn away all your karma to nothing.

Because among all the methods of purification in this world, there is nothing that can compare with wisdom,

Only people who rely on knowledge and reach completeness will be able to purify themselves and make themselves completely good.

People who rely on the power of faith to help their basic faculties and realize wisdom and single-minded devotion,

When wisdom approaches, will immediately experience supreme peace ...

If we rely on yoga and give up our contrived actions, and we use wisdom to cut off the root of doubt and confusion,

The self ends up mastering the self, and no karma can bind it.

Doubts and worries are born from ignorance and lodge in the mind; only by using the sword of wisdom can we cut through ignorance.

Bharata, when you have slain ignorance, then you will cultivate yoga with a focused mind and intent ...

Sukhasiddhi explained: "He is singing of the yoga of wisdom. This wisdom is not the kind of knowledge we talk about; rather, it is the wisdom that can awaken to the fundamental source. The *Upanishads* consider that the root source of the sufferings and the difficulties and the downfall of the human race is ignorance. It is precisely because they have this ignorance, and are ignorant of it, that leads to mistakes in their actions. Only by going through the process of cultivating the yoga of wisdom can practitioners go beyond revolving in birth and death and arrive at the union of Brahman and the self."

I asked: "Ultimately, what is this Brahman they talk about?"

Sukhasiddhi said: "The basic meaning is the power of mantras and prayer. The meaning is that through prayer we can gain a kind of mystic power, and we can reach the basic source of the world, the reality of god and the myriad events and things. Brahman transcends all forms, it has no shape or form. It is 'this shore' and it is also 'the other shore.' It is the original motive power of the secular and sacred worlds. Brahman is the absolute spirit behind the myriad phenomena of the universe, and also the basic source of all the gods. The physical world is a manifestation of Brahman."

I asked: "Isn't the ultimate Brahman what Buddhism calls the empty inherent nature? Isn't their idea of the union of Brahman and the self what Buddhism calls awakening to the empty inherent nature?"

Sukhasiddhi shook her head and said: "On the surface, the two seem to have similarities, but they think that Brahman is a spiritual self, where as Buddhism only accepts that all compound things are impermanent and all phenomena have no self."

That old man's voice singing rose in intensity:

The self can only be saved by the self: the self definitely cannot be dispirited and lose heart.

The self is the self's friend, and the self is also the self's enemy.

If the self can master the self, then the self is the self's friend.

If the self cannot master the self, then the self becomes the enemy.

Once we overcome the emotions of the self, our mental state will be quiet and peaceful,

And the supreme self can look with equanimity upon glory and disgrace, cold and hot, disaster and good fortune ...

Sukhasiddhi said: "Listen, in what he just sang, there are two selves. One of them is the petty self, the other is the great self, that is, the pure self, the self that is Brahman. Only if we can control the petty self and fuse with the self that is Brahman, can we speak of reaching liberation. The liberation they speak of is reaching the point where Brahman and the self merge into one, where we have the same essence as Brahman, the realm of the spiritual self that is merged with the myriad forms of being. Listen to the following content."

This spiritual life and action of mine—anyone who truly understands will agree.

After discarding the physical shell and transcending the cycle of birth and death, anyone is at one with me.

People who have left behind emotional love and hate and fear pray for my protection and focus their attention on me.

*They rely on wisdom and ascetic practice and achieve purification, and
after that they can enter my realm of wisdom.*

*I have included all spirits and transcended the myriad forms of being,
and I have encompassed sacrifices and other rituals.*

*That yoga master of mine who accords with all minds — even when my
life ends will still share the same essence with me.*

Sukhasiddhi said: "The yoga of wisdom, which is explained
above, has some similarity with the Buddhist practice of meditative
concentration. It starts with harmonizing the breath and maintaining
mindfulness, and finishes with stilling thoughts and maintaining
equanimity, and finally reaches the realm of samadhi. Its process
mostly depends on deep meditation. In Brahmanism, the yoga of action
and the yoga of wisdom are not rigidly divided; rather, they intermingle
and often blend."

3 The Four Stages of Human Life in Brahmanism

I asked: "In Buddhism they also have the yoga of action and the
yoga of wisdom. For example, for beginning students, detaching from
evil and striving for good is no doubt a sort of yoga of action; on the
other hand, the yoga of wisdom is more a skill of Buddhist cultivation.
So then, why does the life force of Buddhism in Nepal and India not
compare to Brahmanism?"

Sukhasiddhi said: "There are many reasons, and it is impossible
to explain them all in a few words. However, I think that one of the
reasons is a certain cultural tradition of Brahmanism. In the life of a

Brahmanist, there are generally four stages:

"The first stage in the life of a Brahmanist is the period of pure practice; that is, the stage of studying the religious scriptures and religious theories. The main task for this stage is to study various kinds of religious rites and the Vedic texts.

"The second stage in the life of a Brahmanist is the period of living as a householder. One must get married, have children, undertake ordinary worldly duties. Brahmanists think that although individual liberation is most important, if a person does not leave descendants, and the person cannot make sacrifices to the ancestors regularly, this is immoral. Though during the period when they live as householders with families, they cannot avoid worldly actions, the Brahmanist rules prescribe many ritual forms that must be followed. According to the traditional Indian explanation, in every person's home there are five places where it is easy to commit sins. Because it is easy to kill living beings in these places, they are called the five killing zones: they are the stove, the grindstone, the broom, the water bucket, the mortar and pestle. To eliminate the sins which might be caused by using the five killing zones, the Brahmanist every day must perform five daily sacrifices. The sacrifices to Brahma are studying the scriptures and teaching people; the offerings given to the ancestors are food and water; the offerings given to the gods are burnt offerings of food; the offerings to the good spirits and the evil spirits are various kinds of Pali offerings; the offerings to humans are the good wishes extended to guests. In this way they combine daily life and religious rituals into one. Thus, the Brahmanist religious rites have permeated people's daily lives, and this is one of the basic reasons why the vitality of Brahmanism is so strong.

"The third stage in the life of a Brahmanist is the period of dwelling in the forest, that is, the period of living in seclusion. When a Brahmanist discovers his hair turning white and his face getting wrinkled, and he has raised his grandchildren, he can conclude the period of living at home with the family and enter the period of living in seclusion. At this time he must abandon all the desires of ordinary worldly life, and no longer partake of the prosperous life. He will entrust his wife to his son to take care of, or simply bring his wife with him into the forest. He abandons all worldly implements, and all he keeps with him are ritual implements and things used in religion. He cannot accept offerings, and he must wear animal skins or rags. In his daily life, apart from continuing to carry out the five great offerings as before, he also has to recite the scriptures, nourish the mind of compassion, carry out various kinds of meditation training, and so on.

"The fourth stage in the life of a Brahmanist is the period of withdrawing from the world, the stage of being a holy monk who is a wandering beggar. After a Brahmanist in the period of seclusion has completed the many forms of training, and has genuinely gone beyond the conventional world, he no longer carries out those formalistic sacrifices and rituals. At this point, he can put out all those sacred fires that have visible form, because the true sacred fire is already planted in his mind. He does not read the scriptures any more either, because the scriptural texts have likewise already merged with his life. He has already cast off the last bonds of the conventional world and is approaching liberation. At this point, he must rely on deep meditation for everything. He can move through the world in solitude like a wandering cloud. He no longer clings to a forest retreat: every tree is a hut where he can rest his body. He has abandoned the myriad forms, and he has no more craving for life, nor fear of death. It is as if he is waiting for the agreement of fate: he calmly awaits the inevitable. Relying on the cultivation of wisdom, he can recognize the eternal original substance of things, and he can comprehend his own original face. Any attachment to the sensory world has already been transformed into an attachment to Brahman, and gradually he becomes one with Brahman."

4 The Final Devotion

From Brahmanism's four stages of human life, I discovered where the basic reason lay for its strong vital force. They use the period of pure practice to cultivate a great deal of religious talent, and the period of living as householders also solves the problem of producing successors. That tradition of relying on family succession has a more long-lasting vital force. Besides this, Brahmanism takes religious rituals and integrates them into daily life. In this way, Brahmanism has been a living religion all along. It has continuously won a large number of believers, and even when the upper-level intelligentsia believed more in Buddhism, the ordinary common people still made the many rituals of Brahmanism an important part of their own daily lives. This is because, though the elite in a religion may pursue liberation, the ordinary believers hope to get protection and help from supernatural powers. This is why, beginning in the fourth century of the Common Era, there appeared in India a strong wave of devotionalism, and its theoretical bedrock was devotional yoga.

Listen to what that old man was singing:

(These are the words of the god Krishna speaking to Arjuna in the *Bhagavad Gita*)

You must always cultivate yoga and your focus on me varies, in order to reach the highest supreme faith and generate pure faith.

Only if you act this way, in my eyes, can you be called a practitioner of the highest yoga.

Some people see me as the ultimate meaning, and rely on yoga to meditate on me.

They make offerings to me of many actions, and with pure faith sincerely make offerings to me.

They take their minds and focus on my body, and I become their savior.

I will take those people of pure faith and pull them out of the ocean of revolving in birth and death.

O you who control the six sense organs and have pure faith in me, take your wisdom and offer it to me.

You will forever merge into me — do not have the slightest doubt about this ...

5 In the Peaceful Realm of Samadhi

The voice of that old man was still coming through faintly with the words of the *Bhagavad Gita*, where the god Krishna says to Arjuna:

If you cannot have pure faith in me, you should keep on cultivating the yoga of sincere faith.

Through cultivating yoga again and again, you will be able to get my protection.

If you have no way to proceed with cultivation, then devote yourself to doing actions that benefit me.

After you have done many such things, you may attain the complete achievement.

If you still have no way to do things, you must depend on my miraculous power.

You must strictly control the self, and abandon all the painful results of the various kinds of karma ...

Even if they are Vaishyas or Shudras or low-ranking people or women,

If only they pray to me, they can get the ultimate gain.

How much the more so for those high-ranking Brahmins, for kings and devout immortals.

Since you have come to this painful world, you must have matchless devotion to me.

Concentrate and pray! Make offerings to me!Have pure faith in me! Pay homage to me!

You should look upon me as the highest refuge — then you will be able to become one with me.

Sukhasiddhi said: "The yoga of sincere belief is the part of Brahmanism that has the most religious quality. You are justified because you have faith, and without faith you have nothing. Later devotionalist sects took this as the most important content of cultivating practice. It must go through three stages: the first is worship of external deities, like worshipping Brahma, or Shiva, or Mahakala, worshipping at all the spirit temples and sacred places, and so on. Later, this external worship is gradually internalized — that is, praying to the gods in the depths of one's mind, silently reciting the god's name, chanting sacred hymns praising the spirits, and so forth. The third stage is when form and spirit merge, and the person praying is spiritualized, and cultivates yoga, and awakens to the Atman, the true self that exists within, and reaches the stage of perfection where Brahman and the self merge into one."

Sukhasiddhi said: "Sincere faith is the soul of all religions. This is because with sincere faith a person can reach the perfect human quality — that is the ultimate goal of religious action. Listen, listen seriously to what is in the old man's song below."

He treats all living beings compassionately, his life is compassion and sympathy.

He is not arrogant, he cannot just love himself.

No matter whether they are good or bad, he cannot insult his fellow beings,

And he cannot become angry with them.

He has gotten rid of anger, gone far beyond anxiety and fear —
I fervently love this kind of person!

No matter whether they are enemies or friends, he views them all with compassion.

With the mind of equanimity, he accepts praise and insults; with the same calm, he faces cold and hot, suffering and happiness.

He is far beyond desire, and peacefully observes slander and praise.

In the quiet realm of samadhi, he transcends the eight winds of the world ...

6 The Radiance of the Spiritual Nature

The old man's voice was filled with ups and down, very much like performers in Tibet who sing the *Epic of King Gesar* . I greatly enjoy hearing them play their stringed instruments and sing. The story goes that many of these performers have encountered miraculous events, and they all claim to have received bequests from the spirits. Although many times I too have encountered miraculous events, I understand that miraculous events have no relation to wisdom, and have even less to do with people's moral character. There are many demons whose spiritual powers are vast, but those spiritual powers of theirs usually become a means to injure people.

Sukhasiddhi told me that there are three great guiding principles in the teachings of Brahmanism: the revelations in the Vedas, the power of ritual sacrifices, and the supremacy of Brahman. All these three act to nurture people's roots of faith. Faith is the mother of merit, and without faith, there is no religion. I was moved by the radiance of the spiritual nature emanating from the body of that old man.

Because of your noble nature that does not like to quibble, I am willing to explain the highest secret to you.

If you understand this wisdom and learning, then you can get beyond the deep abyss of wrongdoing.

It is the secret of secrets, the king of wisdom; it is very holy and beyond compare.

But it also understands the ordinary world and follows the rules; it is easy to accept and uphold and it never changes.

People who do not believe in these rules cannot achieve unity with me;

They will enter into the cycle of birth and death and repeatedly tread the Path to death's disasters.

Sukhasiddhi said: "This is the royal yoga which they teach. Among the four yogas, it is the highest yoga. It puts particular emphasis on the inner life of the spirit, on the transformation and control of the deep level of consciousness. Among the four yogas, the yoga of action regulates correct action for humans, and it requires active progress and does not permit lazy passivity. The yoga of sincere faith emphasizes the power of faith and devotion and is the source of a great part of the power of the believers; only through faith can they achieve spiritual peace. The yoga of wisdom makes the cultivation of wisdom the main thing and usually takes meditative concentration as the main form of cultivation. But this royal yoga is the highest and most profound; it goes straight to the inner content of the spirit and emphasizes the inner life. Its main goal is to transform the deep-level consciousness. Its position is similar to that of the Great Mudra in the esoteric teaching of Buddhism."

The practitioner of yoga, going far beyond desires, must definitely control the mind's nature and the self.

Living in solitude in a quiet place, the mind and spirit are always unified with me.

Spread out the meditation mat in a pure clean place; it must not be too high or too low.

Cushion it with soft valley grass, and cover it with a piece of cloth and with leather.

Sit upright on the mat and pacify your six senses, regulate the restlessness of your conceptual consciousness.

Focus your mind and spirit on a single point and diligently cultivate yoga to purify your mind.

Sukhasiddhi said: "Because the human mind is restless and not at peace, false thoughts flying around in confusion constrain the soul's self-mastery and sublime quality. Restless false thoughts are always obstructing the development of the soul's latent ability and the soul's potential to reach the sublime. This is why it is necessary to go through such methods as practising asceticism, restricting desires, developing forbearance, and achieving meditative concentration, to reach the goal of mastering the mind."

The neck and torso must be upright and straight, as peaceful as a mountain, and must not waver;

Rest your attention on the tip of your nose, and do not look around in all directions.

Your mind and spirit should be peaceful and quiet and unafraid; hold firmly to your vow of holy practice and do not abandon it.

As you practice the yoga of controlling the mind, think always of me, sit upright and think of me as the ultimate of human life.

O yogi who practices and upholds yoga, you must control your mind and consciousness and pacify your thoughts.

Maintain it so that it is always in accord with me: only then will you be able to reach the other shore that is peaceful and still ...

Sukhasiddhi said: "Although Brahmanism's four kinds of yoga differ in form, and each has its particular emphasis, for them, I am in you and you are in me and we are fused together, completing each other. Their ultimate aim is always to reach the union of Brahman and the self, and to attain the ultimate liberation."

Chapter 23

A Barrel Full of Demons

1 Return Journey in a Dream

The ceremonial gathering was very successful, but it seemed that many evils had still not been dissolved away. Though outwardly they were adverse circumstances created by the Bonpo guardian spirits, in fact they were the whip of fate, driving me on to realize my destiny.

During that time I was constantly seeing a big red-colored demon, opening his mouth wide and facing me and inhaling. Every time he inhaled, I felt my own vital energy flowing into his mouth. In those days I was constantly feeling very exhausted.

I asked Sukhasiddhi, and she just gave a slight smile and said: "Don't concern yourself with that. You are still on a pilgrimage, aren't you? Hopefully at the next sacred place you will encounter Niguma."

She said she had to go take part in another ceremonial gathering, and she wanted me to go first to the city of Pataliputra.

In Pataliputra, I met a woman who was performing magic tricks in the street.

She was carrying a wooden barrel, and she said she could enable everyone who went into the barrel to enter the Buddha Land.

No one knew the secret of that wooden barrel.

2　North Wind on the High Plain

That day at dusk, I said goodbye to Sukhasiddhi and set off for the city of Pataliputra.

Though I felt a deep eagerness, my mind was still full of a kind of carefree feeling, as if I had been drinking wine—you could call it the joy of meditation. Even though I was on the road traveling, I could still take all forms and merge them into inherent nature. Since I had sought and found the ultimate meaning of life, my mind was full of a kind of dense emotion. This was a feeling that brought together compassion and wisdom in a single essence—you could call this great compassion with no object, the great compassion of sharing the same essence as all beings.

In my mind, there was always a snow-covered mountain which I was headed for. That pure whiteness and grandeur was always the origin of the enthusiasm for life. On the plateau the wind was blowing the dust of the plateau, and over the dust of the plateau the wind of the plateau was roaring. No one would have expected that, along with this wind-blown dust, there would be a very beautiful scene of human culture.

At that time, there may have been wrinkles on my forehead. I was unclear about my own age. In my eyes, this is not at all important. Though there were always people predicting that I would live a hundred and fifty years, I did not feel the least bit of joy about this. I understood clearly that no matter how long the life, compared with the eons of time, it is just like a flash of lightning, like a bubble floating by chance on a boundless ocean. What is important is how you contribute beneficial things to this world during the years of your life.

Compared to the last time I had gone to Nepal, there were certainly more wrinkles on my forehead: these were the marks left by the severe cold north winds on the plateau and the scorching sun of India. You can imagine a monk with a face marked by the ups and downs of life. I was dressed as a monk because bandits generally did not attack and rob monks, so I always let myself be taken for a monk. I still had to go into the world to do many things, and I was afraid I would not be able to scrupulously observe the more than two hundred rules of the monastic code. At that time, I had still not undertaken to observe the full monastic code. Unlike those monks who mix in the world, I was definitely not willing to do things that would violate the monastic code, after I had accepted it.

I went along many mountain roads, and they were as full of twists and turns as a water snake wriggling. In my backpack I was carrying volumes of the scriptures and gold. At this time, among the disciples who were traveling with me, there were two suffering from fever whose lives ended like bubbles. On the journey to India, these two men had almost come to blows due to their incessant wrangling over Buddhist technical terms. They did not know that later on, they would be struck down by a fever sweeping over them in a little village in India. Before they died, those technical terms could not help them at all. They were all agitated and crying. One of them said, "I have not yet married a wife." One said, "After I die, how will my mother manage?" But all their reasoning could not change the final outcome of death. They fell sick while I was out seeking Niguma. They were thrown into a cemetery forest and became part of the heaps of bleached bones. In the cemetery forest the white bones cover the ground, and no one know which ones come from these disciples from Tibet. Life had demonstrated for me in the most direct intuitive way just what impermanence is.

3 Robber Monks

I walked into Pataliputra, walking toward the dakini who was likewise fated to be waiting for me.

More than two thousand years ago, Pataliputra was just a tiny village. There is a place to cross the Ganges River not far from here. One day the Buddha came here with his disciples. He pointed to Pataliputra, which at that time was still an ordinary village, and said: "In the future this place will become a great city."

In the *Great Final Nirvana Sutra* in the Pali Canon, the prediction which the Buddha made at that time is recorded: "Ananda, while the Aryan people are still always coming and going and their merchants gather like clouds, this Pataliputra will become a great city and commercial center. But there will be several dangers for this Pataliputra: one will be fire, one will be water, and one will be conflict among neighbors."

A hundred years later, this place had truly become a famous major city. It was the capital city of the Maurya royal dynasty, which is famous in Indian history. Its splendid culture, its excellent geographical location, and its profitable commerce by land and by water enabled it to have an irreplaceable status.

"Patali" signifies a kind of flowering tree. Long before, there had been forest of patali trees here. One day there was a young man who came to pay homage to a Brahmanist as his teacher. He had studied for a long time, but he had not made much progress. He felt depressed and came to the forest with a group of friends to relax. To dispel his depression, a good friend broke off a flower and made him go through a wedding ceremony with the flower. Amid the mocking laughter of the friends, the wedding ceremony was concluded. Everyone left when the excitement was over, and only the young man himself was still interested, so he was still under the tree savoring the experience. Gradually the sky darkened. Suddenly a great light shone forth, and beneath the tree appeared an old man and a beautiful woman. The old man said he was the father of the flower, and he wanted the young man to make good on the promise he had just made, and get married to his daughter. The young man was both surprised and delighted, and he proceeded with a legitimate wedding ceremony with the flower spirit. A few days later, a team of men came into the forest, and they brought all kinds of building materials, and undertook a large-scale construction project, and from this a beautiful city was born.

This was the origin of the city of Pataliputra.

This is a rose-colored legend. I feel a great poetic quality coming from it.

But in fact, Pataliputra was built by the Maurya Dynasty. At the time, the Maurya kingdom had established good trading relations with various other kingdoms. In the period when it flourished, Pataliputra had sixty-four city gates and five hundred and seventy watchtowers, and every day's revenue was more than four hundred thousand coins.

Pataliputra occupies an important place in Buddhist history. You certainly know of King Ashoka from the Maurya Dynasty period. In his early years, as he struggled to seize the royal throne, he cruelly killed his own elder brother. After he ascended to the throne, he took command of a great army, and campaigned east and west, and unified all the kingdoms of India in a storm of blood. Later on, King Ashoka put down his killing sword and had a transformative awakening, and became the great royal protector of the Dharma in Buddhist history. Within his realm, he used Buddhism to manage the nation. Beyond his realm, he spread Buddhism over the whole of India, sending many monks as emissaries to take the sparks of Buddhist teaching and communicate them to the world. In the traditional accounts, King Ashoka used spiritual powers and in one night built eighty-four thousand shrines containing the Buddha's relics in places all over the world. Besides this, he commanded that a lot of information about Buddhism be preserved by using inscriptions on stone, and these became a memory that has not decayed in a thousand years.

By the time King Ashoka lived, the Buddha has already been dead for more than three hundred years. In that period of time, various currents of thought had appeared on the Indian stage. Some were openly non-Buddhist, and some kept the Buddhist label. Thus it was that within Buddhism, there were many diverse teachings. Some branched off over differences in codes of discipline, some started disputes because of differences in viewpoint. Buddhism was broken into many factions. There was the Mahasanghika sect, the Theravada sect, the Vibhajyavada sect within the Theravada sect, and so on. Later on, when King Ashoka sent emissaries to go out to the various regions to spread the Dharma, due to differences in viewpoints, codes of discipline, customs, and so on, for a time a variety of teachings flourished, and disputes arose, and the internal debates within Buddhism did not cease. In order to gain material support by fraud, many non-Buddhists and people without faith pretended to be Buddhists and wormed their way into Buddhism. Such people were called "robber monks."

The place where there were the most robber monks was a place called Ashuka Garden. "Ashuka" means "undisturbed." This was built by King Ashoka, and he expended a great deal of energy protecting this garden. The monks in the garden were treated extremely well. Because they were greedy for royal patronage, the robber monks swarmed here like bees. They acted as solemn as eminent monks of great virtue receiving support, but they did not keep the rules of discipline, they did not cultivate meditative concentration, and they did not study the scriptural teachings. Every day they argued continuously with each other, and their evil words and deeds multiplied endlessly. According to the Buddha's rules, every month the community of monks had to conduct an *upavasatha (retreat for spiritual refreshment)* assembly and examine their own misdeeds in light of the code of conduct. But because of interference from those evil monks, in seven years the Ashuka Garden could not even conduct a single *upavasatha* assembly according to the rules.

One day King Ashoka sent an emissary to Ashuka Garden to resolve the disputes among the monks. The emissary did his best to admonish them, but those monks went on as before with their wrangling, and even hurled insults at the emissary. The emissary was enraged, and he drew his sword and killed one of them. This provoked a disaster. King Ashoka went in person to Ashuka Garden. Making an apology, he inquired of the monks: "How can I convict the emissary of a crime?" The monks thought that since the emissary had been sent there by King Ashoka, as the killer he certainly must be convicted, and the person who sent him should also be convicted. King Ashoka said: "I just sent him to resolve disputes, I did not send him to kill anyone." The monks said: "If your emissaries are apt to kill people, it must be that you have not always taught them well. If you are not to blame, then who is?"

King Ashoka could not hold back a long sigh. "You each hold to your own views of the Buddha Dharma, and cannot decide which is correct. How can you save people? Are you telling me that there is no one in this world who can resolve the confusion in my mind?"

Unexpectedly, on this question, the views of the monks were surprisingly unified. They told King Ashoka: "Moggaliputta Tissa is publicly recognized as a man of great virtue. He is the fourth-generation disciple of the honorable Upali."

So Moggaliputta Tissa left his mountain and called together a thousand renowned elders, and in a monastery supported by King Ashoka, initiated the Third Council, which is famous in Buddhist history. The substance of the council, which includes teachings and a canon of rules for monastic discipline, is all preserved in a book called the *Kathavatthu* (*Points of Controversy*).

Those elders, numbering more than a thousand, organized into oral examination groups and conducted an examination of all the monastic communities, requiring them to explain their understanding of the Buddhist teaching. After that, based on their points of view, they eliminated the robber monks.

After this, King Ashoka issued a decree that, hereafter, all groups of monks must be harmonious and without disputes, and anyone who created an incident would be expelled from the community.

But no matter how many King Ashokas there are in the world, they cannot keep out those true robber monks. They can preach Buddhist doctrines endlessly, but in their minds the five desires are still blazing, and their greed is unmatched.

They are far more to be feared than those robber monks who hold non-Buddhist views.

4 I Enter the Barrel of Demons

That beautiful woman was performing in a very busy place in Pataliputra.

The place had been a beautiful building several hundred years earlier, and it was called the Council Hall. The building was constructed of the finest stone, with inscriptions and carvings of extremely fine workmanship. It had had eighty stone columns so high they seemed to reach the sky. But by the time I arrived there, I only saw one of these columns — the others had been eaten away by time. In the sixth century of the Common Era, after a great flood, this city had been a great expanse of water, and it had not recovered from that disaster. This had matched the prediction of the Buddhist elders about the flood. Later, the great Islamic army had attacked Pataliputra and destroyed any possibility that the city would revive. Still later, a different ruler mounted the stage, and created an even greater bustling urban center, but that too was a fleeting illusion.

When I arrived beside the ruins of the Council Hall, what I saw were streets full of cows, dogs running wild, pigs defecating everywhere; there were also ox carts and horse-drawn carts, and all kinds of noise seething like boiling water.

The historical glory and splendor was no more. The Maurya Dynasty was like long-gone dust in the wind, lost in the dust of history. All that remained was the myth of King Ashoka.

Pataliputra with its history explains the truth of Buddhism.

I could not help but think of the Pali Canon's *Dhammapada Sutra*: "Enlightened observation views the myriad phenomena as bubbles. Enlightened observation views the myriad phenomena as dreamlike illusions. If one observes the world like this, the demon of death has no way to see him."

Crop after crop of humans dies off, crop after crop of humans comes back. What changes are the countless scenes. What does not change is the light of truth.

In this play of illusory transformation, I saw that woman. The woman was holding a barrel, and I did not know what she was doing. From outward appearances, there was nothing special.

The woman called out: "All it takes is five ounces of gold, and wherever you want to go, I will take you there with this holy barrel!"

She was repeating this over and over again, and there was a certain magnetism in the sound of her voice. It seemed to be a resonance going through the barrel, and it seemed to be an echo coming from within the barrel.

That sound pulled me in like a magnet attracting iron.

By that time, I considered all women as manifestations of Niguma. When I saw that woman on the street, I likewise took her as Niguma.

There were many people around the woman, and they were all looking at the wooden barrel. A man whispered to me: "That wooden barrel is not a holy barrel — in reality, it is a barrel of demons." He said that he had seen people go into it, but he had not seen anyone come out of it. He said: "Look at that barrel. From the size of the opening, it seems it could not hold much." But he had seen with his own eyes five men go into the barrel, and he had not seen them come out.

But I was thinking: "Is she a dakini or not?"

As she saw me approach, that woman smiled sweetly and said: "My holy barrel can go through to anywhere. I am only asking for five ounces of gold, then I can take you to anywhere you want to go. Will you go or not?"

I asked: "Can you also take me to a holy place?"

"Of course. Otherwise, how could it be considered a holy barrel?" The woman said: "Wherever you want to go, that's where you'll go!"

I asked: "Is Niguma there in that holy place?"

"Of course she is there." The woman said: "If Niguma were not there, how could it be considered a holy place?"

I had some doubts. But I thought: "Before, when the dakinis tested me countless times, every time I had doubts, they would create barriers." I immediately regretted having doubts.

I thought: "So is she a manifestation of Sukhasiddhi or not?"

The woman gave a cold smile and said: "Haven't you been seeking Niguma all along? How is it that when you are really called to go see her, you hesitate, thinking of gain and loss?" She shouted in a harsh voice: "Are you going or not? Are you going or not? If you are going, then take out the five ounces of gold. If you are not going, step aside. Do not block the way for others!"

Once she said this, I began to believe. This was because an ordinary woman could not have known the one I was searching for. But I knew that sometimes what the holy ones know, the demons also may know. The one who was truly close to the Buddha was in fact not a disciple, but the demon king Mara. When the Buddha achieved enlightenment, heaven and earth were both dark, and the sun and moon had no light, and no one knew that the Buddha had already realized supreme true awakening. But all his wisdom and attainment could not hide the truth from the demon king Mara. I even considered that the demon king

Mara was the one who was truly close to the Buddha.

I took out a piece of gold that was a full ten ounces. I thought that if I could truly get to the holy place, it didn't matter if it cost ten ounces or a hundred ounces, it was still worth it. I took the gold and gave it to the woman and said: "Keep the change."

She laughed and said: "That's right, that's right. The holy place is priceless. It is filled with wondrous bliss, bliss beyond compare. When you go there, then you will know. That place is the ultimate home for the soul. There are countless people in the world who want to go there, but they do not have the karmic merit and opportunity. You must understand that this holy barrel is the entrance to the holy place, and it only appears once in five hundred years. Sometimes people from the holy place will come out through the opening in the barrel. Those who come out are certain to become kings; this is the secret of the saying 'only after five hundred years will a king arise.' Do not underestimate this pitch-black barrel. Once your body goes through it, your karmic barriers from five hundred years will dissolve away. The original principle is the same as when frost sees the sun and then evaporates in the blazing sunlight."

"Good, good." The woman rocked the barrel. "First get yourself ready. Bring along what you have to bring, and give away to other people what you don't have to bring. These worn-out things will not be of any use in the holy place; instead, they will just seem like an encumbrance."

While the woman was putting the gold into her bag, the same man stealthily poked me and said in a low voice: "Do not go into it. This is not a holy barrel, this is a barrel of demons. Think about it. If this were really a holy barrel, she would not be asking for money. In this world, how can there be a holy person who is greedy for wealth?"

In a low voice I said: "It's not that she is greedy, it's that I am making an offering. What she cares about is not money, it is my attitude."

The man said: "With this barrel, once they go in, I've never seen anyone come out. It is definitely bizarre."

I said: "This is precisely its miraculous quality. Think about it. If it did not lead to a large place, how could it hold so many people?"

The man whispered: "And if it leads to hell?"

I said: "I have not vowed to go to hell. In this world, a correct aspiration will not have negative results."

The man still wanted to keep talking. The woman gave a cold smile and said to me: "Have you ever seen someone barefoot who does not envy the one who is wearing shoes? He wants to go, but ask yourself, does he have five coppers or not? He is so poor that if you pulled something out of his ass, he could not keep his buttocks clenched. You want to go, but you do not have the resources."

The man's face got red, and he whispered: "I am just saying what I have to say. If you want to go, then go ahead."

I patted him and tried to sooth him. I said: "I appreciate your concern. But I know that I must go. I know that there are countless clouds in the sky, but I do not know which clouds have rain. What I can do is hold up my umbrella when I see the clouds fly by."

I smiled at the man, then went into the barrel.

5 A Beautiful Woman

When my body went into the barrel, I felt that it was not a barrel anymore, but rather a tunnel, a pitch-black tunnel. It was as if I had entered into true emptiness, and I could not hear any sounds. In that tunnel there was no time and no space, and of course I did not know how long I was there. When I felt that I had come out, I had already arrived at a place. This was a very dream-like place. The sun I saw here was not the same as outside. It was a design made of multiple rings of light, with seven colors — red, orange, yellow, green, blue, indigo, and violet. It was very beautiful. There were also countless flowers, very much like the ones outside, except that they appeared larger and prettier. The most striking among them were the poppies. I knew that poppy flowers actually are not large and have no scent, but the poppies here were as large as bowls, and they gave off a scent that made me feel intoxicated. I got to the point that I considered this intoxicated feeling to be what in yoga they call the bliss of emptiness, and this association made my faith a hundred times stronger. I thought that I had truly arrived in the holy place. Previously, I had read the books of many non-Buddhist Paths, and they also had this kind of intoxicating teaching, and their descriptions of it were very similar to the bliss of emptiness.

I was very happy. In my mind I thought: "I have truly arrived in the holy place."

I believed that the woman was certainly a manifestation of a dakini.

I discovered that even if I did not cultivate practice, as long as I smelled that fragrance, it would make me forget worldly afflictions and would produce a state of serenity and great bliss. I thought: "The holy place is the holy place."

In that fragrance, I even forgot my goal in coming here.

But in my mind there was still that thread of concern penetrating my spirit, and I began as before to call to Niguma:

Niguma Khyenno

Niguma Khyenno

I was certain I would be able to see Niguma, because I genuinely felt a kind of peace and bliss which I had never had before.

In the sound of my calling out, a beautiful woman appeared.

I discovered that, since she looked like Sharwadi, she also looked like the Niguma of my expectations. I did not know whether or not, in my expectant mind, Niguma would look like Sharwadi. Her gaze was glowing, and she was beautiful beyond compare. The only thing was, she did not have the third eye spoken of in the traditional accounts. But it was precisely this point that made me feel even closer to her. Although I had visualized Niguma all along with three eyes, if a woman who really had three eyes had appeared before me, I surely would have felt something strange. I discovered that this woman's eyes were filled with feeling and flowing with color, and she melted all the accumulated sorrows in my mind.

I asked: "Are you Niguma?"

She gave a clear laugh and said: "Am I not Niguma?"

I also asked: "How is it that you look like Sharwadi?"

She said: "In the eyes of the ignorant, they are separate. But in the eyes of the wise, they are a single essence."

At that moment I firmly believed that she was Niguma.

Niguma extended her hand, and I held it. That feeling of utter softness melted my heart.

6 So You Want to Marry Me?

Niguma took me to an even more beautiful place. There, the flowers were more beautiful, and the masses of flowers put out a mesmerizing fragrance, more like beautiful women smiling at me. My body and mind were surging with intoxication and great bliss—this was the bliss I had been yearning for so long without finding it. In fact, I could not tell clearly if this was meditative bliss or the bliss of desire. It seemed that many kinds of bliss had been blended together.

Niguma asked me: "What did you bring as an offering to me?"

I immediately took out the gold.

Niguma smiled and said: "I don't need this. People here do not use this rubbish. Don't you have anything better?"

So then I said: "Then I will offer you my body, mouth, and mind."

Niguma said: "Do you know the true implication of offering body, mouth, and mind?"

I said: "I do know. It's that from this point on my life and spirit all belong to you."

Niguma said: "Good, then, let's get married."

I immediately thought of the marriage of supreme truth which Sukhasiddhi had spoken of before. I thought: "I cannot hesitate any more. Only a fool can fall down twice in the same place." So then I said very definitively: "Good. My life is all yours. Whatever you want to do, I am willing."

Immediately I saw countless beautiful women gathering around. They were bringing all sorts of rare precious things seldom seen in the world. I had read of scenes like this in the biographies of many holy men. I was very happy. I thought: "Presumably the marriage which Niguma is talking about is another way of saying *coupled practice* ." I already knew that this was a shortcut to experiencing enlightenment. Sukhasiddhi had realized enlightenment in a single night like this. To tell the truth, at that time I was truly longing to get an intimate look from the dakini.

After those women bustled around, a bridal chamber appeared.

There is no way for me to tell you of the beauty of that bridal chamber—it was a beauty that cannot exist in the human world, a beauty that can only be felt, a beauty impossible to describe or relate. The moment I saw it, I was melted by it. I was at the point where I felt that what I had entered into was a realm of the ultimate special excellence. Of course, as to its real form, that you will understand later.

It was in that state of intoxication that I married Niguma.

7 Indulging in Pleasure

I have not spoken of *coupled practice*, but have said "marriage" instead. The reason for this is very simple: what I enjoyed with Niguma was truly the wondrous bliss of the five desires, not the pure bliss of meditation. Of course, at that time I had no way to tell the difference. You should know that when you are talking to someone who has never gone into a labyrinth, if you tell him to explain the way to get out of the labyrinth, obviously this will be beyond him. At that time, all I had was devotion and faith. I thought that since I had offered her my body, mouth, and mind, then whatever she told me to do, I would do.

At first, I could still think of Sharwadi waiting for me, but there were no regrets in my mind. This was because, in my eyes, Niguma was my teacher, and not my wife. It was precisely this religious feeling that dispelled any regrets toward Sharwadi. What's more, in other latent feelings in my mind, Niguma had already merged with Sharwadi. The Sharwadi who was waiting for me gradually faded out, becoming a shadow gradually moving farther and farther away. During the many years in the holy barrel, I never received any information about Sharwadi.

At times I even thought that Sharwadi was in reality a manifestation of Niguma.

In this way, forgetting was a deep snow covering over many traces of Sharwadi. There were only a few chance unexpected moments when I would start to think how, in times past, there had been those intoxicating tender feelings.

Niguma and I lingered in the bridal chamber making love. I could not tell how much time went by. At that point, time seemed to have dissolved away. An alluring fragrance still emanated from Niguma's body. She and I lingered endlessly making love, and afterwards what I felt was only intoxicating bliss—I did not weary of it or get tired. You know that for men, that is truly the most beautiful experience in the human world.

According to our forefathers' teachings, there are various types of women. There are some women who should not be touched. As soon as any man touches them, his vital energy is drained out and lost. And there is a type of woman who is made of jade. When any man makes contact with this type of woman, he will receive the highest benefit. Niguma was this type of woman. Thus for a long period of time— although I did not know how long, that period was timeless—I would join with her, and it would become the traditional *coupled practice*.

Before long, our first child was born. She was an adorable little girl. She was extremely intelligent, and good at understanding people's intentions. She had skin that was as smooth as silk, and golden hair, and the sound of her happy laughter was like a lark calling.

The birth of our daughter gave me great happiness. You do not know how enchanted I was when the child smiled at me, how happy I was the first time she called me papa, how satisfied I was when I held her in my arms. That is truly the bliss that only heavenly beings have.

During that period of time, the joy of having a daughter made me forget all my past experience. It was like a brush wiping away so many traces in my memory.

When our daughter was three, our son was born. I was experiencing the joy of family life, of having my children around me. I felt that in this period my life finally could be considered truly complete and without regrets. Niguma gave me the feeling of being a man, and my children gave me the feeling of being a father. All that my previous experiences had given me was just the experience of life which a religious practitioner has. I had not anticipated that the ordinary worldly life of the senses, which I had previously looked upon as a dangerous road, would finally let me be so enraptured ... yes, enraptured. This expression is really the most fitting description.

But I still had not forgotten my faith. I even thought that I was living continuously in my faith. This was because I was still chanting the sutras, still cultivating the *coupled practice* with Niguma. At that time I really could not distinguish clearly the boundary between *coupled practice* and ordinary pleasure.

I was still enjoying what I took to be *coupled practice* without growing tired of it, and I was filled with a feeling that combined lofty reverence and emotional desire. At that time I had forgotten one standard: that the basic substance of faith is, in fact, to break free of clinging and to bring benefit to sentient beings. I did not know that at that time I had really fallen into another type of clinging and attachment.

I was always using the religious concepts of the past, which seemed right but were actually wrong, to explain my life. I was always entranced with everything as it appeared. In fact, I was engaged in reassuring myself and using the methods I could accept to persuade myself. I got to the point where I was being emotionally moved by myself. I did not know that this being moved was in fact putting on a show, that was a kind of show I was putting on for myself. I was intoxicated in the kind of faith where I was putting on a show for myself to see.

It was just that in the system of terms, which I had already altered, I took considered those two children as reincarnated bodhisattvas. You must know in the teaching of the Esoteric Vehicle, when reincarnated bodhisattvas are needed, you can emit your own semen. Of course, even if it was not to give birth to bodhisattvas, I was willing to give everything I had for Niguma. Almost every time we engaged in "*coupled practice*," I was willing to offer my "sweet dew."

It's just that in this context, although I knew I was indulging in pleasure, there was still a kind of lofty feeling of offering the body out of faith.

8 An Arrogant Son

When the children were very young, I began to teach them some religious forms. I taught them to chant, and I taught them to do visualizations, and I taught them to draw various kinds of mandalas, and I taught them to sit in meditation. I earnestly taught them to cultivate the great prostrations, the hundred-word illumination mantra, the generation stage, and the completion stage. At that time, I only wanted to raise my children. I did not even think of returning to Tibet.

The frightening thing was that Sharwadi had become also a distant dream. Though at some inadvertent moments I still would think of her, I found reasons to persuade myself not to think of her again. I thought that she had certainly already married someone. This was because I had not received any more of her letters. I could even imagine many intimate scenes of her with someone else, to put a stop to my own regrets and to let myself feel some peace.

By the time my daughter was eighteen and my son was fifteen, I had already taken all the esoteric teachings I had gotten and passed them on to them. I passed on all the esoteric teachings from the paternal line to my son, and the teaching lineage of the dakinis to my daughter.

Niguma was still very beautiful. She worked hard on household tasks, and, except for doing the spiritual exercises she had to do everyday, she used most of her time to instruct our children. She was doing a lot of housework, doing those petty chores which, though they consume your life, have to be faced. I was always moved by her unselfish contributions. I firmly believe that my wife was the genuine Niguma.

Under their parents' tutelage, our children progressed very rapidly. Our son quickly completed the eight worldly accomplishments. He had the power of the heavenly eye and could see things people cannot see; he could see all the scenes in all the worlds in the universe. He had the power of the heavenly ear, and could hear the voices of the minds of the sentient beings in any space. He had the power of the spirit foot and could go to any place he wanted to go to. His flying sword made him able to take the head of an enemy a thousand miles away. His accomplishment in medicine for the eye let him see treasures hidden underground. Because of this, our wealth and status were incomparable. Our home was as beautiful as a palace. At that time there were always people from the royal family coming to admire our home. Our family enjoyed unprecedented honor and comfort.

Almost every guest who came to our home wanted our son to demonstrate his spiritual powers to them. Our son was always stomping stones into a mess as if he were trampling mud. He often sat in meditation in the emptiness, and under him a great lotus would spontaneously grow. Our daughter became accomplished in the methods of the angry dakinis, and when she swept her glance across them, she could bring down all the fruit from the trees. All she had to do was call out lightly to the birds flying by in the sky, and they would drop to earth like stones.

They truly were the reincarnations of bodhisattvas. Their accomplishments at that time left me far behind. You must understand that what I was equipped with at that time was just the accomplishment of increasing good fortune, stopping sickness and pain, reconciling enemies, and destroying anger, and I needed to borrow the power of ritual forms and mandalas before I could attain my wishes. But my daughter had almost achieved the power to give life or to kill at will.

But in fact our son had a problem. He thought he had already attained the ultimate accomplishment, and he strutted around with a self-satisfied manner, like an arrogant rooster. He was always employing his spiritual powers. He won innumerable accolades. His biggest problem was that, because he was too familiar with me, he preferred to think of me as his father, not his teacher. This made him unable to get greater support from within the bequest of the lineage, so he could not progress further to break through his own barriers and achieve true great accomplishment.

I was always saying to him: "Son, though you have attained many supreme wondrous teachings, you definitely must understand that the most excellent among all the teachings is the teaching of your own teacher. You still must pray to your teacher. Although I am your father, I am even more your teacher. The teacher's essential nature is all the Buddhas of the past, present, and future, and the Vajravarahi of the holy realm of the twenty-four dakinis. You must understand this point clearly. So besides those mantras you must recite when you are cultivating the esoteric teaching, in your mind, you must not forget to pray to your teacher. You certainly must sincerely recite 'Lama Khyenno.' At the same time, you also must understand that even while you are reciting those mantras, in your mind you must be clear that the essential nature of those mantras is in fact not separate from 'Lama Khyenno.' It has not wandered away to a tutelary deity outside your teacher; it has not wandered away to a guardian of the Dharma outside your teacher; it has not wandered away to a dakini outside your teacher. You must know that those countless dakinis in reality are all manifestations of your teacher. Your teacher is the dharani of the tutelary deities and the dakinis and the guardians of the Dharma. When you chant 'Lama Khyenno,' in reality you are chanting the mantra of all the Buddhas of the past, present, and future, and of all the dakinis. All people with faith in their teacher have only to chant 'Lama Khyenno' when they are facing death, and the Vajravarahi will come welcome them to the Pure Land. You certainly must understand clearly that this Pure Land and that Land of Secret Adornments are not two and not separate, and they are not separate from all the Buddha Lands, and they are not separate from the holy realms of the twenty-four dakinis. For those people who have realized the ultimate, they are not two and not separate. But for those practitioners who have not yet eliminated dualistic thinking and who bring along their karma when they are reborn, they still have the discriminating mind, and so they still can see that in the Pure Land of the dakinis there are many Paths of light going through to the Land of Secret Adornments, and all the Buddha Lands, and the holy realms of the dakinis. All those who are reborn in the Pure Land can get the special support of the Vajravarahi and, according to their vows, rapidly achieve success and go on to any of the Buddha Lands. Of course you must understand that this is just a provisional explanation. This is because, after you have realized the ultimate, then you will understand that the Pure Land is the land of all the Buddhas, and they are truly without duality."

But no matter how I taught him, I could not change his arrogance.

Countless people flocked to my son and became his disciples. He was very similar to me in my youth when I was in Bonpo. He began to instruct disciples. Already he did not much like to listen to what I told him, and he did not go further into a deeper level of cultivating practice. In fact, I knew that his accomplishment was only accomplishment of generating faith in innate enlightenment, and was still within the limits of contrived action. I told him: "Son, you must know that all phenomena by chance are like dreams, illusions, bubbles, reflections, like the dew, like lightning, things you should not cling to." But how was my son going to listen to what I said? You should know that for a person who has attained spiritual powers, the biggest obstacles are those spiritual powers themselves.

My son was always displaying those spiritual powers. From time to time he even engaged in magical contests with other people. At that time, the one who equaled him in renown was a Brahmanist woman. From external appearances, the spiritual powers of the two of them were evenly matched.

But at that time, I already knew that the woman was in reality a flesh-eating raksha demon.

She was already thinking of punishing my son.

Chapter 24

Dearly Beloved Khyung

1 Father Has Grown Old!

While Khyungpo Naljor was enjoying the blessed life of the holy place, Sharwadi was enduring the torments of longing.

The sounds of those sorcerers shaking their dog skins was always appearing in her mind. That eerie sound would often echo and enfold her. Indescribable vexations were always attacking her mind, and she was becoming more and more depressed and timid. She was far from the carefree person she had been in the past.

From the writings she left, I can read a kind of desolation and heartbreak:

I woke up at noon, and I felt as if I was in a trance. In the house it was extremely quiet, and the noisy world seems to have forgotten this little corner. I lay on the bed: my body and mind were still very exhausted. A big blue fly had come in, who knows when, and was buzzing around the room, filling this lonely room with more loneliness. I suddenly got impatient and felt very anxious and unsettled. I listened for anything in the courtyard, but there too was dead silence. I rolled over and pulled myself up, thinking I should get out of bed, but unwilling to move my body. I just let those crazy emotions flow on in my mind ...

Suddenly I thought of Khyung, and that familiar image kept moving before my eyes. How much time will have to pass until my mind does not get agitated as soon as I think of him? At certain moments I think with complete certainty that he must be in some place waiting for me, for sure. He has already waited for such a long time. This thought pushes me to quickly get dressed, to quickly get going, to quickly go see him. But as soon as I put on one shoe, I realize the absurdity of what I am doing. I think, "Maybe he has already forgotten me," and then my mind becomes a lonely, desolate tomb. I am no longer anxious, I no longer hesitate, my upturned face falls, and I lie down again on the bed ...

Suddenly the autumn wind again becomes cool. This sense of coolness fills my father's silhouette with loneliness. I stand by the gate and send my father on his way, and the deep autumn dusk makes me cry even more. I see so much of life's stormy vicissitudes set off by the image of my father's turning sadly to go. My father's unsteady silhouette is hit by the autumn wind flowing cold and cheerless.

Father has gotten old! His hair is white as frost, and it pains my eyes to see it. All I can do is face the accusing autumn wind and turn away, wiping those futile tears which fill my eyes.

2 The Incense Burner Wrapped in Blue Smoke

The sky is damp, and it seems to be about to rain. I like rainy days, cold and cheerless, with the raindrops pattering down, like a sadness that cannot be fully told, like a dark feeling that cannot be cut through. How many past events that went against our will, how many afflictions deep in our minds, are all combed out by the rain?

Rolling up our pant legs, picking up our plain-colored umbrellas, mother and I walk slowly together toward the temple of the female spirits, seeking that dream that has been buried for a thousand years ... Fine rain wets my eyes, my eyelashes are misty, and in the mist your smiling face again appears. Hey, don't think of him.

When I was little, whenever there was a rainy day, my mother would always cook something delicious. We would huddle together and listen to father tell those never-ending stories of the great adepts ... So much rapturous longing accompanied me as I grew up, and in the wind and rain, these memories never lose their color.

Though all my hopes have come to naught, I could not bear to hurt my mother, and I always put on a brave face and sound cheerful.

The temple of the female spirits is very lively and busy, and my mind is even more agitated. Everything before my eyes is all grey shadows. At this moment, I think of those various crazy people who roam the streets. In their brains, is everything in heaven and on earth this way too, intangible and vague, empty and illusory? I think I will soon go crazy.

Beside the incense burner wreathed in blue smoke, my mother's grag hair is especially striking, like the sunlight at dusk.It is the witness to her having experienced the hardships of life. In the temple of the female spirits, the forms of the people are graceful. Mother pulls my sleeve, as though she were pulling along a child, and does not let me get a half step away from her side. By the side of the great hall, while mother was looking up at an old tree for a moment, I mischievously slipped away. Secretly looking back from a quiet place, I saw her look of alarm as she kept scanning the crowd, as though she had carelessly lost a child who had just run off. In the cold wind my mother looked so gaunt and weak, so lonely. At that moment, I understood that I have become my mother's support. When she saw me, she gave a sigh of relief, and a look of joy flashed from her moist, aggrieved eyes. Mother again held tightly to my sleeve, and my tears poured out like water through a breached dyke ... Mother too has gotten old. Now she cannot leave her daughter, and the moment she doesn't see me, the longing pulls at her gut. Right now my mother is most afraid of loneliness and isolation, and as long as I can be by her side, she has an intangible strength. When we were returning home, mother still held my sleeve as if I were a child, and I stayed close by her. An old, eternal feeling was gently tapping at my heart, very far away, and yet so familiar ...

3　A Net That Is Hard to Escape From

... My aged parents have cut off my intention to seek.

I do not know how to explain what kind of feeling this is. Suffering and confusion have been twisted into a net that is hard to escape from. The net is covering the grim smile of fate. I raise my eyes and look far off at the sky outside my window, and there is a black cloud rolling in. As though full of worries, it is pouring down endless rain. Can I take my grief and sorrow and give them to the cloud?

The rain lingers and pours down, soaking the ground, surge after surge, like the sad voice of the dark clouds complaining to a distant lover. This makes me cry sadly. I think of that man who shattered my heart, that feeling ... But finally, all the promises, all the waiting is just a flower reflected in a mirror, just the moon reflected in the water ... Suddenly I feel that hard thing in my mind come crashing down. Every one of my nerves is quickly aging, every drop of my blood is rapidly drying up ...

I have not foreseen that life would end up being so hard to predict. Who would be there on the road? Would it be windy? Would it be rainy?

The vase of fresh flowers on the table had also withered. Every petal had been permeated by the bitterness, like hopeless butterflies sadly staying on dry grass, waiting for the final snowstorm ... My mind hurts. I thought that, although I deeply loved the fresh flowers, I should not ruin their red faces; rather I should put them in the depths of my soul, so they would float and sink together with me, drifting back and forth along with me, until the day my face loses its color and my bloodstream has no rest ...

When I turn back and look at yesterday's story, I finally discover that true love is the conclusion where the lovers come together in marriage. As our wandering feet tramp through so many seasons over and over again, what are you and I seeking? I am used to seeing youthful loneliness. By the bamboo fence, drinking and singing: how many sighs, how many awakenings. The winter season has grown sad and faded away. Let your feet stay here then; there is nothing to be done if your eyes cannot bear it. Put on your bodily form then. Why have your feelings not melted? As for your smiling face at this instant, if you are not careful, it may be blown away by the wind. Hold onto your loving thoughts. The tears in your eyes have no words, let the white hair float.

I have been walking for many days, seeking and searching, but I still cannot find yesterday's cloud ...

O yesterday's cloud, who took you and blew you away in the wind? Suddenly I look back, and all that is left are wisps of injured feeling. In the time when ten thousand families light their lights, in a dream I saw your faded footprints, traveling a road laughing with joy, traveling a road with a mind raining ... O cloud of days gone by, we met by chance in the romantic season of white verbena grass. For this the willow turned green and the white sand got dry.

4 An Emotion Impossible to Describe

In the house it is quiet and still, depressing, empty. I open a window, waiting for your return.

In May sunshine is sprinkled lightly on the jute leaves outside the window. The pure wind is coming and kisses the sunlit leaves with deep feeling, as they dance happily in the sunshine. Seeing them, I feel that I am like an autumn flower that has already withered and died, and when a chance breeze shakes me, I will fall sadly to the ground. I will be trodden into the mud by people's feet, and vanish forever without a trace.

Mother is squatting in the sunlight, taking advantage of the warm clear day to prepare some peppery seasonings. She keeps shaking them and smelling them, checking carefully to see whether or not they have been disturbed by rats. When I see her silhouette, I suddenly sense the emptiness of life, its boredom, and a kind of anxious, crazed feeling surges up at me ...

I am standing in the room, and I extend my head all the way out of the window, and the pure lucid world returns. I stare at a patch of sunlight falling on the peppery leaves, and it flickers unsteadily. I seem to have put myself in an ancient dream from childhood: in it there is a stretch of open country with some broken-down walls, and from the yellow earth here and there some lonely flowers grow. I remember squatting down beneath a low earthen wall with my body and mind all tired out, and digging out of the mud various kinds of small clay bowls, measuring them and measuring them with my eyes.

5 An Emotional Sadness that Cannot be Transformed

The moonlight is dim, and my mind is dreary. My longing

for you still hits my mind under the moonlight. I do not dare look directly at that grey languishing face of mine in the mirror. Sometimes, at night, your searching eyes will appear in it too. I do not have the courage to look at them directly—I am afraid I will start crying. Those two eyes are a pure spring, flowing on forever with a cool purity that never dries up. It is as if they were speaking an everlasting vow. I am afraid of getting tied up by the emotion in those eyes, so I do all I can not to look at them. I keep the expression in those eyes at the end of the night, but my mind is strangely painful.

A tall tree which stands right outside my window has no spiritual energy, and the patch of sky carved out by the window is unexpectedly very attractive. The air is damp, and it seems it is going to snow. As soon as I focus my eyes on something, my mind suddenly gets moist ...

Why must I pursue your up-and-down dreams? These depressing thoughts make a person very tired. Don't tell me I am just doing this for the sake of a casual look back. Or for the sake of a meaningless chance encounter. My mind is like a silkworm's cocoon, wrapped up in a thick shell, and already cannot appreciate the cool purity.

It is always the mind in pain, and always, after the mind in pain, myriad thoughts all in ashes.

O sun, why are you always hidden in your world? O sun, maybe I have been wrong. I really cannot catch up to your up-and-down eyes and wandering mind.

Is your sky also crying? In this winter that has gone through its changes, every word is superfluous. Whenever something crystalizes in the stupidity, it is always your haggard face and solitary mind. O you who are alone hesitating in the dark of night, you should know that in my life you are the song that never stops. My feelings have stayed for you, my mind is waiting for you. Why don't you come back and take my hand?

The wisps of snow are floating by soundlessly, ceaselessly, falling on the ground and melting into water. The snowflakes waited for winter; doesn't it mean that they too have not waited for what they love, and can only just hopelessly cry?

6 Calling Out in the Cold Wind

The winter nights are quiet. They let people doze off. I push open the half-closed little door, and the usual cold flow hits me in the face. Immersed in the black night, with deep feeling I long for you.

If you were still the wind that refreshed me yesterday, the roses that bloomed in my mind would not have withered away. But now, the emotion may be a pure emotion, but whichever way I turn, it hurts. The true love in my life is withering away day by day. Khyung, do you realize, or not, that on the road you are traveling in life, you will lose something?

For months now I often have insomnia, and my soul is tied up day and night by a kind of formless love-hate. My mind is so exhausted, and the events of the past keep pounding at it. Like the Buddha practising austerities, I keep re-experiencing the taste of the hardships and thinking them over. The light of the midnight moon, alone and white, shines on the whole courtyard, and my little room is enveloped in the cold air, broken down and depressing, like a tomb. Life is impermanent. All that was flourishing has gone away, and all that remains is desolation and bitterness. I am the future owner of the tomb.

The warm feeling of the days gone by is excruciating. I think I am dead, but nevertheless still clean. I have earned the status of a lovesick seed, and I have prevailed over sinking into a mental state of loss and misery.

Husband, I have not called you this for a long time. But tonight, exceptionally, I want to call you this, call you this till tomorrow, call you this till forever.

I am a solitary cold star, always calling to you in the bleak moonlight. Beloved one! Beloved one! Where are you? Is my smiling face there in your dreams or not? I think you are very tired, and you have already quietly entered the river of dreams, haven't you?

My Khyung, I want very much to turn into a firefly and fly lightly in through your window and kiss your face that is sound asleep and floating in the spirit light. I want to be there by your ear, to sing a love song to you all night long and dissolve away all your fatigue.

My beloved, when I think of you, the warm tears turn round and round. When I think of you, the dakinis fly around before my eyes.

I am always asking fate: why have you created this lovesickness where there is no way for us to get together? Why has that pact from a past life become in this life a wind there is no way to wait for ...

Beloved one, my Khyung, I am in the cold wind calling to you!

Chapter 25

The Origin of the Dispute

1 Divergence between the Nigumas

Khyungpo Naljor talking to Xuemo:

Son, when Sharwadi was calling out to me in the cold wind on a winter night, I was immersed in a happy life with Niguma.

... Before long, we had fallen into a dispute. The dispute did not come from those outside the Buddhist Path, but rather from within Buddhism itself.

Not far away from our home there lived a master of esoteric mantras with the same kind of cultivation and realization. She and my Niguma both came from the same village, called "Nigu," and people called her Niguma too. What needs to be emphasized is that "Niguma" is not a personal name. Almost all the women of the Nigu clan could be called "Niguma." I already knew that it meant "woman of the Nigu clan." In the same way, all the men of the Khyungpo clan could be called "Khyungpo Ba." Coming from Liangzhou, naturally you could also be called "Liangzhou Ba," which just means "man of Liangzhou." If you stayed a long time in the town of Zhangmutou in Guangdong province in China, people might call you "Zhangmutou Ba."

But you must know that although "Xue" (snow) and "Mo" (sand) are two common words, and combining them is also very normal, when a certain time cames, these two words could represent a particular man. If some other author were to use "Xuemo" as a pen name, you would certainly take him to court. It's the same way with the name "Niguma," and it has a similar nature. Although all the women in the Nigu clan can be called "Niguma," that Niguma in yoga practice is a particular designation, and it only refers to that Niguma who achieved supreme true enlightenment.

Do you understand?

By your present standards, anyone else who called herself "Niguma" would in fact be infringing on her rights, or stealing her name to cheat the public. My Niguma of course could not accept this. At the beginning, she just communicated her dissatisfaction. She had our son tell that other woman of the Nigu clan not to use this name. How could we know that at almost the same time, the other woman was instructing her daughter to come to our house to tell us not to use the name "Niguma" anymore and to switch to another name.

This first dispute was in fact this kind of small matter, hardly worth noticing. But you must understand that this minor matter, in the eyes of worldly people who consider external appearances important, was a big thing and almost involved something fundamental.

So our son was extremely angry.

His mother admonished him saying: "It is not important. Since other people are members of the Nigu clan too, for us to tell her not to use this name seems unreasonable. A name is only a name. Since everything is illusory, what real meaning does that name have?"

"Leave it at that. Whatever she wants to be called, let them call her that." I also admonished our son this way.

But what happened later made me feel it was intolerable. That other Niguma finally made a public announcement that only she was the true source of Niguma Yoga, and she said that we were phonies.

That other Niguma formally became the master of Niguma Yoga. Countless people gathered around her.

Later, I sent a disciple pretending to be seeking her teaching, to go listen to her, and he discovered that her level of perception was not the same as ours. I cannot say whether it was correct or incorrect, but at the very least, what she was expounding was not Niguma Yoga. This is because the basis of Niguma Yoga is the level of perception of the Great Mudra, which takes breaking with external forms and breaking with clinging as the main thing. But what she was teaching was telling people to cling to external forms.

In that period, with my enlightened consort — I preferred to call her "my woman." "Woman" is a very good word. She did not like to call me "husband," but preferred to call me "my man." When she called me "my man," I would feel an immense happiness and satisfaction. I discovered that sometimes names and forms are very important. Though from the bottom of my heart I still considered her as my enlightened consort, nevertheless I preferred to call her "my woman." I did not know whether or not this was being caused by the habit-energy of my previous lives.

"My woman" explained Niguma Yoga to me. I discovered that,

in fact, in my previous seeking of the Dharma I had already found the truths she expounded. Later, my experience proved a truth: in any person's world, nothing is higher than one's own mind.

There were many divergences in the cultivation and realization of the two Nigumas. For example, they diverged on the issue of how to deal with the discriminating mind. The other Niguma emphasized keeping vigilant, and "my woman" — I still like this term — emphasized relaxing. So a dispute appeared over tightening up versus relaxing.

I sent my disciple, who "stole teachings," and he told me what the other Niguma had taught him:

The other Niguma said: "You must consider all the miscellaneous thoughts of the discriminating mind as thieves. As soon as they approach, kill them with one blow. Do not observe them, and do not analyze them. As soon as they appear in your mind, immediately kill them with one blow. When I say kill them, I mean to bring up correct mindfulness. Using the club of correct mindfulness, go and kill those thieves of afflictions. Whenever you notice them appear, then bring up correct mindfulness, and take that power of concentration and maintain it in your linked state. That is to say, as soon as there are miscellaneous thoughts, concentrate on your teacher in your mind. Then those miscellaneous thoughts will naturally disappear. We do not concern ourselves with what kind of discriminating mind it may be. Do not be concerned with whether or not they should arise. You just must actively concentrate on your mindfulness, and the discriminating mind will be gone."

"My woman" explained it this way:

"That is not right. You cannot cultivate practice this way. If you simply emphasize keeping vigilant, you may get tense, and getting tense is the great enemy of meditative concentration. What you need is not to be vigilant, but rather to let go and relax. Your fist must not be clenched that tight, okay? Look at you, your forehead is running with sweat. You are too tense. You definitely must relax. When I tell you to use correct mindfulness to drive away miscellaneous thoughts, this is to tell you to cultivate meditation better, not to tell you to tense up. You definitely must relax. The reason you are tense is that you emphasized vigilance; this means the strength of your *observing* power is too much, and it influences the effectiveness of your *stopping*. This makes the guest try to take over from the host. Your *observing* is basically for better *stopping*. But at this moment, instead, your *observing* is ruining and influencing your *stopping*. Always remember that in *stopping* and *observing*, *stopping* is the leading factor, and *observing* is the auxiliary. Your mental power should be used principally in your mind as your teacher that is not separate from your inherent nature. If you have no discriminating mind and miscellaneous thoughts, that *observing* becomes a continuous vigilance. When your mind is too tense, the power of *observing* is too strong, and you lose the core content of cultivating observation. Because of this, you definitely must relax. Surely you have seen a stringed instrument. The strings should not be too tight; if they are too tight, then it is easy for them to break. When you are tense, the strings of the instrument are too tight. You must relax, but there must be the proper measure in your relaxing. You certainly must not relax to the point of laziness and slacking off. This is because when the strings of the instrument are too loose, the instrument cannot play a tune. If *observing* is too tense, it will damage *stopping*. If *observing* is too lax, the discriminating mind and its muddles will take advantage of that weakness and enter. You definitely must get to the point where there is tension in the relaxation and relaxation in the tension, so relaxation and tension are both there in proper measure. If you go too far with relaxation, your correct mindfulness and correct knowledge and correct thought will have no strength, and you will have no way to arouse the observing mind and the controlling mind. Then it will be very easy for you to flow into scattering and chaos, to flow into muddled confusion, to flow into laziness, to flow into slackness. The situation is as if you were holding a sparrow. If you hold it too tight, you might crush it to death; if you hold it too loosely, the sparrow will escape from your hand and fly away. In that state where relaxation and tension are both there in proper measure, you stay peacefully on the seed mantra in your mind, and enter deeply into meditative concentration."

2 An Open Debate

It was precisely the issue of tension and relaxation which became the fuse for the dispute between the two sides. It directly provoked the later great dispute.

One day, on the initiative of the local nobility, the two Nigumas held a public debate. The focus of the debate was the question of tension and relaxation.

The Niguma who emphasized vigilance considered that all thoughts are thieves, and that we must slay them. She said: "Thoughts are the root of revolving in birth and death, the origin of affliction, the starting point for falling into delusion, and the manifestation of ignorance. With thoughts, there is no so-called positive and negative, right and wrong. Thoughts are actions, and if there are actions, then there would be the reactive force, that is, the force of karma. If there is the karmic force, then there is revolving in birth and death. The basic substance of liberation is wiping away thoughts and all actions as bonds tying down the mind and spirit. Therefore, cutting off thoughts is the number one imperative in cultivating practice. This is the starting point and also the end point. It is the means and also the goal."

But my Niguma said that there is one goal of cultivating practice: to cut off the discriminating mind. Rejecting thoughts in fact was just a type of discriminating mind.

That day her lecture was very brilliant. She almost took the debate and turned it into a session of transmitting the Path. The atmosphere of the scene was full of fervor. Even now, I still remember the content of her lecture. As I remember it, this is what she said:

"It is because our minds are tied up by various kinds of discriminating mind that we cannot get liberation. Because the surface meaning of the word liberation is release from bondage, therefore, we definitely must let go and relax. Only if you achieve genuine relaxing, and relax more, will you be able to achieve meditative concentration. When you are in this condition, and you again observe the fundamental substance of the discriminating mind, then you will discover that the discriminating mind, like any other type of thing in the world, is without inherent nature. In fact, it does not really exist. When you clearly understand this one point, the discriminating mind will dissolve away into the limitless. If you observe this way again and again, you will again and again dissolve away the discriminating mind that arises. You will get to the point that without deliberately counteracting it, as soon as it arises, you will observe its inherent nature, and then after you discover that it is unattainable, you will enter into meditative concentration. This is cultivating the teaching of Prajñāparamita. This situation is very much like a cormorant on the boat of a fisherman. We are comparing your true mind to the boat, and using the cormorant as a metaphor for the discriminating mind. Once the boat is out at sea, although the cormorant flies off from time to time, and flies and flies, no matter how high it flies or how far, in the end it will come back down to the boat. In just this way, all we have to do is take ourselves and concentrate and focus on our teacher's mind that has no discriminating thought, and not grasp it or become attached to it. Then all discriminating mind will dissolve in that mind. This is because, no matter what kind of discriminating mind it is, if we get to its real substance, it is like the moon reflected in the water, like a flower reflected in a mirror. If we seek its real substance, it is ultimately unattainable."

There was one more important divergence in this debate — the difference between goal and result.

In the opposing side, Niguma said:

"All you have to do is cultivate practice this way, and after a long time, you will enter a wholly new realm. It is bright and empty and still, an expanse of light. You will not have any more barriers, and your wisdom will be as boundless as empty space. This light is not different from or separate from your teacher within your mind. But at the same time, you must understand that, although your teacher in your mind is full of light, in its fundamental nature, it also returns to the empty inherent nature. You will not cling to the self anymore, and you will not cling to the esoteric teaching anymore. You will not be deluded by the myriad things of the world, and you will feel the light and empty stillness of the cloudless blue sky."

She thought this was the ultimate goal of cultivating practice.

But my Niguma said:

"Although you will be able to reach that quiet meditative concentration, you must not cling to this. This is because, though you can understand the inherent nature of mind, and you can also abide peacefully in this realm, you still must remember that this is only the first step, and you are still very far away from the ultimate realm. You still have a long road you must travel."

My Niguma thought that the realm spoken of by the other Niguma was only the beginning, not the end result.

In the end, neither one of them could convince her opponent.

Although in terms of the atmosphere of the encounter we had prevailed, there were still quite a few people who supported the other side.

Thus, it was impossible to say who had won and who had lost.

However, at that time I began to have a bit of doubt. I discovered that what they were debating in fact was not the question. But since I loved my woman very much, I knew that their debate was in fact a topic for a trial of strength. It was not important what the topic was. What was important was that they were using this topic to strike a pose.

3 Religious Fanatics

Later on, the two of them also had a big controversy about being and emptiness.

Besides this, the two of them had controversies on almost every aspect of Buddhism: the stage of gradual cultivation, whether wisdom was gradual or sudden, the relative importance of the two stages of generating enlightenment and completing enlightenment, and the difference between emphasizing wisdom (continuation through the mother) and emphasizing skillful means (continuation through the father).

The content of these controversies had emerged in the same way in my previous course of cultivating the Path. I had previously felt that some of these questions had already been resolved, but in this realm of specific terminology, I ended up feeling that this had become a big problem. During certain absent-minded moments, I even considered them to be major matters of life and death.

The two families originally had nothing to do with each other, but now they ended up becoming two enemy camps. Each of the two camps had countless believers. Every day, each family was preaching its own religious ideas.

One day I discovered that the opposing group of followers was getting bigger and bigger. I made inquiries, and was told that the opposing side had invited a great teacher who was an expert in the scriptures. His name was Pema Nam.

Don't laugh. It really was this way. When I heard this news, I did not believe it either. But one day at dusk, while I was out walking, I actually saw that other Niguma walking together with Pema Nam.

"How are you?" As soon as he saw me, he took the initiative and greeted me.

"I am very well." Though he had appeared in the opponents' camp, I was a bit unhappy. But because he was an old acquaintance from back home, I still felt we were on familiar terms.

"What about you?" I asked. "What have you been doing these past few years?"

"I am very well," he said. "I have studied almost all the Buddhist scriptures circulating in India. I have debated with almost all the great teachers. They all lost—no, there was just one that I did not prevail over. Because he had an exceptional memory, he repeated the contents of my arguments without missing a word. Given this, we argued to a draw. All the other debates I won."

"Is that so?" I did not feel interested in what he had said. So I said:

"There is no connection between liberation and intellectual knowledge. What I think is important is the content of cultivating practice, not intellectual knowledge of Buddhism."

Pema Nam said: "How can you say that intellectual knowledge does not guide people in cultivating practice?"

He said: "Those ritual forms that you sought use visualization to influence the mind and spirit. The wisdom that I learned uses knowledge to influence the mind and spirit. The goal of these two types of influences is, in reality, one and the same."

When he said this, I looked at him with fresh eyes.

I said: "With knowledge and real practice, the question is not which is more important, but how you go about it. If that knowledge you learned cannot be applied in your actions, what meaning do your studies have?"

Pema Nam yawned and said: "My learning is my action. Is there any better action than learning?"

While we were talking, the other Niguma was standing by, looking at me coldly. I saw that she too was a beautiful woman, but because she had gone too far with clinging and attachment, it had made her face look a bit hard. On her face where the unique marks of the Nigu clan: a high nose, deep-set eyes, sharp-edged, very beautiful.

A moment later, a little girl came looking for her. That girl gave me a venomous look. I knew that this was certainly the result of what her mother had taught her. In those years, I often encountered this kind of look. They were classic religious fanatics. They thought that only the tripe in their own bowl was the truth, and what filled other bowls was certainly error. They rejected all knowledge that differed from their own point of view. They operated under the banner of protecting the Dharma or defending the Path. They acted righteously and spoke strictly and were lofty beyond compare. They were full of ardor and never compromised. In one hand they held the scriptures they viewed as truth, and in the other hand they held the killing knife to eliminate those who differed from them. In their eyes, the best rouge was the fresh blood of heretics.

At the time, I did not know that it was this little girl who would destroy the good fortune I had at that time.

4 Cursing and Killing

Disputes first broke out among the followers of the two sides.

One day a crowd of believers from the other side came to our door. They were shouting out a slogan: "Out with the false Niguma! Out with the false Niguma!" The sound was like thunder — an indescribable uproar. Our disciples also poured out and began shouting the same slogan. With sides saying the same thing, the sound rose and fell from one side and then the other, shaking heaven and earth.

After that, I discovered that the flowers around our house were all gradually withering and dying. They shriveled up like a disgruntled woman without the nourishment of love. They became stiff as a wax candle without a flame. There were no more birds singing, no more flowers giving off their fragrance. There was only that noise shaking heaven and earth.

That day for the first time, my son made use of an evil curse. One of the disciples from the opposing side started foaming at the mouth and fell to the ground. From the look of it, it was just like what you would later call a heart attack.

I immediately stopped my son. I did not want to let him use the esoteric teaching for cursing and killing.

My son argued saying: "My killing is compassion in another sense. At the same time I am killing him, I am delivering him to the Buddha Land of the dakinis."

"No, don't!" I said to my son. "No matter what the result is, I will not agree to what appears to be killing."

My son was very unhappy with this. I knew I could not convince him. At that time he was almost eighteen. As you know, this is the age when a person thinks he is always right. I just hoped that, no matter what kind of disputes there were, they would not involve murderous intent. I knew that once murderous intent arises, it never stops. When enemies take revenge on each other, when does it ever end?

I do not know what our Niguma was thinking at that time. She had not stopped our son. Perhaps she knew that it would be no use trying to stop him. Faced with a eighteen-year-old son who is sure he is right, a mother's influence is very limited.

Later, I knew that the believers from the other side were in fact being incited by that girl.

Perhaps she thought that if she could make her own Niguma's arguments come true, in the future she could sit back and enjoy the fruits of her success, and with her status as Niguma's successor, she could ascend to the jewel throne.

5 Black Curses Pat by a Woman

Our son's difficulties came on a certain day at dusk. That day he was passing through an orchard. That woman was picking fruit just then. With her, picking fruit, was a large group of disciples. They were picking fruit, and at the same time chanting curses against us. Their method of cursing was to add our names to the end of an evil curse.

What was interesting was that they did not know the real family name of my wife. So all they could do was add the phrase "the false Niguma" to the end of the evil curse.

So our son laughed at them and said: "Aren't you cursing yourselves?"

Those men stopped their cursing and all started scolding our son.

Our son got annoyed, and stamped his foot once, and all the fruit from one of the trees fell to the ground.

That woman was obviously not a modest one. She said hey, and the fruit went back up into the tree.

Our son then let out an evil curse.

The curse from our son was a string of angry thoughts. It relied on words and visualization, and contained a lot of the substance which you would later call dark energy.

Anyone who has cultivated practice with success knows that thoughts have energy. People's thinking has energy in the same way, and it can construct a field of thought that can reach the territory it can reach.

Would you say that an evil curse is a giant wave of energy? You can certainly think of it this way. Would you say that what it sets in motion is a dark energy with a destructive function? You wouldn't be wrong. This world is fundamentally a symbol, which can be interpreted by you as you please. You can interpret it with any language you prefer. As long as your interpretation works, and gets the approval of the world, then you are a great philosopher or a great scientist. As for the true characteristics, that is another matter. The truth of this world is impermanence. In reality, none of your explanations can get away from that truth.

On that occasion, it was our son who first sent out the evil curse, and the force of that curse reached that woman's heart chakra. In that place rests the imperishable point of light. It is the dwelling place of the soul, and the material basis for rebirth in the world. If an evil curses hits that place, it can destroy its original order.

At this point, the woman spit up blood.

Those disciples from the opposing side were frightened and alarmed, and their faces went pale. One brave fellow shouted out: "Hey, you son of Khyungpo Ba, how did your old man teach you to cultivate the mind of enlightenment? How can you treat a woman this way?"

Our son was embarrassed, and immediately withdrew the power of the curse.

But he forgot to protect himself. You must know that many yoga practitioners all must visualize a protective wheel. That protective wheel, when the visualization is complete, is made of a barrier of many diamond clubs emanating from the heart chakra. It is so dense it does not let air through, and burns with a fierce fire. Apart from the wisdom of the Buddhas, no evil demons can come into it. The protective wheel that our son visualized was very strong and solid, like a peerless suit of armor, but at that moment when he was being denounced by that man, he forgot to visualize the protective wheel to defend himself.

Thus he was struck by the black curse launched by that woman.

Our son cried out, vomited blood, and fell to the ground.

6 A Crazy Girl

At that time, I was drawing a mandala with Niguma. We were preparing to shut the gates and perform the fire ceremony for increasing good fortune, in order to increase our own power to influence others. At that time we already felt the crisis. Because our opponents had added to their ranks Pema Nam, who was known as a "great teacher," they had won over countless followers. You must realize that fear of the unknown is one of humankind's basic qualities. The vocabulary that poured out of Pema Nam's mouth made people feel like they had fallen into the clouds, and it left those shallow people stunned and stupefied, like fools or drunkards.

Besides this, he taught a lot of material that went along with their root nature. He used his great fund of knowledge to explain doctrines that were not the same as ours. He opposed the wisdom of the Great Mudra taught by the dakinis without physical bodies. He rejected the human potential for sudden enlightenment. He thought that people cannot become suddenly enlightened, that people must follow the strict forms of study that ordinary people go through. He thought that they must progress in stages, and cultivate austerities step by step, and only then can they reach enlightenment. He adamantly opposed the Great Mudra. He set up a strict system of cultivating study. It was precisely this system that filled up the empty space in the lives of many practitioners. It also satisfied the hopes of people longing to learn all they could of Buddhist knowledge. Thus our opponents won more and more believers.

To be honest, I did approve of Pema Nam's set of teachings. People do not all have the same intellect. Their root sicknesses are not all the same, so of course the prescriptions for them are not the same either. But he was wrong in rejecting the Great Mudra transmitted by the dakinis without physical bodies.

The truth taught by our Niguma came from the same track as what I had learned from the dakinis without physical bodies. I do not know which, ultimately, was the original source. Although I had not completely and finally detached from desire, I had already seen the light of truth, and I already knew what direction to go. Therefore, I was not at all pleased with Pema Nam's methodology of beating everyone to death with the same club.

What made it even more unacceptable was that among Pema Nam's disciples, there were many who specialized in writing, and they were all skilled writers. They produced a large quantity of writings, and they printed pamphlets which were sent everywhere. They even used kites to scatter their pamphlets in the sky above us. Every morning, the pamphlets descended into our courtyard like snowflakes. These writings cited all kinds of authorities and made precise arguments and had a very strong provocative power. Before long, more than twenty of our disciples had lost their faith in their own family's teachings. There were even more disciples who could not abandon our esoteric teaching, but who became willing to accept our opponents' philosophy. You know that a religious teaching must have a religious worldview to support it. The Great Mudra has the level of perception of the Great Mudra, but Pema Nam's philosophy only suited those who practiced Pema Nam's teachings. Due to the interference of Pema Nam's philosophy, many of our disciples had already lost the perceptions they had when they practiced. Those perceptions were as precious as jewels, and once they were lost, it was really a pity. If they gave rise to doubts about their own family's teaching, this was the same as ruining the root of faith. From a religious point of view, that disaster was truly ruinous.

When we wanted to perform the fire ceremony for increasing good fortune, we were thinking to use the power of the fire ceremony to mobilize the mystic power protecting the teaching, and block the momentum of our opponents' craziness.

At that time we also knew that our opponents were chanting a kind of ritual form. In their own way, they too were praying to a power greater than human.

We also knew that crazy girl was also stirring even more power. She wanted to use violent means to wipe us out, or drive us away. They had many people on their side, and they were extremely fanatical. Waving the banner of truth, they called together a lot of hot-blooded young men, and they got their clubs and knives and whips ready. In terms of numbers, we could not compare with them.

All we could do was to rely on the power of the realm of truth. We prepared unusually abundant offerings. You surely must know that any of the spirits of the realm of truth, from bodhisattvas to Buddhas, are sure to like such abundant offerings. Some care about the actual things, some care about your attitude. No matter what, your offerings must be very abundant: only then can they express your appropriate devotion. Don't think of giving a copper coin to get a mountain of gold. That is not called making offerings, that is being greedy.

But just as we had finished drawing the mandala to increase action, our son came staggering into the room, holding his stomach.

Blood was flowing from the corners of his mouth, and his face was purple, and he was in great danger. I performed the rite for stopping disaster, and although it mitigated many of his symptoms, I still could not totally get rid of that evil curse.

My wife entered into meditative concentration to examine him, and discovered that in this world there was only one person able to rid him of that kind of black curse. This was a dakini whose name was Bandi. I did not know whether or not this was the same person that Sharwadi had spoken of. In her outer form, she was a seamstress. She was a great teacher who had succeeded in her esoteric cultivation, and she was most skilled at stopping disaster. For those who had a karmic affinity with her, she was able to prolong the life of wisdom and the lifespan that had already been cut off.

My wife told me that the dakini was at Vaishali. That was the place where the Buddha had first received women leaving home to become Buddhist nuns. Because of these karmic conditions, countless dakinis gathered there.

So I told my wife to look after our son, and my daughter and I went together to Vaishali.

Chapter 26

The Prostitutes of Vaishali

1 Women Pursuing the Sangha

Khyungpo Naljor talking to Xuemo:

I hurried along to Vaishali, walking fast. Though I did not remember clearly how long I walked, my impression was that the journey was long.

I saw another group of people who were walking just as fast. They were a group of women, made up very beautifully, but they seemed to be in a terrible predicament. They had come from the royal palace of the Sakya clan and were of noble descent. They had heard the Buddha's teaching with their own ears. They already understood that everything in the worldly realm is like an illusory transformation, and they were fleeing toward an unknown emptiness like flood waters in a spillway. They had seen through those empty illusions, and they did not want to drift along lazily through the days any more. They were like that woman called Zixiao that you wrote about in your *The Grey Wolf of Xixia*: they did not want to keep on muddling along through life. Though they had experienced the wondrous pleasures of the five desires, they did not feel the least bit happy, and they could not find any meaning at all. They wanted to lead a different kind of life. They understood clearly that this kind of life would be unspeakably painful in the eyes of ordinary worldly people, but they left that glorious palace resolutely, without looking back.

I discovered an older woman in the group. She was the Buddha's aunt, and her name was Mahaprajapati, which means "Path of Great Love." After the Buddha's birth mother died, it was this woman who raised Buddha, and she was his mother in the true sense. She had a gentle way of acting and a good nature, and she could truly be the model of motherhood for the whole realm. When her husband, King Suddhodana, died, she lost interest in drifting on through ordinary life. She wanted to leave home. She wanted to detach from the wondrous pleasures of the five desires and follow her own beloved son and revered teacher.

One day the Buddha came home to preach, and Mahaprajapati, along with many women in the palace, heard the sound of the Buddha's lion's roar. The clear sound of the Dharma dispelled the dark clouds from her mind: she developed a powerful intention to leave, so she wanted to leave home and become a Buddhist nun. She mentioned her wish to leave home to the Buddha, but the Buddha refused her. She brought it up three times, and the Buddha refused her three times. The Buddha said: "You women cannot leave home. You must cultivate practice at home with a pure mind, and you will be able to detach from suffering and find bliss in this way."

I know that at the time that Princess Mahaprajapati asked to leave home, the conditions for women to leave home were still not fully prepared. The Buddha and his disciples alike were traveling most of the time, traveling through the wild countryside, staying in burial grounds. If women were living like this, it would have attracted countless evil men. Besides this, in India at that time, the position of women was low, and they were the dependents of men. *The Laws of Manu* sets the guidelines for women's behavior like this: "When women are young, they are under the control of their fathers; when they are in their prime, they are under the control of their husbands; and when they are old, they are under the protection of their sons. Women definitely cannot act as they please." If Buddha had taken in women who had left home, vehement indignation would have overwhelmed the monastic community.

Therefore, the Buddha did not permit women to leave home to become nuns.

Mahaprajapati called together several hundred women who wanted to leave home and become Buddhist nuns. They wanted to go together to where the Buddha was staying and make their request to the Buddha. But when they got there, the Buddha had already left.

What I was seeing was precisely these Sakya women pursuing the Buddha. Their delicate footsteps were stirring up endless dust, blurring the more than one thousand years of historical time separating us. I heard their gentle huffing and puffing and saw them sweating through their makeup. I was very moved. My daughter of course did not budge and acted nonchalant, but she was immersed in hatred and anger. She was angry at the woman who had injured her brother. Anger is always very short-sighted, and of course it cannot penetrate a thousand years of misty rain.

I also saw a beautiful woman called Yashodara. Though this name may be unfamiliar, if I give a different explanation, you will certainly remember her story. She was the Buddha's wife before he left home. Whenever I think of her waking up one clear cool morning and discovering that her beloved husband had left for parts unknown, the pain pulls at my heart. I can always experience this woman's gut-wrenching, heart-shattering pain. At that time she was only in her twenties. Though Chandaka brought her the news that her husband had left home, she continued to wait for him with undying affection. Every day she strove to preserve her appearance, washing her face with milk, and cleansing her body with fragrant herbs. She expected that she would wake up some morning and see her husband's handsome face by her side.

She spent many years in this state of expectation.

One day, she heard tell that the Buddha had achieved enlightenment, and would return home. She was very happy, and her heart was overflowing with honey. At that time she still did not clearly understand the implications of achieving enlightenment. She felt that after her husband had found the thing he was looking for, he must surely return home. Just like a fisherman who has gone fishing always returns home with his catch, after her husband had found what he needed, he would return home to enjoy the pleasures of family life. So her honey heart was overflowing with euphoria and expectation.

At that time there was still a jewel in her hand — that was her son. The son was very lovable. He had an angelic quality, and in his pure eyes was stored the mother's endless happiness. She believed that the Buddha would surely like his son. Certainly that was right. She thought that the Buddha might not care about her, but it would be impossible for him not to care about his son — he was such a lovable son.

She even believed that after his son called him, her husband would give a long sigh and be done with that dream of traveling to distant places.

When she finally saw the face she had dreamed of countless time, it was filled with compassion. She was delighted by this breath of compassion, but she could not find the thing she had been expecting. She hoped to see a secret indication of tacit understanding, no matter how small, but there was none. The slight smile on this handsome face was pure and bright as the clear sky. At the same time, she heard a voice she had never heard before, a relaxed and composed voice, and though she did not understand fully what it was saying, she felt the incomparable purity.

She gently exhaled and turned her gaze toward her son. The son was very obedient and rushed to his father. She expected that his father would open his arms and embrace their son. She hoped that he would be like countless fathers, lift his son up over his head, and come out with murmuring sound of vague happiness. She certainly did not imagine that when her son rushed over to his father, he would unexpectedly have another kind of thought.

The son knelt down a few yards from his father—just like countless people who came to pay homage to the Buddha. What surprised her the most was that her son came out with a request:

"I want to leave home!"

I saw her at that instant, thunderstruck.

At this instant, I too was thunderstruck, suddenly thinking of Sharwadi. I thought that the pain of longing that Sharwadi had gone through would certainly not be lesst han Yashodara. My mind was wrenched by the pain.

I do not know how Yashodara lived through those days when her son left her. When she too decided to take the initiative and leave home, I finally heaved a sigh of relief.

I discovered that among the group of women pursuing the Buddha, she was very striking. She truly was incomparably beautiful. Along the side of the road there were countless non-Buddhists looking at those women. When they found out that the women's goal was to follow after the Buddha, the non-Buddhists were making a clamor. These of course were catcalls. Buddhist monks at that time mostly lived in the same places as the non-Buddhist ascetics, in dense woods or cemetery forests. Even in your time, how do you think people would regard you if several hundred women were madly pursuing you, Xuemo? At that time two thousand years ago, it would be even worse. The sound of those derisive catcalls was earth-shattering.

Sweating profusely, those women pressed on. No matter how much effort they made, they were always a day's journey from the Buddha and his group of monks. Their bodies where covered with mud. Their hair had become disheveled and was dancing around in the wind like comets. When they got hungry they ate a few morsels, and when they got thirsty they took a bit of rain water. They followed the Buddha for thousands of miles, they followed him for thousands of years. Finally, in a certain moment, they followed him into history. They only hoped that history would grant them an unfamiliar name—bhiksuni, Buddhist nun.

I saw the Buddha's compassionate face filled with indifference. That indifference was the earth's crust on top of the magma. He too had heard the mocking catcalls of the non-Buddhists along the road. He had heard this kind of sound many times, and the loudest mockery of all was when he accepted Upali as a disciple. Upali was born a lower-class person, an "untouchable." According to the standards of that time, if a lower-class person stepped in the shadow of an upper-class person, he would get the death penalty. Those whom the people of the time considered "untouchables" were the unluckiest living beings in the world. To come in contact with one of them would bring a lifetime of bad luck, and even send you to hell. Thus, when the Buddha accepted Upali as a disciple, the whole world was in an uproar, and some disciples even left the Buddhist monastic community because of this.

This time, if the Buddha accepted a woman as a disciple, that would truly be an even more scandalous.

Princess Yashodara felt the situation was utterly hopeless and cried out in pain. The hundreds of Sakya women with her lost hope too, and were wiping away their tears.

At this time a monk walked over. Even today, a thousand years later, he is still venerated by countless Buddhist nuns.

This was Ananda.

"I will go try to ask him," he said.

He went to the Buddha.

Again and again he used his unique wisdom and verbal skill to get the Buddha to change his viewpoint. The Buddha at first refused, but in the end he gave his consent. After he had established a system of very strict rules of conduct, he permitted those women to become Buddhist nuns.

For this reason, Ananda is the person my daughter most respects.

Although what she cultivates is the esoteric teaching that I passed on to her, the one she usually makes offering to is Ananda.

2 The Protector Spirit of the Mango Tree

I also saw a courtesan. The city of Vaishali showed a different kind of gentleness because she existed. That woman was as dignified as a goddess, and had no equal in the world. There was not a man who could resist the fragrance of her body, there was not a man who could stand up to her gentle words. When she sang in her clear voice, the hundred lark would all go mute. There were countless carriages in front of her gate, and all kinds of well-dressed gentlemen came and went.

There was no one who did not know here name. She was called Amrapali, which means "Protector Spirit of the Mango Tree." She lived in a mango grove, about an hour's journey from Vaishali. In your present way of calculating, it was probably about eight kilometers from the city. Her home was very opulent and grand and incomparably luxurious. At that time, all the local women bitterly hated this woman, because they were always hearing their husbands saying things in their sleep connected to her. The story goes that even the kings at the time all wanted to die drunk in that mango grove. At the very mention of this woman, the queens would spew out endless jealous remarks.

Nobody thought that this woman, who was a filthy prostitute to the eye of people world, had the purest mind in the world. One day, when she had gone out, the Buddha came on foot to her mango grove. In that period, the Buddha was already past eighty, an old man. When the woman heard tell that the Buddha had come, she immediately went out and hurried to the mango grove, wanting to hear the Buddha's teaching. The Buddha smiled upon her like a father, and explained to her the ultimate truth. The courtesan felt completely purified, and generated the greatest faith. Thus, she hoped that the Buddha would give her a chance, and allow her to make offerings to the Buddha and his group of monks the next day at noon. The Buddha silently consented to this request.

After news of this got around, there was another uproar of the same sort. How could the supremely honorable Buddha accept the offerings of a prostitute? Many people were infuriated. They thought of many ways to deal with the situation, and finally they proposed a plan. Their hope was to have the noblemen give the courtesan a hundred thousand gold pieces in exchange for giving up this opportunity to make offerings to the Buddha.

But Amrapali refused.

In this refusal, I saw her incomparable nobility.

Amrapali cleaned her beautiful home until it was spotless, and bought many kinds of delicious food. She expended great energy, converted her devotion to the Buddha into fine food and positive action, and left behind a beautiful moment in history.

The Buddha accepted her delicious food. She accepted the Buddha's truth. She finally understood that her beauty in fact would be as evanescent as droplets of dew in the hot sun. So she went toward a more lasting truth. She took what she loved most, her grand house, and offered it to the Buddha, to be used as a monastery for nuns to cultivate the Path. Before long, she cut off her beautiful hair, which was like a black cloud, and became a legitimate Buddhist nun.

According to the story that was circulating at that time, this nun was the previous incarnation of the dakini Bandi whom I was seeking.

Although Amrapali achieved the result of becoming an arhat while the Buddha was in the world, she made a great vow: for immeasurable eons, in the form of a woman, she would deliver sentient beings.

My daughter and I wandered along every street and lane in Vaishali, looking for Bandi. According to the story, after the Buddha delivered her, she saved sentient beings, lifetime after lifetime, in the body of a woman, but she never again sold sexual favors — she made a living as a seamstress. You have seen many seamstresses in the streets of Liangzhou, right? She was that kind of seamstress. They live on the streets, and when the blazing sun is in the sky, they put on gauze masks to cover their mouths. But in India a thousand years ago, people did not have the custom of putting on gauze masks, so since she was out in the wind and the hot sun, Bandi's complexion became very dark.

As we walked one street after another, we observed various seamstresses. They were all ordinary seamstresses. My daughter was also searching, and although she possessed many spiritual powers, in essence she was still a child. She had not experienced the vicissitudes of the human world, and a child is always just a child.

Finally, I saw a special sign of the spiritual on one of the seamstresses. That so-called special sign of the spiritual would in fact have been very easy to overlook. I had seen that, when their thread broke, all these women would use their hands to fix it. But this one scrawny woman simply moved her eyes across the broken thread, and it would be joined together again.

I went up to her and bowed down with my head at her feet. The woman gave a cold smile and said: "O patron, why do you need to bow down like this?"

I said: "O Bandi the dakini, I have finally found you."

She said: "Why are you looking for me?"

So then I explained what had happened to my son. She smiled coldly and said: "In this world there is a rule which says 'self-made, self-received.' No one can escape from this rule. You son must receive the consequences of the actions he did."

I knew that what she said was very correct, and I did not try to offer a justification for my son. You must understand that when you are face to face with this kind of dakini, any justifications and excuses are meaningless. I was just ashamed: ashamed for my son, and ashamed of myself for not teaching him better. But apart from this, I did hope she would generate the mind of enlightenment, and clear away my son's difficulties.

Then the expression on her face gradually became more gentle.

She entered meditative concentration for a moment and observed the set of karmic causes and conditions. She said: "Your son's difficulties in life are not ordinary and cannot be cured by the ordinary antidotes." She said: "I must go to the foot of Spirit Mountain, and look for a giant stone. In that stone, there is a golden toad which has not seen the sun for a thousand years. Under its belly it holds three hailstones. I must kill that golden toad, take those hailstones and put them into the belly of the golden toad, and bring it back for your son to eat. Only then will his difficulties be resolved. In fact, your son only has a hundred days left. In that hundred days, I have to hurry there, open up that stone, and hurry back. I wonder if there will be enough time to do that."

She saw the dismay on my face, and she reassured me: "You mustn't worry. I'll do all I can. You may not know that your son has already been my son three times, and I have a karmic connection with him. I have to be concerned about what happens to him. Within a hundred days, I will find your house."

When she finished speaking, she left us.

3 The Cooperating Cause of the Poison Mushrooms

I told my daughter to go home and, together with her mother, take care of her brother.

As for me, I kept looking for wonder-workers in Vaishali. I was thinking that the more wonder-workers were protecting him, the safer my son would be. Perhaps you can understand the mentality of being a father.

I really did discover a few mysterious people in Vaishali. I saw a headless man: his eyes were his two nipples, and from his belly came the sound of chanting sutras. I could even hear the *Mahaprajna Sutra* coming from him. I also saw a strange man who had a wooden stopper in his solar plexus, and when he pulled out the wooden stopper, I could see a Buddha Land in his heart chakra. When he lit a lamp, he did not use a match; he just pulled out the wooden stopper, and a beam of light would radiate out and light the lamp. There was another mysterious man who had a mirror hanging in front of his chest, and anyone could see his own future in the mirror. If you felt dissatisfied with that future, you could go into the mirror, and change the course of events … There were many others, too; I will not describe them one by one. Do not ask me if they were real or not. In my eyes, nothing was real any more. Everything was real, and everything was an illusion.

When I begged them to protect my son, they all said that the causal conditions were not there with them.

But the one with the jeweled mirror on his chest agreed to let me return to my past. He did not ask me for gold. He said that on a certain day a thousand years earlier, he and I had been together in the same community of monks, and because of this karmic connection, he would not demand anything from me.

I went into that mirror.

I discovered that I had entered the Vaishali of a thousand-year ago. There were many monks traveling with me. I saw that there was a hammock hanging between two trees, and the Buddha was lying in it. As I saw him, the Buddha had already become very feeble. At that time, he was always saying: "Ananda, my back hurts." Whenever you see this period, you will always cry. This is a story that is often seen in the *Agama Sutra*. Although you also like the Buddha with vast spiritual powers, you like even more this old man who still keeps traveling on foot to teach, even though he is bothered by back pain.

I saw that Ananda was crying. At that time, he had not yet detached from desire. He was always worrying that the Buddha would leave him. He was like an immature child, and what he feared most was that the Buddha would depart without saying goodbye, and pass away. As he looked at the Buddha, Ananda could not stop crying. He said: "O Buddha, when you are sick, what I most fear is that you will leave us. But then I think that the Buddha will definitely not leave us without imparting some final teachings. It is precisely this point that accompanies me through these fearful days."

At that time, I too had the same emotions. Every time I thought that the Buddha would ultimately leave us, I felt the sun and moon no longer had light. I could not imagine days without the Buddha. I think the other monks all certainly felt the same way; their eyes were filled with expecting. They hoped, of course, that the Buddha would be able to rerwain in the world forever. But at the same time, they understood that in this world there is only eternal truth, there is no eternal life.

The Buddha looked at Ananda with compassion, and looked at us. He knew, of course, what we were thinking about. At that time the Buddha gave a long talk, which is preserved in the *Great Final Nirvana Sutra* in the Pali Canon and is also preserved in our relatively everlasting memories.

In his old age, the Buddha displayed his incomparable compassion more and more. His voice was increasingly kindly, like the light touch of the sunlight at dusk. This was the time at Vaishali that was hardest to forget. The Buddha left behind his final instruction here.

The Buddha's voice was relaxed and soft. He said: "Ananda,

although you hope I will leave a final teaching, I want to direct you to detach from the sea of suffering, and directly arrive at the citadel of nirvana. I understand your minds. You must know that my truth has already been explained to you in its entirety, implicitly and explicitly, and I have hidden nothing. I have not been the least bit stingy in communicating the truth.

"Ananda, in the world there are people who will think that they themselves can be what the sangha relies on forever, but I myself have certainly never thought of this. You must know that the physical body of the Tathagata is also impermanent. Now I have grown old, and my body is weak, and my life will soon be over. My body is like a broken cart that will soon fall apart, and even if I make every effort to tend to it, I won't be able to use it much longer. Ananda, if even the physical body of the Tathagata is like this, how can you find something to rely on forever?

"Ananda, you must take your own true mind as the bright lamp; you must rely on your own true mind; do not rely on external things. You rely on the truth; you must not rely on other impermanent things. As long as you rely on the truth, on the true mind, and on the Buddha Dharma, you will then have a genuine refuge to rely upon. Apart from this, you cannot find anything in the world that you can truly rely upon forever. You must abide in true mind, and make progress in your practice. Only then will it be possible to reach the peaceful and blissful Other Shore."

But the Buddha's instruction still could not dispel Ananda's fears. At that time Ananda still had not yet detached from desire, and whenever he thought of the Buddha leaving him forever, he would cry in pain. He did not dare imagine days without the Buddha. He was right: would the sky without the sun still count as the sky? Ananda kept crying and crying. So the Buddha thought: "It's still this way even for Ananda, who has been continuously by my side as my attendant. The monks who have not been Buddhists for very long, and who have still not discovered the Path for cultivating realization, will not know what to do." So the Buddha had Ananda call together all the monks who were in the vicinity of Vaishali, and he gave his last teaching session.

Thus Vaishali is remembered in history as the site of the Buddha's final time turning the wheel of the Dharma.

The Buddha said: "All you monks, in three months I am going to enter final nirvana. The teachings I have given, you must consider well, cultivate well, practice well, and pass on well, so the wheel of the Dharma will endure for a long time and benefit countless sentient beings. You must understand that all worldly phenomena are phenomena that result from the combination of causal conditions, and they do not have any eternal inherent essence. They are certain to decompose and come to an end, and you must not cling to them. Now my life is coming to an end, and I will finally leave you. You must rely on your own true mind, make progress in cultivating practice, uphold discipline, and contemplate the truth. Then you will be able to transcend the sufferings of revolving in birth and death and realize the quiet bliss."

I saw Buddha's compassionate face filled with expectation.

In order to commemorate Buddha's teaching at this final assembly, many years later King Ashoka of the Maurya Dynasty erected a stone pillar here. It was several dozen feet high, and at the top of it was carved a lotus flower, and a lion on the lotus flower, facing the northwest, giving forth a mighty roar. This stone pillar has already stood tall for more than two thousand years. Because its workmanship is very beautiful and out of the ordinary, it has provoked countless speculations from later day people. Some scholars even think that India at that time could not have had such a high level of sculpture.

The wind of Vaishali was swirling through the fallen leaves. In the sky, so high and far away, there was a white moon shining in the air.

Not long afterwards, a blacksmith found some very beautiful mushrooms. He could not bear to eat them: he wanted to offer them to the Buddha. The Buddha could not bear to refuse the good intentions of the blacksmith, so he went along with him and accepted the offering, but he gave instructions not to let the other monks eat the mushrooms. Later, the Buddha passed blood in his stool. I saw that the blacksmith was devastated with regret, and the Buddha comforted him saying: "In this world there are two kinds of people whose merit is the greatest: one kind are those people who give offerings to the Buddha when he achieves enlightenment, and one kind are those who give offerings to the Buddha when he enters nirvana and dies."

Relying on the cooperating cause of the poison mushrooms, Buddha passed away into nirvana.

4 The Venerable Yasas

In that mirror that could penetrate through time and space, I saw an old man. He was the Venerable Yasas. He was a Theravada elder, famous for his lofty virtue, with extraordinary spiritual attainments. He traveled around while preserving the purity of the enlightenment in his mind.

Following that old man's footprints, I saw the scenery of Vaishali. I discovered that it was a village on a plain, under a clear sky with pale clouds, a wide expanse of flat land. You may have heard of a historical epic called the *Ramayana*. In it there is a good king called Vishal, who was from Vaishali.

Although Vaishali was one of the six great ancient kingdoms of old India, when I saw it, it had already lost the prosperity of days gone by. It was more like a grassy plain, and its former glory had already become a ruin. There were many ancient ruins here, but nobody cared. The donkeys were grazing on the grasslands, and to prevent them from running off, the owners had tied hobbling ropes to their back legs. This way they could only lower their heads to eat grass, and it was very hard for them to run away.

The Venerable Yasas also saw those donkeys. He thought of the countless donkeys in the world who were hobbled by their desires. Those ropes were very much like revolving in birth and death.

The old man walked past a giant pond. It was rectangular, and the water was very pure, and it mirrored the white clouds in the sky. When a slight breeze swept across it, the water rippled and revealed an infinite cool purity. Many kings had passed by here. Before becoming kings, they had to have a coronation ceremony. First they washed themselves clean in the pond, then they were anointed with fragrant oil. Then after being crowned, they held the lawful power recognized by worldly people.

The old man saw a Buddhist stupa. This was just a small stupa, built of bricks, shaped like an inverted bowl, about twenty feet high. The old man joined his palms together and bowed down to the Buddhist stupa. I know that this was a stupa containing relics of the Buddha. More than a hundred years earlier, eight kingdoms had divided up the Buddha's relics, and the Licchavis also received a share. They had built a stupa here dedicated to the relics of the Buddha. The old man certainly did not know that, many years later, this stupa would be destroyed by the flames of war. Still less would he have thought that a thousand years later, Buddhism itself would be verging on extinction in this wondrous land.

The old man also bowed to another small stupa. This was the stupa containing the cremains of Ananda. For many years after Buddha died, Ananda still traveled all around disseminating the truth. One day, as he was walking somewhere, he heard a novice monk reciting the text of a sutra, confusing the text's meaning, and making all kinds of mistakes. Ananda corrected him, and he reprimanded the novice, disliking the way he was always getting mixed up. Then Ananda thought: "Sentient beings are ignorant and hard to teach, and they cannot clearly understand the true teaching. Of the many people I practiced with before, many have died, and I am the only one left, a decrepit old man. Rather than be a bother, it would be better to die." So he left behind the kingdom of Magadha where he had been traveling and teaching, and intended to cross the Ganges River and go to Vaishali. Unexpectedly, the kings of the two countries got word of this, and each of them posted cavalry on his side of the Ganges; they both wanted to invite Ananda to come to their country for his final nirvana. Ananda was afraid of provoking a war. So using his spiritual powers, he flew up into the sky above the Ganges and using the true fire of samadhi, he burned up his own body. He also took his relics and divided them into two portions: one portion descended into the kingdom of Magadha, and one portion descended into Vaishali. The kingdom of Vaishali then built a stupa dedicated to him.

The old man Yasas also passed by a pond. This was the Macaque Pond spoken of in the Buddhist scriptures. The Buddha had sat in meditation here. All the macaques were happy, and they all worked together to dig into the ground and make a pond, which they offered to the Buddha. One of the macaques also took the Buddha's bowl, gathered some honey from a tree, and presented it to the Buddha. After the Buddha accepted the offering, the Macaque was very happy and was jumping up and down. Unexpectedly, it lost its footing and fell to the ground and died. But because of the merit it had earned by making an offering to the Buddha, its spiritual consciousness immediately went up to the heavens, and it became a heavenly being.

The old man finally ended his journey and stopped in front of a large monastery.

He saw something he had not anticipated: a monk was asking a crowd of believers for money. The monk had filled his begging bowl with water, and he told the people that if they put their money into the water, it would be a pure donation, and they would receive a big reward.

The old man became angry.

This was because in Buddha's rules of monastic discipline, it is absolutely forbidden for monks to accept money.

The old man walked on rapidly and traveled all over. He criticized this obvious violation of the rules, and the monks who accepted money, but he met with mockery from many people. He also discovered ten unpardonable practices. In Buddhist history these are called "the ten practices."

More than seven hundred Buddhist monks came to Vaishali at the behest of the Venerable Yasas and held the second council in Buddhist history. The Theravada elders judged the ten practices, including the "pure donations," to be in violation of the Buddhist Teaching, but the ordinary monastic communities were unwilling to submit to this. After this, Buddhism was divided into two great systems: the "Western Theravada" and the "Eastern Mahasanghika."

This was the first great schism in Buddhist history. After this,

Buddhism entered into its sectarian period. Plain, original Buddhism gradually faded from people's field of vision.

5 The Drug of Immortality

I had searched around Vaishali for many days. Though I met some unusual people, I did not find anyone who could genuinely remove my son's difficulties.

All I could do was return home. My son was still listless and looked like he had lost his spirit. My daughter was very angry, and at times she was ranting. She very much wanted to go get revenge, but my wife and I persuaded her not to. I thought that at the time what had to be done first was not to exact revenge, but to save our son's life.

I fell into a state of great anxiety. This was something that had not happened for the last several years. My son's illness occupied the space and time of my life.

Before I encountered this situation, I still thought that I had succeeded in cultivating practice. After Sukhasiddhi instructed me in the inherent nature of mind, I have felt I could control my own mind. I even considered that state of calm composure to be the cessation of affliction that comes after succeeding in Buddhist practice. I had not thought that when something happened, I would still be unable to control my mind. This in itself made me feel terrible.

All along I kept performing the fire ceremony for halting disasters, hoping I would be able to put an end to my son's difficulties, but I found the results I got were minimal. My son had a kind of listlessness, as if his life essence had been drained dry. He sat there inertly, and his eyes did not seem to move. The son who used to be so mischievous and arrogant had disappeared, and all that was left was a bodily shell that seemed like a living dead man — this phrase jolts my heart .

In addition to performing the fire ceremony for stopping things, our family was impatiently awaiting the arrival of the dakini Bandi.

During that period of time, with sorrow and anxiety enveloping our whole family, I finally truly understood the saying, "the world of mortals is like a fiery prison." Day and night I thought only of my son's illness. I was thinking: I cannot be without my son, I cannot face my beloved son withering away and dying right before my eyes. I did my utmost to cultivate the methods I had previously found for stopping disasters, but because I had lost my purity of mind, none of the methods I cultivated got a response. My wife and my daughter were also performing fire ceremonies for stopping disasters, and the house was always full of smoke. This added to our sense of affliction and depression.

Very quickly, my illusions were shattered.

The dakini Bandi had truly found a remedy. She crossed ninety-nine rivers and streams, turned over eighty-eight mountains, and ended up finding a drug of immortality that could remove mortal problems. It was hidden in a rock that had been left in the wilderness since ancient times. It was a hard holy stone like the diamond seat. It had the hardness of granite, the precious quality of diamond, and the exquisite nature of crystal. The stone did not have any cracks — it was a natural seamless whole. There was a depression on the stone, and in the depression there was a golden toad. That golden toad had been in a state of meditative concentration for a billion years. Under the belly of the golden toad were three doses of the drug of immortality in the shape of three hailstones.

I had heard it said that to be able to open up that stone, one had to be a holy sage who had awakened to the empty inherent nature. In the eyes of the holy sages, no matter whether it was granite or anything else, everything was like a dream, like an illusion, without the least real substance. When worldly clingings and attachments dissolved in the wisdom of the holy sage, and when the causal conditions were all sufficient, only then could this stone be opened.

That is how the dakini obtained the three doses of the drug of immortality.

The dakini took the drug and put it into the belly of the golden toad. Holding a jewel vial of energy, traveling a thousand miles a day, she came to us. She found our village. But that day the causes and conditions were not favorable. We had just gone to a spirit shrine and made a vow. I had never done this sort of thing before. To my eye, all vows seeking favors from the spirits were, in fact, a kind of clinging and ignorance. But after my son got sick, I too changed. I discovered that if there is someone you love, there will be someone you suffer over. When the Buddha proposed that monks leave home, he had this in mind. Ever since I had had a wife—even if she had the label "Niguma"—I had had many worldly afflictions.

You can certainly understand my feelings.

For this reason, the dakini did not see us.

I do not know how my life would have changed if she had found us and saved my son.

That's right. You might ask: If my son had not died, if my daughter had not met with disaster later on, if my family had not gone through subsequent unforeseen misfortunes, would I still have been the Khyungpo Naljor you know so well, or not?

Child, I do not know. Ask yourself, if after you graduated from high school, you had gone to Peking University, would you still have become the present Xuemo or not?

You do not know. Right?

Everything can change. Everything in the world is always changing. Sometimes, what some little thing controls, can be a person's whole life.

Many times even world historical changes originate with some minor matter.

Aren't you always telling that story? One time, on the eve of a great battle, a groom goes to shoe the horse the king rides. Because the groom is impatient, he does not attach one of the horseshoes properly. In the heat of battle, the horseshoe falls off, and because the horse breaks stride, the king falls off the horse. The soldiers think the king has been slain in action. They scatter and are routed. The army being defeated is like a mountain falling, and the nation perishes because of this, and world history, too, is changed by this.

That's right. Many things are this way. A dyke a thousand miles long cracks because of a hole made by an ant.

I think that, if not for these unforeseen events, I certainly would have sunk into that gentle village home life, and I would not have been able to wake up. I certainly would have thought that I had already found the ultimate truth. We must realize that finding the ultimate truth implies changing one's mind and behavior; it is not just a theoretical understanding. Although those many dakinis explained many truths to me, if they had not been able to shed light on my life, and illuminate my human life, then all those so-called truths would have been just a kind of intellectual knowledge. No matter how much intellectual knowledge a person has, if that intellectual knowledge cannot become his wisdom, he is just a bookcase or library. No matter how big the library, after a great fire, it can all become a ruin. That great fire can be greed, it can be ignorance, and it can be hatred. That's why our ancestors said: "Fire burns the forest of virtue."

Because of the existence of forgetfulness, all the intellectual knowledge that you can put into your mind may one day leave you. Only when you take intellectual knowledge and transform it into wisdom, and it becomes your breath that is inseparable from you, only then will it merge with the very essence of your life.

That's why, in terms of my life, the dakini missing us that time can hardly be called a tragedy.

6 The Lion-faced Dakini

Xuemo, following the pure light of my mind and spirit, you have entered with me into that time and space.

Right. That extremely ugly-looking woman that you see is the dakini Bandi. She was called the lion-faced dakini by the local people. Later, in the religious paintings circulating in Tibet, you can see that image. She was the great protector of the Dharma for many accomplished adepts. Someday later on, she will obey you the way a little maidservant treats her master. Do not be confused by her external appearance ... That's right, she appears to be very fierce, but that ferocity is in fact a kind of fearless feeling.

That's right, she appears ugly, but those concepts of beauty and ugliness are in fact people's discriminating minds. To my eye, she is really as beautiful as a female celestial. In the eyes of the countless people whose lives she saved, she is radiant with light and beautiful beyond compare.

She belongs to the worldly dakinis. Of course, this does not mean that she has not been able to awaken to the empty inherent nature; rather, it means that she has taken a vow to use the form of a worldly dakini to benefit sentient beings.

She is just now going to our house.

Look, that wooden house hidden in the beautiful clearing in the forest was my home at that time.

Do not ask me whether or not it really existed. For me at that time, it certainly did really exist. But for our narrative at this moment, it is just a memory.

You must know that all that exists in the world can change into memories.

Even now, I still have feelings of gratitude toward that wooden house. Although in my life it represents a kind of past, and to the eye of many people in the world this past was a kind of negative experience, nevertheless, it was always another cooperating cause that made me understand clearly. Without this experience, I would not be Khyungpo Naljor. In the same way, without those experiences where you were disparaged by other people, you would not have become Xuemo.

One day, your wife might say to you that you are the most "evil" man in the world. She may say that when she was twenty, you made her wait, and now that she is fifty, you are still making her wait. You may say: "This was your choice. The one you chose was not a man who did not have to make you wait." When she chose Xuemo, she chose the whole of Xuemo. That's right, it really is this way. In the same way, when your disciples choose you, it is the same as choosing the whole of you. They chose your glory and brilliance, and at the same time they chose the disparagement which other people direct at you. These two sides, the light and the dark, form your life as a whole.

It is the same way with me. When you are facing Khyungpo Naljor, in fact you are facing my life as a whole. When you chose me to be your teacher, you also chose the whole of me. This whole contains that part of my life in the wooden house. Though that was a period of time I regret very much, still, you must know that many times I truly had no other choice.

We continue to look at that pure light.

Look, that lion-faced dakini has encountered a woman from the enemy family.

The dakini asked: "Do you know where the family of Khyungpo Ba has gone?"

The woman lied and said: "The whole family has gone to the cemetery forest. Their son died three days ago. They went to take his body there."

When the dakini heard this, she cried out hopelessly: "I have come too late." She got upset and threw away the golden toad. The golden toad flew up in an arc and as soon as it was in the air, it was swallowed by one of the surrounding non-human onlookers.

In India at that time, such things were always happening. In that period, the esoteric teaching was circulating in the world, and there were many legends in circulation as well. Of course, you can take my experience as a kind of traditional story. Sometimes legends are true. After many scenes of life that really did exist have faded away, legends then occupy the time and space. Legends, in fact, are more real than real life, and more powerful. If a kind of life was not able to become a legend, then in terms of the world, it never existed. What circulates in the world and can be passed down can only be legends. In many forms—oral tradition or written texts or images and so on—they carry, in the form of "legends," the existences that have passed away.

So do not ask if that golden toad was real or not. In this world, legends are real. Of course, I never saw that golden toad. But the lion-faced dakini said that she saw it, so she saw it.

How can we say she didn't?

I remember one day a journalist said that the local dialect in your book *Desert Rites* was not necessarily accurate. You said: "No matter whether it is accurate or not, in the future they will take mine as the standard." ... Ha-ha. It really is like this. After all the many existences of Liangzhou have faded away, what will be left will only be your texts. The people of the world cannot find existences that have passed away. What they can find is only your texts. They will certainly take your texts as the standard.

The story of the golden toad and the medicine of immortality is also like this.

If there are people who want to ask if these stories are true or false, the people asking are certainly fools. This is because the wise ones all know that everything in this world is all a giant play of illusion. Birth, death, everything that flows and moves — all of it reveals an empty falsity that flies by and quickly dissolves. Everything in the end will become a memory. The greater part of it will be forgotten, and what remains will become legends.

7 The Collapse of the Hall of Faith

And later?

Later, there was a series of bloody incidents. The dakini Bandi killed that woman, and that woman's clan tried to take revenge. The enemies retaliated against each other, and the smell of blood filled the air. My dearly beloved daughter also died, as the two sides sent curses at each other.

You have already left a lot of writing about those curses. Of course, you have a thorough knowledge of the ritual forms of those curses. I remember that you said that, although the different religions have different curses, their real substance is mostly to rely on some spiritual rituals to stimulate the hatred in the practitioner's mind and spirit, and to mobilize some dark energy in the universe so it can match its frequency and resonate with it. This, of course, is your explanation, which I know is an expedient to accord with the world. You will think that since scientists recognize that in the universe there is ninety-six percent dark matter and dark energy, you might as well explain it this way. But you must remember that all the explanations in the world, including the scientific ones and the religious ones, are just explanations. Explanations can never take the place of the true characteristic. The function of explanations is to help people fully understand the true characteristic. Explanations are not the true characteristic. In every person's mind there can be different explanations, but the true characteristic is formless. That true characteristic is also called the characteristic of reality.

Remember, what can be explained clearly will never be the true characteristic.

The true characteristic will never be explained clearly, but you can use wisdom to approach it, and even to merge with it.

I have nightmarish memories of what happened with those gory curses.

First of all, my son died.

My son died very cruelly. His face was like charcoal, he was emaciated as a skeleton, and his body was bent. After having convulsions for several days, he finally stopped breathing.

My wife cried until she almost stopped breathing too.

Though my wife had the appearance of a heavenly being, she looked very much like the Niguma in my mind—before the curse was placed on our son, I had always considered her to be Niguma. You must understand that my wife, in my mind, was in reality shaped according to the needs of my mind and spirit.

Haven't you often encountered this kind of thing in your life? The girls who are good at imagining things always take swindlers and petty people and fashion them in their minds into artists or religious practitioners. Swindlers who are completely idle and ignorant do not need to work to support themselves. They depend for their livelihoods totally on the hard work of their girls. These lovable and pitiable girls think they are making a contribution to the arts or to faith. But they basically do not know that the ones they are supporting with their youth, their lives, and their love — and they take the control and possession these guys exercise over them as love, to intoxicate and console themselves — they do not know that these are in fact shiftless guys and swindlers. If a woman meets an irrational thug, or if she discovers she has been cheated but cannot save herself, or if she discovers the true situation and depression enters her mind, or even worse, some evil disease troubles her and she loses her health — her such life is wasted. You have looked on helplessly as those women, filled with yearning, rush into the arms of swindlers waving the banner of "faith" or "love." Your mind hurts as if it is being cut with a knife, but there is nothing you can do about it. You know, after their brains are besotted by the wine of "faith" or "love," they get so that even their grandmas don't want them. Even if you shout so loud you wreck your throat, there is no helping it. When the true situation becomes clear, when the raw rice has already been cooked, when they have children at their knees, and the vicissitudes of life have entered their minds, all they can do is acknowledge the sufferings of life and drink the bitter wine. Or if they are unwilling to do this, and they choose divorce, then they are taking the bitter fruit of faith and throwing it onto their pathetic children.

This world is always filled with these kinds of regrets. These regrets become an excellent footnote to the truth discovered by the Buddha, that "all defiled things are painful."

That's right. At that time, I was also this way. In my eyes as I was at that time, Niguma was radiant with light and her wisdom was matchless. I even took the ordinary things she said as wondrous words of wisdom. She and I undertook what we considered to be *coupled practice*, and we produced a pair of lovable children... Ha-ha. Don't laugh.

Only after our son became sick, did I discover that this Niguma was definitely not the Niguma I was seeking, because she had not detached from desire. She suffered intense pain from our son being cursed. She wore out her eyes looking to our son's health to be restored. She also performed many fire ceremonies to pray for good fortune and to neutralize disaster. Because I too was doing this, I did not realize what was inappropriate about her. I was only aware of the fact that she seemed to some extent to be unable to control her own mind.

But on the day our son died, I had doubts about her. As soon as he stopped breathing, she rushed forward and starting clawing at our son like a mad woman, as if she wanted to pull back the life which had just departed from him. You know that this was not right. At that moment in time, what she should have done was to remain peaceful and calm. Our son needed peace and calm to have a dignified departure. At that point, any action on his physical body, for him, was close to being slaughtered. Though he had stopped breathing, his spiritual consciousness had not yet left his body, and every time he was touched, it was like being cut with a knife, painful beyond compare. And that pain would certainly make him give rise to the mind of anger.

And that mind of anger would impel him to descend into hell. But my wife, besides clawing at him, was also crying out in a loud voice, and her tears where falling on our son's body. All of these were evil karmic conditions that would allow our son descend into the evil planes of existence.

If she were really Niguma, she could not have not known this.

I was also thinking, if she were truly Niguma, she definitely would not have forgotten herself this way. The reason she forgot herself was because her mind could not control itself. If she could not control her mind, could she still be Niguma?

At that instant, the rivers and seas turned upside down in my mind. For me, the shock that this discovery gave me was heavier than my son's death.

The Niguma, whom I had wasted so many years to find, was actually not Niguma after all.

At this, my thoughts turned to ashes. I thought: Is there anything more fearful than the collapse of the hall of faith?

Amidst this end of the illusion, I took my son's body to the cemetery forest. After those wolves swallowed my son's body, I suddenly felt faint: had I really had a son or not?

8 The Fearful Curse of the Barrel of Demons

And later?

Later I was like that man Tolstoy you always mention: I fled from my home.

What must be emphasized is that my fleeing originated in the first instance from my discovery. At the same time I discovered that empty illusion, the fleeing started.

As if wandering in a dream, I left that village. The myriad forms were empty and hazy, and I too was empty and hazy. The I who was empty and hazy left the empty and hazy world. But the strange thing was that, at the same time, I realized I had never left anything. In that instant, I suddenly discovered that the basic substance of inherent nature in fact has no coming and no going.

You must know that genuine fleeing has two stages: first is discovering the empty illusion, and second is beginning to search.

So I again began a new search.

As for that Niguma, this may have been a bit cruel. But I told her that after I had found the real Niguma, I would first come back and save her.

I did not know whether or not she would turn into another Sharwadi. Likewise I did not know, if I really got married with Sharwadi, whether or not I would drop into a barrel of demons in a different sense.

When I started to search, Sukhasiddhi found me.

She told me that the prerequisite for the teacher finding the disciple was that the disciple has already begun to search. During the time when I had abandoned the search, she did not want to look for me. Faith only exists in the mind of the one who is seeking faith. That is why the ancestral teachers said: "The Buddha does not save people with no karmic connection to him."

She told me my true situation. Then I finally realized that what I had fallen into was a fearful curse of the barrel of demons. In the illumination of the light of the teacher's wisdom, I discovered that the Niguma who had lived with me for twenty-two years was, in reality, an ordinary woman. Our *coupled practice* was desire labeled as faith. Later, I did not achieve the rainbow body like the real Niguma, because during this period of time I had lost too many points of light.

Within the demonic power of that curse, I had created what seemed to me to be a life of faith.

In that fearful barrel of delusive demons, I had passed twenty-two years of time.This differed from a daydream where what seems like several decades to the person in the dream is really only a short time. That is to say, though the person has several decades of illusory dreamlike experience, he has not been wasting his life. But what I went through in the barrel of demons really did take twenty-two years.

My hundred-and-fifty-year lifespan of course included this twenty-two years. Luckily, I had my teacher Sukhasiddhi, and I finally escaped from the barrel of demons. If I had not been able to escape from the barrel of demons, my whole life would have been wasted. The story goes that none of the people who had entered the barrel of demons before had come out again. They wasted their entire lives in the barrel of demons of seeming faith.

Even now, there are still countless people who live within the barrel of demons.

Xuemo, my child, do not look at me that way.

You cannot make demands on an ancient man based on your intentions as an author.

You must realize, at that time I did not know what was going on in Sharwadi's mind. My mind was filled by life in the barrel of demons, and there was no room left for the past. This is certainly very frightful. But many times, we cannot control ourselves. We are always wrapped up in certain fated habits, and, like rocks rolling down a hill, we cannot help ourselves.

Many times I even took that Niguma as Sharwadi.

You can certainly look at me with resentful eyes, but you must know there is no way for you to change the past. Likewise, you cannot change the future either. All you can control is the here and now.

You have surely read of Sharwadi's pain — my mind is also in pain. Although that pain has already become the past, every time I think of it, my mind still feels a sharp pain, as if it is being pulled apart. But, you must know, it is precisely this pain which built the great poetic sense in my life.

In the same way, those friends who can read and understand what you write will certainly produce a similar feeling. We can use another expression for that pain: being moved emotionally.

9 The Most Excellent Mantra

Sukhasiddhi told me: "Though that barrel of demons appeared because of curses with external power, in its real substance it still belongs to your own ignorance. People who consider themselves intelligent always deceive themselves due to their apparent faith. This barrel of demons which wastes lives is born from this.

"In the barrel of demons, you used the intelligence of your apparent faith and recreated that woman. Everything about her was actually your own expectations. In this world, the search which many people look for has, in fact, already been made into something else by their expectations.

"Remember, do not take a woman in life and make her the object of your yearning. The basic substance of faith is yearning. The object that can make you yearn must be a being that cannot be treated disrespectfully.

"Faith must be sublimated love. If there is no sublimation, there is no love.

"Child, above all, do not take the Niguma you seek and make her into an ordinary woman. Even more important, do not take an ordinary woman and build her into Niguma. Niguma is Niguma: she is in reality a being that cannot be treated disrespectfully.

"In the future, when your cultivation reaches a certain realm, you will need an enlightened consort. At that time, I will be able to be your enlightened consort, but Niguma will not. This is because, if you are too close to Niguma, you will damage your respect for her. Although the root capacity of Yeshe Tsogyal's husband Atsara Sale was very good, because he got too close to his teacher, he became too disrespectful, and in the end he was unable to realize great achievement. Milarepa's glorious disciple Rechungpa had a very good root capacity. It was because he was on overly familiar terms with his teacher that he repeatedly disobeyed his teachings, and although he practiced austerities his whole life, he still had to be reborn and practice some more.

"Child, you must not be on overly familiar terms with Niguma. You must be respectful, and you must pray to her. In your mind you must not depart from 'Niguma Khyenno.' Your teacher is the sun. If you come too close, you may get burnt. If you get too far away, you will not get the light of wisdom. The distance between you and her must be adjusted properly: you can be close, but you cannot be disrespectful.

"Child, among all the people who cultivate practice, there are two types who most easily find deliverance: one type are the people of superior wisdom, and one type are those who may be ignorant but are respectful and sincere. The people of superior wisdom have only to focus their energy on cultivating the yoga of wisdom, and then they will be able to experience reality and attain liberation. Many of the adepts of the Great Mudra are this type. Although the ignorant people do not have enough wisdom, and do not easily illuminate mind and see its inherent nature, their so-called 'ignorance' is in reality a type of clinging. When this clinging and attachment are changed into respect and sincerity, it is easy for them to merge with the yoga of faith. Those with good karmic connections can also see reality, and those whose karmic connections are weaker can still achieve deliverance on the basis of faith.

"Thus, those who generate faith in Niguma will also be in these two categories. The people of superior wisdom easily understand the ultimate truth and focus on 'Niguma Khyenno,' and easily come into accord with the teacher. They get the added support of the teacher's enlightened attainments, understand reality, see the empty inherent nature, and merge with the Great Mudra and finally realize the ultimate. Those so-called ignorant people are in reality not ignorant. Often, this kind are actually people of superior wisdom, but they are called ignorant because they are not willing to use what worldly people call strategies and schemes, and they do not know that they are truly wise but seem ignorant. They are not willing to be opportunists, not willing to play tricks, not willing to be calculating, not willing to take shortcuts — instead they always act with simple honesty. They can control the six sense faculties and purify their thoughts continuously. Because of their pure faith, they pray to their teachers. On the basis of faith, they develop meditative concentration, and from meditative concentration, they develop wisdom. They may see the empty inherent nature, or they may get to go to the Pure Land to be reborn. Child, although you are a person of superior wisdom, you surely must imitate the conduct of those ignorant people, and truly work at it, and often chant 'Niguma Khyenno.' Only then will you be able to be in accord with your teacher. You must understand that without a teacher there will be no achievement.

"Child, many times faith is more important than anything. If there is no faith, there is no religion. That's why I call those who have wisdom but no faith people with crazy wisdom. On the surface, what those with crazy wisdom lack is the power of concentration, but in reality what they lack is the power of faith. This is because it is very easy for those who genuinely have faith to achieve concentration. Thus, if you pray to your teacher a lot, and chant 'Niguma Khyenno' a lot, this is better than cultivating meditative concentration thousand or ten thousand times. This is because over the centuries those who have found deliverance through faith are as numerous as hairs on a cow, while those who are not on the Buddhist Path who cultivate meditative concentration still go on as usual, clinging to illusion as reality and accepting the false as true. Even if they experience the four meditations and the eight concentrations, they still cannot transform their basic substance as people who are not on the Buddhist Path. This is why I say that reciting 'Niguma Khyenno' is better than cultivating meditative concentration thousand or ten thousand times.

"Child, you might ask why I do not tell you to recite 'Sukhasiddhi Khyenno.' I am telling you that, although on the surface there are obvious differences between Niguma and me, in reality we are a single essence. All the differences in name and form, to the eye of those who have realized the ultimate, are all one flavor. Thus, when you are chanting 'Niguma Khyenno' it is the same thing as chanting 'Sukhasiddhi Khyenno,' and naturally you will also receive the support of me, Sukhasiddhi. In the same way, among your heirs in later generations, when we are arranging successors for the teacher's position, sometimes this will be done by the image of Niguma appearing, and sometimes this will be done by the image of

Sukhasiddhi appearing. Though in name and form there are two of us, our inherent nature is one. Do you understand?

"Besides this, let me tell you a secret for cultivating realization. When you are cultivating the yoga of wisdom and you do not get the gist of it — or, shall we say, it is hard to reach accord with it — then cultivate the yoga of reverence and faith. In other words, when you are cultivating the tutelary deity and it is very hard to reach accord with it, it is better to pray many times to your teacher. This is because, although seen from the point of view of ultimate truth, your teacher and the tutelary deity are fundamentally a single essence. Nevertheless, sometimes, because the practitioner's discriminating mind is making trouble, it carelessly considers them to be two. If you look upon your teacher and the tutelary deity as two different entities, it is very hard to reach accord. If you encounter this kind of situation, pray many times to your teacher. Therefore, 'Niguma Khyenno' must merge like air with the space and time of your life.

"Nevertheless, though you are constantly cultivating the yoga of reverence and faith, you certainly must clearly understand that when you recognize true mind and realize the empty inherent nature, there is no duality and no separation between you and your teacher and the tutelary deity. In many of the teachings, they term this kind of action 'focused attention,' but this term is just a very forced kind of expression. The true correct behavior is not 'attention,' but rather 'firm faith without doubt,' to the point that it is 'fundamentally like this.'

"Child, you may run all over India, and all the teachings which you find will not be more excellent than what I am telling you.

"If you do not understand this truth, you have not merged with the true Esoteric Vehicle.

"Therefore, you certainly must tell all your disciples that all they have to do is recite 'Niguma Khyenno' or pray to me, and they will surely receive my support, as a shadow follows a form. Like the Bodhisattva Guanyin who saves people from suffering when they call upon her, this is the Great Diamond Vow I have made, and as long as the cycle of birth and death is not empty, the power of my vow will not fade away."

Khyungpo Naljor addresses Xuemo:

Thus, in your book *The Great Mudra of Light: the Heart of Real Practice* you wrote this about great vow of the dakini Sukhasiddhi: "In the teaching of Shangpa Kagyu, Sukhasiddhi has the same position of virtuous teacher as the dakini Niguma. She and Shangpa Kagyu have a great karmic connection, and those who have gotten her support and achieved enlightenment are countless. She has handed down the heart's blood of the dakinis, the 'Six Methods of Sukhasiddhi,' and if those with superior potential go into seclusion for eight months and cultivate them, they can succeed. Besides this, she has vowed to help all sincere disciples succeed, and whenever she encounters a sincere prayer, she always goes to work with her full power." I said: "Disciples with a karmic connection, if they seriously ask, maybe for seven days, maybe for a hundred days, will surely be able to see the dakini of wisdom."

Xuemo says:

"That's right, Teacher. In the real cultivation of realization, praying to Niguma and to Sukhasiddhi is in fact the same. I have never separated myself from them. Thus, I realized I was always able to be in accord with them. Many times a great good can be achieved through this kind of influence."

Chapter 27

Sharwadi's Longing

1 By Myself in the Loneliness

Beloved Khyung, though I have no way to send letters to you, I am still enduring the pain, and I will keep on writing letters to you — this is the pilgrimage of a solitary old woman.

I feel I have grown old, at least my mind has grown old. I feel that I cannot go on any more.

In the middle of the night, I am still being woken up by the noise in dreams of the cursing voices and the shaking dog skins. In my recent nightmares, those sorcerers are always coming into my dreams. In the dreams they are always shaking those dog skins, and the sound is very hard to take.

These days it is always this way. My mental state is bleak.

It rained, and my spirit froze as I listened to the sound of nighttime rain hitting the roof tiles.

Another night of wind and rain, prompting me to cry, making the pillowcase wet. That familiar sound of the rain gets louder and more urgent, and I am a bit frightened. Do you remember? It was during this kind of rain that you once let go and sang a sad but beautiful Tibetan song to me.

By chance, I think of yesterday's story, and again I cannot prevent the tears from covering my face. Two hands without strength twist the long thread of thoughts of you. My love, are you still well in some other town?

It was also in this kind of rainy season, in this kind of rain, that I looked on with joyful eyes, nibbling sweet rose petals, and passed that most happy, most fortunate time ... A feeling impossible to express floats in the midnight rain.

The twilight is deepening, the flying snow is fluttering down, I am walking in a bleak, cold wind, wandering around by myself in the loneliness.

Beloved one, why have you not come back? Can it be that you want me to turn into a cold plum tree on a snowy night? Your tender feelings will not appear in my dreams. Maybe there will still be a bit of warmth waiting for you in my eyes. Beloved one, when I think of you, it will make me think of a song, think of the time you and I were together. In these fragmentary recollections, I force myself to go on living ...

I am a snowflake drifting in the night, a journey seeking a familiar form, a journey of longing thoughts, a journey of expectation ...

You are a mark cut deeply into the depths of my heart,

you are the only silhouette in my mind, you are the story that keeps repeating in my dream, you are the exhortation that rolls by my ears ... You have gone, you are always letting me wait. When will this uncertain waiting finally come to an end? My love, will this lifetime of mine be like being a canary tied up with threads of gold in an elegant cage, waiting my whole life, forever alone?

2 Prelude to Exite

The sound of the zither moves melodiously on the night of New Year's Eve, elegant and calm, sorrowful, like an exile's prelude for the feelings frozen in my mind.

My mind is like a kite with a broken string, floating along, moving up and down with the wind. The scene pulling my heartstrings is very depressing, very painful. In the twilight, I look to the sky so far away: the moon is like a sickle, the stars are like silver powder. It seems that everything has been tired out by longing thought. All is sad, solitary, quiet. Matching the tracks of my tears, everything has died sitting in an eternal wait.

My love, do you still miss me? Can your mind come to a tacit understanding with these warm words I am saying?

In the twilight, I am snuggled up in that familiar little house, but my mind is blank, and that pitch-black window frame is still like your haggard eyes. An unnamable listlessness makes my mind an expanse of suffering, and the tears surge forth as if a dam has broken. Having parted from you, I have almost become a prisoner of loneliness. I can't think of swallowing a mouthful of light tea. Only if I sit tight in this warm little house will I feel a bit of peace. O little house of mine, you have embodied so many of my dreams and illusions, so many deep feelings! In your smile I have passed more than twenty years of longing. In the crook of your arm, I have laughed with joy and cried in pain. It is you who shielded me from the storms of the conventional world. It was you who rolled out the long hair of springtime for me.

O little house of mine, you and I breathe each other's breath, no matter how the human mind shifts. When I am lonely, I just have you to silently accompany me, to give me support, to give me warmth. When I am alone, it is only to you that I tell what's in my heart. O little house, your bosom overflows with a gentleness that cannot be cut off, a warm sweetness that cannot be refused. Even in winter when the snowflakes fly, you are still as splendid as ever. I cannot forget your eyebrows, your eyes, your ups and down and changes. Little house, you are always smiling in my life!

3 The Hesitating Mind and Spirit

This sadness, this lingering, floating by outside the window is pure, clear rain.

Pain has become the nightmare I cannot break free from.

Enduring a pain like having my physical body torn apart, I slowly walk out of the house with my mind cold and clear. Whenever this soul-ending pure clear rain begins, I am a person in the rain with my soul cut off. I walk into the curtain of rain, and I focus my eyes and look all around: I am looking for my spirit in the rain and fog.

In this lifetime, will you come again or not? My perfectly real, perfectly pure lover. You have walked through the windblown dusts of history and entered into another peaceful land, a Peach Blossom Spring, beyond the world. I too have gone through the cycle of birth and death a thousand times. You certainly must understand my feelings as I wait for this lifetime, right?

Beloved one, please come quietly then. During these three months of pure, clear rain, come to the south window and take a look at me. You have already let my beauty wither in the springtime light. Even though I know you are strong as a mountain cliff, I still love your furrowed brow and your haggard mind.

The atmosphere is so depressing, I go back and forth in the courtyard restlessly, and my tears slowly flow down. When will I finally be able to put an end to this kind of life? My little house is empty, and I still go to take a look at it — my deepest love is hidden there. I open the door, and the familiar atmosphere welcomes me, makes me happy and makes me sad. The flowers and plants I love will not be here any more, the handy little desk will not be here any more, the simple bed ... Where have you gone, the you that was here? There will not be another warm, sweet man to give me a cup of fragrant clear tea. There will not be another man to read with me for those years and months that were light as clear tea. I stand here in this little room, and countless beautiful days and nights of the real world surge up all at once and fill my hesitating mind and spirit ...

The tide has gone out
The shells on the beach
Are already being picked up by people
From this
The things of the past transformed by that wind
Will you pick them up too ...

Chapter 28

Niguma's Mandala

1 The Mind-Marrow of the Dakini

After a rough draft of this book was done, I asked a great worthy who is proficient in both Tibetan and Chinese to read through and check it. When he saw what the book contained, he turned pale with fright and asked: "A lot of the content you wrote is the mind-marrow of the wisdom of the dakinis! How did you get that?" So I told him many stories that had happened in my life. I told him about my encounters with the Vajravarahi and with Niguma, and I told him about that wondrous book which had appeared in the light of wisdom. I told him about the song of the dakinis that filled the time and space of my life. I also told him about many things I' d been through that I called religious experiences, but that could be dismissed by worldly people as "mental disorders."

The road of life has been like an arrow flying by behind me. Sixteen years have passed by since that time, and I am not the same person I was then. The sparks that were planted in the field of my mind then have already set the prairie on fire and become a great fire of wisdom. No matter what kind of evil winds I encounter, nothing can blow it out. On the contrary, the wind adds to the force of the fire, and the fire extends and becomes an epochal fire that fills the universe.

In the pure realm, I often encounter Niguma and Sukhasiddhi and the Vajravarahi. They are radiant as rosy clouds and have an unusual appearance, but in their essential nature, they are not apart from my own inherent nature. They are the source of great goodness, the source of my life's passion, and they are the sun in my life. It was being under their motherly oversight that allowed me to finish writing this book without being afraid of being slandered by people. Even though this world is filled with falsity, as long as there is only one person who understands the true mind of this book, then I have not written it in vain.

As for the contents of this book, the believers will believe and the doubters will doubt. Its myriad images are complex and, according to karmic conditions, will be understood spontaneously in the here and now. Even samsara and nirvana are both vast, dreamlike illusions. Why should we fight over whether a bit of writing is real or not, and influence the pure light of your inner mind?

Khyungpo Naljor and Niguma encountered each other more than nine hundred years ago.

Later the author also became an important link in Niguma's chain of transmission.

Time and again in the pure realm of the ultimate truth, I have experienced the same kind of encounter with Khyungpo Naljor.

Thus, there is no way for me to distinguish clearly: is the "I" in the text that follows ultimately Xuemo, or is it Khyungpo Naljor? This is because in this book "his" wondrous encounters in fact also come from the secret realm of "my" life. In the eyes of the wise ones, these two names in fact have their source in one essence.

After a river merges into the great ocean, it becomes the great ocean itself.

You must know that the "he" and the "I" in this book are in fact the two sides of a single brocade.

2 Strange Transformations

I came back to that bend in the river. I decided not to go searching all over again. I believed that the reason I was unable to see Niguma was my karmic barriers. I thought: "I had better clear away my karmic barriers." So I was chanting "Niguma Khyenno" and also doing great prostrations.

I was praying and bowing down day and night, and I cannot say for sure how many days went by. Gradually, I no longer had clingings and attachments. I thought: "No matter whether or not I can see Niguma, I will never again cling to or become attached to anything." I thought that I would keep praying this way. I discovered that what this praying brought me was a different sensation than chanting rituals. My mind changed and became like the sky, a vast expanse of blue, undisturbed by the slightest dust. I felt a pure clarity that I had never had before.

In this ultimate purity, I prayed: "O Niguma, please show your secret realm!"

Suddenly, I became aware of a strange transformation appearing.

This transformation started first from the body. I found myself turning into a crystal body. I saw millions of rays of light from the sky entering into me, and I too was radiating an incomparable light. Though I felt the light, I also discovered that this light was not physical light, but originated from the mind and spirit.

At this time that secret realm had appeared.

3 What Is the Resource?

The secret realm appeared in the sky above my head. It had seven banana trees that were so tall, and they sparkled like rosy clouds — it was like a dream, like an illusion. I suspected this was a dream scene, so I pinched myself, but I did feel pain.

At first, the secret realm was like a dream or an illusion, but gradually it became clear and distinct. I saw a woman, as dignified as a heavenly being, beautiful beyond compare. That woman seemed to be Sharwadi, but she also was vaguely Sukhasiddhi.

I asked in a loud voice: "Are you Niguma?"

She smiled happily and said: "Am I not Niguma?"

I also asked: "Previously in my life there have appeared women who called themselves Niguma. What is the difference between you and them?"

The woman answered: "Those women were just illusions in your mind. Their basic substance was your false thoughts. All their wisdom could not be higher than you yourself. Their level of perception and their knowledge, in fact, already existed in your own mind. Their appearance and their manifestation was only a repetition of you yourself. What you knew, they also knew. What you did not know, they did not know either. They were just another manifestation of your desires. Your contact with them, no matter what names and forms you had for it—for example, *coupled practice* or faith—gave you no way to break your clinging, no way to eliminate your affliction, no way to purify your habit-energy. The way they appeared was just your afflictions putting on another face. It was impossible for you to attain true purity. Since they could not go higher than you yourself, they had no way to help you attain genuine transcendence. But what I bring you is a precious treasure which you have never before discovered. What you have attained is a purity which you have never before experienced. What you are tasting now is the calm and serenity and the light that comes after your clingings and attachments have been smashed.

"Do you understand?"

I opened through with enlightenment.

"Sometimes you might meet some delusive demons impersonating Niguma, appearing in the time and space of your visualization practice. You can ask about your genuine doubts and see whether or not you can get a final answer. You can also take the fire of wisdom from the protective wheel and burn up the illusory forms conjured up by those evil demons. A genuine enlightened one does not fear the fire of wisdom. The false ones, like frost in the blazing sunlight, will quickly melt away.

"Do you understand?"

4 Interesting Conversations

Khyungpo Naljor told me that there had been very significant dialogue between him and Niguma.

The first dialogue:

Niguma asked: "Where have you been?"
Khyungpo Naljor: "To a sacred land."
Niguma: "What have you done there?"
Khyungpo Naljor: "To seek the Dharma."
Niguma said: "Seeking the Dharma is of course very important, but even more important is genuinely cultivating practice."

The second dialogue:

Niguma: "What did you seek the Dharma for?"
Khyungpo Naljor: "To cultivate visualization."
Niguma said: "Cultivating visualization is very good, but even more important is genuinely cultivating practice."

The third dialogue:

Niguma asked: "What did you cultivate visualization for?"
Khyungpo Naljor: "To achieve enlightenment."
Niguma: "Seeking to achieve enlightenment is of course good, but what is important is genuinely cultivating practice."

The fourth dialogue:

Khyungpo Naljor: "What is genuinely cultivating practice?"
Niguma: "Genuinely cultivating practice is leaving behind all clingings and attachments to this life."

5 The Infinite Pure Realm

In that infinite pure realm, Niguma picked up a bowl made from a skull, and a trident, and looked at me with a faint semblance of a smile. As if in a dream, in that illusory light which was like reddish clouds, I saw that suddenly she was Sukhasiddhi, suddenly she was Sharwadi, suddenly she appeared to be standing, suddenly she appeared to be sitting. Though she had various manifestations, my wisdom told me she was Niguma.

You look for someone in the crowd a thousand times, and suddenly you turn your head and that person is there where the light is waning.

I was overjoyed and began to cry. I bowed down many times, and joined my palms to ask her to please pass on the wondrous teaching.

With a faint smile the woman said: "You have mistaken me for someone else. I am surely not Niguma. I am a demon woman, a flesh-eating dakini, accustomed to sucking human blood and eating human flesh. You had better hurry up and run away. Otherwise, when my companions come, it will be hard to save your little life."

I said: "To attain the wondrous teaching, I will not spare my life."

The woman gave a slight smile and said: "I can pass on the teaching. But this teaching cannot be passed on lightly. Do you have any gold? If you do not have gold, you will not be able to get anything."

I quickly said: "I do, I do." I took out the gold and threw it into the air. The woman caught it and gave a slight smile. She waved her hand, and that gold flew into the depths of the secret forest.

This time, it was obviously a duplicate of Sukhasiddhi.

As soon as I saw her, I was delighted. I thought: "If she were really a flesh-eating dakini, she would have been greedy for the gold." But at the same time I also thought: "Why does she not value my offering?"

The woman laughed delicately, and her eyes wandered: wherever she looked, everything — the mountains, the rocks, the earth, the trees — all turned to gold and gave off a golden light. I thought: "Is this a magical illusion, or not?" The woman laughed and said: "Real gold is also an illusory transformation, and illusory transformations are also real gold. Samsara and nirvana, all phenomena, are like dreams or illusions. If you can understand this principle, then everything in the world is gold, so why would I need to value this bit of gold you offered?"

At this point I was certain that she was Niguma.

I asked: "Teacher, I have been praying to you for so many years, why do you finally appear now?"

Niguma laughed and said: "I have been with you all along, but your karmic barriers were deep and heavy, and you could not see me. The many years of searching and practising austerities which you have gone through have dissolved away the karmic barriers, so finally you see me."

She said: "From the first time you recited 'Niguma Khyenno,' I have been with you. In the same way, for a thousand eons after this, if anyone recites this with complete sincerity, I will always appear according to karmic conditions. But what that person sees then may be a pure wind, or may be a colored cloud, or may be an unexpected good thought, or may be a bird song far up in the clouds. But you must recognize that those are Niguma."

She said: "The genuine Niguma, for those who have a karmic connection, will always be with them, like a shadow following a form."

She told me: "Only if you have purified yourself of all defilements and accumulated the provisions will you see the true countenance of Niguma."

I asked: "What are the provisions?"

She said: "The provisions are the mind of faith. There are three aspects of the mind of faith. One is faith toward your teacher, pure faith that your teacher is like the Buddha. Second is faith in the teachings, pure faith that if you rely on the excellent teaching, you can achieve the result of Buddhahood. Third is faith in yourself, pure faith that you are fundamentally the Buddha, but because you are covered by karmic barriers, it is hard to see your original face."

She also said: "The one who travels a hundred miles only prepares provisions for a few days. The one who travels a thousand miles must prepare provisions for a few dozen days. The one who travels ten thousand miles must prepare provisions for several years. The *Five Great Diamonds Teachings of Niguma* cannot be compared with the usual esoteric teachings. For people with insufficient provisions, it is hard even to hear the name."

Them I asked: "Teacher, why do you all appear in the form of Sukhasiddhi?"

Niguma laughed and said: "Son, I am Sukhasiddhi, and Sukhasiddhi is me. The people you have met and events that you have experienced are all my manifestations. You must know that Niguma is a realm. She is the goal, and even more, she is the search itself. From the instant you generated the intention to seek, you encountered me."

Suddenly I had a great awakening. I tapped my forehead on the ground again and again, asking her to pass on the wondrous teaching to me.

Niguma said: "You have already ripened the inherent nature of mind, and you no longer need any teaching from outside. But out of consideration for the process of karmic causation, I will still teach you a kind of teaching with form. But you must know that the genuine Niguma Yoga is formless. Its highest essential nature is a teaching without contrived action. It is the truth itself. You must know that the real truth is formless and transcends language. It is the Great Mudra of Light. It is a realm that is far beyond all concepts, far beyond all discriminating thought, far beyond all names and forms."

As she was speaking, she looked around in all directions, and countless dakinis had gathered.

Niguma instructed them: "I have found a disciple with a karmic connection. Prepare a mandala as quickly as possible."

6 The Five Great Diamonds Teachings of Niguma

While the dakinis were making the mandala, Niguma said: "Although the *Five Great Diamonds Teachings of Niguma* are a kind of yoga with form, they are not the same as those kinds of yoga which you sought and found. They are a kind of mystical supreme yoga."

She said: "Although you studied the teachings of more than a hundred teachers, the methods of the Buddhist teachings are countless, and they are very excellent. But the *Five Great Diamonds Teachings of Niguma* are even more perfect. These teaching are not to be compared with the ordinary esoteric teachings. They are the heart and marrow of all the Buddhas. Their starting point is very lofty, and their merit is incalculable. They are like a big tree that contains all the esoteric teachings. Their roots are the Six Methods of Niguma; the Great Mudra is the main trunk of the tree; the methods of the three branches are the branches that adorn the tree; the methods of the white and red dakinis are the blossoms that adorn the tree; the methods for cultivating immortality of the body and mind are the seeds that adorn the tree."

Niguma said: "All the many teaching methods have their perception and their practice. The level of perception of the *Five Great Diamonds Teachings of Niguma* is the Great Mudra of Light. Its teaching method is the cultivation of practice under the direction of the level of perception of the Great Mudra. Any cultivation of practice that departs from the level of perception of the Great Mudra makes it hard to genuinely merge into the *Five Great Diamonds Teachings of Niguma*.

"This is the special excellence of the *Five Great Diamonds Teachings of Niguma*, so we call the Great Mudra the main trunk. The main trunk is what runs through it from beginning to end.

"So then, what is this perception? Perception means correct perception. The Great Mudra takes the *Prajna Sutra* as the main theoretical basis, and takes the empty inherent nature as the ultimate: it eliminates all names and forms. Though there are many kinds of yoga with form in the teaching, they are appearance and have no intrinsic nature. Though there are many kinds of appearances, they are all in accord with the Great Mudra's perception of the empty inherent nature. If you do not understand this principle, it is very hard to merge into the *Five Great Diamonds Teachings of Niguma*."

Niguma said: "I do not consider your conduct important, I consider your level of perception important. Someone without a transcendent level of perception will certainly not have transcendent conduct."

The moon was gradually rising in the sky, and the cemetery forest appeared very tranquil. The secret realm became more bright and beautiful, sending out light in all directions. The dakinis had already finished making the mandala and they came to report that they had completed their task. Niguma smiled and said: "The karmic conditions are very good, and my transmission and wisdom will certainly be like the full moon, bringing unlimited light to the world."

I felt myself trembling. That mandala was incomparably solemn and extremely colorful. Niguma was standing on a majestic gold mountain, and a clear spring flowed down from the gold hill, giving a gurgling sound.

I asked: "Teacher, is this golden hill real, or is it something manifested by your spiritual powers?"

Niguma gave a loud laugh and said: "Son, when the great ocean of revolving in birth and death is overturned, when all cravings and clingings and attachments are changed into mist, there is no place in your life that is not gold. At that point there is no difference between emptiness and the palm of your hand, cow dung and gold are similar to each other, defiled and pure are a single suchness. You have eliminated duality: the myriad forms are all true thusness, and true thusness is not apart from the myriad forms. All revolving in birth and death and all kinds of apparent forms are no more than the play of dreamlike illusions. When you realize this experience of forms, you have already transcended the great ocean of revolving in birth and death. Son, if you want to have this achievement, there is no other way: all you need to do is have the greatest sincere respect for your teacher. When you really and truly look upon your teacher as the Buddha, that flower of enlightenment will smile at you. Son, right now close your eyes and go catch your dream!"

Following Niguma's instructions, I gradually and entered the pure realm. That pure realm was clearer than the apparent reality. I entered into the mandala. Around me were many colorful things belonging to the teaching: I saw eight lucky signs, I saw many kinds of offerings and vessels of the teaching. At the same time I also saw the cemetery forest. The Soshaling cemetery forest at this time had already become an indistinct illusion.

7 The Mandala of Life

Niguma said:

"My child, please enter into your mandala of life.

"Take your body and mind and transform them into the pearl of the cosmos and offer it to our great Buddha. Without his austere practice and his enlightenment, there would be no purity in our lives. Son, if the world had not had the Buddha, through the ages it would have been like an eternal night. I offer my body, mouth, and mind to the Great King of Medicine. Because the Buddha was there, the sea of suffering became the Pure Land, and there is a stream of sweet water in the barren desert. We bow down to him, we praise him, we take our lives and turn them into a beam of light, and we use that light to adorn the Buddha Land.

"Look, in the light the teacher has appeared, the tutelary deity has appeared, the dakini protecting the Dharma has appeared. They are fundamentally a single essence: why must we differentiate them? We take refuge in them, we take refuge in the three precious jewels: Buddha, Dharma, and Sangha. We take refuge in the scriptures of the most excellent teaching. We take refuge in those dakini warriors of the twenty-four realms. After this, all the disciples in your lineage have already become members of the Buddha Lands of the dakinis. As long as we are fully equipped with the mind of faith and do not fall from basic discipline, we will all be reborn in the twenty-four Buddha Lands of the dakinis.

"Look, my three chakras are emitting light: white light from the chakra on the top of my head, red light from the chakra in my throat, blue light from the heart chakra. The lights are moving, and they have entered into your three chakras. Those three chakras represent your body, mouth, and mind. When the three lights merge, then you will no longer be separate from me. Your three kinds of karmic barriers will already be purified, and your root intellect for the Esoteric Vehicle will already be complete. The bright moon will begin to appear over the lotus flower in your mind: that is your mind of enlightenment for the ordinary world. The light from that lotus flower shows seven colors and is pure beyond compare. That moonlight is pure and clear and untainted by dust. A five-legged diamond club stands on the lunar disk, emitting a five-colored light which shines into the three realms (the realm of desire, the realm of form, and the formless realm) : that is your mind of enlightenment for absolute truth. Child, from this point on your mind of enlightenment will be hard as a diamond, unshakable, indestructible. Child, that is your diamond mind that will never be lost.

"My child, come with me into the mandala of life. This mandala is named the Five Great Diamonds. Come with me, and we will enter through the east gate. Our footsteps are flashing light, and in the light there are lotus flowers. We go to the north, go to the west, and go to the south, and we salute our parents one by one. Look, they are at the three gates giving their support, and those lights of wisdom and just now entering our three chakras. Look, your footsteps are flashing light, and that light comes from distant ages past: that is the light of pure wisdom. We are bathed in the light, as we sit upright on the five-colored lotus at the east gate. Your mind is overflowing with happiness, because you know that from this point on, you have become part of the family of the Five Great Diamonds.

"Don't ask what family means — family is family, and it is a term that is not at the level of ultimate truth.

"The way to explain this at the level of ultimate truth is this: From this point on, you and the tutelary deity are not two, not separate. You have already become a practitioner of the ultimate yoga tantra (Anuttarayoga Tantra). When you strictly uphold the rules of discipline, the protectors of Dharma will support your work. Look, those are the hundred Mahakalas, those are the five dakinis — they are all looking at you fondly, like a mother looking at a wandering child who has returned from afar.

"I am giving you something refreshing, but it is called hell water. Do not be afraid: as long as you strictly uphold the rules of discipline, this water will be sweet dew, and with its help, spiritual achievement will be a jewel in your bag. But it is also a gauge of your fate. The rules of discipline are the dividing line between ascending into the Buddha Land and falling into hell.

"Son, I have already become your teacher. Listen: 'teacher' — such a term of veneration. I am the vehicle for the spirit of all the Buddhas of the past, present, and future. My body bears the spirit of benefiting sentient beings; my mouth transmits the teachings of wisdom; my mind, my intent, is entirely to benefit sentient beings. I am a compendium of all the Buddhas of the past, present, and future. If there is no teacher, spiritual achievement is just a word off in the distance.

"Look, I have already invited all the Buddhas to merge with your fully developed pure essence. Son, like a heavy rain, they are already soaking into your pure stainless mind. Like a sudden wind, they have already blown away the afflictions from your mind. They are the teachers, they are the tutelary deities, they are the dakinis, they are the protectors of the Dharma. They come from the Buddha Land, bringing all the merit and compassion of the Buddhas. Look, your three channels and five chakras, all your pores, have become a Pure Land of their mandala. Son, you are no longer only my son.

"Open your eye of wisdom, my son. Then you will see a golden stupa. It was built of rice and reaches to the sky. On top there is a mandala, which is the dwelling place of your tutelary deities, the Five Great Diamonds. You see that glittering light. When the karma of your eyes is purified, you will see the infinite, boundless tutelary deities."

8 The Bequest of the Five Great Diamonds

"Son, keep on making your mind reverent and purifying your intent, and receive your mother's bequest.

"You see the tutelary deities flying toward you — there are five of them. You have seen them before, in the lineage of the teaching you were seeking. At that time, they were acting singly. Each had his own teaching lineage and transmission. But this time, they have come together, and they are carrying the precious pitcher of sweet dew. You surely know that in that pitcher there are five kinds of sweet dew. When the sweet dew enters the chakra on the crown of your head, your crude karmic barriers will be dissolved away. Son, this indicates that you will get a rough view of success in the stage of generation.

"I have seen the joy in your mind. I too am joyful. In your mind it has become a white light, making offerings to the Buddhas in the mandala. Look, the sweet dew is being produced in their minds, giving forth the sound of a pure stream in which emptiness and bliss are not separate, flowing into the vessel in my hand and flowing into your throat chakra. Child, it has purified the crude portion of your karmic barriers of speech. Thus you can see a Mudra Mother. She looks very much like Sukhasiddhi. She is your wife who transcends the world. When you merge together, it will produce great bliss, and that great bliss will merge into the great voice, and that great voice will manifest great bliss. Within that great bliss, the crude portion of your karmic barriers of intent will dissolve away. By means of these causal conditions, you will realize the body of illusion.

"Do not lose that emptiness, do not lose that bliss. That is the bequest of the Five Great Diamonds. They have no dualism, they have no separation, they are fused into one. When your three kinds of karmic barriers are then dissolved away, the light will suddenly appear, incomparably pure.

"Child, you are the child of my heart. You must look upon my teachings as the root of life of all the Buddhas.

"Look, in the center of that mandala, all the dakinis of the twenty-four holy lands have appeared. They are dancing, and they have come to the emptiness right in front of you. Flowers are raining down from the sky, and a rainbow extends like a road. The dakinis are holding various musical instruments in their hands, and they are giving a prediction of enlightenment, saying: Your disciples, and the sentient beings who have faith in Niguma, always invoke 'Niguma Khyenno,' so that when they are at the point of death, we will surely come to welcome them and receive them, and take them along that rainbow road to the Buddha Land of the dakinis."

Chapter 29

Sharwadi's Pain

1 After the Bleak Rain

Just when Niguma was initiating Khyungpo Naljor, Sharwadi was contending with the most fearsome pain in her life. It joined with her longing and, like an evil demon, charged at a weakened Sharwadi.

Khyung, last night it rained again.

I woke up at dawn, and the color of night had still not dispersed. Outside my window it was all gray, but I knew the sky would soon brighten, because the pain-relief medicine had already worn off a while ago. That pain is like a rising flood, which comes on gradually without my knowing it, and gradually drives off my drowsiness. I am already used to waking up this way every day. Every day at this time I know a new day has begun.

Outside my window a pure gentle autumn wind is blowing from time to time, and the curtain in the window is fluttering, like an old woman's trousers moving with the wind, following the rhythm of the wind rising and falling at random. It is really very comfortable. If it were not for the sickness and pain, what a fine, beautiful morning this would be! But even though there is sickness and pain, this kind of morning is still extremely beautiful. If it were before, this would be the time when my drowsiness was thickest. If this cool wind had blown across me a few times while I was still bleary-eyed, I surely would have wrapped a blanket tightly around my body, and turned over and gently smoothed out the covers to let my skin get some warmth, and then contentedly gone back into another dream.

But this has already become the past. Now I must hurry to get out of bed, to begin my busy and hectic day. The sickness makes me truly conscious that life flies by and vanishes at lightning speed, that time is fleeting. Time is like a stream of water I try to hold in my hand: no matter how tightly I clench my fist, I cannot catch it or keep it. I do not want to wait till the day comes when I open my eyes and suddenly discover that I have become a pure wind among the shadows, and regret having wasted my time.

There are many things I want to do. The most important is to let myself get healthy. Only this way will I be able to accompany you through a lifetime. I think that when my body is well again, when the season comes when spring is warm and the flowers bloom, you will surely have returned, and we can go together to the high plateau of Tibet—this is such an enticing dream. In my expectations, there are still many many places waiting for us.

Therefore, in order to defeat the demon of sickness and let myself get healthy again, I have abandoned almost all other pursuits and objectives. I will no longer be the way I was in the past, demanding that I must become so special and perfect. I am taking all my life and energy and pouring it into extending life. Every day I am very busy, but all I do is brew medicines, drink medicines, do exercises, cook, eat, sleep, and read.

Every day these days I repeat the same monotonous and trivial things over and over again. When my mind is still dissatisfied, I think of accompanying you through life, and then I am satisfied again. Is there anything else that cannot be abandoned? Isn't my intention to take the whole world and erase if from my mind, so only you alone are left?

You said that benefiting beings starts with the people around you—first let the people around you be happy. You genuinely acted this way. I saw everyone around you, because of your compassion and wisdom, reach a state of feeling refreshed and happy and satisfied. When I was waiting at your side, I too always felt that I did not have any trouble and was at peace; that I was not thirsty and was refreshed; that I did not have any expectations and was brimming with joy. I believe that in this world, no matter whether inside or outside the mind, there is no more excellent Pure Land than this.

After the rain, the beauty of autumn is a bit bleak: clear and bright, but also sad; soft and gentle, but also hard and strong. How is it that I seem to be talking about myself? Ha-

ha, when we look at it, the world is, after all, a reflection of our minds. When people's minds differ, the worlds they see will surely not be the same. I wonder, at this moment, what kind of autumn are you seeing?

Lingering in my ears is the elusive sound of the Medicine Buddha mantra. The sound of this mantra has already gradually followed the wind and hidden in the night, and it is always sneaking into my dreams. Deep in the night, when I am half asleep and half awake, and especially when the effect of the medicine on my body is heaviest, all the breath of life is extinguished in loneliness, and there are only two kinds of life force. I can feel them like hidden streams underground, gurgling and wriggling along. One comes from that evil demon of pain; it cannot be eradicated, only forced to go to sleep temporarily. The other one is following the Medicine Buddha mantra, which seems like the call of love coming from some place very far away.

This is a mantra you are sending to me. In my mind, there is no duality between you and the Medicine Buddha. In this world, there is no medicine better than your love. In my empty silent world, the mantra and that lotus flower lamp with its indistinct red light have already become the breath which you left behind for me, to accompany me through one long endless night after another.

Remember before, you always told me to be happy. Even though for me to be happy is not an easy thing, every time you said this to me, I always felt very sweet, because I knew that there was someone in the world who genuinely cared whether or not I was happy.

*Thank you for all that you have done for me! This includes
everything I know about and everything I don't know about.
Every time I think of you, my mind feels pain ...*

*Being healthy and happy would be the best way I could
repay. Also, I'll love you forever!*

2 The Breath of Death Closing In

*Today I am still thinking of you very much, thinking of
writing a letter to you. I am afraid that if by any chance, before
I go, I do not have time to write you a letter telling you what is
on my mind, I will regret dying. Suddenly thousands of words
well up in my mind, gushing out without the slightest logic or
order, and then I know that actually I have so much I want to
tell you. Then I think of these many years of waiting, and I still
haven't written anything, and I cannot hold back a big outburst
of crying. I know that never in my whole life will I be able
to part from you. If I am not wrong, you have said the same
thing — these were the words that entranced my mind.*

*In reality, I don't know what I should say to you. I have
said everything that had to be said. Now I want to say that the
period of time when I was with you and loved you was the most
fortunate and joyful time of my entire life. Before, I felt that the
most fortunate and joyful time was when I was young, but now
I no longer think so. My youth certainly did not have that kind
of satisfaction and sweetness. Whenever I think of you talking
and laughing, whenever I think of any time we were together,
it's always enough to make me intoxicated for a long time.*

Thank you! You let me taste the most beautiful sincere love in the human world. I now understand that if one lives one's whole life without ever having genuinely loved, that is truly very lamentable, that is truly having lived in vain. People who have never loved do not know the beauty of love. However we live, however we die, it is all worth it for the sake of this beauty.

Meeting you let me recognize the romance in life. What brought about this romance was a karmic connection. It let us end up crossing over such a long, broad time and space to meet each other, and to love each other. A "karmic connection" is truly a link between lives that is inconceivable and filled with limitless possibilities. It says to me that it even counteracts the passivity and melancholy of "everything quickly passes away," because a "karmic connection" has its own trajectory of being born and growing, and does not pass away along with "everything" passing away. It is precisely because of this that I have expectations and yearnings toward fate, and I am no longer afraid that death will separate us. I believe that the "karmic connection" will surely let us be together forever. But even if I do not fear it, I think of death approaching—I can feel more and more the god of death eyeing me and his breath closing in. Maybe this will allow me to let go of my clingings and attachments as quickly as I can, and to value every moment's reminder. It also will make me very disappointed, because no matter in what form I am separated from you, I will never be able to let you go.

You once told me that if there are bonds, then we cannot get away. Please tell me, how can I let myself abandon my bonds to you and happily part from you? Will I be able to do this?

Now I know that falling in love with someone can make me feel an unbearable pain at any time. When I think of certain things you said, certain looks you gave me, or when I imagine how you would think, and it always produces this painful feeling, then I know that I am truly in love with you.

This painful feeling is too familiar, but before, it just appeared in my illusions, and its object then was always empty and illusory. When it was empty, I thought that to let that painful feeling appear was very easy, and to put an end to it was also very easy—as easy as blowing out a candle. These feelings never before occupied my inner mind; they were just passing emotions, that's all. But now it is completely different. My inner mind has been totally occupied by this feeling, and this occupation is like a forcible seizure. It wants to occupy so much space and so much time, and no matter how I struggle, it is totally beyond my control.

After I fell in love with you, apart from the pain, I also tasted a kind of sweetness I had never experienced before, and this let me have the feeling that I existed. I finally understood why it is said that after a person has found true love, in this lifetime she can die without regrets. Only a person who has loved deeply can understand the great satisfaction and good fortune behind those words. I took this love and relied on it like the air I breathed. I did not know what the outcome of this reliance and addiction would turn out to be. Of course, I do not want to think about the outcome. I do not want it to kill the sincerity and sweetness of this love. But, as usual, I am afraid I will lose control. Always accustomed to being rational and to suppressing myself, I am always worried that I will lose control

in my love for you and it will bring me pain and suffering—
a kind of pain and suffering I have no way to control and put
an end to. You said that, behind my back, I always bring along
a pair of spying eyes. You are right, I have seen it too. But
in reality it is a child pretending to be strong. Its pretended
coolness and sophistication are only there to conceal its
weakness and lack of courage. I know it is this rampart of
self-protective consciousness that separates two minds which
actually could freely embrace each other.

Suddenly, I want very much to have a good cry. I cannot
explain why. Maybe I want to release these feelings, this long
suppression. Maybe it has no purpose—it's just because my
breast feels tight, and the tears themselves are seeping out, and
they are caught in the contradiction between suppression and
release. I've taken a few deep breaths, trying to take the sour
feelings they have pulled out and suck them back into my mind.

I don't know if this counts as a love letter or not—though
I still feel emotionally suppressed, I don't know how I will
finally be able to completely release the feelings in my mind,
because my rational nature is like an invisible string that from
time to time reins in my mind. I believe that you are better able
than I am to understand the unbearable feeling of this kind of
suppression, especially that there is no place to release it, no
way to release it, and that when facing the ultimate limit, it will
soon make me suffocate.

I love you! Let me say it, let me wholeheartedly enter into
this love, let me totally lose control—this is the cry from the
bottom of my heart. Maybe I still must conquer this rational
nature that imprisons my real nature. You were right when you

said this is a kind of habit-energy, this is the habit-energy left with me by my career as a female spirit. When I am conscious of this point, the flame of great joy of the surging infinite breath of life flies before my eyes.

Let me continue saying I love you. I have discovered that every time I have the courage to say "I love you," I can always draw out the sweet honey rippling in my mind. Though I am constantly suppressing that terrible pain because of my contradictions and pressures, in order to accept my openness to you and my uncontrolled love for you, I have decided to let myself leap into that joyous fire of desire—from now on, I am willing to fall into it anywhere, anytime.

I really expect that the joyous fire of desire will burn me to ashes.

This is something that is not easy to divulge, but now that I have let it out, I am recording it, and it will be the evidence that I love you.

I love you, birth after birth, lifetime after lifetime.

3 Endless Pain

My Khyung, every evening I lie quietly in bed and patiently wait for the medicine to take effect. Sometimes I think, if the medicine does not take effect tonight, what will I do?

Behind this question is a bottomless abyss in my mind, and in it is hidden the crazy laughter of the demons of sickness having their way.

I certainly do not want to look into that pitch-black abyss,

which will only reduce my faith that I can conquer myself.
You always told me to think of my health, and to think of our
promises. What can I do — the distance is so far between me
and health and promises. Not only is it far, I feel that they are
running in the opposite direction from me. Their laughing
voices like bells that delight the ear will only become tangible
when you are there at my side. But pain and death are always
flashing in front of my eyes, like two dark oppressive mountains
blocking the way in front of me, taking health and promises
and all forms of joy and blocking them off somewhere I
cannot see.

When the pain roars in like the roar of the ocean spreading
over the sky and the earth, I often will fall into a pessimism I
cannot pull myself out of, because this time I have nowhere to
hide and nowhere to run. I am like prey caught in the net of
the god of death. I tried visualization, but I cannot focus on
anything. That pain which dims my brain twists me up so my
mind and spirit are not at peace. My mind feels so constricted
by the pain that soon I will be unable to breathe, and half my
body is boiling hot. I think of you saying that everything will
soon pass. When I was together with you, no matter how I
valued and tried to hold onto each moment, the joyful times
always flew by quickly. Everything except for this pain seems
to be unreliably momentary; but with this pain, time seems
to come to a stop, and though it is just a moment, it becomes
extraordinarily drawn out ...

How I wish you were by my side at this time. Even if you
could not get rid of the pain, at least I would not feel alone. But
I do not want to keep telling you my troubles. I hope that what

I bring you will always be happiness and good fortune.

I am always caught in contradictions. Like with taking the medicine — on the one hand, I have to take medicine to cure the sickness, and on the other hand, I have to take an herbal medicine to stop the pain that is as damaging to the body as a slow-acting poison. It has already made me addicted, but I have no other choice. Fate is this way. When I can choose, I am like many other people, and I choose without understanding. When I do understand clearly, usually there is no more room for choice. When I see the people around me still squandering their bodies and wasting their lives, I truly feel a sense of worry and heartache on their behalf. I think I will finally be able to understand your solitude. When there is only one person who is lucid in this world, the other people cannot hear, even if you shout at them till you wreck your throat.

As endless pain becomes more and more the constant situation in my life, I think always of death. I cannot bring anything along, including all that you gave me, everything that I view as more precious than life itself. No matter how much I may cherish these things, I am only keeping one passing traveler from among them. Thus, with all these external objects, I am taking them from my mind and discarding them. The only thing I cannot discard and cannot give up is you. But do you count as something external? But what can I leave behind? Life has been long enough to let me leave some traces behind for the world, even if they are just the traces of loving you. As for me, the most meaningful feeling right now is to let myself take root in your life.

The suffering of being sick has let me see how close the

god of death is to me, but isn't it always this close to everyone? Just as you said, the god of death shadows every one of us. From beginning to end it is with us like a shadow following a form, but only when the light appears can we finally see its existence. Every time the god of death and those other demons from the death-dealing mandala appear before me, and I see them grinning at me and laughing, I immediately start to think about what things I have not done and must urgently go do. I have discovered that I have to appreciate the god of death, and I especially have to be grateful to it for letting me have moments of lucidity in this present pain. The god of death is constantly being pulled out by this continuous pain.

The painkiller is beginning to take effect, and I am slowly feeling my body getting a bit calmer. The fierce pain that I was just feeling—who knows when, it has started to gradually retreat, like the tide going out. This feeling is really good, like after an ocean wave has gone by, and the bright moon rises on the surface of the ocean. Only at this time does my mind begin to feel at peace. I let the dark night flow comfortably over my body, and my body then becomes heavier and heavier, as if it is sinking right to the bottom of the ocean ...

4 The Road Ahead Is Boundless

Khyung, now my throat has become so fragile I am like a child.

Any food that is the least bit hard, like grains of rice or cabbage leaves, can irritate my throat and bring on great pain. Every time I swallow, I have to prepare to resist the pain, because the smallest motion of swallowing is a major upheaval for my throat. Even a light flow of saliva brings on terrible pain, so I cannot talk very much; I cannot talk too quickly or loudly. I have to pay attention then to doing all I can to let the saliva slowly flow in my throat. But even if I do not swallow anything, the pain will still not go away. It will stay with me in a certain part of my chest, too deep to probe, and come forth again and again and make me feel sick. At times, with no advance preparation, that pain, which was originally mild, will suddenly hit several times with a stabbing pain — I have no way to describe that feeling of "evil pain." It is a sudden, violent, stabbing pain, like a wound from a piece of flesh suddenly being pulled open with pliers. But it is far from this simple — the nerves in my whole body are all being tugged at by this evil pain. At these times, better feelings are all obliterated by the pain.

As for the pain, ordinarily all I can do is to lightly press on my ears, to soothe the pain as if I were comforting a small child who had done something wrong. I don't know if this is a psychological function, but it has a real effect. At a minimum, after each time I rub my ears, I feel that the pain has let up a bit. So I am constantly rubbing my ears, and this has become a kind of communications channel between me and my body.

Now I can no longer yawn when I want to. Even when I am extremely tired, when I feel a yawn coming on, I must immediately mobilize the strength of my whole body to resist it. It is best if I can hold it back. If I cannot hold back the yawn, then the bit of energy that was not easy to preserve will be consumed in a crushing, burning pain that feels as if my whole skull is being ripped apart, which comes after the yawn. Besides yawning, the results of coughing and sneezing are the same. But if I compare them, the hardest to bear is sneezing, because yawning and coughing can be controlled, and sometimes even can be suppressed, but this does not work for sneezes. So I am always worried I will catch a cold. I don't dare imagine what the results of continuous sneezing would be.

Besides this, I am developing a resistance to food, and sometimes I don't even want to drink water. Whenever it is mealtime, I feel there is pressure. This is not only because the pain has dispelled my desire for food—though in the past I was very fond of food. The process of eating itself is torture for me. From putting the food in my mouth, to chewing it, to swallowing it, I must be extremely careful with every little movement. But even if I am very careful, there is no way to avoid the pain that is brought on every time I swallow. And if I am not careful, if one day a bit of food gets caught in my throat, then for many days I would not be able to get it down or bring it out, and this could bring about a new wound and continuous severe pain.

Beginning several months ago, every evening when I go to sleep, I must take two doses of painkillers. When I had just started with this, the painkillers seemed to have some effect, but now it seems they are less and less effective. What's more, I cannot sleep on my side, because the wound is on the right side of my throat, and if I sleep on my right side, this puts pressure on the wound. And I cannot sleep on my left side either: if I sleep this way my right nostril gets blocked, and the air coming in through the left nostril cuts like a knife into the place in my throat that hurts. All I can do is lie down flat on my back, but sometimes after lying flat on my back for a long time my throat will begin to itch, and I desperately want to cough ... So when I sleep at night, I am not at all peaceful, and almost every night my sleep is very shallow.

In the past I always heard people saying, "If you can eat and you can sleep, this is the greatest good fortune." I never took this to heart; only now do I truly appreciate the great wisdom in this saying. But I don't know if the people who said that were having the same feelings and helplessness as me.

When even basic existence is all very difficult for a person, a sense of faith and a sense of purpose will really be very easily destroyed. I am also always thinking: what meaning is there in living this way? If not for the strength of faith and of love, I think I would have already surrendered a hundred times to this inhuman torture.

I know at a deep level that you certainly hope I will go on living well. Kumari and others also hope I will continue living well. I do not have the power to bring an end to this life that bears the expectations of countless people. Whether or not life has meaning is not important, because living itself is the greatest meaning.

It's just that the road ahead is boundless, and I am really afraid I will not be able to endure it.

5 The Solitary Light in the Darkness

... In the darkness, I am awakened by that familiar pain.

*It drags me roughly from my dream back to reality. The pain
has already entered into the depths of my subconscious,
and probably in my dreams I also remember its everyday
ferocious look. Many times I am startled awake by the illusory
appearance of pain.*

*I've forgotten when it started. I began to get used to this
rough style and think of it as normal. Because it always wakes
me up many times every night, slowly I learned to distinguish
time in the dense darkness.*

*I like it most after I wake up, when it is still deep in the
night. The pain is still deadened by the effect of the painkillers,
and I am drowsy. I am like a prisoner in shackles all day long,
and there is just this short moment when I can enjoy being
released from the shackles, and freely relax my body and
mind, and let every pore in my whole body enjoy the beauty of
breathing freely. However, at times like this, the effect of the
drug makes my whole body as heavy as stone, and even to turn
onto my side takes a lot of strength. My body almost does not
obey my commands, and it seems it has totally separated from
me. But being this way is good too: this feeling of not being in
pain and not being easily moved fills me with the joy of feeling
peaceful and secure.*

*In this state of oblivion, it is as if my soul has left my body
and drifted off, and, without sound or form, has merged into
the dark night, which is so thick and dense that it seems to have
solidified. Compared to the soul, I finally realize, a person's
physical body is actually very coarse and heavy.*

*Borrowing the body of the night, the soul goes wherever
it wants to go. It returns to the past, it goes to the future, or it*

stays at your side.

I am quietly telling you that I am always taking advantage of the dark night to hasten to your side. When I am by your side, I watch you as you are deep asleep, and I wrap you with my body, and I hold you tight and cuddle you. You are like a child sleeping in its mother's embrace; the faint sound of snoring is regular and light, and as I look at you, you look fortunate and satisfied. But in reality, the most fortunate one is me, as I gaze upon you. If you opened your eyes at this time, you would see my entranced smile.

I lightly summon the pure wind and let it gently brush across your face — do you feel even more pleased? I also summon the fine rain and transform the words in my mind into the sound of pattering raindrops dripping into your dreams. When you wake up, I have already gone, lightly, not leaving any trace. Did you suspect I have been coming to you, or not? In dreams there are no traces, and there is no way for me to leave footprints.

Maybe, after many years, there will be a day when you suddenly think that we have always been meeting in dreams, and holding each other in the dark night.

What is really waiting for me is not just the god of death, it is also you!

Though the long road is boundless, in the endless darkness you have left a solitary lamp for me, and it warms my heart.

Chapter 30

Niguma's Sweet Dew

1　Good Medicine to Save Minds

Khyungpo Naljor is talking to Xuemo:

Child, you must realize that Sharwadi's pain in fact is also my pain. For many years after this, whenever I think of Sharwadi, my mind would always be in pain. Do not think that accomplished adepts have no pain. No, accomplished adepts are not made of wood or stone; they too feel pain. It is just that the pain cannot bring them affliction any more, that's all. This is because they are already dwelling at peace in that place inside which does not have pain.

"This is the way it is.

"Let us go ahead and speak of Niguma's pure land.

"In that pure realm of light, I received the complete set of empowerments into the *Five Great Diamonds Teachings of Niguma*. These are the empowerment of the precious vessel, the empowerment of the secret, the empowerment of wisdom, and the empowerment of the Great Mudra. Besides these, there are still the empowerment of Niguma's Six Methods, the empowerment of the method of the three branches, the empowerment of the red and white dakinis, the empowerment of no birth and no extinction …

"When I left the pure realm, I still could see before my eyes the gold hill and Niguma on the gold hill. My body and mind were full of joy, and I was extremely happy. I asked: "Teacher, is that pure realm I just saw a kind of dream or not?"

Niguma smiled and said: "Son, in this world, is there anything that is not a dream?"

As she spoke, she handed me a bowl of sweet dew. I took it and drank it down. This sweet dew comes from the Buddha Land, and its essential nature is the joy of emptiness without distinctions. Niguma said: "In the pure realm, you received the full empowerment, but to dispel your doubts, I can do three more empowerments for you."

So then Niguma both gave me the empowerments and transmitted the teaching, giving detailed explanations of the essential points.

She said: "Son, this teaching comes from the sacred Vajradhara and has never been widely transmitted. You must receive it and uphold it well. You will transmit my teaching widely, and it will be able to benefit countless sentient beings. I will be concerned for all your disciples who inherit the teaching and will support them in attaining the ultimate achievement. Any sentient beings who have faith toward me only have to pray to me, and I will surely work for them with all my power. As for any sentient beings who are facing the end, if they have sufficient faith in me and chant 'Niguma Khyenno,' then

I will bring many dakinis and receive them into the Soshaling Pure Land. Though this land is a realm that appears by transformation, it is connected with the Land of Esoteric Adornment, and any who go to be reborn in this land are sure to attain the ultimate achievement. Son, the content of what I just said is my great vow, and you must transmit it widely. It will make those who do not believe develop faith, and it will make those who already believe have stronger faith. I have already realized the ultimate fruit of enlightenment: with wisdom, I do not enter into the cycle of birth and death; with compassion, I do not enter into the extinction of nirvana. While the cycle of birth and death is not yet empty, I will always be concerned with sentient beings who have a karmic link to me.

"Son, though the *Five Great Diamonds Teachings of Niguma* have special excellence, what is even more excellent is the spirit of benefiting sentient beings, which has been passed on in the lineage of the teaching. It is like a snowy mountain, lofty and pure. It is like a sandy desert, vast and unbounded. You must remember this well. Without the mind of enlightenment, by cultivating the teachings, you will not be able to reach the ultimate benefit. Son, you must always remember, the true aim of all the teachings is to attain purity, is to detach from suffering and find bliss, is to attain the ultimate liberation. Above all, do not mix up the root and the branch and make the great Esoteric Teaching into one more rope binding the mind.

"Son, you have received all my teaching lineages as if they have been poured into you. After this, your work will be like the sun in the sky. The accomplished disciples in your lineage will be as numerous as the stars in the sky. All my teaching lineages are like a treasure chest which you brought out from the depths of the ocean in the light of your dream. Once you open it up, then it will send out infinite light. But the

Path is a foot tall, the demons of delusion are ten feet tall. Because the demons of delusion will make mischief, there will be countless people who defame you. Sometimes the thick fog created by the demons can even conceal the sun. Just as darkness always accompanies light, adverse circumstances will always accompany your teaching lineage, but they will not be able to influence the purity of the teaching lineage. Just as Devadatta's evil deeds highlighted by contrast the great human character of the Buddha, all the adverse circumstances in life will act to perfect your immeasurable merit.

"As the minds of worldly people day by day become more and more dangerous and evil, my teaching lineage of wisdom will become a good medicine to save minds.

"Son, my teachings will certainly carry on and flourish. Do not get stuck in the old ways: you must advance with the times. In the defiled evil world of the future, the attraction of material desires will be greater and greater, and disciples with a karmic connection to us will be rarer and rarer. Above all, you must not establish a lot of barriers, reject people and leave them outside the gate of liberation. Tell the worldly people that as long as they have faith in me, and can recite 'Niguma Khyenno' every day, they will receive my immeasurable support. My body of reality is everywhere in the realm of reality and transcends time and space. Any sentient beings who sincerely ask it of me will surely receive my immeasurable support and will advance and merge into the Great Mudra of Light.

"Tell all those who have a karmic connection that reciting 'Niguma Khyenno' does not require them to be initiated. You must know that all the Buddhas and bodhisattvas definitely do not place any barriers in the way of sentient beings detaching from suffering and finding bliss.

"Anyone who has faith in Niguma is my disciple."

2 The View of the Great Mudra

"Son, you must know, that there is nothing in the universe that is eternal: all phenomena have no inherent nature.

"So why is it that all phenomena have no inherent nature? What I am calling inherent nature here means an independent, unchanging basic essence—it exists forever, never changes, never perishes, endures forever. The myriad things and events in the world when viewed superficially are really there, but you cannot find in them an independent, unchanging basic essence. No matter what it is, all things are a combination of causal conditions:this exists, so that exists; this is born, so that is born; this perishes, so that perishes. They exist based on causal conditions: suddenly born, suddenly perishing; suddenly existing, suddenly gone; suddenly good, suddenly bad; illusory transformations, like bubbles. This is why their basic substance is empty. Moreover, this is not emptiness based on our acknowledging it, nor is it emptiness that only appears later: rather, it is fundamental emptiness. This emptiness is the emptiness of basic substance: that is to say, only emptiness is the basic essence of the universe.

"Son, since emptiness is the basic essence of the universe, all the many apparent contrived phenomena are of course empty and without inherent nature. Though in appearance they have birth and extinction, they still are not apart from the basic essence of emptiness. All events, all things, all people, all states, including birth and death, including samsara and nirvana and so on, are all like this. They are lightning in the sky; they are bubbles in the water; they are dew drops in the sunshine; they are locusts after the autumn ends. Although they put on a show of illusory starting and ending, that fundamentally empty basic essence never moves. The myriad phenomena are the play of wisdom of that spontaneous basic essence. Seen from the surface, it has many kinds of wondrous functions, many kinds of adornment, but those numerous manifestations cannot last forever. With them, what appears is not different from emptiness, and emptiness is not different from what appears. Those numerous manifestations are all sea spray floating up from the empty, still, fundamental essence. All actions, all the phenomena that are manifested by external objects, are all instantaneous and impermanent: their inherent nature is fundamentally empty, and they are like illusory transformations.

"Though the enlightened inherent nature of the fundamental essence can, in its manifestations, show samsara and nirvana, from the point of view of the ultimate truth, no matter whether it is samsara or it is nirvana, nothing is apart from the empty inherent nature of the fundamental essence; that is to say, everything is ultimately unattainable.

"Son, the enlightened inherent nature is the empty inherent nature. All the many manifestations are, in reality, the action of the wondrous function of the enlightened inherent nature. It manifests samsara and nirvana; it manifests the play of all the many illusory transformations; it manifests the grandeur of the enlightened inherent nature. But in their fundamental substance, these have no birth and no extinction, and are not apart from the fundamental essence. Therefore, the enlightened inherent nature must go beyond good and evil, go beyond cause and effect, go beyond delusion and enlightenment, go beyond suffering and happiness. This is because the enlightened inherent nature does not need to be cultivated: it is not defiled or purified, not added to or diminished. It is fundamentally of itself liberated, and abides in the realm that is everywhere equal.

"Thus the true enlightened nature in its basic essence is empty and still, and is not attached to forms, and is completely without anything to attain. It does not necessarily recite the scriptures, or focus on mantras, or cultivate the tutelary deity, or visualize mandalas. For people who clearly understand that the inherent nature of mind, the enlightened nature, is fundamentally empty, the two procedures of generating enlightenment and perfecting enlightenment both belong to the category of teachings with form, and the entire Buddhist Canon is spare furniture.

"Son, I am saying that the enlightened inherent nature is the empty inherent nature. The wondrous enlightenment of its spiritual light is spontaneously complete. If illumination and emptiness are not one, the fundamental purity has not been achieved. That basic essence, the inherent nature of mind, is fundamentally pure, fundamentally without anything. If we understand this truth, and abide peacefully in it, being as it is without moving, this is called cultivation. We observe the myriad phenomena as if we are observing flowing water. Our eyes see all forms, but our minds do not stir. We are not attached to diligent practice, and we are not attached to the duality of being and nothingness. We do not engender clingings and attachments, and we do not engage in discriminating thought. All forms are like the water of a great river flowing along endlessly. Our minds are like a bright mirror, untainted by dust, with no worries remaining. When our minds encounter the forms of external objects, then you must understand that all the many manifestations are in reality the wondrous function of mind. When you understand this point clearly, and you know that the myriad phenomena are all the wondrous functioning of the enlightened inherent nature, then your mind does not turn following objects, and mind and objects both fade away.

"Son, how can you take this theoretical idea and make it run through all your activities? I am telling you to abide peacefully in the empty inherent nature, to clearly understand its reality, to take the realm of desire and the realm of form and the formless realm, and fuse them all into the enlightened inherent nature that is clear as empty space. All the forms which the eyes see, all the sounds which the ears hear, all the odors which the nose smells, all the flavors which the tongue tastes, all the touches which the body feels, all the thoughts which the conceptual mind stirs up, the mountains and rivers and land, the buildings and beautiful scenery, the rivers and lakes and oceans, the flowers blooming, the animals leaping with joy, that complex variegated world … all the external objects, all the internal states of mind, all the clingings and attachments, all the worries and concerns, all the forms that start and end — all of them are included in the spontaneous wisdom of that empty inherent nature. The various kinds of realms outside the mind, the consciousness that starts and ends inside the mind — they are all contained in the spontaneous wisdom of that empty inherent nature. You must know that this spontaneous wisdom of that empty inherent nature is not to be sought outside the mind. It is something that is fundamentally present in the inherent nature of the minds of sentient beings. It does not depend on cultivating practice to attain it. It is fundamentally fully complete. It is equivalent to the Buddha's Body of Reality.

"Son, at all times, you must not cling to contrived exercises and practices. This is because the pure enlightened inherent nature does not use external seeking, does not depend on what is gained by cultivating good deeds and adding merit — it is an uncontrived reality. For the correct way to proceed, you must take your body, mouth, and mind and fuse them into the enlightened inherent nature. You must understand that the enlightened inherent nature is uncontrived, that the empty inherent nature has no clingings, that inherent nature has no obstructions. If you want contrived action, then there will something you cling to. If there is something you seek, then there will be something you suffer. If there is something you crave, then there will be something you lose. All contrived action, whether creating evil or doing good, is all the root of revolving in birth and death. Therefore you must transcend the dualism of good and evil, and let go of everything, and not have the slightest attachments in your mind. Let your mind be independent, and go along with uncontrived action. Son, you must know, all contrived action returns to interdependent origination. All phenomena that come from interdependent origination all return to birth and extinction, and they are all like illusions and without reality. Thus, we need uncontrived action: no contrived action, but nothing left undone.

"Son, ultimately what is having no contrived action? No contrived action means lucidly deciding that all phenomena have no inherent nature, that you must not abide in being and you must not abide in non-being, that you must not abide in the view that everything is eternal and you must not abide in the view that everything is annihilated. You must not debate right and wrong; you must have no grasping and no rejecting, no dividing and no separating. It is precisely because the ignorant people in the world have all kinds of contrived biased views, that they generate clingings and attachments, cling to the illusory as real, accept the false as true, grasp forms and become attached to forms. Thus, they drift in the great ocean of samsara, revolving in birth and death. You must know that only with the rule of having no contrived action, you can transcend cause and effect.

"Do you understand, son of my heart?"

Niguma said: "Son, pacify your mind, concentrate your spirit, put aside the myriad phenomena, and come listen to our song."

3 The Warm Sunshine After Awakening

Then the dakinis sang together:

In the mundane world there is a most exalted substance, called the holy thing or the sweet dew.

Those outside the Buddhist Path may have different names and forms for them, but in reality they are substances that aid the Path.

The true most exalted substance is the experience of enlightenment; like a warm sun in winter, it can bring you peace and comfort.

You calmly relax as if the sun is shining in winter, but at the same time you do not lose that enlightenment.

You must bathe forever under the warm sun of enlightenment; do not pursue questions and do not have expectations.

You must experience that relaxation after enlightenment, but it is not oblivion or ignorance.

In relaxing, you must experience the sunlight of awakening, and use the light to deal with everything before your eyes.

Though the light is bright and shines everywhere in the world, do not abandon that warm bath.

What the bath warms is the body and the spirit; body and mind both receive the light of awakening.

Light rays flow in through every pore, calmly permeating everything from inside to outside.

Do not go on looking for holy things outside of mind; there are many
real deceivers in the world.

They play with empty illusions and waste the mind's potential; their
purpose is to use holy things to satisfy selfish desires.

The true holy thing is of course enlightenment; do not cling to it and do
not lose it.

It is like walking through the countryside under a clear blue sky;
though you do not cling to it, you still enjoy the bright sun.

The source of that bright sun is still the inherent nature of mind;
outside of mind there are no especially excellent material things.

Because the light of awakening is there, all forms then have brilliant colors.

Walking under the bright sun, you are calm and relaxed, and your mind
is clear and bright as a mirror.

In the mirror, all the worlds in the universe can be reflected, but the
essence of the mirror is still as it is, unmoving.

When all the objects come near, the surface of the mirror seems
complicated; when all objects depart, the mirror is again clear and still.

Though the bright mirror welcomes the new and sees off the old, the
surface of that mirror of light has no traces of anything at all.

Again: it's like a sharp sword piercing the surface of the water: for an
instant there is a ripple on the surface of the water.

When you pull the sharp sword out of the water, no trace can be seen in the water.

The way practitioners who have realized enlightenment act in the world is like that sharp sword cutting into the surface of the water.

Though they act in many ways, walking, standing, sitting, and lying down, the essence of mind does not move in the slightest.

When we face external forms with their complex diversity, we must understand them like the bright mirror.

External objects themselves can go through many strange changes, but the essence of mind should not follow them.

When you have clearly understood this truth, then you have the most exalted substance.

Though you see it as quite ordinary, in reality your mind now holds the Pearl of Spirit Peak (the ultimate truth of Buddha's teaching).

The light of that precious pearl shines brightly through heaven and earth, and under the bright sun, the shadows of the six planes of existence are no more.

Pain and suffering and affliction are the shadows of frost on a summer day; if there is no clinging and attachment, then there is no ignorance and delusion.

The light is sparkling, the spirit is clear, like the white ox on the open ground; the emptiness is vast, the brightness is dazzling, like the lotus torch in the fire.

The light is pure, the brightness is endless, like the bright moon in the mind; the blue is vivid and the purity is pervasive, like ten thousand miles of clear sky.

When you reach this point, you will not seek anything else in the human world, and there is no more wondrous message in the heavens.

Intoxicated, ecstatic, you forever nurture the embryo of holiness; having swept away the myriad appearances, the self too is gone.

At this time you do not need to seek the Buddha Land anymore: the pure lands and the holy places are all in your mind.

The Dharmakaya, the Body of Reality, is in all places at all times, and when you arrive at this moment, what meets your eyes is all the Pure Land.

Niguma taught me, saying: "Son, you must be sure to remember that in the world there are many excellent material things that help the Path to Enlightenment. They are taken as sacred objects by people. They can be precious herbal medicines and things used by the holy people, but they are the things of samadhi, and they are only useful for those who uphold their vows. True holy things let you enter deeply into the truth of the teaching and awaken to the fundamental. When you are bathing in the fundamental, that is tantamount to obtaining the nourishment of the most exalted substance. You must know that the bright emptiness you awaken to is not empty nothingness, but rather is filled with clear, living, inherent nature.

"After you recognize the fundamental original mind, it will magnetize your human life. From this point on, you will have no more worries and no more fears. Your mind will already have become like water, so even if it is stabbed by a sharp sword, it will not harbor expectations and it will not give rise to fears. Though there will be ripples on the surface of the water that has been stabbed, they will quickly settle and cease, and no marks will be left behind.

"Son, you must recognize that the fundamental substance of all that you have experienced is equally unborn, and you must not have hopes or fears, or keep on having expectations or anxieties. Even if you become a king one night, you must not be overjoyed. Even if you are transformed into a beggar in an instant, you must not be worried. This is because, no matter what happens, the basic substance of the inherent nature of your mind is always without birth and without extinction.

"You do not need to cling to those who are close to you, and you do not have to hate your enemies. You act according to circumstances and help them, but you must not bring along any clingings or attachments or expectations. There will be a day when someone close to you dies, and you will not have to cry with grief, and you will not have to depart from that realm of light you have realized. You can do meritorious deeds according to circumstances, and bring benefits to the mind and spirit of the departed ones. But remember, their fundamental substance is still without birth and without extinction.

"Those who truly achieve the Great Mudra are like lofty snowy mountains. Though they do not move or waver, in the light of the sun of faith, they can let the water melting from the snow flow down to nourish the myriad things. They can manifest all sorts of realms according to conditions, and they can do this without leaving the fundamental for an instant. No matter whether they become kings or beggars, they can never be startled by external changes, and they calmly enjoy the circumstances they encounter. Their actions are adaptive and spontaneous, and they do not fabricate or imitate. In the fundamental condition, they will be aware of what they do and how they act in daily life: they are self-confident but also skillful, and thereby avoid unnecessary misunderstandings.

"When a person fully awakens, he no longer worries about revolving in the cycle of birth and death, and no longer yearns for nirvana. In his true mind, the myriad phenomena have one flavor and one source: there is nothing that has to be accepted or rejected. His mind is like a mirror that can clearly reflect the myriad things, but without using good or evil. At this point, for him there is no longer the subject doing the cultivating and the object being cultivated, because he is in the fundamental source every minute of every hour."

The dakinis sang together:

The function of words has totally dissolved away, so it is like a blind man seeing and a deaf man hearing.

Like the silent sound of a mute's words, there are no words that can describe what is what.

There is no way to describe that most wondrous great flavor in terms of sensations of flavor; there is no way to represent that most wondrous sound using musical notes.

That most exalted form has no colors any more; that greatest realm has no physical form.

Even if you could swallow all the water in three rivers in a single mouthful, you could not express the flavor your mind wants to describe.

Even if you could spit out a vast expanse of waves, there would still be no way to express that still, silent sound.

*Though we have sung many songs, the wise understand completely,
while the deluded are still deluded and confused.*

*Even if there are a million words, the enlightenment in the mind is still
beyond the scope of words.*

*Only if you have tasted the flavor of that wondrous truth, will you be
able to awaken from your dream and suddenly become enlightened.*

*Only then will you know that all truth is not words: truth is the
fundamental essence beyond concepts.*

*Babbling Xuemo, or is it Khyungpo Ba: your mind's light of wisdom
has already begun to appear.*

*You must go beyond the trap of dualism: this going beyond is the basic
substance of liberation.*

*Though your candle of wisdom has not set the prairie ablaze, and that
seed still has to grow into a great tree,*

*Still, you have already glimpsed the road for cultivating the Path, and
you have already emerged from the worldly and suddenly gone beyond
ordinary sensory life.*

*Although you still have a long road ahead of you, the light has already
appeared, and you will not mistake the road again.*

*You will not rush around everywhere seeking the Dharma outside of
mind, and you will no longer accept the false as the true and cling to
the illusory as real.*

You have discovered that, in fact, your realization has nothing that is realized, and that you are already equipped with that light.

The true goal of your long travels is to discover your own precious jewel ...

4 Awakening Revealed

Khyungpo Naljor said that he emptied through in great enlightenment, and was so happy he began to cry. Everything he had studied before had suddenly come alive. He said: "The dakinis all referred to the essence of all the teachings I sought before, and it has become more simple and clear."

He was crying tears of joy as he bowed down many times.

Niguma said: "Good, good. You have truly understood."

Khyungpo Naljor smiled, and I smiled too.

He asked me: "What are you smiling for? Can it be that you too have understood?"

I smiled and said: "Understood what? I am slow-witted, and I don't know whether or not I have awakened to such a lofty and profound truth. But I would like to reveal my own awakening and ask you, Teacher, to verify it:

Cutting the bonds of the mind, becoming fully developed and liberated;

Not subject to the mind's deceptions, and beyond this, no clinging or attachment.

Preserving samadhi, examining the bright mirror of my mind;

Without thinking of observing all phenomena, fundamentally without doubts or confusion.

Cultivating the vital energy and its channels, giving it the life-force;

Purifying all the energy channels, diligently cultivating the subtle body.

When I calmly cultivate great bliss, and preserve the jewel of wisdom,

Great bliss blends with all states of mind, and I awaken to all enlightenment.

Quietly observing the mind of clear wisdom, the light of fundamental enlightenment shines;

Emptiness is not dead, still nothingness, it is bright as a crystal.

In the place of spontaneous liberation, the Great Mudra is what I rely upon;

Like a snake uncoiling, I am spontaneously liberated.

The most lofty material substance bathes in the warm sunshine of enlightenment;

In emptiness it is not empty nothingness, it is clear and full of living inherent nature.

As for cultivating practice, it is like a sword piercing water;

Going beyond the eight winds of the world, there is no worry and no fear.

As for the semblance, I observe the mirror of external forms.

I revel in the fundamental uniform flavor and transcend dualism.

"That's it, that's it." Khyungpo Naljor smiled with delight. He said: "Son, I have already illuminated you, and you will go on to illuminate them!"

I asked: "Who do you mean by 'them'?"

He said: " 'Them' is just a word."

Chapter 31

The End Is Also the Beginning

1 The Silhouette Becoming Gradually More Distant

After many years of genuine cultivation according to the teaching, Khyungpo Naljor started on the journey back from India to Tibet.

No one knows how many years he cultivated practice. We must understand that in the realm of clear emptiness, there is no time. Seven days in the cave is already a thousand years in the ordinary world.

The journey coming was long, and the journey going was far. But the mind has changed. This is because with each further experience, the mind gets a bit more clear and enlightened.

In the same way, no one knows how many years Khyungpo Naljor was searching in India. This is not recorded in the *Secret History of Khyungpo*, and it is really not important. In Khyungpo Naljor's hundred-and-fifty-year lifespan, whether he stayed a few years less or a few years more is not such an important question. What is important is what he did while he was there. When he went to India, he had only an expecting and seeking mind. When he returned to Tibet, he had become the carrier of many esoteric teachings. He had already seen many tutelary deities and had already realized the illusory body and the light, and he had gone through coupled action that is learned and arrived at coupled action without study, and he had realized the ultimate achievement of the Great Mudra.

Of course, in the life of a teacher of great achievement, the most important thing is still his mind of enlightenment.

Khyungpo Naljor's face was marked by his journeys. There were already light wrinkles on his forehead—this is very normal. Everyone gets wrinkles. It's not possible that time would not leave the marks of impermanence just because of his faith, just as those who discover the laws of cause and effect cannot escape from cause and effect. But I understood that for Khyungpo Naljor, there was still a very long road he had to travel. Of course, speaking of him as an individual, he lived in the world for a hundred and fifty years, but compared to the great wilderness that has lasted through the ages, his life is like a ripple that arose for a moment on a boundless ocean.

Khyungpo Naljor saw the mountains stretching off into the distance, and he saw those misty, colored clouds. The wind was blowing gently and wafted into his mind. His mind had not left those women in his life who had given him enlightenment. He believed that no matter where they were sojourning, they would be silently watching him. He heard a long-drawn-out boundless call coming down through the ages. This was his reason for living this life.

Hasty steps stirred up endless dust. A benighted mind had already welcomed the light of wisdom. Though he was fatigued, even though he was walking toward the home he had long parted from, he was thinking: "I have never left those women, and I have never left those women whom people call the dakinis of wisdom."

"Niguma, my teacher lifetime after lifetime!"

"Sukhasiddhi, my enlightened consort lifetime after lifetime!"

"Sharwadi, my beloved lifetime after lifetime!"

Such calls would often echo in Khyungpo Naljor's mind.

It was always by chance: he would see a pair of eyes. They were gazing fondly, they were fascinating. Don't think I am using the wrong word. That's right, they were fascinating. That fascinating quality is the wisdom of the dakinis. They use that wisdom to look upon sentient beings. You must not think of them as mute idols. No, they are vibrant life. They are surging with the passion of life, like the billowing waves of a great ocean. They reveal bodies filled with great bliss, like towering mountain peaks. I can always feel that gentle breathing overflowing with life. They have become a light that is present everywhere in my life. Niguma, Sukhasiddhi, my teachers lifetime after lifetime! Sharwadi, my spouse lifetime after lifetime!

Every time I think of these three women, I weep. The tears blur my eyes but burnish my mind. In my life there is a kind of atmosphere that cannot be wiped away, a kind of emotion that is calm but so dense that it cannot be changed, a kind of bright emptiness that includes everything and is present everywhere.

Khyungpo Naljor told me that what is always flowing in his mind is not the mantra of the tutelary deities which his teachers passed on to him, but rather is "Niguma Khyenno." Although he received a thousand teachings from a hundred teachers and learned countless mantras, what constantly echoes in the space and time of his life is "Niguma

Khyenno." This is because all his teachers told him that reciting the mantra of the tutelary deities ten thousand times is not as good as praying to your teacher once with total sincerity. He took the tutelary deities of all his teachers and fused them all into Niguma's great ocean of wisdom.

I once asked Khyungpo Naljor: "How did you come to have such great achievement?"

He answered: "It is because I am praying to my teacher every minute of my life."

One night nine hundred years later, he took the most important mantra in his life and transmitted it to me.

Niguma Khyenno!

Khyungpo Naljor said: "Niguma has achieved the ultimate result of enlightenment; she is not separate from all the Buddhas; her Dharmakaya (True Body) is everywhere in the realm of reality. All that is necessary is to pray to her with complete sincerity, and she will always give her support according to karmic circumstances."

However, before this moment arrived, this moment that had seemed far away beyond the sky, Niguma was only a concern in Khyungpo Naljor's mind that he could not get rid of. He of course did not know that this concern itself was a manifestation of Niguma.

The phrase "Niguma Khyenno" accompanied Khyungpo Naljor all along, during the time he traveled for so long seeking the Dharma, and it also accompanied him as he returned to the snowy regions, to Tibet.

In the faraway dust, I see Khyungpo Naljor's silhouette gradually getting farther and farther away.

Faintly there comes the sound of a song:

Though the mountain towers up,

It is not higher than the radiant spirit.

Though the road winds into the distance,

It is not longer than the footsteps of the trek.

Though my steps are labored,

My faith is solid as a rock.

Because in my spirit the light is gleaming,

It will become the lamp in the hand of the nighttime traveler.

That fire of wisdom which has been passed on for a thousand years

Will go on from our hands

To set the prairie ablaze, and become the most beautiful scene in history ...

2 The Sad and Moving Song of the Heart

Before Khyungpo Naljor returned to Tibet, he also went to Nepal, looking for Sharwadi.

At that time, the average lifespan of people in Nepal was less than forty years. There was not any woman who would have been able to hold on through his long search. What's more, Sharwadi had met with difficulties in her life, and everyone said they were brought on by the power of those evil curses from the death-dealing mandala. Many people fully believed this explanation.

In that little temple where he had previously studied, Khyungpo

Naljor saw Kumari. Earlier on, she had provided Sharwadi with much information on those sorcerers. By now she was very old. In order to wait for Khyungpo Naljor, she had sought from Bandi "Niguma's esoteric method for prolonging life and holding to the light," and she had diligently cultivated it, keeping it up day and night. For this reason, she lived for a hundred years.

Kumari delivered some documents to Khyungpo Naljor, and she said that Sharwadi had converted all her wealth into gold and stored it away in a storage depot. A storage depot was an organization that specialized in storing and protecting valuables. According to these documents, he could take this wealth and use it as a resource for his future work spreading the teaching. All he had to do was pay a very small fee, and the storage depot would help him transport the wealth to Tibet. Their caravans could pass through the commercial outposts of many countries.

In what Kumari passed on to Khyungpo Naljor, there were also letters that he had previously written to Sharwadi. Besides these, there were also some of Sharwadi's writings.

From these writings, he finally knew what kind of longing and pain Sharwadi had suffered.

Later, after he had realized enlightenment, Khyungpo Naljor asked the dakinis to preserve these writings in the scripts of the dakinis. He gave instructions requesting them to give these writings, after a thousand years, to someone who had fully realized the empty inherent nature, and who knew the scripts of the dakinis.

With the help of that dakini scripts, I saw Sharwadi as she was dying:

During a break in the pain from the evil demons pulling me apart, the sound of knocking at the gate came again, making me feel how heartbroken I am, and making my blood race.

Though I knew you would not be coming back, my heart was still beating fast. Before, whenever I heard the distinctive sound of your knocking at the gate, my mind would be like the water of a pond rippling in the spring wind, like a great ocean surging. It could wake me up after I had been sunk in sleep for a thousand years, and could summon forth a beautiful rosy dusk. Khyung, was it yesterday's you bringing me another cup of excellent tea again and inviting me to taste it? Was it yesterday's you bringing a book for me to enjoy? Was it you eagerly inviting me to go bathe in the starlight?

When my body permits, as soon as I hear that sound, I jump up and eagerly open the door, then return dejected.

My sunshine, why can't I get beyond those dusty things of the past? Is it that you were too beautiful, or that the time was too beautiful? Traveling in the moonlight, we have both gotten old, but my feeling toward you is still so young, and can bear to leaf through the pages of time.

Yet you ended up leaving, and entered into your dream. My grief is as it was before, the little lane is as it was before. Once you had gone, who would stand at the entrance of the street gazing at me? Once you had gone, when would we be holding hands in the spring light, taking my wavering gaze and merging it into your limpid eyes?

Tonight's snow is floating down as usual without stopping. But in the end, the weather of these three months, with its cool breath, has evoked a lonely and dreary longing. How much I miss you! On this kind of peaceful evening, I unwittingly pass by that little house, which once was full of the warm feeling of springtime, but is now chilly in the wind and rain, and a feeling that seems to be from ages ago wells up in my mind. If there had been nobody in that little courtyard, I certainly would have started to cry. I must let that warm little house never forget that true and beautiful story of sensory experience.

I stood under the window where we had once made a pact, lightly rubbing the simple window curtain, and the feelings in the depths of my mind were faraway but clear. My love, where have you landed tonight? Here on my cliff looking out for my man, I have already seen you not returning, leaving behind beauty and loneliness!

My love, you can see the stars filling the sky, glittering in the cold light, leaping up in my mind, receding, bringing on that season of rustling uneasiness. That winter moonlight is telling me: "He is late arriving, late arriving; late arriving footsteps are pursuing a beautiful mistake."

My love, the moon is clear and bright — are you wandering in difficulty and confusion? Do you also hear the language of the moon? Can you see that mind like a bright moon on the horizon? It always wants to soothe your tense brow, it always wants to hold onto your soul which has gone so far away. Who says we are late arriving? Who says we made a mistake? There is no distance from heart to heart, from mind to mind.

The snow is coming down hard, and the snowflakes are hitting my mind, which is already riddled with a thousand wounds. Facing the cold, clear, empty space, I do not know how there can be fewer wounds.

Outside the window, the snowflakes are drifting down as

*usual without stopping, continuously, like the inexhaustible
endless longing deep in my heart. I long to see that familiar
silhouette, but before my eyes only an expanse of snow fills the
sky and covers the earth, blocking the meeting of heart with
heart, of mind with mind.*

*I lean against the corner where two walls meet, letting
the cold wind brush over me. A jackdaw passes by that stretch
of blue sky marked out by the red wall, appearing carefree in
my eyes. Then the feeling that seems to be from ages ago, that
things are the same but people have changed, strikes me and
my tears quietly start to fall. Under that low, ocher-colored
wall, I used to be there, standing, facing the wind, looking out
toward that beloved corner. In the wind and snow, I would
cover my forehead with one hand and hold steady in the corner
of the wall with the other hand. With an ordinary posture, I
would stand as a unique part of the scenery and look to the
end of the lane where you would come meandering along, so
carefree and lovable ...*

*A person walks in a long long dream, mulling things over
and sighing, relying on faded things of the past, fiddling with
the white hair on her shoulders. It is the same sky, the same
wind, but I am all haggard as I look around in a trance, and
I can no longer find the road home. Your eyes shine in the
brightest place in the sky, and in the look in your eyes is written
something I have no way of understanding. Maybe yesterday's
wind of many feelings played a lovable game with me, and
played tricks on me, and played tricks on you, and played
tricks on the pink summer.*

My mind is lost in a reverie, and my footsteps are so heavy that there is no way to move forward. I do not know how I can finally free myself. All along, I have been expecting you to keep your promise and come back, but the wind rises and the clouds move, and I am still waiting for the loneliness after the daydream.

My mind has fallen like a yellow leaf drifting on a vast ocean. On shore, the fishermen's songs are sounding in the evening sun, as if in a dream.

The sound of the songs is all around, striking the empty ocean in my breast. More than twenty years of waiting has finally frozen the plaintive song in my heart ...

As I finish gathering up the last few leaves of my life, my mind and spirit end up flying out to those longings that are withered yet sweet, happy yet heavy.

It has gone far away, other people mocking me ...

That chunk of ice in the depths of my mind is gradually melting ...

3 A Secret Encounter

On a certain day almost a thousand years after Khyungpo Naljor returned to Tibet, I too encountered Niguma. Our encounter started where the search had started and ended at the first light of dawn at the crossing point.

At the crossing point in that realm of light, I saw Niguma. She was an ordinary woman. She was not as beautiful as in the traditional accounts; she was ordinary and not like a legend.

I do not know whether or not the Niguma I met was the same person as the Niguma that Khyungpo Naljor met.

But I think that the truth appears with different names and forms, and it is the same way with Niguma. She could be a pure wind, or a red evening sky, or the sun at sunset, or a morning cloud, or the bud of a flower shyly waiting to bloom, or the sound of contented breathing. Even more, she could be a woman like Sukhasiddhi, both crafty and wise.

An encounter a thousand years ago and an encounter a thousand years later can be assumed to have differences of the times. But I do not care about the cup: what I need is the sweet dew in the cup. No matter what kind of external form she has, I will always see through the temporary appearances and see the true substance.

We met in an extremely quiet realm. She said she was waiting for someone. I did not know who she was waiting for. At that time I thought that if she truly was Niguma, then in fact she did not have to keep waiting, because she had been waiting for me.

That woman told me that the genuine Niguma was, in fact, a process of seeking. In the book, Sukhasiddhi, Sharwadi, the countless holy places visited, the Bonpo spells, and also that spirit swallowing the sky, those countless demonic barriers, that endless longing—all the scenes on the journey, all the people, all the events—it all was Niguma.

She said: "If you do not understand this point, then that Niguma is really a legend."

I smiled and posed a question: "So then, am I Niguma too?"

"How can you not be?" She laughed, and the sound of her laugh was the lingering sound of a diamond bell.

I asked: "Are you waiting for someone?"

I also said: "In fact you do not have to keep waiting, because you have been waiting for me."

She laughed, and the look in her eyes was full of charm and grace.

She said: "I am not still waiting. I am just being with you."

I told her that at this crossing point shining with pure light, she was not waiting for me, but I was waiting for someone. Though I was also searching, I did not know when my search had started, and it had already become my waiting.

We both knew that at the end of this long journey, the person I was waiting for would come.

We waited in the vast quiet. From the deep red dusk, we waited till the night was waning. Because we had had this encounter, our minds were overflowing with great bliss. In this great bliss, there was no self and no things, no boundaries and no end, no grasping and no rejecting, no time to rest and no place to take shelter. It was like a wave of light, flowing out to the horizon.

Though the night was very long, because there were several stars with a very strong sense of reality, we felt that the light was infinite. Under the starlight, that woman was still and silent, but I knew she was the sun. Because she was there, I was not expecting some other sunrise.

We were immersed in a great implicit meaning, and in the still silence, we said what we wanted to say.

In the smile of the pale dawn on the horizon, I finally discovered that there was someone walking right toward me. I could not see his or her face. I could not even make out his or her gender. Behind him or her was the light before the dawn. In the faint light of the sky, there were the silhouettes of countless people. In the still silence, I asked a question: "Are you my escort?" They did not answer. But to my speech in the silence, they gave a round of applause. In fact, I understood that the applause was an even greater silence.

At that instant, I suddenly had doubts: I did not know whether I had been waiting for them, or they had been waiting for me.

In that waiting which had come so far, Niguma laughed with delight. We looked into each other's eyes, and it was sweet beyond compare—I am not wrong in using this word "sweet," I truly felt very sweet. Besides "sweet," I cannot find any other word to express the feeling.

From that meeting until now, I have never asked her any question. This is because I basically have no questions.

In this infinite sweetness, the light of my mind and spirit shone forth. I clearly saw that the woman called Niguma was, in reality, I myself. All my seeking, all my encounters, all my expectations, all my experiences, all the silhouettes in that light in the sky, were in reality I myself.

In my life of wisdom, the true Niguma appeared at this time. Because of this, that pure light in my mind flowed forth in the light of dawn in all directions.

A voice gently said: "You have finally discovered the true characteristic of reality."

Right. I said, "Now I can finally say it: the I who was waiting, the she with whom I had an agreement, the you for whom we had to wait—in reality they all are I myself. In the great play of illusory transformation, Niguma and I are together, and all along we are performing another kind of play."

Nigumahad never left me, and we had no so-called meeting. In my undefiled purity, even that process of seeking was not necessary. Although that process was also Niguma, the genuine seeking did not need a process.

But if there had not been that process of seeking, I might have been seeking forever.

Precisely in this infinite seeking, I finally discovered that fundamentally I did not need to seek.

The woman laughed. She said: "That's right, that's right. However, your level of perception only belongs to you yourself. It is what you experienced after you realized transcendence, not the crazy conceit of an ordinary person. As for the people who have not traveled the road of seeking, who have not experienced the sufferings of seeking, who have not undergone spiritual cultivation, who have not realized the ultimate transcendence—they still have a long road they must travel. Without seeking, without experience, without cultivation, without many years of genuine practice, you would not have been able to be Niguma."

She said: "Only after you reached the stage of the objective is that Niguma your final self."

Then we looked at each other, laughing, and embraced each other contentedly, with no this and no that, and merged into each other's lives.

In the sound of laughter, a song quietly sounded:

Has a thousand years of wind and frost entered your belly?

Has a hundred generations of longing made your spirit break down and weep?

Has the windblown sand of the great desert cut off the camel bells in your dream?

Have the misty clouds passing before your eyes made you confused about the road of your long travels?

Such a vast ocean from this, without a trace of spring color

What wets the clothes will no longer be laughter bringing tears

The roaring swirling sand and dust

Rise up every time in dreams

You always say that your seeking has already come to an end

Ascetic monks are the enemies in life

That arrow does not have to come slowly

Amid the sighs

The white hair has already replaced the dark hair

Who is telling you to be longing to play games in heavenly realms?

The flow continues

So you arrive five hundred years late

You always say that in the icy cemetery forest there is no warm feeling

That tunnel they call the world of mortals, the life of the senses, is certainly windy and rainy and cold

Is it because you fear loneliness that you laugh so heartily?

Do you know or not?

The life of true love has no end

Love is the eternal title

You always say the next lifetime will come

To fulfill the dreams you have looked forward to for a hundred lifetimes

Whoever wants to achieve enlightenment, let them achieve it

Your true result is called the concubine

By the side of the tyrant's black steed

Ask the whole world who is the hero

The hero's name is also Loneliness

The road through the land of the rivers and lakes is long

Even longer-lasting, are the hero's feelings and thoughts

That great bow for shooting eagles

Confused for a thousand years

Windblown sand arises from it

The sand swirls in confusion and the stones wait in ambush on all sides

The wilds are barren

The hero's road is in the howling winds

The frosty wind whitens your dark hair

It cannot make your search get old

Plum blossoms one by one

Night after night shooting toward the edge of the sky

The husband is not there on the road to the horizon

The husband is the rain and snow that comes and goes

It all comes quietly

And quietly it goes

Can it be that you are sick because of this?

That moon has lost its color

The natural dog keeping watch is surely whispering secret words

Or is it entering a dream?

In the dream you are a skinny moon

In the dream you are a crab apple tree

In the dream you are an ancient zither with a sad chant

In the dream you are a cuckoo crying blood

The world of mortals

Never sees the magpie with feathers in its mouth

The Queen mother of the west's hairpins flutter without stopping

A light stroke

Then there is a meteor bringing hate

Last night the west wind rose again

A great blood-red banner

Making a fluttering sound in the evening glow

The black horse gives a long whistle

Drawing the misty rain that's blocking it

The soul is in the west wind

Calling again and again—

Come back, come back,

O you who wander to the far horizon ...

First draft at Liangzhou, 2005

Final version at Dongguan City, Zhangmutou Township,
"Xuemo Zen Forum," June 2011

Postscript

One Must Establish One's Own Rules

1

If people ask: "Xuemo, of your novels, for you, which is the most important?" I will say: "*The Holy Monk and the Spirit Woman.*"

If people ask: "Xuemo, among your novels, for your readers, which is the most important?" I will still answer: "*The Holy Monk and the Spirit Woman.*"

Why is this?

It is because my usual novels may move you or change you, but *The Holy Monk and the Spirit Woman* can enable you to achieve enlightenment. This book is fertile soil. All you have to do is make an effort to pull on the "finger of wisdom" that is showing through the surface of the soil, and you will be able to pull out "a person who has achieved enlightenment" who is bursting with life force. That is to say, if you are able to go through experiences like the main character of the novel, you will definitely achieve enlightenment and become a holy person.

However, in the eyes of people in general, *The Holy Monk and the Spirit Woman* may be a strange anomaly. Basically, it is not like a novel, but I still could not but cast it as a novel. It is not the kind of novel contemporary people are used to or recognize as such, but because it describes a kind of mystical experience, I could not say it is a "true record," and I could not say it is "an experience." All I could do was give it the name and form of a "novel" or "traditional tale."

What needs to be explained is that I too traveled the Path that Khyungpo Naljor traveled. The protagonist's process of enlightenment and spiritual journey also truly exist in my life.

That's right. A clear-eyed person of wisdom can see that I have written about the most real existence. Real to what degree? Real to the point that if a person proceeds according to the protagonist's Path, that person will become Khyungpo Naljor in another sense.

How could there be a more real novel in the world than that?

2

The Holy Monk and the Spirit Woman goes far beyond people's understanding of the novel, but among Xuemo's novels, it is the one that it is most necessary to read—in fact, it should be called "great narrative." (In Chinese, the word for "novel" literally means "little narrative.") Thus, you should not make demands of it based on the standards of the "novel." You should appreciate it according to the standards of the "great narrative." In the "great narrative" I have written, there is a great deal of wisdom, thought, and "teaching" that novels in general do not have. Though sometimes it also has touching sentiments like an emotional novel, more of the chapters are like roots carved out with an axe, very coarse, but strong. I have a student named Luo Qianman; she designed the covers of *Curses of Xixia* and *The Grey Wolf of Xixia*, and I liked them very much. When she was first reading my draft of *The Holy Monk and the Spirit Woman*, to facilitate designing the cover, she said it had absolutely no literary quality. But after she had finished reading it, she said: "If Teacher Xuemo's writing has reached this level, is a literary quality still necessary?" She even thought that it was precisely that rough-hewn quality that enabled the text to appear so very forceful; although it was a bit crude, it still had a kind of power that other reading materials do not have.

At that same time, another publisher's editor also read the draft. After he had patiently finished reading the draft, he said that a novel cannot be written this way; he said there should not be so many incomprehensible religious ideas in it. There were also some good friends of mine who went so far as to warn me to stop at the brink and put on the brakes, and immediately go back to writing more works like *Desert Rites*, *Desert Hunters*, and *White Tiger Gate*. But I thought, if I really turn back, then won't my writing just be repeating itself? If I' m going to do that, I better throw away my pen and my computer, and go do something more meaningful.

There were also some knowledgeable friends who, with good intentions, passed on the news: a novel cannot be written this way. Of course I know they meant well, because when I first started my creative work, many editors had given me this kind of advice.

That's right, a novel cannot be written this way, but Xuemo's "great narrative" certainly must be written this way. A novel cannot have a lot of theoretical discussion, but Xuemo's "great narrative" certainly must have theoretical discussion. A novel cannot describe religious wisdom, but Xuemo's "great narrative" certainly must describe it. There are a lot more things that a novel, a "little narrative," cannot do, but in Xuemo's "great narrative" these definitely can all be done. What I wanted to write was this kind of "great narrative," the kind that nobody else can write except "Xuemo."

Thus, I have my own standards.

For example, Chekhov said that if a gun that appears in the beginning of a novel is not fired in the later scenes, then it is superfluous. He means that in a novel, there has to be correlation.

But Xuemo says, why does that gun necessarily have to be fired? Why does there have to be something correlated with that scene? I might have to describe some characters and scenes that are not correlated with anything later in the text — as long as they are necessary materials or nourishment needed when I am "speaking." In my rules, it is not that I must correlate anything with them, but that they must correlate with me. With many things in our human life, there is in fact no way to plan or correlate. Many times we basically do not need "creativity," but that still does not influence the wonder of our human life. Many times contrived "creativity" instead appears contrived and constrained. The Great Path is simple and spontaneous. It does not say "this doesn't work, that doesn't work," but rather operates according to circumstances, acts in harmony with situations; it is wholly natural, and without any contrived action. As in the poetry of Li Bo (a renowned poet of the Tang Dynasty), there are many unexpected "natural sentiments" that just come out smoothly and spontaneously. Though these are not as deliberately crafted as his contemporary Du Fu's poems, but we perhaps like Li Bo's poems precisely because of that spontaneous outflow of unconstrained "vital energy." It is this way with novels too: sometimes careful crafting or planning appears instead as empty and false. For example, in the novels of Dostoyevsky, there are many scenes and characters that are not correlated with anything else. Turgenev criticized this as "diarrhea," but this had no influence at all on Dostoyevsky's greatness as an author. Dostoyevsky, who is not delicate, may have been even greater than Chekhov, who emphasized "delicacy." This is because what we feel in the writings of Dostoyevsky is his natural talent pouring out, his thoughts and his passions.

The Holy Monk and the Spirit Woman is the product of this kind of thinking on my part.

The Holy Monk and the Spirit Woman is so crude that it is very powerful; so plain and simple that it is like a meteorite; so coarse that it is like a cave painting carved out by a prehistoric human with a stone axe; so mystical that it is like a deep dark valley filled with mist. If it were not for the romantic love in it that is so tender and lingering, the reader would think that the author was some withered Buddhist ascetic who had practiced "dead-tree Zen" for a thousand years. But if you patiently read it through to the end, you will surely discover the scenes from Xuemo's pen are truly "a limitless vista from a perilous peak." If you seriously read it all the way through—if you read it without understanding it, why don't you read it a few more times—you will surely heave a sigh of relief and say: "I have not read it in vain." It really has something that the ordinary novel definitely cannot give you, and this is enough.

I discovered that, even if I had gone ahead and polished up some of the language in it which people called "simple," then I would have desecrated this book. In this superficial simplicity, there is in fact the "energy" of a great skill that appears clumsy. Every time I polished it, I would discover that this "energy" had been damaged. Just as we do not hope that a simple monk will become a talk show host, sometimes clumsiness is in fact great skill; sometimes what is simple and low is in fact genuine and real; sometimes what is crude and coarse is in fact a return to the original and the real; sometimes what is simple can be even greater.

So I think I might as well let the book keep its "original face."

Look at that, scruffy as a barbarian, with a head of wild hair, Xuemo.

In the coarseness, there is no lack of wisdom and strength.

Quite a laugh, isn't it?

3

Therefore, you definitely should not hope that Xuemo will pretentiously write an overly cautious, utterly conventional novel. Such things are everywhere, and if you want to read them, you can go into any bookstore and pick a novel as you please, and they will all be able to meet your expectations.

But if you want to read a "great narrative" like *The Holy Monk and the Spirit Woman*, I'm sorry, but you first must look and see whether or not the author is "Xuemo."

In the last few years, there have been people with all kinds of things to say about my works. Some say I am a great writer, some rebuke me for not being able to write novels, and there are also others saying various other things. In fact, if we judge by the standards that are current at the moment, I really do not know whether or not I can be counted as an author. Those who love my novels love them to death, and those who hate them hate them to death. Though they do not fit the current fashion, strangely enough, there are many stalwart "Xuemo fans." It is like the way they treat me: some say I am a Buddha, some say I am a demon. In fact I am just a mirror, and what everyone sees when he looks at me is, in fact, always himself. It is the same way with my novels: those who like them always find in them the things they themselves need.

Of all my novels, *The Holy Monk and the Spirit Woman* is the most unlike a novel: it is a "great narrative." Perhaps it violates many taboos which novels cannot violate — for example, it is filled with truths and ideas between the lines. In terms of the traditional rules of the novel, writing ideas violates a taboo. Ideas will decay, but the tree of life can be green forever. But in my books those ideas are precisely the things I am making an effort to spread. If I did not violate those "taboos," then I would not be writing. This is because, in my eyes, those "taboos" are the "souls" of my works. If my books did not have those "souls," then I would not be able to find any meaning in writing, and it would be better to discard my pen or computer and go lie in the sun. The things that I write must be useful for people's minds and spirits, and even have a great function. No matter what the rules, if I cannot accomplish this, then I will destroy that piece of writing.

I will also say that certain ideas do indeed rapidly decay. But there are some ideas which must continue to exist along with the human race, like the ideas of Laozi, of Zhuangzi, of the Buddha, of Jesus. If someday these decay, then the human race will surely perish too.

The ideas, or wisdom, which I write about is, in my eyes, precisely this kind of thing that cannot die. For this reason, my writings will surely have a longer life than my physical body. My teacher Lei Da even thinks that my *Great Mudra of Light* series (published by Central

Compilation and Translayion Press) will surely be more influential than my novels… Hey, my teacher Lei Da really was correct: as soon as that book came out, there was a wave of good reviews. When I was invited to the National Library, Chinese Academy of Sciences, Minzu University of China, Central University of Finance and Economics, to lecture on the Great Mudra, there were scenes of enthusiasm that my previous novels had never brought about. There were many people who came to Beijing from other places in order to hear my Great Mudra lectures. My *Great Mudra of Light* series truly won me even more "Xuemo fans." It even changed the minds of many readers. We must know that, many times, if they can change their minds, then they can change their lives.

For writing, I have my own standards. I am not willing to waste my life trying to adhere to other people's standards, even if those standards have already been acknowledged by the whole world and have become the rules that literature must follow. I still want to establish my own rules. In my eyes, the novel must be a way for me to speak. Even if this world does not approve of it, as long as it lets me be happy or fulfilled, then I am willing to write it.

Chen Yanjin, a Peking University Master of Literature and senior editor of the People's Literature Publishing House, said in an article in the journal *China Talent* that Xuemo is an "anomaly" on the literary scene, because he is generally "not in accord with the standards of the time" — and cannot "get in step" with the time. She said:

> In 1988, when Lu Yao's Ordinary World came out, Xuemo had just published his first novel, Where the Sun Goes Down in the Eternal Mist, in the journal Fei Tian, and had received the Gansu province award for excellent literary work. After

winning the award, Xuemo wanted to write a major work for his fellow countrymen, the poor common folk of the western desert, and so he began the work The Trilogy of the Desert. He did not anticipate that this idea would consume twenty years of his life. When Desert Rites came out, it was already the year 2000, and when the third part, White Tiger Gate, was finished, it was already 2008. The 1980s had brought styles from western China and from rural areas into literature and film and television and music, but by the twenty-first century, these had already been made unfashionable and passé by the great wave of urbanization and commercialization. But in his work Curses of Xixia, Xuemo took up the narrative of the avant garde of the 1990s, and so there were critics who pointed out that Curses of Xixia was "China's One Hundred Years of Solitude " and was "a powerful work of the avant garde become easternized." With The Grey Wolf of Xixia, Xuemo for the first time directly confronted the metropolis. But with The Holy Monk and the Spirit Woman, Xuemo has returned again to the "narrative of nightmarish chaos" in the style of Curses of Xixia ... We must know that avant garde narrative was already declining in the 1990s, with urbanization advancing by leaps and bounds. At present, what is flourishing on the literary scene are commercialized works that hope to fit into the search for novelty. In this kind of environment, Xuemo still firmly upholds purely literary works in the avant garde style. In particular, in an era where everybody only cares about economics and vulgar pleasures, he turns his eyes to the peasants of the barren lands of western China, who have been forgotten by the great majority of people. His books describe their existence "living like animals," and he investigates the "soul" that they stubbornly distill from the earth. He investigates the whole of humanity's "soul transcendence" of worldly desires and the evils of history. This pursuit is without a doubt totally against the tide of the times.

That's right, I admit it, my writings really "do not fit the standards of the time," because I have never cared about "the standards of the time." "The standards of the time" are this world's rules for what is good and what is bad and what is fashionable. In this world, there are already so many writers who follow the rules, it won't miss one me. The things I write are certainly not novels in the eyes of some people. I just write the kind of things I "must" write. Maybe they "do not fit the standards of the time," but they are the simple and sincere things that flow from my mind and spirit. Everything in this world, from the point of view of its basic substance, is all a kind of play. Different social groups establish different rules for the play, and they are followed by different people. It is the same with novels. So why should I have to cater to other people's rules?

Though in terms of its theme, my work *The Trilogy of the Desert* fits in with the "rural style" that was flourishing then, in the way it is written, it is far away from the rules for novels in the eyes of the critics, where story and plot must prevail. When an editor read my *Desert Rites*, she said that when she had read a hundred thousand words, I still had not come to the real subject of the book. I said: "As soon as a novel begins, it has entered the real subject!" Actually what she wanted to find was a story, but what I wanted to write was a kind of existence. What I wanted to depict in freeze-frame in *The Desert Hunters* and *White Tiger Gate* was a way of life that was about to vanish from the field of vision of the human race. It is the same with my books *Curses of Xixia*, and *The Grey Wolf of Xixia*, and *The Holy Monk and the Spirit Woman*. Because they touch on the spirit and belief, I call these three works "the trilogy of the spirit." They let people see a new Xuemo. These are not novels according to the narrow standards of contemporary critics; they are just another life essence that pours out of my mind when I want to talk.

After *Curses of Xixia* was published, it provoked many controversies. Some called it good, some rejected it. It was the same way with *The Grey Wolf of Xixia*. One can foresee that after *The Holy Monk and the Spirit Woman* is published, it will certainly provoke some hisses and some applause. That is not important: those who criticize it will criticize it, and those who praise it will praise it, each according to his circumstances—I do not have time to care about this. Life is too short, and we should not care too much about how the world views us. I have said, even if everyone in the world cared about you and praised you, after this generation of people dies off, you will still be a stranger to the next generation of people. What is important is whether or not you can truly leave behind something that can let the next generation of people remember. Of course, I don't even care about "leaving something behind," because what I most care about is happiness and understanding here and now.

I have said that when I wrote the *Desert Rites* books, I wanted to capture a view of a kind of existence that was just then rapidly passing away. It was just that I wanted to say what I wanted to say to that long-gone land. But after I finished *White Tiger Gate*, I suddenly wanted to say some other things, and so there was the set, "the trilogy of the soul." A few clear-eyed people saw the symbolism and parables in the writing of these three novels, and there were also people who saw the narrative and the "penetration" that were current at that time. But as for me myself, in fact there were no such concepts in my breast. These were just words that erupted from my mind, that's all. When I was writing, in my mind there were none of those rules for novels; I was just enjoying the happiness of that eruption of words, just this, that's all.

4

What needs to be emphasized is that my state in doing that kind of writing cannot be separated from my cultivation of the Great Mudra, where twenty years has been like a single day.

During the second session of the Shangpa Culture Forum, I had a dialogue with several scholars at the Peking University's Department of Chinese Language and Literature. I spoke of the influence the culture of the Great Mudra has had on my writing:

> *My novels are not composed. Rather, being within the pure light of merging into one body with a greater existence, lets words flow forth from my inherent nature itself. When they are flowing forth, my mind is like a clear emptiness, and though my fingers are moving, in my brain there is not a single word. I do not know which scene will flow out at which time. I just feel there are countless lives, countless stimuli flowing at me, pressing in, and the words flow out by themselves — it is as if it is not me writing, but rather an existence greater than the human race, which streams through my pen into "another kind of life." Professor Chen Xiaoming of Peking University put it very well: he said my writing is a kind of "being possessed."*

Of course, I do not necessarily accept that this is "being possessed," but I genuinely feel that there is a kind of force that flows out from my life. That force emerges, surges up, rumbles, flows forth from the depths of my life, and brings me an enormous happiness. It is a kind of great happiness that surges from within toward the outside, and the whole universe, the whole world, rejoices along with me. But at the same time, my mind is like a clear mirror, that is as it is and does not move, yet still shines on the myriad things. You might wonder, when writing in such conditions, how can I think of themes, of structure, of characters, of sense ... But there is none of this, everything just gushes out. My "The Trilogy of the Desert" and "The Trilogy of the Soul" flowed forth in this kind of bliss.

On this point, it was similar when I wrote out the "Great Mudra" books: "When the spirit light appeared, I was far removed from all concepts of how to write, I forgot pen and ink, I forgot aesthetics, and I just let my recollections go on their way, without clinging and without rejecting. Wondrously using this empty, spiritual, clear mind, having it control the pen that followed what the mind wanted, getting rid of mental machinations, not employing contrivances, returning to the simple, with objects and self both forgotten, going ahead and writing of the great good and great love in the mind ... Those words 'the Great Mudra' were like an infusion of spiritual power, surging out with infinite spiritual harmony. An old calligrapher exclaimed: 'Good! The epitome of crude and plain, but also secretly surging with infinite power.' I only get rid of contrivances, get rid of mental machinations, get rid of all empty embellishments, and out flows the great love of my own true mind without falsity." (from *A Talk on the "Light" of True Mind from My Experience as a "Calligrapher"*)

To put it simply, my secret for writing calligraphy and composing texts is this: "Get rid of the calculating mind, serve fundamental enlightenment, follow the natural course, and illuminate the Great Path."

My goal in studying and cultivating the Great Mudra has been to remove my own desires, let myself have no mental calculations, and just let the text flow out from my own soul in a simple, unaffected way. After you break up your desires and cravings and hatred, and all the bonds that external realms have tied you with, and you let the light of your mind and spirit shine forth, and you are not subject to the bonds of the various concepts and theories that are current in the world, then you will be able to enter into a realm of freedom.

Writing that is done with the light of true mind is able to "exchange mind for mind." So I am able to use my true mind to stimulate and bring to life the reader's true mind. That is why, when they read my books, many people will feel very refreshed.

If we look at it from the ultimate level, all my writings in fact are a data line into the reader's mind and spirit. What I want to transmit is that refreshing purity and wisdom. I have said, when the words come from the true mind, when they hit people, it hurts. Writings that flow from the true mind, when they are loosed on the reader's mind, will start resonating … Go ahead and try it: as long as you have a truly sincere mind, then when you are reading my works, you can feel that true mind aroused and throbbing behind the written words.

What needs to be explained clearly is that the works I am speaking of also include the novels. A doctor at Fudan University was feeling terrible after losing his credentials and his money and goods, but when he read a novel of mine, he felt incomparably refreshed, and all his unhappiness was swept away, so he said: "I salute Xuemo!" There are many other readers who were also like this. My writings have always been able to offer them nourishment for the mind and spirit. Thus, we do not necessarily insist that writings which have their source in the true mind have a religious name or form. Those writings themselves can convey wisdom and spirit. No matter whether they are labeled "religious" or "cultural" or "literary," nothing can cover over the light of true mind flowing from these writings.

In recent years I am always receiving email from readers. They hope that I will be able to publish those writings which have come from the true mind in the same way, but have different names and forms, anticipating that they will bring refreshing clarity to more people.

These requests became the causal basis for my last two books. Because they also convey the wisdom of the Great Mudra of Light, I have titled them *The Great Mudra of Light: Penetrating through Birth and Death*, and *The Great Mudra of Light: A Literary Pilgrimage*. At present, these two books are already completed in draft form, and will soon face the world.

5

It is precisely because the wisdom of the Great Mudra can smash the bonds which concepts put on people that, in my writing, I never care about any "isms." I do not want to let any shackles bind the light of my true mind.

The strange thing is, I do not need any "isms," but despite that, it seems I have many "isms." For example, different specialists have different views of my book *White Tiger Gate.*

The vice head of the Fudan University's Institute of Humanities and renowned critic Chen Sihe considers it a symbolist novel. My teacher Lei Da calls it a realist novel. Mr. Mu Gong, assistant editor-in-chief of the *Literary Gazette*, considers it a romanticist novel. At the third Beijing Literary Forum session on "The Eight Champions of the Gansu Novel," Mr. Gao Hongbo, vice chairman of the Chinese Writers Association, said I am "doing spiritual writing" ; Li Jianjun said I was doing "narrative with mantras" ; and others said it was "psychic narrative." Some critics focus on a major shift in my writing and have published different views of it. Ekber, Hu Ping, and others offer me advice and suggestions and expect I will have a new breakthrough. Selections from *The Holy Monk and the Spirit Woman* in the journal *Chinese Writer* became a hot topic for that discussion: some critics praised it, and some panned it, and there was endless controversy. But in the discussion meetings held by the research section of the Chinese Writers Association on *White Tiger Gate* and *Curses of Xixia*, the critics also divided into several factions. Professor Chen Xiaoming of the Department of Chinese Language and Literature of Peking University said I was a great author who was being "seriously undervalued," while others said I was a "cultural criminal." Controversy of that degree of intensity, with such explosive rhetoric, has seldom been seen in recent years.

After one explosive discussion, Mr. Ma Shaoqing of the Gansu Federation of Literary and Art Circles said to me: "Xuemo, in your work you must firmly believe in your own road, and resolutely keep going. The light will always appear. Don't go along with the crowd, saying what everyone else is saying. The value of literature lies in creativity, in blazing a new trail. Many times the seeker who succeeds is the first in the world."

He was right. Even though I did not necessarily want to be the first in the world, I was determined to be a "different kind." If other people could also write the things I write, why should I waste my life?

Though I stood fast and defended myself all along, I also appreciated all the criticism directed at me. Not long ago, the *Literature* published a continuous series of essays critical of me. I expressed my sincere thanks to Chen Xingeng, the director of the *Literature*, thanking him and his readers for paying attention to me. Later, in a piece in the *Xinmin Evening News*, he said: "Some writers even welcome and praise those who criticize their work. For example, the Gansu novelist Xuemo. *New Criticism* published an article by Li Jianjun criticizing his full-length novel *Curses of Xixia*, and recently also published an article criticizing his short novels. Recently I went to Beijing to take part in a symposium on 'The Eight Champions of the Gansu Novel.' Xuemo was one of 'the eight champions.' since we were 'meeting on a narrow road,' I originally thought that Xuemo would have some sarcastic response for me, or look at me coldly, or even make a more vehement emotional response. I did not expect that, instead, he would amiably take the initiative and bring up the recent article criticizing him, and even say 'It was well written, well written indeed!' He went on to say: 'This is effective transmission. Criticism is one of the effective means in the contemporary diffusion of information. This is because now nobody reads articles that say good things; the critics are better able to attract people's attention, and expand the influence of a piece of writing.' Xuemo was able to be so magnanimous in permitting other people to make carping comments about his works—this is rare and commendable."

After I read this article, I responded to Director Chen like this: "I still welcome all criticism of me. Not only is it necessary for spreading the word, but also because criticism is also a form of good intention! We must appreciate all good intentions! I will always be grateful for the good intentions of the *Literature* and those friends who criticize me! I am also willing to continue to serve as a specimen for people to dissect and criticize — this will certainly be beneficial to the contemporary literary scene."

I know that the approval of well-intentioned criticism and analysis is also worth valuing.

In reality, what is most worth valuing in this world are those good intentions.

6

Although I understand and feel grateful to those people who criticize me, and I understand that subjectively they mean me well, still, I do not want to lightly abandon my search.

This is because I understand that the fundamental substance of all rules and all language is a play of concepts. Play has a short lifespan, but the true mind remains forever. The world is fundamentally a play of concepts.

Therefore, I do not care about the world's value system — when we care about the value system that is current in the world, then we are "controlled" by it. When we fully understand that play, and we can preserve the independence of our mind and spirit, then we are able to detach from the play, and find freedom. I have two phrases to express that kind of detachment: "In a quiet place, observing things move; at leisure, watching people be busy." All of my works are just for the purpose of experiencing and passing along this happiness and understanding.

Chen Yanjin expressed this in her essay in *China's Talents* when she wrote:

> *"It is precisely this 'not matching the standards of the time' that enables Xuemo to reveal some of his unique writing style, and become a presence on the current literary scene who cannot be overlooked. Of course 'not matching the standards of the time' does not only mean in terms of subject matter and writing style. Behind it is Xuemo's concept of literature, which has not changed since he embarked on the literary road ... Xuemo's writings have never considered the world's superficial aspects. He just wants to contribute everything he has, and sing a most beautiful song — he says, 'World, I do not cater to you' because 'I care about the world's people, who are put in bondage by the world.' While he does not pay attention to other people's superficial writings, and only cares about whether or not he will bring the world understanding and refreshing clarity, he has nevertheless won over the world. Not only are Xuemo's works more and more respected in the world of literary criticism, they have won honor and recognition for that place where he lives, and have won a large number of ardent fans. In Liangzhou, Desert Rites was widely known. At that time, when his young son and his classmates were out on the street, when his classmates told people that he was the son of the author of Desert Rites, the cab drivers and the popsicle vendors would not take his money. Among Chinese authors, Xuemo is also the one with the most web pages, and these were all put up by his loyal fans. In the eyes of these*

readers, reading Xuemo's works is a kind of action to 'rescue the mind.' The minds and spirits and lives and fates of many people have been raised to a higher level, and changed, and saved, by Xuemo's works. They have wanted to let more people encounter Xuemo's works, and so they have put up web pages, and organized reading groups, and voluntarily purchased all Xuemo's works to donate to various major libraries all over the country. So the scholars say that Xuemo's influence is not only on the western part of China, and not only on literature; 'Xuemo' has become a cultural symbol, and he has influenced people's minds worldwide. As Gabriel García Márquez, the author of One Hundred Years of Solitude, said: 'The truest, most important influence an author can have is that his work can enter deeply into the human mind and change some of the readers' concepts of the world and of life.' Xuemo's works have truly gone beyond influence in the usual literary sense. Today, when values are in confusion, and writing has become too commercialized, when many writers write motivated by economic gain, Xuemo's writings, which hold fast to 'saving minds,' are no different than singing songs of 'soul purity' on the literary scene."

Indeed.

I genuinely do want to travel the road that I want to travel, and I certainly can go all the way on it.

7

In this text, I also want to make a point of thanking two people, because they have an intimate connection to my work and fate. While

I still have the power to be able to speak for myself, I want to say what I want to say, and I want to thank those people I want to thank. There will be a day in the future when I have become a soul in the museum in *The Grey Wolf of Xixia*, and if I want to express feelings, there will be no vehicle for doing so, and that would be very regrettable. So, making use of this chapter, I have written the following text.

The first person to thank is my benevolent teacher, Lei Da.

Lei Da was my mentor when I was at the Lu Xun Institute of Literature. He was my "patron" in literature; if he had not discovered me and recommended me and spread the word about me, I would not have been able to have the influence I have today. He directly changed my literary fate. The fact that my novels were included in the list of top-ranking Chinese novels of Association of the Chinese Novel for the year 2000 was due to his recommendation, and only then were they discovered and acknowledged by the review panel.

After *Desert Rites* was published, Lei Da published an essay evaluating *Desert Rites* in the *Guangming Daily*. Before long, I received the Feng Mu Prize for Literature. Afterwards, Mr. Tao Taizhong said: "When it was first evaluated, *Desert Rites* was not on the list. Lei Da recommended it very forcefully, and when the other jury members read it, they thought it wasn't bad, so it was added to the list. At the end it passed by a unanimous vote. At the awards meeting, the jurors told me that it was lucky that Lei Da recommended it." Subsequently, to introduce me to the whole country, Lei Da also published many articles in newspapers and periodicals like the *People's Daily*, and the *Literary Gazette*, and *Critical Discussions of Novels* .

When he was promoting me, Lei Da spared no effort. At that time, besides publishing many essays, he would recommend me whenever he had the opportunity, and he was always talking about *Desert Rites*.

Later on when he was writing other essays, he would always mention *Desert Rites.*

One writer said to me: "On the current literary scene, there are many writers, but they lack someone like Lei Da to push them forward. When he was promoting you, Xuemo, it wasn't that he just wrote one review; rather, he talked about you whenever he met someone and whenever he got the opportunity. How could a contemporary critic be so sympathetic and warm-hearted?" Later, when I got to Beijing, whenever I saw literary friends, they would say: "Lei Da treated you so well!" But at that time Lei Da and I had barely met in passing. When I went to receive the Feng Mu Prize for Literature, Lei Da, as though he felt "wronged," said: "Other people think there is some kind of relationship between you and me, but you have never even come to my door." In fact, when I had gone to the capital to receive the Feng Mu Prize for Literature, I had not gone to Master Lei's home. At that time I thought, who knows how many people in China like me all go bother him, to get him to tell them how to write essays. The first time I went to Master Lei's home, it was after I had gone to the Lu Xun Institute of Literature, and I had gone from being an unknown minor author to "becoming a name" overnight. I was now a professional writer, and I had become the "myth" which Mr. Li Xing, the editor-in-chief of the journal *Critical Discussions of Novels,* spoke of in an article he wrote about me.

At the Lu Xun Institute of Literature, every student had to choose a mentor. Master Lei urged me many times to pick someone else, hoping I would be better able to get acquainted with a knowledgeable editor who could help me. He said to me: "Xuemo, whenever you need me, I will help you. Now you must select a knowledgeable editor and let him give you detailed guidance on your work. We should not care if there is the mentor-student relationship or not between you and me." I remember at that time I said something very arrogant: "Master Lei, of course you do not care, but history cares. Think how proud you will be in the future for being Xuemo's teacher." From this statement, the reader can see that at that time I was truly very self-confident. But this was also an expression of my innermost feelings, because I would use a lifetime of effort to enable all my teachers to be proud of me.

After Master Lei Da became my mentor, I discovered that he is a very serious person. Every time he meets with a student, he is always very earnest in systematically investigating the subject at hand, and he mercilessly points out the flaws in the student's work. He does not care at all whether the person he is talking to is happy about it or not. It is as if when there is something to say in his mind, he is not happy unless he comes out with it—he is always completely sincere. Just as Wang Jiada says: "Lei Da's fundamental substance is to be a scholar; he cannot be a politician."

Master Lei had a special quality: he helped me, but he did not tell me what to do. After he published the review article in the *Guangming Daily*, for a long time I did not know this had happened. When *Desert Rites* was included in the list of top-ranking Chinese novels, and when I won the Feng Mu Prize for Literature, both times it was other people who told me. When I offered my thanks to Master Lei, he unexpectedly pretended not to know what had happened. He always would say: "The best thanks you can give me is to produce better writings." Every time we exchange email, he always inquires about how the latest piece of writing is progressing, and he always orders me not to dare to get lazy. One day Master Lei Da said to me: "The reason I promoted *Desert Rites* was not only because you were a native of Gansu. The main reason was its connection to the direction Chinese literature takes. This was not a personal issue with me."

After the publication of *The Desert Hunters* and *White Tiger Gate*, Master Lei Da said to me: "Xuemo, you must make an effort on the narrative. Your powers of description are very deep; they have the charm of the classic nineteenth century novels. If you also draw nourishment from the contemporary era into your narratives, the road ahead is limitless."

My subsequent explorations as a writer have benefitted from Master Lei Da's advice.

Of course, my explorations are still just getting started, and later I may produce even better works.

8

The second person I want to make a point of thanking is my wife, Lu Xinyun.

As for Lu Xinyun, I always call her "Boss Lu." She has never let me write openly about her. But many people who understand inner feelings say, you must write about your wife, don't let the facts be buried by the passage of time.

I have said that for the past twenty years, I always get out of bed before daybreak, around 3 a.m. Later, our son Chen Yixin was also this way. But nobody knew that in our home at that time there was someone else who got up even earlier than us, and that was Lu Xinyun. Before I would go out and meditate in solitude, I had gone through several years of practice, until this developed into the later habit. During that period, Boss Lu would always get up before daybreak at 2 a.m. and prepare some boiled water, and something good to eat, and then wake me up. Having taken me from being an elementary school teacher and made me become a "famous" writer, she has begun again to make our son one.

Later on, many people liked my calligraphy, and there were more and more people who collected it. According to the explanation in the article by Buddhist Master Xinyin, it amounted to "ten thousand gold pieces per word." But other people did not know that every time I picked up the writing brush, Lu Xinyun was always finding fault, always wanting to turn stone into gold. And it was just because of Boss Lu's nitpicking and "corrections" that the characters I wrote got better day by day. One day, she said half-jokingly, that she had the best disciple, not the best master. The one writing the characters became famous, but the person who taught him to write characters, nobody knows.

Lu Xinyun is one of the original models for Sharwadi, the main female character in *The Holy Monk and the Spirit Woman*. Because I have cultivated practice in seclusion for the last twenty years, beginning from when we were young, "waiting" has become an accomplishment she has cultivated, and she has extended this accomplishment to her whole life. Though sometimes there are grievances, there is no resentment or regret.

In an essay our son Chen Yixin wrote when he was in the sixth grade, he mentioned his mother's waiting during the time when I was cultivating practice behind closed doors and writing *Desert Rites*. But her waiting did not end when *Desert Rites* was published. The subsequent works, *The Desert Hunters, White Tiger Gate, Curses of Xixia, The Grey Wolf of Xixia,* and the *Great Mudra of Light* series, for me, were almost all written in the intervals of free time while I was cultivating practice behind closed doors. Every time I shut the door to cultivate practice, for Lu Xinyun it was a new round of waiting. In *The*

Holy Monk and the Spirit Woman, I use the voice of Khyungpo Naljor to make a statement like this: "One day your wife will say to you, you are the most 'evil' man in the world. She will say that for twenty years you made her wait; and now when she is fifty, you are still making her wait. You will say to her: 'This was your choice. The one you chose is not someone who did not need to make you wait.' She chose Xuemo, and so she chose the whole of Xuemo. Yes, it truly is like this. In the same way, when your disciples chose you, that was the equivalent of choosing you as a whole. They chose your glory and your renown, but at the same time they chose the slander that other people direct at you. These two sides, the light and the dark, form your human life as a whole."

I described the constant condition of my life in a poem:

A hand waving

Are you still going to the mountains, then?

The mountains are high

So high they go up to the sun

In the sun there is a Vajravarahi cave

The cave is the happy song in my life

Holding the prayer beads in my hand

The signal sounds in my mind

The black night is the monk's robe for this life

The high house is the cave on the cliff of previous lifetimes

It is truly like this. The reporter Yan Shide wrote an article, *Approaching the Ascetic Monk Xuemo,* and recorded my life as an "ascetic monk." In Liangzhou, I kept a closed room for twenty years. It was far from the center of town, and few people knew of it. There, I cultivated practice, read books, and wrote. In circumstances in which I was virtually cut off from the world, starting from when I was twenty-five years old, I passed twenty years of the most solitary and wondrous life. Since I moved in recent years to Zhangmutou Township, Dongguan City, Guangdong, I have had a new closed room near a dense forest in south of the Five Ridges of southern China.

While I was behind closed doors for the last twenty years, my wife, without resentment and without regret, managed the family's affairs and brought up our son. She is a woman who stands in the fire herself, while warning me, "Be careful, the cup will burn your hand." In her life, she herself is not there. Without her sacrifices, I would not have emerged. She has given almost half her life for the sake of my work — the other half she has kept for Chen Yixin, our son.

9

During the process of bringing *The Holy Monk and the Spirit Woman* into the world, there were also many other friends who offered their help: He Yan, An Fengying, Dong Wei, Buddhist Master Xinyin, Cai Tianyi, Chen Yanjin, Yin Xiaoming, Lin Wenqiao, Tao Qingxia, Zhan Jiazhen, Qian Hongbin, Zhuang Yinghao, Tian Chuan, and others. Some did planning, some did editing, some did proofreading, some helped print, some offered suggestions — all of them represented fortunate favorable karmic conditions. I am also grateful to Madam Li Yang of Zhangmutou's "99 Guild," as well as to Chen Yixin, Chen

Si, Wang Fei, Gu Zhicao, Wang Jing, Chen Jianxin, and many readers and friends for supporting me. There were so many people I cannot list them individually here. But their names are inscribed on my heart.

I am grateful to all my teachers, grateful to all my readers, grateful to all my friends who have shown their concern for me. I take the merit of writing this book and transfer it to them; I wish them good fortune, happiness, understanding, cool clarity. I wish them to have healthy and abundant lives.

After I finished a draft of this book, on New Year's Day 2012, I wrote a "New Year's Message," to express some of my feelings. With some slight revisions, I record it here below, to serve as the ending for this book.

As we look back on 2011, a phrase has been added to the world— "Xuemo fans." This is my favorite phrase. It leaves behind religious names and forms, and approaches the spirit of helping people; it conveys incalculable fascination, and is suffused with endless sincerity.

Starting with the new year, can we agree on "spiritual writing"?

What is "spiritual writing"? Let's say it is detaching from our animal nature, conquering desires, going beyond the petty self, realizing wisdom.

I hope that when we pick up our pens, we will use the most sincere language, and write of yearning, communicating true feeling, contributing true love, portraying true beauty.

Below, I spin out some doggerel, and offer it to the more than two hundred thousand "Xuemo fans."

Xuemo fans are not Xuemo fans, there is dust in the light.

True mind waits for the myriad things, and does not abandon action that benefits living beings.

Knowledge and action are even more merged into one, awakening to emptiness does not mean one-sided emptiness.

Accumulating good, you achieve great virtue, so it is never without the Light.

A message to all the friends of Xuemo: there are beautiful scenes on all sides.

We must transform the myriad things, and accompany the noble sages on their journeys:

Xuemo is a pair of shoes, put them on and you will not be so short;

Xuemo is pulling a donkey, and you can ride it too.

Xuemo is a wind, and it will clear and cool your mind;

Xuemo turns into a ball of fire, so you do not huddle up in the cold.

Xuemo becomes a fine rain, which secretly enters you with the wind.

Xuemo is a piece of earth, which lets you open a road.

Xuemo is also you, and in the purity the two match.

You will merge into one flavor, and the drop of water will enter the great pond.

My fine chattering brothers and sisters and fathers and mothers:

Human life goes by in the blink of an eye, do not rigidly cling to forms.

The long night needs a long song, happy and joyous and without worries.

The bright moon shines in the great night, and speeds through a thousand miles in a single night.

A thousand miles beneath our feet, the bright moon shines like a great banner.

Alone, singing the song of the great wind, laughing at the floating clouds as they arise.

A noble spirit transforms cultural bravery, picking up the pen the wind is strong.

A single laugh sweeps away the leftover clouds, fusing me and you.

This time is bright and clear, without self and without others.

The noble mind is like the moon, reflecting on me and the donkey.

January 2012, written at "Xuemo Zen Platform,"
Zhangmutou Township, Dongguan City

Appendix

My Father Xuemo and I

Chen Yixin

1

From the time I first understood things, I knew that my father was writing a "great book." I did not think that this writing project would end up taking twenty years. When he first started, he was a young man in the full bloom of youth; when he finished, he was already approaching fifty. Many things happened during the course of writing this "great book," and now as I think about it, they were interesting indeed.

When we first moved from our native place to a small city, our whole family lived in a bachelor quarter. The room was very small and just had space for a single bed and a sofa. Later we added a bookcase, and the bookcase took up one wall. Now when I think about it, our life at that time must have been impoverished and difficult. But in my memories it is as if we were the wealthiest and happiest people in the world. At that time, there were no feelings related to "poverty" or "hardship" in my brain, because my father and mother never communicated any information about that to me, and so I grew up very arrogant.

Our whole family was always engaged in lively conversations: We discussed heroes, we discussed love, we discussed history, we discussed success and failure ... When my father was talking about such things with a seven-or eight-year-old child, he did it with all respect and sincerity. He often told me stories of literary people. By the time I went to kindergarten, I already knew the names of many great authors: Tolstoy, Cao Xueqin, Dostoyevsky, Balzac, Victor Hugo ... I was full of yearning for these people. They were like my friends from another time and place, great yet close friends. From that time on, I aspired to be an author, an author like my father. In my mind, he was a writer like Tolstoy.

A lot of the time, we were more like friends. The year I was eight, I questioned my father like this:

"Papa, does eight years count as many years?"

"Eight years? It must count as many years."

"Ha! Then from now on the relationship between us is no longer father and son, but elder brother and younger brother!"

"Why?"

"Aren't you always saying: 'Over many years, father and son become elder brother and younger brother'? Since eight years counts as many years, we must be elder brother and younger brother!"

My father laughed. Later, he always told this story to friends.

Every morning my father would get out of bed at 3 a.m. After getting up, he would first sit in meditation, and afterwards he would write. When I opened my eyes, I would always see him looking very energized. Starting from when I was in kindergarten, he insisted that I get up every day at 5 a.m. He would say: "The lamp is lit at three and the cock crows at five, that's the time a man studies." Many people, when they hear that I got out of bed at five in the morning, laugh at my father's "cruelty," and are full of sympathy for me. When that happens, I secretly laugh at them: I have three more hours every day than you, and in a year that is a lot of days, and this is equivalent to me living more days than you.

When I was eighteen, I began to try to write a long novel, and I learned from my father to get up at 3 a.m. every day, too. That is the time in my life that is hardest to leave behind. I was totally immersed in a world that I was creating myself, whether happy or sad or love or hate … I took my soul and transformed it into a cloud, into wind, into snow, into a song, and they were interwoven together, pure and clear and beautiful, expressing the ups and downs of loneliness. Outside the window, the whole country was starlight.

As soon as I began to get tired, I would say to myself: "Father can go on this way, and if he can do it, so can I." It was this thought that helped me persevere through countless difficult predawn sessions. That year, I was still going to school, and I slept less than four hours a day, but it was then that I wrote many pieces that made my father praise me. During that period of time, I felt that my mind and spirit were in communication with my father, because I could always find everything I needed in the expression in his eyes.

Later, I loved getting up early, and my mother said that I loved the feeling that "the whole world is asleep, and I alone am awake."

When the first draft of my father's *Desert Rites* was complete, we moved to an apartment building, and we had a lot of debts. Under these pressures, my father came out of his closed room where he practiced meditation and wrote, and opened a modest bookstore. When it began to get busy, my father would cultivate practice in the early hours, then write in the morning, then take care of business matters in the afternoon. He later told me that when he was dealing with business in the afternoon, that was his best opportunity to fine-tune his mind. He said that no matter what he was doing, whether walking, standing, sitting, or lying down, he never left his tutelary. He did not use prayer beads, but he could remember all the mantras that he chanted in a day. He always had a pad of stiff paper with him, and on every sheet he was always writing poems from the Tang and Song periods. Whenever he had a little free time, he would take out a piece of paper and memorize the poems. Later he said that most of the poems he learned by heart, he learned this way.

After the bookstore business stabilized, my father again went into "seclusion." He shaved his head and shaved off his beard, and went into a farmhouse on the outskirts of the city, and began again to meditate behind closed doors. I did not know where his retreat was, and from that time on, I saw very little of him. Besides taking care of the bookstore, my mother brought my father a meal every day. Before this, for four years, my father had cut off contact with the world, and made his own food, and did not ask my mother to bring him food. At that time, what my father left for my mother was endless waiting. When I was in the sixth grade in primary school, I wrote something like this:

I will dare to say that without my mother, the achievements my father has today would not exist. Without my mother, absolutely no one would have seen the book called Desert Rites. For my father's sake, my mother has paid too much.

Countless evenings and nights, my mother is always bent over at the window, looking out, waiting. I know that my mother is missing my father. My father is somewhere far from the city cultivating practice and writing. He has spent a full four years cut off from the world.

My father has gone. My mother takes responsibility for everything in the household, and maintains this family. She gets up at 5 a.m. She goes to sleep at midnight, and is busy rushing around all day on behalf of the family. She does not let my father worry about this, and she lets him stay there writing with his mind at peace.

My father has gone. The house is empty, and there is no longer the sound of laughter as in the past, no longer the warmth. The house has become cold. My mother patiently bears the solitude and loneliness. But my mother is vey strong-willed. She firmly believes that father is certain to become someone glorious. Since he has paid for it, he is sure to get it; since he has ploughed and sown, there is sure to be a rich harvest; since he has made the effort, he is sure to succeed. She supports her husband with all her strength, and she is not afraid of more pain and more fatigue. She is willing to give her all for the sake of her husband.

My mother's body was originally already very thin, but she overcame all difficulties with her startling courage and strong will. To be honest, I truly admire her. She is a strong woman.

Every night the house is so deserted and so quiet it is frightening. Without a bit of warmth, the air seems frozen solid. But my mother passes the solitary nights like this, one after another. In the few years that my father has been writing Desert Rites, my mother has aged a lot. In this time, she has been concerned for my father like a kindly mother. Without the pain of this waiting, she would at least be a lot more youthful than she is now. She has been able to do everything that ordinary women cannot do.

During the four years my father was meditating behind closed doors, my mother seemed to have aged ten years.

Again and again, dusk; again and again, a solitary silhouette.

I remember one time when I had developed a high fever, and for a whole week there was no way to bring it down. My mother was running back and forth between the hospital and our house by herself the whole time. For those several days and nights, my mother could not sleep. She kept applying a towel soaked in cold water to my forehead, to help bring down my fever. She did not tell my father, for fear of disturbing him. But I cannot forget her hair all blown around by the wind, and how utterly lonely she was.

By now, she began look after me the same way that she had looked after my father at first. She helped me complete all the petty tasks of living, to allow me to have more time to write and to read books. She always said she was using her life to conserve the lives of me and my father, and let us have more time to do the things we wanted to do. When she said this, she always appeared matter-of-fact and resolute.

At times, when my inspiration for writing dissolved away and was almost gone, I was very upset. Every time this happened, my mother would say: "How can there be no future prospects for a lad who gets out of bed at 3 a.m. to write?" When I heard this, all the haziness and upsetting feelings in my mind would dissolve away.

Whenever I was writing something, the house was extremely peaceful and quiet. My mother moved around quietly and spoke softly, for fear that any careless sound would scare off my inspiration, which was fragile as a bubble. My mother never actively demanded to see the pieces I had written. Every time I rapturously lectured her on the composition and selection of materials for the novel, what she gave me in return was a satisfied smile and a look of praise and approval.

Giving her support to my father and giving her support to me, without being aware of it, my mother had aged, and was already past forty. The grey hair on the top of her head could no longer be avoided, and the wrinkles she had been shy about now covered her forehead. As I write this, I especially want to cry: I do not know how to pay back my mother. All I can do is write well.

Mention my father, and I am filled with pride. Mention my mother, and I am filled with gratitude.

In order to write that "great book"—in my eyes, this great book even includes my father himself—my father gave up what were, in other people's eyes, many great opportunities. Whether opportunities to rise to official position, or to get rich, he gave them all up. Colleagues laughed at him for being foolish. Relatives worried but could do nothing. As a young man I did not know why, either, but I supported my father's decisions, just as later on he supported my decisions.

Every day my father was in that dilapidated closed room, meditating, reading books, writing: a day, a month, a year... One day, after more than ten years, I went to my father's closed room. It was a small and narrow room, and in it he had only put a single bed and a writing desk. The writing desk was piled with books. That room was like a cave: very dark, very damp, without any windows in the strict sense, just a narrow skylight. My father joked that he was "sitting in a well observing the sky." On the wall of the room hung a piece of calligraphy that said: "One who can endure loneliness is truly a good fellow. One who does not encounter the jealousy of others is a mediocre person."

In October 2000, one of my father's "great books" was finally published. This was *Desert Rites*. This book was a big hit, not only because the book itself was excellent, but also because everyone was delighted to talk about the author's spirit of "sharpening a single sword for twelve years." Many people were very surprised that in this era of impulsive utilitarianism, there would finally be someone who took ten years to write a book, while revising it over and over again. But I understood that my father was not only writing a book, he was completing himself, breaking himself up again and again, and rebuilding himself again and again. He used a pen to reshape his spirit and complete his metamorphosis.

Not long after *Desert Rites* was published, my father sold off the bookstore at a low price, and still had thousands of books left. Several friends in official posts wanted to help him manage this, but my father did not respond: he donated the whole inventory to the children of the farming villages. He again went into seclusion, where he cultivated his Buddhist practice and began writing *The Desert Hunters, White Tiger Gate, and Curses of Xixia.*

2

My father used his experience of half a lifetime to teach me one thing: Choosing. He has told me three points about "choosing: " First, every person's fate is chosen by that person. Second, every person at any time can always choose. Third, whatever kind of person you choose to become, as long as you make the effort, you will surely become that kind of person.

I firmly believe this, without a doubt. So when I was in my junior year of high school, I chose to write a novel, and I chose to withdraw from school. At the time almost everyone was against my withdrawing from school. Some of them expressed regret, some ridiculed me, some did not understand, some blamed me. Everyone lectured me on some great truths, trying to persuade me. I would give a slight smile and shake my head. Seeing that I was not moved by this, they turned their spear points toward my father: "How can you let a young kid decide this? Later on he will blame you!" But my father did not stop me. He said: "Have you chosen well or not? If you have chosen well, then go ahead and do it."

In fact, the other people could not understand the situation at that time. In those days, I got up every day at 3 a.m. to write the novel, and then at 6 a.m. I went to school. Because I was about to enter my third year of high school, the pressure to study was very great. But there was no longer any way for me to put my energy into studying; what filled my mind was the novel, and every day I was immersed in the atmosphere of the novel, and I was annoyed by not having enough time to write. A year of time had rushed by in struggle and confusion, and the novel had been written up to the point of its climax, but every day I was unable to bring it off vividly. The trifling three hours would pass in a flash. I seemed helpless, my body and mind were exhausted. Many nights I could not fall asleep, and my eyes stayed open until the alarm sounded at 3 a.m.

Either to write the novel, or to go to college.

If I went to college, then for the whole of the senior year in high school there would be no way for me to write, and my novel would come to an untimely end. It was very clear to me that within a particular period of time, that particular feeling could only appear once. It was like springtime: once it goes by, there is no way to have it again.

I truly could not take this suffering and torment, so I chose to leave school. This choice was very difficult: it implied that I would lose many opportunities. If I could not succeed in becoming a writer, later on even surviving would become a problem. But I thought, if I don't succeed, then I'll perish for a righteous cause. Surely I would rather live in poverty than live a life of regrets. I said: I must cut off all avenues of retreat behind me, and not turn back, and not turn around, and not retreat.

On the afternoon of June 29, 2006, I handed in my request to withdraw from school. I remember the day. The sun was shining bright.

My request to withdraw from school was written like this:

Under my father's influence and tutelage, I came to love reading books and writing. Moreover, I understand clearly that time is flying by, and no one knows whether or not he will live another second, and I am running a race with death. This is not a useless effort: I need more time to concentrate on reading books, and to consider these questions, but when I am in school I can never quiet my mind down. Starting last year in June, I have been getting up every morning at 3 a.m. to work on my writing, until I go to school at six o'clock, but this is far from enough, and a mere three hours cannot fulfill my requirements. Even more alarming is that at school I cannot wholeheartedly enter into the studies, my physical strength will not permit it. Thus, in the nearly ten or more hours at school, I virtually waste half the time. As long as a person does one thing well in his lifetime, that will do. I follow this principle, and I must be responsible for myself. This is one of the reasons I have decided to withdraw from school.

A person's life only lasts a few decades, and the essential time, the time for achievement, is no more than ten or twenty years. Every day that goes by means one day less to live. I must gather together my energy and do a good job with the work that I must do. I cannot go on any longer living by just drifting along, going through the motions. I believe in my own ability. I respect every person who has a dream, including myself.

Of course, I know the importance of a college education, but as who I am right now, I cannot abandon reading and writing. I have chosen another Path, and perhaps I will pay the price for my choice, but I respect myself, and I will do all I can to realize my own value. I am full of faith in myself. This is not a rash decision, and I believe time will prove it all!

Looking at this now, I could only have written such a flighty text when I was at that flighty age.

The strange thing is, after I withdrew from school, I ended up not being able to write a single character. During that period of time, I lost my spirit, and I was like a ghost wandering apart from the human crowd, feeling the world had suddenly left me far behind. All the voices faded away, and all the hubbub left me behind. I was no longer busy every day at school and at home, and I no longer pondered the connection between parabolas and coordinates, and I no longer imagined what kind of life I would lead after I entered the university.

Every day I sat in front of the computer: this was my whole life.

In my diary, I expressed it like this:

After leaving school, a kind of nameless emptiness has suddenly attacked me. It is as if I have had my backbone pulled out, and in my confusion I cannot find myself, and even my dreams are as murky as mudslides. I wander around all day half asleep and half awake, enduring the time with a heavy head and light feet ...

This was a frightening period of time, and I ended up understanding that "loneliness is more fierce than a tiger." I finally understood why my father had hung on the wall of his closed room that epigram: "One who can endure loneliness is truly a good fellow. One who does not encounter the jealousy of others is a mediocre person."

After a few months, I recovered my normal state of mind and began to write calmly and quietly. I immersed myself in the novel again, and every day madly proclaimed that I was a genius.

In fact, I very much missed my former life at school, and longed for the college life that I would not have. More than once I dreamed that I had returned to school, and I was having fun with my classmates on the sports field, or in the classroom listening to the teacher giving lessons. In my dreams I could always clearly feel this longing, to the point that it was etched in my memory. I have never told this to anyone else, including my parents. I have stubbornly traveled the Path I myself chose, and I will not turn back.

Later, many people asked me: "Do you regret abandoning going to the university?"

I may have had some misgivings, but I do not regret it. Because this was my choice.

3

There is nothing my father likes more: he only loves books, he loves books like life itself.

When friends visit from afar, when they enter our house they are sure to exclaim: "So many books!" It's true, wherever you look, it's all books. In our family we have a custom: to save space, we always make walls of books. In addition to this, the living room, the bedrooms, the hallways, the beds, even the toilet, are all piled with books. Our family has a two-story house in Wuwei, and each room has books from floor to ceiling. Now it's been two years since we came to Dongguan, and our place there is also filled with books. As my mother says, "It's so full of books, it's a disaster."

My father loves books, and he truly loves them to his bones. When I had just learned to turn pages, he told me that whenever I read a new book, first I should properly arrange the book jacket; and before reading the book, I must first wash my hands. I must not rip the pages, I must not fold them, and I must not scribble on them. After I finished reading it, I must put it back in its original place. I must revere every good book.

Every time my father goes anywhere, he always looks for the bookstores first. He cannot pass up any of the bookstores he has been able to find out about, no matter whether they are grand-scale book malls or bookstalls deep in the shabby backstreets. Many times I have gone to strange cities with him, and he always readily locates the bookstores. I am very puzzled by this: there are many things he looks at without seeing, so why does he find bookstores so easily as if he knows them well?

When our family goes traveling, he would rather give up the

opportunity of seeing the famous sites, and go to bookstores. At first, I had a lot of veiled criticism. Seeing that I was not happy, he laughed and said: "We will still be able to see the scenic spots later, but if we miss a good book, then we have missed it." Though we travel every year, as my mother says, our travels are from bookstores here to bookstores there.

My father is very generous, and gives his friends a lot of treasures as he pleases, but he rarely lends out books. When our whole family was still living in bachelor quarter, he stuck a strip of paper on the bookshelf that said: "Keep your mouth shut, and never lend these out." In earlier years, he was always lending people books, and later many of these people did not return them. There were also more than a few people who borrowed books just to keep up appearances, and in fact did not read books, so my father would not lend books to these poseurs. Later, my father bought a lot of books specially to give to people, and if he felt a certain book had a karmic connection to you, he would give it to you without the least hesitation. His giving books and not lending books had significance.

My father reads a wide range of books: he reads books from all fields. When he reads books, he has his own principles. The three most important of these are:

1) Read those books which are most worth reading in this present life.

2) The content of the book must be fully absorbed and digested, so it can be put to use; it must not be made into fetters.

3) When you read a book, do not always go looking for the book's defects and shortcomings; you must discover its strong points, and learn from its strengths. Reading books is not done in order to search for their defects, but to absorb nourishment.

When my father reads books, he reads those books that he would regret not having read in his life. He never reads dead books, and he has not turned into a bookworm. As for the third principle, later he used this in his interchanges with people. He says that the eyes are used to discover beauty, to discover strong points. You should not deliberately go looking for other people's shortcomings and defects; if you act like that, then you will only bring yourself and others unhappiness and pain. He says you must be like the great ocean; you should not be concerned with how much mud and sand there is in the flow of some rivers. What you do is do your utmost to take in nourishment, and let yourself grow.

Under this constant influence, I too fell in love with reading books. From the time I was little until I grew up, I never lacked for books to read. Before I went to elementary school, I had read almost all the world's famous children's stories. While my companions were immersed in playing games, I was wandering far and wide in the beautiful, wondrous world of children's stories, completely entranced: I was battling the wolf men in the forests of Northern Europe; or marveling at the cunning of Reynard the Fox; or quietly listening to Münchhausen boasting; sometimes I also wanted to have a Puss in Boots ... I had so many roles — in every children's tale I was the main character.

Since I've brought up books of children's stories, there is one story I must tell.

Ten or more years ago, our whole family had just moved to the city, and we were living in my father's bachelor quarter. At that time, wearing leather shoes was a very foreign-style thing, and my mother had never worn leather shoes, and always wore handmade cloth shoes. My father very much wanted to buy a pair of leather shoes for my mother. Finally, one day my father received a payment, fifty-five *yuan* in all. So the whole family happily went shopping, to buy a pair of leather shoes for my mother. On the way we were all discussing what color and what texture shoes to buy. When we got to the square, my father stopped: there was a bookstore here that he often went to. Father said: "Let's take a look and then we' ll go. It' ll be quick."

The whole family went into the store, and my father went to look at books of social sciences, mother went to look at books on healthy living, and I ran over to the children's shelf. Right away one set of books attracted my attention. It was a set of picture books called *Famous Children's Stories of the World,* in eight volumes. It contained almost all the classic children's stories in the world. Most important were the beautiful illustrations inside. I loved it and would not let go of it. Very quickly my father and mother also discovered this set of books. My father said: "This is a set of good books." He looked at the price, and it was exactly fifty-five *yuan.* My father and mother looked at each other and laughed. My mother said: "It's better to wear cloth shoes; if I wear leather shoes, my feet will hurt."

That day I was delighted as I brought the set of books back, but hidden in my heart I felt I could not face mother. But this feeling of regret was soon diluted by the joy this set of books brought me. I read this set of books countless time — it was my most important treasure, and now it still sits there squarely on my bookshelf.

This was a minor event, nothing heart-rending, nothing earth-shaking, but I cannot forget it.

Later, we opened a bookstore, and during that period of time I read a great many books. In front of the bookshelves I sat, crawled, stretched out, lay down, reading till it got pitch dark, and often I forgot my writing work. My father did not blame me; instead he made a telephone call to my teacher, saying they should not assign me homework. Many people find this inconceivable, and I laugh—this is the kind of special person he is. Later, when I entered my first year in middle school, I truly could not bear the endless repetitive school work, and my father again made telephone calls to the teacher, telling him not to assign me school work. After this he began to arrange my reading according to a plan. While my age-mates were doing the same topics over and over again, I was avidly reading the world's most beautiful writings. For this I feel very fortunate.

The direct result brought about by my father's love of books was that I very seldom bought books. This was because I could find all the books I needed on my father's bookshelves. I thought, I will conscientiously read the books, and as for the happy feeling of strolling in bookstores buying books, I'll leave that to my father!

4

When my father was a teacher, any time there were holiday periods, he always asked to "keep watch on the school"—to be on duty at the school. This was because when he went home, there were many social engagements, and this wasted time.

One time over the Spring Festival, my father put a set of couplets over the door of the school dormitories. The top one read: "Hey, who set off the firecrackers?" The lower one read: "Wow, they are celebrating the Spring Festival!" A horizontal scroll read: "It has nothing to do with me."

Many people took these as a joke, but I knew the steadfastness and hardship behind the joke.

Our hometown, Liangzhou, is a classic small city of Western China. The people of Liangzhou are very interesting, and particularly content with their lot and always happy. The urban area of Liangzhou city is very small, and it takes no more than ten minutes to drive from one end of the city to the other. It is this small a city, but it has several thousand small-scale teahouses. Besides these, when summer comes, the parks and gardens are full of people. Everywhere there are simple restaurants, with people sitting under the shade of the trees, ordering a big plate of chicken and two cold dishes. Later, they bring out a couple of cases of beer, and they play the finger-counting game, or play cards, or chat … On the walking streets, in the squares, on the tops of the high-rise buildings, wherever there are open spaces with people passing—they are all full of beer stalls and barbecue stalls. If something happens in their family, no matter whether it is important or not, they must have a party, and the sound of the finger-guessing game fills the air, and the party does not break up until they are so drunk they cannot recognize their parents.

One year, a program on China Central Television (CCTV) asked this question: "Where is Asia's biggest open-air casino located?" The respondents all went to Macao to pick one, but who knew that the answer was actually the Liangzhou East Gate Botanical Garden in Gansu? This is because it can hold ten thousand people playing mahjong at the same time. After the Liangzhou people found out about this, they laughed out loud: "What does this matter? It's just the tip of the iceberg."

The people of Liangzhou are this way: they love to feel contentment, and they are experts in enjoying pleasures. Among this kind of Liangzhou people, my father is an anomaly—he even seems like a freak. He never gets drunk or plays cards, and he does very little socializing. My grandmother always says: "Everything about your father is good, it's just that he does not understand people's feelings and the ways of the world." When grandmother says "people's feelings and the ways of the world," she means running around a lot visiting relatives, creating good connections with a lot of people, and, when necessary, currying favor with the leaders. Years ago, when it came to making good connections, my father was not successful. His character was honest and frank, and he would not play up to people, and he would always arouse the ire of the leaders. He was not good at socializing, and his friends were few. In the eyes of many people, he was obstinate and rebellious and too independent.

Speaking of this, there is a little story that is still fresh in my memory.

A long time ago, my father was teaching school in a village. He was an impoverished teacher. Later on, he went through an examination and was chosen to come to a school in the city. At that time, he already had grown a beard. While managing the transfer procedure, the cadre in charge of personnel matters for the Board of Education said to him: "Either you shave off the beard, or you can return to the village to teach." What astounded everyone was that he actually returned to the village to teach. Some people shook their heads, some laughed derisively, some felt regret. At that time, the village teachers were all jostling to find a way to get to the city, but he was abandoning such a good opportunity for the sake of a beard. Many years later, when he was working for the Board of Education, the leadership again let him make a choice between the beard and working for the education committee, and he still chose to keep the beard. Luckily, he met Pu Long, the chairman of the Board of Education, who appreciated him, and so finally he was kept on at the Board of Education. Later on, Pu Long and his successors did not assign any concrete duties to my father, so he had many years to go off and cultivate practice in seclusion.

Years earlier, we always celebrated the New Year in the old house with grandfather and grandmother. As soon as we got to the old house, he would crawl up on the heated sleeping platform, and read. In the courtyard, the kinfolk would be drinking liquor, and playing the finger-counting game, and playing mahjong. Although it was very loud and lively, basically this could not influence him. He kept on reading as always. He would keep on reading till the third day of the New Year festivities, and then we would leave and go back to the city.

When grandmother saw him like this, she explained to me: "This child was always like this. As long as he had a book, that book never left his hand no matter whether he was eating, or drawing water, or lighting the fire."

When we returned from the old house, my father would say: "In these few days I read a few books. What about you? What did you do in the same time?"

I would feel embarrassed.

During the four seasons of the year, our house was peaceful and quiet, and very few visitors came, and we never had parties.

When I was little, I did not understand. Other people's houses were always very noisy, but our house was always so quiet. At that time, I thought my father was reclusive and arrogant. Only later, when he and I settled accounts, did I finally understand the reason for all this.

One afternoon when the sun was shining bright, my father had a talk with me, and we worked on an arithmetic problem: Suppose a human life is seventy years long; sleep occupies one-third of this; going to school occupies sixteen years; eating and drinking and going to the toilet takes two hours a day, or about five or six years; falling in love also takes up several years; having children, educating children, studying for the sake of the children, working, getting married, worrying about the children also takes up several years; there is also doing one's duty toward parents; watching television; being online; exercising the body ...

On that afternoon, my father was like an elementary school pupil doing an arithmetic problem. How many hours, how many days, how many years — he seriously added them up and carefully calculated them. At last, the conclusion we got was that the human lifespan yields a negative number! If we suppose that one person does all these things well in the prescribed way, seventy years' time is basically not enough!

My father stared at me pointedly and said: "The timespan of a human life is limited. If you want to achieve something, you must learn to value the time, and you must learn how to give up things. Only this way will you have enough time to do what you want to do." My back and my hands were covered with sweat. This arithmetic lesson made me frightened and uneasy. I finally understood clearly why my father was a "freak," why he didn't go out to eat and drink and have fun, why our house was always so "deserted".

I have searched my memory for a long time, but I have never found one picture of my father wasting time. When he was in the car, he would be reading books. When he was soaking in the tub in the public bathhouse, he would be reading newspapers. When he brushed his teeth, he would exercise his body by squatting down and standing up. When he was reading a book or writing, he would always be maintaining the cultivation of the energy of the precious vessel ... He seemed never to do things one at a time, and this discovery made me apprehensive: I seemed to waste too much time.

Later, when some television station interviewed me, they asked: "How did your father educate you? Tell us what you gained at your father's side."

I said: "The best education is personal experience, to provide the child with a model. My father established a model for me. Through all his actions he was telling me how I must act if I wanted to become a man like him!"

Later I began to enjoy the "deserted" quality of the house. Every day the bright sunlight came in through the glass windows and spread over the bookshelves, serene and calm.

Time did not pass, and everything seemed to come to a stop.

5

People always say that special people must have a different look. Whether or not my father is a "special person," I would not presume to say. No matter where he goes in China, there are always people who say that with his bushy eyebrows and deep-set eyes, my father looks very much like a foreigner. As for my father's appearance, I am very puzzled: our ancestors all looked very ordinary, and our blood relatives now are all very steady. He is the only one who is "a fierce fellow with leopard's eyes, a dark spirit with tiger's whiskers."

People who have met my father are almost all struck by his appearance, especially his beard and the cinnabar-colored mole between his eyebrows. Someone once said: "When you look at his beard, Xuemo looks like a demon king. When you look at the mole between his eyebrows, he also looks like a Buddha." When my father heard this, he laughed out loud and said: "Xuemo is neither a demon nor a Buddha. He is just a crazy old guy."

But our whole family believes in Buddhism: can it not be because of the cinnabar-colored mole on father's forehead?

According to my grandmother's account, when my father was

little, he believed in Buddhism, but he was not one of those people who always have "Amitabha Buddha" on their lips. Only later, when I was organizing my father's diaries, did I come to know that when he was seventeen he had already paid homage to Buddhist Master Wu Naidan of Songtao Temple as his teacher. When I was little, he often told me Buddhist stories. He told me that I must not step on ants and bugs, that I must not deceive people, that I must help people, that in the future I would be a good person.

In our native village there was a Vajravarahi Cave. My father said that this was a famous place, but was unknown to the people of Liangzhou. When I was little, our family often went there. At that time, that mystic cave had not yet been sealed off, and it was very dim and dark inside. In the cave there were many passageways of different sizes, twisting and turning and uneven, going up and down and right and left. Every time we went there, our family would spend a long time with old man Qiao, who watched over the cave. My father would rub the minerals on the walls of the cave sparkling like crystal and say: "This is a great being!" Associated with the Vajravarahi Cave, there was also the story of Zhang the butcher and his five daughters. This story was passed along by oral tradition, and communicated from the Western Xia kingdom (which ruled in this region 1038–1227 C.E.) up till today. A veil has already been cast over the Tangut people who founded the Western Xia kingdom, and they have disappeared into the mists of history. But the Vajravarahi Cave, along with this story, still tells the tale of those special causal conditions. Later, this went into my father's novel *Curses of Xixia*.

When I was seven, under my father's guidance, I began to cultivate Buddhist practice in a full-fledged way. Every day I would do prostrations and recite the *Hundred Word Mantra*. Before dawn, at 5 a.m. when the world is all quiet, I would silently recite the holy sounds that have been handed down for a thousand years, and peacefully listen to the obscure, hard-to-understand texts of the sutras. I do not know whether doing this increased my wisdom, but it truly softened my heart. I began to hate the way I had grabbed the wings of bees before. I began to stop my companions from slingshotting at birds. I began to put my spare change in the bowls of beggars … Later, I slowly came to understand that it was during this period that I learned respect and a sense of gratitude. Although at that time, I had still not memorized any scriptural texts, and I did not recognize the special characteristics of the different Buddha images, nevertheless, it was enough to have influenced my life.

Not long after this, our family went on a pilgrimage to Wutai Mountain in Shanxi Province. This was a pilgrimage in the true sense. For a period of more than a month, we set out early in the morning and returned at dusk, and visited every peak on Wutai Mountain. In my memories from that period, apart from the temples and the mountain Paths, are memories of us constantly walking. Sometimes, in order to go to a temple hidden in the folds of the green mountains, we had to walk several dozen kilometers in a single day.

During that time, we made pilgrimages to all the temples of Wutai Mountain, and knelt before all the Buddhas' images, and turned all the sutra wheels, and circumambulated all the stupas. We left the footprints of all our yearning, and we used all our sincere reverence to feel the atmosphere of every blade of grass and every tree that was there.

My father later said that the great vows he made on Wutai Mountain during those days were later all fulfilled.

Those days were serene and happy. We put all worldly complications behind us, and on one little Path after another, on one quest after another, we savored the simplicity and cleanness of the mind and spirit. Every patch of sky was clear blue for you. Every mountain breeze was pure for you. Every tree was fresh and strong for you. Every temple was waiting for you to keep your appointment.

Keep going and going, from the previous lifetime to the next lifetime!

With my father, I made pilgrimages to many holy sites, like Labrang Monastery in Gansu Province, Ta' er Temple and Xia Qiong Temple in Qinghai Province, Xiang Xiong Temple … Almost every one of these places became a pure land in my mind.

Our family's most recent pilgrimage was to Tibet.

This is a place that I had dreamed of but had never dared to encounter directly.

In the book *The Alchemist*, by Paulo Coelho, known in Chinese as *Fantasy Travels of a Shepherd Boy*, the shopkeeper of the crystal shop said it this way: "Because Mecca supported my hope to keep on living, and enabled me to bear the ordinary times, and put up with the crystals in the cabinet that could not talk, and put up with those lunches and dinners in awful restaurants, I was afraid to make my dreams come true. After they came true, I would have no more impetus to keep on living … So I would rather just hold onto it as a dream."

I had this kind of feeling about Tibet. I was afraid I would lose hope and I would destroy the dream that I had built up for so long. The Tibet in my mind belonged only to me; it was my sacred land, with no connection to anyone else, no connection to the outside world, and no connection even to the real Tibet.

But I had decided to go on a pilgrimage. This world has no lack of dreamers. What is lacking are people to revere the truth with their actions and to put the truth into practice. What's more, many scenic places require you to go there in person and touch them, and only then can you feel their soul.

Thus, snowy mountains, Buddhist temples, holy lakes, like old friends keeping an appointment, forced their overflowing natural energy into my life.

When I returned from the pilgrimage, I suddenly became conscious of that fact that the destination of the pilgrimage may not be what is most important. What is most important is that you must have the mind of pilgrimage, and then use the action of going on the pilgrimage to purify your own spirit. Later, my father said that, from the point of view of the ultimate truth, all his activities were in fact being on a pilgrimage.

Some time later I read *Biographies of Eminent Monks and Great Worthies through the Generations*. Many of the eminent monks and great worthies in it climbed mountains and crossed rivers in order to spread the Dharma, or to get the Buddhist sutras. I thought: these arduous journeys are a part of cultivating practice.

The years flow by like water, and the things of the world change and shift. After I grew up, I had my own understanding of the Buddha Dharma. What was muddled at first became a clear, lucid yearning. I particularly like a statement of my father's: "Genuine faith is unconditional. It is just a certain spiritual reverence and yearning. Faith is not a means for seeking merit and reward, faith itself is the goal."

I have spent two years editing the text in such books as *The Great Mudra of Light: Real Practice, Sudden Entry*. These books are a recording of my father's everyday conversation. He explains to me a thousand years of wisdom which Buddhism has passed on, and he resolves all the questions in my mind about death and life. It was as if I turned around for an instant, and suddenly everything before my eyes emptied through and was clarified, and I saw a scene which I had never seen before.

The road I must travel from here on is even more clear and solid. I think back on the scenes from when we were on pilgrimage, and at the end of a faraway, rugged mountain road is a temple smiling into the wind.

6

My father and I have gone through several important deaths together. Every time I went through one of these deaths, I was always left feeling utterly exhausted. They were like an evil laugh behind me on a dark night. They were rope in a deep seam in the earth. They were a fierce fire burning up people's hearts and lungs. They left me afraid and uneasy. They made me feel a wrenching hopelessness.

The first to leave the imprint of death on my life was my uncle. He was a young man of twenty-seven when he was buried in the yellow earth. His name was Chen Kailu. What he left me was only a few fragments. I couldn't imagine anything that he had completed. His existence was like a dream from which a person is awakened with a start halfway through.

My earliest, clearest memory of my uncle is after he became ill. At that time, the operation for his late-stage liver cancer had failed, and so he had returned home. He lay on the heatable brick bed, and his whole face was a waxy yellow, and his stomach was growling loudly. I stood in the corner, having just come in, and looked at him from afar, and did not dare come closer. He waved to me, and asked me to come over. I shook my head no, because I was trapped by a nameless fear. I saw that when anyone mentioned my uncle's sickness, there was always a look of catastrophic terror showing in their eyes. Later on, no one wanted to mention it, and this was like a wound that there was no way to heal, and even if you lightly touched it with your finger, it would release a pain that made people tremble non-stop. When my uncle saw that I would not go over to him, there was a look of gloom in his eyes, and I saw that he was very lost. When I think back on this moment, it is very hard for me to bear. Even now, I cannot forgive myself for this behavior, and I don't understand why a five-year-old child would be so cold and indifferent.

I looked at him again, and we were already worlds apart.

In an essay I wrote this:

> *I remember that morning very clearly. In the clean glass of the window of the kindergarten, my mother's grief-stricken face appeared. She had a few words with my teacher, and after that the teacher turned around and said, "Chen Changfeng, collect your book bag, and go home with your mother."*
>
> *As soon as we entered the gate, the sound of crying filled the courtyard. I was scared stiff and stood terror-stricken where I was, and for a long time my soul did not return. With these adults I had originally seen as big and strong all crying with grief, I was terrified. Later, when my uncle was put in his coffin, I saw his discolored face. That face was branded on my soul from then on.*

When I think about this now, what had the greatest impact on me then was not my uncle's death in itself, but rather how people looked after his death, or to put it accurately, how my father and my grandmother looked.

My father had been with my uncle during the last few months of his life, and he watched helplessly and saw how a strong man could be buried in the ground. The look of grief on his face brought a deep stabbing pain to my heart, because I had never seen him this way before. The day of my uncle's funeral, my father shut himself up in a small room, and wrote a long eulogy.

My uncle's early death directly changed my father's life. For a few years afterwards, he began to ponder death, and he put the skull of a dead man in his bedroom, to constantly alert himself to how easily life passes away. Once he pointed to that skull and said to me: "He or she may have once had talent, or may have been rich, or may have been good-looking and elegant, but now none of this is important anymore. What is important is whether or not he or she completed the work that he or she had to do, before god of death caught up with him or her."

If my father's appearance alarmed me, then my grandmother's appearance terrified me.

I wrote about it like this:

The night before my uncle was buried, it was very windy. A Taoist priest brought nails and began to nail up the coffin in the courtyard. Grandmother, who by this time had already become feeble, suddenly rushed like the wind over to the coffin, desperately wanting to open it up and see my uncle. People forcibly picked her up and carried her into the house, but where her fingernails had scratched the coffin, it left deep marks.

The next few nights were hopeless and endless. Grandmother's mournful howling went on without stopping, and this howling was magically transformed into all of life's hopelessness and helplessness, and floated out into the dark wilderness.

For several days I did not dare go into my grandmother's room, or dare to look at my grandmother's face. I stood in the bustling courtyard, and her hoarse cries came out through the window, blending with the noisy sounds of the horns, and became a drill piercing my mind again and again.

Though the courtyard was full of people, it exuded a kind of desolation it had never had before. I was constantly feeling a vague pain in a certain place in my body, as if there was a wound that was deep, though not bleeding. I do not remember what the weather was like then, but in my image of it, the whole sky was yellow, the sun was pale and dim, and a cold wind was blowing in the sky. No matter how thick the clothes I put on, I was chilled to the bone.

The next day, I went with my father and mother to the gathering at the grave. In the flight of the yellow earth as it was shoveled into the grave, I realized that this was the end point of every life, and no matter how you try, no one can escape it.

If my uncle's departure gave me my first impression of death, the demise of Master Wu was my most close-up feeling of death.

Master Wu's original name was Wu Naidan; he was the abbot of Songtao Temple in Liangzhou. My father was his disciple for more than twenty years, and received from him many precious teachings of Shangpa Kagyu Buddhism. When I was little, I would often go play in the temple courtyard, and from time to time he would teach me a few things.

Songtao Temple had previously been a temple in name only, and there were just a few mud brick houses. I had heard my father say that the great hall and the Buddha-images had been destroyed during the "Cultural Revolution." So Master Wu's greatest wish was to rebuild Songtao Temple.

Master Wu's master was called the "Stone Monk." He was a famous martial arts master in Liangzhou. His level of attainment was high, and he was very fierce. He was the real-life prototype of "Papa Jiu" in my father's novel *Curses of Xixia*, and also of the "Stone Monk" in *The Grey Wolf of Xixia*. Even today, the old men in the streets of Liangzhou still take delight in telling wondrous tales of his martial arts prowess. When I was eighteen and an admirer of the martial arts, I visited a famous martial artist in Liangzhou and heard many stories about the Stone Monk. In theory, Master Wu must have been a martial arts expert too, because he was the only disciple of the Stone Monk. But in fact it was just the opposite, and Master Wu knew nothing about martial arts. And this was not because the Stone Monk had been stingy about sharing his knowledge, but rather because Master Wu thought that studying martial arts was without meaning, and was not the ultimate level, and would waste his life. I felt sorry about this for a long time.

In order to repair the temple, Master Wu subsisted for years on boiled water and dried buns. These buns were donated to the temple by the congregation twice a month.

When Master Wu was nearly seventy, Songtao Temple finally began to take shape.

Before Master Wu died, our family went to see him.

Songtao Temple was serene and quiet as usual, and the great hall was empty and lonesome, filled with the atmosphere of Zen study. On the floor in front of the Buddha-image there was still that worn-out meditation hassock. The hundred-year-old pine trees in the courtyard were still vigorous and strong, standing upright through the vicissitudes of time. They had seen through the human world, with its sorrows and joys, it separations and meetings, and were already indifferent: they had become Bodhidharma facing the wall.

Master Wu used all the money he had to repair the temple, and basically paid no attention to the fact that he himself was already a seventy-year-old man, and paid even less attention to his undernourished body. He had truly achieved a selfless state.

On the way home, my father told me: "A person's value is the sum of his actions, and Master Wu is an amazing eminent monk."

One week later, in Songtao Temple, Master Wu went to sleep forever. Every hall he had built, every wall, every stair, silently accompanies him, and tells of his greatness.

On the day Master Wu was cremated, my father and I came early to the site. The sky had not yet fully brightened, and a fine drizzle was coming down. Before, I had thought that the cremation ground must be very gloomy, and I had not realized that it would be extraordinarily quiet and still, and there would actually be the feeling of being in a temple.

At daybreak, the other masters from the temple came to perform the ceremony, and the sounds of the music and the chanting and the crying all blended into one, and fused into the empty spirit in my mind.

When the ceremony was completed, the cremation began.

There was a small opening in the crematory oven, and you could see what it was like inside the oven. My father with me stand in front of that small opening and watch what a life returns to.

This let me understand that life is a joke, a joke played arbitrarily by the gods.

I felt heaven and earth turning, and it was like falling, falling endlessly...

For a month after this, I was dispirited and wandered around like a ghost. Burning bones appeared constantly before my eyes. At that time the sunlight was covered by black clouds, and my emotions were withered by the cold wind. The world was an abandoned orphanage, dark, dead quiet, boundless, for a thousand years.

I suddenly understood the "impermanence" which the Buddha had spoken of, and felt the hopelessness behind the impermanence that makes heaven and earth collapse. That's it then: the myriad things, heaven and earth, finally come to the same end.

At that point in time, I could not find a reason for living, and I felt that the world had no meaning, and life had no meaning, and nothing had any meaning. During that time I did not write anymore, I did not read books anymore, I did not cultivate Buddhist practice anymore, I did not have joy and anger and grief and joy anymore. I had seen the end: the end of heaven, the end of life, the end of the world.

My father saw all this in his eyes. He explained to me the *Verses on the Genuine Cultivation of the Great Mudra*, and had me put the draft of his book in order. My father's Great Mudra wisdom let me realize a true spiritual advancement.

After several months, I slowly emerged from the morass of hopelessness, and I was no longer tangled up innihilistic empty nothingness. Having gone through this experience, I again saw this familiar world as especially vivid and clear.

Yes, Master Wu had died, and his remains had been cremated. But the temple that he had repaired was still there, and the spirit that had repaired the temple was still there, and the teachings and wisdom that he had imparted to my father were still there. This spirit would be passed on, and this wisdom would be passed on, and would influence more people. Maybe this would become my meaning and purpose for living.

That fire also burned up many clingings and attachments of mine, and let me seriously ponder my own life. I'm always wondering whether or not, many years from now, when my own body enters the flames to be cremated, I will be able to leave something behind that the fire will not burn up.

In later years, when I was wasting my life or criticizing myself or others, I would think of that crematorium. When I was entangled in clingings and attachments, I would think of that crematorium. When I was at a fork in the road and unable to choose, I would think of that crematorium even more. Though it does not make a sound, it is always rumbling in my life.

At this point, my father had taught me something he had wanted to make me learn—using his wisdom and his actions.

I will follow in my father's footsteps, and go forth on my own path.

图书在版编目（CIP）数据

无死的金刚心 = The Holy Monk and the Spirit Woman：英文 / 雪漠著；
（美）柯利瑞（J.C.Cleary）译. —北京：中国大百科全书出版社，2018.10
　　ISBN 978-7-5202-0279-4

　　Ⅰ.①无… Ⅱ.①雪…②柯… Ⅲ.①传记小说-中国-当代-英文
Ⅳ.①I247.5

　　中国版本图书馆CIP数据核字（2018）第102294号

出 版 人	刘国辉
特约编审	阿去克
策划编辑	李默耘
责任编辑	姚常龄
特约编辑	王人龙　刘　琦
英文校对	石学亮　周令钧
责任印制	邹景峰
封面设计	画欣 Cindy
出版发行	中国大百科全书出版社
地　　址	北京阜成门北大街 17 号
邮　　编	100037
网　　址	http://www.ecph.com.cn
电　　话	010-88390739
印　　刷	环球东方（北京）印务有限公司
开　　本	880 毫米 ×1230 毫米　1/32
字　　数	603 千字
印　　张	28.5
版　　次	2018 年 10 月第 1 版第 1 次印刷
定　　价	152.00 元